The White Tecumseh

Also
by
Stanley P. Hirshson

Farewell to the Bloody Shirt
Grenville M. Dodge
The Lion of the Lord

The White Tecumseh

A Biography of General William T. Sherman

Stanley P. Hirshson

John Wiley & Sons, Inc.

New York • Chichester • Weinheim • Brisbane • Singapore • Toronto

To Janet and Scott

Published by John Wiley & Sons, Inc.
Published simultaneously in Canada.

This publication is designed to provide accurate and authoritative information in re-gard to the subject matter covered. It is sold with the understanding that the pub-lisher is not engaged in rendering legal, accounting, or other professional services. If legal advice or other expert assistance is required, the services of a competent pro-fessional person should be sought.

Library of Congress Cataloging-in-Publication Data

Hirshson, Stanley P.
    The White Tecumseh : a biography of General William T. Sherman /
by Stanley P. Hirshson.
      p. cm.
    Includes bibliographical references and index.
    ISBN 0-471-17578-1 (cloth : alk. paper) /
    ISBN 0-471-28329-0 (paper : alk. paper)
    1. Sherman, William T. (William Tecumseh), 1820–1891.
2. Generals—United States—Biography.   3. United States—Army—
Biography. 4. United States—History—Civil War, 1861–1865—
Campaigns. I. Title.
E467.1.S55H65   1997
355′.092—dc20   96-29477

Printed in the United States of America

10 9 8 7 6 5 4 3 2 1

"Put 'Faithful & honorable; faithful & honorable!' "

> —William T. Sherman's deathbed request to his
> daughter Minnie about his monument inscription

"So ends the family distinction. There is no one in the next generation to revive it. I doubt if the third generation can produce anything better. You Adamses transmit your energy and strength as few do. But I suddenly feel old and gray."

> —Elizabeth Sherman Cameron to Henry Adams
> upon hearing in 1900 of the death of her uncle,
> John Sherman

Contents

Maps

Preface

THE PAST TEN YEARS have seen such a revival of interest in William T. Sherman that they might well be termed Cump's Decade. In rapid succession we have seen the appearance of studies by Charles Royster (1991), Albert Castel (1992), John F. Marszalek (1993), and Michael Fellman (1995), each devoted partly or totally to Sherman. Strangely, during the many years I have worked on this book, I never came across any of the others and knew of each work only when it appeared.

The reader will find my volume far more sympathetic to Sherman than any of the others. Naturally, I feel that the Sherman I present in these pages—a brilliant but unhappy and tormented soul—is the true Sherman, but I have profited from the works of my predecessors and feel fortunate in being the last in this series of Sherman authors. But I must say that my experience in seeing the works emerge one after the other has been the academic equivalent of having the contents of a six-shooter slowly emptied into one's body.

Of the previous biographies the two best are those by Lloyd Lewis (1932) and Professor Marszalek. But I strongly disagree with their interpretations of Sherman, revealed by the subtitle of each. To Lewis, Sherman emerged as a "Fighting Prophet," a forerunner of modern war, to me an exaggeration. Marszalek's work has many strengths, but he never even begins to prove his thesis that Sherman, after the death of his father, spent his life developing "A Soldier's Passion for Order." Indeed, I can think of few American generals whose lives were more confused and disorderly than Sherman's. Perhaps because Professor Marszalek was trained in religious schools and I in secular, I have looked at religious issues, tremendously important in Sherman's life, far differently than he. This, in turn, has led to vastly different views of Sherman, Mrs. Sherman, and their son, Father Tom Sherman.

The theme of Sherman's life, it seems to me, is readily discernible. From his early days Sherman emerged as a brilliant but tormented soul. His troubles, I suspect, came not from the loss of his father but from the realization that mental instability plagued his mother's family. Sherman's maternal grandmother, his maternal uncle, and his son Tom all died in, or spent years in, insane asylums.

His brother Jim died a drunk, and his most famous brother, John Sherman, died mentally unstable.

Sherman indeed seemed tormented. As a cadet at West Point he was a superb student, but he went out of his way to defy the academy's rules and amass demerits. General William S. Rosecrans remembered him as "by no means a goody-goody boy." Sherman's unhappiness also showed itself in a life of domestic uneasiness, with a wife and family of a different religion; in his poverty and his struggles to make a living; in his decision to fight against the region he loved; in his breakdown in Kentucky; in the death of his favorite son; in his destruction (Sherman argued the Confederates destroyed even more) of Southern property; in his squabbles with army associates—Ulysses S. Grant, George Thomas, Joseph Hooker, and Henry Halleck; in his misshapings of many events in his autobiography; and in a dozen other things related in this study. He knew much sadness and only occasional happiness.

In this volume I take sharp issue with the way recent historians have evaluated Sherman as a general. My complaints against them are twofold. First, two of them have studied only a portion of Sherman's career, not his entire Civil War experience. Their evaluation of Sherman is at best questionable, at worst spotty. Second, Professor Marszalek makes no use of regimental histories, which, with the *Official Records,* constitute the most important source on Sherman as an army leader. Fortunately, I had complete access to what I estimate to be the fifteen hundred regimental histories on the open shelves of the United States Military Academy Library. Of this number, I calculate that about six hundred contain references to Sherman. And of these, I think I have cited and gotten material from close to two hundred. I consider it impossible to understand Sherman without these volumes. It is a mistake to assume that American soldiers, whether they fought in the Civil War, World War Two, or any other war, were fools. I do not believe that I have seen in regimental histories more than three or four comments critical of Sherman. For decades men bragged about serving under him, just as today they brag about serving with George S. Patton Jr. in World War Two. By ignoring regimental histories and the comments and reports in the *Official Records* and in the dozens of volumes of patriotic speeches, recent historians have blamed Sherman, to cite just two examples, for the defeat at Chickasaw Bayou and the withdrawal from Meridian, both clearly not his fault. And they have forgotten such remarkable achievements as the chase after Joseph E. Johnston across Mississippi, without water, in the broiling sun of July 1863.

As for Michael Fellman's recent study of Sherman, *Citizen Sherman,* I must say that I disagree with it completely. I do not see Sherman as a racist, an anti-Semite, and a philanderer. Anyone who, for example, has read the regimental histories cannot help but notice Sherman's frequent kindnesses towards African-Americans. I strongly disagree, moreover, with the deemphasis of Sherman's military career, which is, after all, the reason why he is today remembered. Reading Professor Fellman's work, I was reminded of the comment of the late social historian, Dixon Ryan Fox, who used to say that he much preferred drum and trumpet history to bum and strumpet history.

Perhaps because I am an Easterner and have had daily access to the vast collection of regimental histories and patriotic speeches, absolutely essential in understanding Sherman, at the West Point library, I have devoted far more space to his battles and marches than has any previous biographer. Assessing Sherman as a soldier is not easy. He won few battles. Often, Sherman avoided conflict. At other times, such as during the Battle of Atlanta, he deliberately stayed out of things and let his subordinates—in this case his beloved Army of the Tennessee—fight it out. Sherman's chief accomplishments, I am convinced, were his superb marches, especially the ones across Mississippi in the heat of 1863, to Knoxville in the cold of late 1863, and through the icy Salkehatchie swamps of South Carolina during the early winter of 1865. Coupled with these was Sherman's great mastery of logistics, admired, just as an illustration, a half century later by the youthful West Point cadet George S. Patton Jr., to whom supply lines remained forever a mystery. More than anything else, these justify America's interest in Cump Sherman.

Acknowledgments

THIS VOLUME stems from an incident that took place over thirty-five years ago. During the summer of 1956, when I was a graduate student at Columbia and was working on what became *Farewell to the Bloody Shirt*, my adviser, David Herbert Donald, kept urging me to go down to the Manuscript Division of the Library of Congress, where, he was sure, I would get the inside story relating to my topic. In mid-August I followed his sage advice.

My first morning in the library brought me face to face with the huge collection of John Sherman's papers. About ten o'clock, as I was acclimating myself to the job of reading letters, I noticed a half dozen people going over to someone who had just entered. They introduced themselves to him and shook hands. I later learned that the person who had entered was Roy F. Nichols, then working with his wife on a biography of John Sherman.

In my own patented antisocial way I refused to glance at Professor Nichols, but he did not ignore me. After a few days, seeing me struggle with the John Sherman Papers, he came over, introduced himself to me, spoke of the Shermans, and encouraged me to stick to it. Just before Labor Day, about to return home, he again came over, said good-bye, and once more encouraged me. I think that at that moment I vowed someday to write a book about one of the Shermans. Not until ten years ago did I begin this venture, but I still like to think of Professors Donald and Nichols as its godfathers.

During the years I have worked on this book I have received nothing but help from librarians around the country. I should especially like to thank the following: Susan Ravdin of the Bowdoin College Library; E. Cheryl Schnerring and Dennis Suttles of the Illinois State Historical Library; Gary J. Arnold of the Ohio Historical Society; Leona Schonfeld, Kelli Ann Bronson, Frances Rouse, Brita Mack, and Dr. Bill Frank of the Henry E. Huntington Library; Martha Clevenger of the Missouri Historical Society; David Crosson, Ellen Sulser, Laura Bloom, and Sharon Avery of the State Historical Society of Iowa in Des Moines; and William Kevin Cawley of the University of Notre Dame Archives.

My home base during the writing of this book has been the library of the United States Military Academy at West Point. At least three hundred times I got into my car and drove up the Palisades Parkway to that magnificent institution, where I was allowed to roam about the library, working with manuscripts, regimental histories, and reminiscences, or just picking books off the shelves, seeing what tidbits I could unearth.

I am most deeply grateful to many people at the academy library. Alan C. Aimone, the director of Special Collections, has been a constant source of encouragement, as well as of materials. Greeting me on almost every visit with the words "I have something for you," he would hand me a bunch of documents that immeasurably added to my understanding of Sherman and of the Civil War period. For helping me in various ways I also wish to thank Gladys Calvetti, Dawn Crumpler, Angela Kao, Carol Koenig, Susan Lintelmann, Debbie McKeon-Pogue, and Judith Sibley. I am also happy to acknowledge the assistance given to me by Sheila Biles, who spent three weeks helping me to select the illustrations and the maps.

I should like to mention others. My close friend and fellow West Point researcher, John Shelter, taught me much about army life and battle tactics. I have enjoyed immensely our numerous talks. During all the years I have known them, two of my former teachers, David Donald and William E. Leuchtenburg, have done me so many favors that I hardly know how to begin to thank them. I hope that this volume is some, if indeed small, recompense. The late William J. Chute, Arthur Moskowitz, and Edgar McManus read the manuscript and made several suggestions. David Syrett shared with me his mastery of American military and naval history. Olive and Ari Hoogenboom, Grady McWhiney, and Charles Calhoun looked out for, and told me about, Sherman material. Debbye, Marci, Staci, and Bruce Feldman made me welcome during my many trips to Washington. My friends from the summer I spent at the Huntington Library, J. J. Humphrey, Michael Green, Wang Xi, and James Long, frequently talked with me about the Civil War and about history in general. And my favorite correspondent, Sharon M. Moody, the world's greatest Sherman fan, encouraged me and graciously pointed out to me mistakes in other books, thus helping me to avoid them.

I should especially like to thank three people who engineered the publication of this volume. To me, Hana Umlauf Lane, my editor at John Wiley & Sons, is indeed a wonder. Deeply interested in the Civil War, she actually sat down and read every word of the manuscript. I suppose there are other senior editors who critically read entire manuscripts, but I have never before met one. Next comes Benjamin Hamilton, who supervised the production of the book. From the beginning I have found my conversations with him to be cordial and informative. The third person, James Gullickson, went over the manuscript with great care and prepared it for publication.

Finally, I should like to thank my wife Janet and son Scott for their patience and understanding.

The White Tecumseh

1

Of Raymonds and Streets, Hoyts and Shermans

— I —

IN GEORGIA AND SOUTH CAROLINA he is detested as a fiend and destroyer. In Louisiana he is—or should be—revered as a father of the state university. Everywhere he is looked upon as an innovator and a soldier of dedication and determination. He was William Tecumseh Sherman.

The origin of the name Sherman, forms of which appeared in England during the Anglo-Saxon period, is unknown. According to some authorities, it stemmed from the occupation of wool stapler, or shears-man. Others believe the first bearer of the name to have been a cunning or knowing fellow, a sheer man. Or the name might have the same derivation as sheriff: a shire, or county, man. The initial written appearance of the name occurred in 1164, when an Anglo-Saxon monk named Sharman fled from the Council of Nottingham.[1]

The first Sherman to come to America was Edmond Sherman, a Puritan who in 1634 escaped from the religious tyranny of King Charles I. In 1636 Edmond Sherman returned to Dedham, in Essex County, England, but his sons, the Reverend John Sherman and Samuel Sherman, and his nephew, Captain John Sherman, remained in the New World. Eventually settling in Watertown, Massachusetts, Captain John produced descendants famous in American history. They included Roger Sherman, who signed the Declaration of Independence and the Constitution; Roger Minot Sherman, a participant in the Hartford Convention of 1814; William M. Evarts, who became secretary of state in 1877; Senator George Frisbie Hoar of Massachusetts; and Chauncey Depew, the president of the New York Central Railroad.

It took six generations, but Samuel, too, produced descendants of national stature. William Tecumseh Sherman became a noted general, his brother John a congressman, a senator, a secretary of the treasury, and a secretary of state.[2]

In an informal genealogy written when he was twenty-three years old, John Sherman noted that "in the Sherman family every one was a lawyer." For

1

thirty-seven years his great-grandfather, Daniel Sherman, presided over a probate court. His grandfather, Taylor, also served as a judge.

At first, Taylor's son Charles Robert Sherman, the father of the general and the senator, seemed destined to wander from this path. Born in Norwalk, Connecticut, on September 26, 1788, he was, John remembered, "a wild boy. . . . If any mischief was done in the town it was laid on him & Thaddeus Betts—a neighbors son—& a companion of father from boyhood up." Betts later became a Connecticut Supreme Court justice and a member of Congress.[3]

Charles Sherman never attended college. He was educated at the academy at Norwalk, there becoming familiar with Latin, Greek, and French. But the year 1810 would prove adventurous for him. Early in the year, after studying law in the office of a Mr. Chapman in Newtown, Connecticut, he was admitted to the bar, even though he had not yet reached his twenty-first birthday. Then, on May 8, he married Mary Hoyt, whom he had known in Norwalk since childhood. Mary was nine months his senior.[4]

The Hoyts, too, were an old family, going back in America seven generations and being among the first settlers of Norwalk. During the Revolutionary War the sons of the family split their allegiance, half supporting the king and half favoring the rebels. One son, Jesse, even accompanied the British through Norwalk, pointing out the patriot homes and churches that were to be burned. After the war, he wisely migrated to Nova Scotia.[5]

The Shermans tended to be lawyers, the Hoyts merchants. Early in life Isaac Hoyt, Mary Sherman's father, followed the usual occupation, but severe asthma forced him to seek a cure at sea. For twenty years he was the captain of a vessel. In 1804 he died at sea and was buried at Gibraltar.[6]

For a good reason neither John Sherman nor his brother ever publicly mentioned Isaac Hoyt's wife, their maternal grandmother, Mary Raymond Hoyt. In 1928 a genealogist hired by General Sherman's son, P. Tecumseh Sherman, could find out nothing about her, noting simply that she died after 1804. A history of the Raymond family published in 1970 also recorded nothing.[7]

Fortunately, however, a dedicated researcher, Francis F. Spies, has deposited in the Genealogy Room of the New York Public Library a typed copy of his unpublished three-volume study of tombstone inscriptions in Norwalk. It reveals that among those buried in the graveyard encircling St. Paul's Episcopal Church is Mary Raymond Hoyt, who died on October 1, 1828, at the age of seventy-three.[8]

In later life Mary Raymond Hoyt suffered mental incapacity. Although buried in Norwalk, she did not die there; the most educated guess is that she spent her last years in an asylum. Her exact ailment will never be known, but she transmitted whatever she had to the youngest of her two sons, Charles Hoyt, a prosperous New York merchant. One of General Sherman's sons and perhaps John Sherman later seemed to have suffered from the affliction.

With each other, the Shermans several times discussed the malady. In 1860 Ellen Ewing Sherman, General Sherman's wife, mentioned Uncle Charles's stay in "the Asylum." Two years later she reminded her husband of "the melancholy and depression to which your family is subject," particularly "your Uncle and Grandmother." Early in 1862 Ellen Sherman again wrote of the "more serious melancholy that afflicted your Uncle Charles." And in 1869, when Charles Hoyt died, John confided to his brother: "He had many good qualities, but his visionary recklessness dissipated his Fortune & led to his insanity. The latter is Hereditary in our branch of the Hoyt family."[9]

A student of the Sherman and Hoyt families can only guess at the nature of the affliction. It might have stemmed from Mary Raymond's parents, Eliakim Raymond and Hannah Street, who were second cousins (Hannah's maternal grandfather, John Raymond, was the brother of Eliakim's paternal grandfather, Samuel Raymond). This marriage might possibly have triggered a genetic weakness in the family.[10]

Late in the Revolutionary War the burning by the British of several coastal towns in Connecticut provided the catalyst that drew Charles R. Sherman west. In 1800, Connecticut allotted to the victims of these burnings a half million acres of its land in Huron and Erie counties in northern Ohio. Taylor Sherman was appointed one of the commissioners directing the surveys of this territory, then in possession of Indians. For his labors he received title to two sections of land. Enticed by this grant to his father, Charles R. Sherman left in July 1810 to look for a place in Ohio. He stopped in Zanesville, but finally selected Lancaster, a town of three hundred people southeast of Columbus in Fairfield County.[11]

In September 1811, Charles R. Sherman, having returned to Norwalk, departed with his wife and infant son, Charles Taylor Sherman, then six months old, for Lancaster. For twenty-one days the couple traveled, most of the time on horseback, carrying their baby on a pillow before them.

In Lancaster, Charles R. Sherman began the practice of law, rising, according to John Sherman, "with unexampled rapidity to the first ranks of the profession." In those days lawyers spent much of their time on horseback, for they covered the circuit, usually Marietta, Cincinnati, and Detroit.[12]

Charles Sherman was hardly established at Lancaster when the War of 1812 broke out. The British crossed the Canadian border and captured Detroit and the land around Lake Erie to the Maumee River. Indians still occupied most of Ohio. Until Captain Oliver Perry defeated the British on Lake Erie and General William Henry Harrison's victory at the Thames River in Canada, in September and October 1813, the West seemed at the mercy of the British and the Indians.

Charles R. Sherman's part in the war was limited to giving patriotic speeches and to serving as some sort of commissary. But like many settlers in the Old Northwest, he took a fancy to the gifted and literate Shawnee chief, Tecumseh, who had organized a confederation of Indians from the Great Lakes to the Gulf of Mexico and had been killed by the Americans at the Thames River. A daughter, Mary Elizabeth, had arrived just as the war began, but Charles Sherman was determined to name his next son, born on December 12, 1814, for the great chief. His wife, however, objected. She had named their first boy for her youngest brother, Charles Hoyt, and insisted on naming this one for her other brother, James. In 1816 the Shermans had another daughter, Amelia, and in

1818 a third, Julia. When the next boy came along, on February 8, 1820, Charles finally fulfilled his desire.[13]

After the death of Taylor Sherman in 1815, his wife, Elizabeth Stoddard, and daughter Elizabeth joined the family in Ohio. Throughout his life, Tecumseh, or "Cump" for short, never discussed Mary Raymond Hoyt, but he spoke with pride of this other grandmother. "Oh what a flood of memories come up at the name of Betsey Stoddard," he reminisced in 1886, "—daughter of the Revd. Mr. Stoddard, who preached three times every Sunday, and as often in between as he could cajole a congregation at ancient Woodbury, Conn." Betsey Stoddard

> came down from Mansfield to Lancaster, three days' hard journey to regulate the family of her son Judge Sherman, whose gentle wife was as afraid of Grandma as any of us boys. She never spared the rod or broom, but she had more square solid sense to the yard than any woman I ever saw. From her Charles, John and I inherit what little sense we possess. . . . If I could I would not awaken Grandmother Stoddard because she would be horrified at the backsliding of the servants of Christ.[14]

Nearly six feet tall and imposing looking, Betsey Stoddard remained a constant reminder of the family's religious tradition. In England, the Shermans had been Puritans, but in Connecticut they belonged to the Congregational church of the Reverend Anthony Stoddard, the Harvard graduate who was Betsey's great-grandfather. Both Judge Daniel Sherman and his father were deacons in Reverend Stoddard's church, and throughout her life Betsey Stoddard remained a devout Congregationalist.

The Hoyts, as shown by Mary Raymond Hoyt's burial in St. Paul's churchyard, were Episcopalians, but when Mary Sherman arrived in Lancaster she found no Episcopal church there. She therefore, John noted, "joined the Presbyterian church under the patronage of Rev. John Wright, who baptized all her children." When an Episcopal church was finally established in Lancaster, she became a member. Moving to Mansfield, Ohio, in the summer of 1844 at the urging of John, who lived there, she joined the Episcopal church there.[15]

For Charles and Mary Sherman five more children came. Lampson Parker Sherman was born in 1821, John in 1823, Susan in 1825, Hoyt in 1827, and Frances, or Fanny, in 1829. During these years Charles R. Sherman's fortunes skidded downward. In November 1813, President James Madison appointed him Collector of Internal Revenue for the Third District of Ohio. In that office he took for payment of taxes on such items as distilled spirits, salt, and sugar the notes of local banks, the only currency available in Ohio. But in July 1817, the government suddenly refused to accept these notes, demanding instead the bills of the recently chartered Bank of the United States. The loss fell heavily on Sherman's deputies, who held large amounts of local notes. Assuming this obligation, Charles Sherman mortgaged all of his property and spent the remainder of his life trying to pay off the debt.[16]

Within the wilderness called Ohio in the 1810s and 1820s, the Lancaster members of the bar excelled. One attorney, Philemon Beecher, had practiced law in the town since 1801, was a general in the militia, and lived in a large brick house in the center of town. Another lawyer, William Irvin, rode circuit with Charles Sherman.[17]

The most imposing of all was Thomas Ewing. The son of a Revolutionary War lieutenant, he had been born on December 28, 1789, in West Liberty, Virginia. Reared in the wilderness along the Muskingum River, where Indian raids were common, he was taught to read by an elder sister and studied the Bible so assiduously that he came to be known as the Bishop. Six feet tall with a massive head and broad shoulders, the young man attended the new college at Athens, Ohio, now Ohio University, from which he was graduated in May 1815. He then came to Lancaster, where he read law in Beecher's office.[18]

In Lancaster, Ewing found a wife as well as a profession. His future father-in-law, Hugh Boyle, had been born in County Donegal, Ireland, in 1773. Becoming involved in political troubles, he fled, reaching Virginia in 1791. Settling first in Martinsburg, he moved to Brownsville, Pennsylvania, where he met and married Eleanor Gillespie, whose half sister, Maria Gillespie, became the mother of the politician from Maine, James G. Blaine. He moved on to Chillicothe and finally to Lancaster, where he served as clerk of the Fairfield County Court of Common Pleas from 1803 to his death in 1848.[19]

The union of Hugh and Eleanor Boyle produced two daughters, Maria and Susan. When Eleanor Boyle died in 1805, a few months after the birth of her second daughter, her sister Susan, who despite being twenty years his junior had married Philemon Beecher, took in both girls and reared them. Although devoted to her father, Maria always referred to her Aunt Susan and her Uncle Philemon as Ma Beecher and Pa Beecher.[20]

Reading law in the back room of the Beecher house that constituted the office, Thomas Ewing would often gaze out the window at Maria. While he was tall and stately, she was small but very pretty. On January 7, 1820, in the parlor of the Beecher home, they were married by Father Edward Fenwick. Their first son, Philemon Beecher Ewing, was born that November 3.[21]

Like her parents, Maria Boyle Ewing was an ardent Catholic. "She was so staunch to what she believed the true faith," General Sherman later observed, "that I am sure that though she loved her children better than herself, she would have seen them die with less pang, than to depart from the 'Faith.' Mr. Ewing was a great big man, an intellectual giant, and looked down on religion as something domestic, something consoling which ought to be encouraged; and to him it made little difference whether the religion was Methodist, Presbyterian, Baptist, or Catholic, provided the acts were 'half as good' as their professions."[22] Destiny had in store for Maria a harsh blow, for she lived to see her son Thomas Ewing Jr. marry the daughter of a Presbyterian minister and convert to that religion.

As with the Shermans, the years brought more children to the Ewings, who lived in a stately house just up the block from the Shermans, on the hill overlooking the town. Added to Philemon were Ellen Boyle, born in 1824; Hugh Boyle, born in 1826; Thomas Jr., who arrived in 1829; Charles, born in 1835; and Maria Theresa, nicknamed Sis, who came along in 1837. Thomas Ewing loved all his children, but Ellen always possessed a special closeness to her father, who in 1827 lovingly described her as "a fat clumsy little puss."[23]

In 1823, meantime, good fortune smiled upon Charles R. Sherman. The state legislature appointed him one of the four judges of the Ohio Supreme Court. During winters the court met in Columbus, but at other times of the year each judge—accompanied, John Sherman remembered, "by a bevy of the leading lawyers of the state, all mounted on horseback and always ready for fun or frolic"—rode circuit around the state.[24]

Then, in 1829, tragedy hit the Sherman family. Charles Taylor Sherman was attending the college in Athens, and James was working in a store in Cincinnati. The rest of the children were either at home or at school. One day in June, Jane Sturgeon, a neighbor, came to the school, called out the Sherman children, and told them to go home. There they learned that their father was seriously ill. Away at Lebanon on circuit, he had taken his seat in the afternoon before suffering a severe chill. For three days he seemed to fight the fever, but on the fourth he grew much worse. James and a cousin, Henry Stoddard of Dayton, reached his bedside before he died on June 24. Mary Sherman arrived too late. Stoddard later told Cump that cholera had killed Charles, but the family always attributed his death to typhoid caused by exposure to the hot sun.

Charles Sherman died in debt, leading to the breakup of his family. His children went every which way. Charles Taylor Sherman had nearly completed his course in Athens and decided to study law in the office in Mansfield of his uncle, Jacob Parker, the husband of Charles Sherman's sister, Elizabeth. The oldest girl, Elizabeth, married William J. Reese, a graduate of the University of Pennsylvania who came west to practice law. Unable to make a living at it, he became a merchant. Though possessing slight military training, Reese rose to become the major general commanding the state militia and was called "General." John Sherman eventually went to Mount Vernon to live with his namesake, a merchant and cousin of his father.[25]

Of all the children, Lampson was shipped the farthest. Described by Ellen Ewing as a "pleasant, handsome boy, very shy and modest," he was sent to Cincinnati, where he was taken in by Charles R. Sherman's friend, Charles Hammond, a lawyer and the first editor and owner of the *Cincinnati Gazette*. Hammond would often come up to Columbus to attend court and would bring Lamp along so the family at Lancaster could see him. But years after Lampson informed one of Cump's daughters: "I don't think that I have ever seen him a dozen times since I was eight years old."[26]

In contrast to Lamp, Tecumseh, a flaming redhead, had a short trip to his new home. Taken in, but never formally adopted, by the Ewings, he moved up the block from his family's two-story brown frame house on the north side of Main Street to the large Ewing home on the corner of High and Main streets.

Welcomed into the family, Tecumseh was treated as an equal. Religion was among the first things attended to. In those days Lancaster contained no Catholic church, but a priest would come over at intervals from Somerset, just to the northeast, where Dominicans ran a college. During these trips to Lancaster, the priest invariably stayed at the Ewing home, sometimes for a week or so, holding classes for the children. At one of these, someone mentioned to Father Dominic Young that Cump had never been baptized. In reality, as John Sherman attested, all of the Sherman children had been baptized as Presbyterians by the Reverend John Wright, but as Father Young was leaving, someone ran down the block to ask Mary Sherman if Cump might be baptized by the priest. His mother having no objections, Cump was taken into the front parlor. Ellen, then five years old, stood in back of the group, in front of the mantelpiece, as Father Young asked the boy's name. Told it was Tecumseh, he pointed out that a scriptural or saint's name had to be used in the ceremony. Since it was St. William's Day, Tecumseh was baptized William. Ellen later thought the day was June 8, 1830, but Philemon's daughter, Ellen Ewing Brown, believed it to be June 25. After that, Cump always signed his name W. T. Sherman or William T. Sherman.[27]

After Charles Sherman's death, his relatives and friends helped his widow with money. From New York her wealthy uncle, Gould Hoyt, contributed $1,000, a large sum for that day. Stoddard, Parker, and Thomas Ewing gave smaller amounts. Ewing, "the almoner" of these funds, loaned the money out in Cincinnati at 10 percent a year, the proceeds going to Mary Sherman.[28]

Cump, meantime, became inseparable friends with Philemon Ewing, eight months his junior. The valley of the Hocking River, in which Lancaster nestled, was noted for its beauty. In winter the boys had snowball fights and went sliding on the ice. In summer they roamed the Hocking hills, fished, and swam. With great interest, they went down to the river and watched as the canal boats came in and unloaded their cargoes.

Phil and Cump spent one summer on the farm of Thomas Ewing's sister, Aunt Hannah Clark, just outside of Lancaster, where they grew watermelons. Long before dawn the two boys would rise, place their crop on the market wagon, and in the cool starlight ride to town to get a choice spot in the markethouse. Usually the boys slept as the horses jogged into town.

Their only other business venture failed. Sitting on the hillside, they noticed red sumac all about. Thinking that the plant was pronounced "shoemach," they convinced themselves that it was used to color the leather of the redtop boots then in style. They gathered it and took it to town, only to find that the bootmakers did not want it.

As the boys grew up, Thomas Ewing rose in his profession. Admitted to practice before the United States Supreme Court in 1829, he joined the nation's most eminent lawyers. Then, in 1831, he garnered a choice plum. The Ohio legislature elected him a United States senator. A Whig who loved Henry Clay and Daniel Webster and hated Andrew Jackson, Ewing spent most of his time in Washington. But when he was home, he was always up late, working in his office, which was off by itself at the end of the yard. One night he asked Phil and Cump to stay up with him to tend the fire as he worked. To entertain themselves the boys bought and began to read by the firelight three small volumes bound in red leather and entitled *The Spanish Cavalier*, a blood-and-thunder novel about battles and ghosts, all of which they thought they saw when Ewing sent them outside for wood. The next day the boys returned the volumes to the bookdealer, who to their relief cheerfully took them back.[29]

Years later Sherman, with great frankness, shared with his friend Major Henry S. Turner, then entertaining Phil in St. Louis, his thoughts about the Ewing sons, Philemon, Hugh, and Tom. Hugh was "of good parts but lacks industry & system," he revealed. "He is likely to get into Company to drink & smoke to excess especially if the tide sets him that way—. . . . The eldest son whom you saw is very different, being more fixed in his notions & habits, actually older than the Old Gentleman himself. . . . Hugh has some of the wit of his father but not much of his industry. The third son Thom is regarded as the brightest but for my part the one now in St. Louis was always my favorite."[30]

Even at this age, Cump and John were becoming the closest of the Sherman children. During his stay with his father's cousin, John engaged in some wild escapades, including carrying a dead sheep into a classroom and placing it on the teacher's seat. By 1835 Cousin John and his wife had children of their own, and young John came to believe that the wife no longer wished to put up with him. He returned to Lancaster. John remembered:

> My brother, William Tecumseh, was three years my senior, and he and his associates of his own age rather looked down upon their juniors. Still, I had a good deal of intercourse with him, mainly in the way of advice on his part. At that time he was a steady student, quiet in his manner and easily moved by sympathy or affection. I was regarded as a wild reckless lad, eager in controversy and ready to fight. No one could then anticipate that he was to be a great warrior and I a plodding lawyer and politician. I fired my first gun over his shoulder. He took me with him to carry the game, mostly squirrels and pigeons.[31]

At the school run by two brothers, Samuel and Mark Howe, John displayed his temper. One day, during an argument over geometry, Sam Howe hit John's right hand with a ferule. Mustering all his force, the boy struck his teacher with his left hand. Expelled from school, he was allowed back only after pleading by his mother and his sister, Elizabeth Reese. At school the future politician displayed another characteristic. "John was very fond of the girls," Ellen Ewing later recorded, "& paid great attention to them by turns. He really was gallant and a gentleman at heart, as manifested in many ways at that early day."[32]

Philemon, Cump, and Ellen also attended, Ellen later wrote, "a select & quite expensive French school. . . . I do not remember how often these lessons were nor whether they conflicted with the school of the Howes." But Ellen did recall that on the morning of visiting day Cump and Phil suddenly became sick and stayed in bed. "Father gave them each a dose of medicine certainly not as a curative, therefore it must have been as a punishment or a joke—He treated the affair as a good joke & I think he did not press them to study French after that."

The fall of 1834 and spring of 1835 saw Cump working as a rodman on a party surveying from the Great Ohio Canal south through Lancaster and the Hocking Valley to the Ohio River. One of four boys selected from the Howe school for the job, he helped mark two routes, receiving for his toil a silver half dollar for each day's work. "His being called to start out on business or to work before daylight," Ellen noted, "made a great impression on me and I thought he was a great fellow because he liked it."[33]

—— II ——

As a United States Senator, Thomas Ewing tried to look after his friends. In 1835 he appointed to the United States Military Academy at West Point, New York, young William Irvin, the son of Judge William Irvin, Maria Ewing's uncle by marriage. Approaching sixteen, the age required for admission, Philemon showed no interest in the military academy. As religious as his sister Ellen, who, when her mother was keeping her father company in Washington, spent winters with the Dominican Sisters at Somerset, Phil briefly toyed with the idea of entering the priesthood, but he decided instead to study law.

Philemon's choice made things easier for Ewing, who was now able to fulfill a request of Charles R. Sherman. "It was his fathers wish," the senator informed the secretary of war in a letter regarding Cump on August 1, 1835, "often expressed before his death that he should receive an education which would fit him for the public service in the army or navy—the situation of cadet at West Point coincides better with the wishes of his mother than that of midshipman in the navy." Ewing praised his foster son as "a stout athlete . . . a good Latin, Greek & French scholar & very good . . . in the Mathematics."[34]

Appointed to the academy on March 4, 1836, Sherman left Lancaster for West Point, via Washington, in late May. Ellen Ewing later noted of the new cadet's final meeting with Mary Sherman: "His mother was with him alone in the parlor at our house for a long time before he started."[35]

Sherman found the journey to Washington "pretty fatiguing." He was the only passenger as the stagecoach crawled over bad roads to Zanesville. From there he went to Wheeling, Virginia (now West Virginia), and then, one of eight passengers crowded into a small coach, to Frederick, Maryland, in a pouring rain. Not trusting the newly built railroad, Sherman there climbed aboard a two-horse hack to Washington, reaching Gadsby's Hotel in the capital about nine o'clock in the evening of June 1.

The next morning Sherman found Thomas Ewing "boarding with a mess of Senators at Mrs. Hill's, corner of Third and C Streets." Spending a week in Washington, he "saw more of the place in that time than I ever have since in the many years of residence there." Peering for a full hour through the wood railing around the White House, he spied President Jackson, looking smaller than Sherman expected, pacing over the gravel walk on the north side of the White House. He also saw Vice President Martin Van Buren, Webster, Clay, and John C. Calhoun.

Departing for West Point, Sherman stayed a day in Philadelphia visiting the Reese family. Then it was on to New York City, where Cump spent a week with his mother's brothers, Charles Hoyt of Brooklyn Heights and James I. Hoyt of White Street, both prosperous merchants. He also met Uncle James's beautiful daughter, Louisa, and her wealthy husband, William Scott, "a neatly-dressed young fellow, who looked on me as an untamed animal just caught in the far West—'fit food for gunpowder,' and good for nothing else."[36]

— III —

In June 1836, when Sherman registered in the office of Lieutenant Charles F. Smith, the adjutant of the military academy, he was stepping into a new world. A visitor to today's spacious campus would find the West Point of the 1830s confined. Cadets roomed together regardless of class in two stone buildings. Half lived in the North Barracks, a four-story rectangular structure with plain walls. The South Barracks was three stories and also contained offices and the officers' quarters. "The rooms in the South Barracks were severely cold," remembered Professor Albert E. Church, who supervised the teaching of mathematics at the academy, "and many a winter's night were we obliged to sit at our tables with blankets at our backs, scorching on one side and freezing on the other."[37]

The remaining buildings were few. Most of the academic departments and the library were in a two-story structure directly west of the South Barracks. In 1838 a fire destroyed one section of the building. Farther west was another two-story, plain stone building. On its first floor rested the cadet mess. The upper story contained the drawing academy.

Cadets at West Point hardly got rich. Their monthly pay was sixteen dollars. For rations they received an additional twelve. For years Mr. Cozzens, whose family ran the hotel, fed the cadets for ten dollars a month each. "Give young men plenty of first-rate bread, butter and potatoes," he preached, "and they will require little meat, and never complain of that." In accord with this philosophy, mess fare was plain.

The uniform of the cadets remained almost the same throughout Sherman's lifetime. The cloth pants contained sides trimmed with black silk braid and a front decorated with an Austrian knot. In cold weather cadets wore any overcoats they wished. On parade in winter they looked as motley as any military group ever assembled.[38]

From its inception in 1802 to the turn of the century, the course of study at the academy changed little. Emphasis was put on mathematics. Engineering and military tactics were taught in Sherman's time by Dennis H. Mahan, natural philosophy by William H. C. Bartlett, and French by Claudius Berard. Most of the assistants were cadets of the upper classes. Without teaching experience and with their own assignments to worry about, many were inadequate.[39]

While few things at the academy seemed to change, one innovation was destined to plague Sherman. Until 1831 or 1832 cadets were allowed a limitless number of demerits. The system was then changed so that two hundred in any single year brought dismissal.[40] At least once during his stay at the academy Sherman approached the limit.

To Hugh, who later attended the academy, Sherman described his baptism there:

> When a cadet first lands on the wharf at West Point the first thing he sees is a soldier with his dress and sword and a slate in his hand—whereon he records the name of every person who lands—he then toils up a winding road that mounts to the plain whereon are arranged the Barracks, and the professors buildings—to the former he bends his steps and of the first person he meets, he inquires for the "adjutant's office"—This is a magnificent stone building beyond the Barracks on the second floor of which is the office sought. He knocks, enters and sees a fat individual with some clerks around—To the fat man . . . he makes known that he is a *new* cadet.

After the fledgling deposited "his spare cash" in the treasurer's office, he was shown his small room, which he shared with "half a dozen others." Then he met the superintendent, "who is King, yea Emperor, in those dominions." He was issued an arithmetic book, a lamp, a bucket, a broom, and two blankets, "the sum total of a Plebes estate whereon he has to build his fortune." Soon came the command:

> "Turn out new cadets." He tumbles out of his room runs down stairs and first meets his comrades for life, country boys from Maine to Louisiana and from Iowa to Florida—he has hardly a chance to observe these things well before he hears the word to "Fall in" which he obeys instinctively—along with the rest and is marched round the corner of the South Barracks to view for the first time the evening parade.
>
> Then he will feel the beauty of Military parade and show—the fine music, the *old cadets* marching by companies, stepping as one man—all forming in line—he hears the echo of some commands—hears the roar of the evening gun and sees the flag fall and the parade dismissed—then his highest ambition is to be an *old* cadet.[41]

From his earliest days at West Point, Sherman flouted its rules but took to its academic life. At first his class contained about 115 cadets. "There are some in our class who have graduated at other institutions," he informed Thomas Ewing in September. "Some who have studied Mathematics but little and some who have been studying this same course for the last two or three years. . . . Our lessons are such as to keep us studying. Since we began to study three belonging to our class (I am sorry although obliged to say) have deserted & about 20 others are thinking of resigning for fear they should be found deficient in January & dismissed."[42]

The hazing and segregation of plebes later associated with West Point were absent in 1836. For all of his four years at the academy, Sherman mingled with men of all classes. The class of 1837 contained several cadets destined for fame.

Three—Braxton Bragg of North Carolina, Jubal A. Early of Virginia, and John C. Pemberton—became Confederate generals. Always drawn to Sherman, Bragg, a top student of mathematics and engineering, prided himself on being the ugliest man in the corps, a boast to which his plain, long face attested. He was noted for his nightly visits to Benny Havens's tavern and food emporium, two miles from the barracks. Pemberton, on the other hand, was handsome, with a perfect grade in drawing that led to the conclusion he was a better artist than soldier. A Philadelphian, he married a girl from Norfolk and linked his fortunes to those of the South. The northerners in the class included the dashing Joseph Hooker, whom Sherman never liked, and Edward Townsend, long the adjutant general of the army.

The junior class contained three men later important to Sherman. Second in the class was the Creole perfectionist Pierre G.T. Beauregard of Louisiana. An assistant teacher of French, he looked French and acted French. Seventeenth in the class was William F. Barry of New York, for years Sherman's chief of artillery. Further down the list was someone Sherman had known since childhood, Irvin McDowell of Columbus. Nicknamed the "fat boy," McDowell would lead Sherman into his first battle.[43]

In addition to William Irvin, with whom Sherman roomed for three years, the class directly above his contained three cadets who would play roles in his life. Henry W. Halleck of New York ranked third in the class. Studious and scholarly, his owlish face made him look old beyond his years. In the middle of the class stood Sherman's lifelong friend, Edward O. C. Ord. In his hometown of Cumberland, Maryland, people believed Ord to be the grandson of King George IV of England and a Mrs. Fitzherbert, whose marriage Parliament had refused to sanction because she was a Catholic. Ord's father, their son, had studied to become a Jesuit priest but had left the order, served as an officer in the War of 1812, and married the daughter of a wealthy landowner in Cumberland. During Sherman's first year at the academy, Ord came within thirteen demerits of being thrown out. The third friend gave at West Point no indication of his ability. Edward R. S. Canby of Kentucky graduated next to last in his class, but during the Civil War he proved competent and reliable. In 1873, his murder by Modoc Indians at a peace conference shocked the nation.[44]

Sherman often talked about the members of his own class. He remembered Job Lancaster of Ohio, "6 feet 5 inches in his stockings, a yard across his shoulders, weighing 260 pounds, with hands hard with toil on his father's farm." Despite never having seen an arithmetic book before arriving at the academy, he graduated seventh in his class. A year later he was struck by lightning in Florida and killed. Then there was Stewart Van Vliet of New York, like Ord never much of a general but Sherman's lifelong friend.[45]

Even then, the cadets talked about a gentle, slow-moving member of Sherman's class, George H. Thomas. Sherman later romanticized:

> He came to us from the region of the dismal swamp of Virginia,—Newsome's Depot—which we in boyish mischief translated into Nuisance Depot. He could blush like a girl, but never resented the insult to his

birthplace by angry words or gestures. As a cadet, his life was normal and uneventful but it was told of him that, during the Nat Turner insurrection, he had displayed a courage which attracted the notice of General Jackson, which secured him his appointment to West Point.[46]

Thomas's actual role during the insurrection amounted to helping his mother, brothers, and sisters hide. And his appointment came not from Jackson but from Congressman John Y. Mason.[47] But after the Civil War there were those who called him its greatest general.

Rooming with Bill Irvin brought out the worst in Sherman. Beginning his second year at the academy, Cump wrote Phil, now attending the college (now Miami University) in Oxford, Ohio:

> There is such a perfect system of cooking here although strictly prohibited . . . that is not a dozen in the corps except the plebes that are not good cooks. It would do you good to see one of our night meals; five or six fellows around a pan of smoking potatoes swimming in butter each furnished with a knife or flat piece of pine going it real dutch fashion all eating out of the same dish or rather pan in which they were cooked.

For these nightly feasts, roasted in the fireplaces in their rooms, Irvin got provisions any way he could. Early in Sherman's plebe year Irvin was arrested for taking food from the mess hall. A year later, on a dark night, he was on his way to Benny Havens's to buy oysters and beefsteak when he stumbled off a precipice and ended up in the hospital. Reported by the doctor for being off limits, he was punished with six extra Sundays of guard duty. But the penalty failed to stop Irvin. "Bill, another fellow cadet, and myself went to Benny's last evening," Sherman reported to Philemon in November 1837, "and got about a half bushel of oysters in the shell which together with potatoes bread and butter made an extraordinary supper. Our currency is neither hard money nor is it paper but dollar bills in the shape of blankets."[48]

William S. Rosecrans of Ohio well remembered Sherman's antics as a cadet:

> Sherman was two classes above me, but he was one of the most popular and brightest fellows in the academy. I remember him as a bright-eyed, red-headed fellow, who was always prepared for a lark of any kind, and who usually had a grease-spot on his pants. These spots came from our clandestine midnight feasts, at which Sherman usually made the hash. He was considered the best hash-maker at West Point, and this, in our day, was a great honor. The food given the cadets was then furnished by contract; it was cheap and poor; and I sometimes think that the only meals we relished were our midnight hash lunches. . . . After the materials were gotten, one of the boys who had a retired room, where there was least danger of discovery, would whisper invitations to the rest to meet him that night for a hash feast. When we got there "Old Cump" would mash the potatoes and mix them with

pepper, salt, and butter in such a way as to make the most appetizing dish. This he would cook in a stew-pan over the fire—we had grates in those days—and when it was done we would eat it sizzling hot on our bread, which we had toasted. As we did so we would tell stories and have a jolly good time; and Sherman was one of the best story-tellers of the lot. He was by no means a goody-goody boy, and he was one of those fellows who used to go down to Benny Havens's of the dark night at the risk of expulsion to eat oysters and have a good time.[49]

Professor Mahan once described Cadet Sherman as

eager, impetuous, restless. If he wasn't at work he was in mischief. If, while explaining something to his class at the black-board, I heard any slight disturbance, denoting some fun, I was seldom wrong, in turning round, in holding up my finger to Mr. Sherman. But one was more than repaid for any slight annoyance of this kind, by his irrepressible good nature, and by the clear thought and energy he threw into his work.[50]

Sherman did well in his studies. In January 1837, after his first semester at West Point, he ranked twelfth in mathematics and fourteenth in French among the ninety-seven cadets still left in his class. After the general examinations in June 1837, he stood thirteenth in mathematics, with a score of 174.1 out of a possible 200, and fourteenth in French, with 93 out of 100. Overall he ranked ninth. By June 1838, after a year of drawing, in which he achieved a perfect score, Sherman jumped to sixth in his class. Among his classmates, Van Vliet ranked seventh, Richard S. Ewell, later a Confederate general, thirteenth, and Thomas fifteenth.[51]

In later years, explaining why, unlike Van Vliet and Thomas, he remained a cadet private during his days at West Point, Sherman pointed to his demerits, which, he insisted, averaged 150 a year. Actually, his demerits totaled 109 for his first year, 66 for his second, 57 for his third, and 148 for his fourth, an average of just 95. But unlike Van Vliet, Halleck, and Beauregard, who went entire years with no demerits, Sherman seemed to go out of his way to amass them, especially in his final year. He wore dirty clothes, talked in ranks, loitered about during study hours, and failed to police his room. He missed roll calls and was in other rooms when he should have been in his own. Once he left church without permission. Another time he neglected to salute an officer. On a third occasion he saluted improperly when passing in review on parade.[52] One of the youngest members of his class, Sherman also seemed to be among the most immature.

During the summer of 1838 Sherman was able to go home for the first time in two years. Ellen, now fourteen years old, described him as looking "very grand" in his uniform. Taylor, now practicing law, and Mary Hoyt Sherman came down to see him. With Lamp, Sherman went to Oxford to visit Phil, then to Columbus to see Thomas Ewing, who had failed to win reelection as senator. Next it was on to Mansfield and from there his first visit ever to his father's brother, Uncle Daniel Sherman. "He is a very fine old man," Cump wrote John, "but I do not think he resembles father (if you recollect him)."[53]

Returning to the academy, Sherman found in the classes below his—and later, in the one destined to arrive in 1839— more cadets whose lives would intertwine with his. In the class of 1841 were the ill-fated Nathaniel Lyon, whom Sherman later described as a "white-haired, white-eyebrowed, lymphatic boy, who didn't seem to have energy enough to make a man," and Don Carlos Buell, first Sherman's friend, then his enemy. In that class also was Sherman and Ellen's beloved Julius P. Garesché, who in a horrible episode was decapitated by a cannonball at Stones River in December 1862. The class of 1842 contained James Longstreet, the Confederate general destined late in life to become Sherman's warm friend. The class of 1843, not yet arrived, would include George Deshon of Connecticut, who despite graduating second in his class spurned military life, became a Paulist, and participated in Sherman's private funeral service, and a plodding cadet from Ohio who did abominably in French. His name was Ulysses S. Grant.[54]

Opening his third year at the academy, Sherman felt overwhelmed. In October, he lamented to Phil:

I wish to God we could be as independent as you, that is recite when we please, and study when we please, and what we please, but we drill & recite all day, bone which means in our vocabulary study all night or take the "consequences" curse them. I have been cursing for the last month all Philosophers & all Chemists that ever did exist—not the philosophers but our Academic board. They have selected the most difficult text books they could find. Our Mechanics contain 400 and odd pages which we will be examined upon next January every little law is deduced Mathematically. I ought not to have included all Chemists for our professor is a perfect Gentleman renders Chemistry as interesting as *possible*. I begin to agree with the cadet who gave the following toast—some time since. "West Point tis distance lends enchantment—to the view."[55]

What Sherman believed to be true in October, he knew to be so in May. He told Phil:

This Academic year is thank God rapidly drawing to a close, and when it will have passed I think I will be safe in saying that it was a little the hardest time I have ever before experienced or ever expect to. Indeed the Second Class course has always enjoyed the reputation of being a little the "D—est of the d—d" and well does it deserve the title but one consolation is that it will be followed by a year a little more instructive and amusing. Heretofore we have been attending to the duties of a soldier but shortly will be instructed in the theoretical and practical duties of the officer.

Still, when the year ended, Sherman, of the forty-six cadets remaining in his class, ranked seventh in natural philosophy, sixth in chemistry, third in drawing, and sixth overall. At this stage Thomas stood seventeenth, Ewell fifteenth, and Van Vliet eighth.[56]

Sherman found his final year at the academy far different from his third. "We have very easy times nowadays," he reported to Phil in December 1839, "and have had all this academic year the studies being very easy as also the military duty." After the January examinations, Sherman found himself sixth in mineralogy, sixth in ethics, and fourth in engineering among the forty-four members of his class. Of the seventy-three cadets in the plebe class, Grant ranked twenty-third in mathematics and sixty-sixth in French.[57]

Meantime, John was engaged in his own adventures. In 1837, at the age of fourteen, he began working as a junior rodman on a crew surveying the Muskingum River from Zanesville to Marietta. But when the panic of that year halted the project, John turned to law. In Mansfield he began studying in the office of Taylor and Uncle Jacob Parker. John considered Parker to be "perhaps the best land lawyer and special pleader in that part of Ohio." But he stuttered so badly that he could not appear in court. Taylor was also developing a lucrative practice collecting debts for eastern merchants. But he was shy and contested few cases. Young John therefore found himself arguing cases in court for both of his relatives.[58]

John's selection of a profession perplexed Cump. "It would be my last choice," he advised his brother. "Every body studies Law nowadays and to be a Lawyer without being exceedingly eminent which it is to be hoped you will be some day is not a sufficient equivalent for the risk and immense study and labor."[59]

In his last examinations at West Point, in June 1840, Sherman did exceedingly well. He ranked twelfth in his class in infantry tactics, eighth in artillery, seventh in both engineering and ethics, and fourth in mineralogy. His French and drawing grades were each 96 out of a possible 100 points.

But throughout his final year Sherman scoffed at discipline. With 148 demerits he ranked in conduct two hundred and sixteenth out of 233 cadets. Translated into points and added to his other grades, these demerits pulled Sherman down. Receiving but 205 out of 300 possible points for conduct, he amassed a total of 1,832.3 points for the year and ranked sixth in his class. In contrast, Van Vliet, who received no demerits during his last three years at West Point, scored 297.5 points in conduct. Well below Sherman in every academic discipline, Van Vliet was thus able to pull up to ninth in class standing. Even Thomas, perpetually ridiculed for slowness, accumulated but 21 demerits. His 278.3 points in conduct enabled him to finish twelfth in the class.

For his behavior Sherman paid dearly. Instead of being recommended for the engineers, considered the army's elite branch, Sherman upon graduation was forced to choose from among the artillery, infantry, or ordnance.[60]

Just before graduation, Sherman again showed his immaturity. Visiting Ewell's room, he was reported absent from quarters for an hour and a half. His punishment, three Saturday afternoons of guard duty, meant that he would be detained at the academy after graduation. Sherman appealed to the superintendent, Major Richard Delafield, and the punishment was changed to five demerits.[61]

Just before graduation, Thomas Ewing and Phil, now reading law in his father's office, visited Sherman at West Point. With the country in the midst of the Log Cabin presidential campaign, Thomas Ewing was stumping for the Whig, General William Henry Harrison, who was challenging the Democratic president, Martin Van Buren. The Ewings found the academy a beehive of activity. The plebes had just arrived, the second class was about to go on furlough, and the graduating class was preparing for commencement.

From the academy father and son headed down the Hudson. "The night of our arrival in NY City," Phil informed his mother, "Father addressed some two or 3 thousand Whigs at the dedication of a *log cabin* in the heart of the city. . . . We dined and passed a pleasant afternoon at Mr C Hoyts in Brooklyn."[62]

Graduating on July 1, 1840, Second Lieutenant Sherman left West Point. He visited Ellen, for the past two years a student at the Convent of the Visitation in Georgetown, in the District of Columbia. He then went on to Lancaster, where he whiled away two months. Late in the summer he finally received orders to report to Fort Columbus on Governor's Island in New York Harbor. From there he was to be shipped to Florida, the scene of an Indian war.[63]

On the way to Governor's Island, Sherman decided to visit his friends still at West Point. Discovered in the cadet barracks, he was arrested for violating the rule prohibiting the association of officers and cadets. Delafield recommended that he be court-martialed, but Sherman's pen saved him. "I do not think I thought of regulations at all," he explained to Delafield, "but acted in accordance with my feelings, which prompted me to do a common & friendly act, bid my friends a farewell upon parting with some perhaps forever." Satisfied with the explanation, the secretary of war dropped the charges against Sherman.[64]

At Fort Columbus, Sherman was anxious to leave. "I have a natural curiosity to see strange places and people," he wrote Maria Boyle Ewing, "both of which exist in Florida. Also I wish to pay the debts I was compelled in common with all graduating to contract as soon as possible. This I can do by staying in Florida one year whereas it would take two or three here or at adjoining military post." His regiment, the Third Artillery, had been fighting in Florida for three years. For companionship, Sherman was taking along "a most beautiful black pointer."[65]

Sailing first to Savannah and next to St. Augustine, now commanded by Bragg, Sherman then boarded a little steamer that took him down the east coast of Florida. Arriving off the bar of the Indian River, he transferred to a whaleboat, which chugged inland. A smaller vessel ferried him into a lagoon and across to Fort Pierce. Met on the tiny wharf by two of the post officers and the surgeon, Sherman walked up a steep sand bluff to the fort, whose buildings consisted of logs.[66] The twenty-year-old lieutenant had entered the strange universe of the regular army.

2

Beside the Still Waters

— I —

THE SEMINOLE WAR in Florida was an intermittent series of minor incidents, preparing its participants for neither the Mexican War nor the Civil War. Hot sun, fever, and swarms of mosquitoes in the summer limited activity to the cooler months, and even then guiding small boats around the Everglades proved too arduous to be sustained for long.

During the prolonged periods of inactivity, Sherman and the others occupied themselves as best they could. They speared sharks, trolled for redfish, fished for sheepshead and mullet, and hunted deer and wild turkeys. The members of the Third Artillery also caught in nets large green turtles. These were kept alive until cut up for steaks, providing relief from the usual army fare of low-grade Florida beef, barreled pork, and beans. " I do not recall in my whole experience," Sherman related, "a spot on earth where fish, oysters, and green turtles so abound as at Fort Pierce, Florida."[1]

These fruits of the sea provided gifts when visiting. Captain Erasmus D. Keyes remembered Sherman bringing down

> two fat turtles and some fine oysters as a present for our captain. I had not met Sherman before, though we belonged to the same regiment. At that time he was thin and spare, but healthy, cheerful, loquacious, active, and communicative to an extraordinary degree. . . . He gave me a good idea of the country and described the difficulties of campaigning in the swamps and jungles, where the Seminole Indians had so long evaded pursuit.[2]

In Florida, Sherman believed himself "cast into a new world. The ground is different," he explained to Phil, "and all the vegetation—They boast of the largest rattlesnakes, alligators, sharks &c—cranes & pelicans on the coast and we have been waiting for a proper breeze to sail down to the bay to spear sharks. . . . We live here in a most primitive style. Log cabin thatched with palmetto—rough bedstead table & chair constitute our whole—these are ornamented by fawn skins—feathers & wings of birds & the head & teeth of the shark the nose of the saw fish skin of rattlesnakes & the like." The fort consisted of three rows of cabins, two parallel to each other and the third perpendicular to the others. Like blockhouses constructed during the Civil War, each cabin contained holes from which to fire out at an approaching enemy. "So if the Indians were to take a notion of a very dark night to pounce upon us we might get the worst of it, but we rely upon their cowardice."[3]

Sherman's most exciting adventure in Florida came in May 1841, when he was ordered to bring in the Seminole chief Coacoochee, or Wild Cat. Riding into the Indian camp, Sherman soon faced the handsome young leader. Preparing to make a grand entrance into Fort Pierce, the chief washed in a pond and dressed. He put on several vests, including one containing a bullet hole and bloodstains above the pocket. Sherman assumed Wild Cat had killed its owner. Finding a bill in the pocket, "the rascal had the impudence to ask me to give him silver coin for that dollar."

All attempts at negotiation between the Seminole chief and the army failed. After Colonel William Jenkins Worth threatened, Sherman told Phil, to "string up" Coacoochee, the Indian finally agreed to move his people west. But his answer to Worth might have been uttered by any of hundreds of Indian chiefs:

> I was once a boy; then I saw the white man afar off. I hunted in these woods, first with a bow and arrow; then with a rifle. I saw the white man, and was told he was my enemy. I could not shoot him as I would a wolf or a bear; yet like these he came upon me; horses, cattle, and fields, he took from me. He said he was my friend; he abused our women and children, and told us to go from the land. Still he gave me his hand in friendship; we took it; whilst taking it, he had a snake in the other; his tongue was forked; he lied, and stung us. . . . I was put in prison; I escaped. I have been again taken; you have brought me back; I am here; I feel the irons in my heart.[4]

From Florida, Sherman observed the successful career of his stepfather. Appointed secretary of the treasury by President Harrison, Thomas Ewing almost immediately proposed the reestablishment of the Bank of the United States. Scoffing, Cump lumped "bankers brokers & hangers on" into one group. "If one ever assisted an honest man without exaction & usury," he complained to John, "I would like to hear of it. . . . Self interest is the only motive." Ewing's time in office proved brief, for Harrison died on April 4, 1841, and the secretary resigned to protest the policies of the new president, John Tyler.[5]

Promoted to first lieutenant, Sherman was ordered in December 1841 to St. Augustine. The oldest town in the United States, it contained, in addition to old American families, numerous Spaniards, whose daughters, Sherman teased Ellen, were "ignorant but very pretty, with beautiful hair and eyes." The girls had thus far enticed between a dozen and twenty army officers into marriage. Watching the beautiful Spanish women at a gathering at the barracks one evening, Sherman vowed to "make an attempt to learn the Spanish dance."[6]

As much as Sherman admired the looks of the women in St. Augustine, he detested its people. As he informed Phil in February 1842,

> The spirit & enthusiasm were for the first part of the campaign too warm & unnatural to last and is now resulting in every body becoming thoroughly tired. It is not ended by a d——d sight but about as near to it as we can come unless a population be got to fight for themselves, not only to repel the attacks of the maurauding bands but to follow up & drive them out of their settlements—this the way in which the indians were always conquered in the west should have been done here but the citizens are a most dastardly cowardly set and have never made a shadow of defence or attack no matter how few or insignificant party of indians there may have been.[7]

The spring and summer of 1842 brought to the Third Artillery a welcome change. Transferred first to Fort Morgan, at Mobile Point, Alabama, the regiment was next sent to Fort Moultrie on Sullivans Island, at the entrance to Charleston harbor. "We are all here now," Sherman wrote Phil in August. "Three companies with a Colonel, his adjutant, two captains, one doctor and six young lieutenants with nothing to do but keep our men in good discipline and abuse Congress for their economy and threats to reduce the Army."[8]

The eleven officers who ate at the Fort Moultrie mess in 1842 and 1843 were capable enough to conduct a war successfully. "It resembled," recollected Keyes, "a garden in which there were many young trees covered all over with blossoms. I was the oldest of all, and highest in rank, being a captain, and consequently called old." Of the others Sherman, "then as bright as the burning bush" and an incessant talker, became a four-star general and commander of the army. Bragg, "morbid" and "vitriolic," became a Confederate full general. Thomas, a teller of "humorous stories," John F. Reynolds, who died at Gettysburg, Thomas W. Sherman, a man of "morbid sullenness" who lost a leg at Port Hudson, Louisiana, in 1863, and Keyes became major generals. But most of the eleven died young. Writing in a San Francisco paper in 1879, Keyes lamented that only he, Sherman, Colonel Henry B. Judd of the class of 1839 at West Point, and Colonel William Austine of the class of 1838 still lived—"the ruthless sickle of death has clipped all the others."[9]

Of the eleven, Bragg was the most unpredictable. Sherman recalled a Fourth of July celebration at the fort during which John A. Stuart, the fiery editor of the *Charleston Mercury*, referred to North Carolina as a "strip of land lying between two states." Indignant at this affront to his home state, Bragg challenged Stuart to a duel. Only the peacemaking of Sherman and Reynolds stopped it. "I think I knew Bragg as well as any living man," Sherman later observed, "appreciated his good qualities, and had charity for his weaknesses. His heart was never in the Rebel cause."[10]

Though Sherman and several of the others came from the North, none of them questioned the plantation slavery they saw around Charleston. Indeed, when Keyes's wife could not find a cook, her husband bought for $350 "one wench, aged 23 years. . . . No sooner was my purchase known," observed Keyes, "than I was admitted to the society of Charleston with a stamp of merit above my value."[11]

Like Keyes, the popular and lively Lieutenant Sherman found himself mingling with the elite of Charleston, many of whom left the disease-ridden city during the summer to vacation on Sullivans Island. Twice during the latter part of the Civil War Sherman's old South Carolina friends wrote him decrying his cruelty toward the people he once loved. The first letter came to Sherman, then nearing Atlanta, in 1864 from Mrs. Annie Gilman Bowen, the daughter of Caroline Howard Gilman, the author of dozens of volumes of poems and women's stories. Sherman responded:

> Your welcome letter of June 18 came to me here amid the sound of battle, and, as you say, little did I dream when I knew you playing as a schoolgirl on Sullivan's Island beach that I should control a vast army pointing like the swarm of Alaric toward the plains of the South. Why, oh, why is this?
>
> If I know my own heart, it beats as warmly as ever toward those kind and generous families that greeted us with such warm hospitality in days past, but still present in memory; and today were Frank and Mrs. Porcher, or Eliza Gilman, or Mary Lamb, or Margaret Blake, the Barksdales, the Quashes, indeed, any and all of our cherished circle, their children or even their children's children, to come to me as of old, the stern feelings of duty would melt as snow before the genial sun, and I believe I would strip my own children that they might be sheltered; and yet they call me barbarian, vandal, a monster, and all the epithets that language can invent that are significant of malignity and hate.[12]

At Savannah a half year later Sherman again reminisced about his Carolina friends, especially the young ladies. To Mrs. Simeon Hawkins Draper, he wrote:

> I was much pleased to receive at the hand of your son Hamilton Hawkins your kind letter of Jan 4. I had not seen him since he was a little fair haired boy of 10 years in 1845, and now he is a tall fine handsome looking officer. . . . Indeed it feels strange to me to lead a large army through the Land, and ride through the streets of Savannah as its enemy. . . . You and I remember how Bragg used to ridicule the pretensions of the "Mac tabs" of Charleston to dominion over us, how he resented their pretensions to excellence over us of ruder habits and born in distant lands and now forsooth he joins his fortunes to them, demands that our Country shall sink into ignominy at the demands of

those Self Same, Self Constituted Rulers. . . . But I know when the truth is made manifest, that our Country will rejoice at its escape from the doom prepared for us. And that even our Old Charleston friends, the McBeths, the Hayeses, the Barksdales . . . etc will praise us for rescuing them. So terrible however is the Animosity to South Carolina that I fear my old attachment to Mary Lamb, Mary Johnson, the pretty Miss North and others of the Charleston girls will not hold back the Strong Arms and Eager Minds that led to her destruction. But how Strange! is it not? that I who used to ride all night to dream with Hardy or Sally Quash up on the Cooper or to hunt all day with Jim Poyas should now be the Leader of the bandit horde that has made its mark from the Mississippi to the Atlantic. I feel little changed but must be more than I realize; yet if the present dream could vanish, and the Night Spring should place us amid the sweet Jassamine of Mount Pleasant I could forget the Shouts of battle and the hissing shell and ever more gather the Magnolia blossom for some fair girl or drape the scene to make a picnic. But I forget, you are no longer the good kind Mrs. Hawkins whose dreams I used to borrow. . . . Nor am I the red headed Sherman of Sullivans Island.[13]

While at Moultrie, Sherman grew so attached to Mary Lamb that in March 1843 Ellen asked if he intended to show her off in Lancaster. "As to *Mary*," he answered, "I see her frequently. She is quite well. I do not intend to bring her home with me next summer—I thank the Lord I am not so far gone as to commit so foolish an act."[14]

Keyes characterized Sherman at Sullivans Island as "ambitious without asperity, and surprisingly active and always attentive to duty." Unlike Keyes, Sherman spoke and wrote plainly. Irritated by his ill-tempered dog Carlo, Keyes once yelled to his company clerk: "Waterbury, conduct this quadruped to my dwelling." Perplexed, Sherman suggested that Keyes might better have said: "Waterbury, take this dog to my house."[15]

Holding no particular religious belief, Sherman spent some of his weekends exploring the churches of Charleston. A priest sometimes came to the fort to conduct services for the men, many of whom were Catholic, but, much to Ellen's annoyance, Sherman never felt drawn to the religion. The young lieutenant sometimes found comfort in the Presbyterian church in Charleston, but did not attend it regularly. Captivated by the beauty of the building, he even wandered into a synagogue. Inside, Sherman wrote Ellen, men and women sat separately, the men with their hats on. The rabbi, "a reverend old gentleman," read "Hebrew through his nose" while those in his congregation "were laughing & talking."[16]

Having served continuously for three years, Sherman received, in the fall of 1843, a three-month leave of absence. He spent much of it in Lancaster, and by its end was engaged to Ellen, then nineteen. Mary Lamb, Mary Johnson, Miss North, and the other Charleston flames were now relegated to the past.

Returning to his post via St. Louis, Sherman was enchanted with the city. There he visited Colonel Stephen W. Kearny, in charge of the arsenal at Jefferson Barracks, Pacificus Ord, the brother of his close friend Edward Ord, and Lieutenant John McNutt, his classmate at West Point. But the city, then containing forty thousand people, was to Sherman the chief attraction. At its levee he counted thirty-six steamers either loading or unloading cargo. Sailing down to New Orleans, he saw for the first time the expanse that seemed to enter his soul, the mighty Mississippi.[17]

Back again at Fort Moultrie, Sherman soon got a letter from his betrothed on a theme she pursued as long as she lived. "I will not attempt to describe my feelings of delight upon receiving your last," he answered her, "and reading therein, not my doom, but the assurance of your love, and a desire that I should with an honest heart, and a wish to believe, if possible, the doctrines of your church. I snatch at the opportunity, and will do so at once—but does it not seem that the Fates are arraigned against me. . . . I am ordered into Georgia and Alabama where Religion except of the Rudest species is never found."[18]

The new assignment not only provided Sherman with an excuse for not adhering to Ellen's request, but later paid unexpected dividends. Shortly after arriving at Moultrie, he was selected by Colonel Sylvester Churchill, the inspector general of the army, to help investigate the claims for money by the 1,500 militiamen from western Georgia who in 1837 and 1838 had been sent to fight in Florida. "They were about the d——dest rascals that could be found in the United States," Sherman explained to Phil and Hugh. Most of them claimed to have lost one or more horses while in service. "All I have to do is cross question the claimants to see whether the old horse (killed in Florida) is not still working in his cornfield at home. We have many a rich scene and I have unfolded some pretty pieces of rascality for an honest and religious people."[19]

Taking depositions, the party, which included Churchill's family, stayed six weeks in Marietta, Georgia. It then moved for two months to Bellefonte, in the northeast corner of Alabama. "Thus by a mere accident," Sherman observed, "I was enabled to traverse on horseback the very ground where in after-years I had to conduct vast armies and fight great battles."[20]

By June 1844 Sherman was back at Fort Moultrie. "After being seated in my old arm chair for a few days," he commented to Phil, "I could scarcely realize that I had been away among the Barbarians and heathens, robbing them of the pleasing dreams of Gold and Silver for their poor horses sacrificed to an ungrateful Government." The trip whetted Sherman's interest in the law, and he read Blackstone, James Kent's *Commentaries*, and volumes on evidence, finding none especially difficult.[21]

In mid-1844 Sherman looked forward to getting married. "I am entirely out of debt," he revealed to Thomas Ewing, "have within the past month sent mother fifty dollars and have on hand for the purchase of books more than a hundred more." In the presidential election of 1844 Sherman favored Henry Clay, the Whig, over the Democrat, James K. Polk. If Clay were elected, Ewing would surely be in his cabinet. Sherman might then be transferred to Fort

McHenry in Baltimore, from which he could see Ellen often. "Hope whispers that I might at the end of that eventful year throw off the Selfish and hypocritical garb of old Bachelorism," he fantasized to his betrothed, "and share my future life with one whom I have so long loved as a sister, yea more than any that now live. Is that picture either absurd or delusive?"[22]

Yet in October, when John, at a Whig rally, was pressed into service and made his first political speech, Cump raged:

> What in the Devil are you doing? Stump speaking! I really thought you were too decent for that, or at least had sufficient pride not to humble and cringe to beg party or popular favor. . . . As an assistant to leering dissimulation & declamation so necessary to a Lawyer it may be well enough but it be so humbling and disgusting to a man of honor or honesty that I trust never to see your name mentioned in connexion with traveling demagogues again.[23]

Like many lawyers, however, John was slowly but irresistibly drifting toward politics.

While John was thus engaged, Hugh Ewing was aiming, despite Cump's warnings, at a different career. "I have often regretted that your father did not actually instead of sending me to West Point, set me at some useful trade or business," Sherman advised him. ". . . If I were in your place I would study hard now, all the time, go from home for that purpose either to a College or School, learn to write and draw well. . . . If in addition to that you get a knowledge of some profession, Medicine or Law, besides a practical insight into the methods of keeping accounts like the Storekeeper, by the time you are 23, you will be richer and actually better off than any officer of the army."[24]

Entering West Point in June 1844, Hugh, nicknamed "Monk" by his classmates, found it difficult. "Napoleon did not stand at the head of his class," Sherman consoled him, "nor did Wellington though they were great men. . . . You are capable of getting along well at the Academy and I have no doubt but that you will if you do not permit yourself to *fear* for the result. . . . If you can get high in your class I shall rejoice, if in the middle I will encourage you to persevere, and if lower my love for you shall be none the less."[25]

—— II ——

An injury to his arm, incurred while hunting deer with Reynolds on the plantation of their friend, James Poyas, up the Cooper River from Fort Moultrie, enabled Sherman to go home again in January 1845. Returning via New York, Sherman sailed up the Hudson to West Point, where he visited Hugh. Sherman reported to Thomas Ewing:

> He was in good health & spirits, about 5 feet 9 inches high, well set up, square shoulders, full in the chest and withal a fine looking sol-

dierly fellow—in manner & conversation much more manly than when at home. . . . Since you advised him of his narrow escape from military execution for his neglect of a sentinels high duties & responsibilities, I refrained from further warnings about the demerit list. . . . He says he is not homesick and that each day he becomes more attached to his books and duties.[26]

By the time Sherman reached Fort Moultrie, the United States had annexed Texas, but Mexico still claimed it. In anticipation of war, Bragg's company, with Lieutenants George Thomas and Reynolds, was ordered from South Carolina to General Zachary Taylor at Corpus Christi. "I would give any thing in the world to go down there," Sherman told Ellen in June, "and seriously contemplate exchanging into an infantry Regiment now in Louisiana. I could easily effect a transfer but I feel loth to quit the 3rd to which I feel most attached, besides I feel a decided preference for Artillery to Infantry service in time of actual war."[27]

By November, Sherman was sure his entire regiment, which had been stationed in the South since 1834, would be sent to Texas. Sherman wrote Ellen:

> You have often desired me to leave the Army, probably without thinking that I am perfectly dependent upon it for a living—that I have no profession that would command employment in civil life and that if I should leave the Army I would have to begin where I was ten years ago. . . . What shall I do? I want no one's advisement but your own and wish you not to breathe a syllable of what I write to Phil or your father. I then propose next spring about May to get a long leave of absence, go to the northern part of Alabama, select some pretty place and then see what may be done as a surveyor or draughtsman, in each of which I am fully competent—should I meet with partial success then I can complete what I have begun at the Law which I can master sufficiently by one winters study in a Law office. . . . Now Ellen think well about it and do not ask any questions of any persons that may give a clue to your thought, but barely think of the trials we have to endure, and the resolution I have made of never living in Ohio, or accepting ought from any one there.[28]

Ellen's answer surprised her fiancé. Of all places, she preferred to live in the frontier town of Memphis because the revered Dominican prior of Somerset, Bishop Richard P. Miles, was now there. Cump gently argued:

> Indeed, you would not like it yourself nor would it be politic to select it to enjoy the presence of a favorite bishop—he may be there one year or fifty—at most the prospect of his proximity would be so much a matter of chance as not to enter into serious calculation. Wherever we may go there is no doubt we will find kind and good men, equal if possible to your favorite Bishop Miles—I still have my eye on North Alabama but will not make a definite final choice for some time.[29]

___ III ___

During the last half of 1845 and the first of 1846, Sherman whiled away his time at Moultrie. He went shopping in Charleston with the wife of his commander, Captain Robert Anderson, attended Mrs. Anderson's parties, and, he teased Ellen, flirted with "a Miss Elliot of Georgia that by Mrs A's request I escorted down from the city."[30]

John Sherman later recalled the excitement that swept the country when war broke out with Mexico in April 1846. Cump soon found himself transferred to Pittsburgh for recruiting duty, from which he stole chances to visit Lancaster but inexplicably not Mansfield, to which his mother had moved to be near John. "That I should be on recruiting service, when my comrades were actually fighting," Cump later observed, "was intolerable." Impulsively Sherman wrote to the adjutant general in Washington asking to be sent anywhere. He then brought his twenty-five recruits to Cincinnati, from which he expected to be shipped to Texas. Instead, the commander at Cincinnati, a one-armed colonel named Fanning, "cursed and swore at me for leaving Pittsburg."[31]

Returning to Pittsburgh, Sherman found orders to report to New York, from which he was to sail not to Mexico but to California. "Farewell, God bless you," the dejected soldier told Ellen as he was about to leave Pittsburgh. "I'm glad I didn't know of this when in Lancaster for I should have made a fool of myself. Even here the tears start at the thought my wayward life has already given you. . . . You will think of me will you not? but you cannot answer—farewell Ellen, I must now write to mother. Cant you do something to allay the feeling of grief she must feel at my unaccountable conduct in not going to Mansfield."[32]

From his stateroom on the *Lexington,* which he shared "with my old friend Ord," Sherman wrote Ellen two days before sailing:

> Up to this moment you must admit that I have been constant and per-
> severing almost to a fault, almost to pertinacity—that I left my friends
> at Charleston to be near you, and that it was only upon the unfortu-
> nate feeling that ensued my first visit to you that I urged upon the Adjt
> General to send me upon any expedition however desperate. I am paid
> for it—in being sent around Cape Horn to a distant land without mails
> or any thing else for an unlimited period. It is not in this view that I
> must regard it but as a military expedition that must produce a result
> favorable or otherwise to all that are engaged. The time it must nec-
> essarily occupy will cut off from me all hope of afterward abandoning
> this my profession for any other. It will then be too late, by any fash-
> ionable means, to convert me into a youth, a law student. The future
> must take care of itself and I must do the best I can under the cir-
> cumstances.

While visiting Elizabeth Reese in Philadelphia, Sherman had seen a letter from his mother "from which I learned she knows I was ordered off—she felt it keenly that I have been to Lancaster three times—purposely avoiding Mansfield."[33]

Leaving New York on July 14, 1846, the *Lexington* plodded toward the bottom of South America. "After sixty days of absolute monotony," the ship approached Rio de Janeiro. Pulling into a "perfect harbor," it lay there for a week, as its passengers, delighted with the feel of ground, explored the area. With Halleck, also on board, Sherman saw much of Rio, including the city's source of water. "The Emperor is about 22 years of age," Cump related to Ellen, "and a real booby—is married to a princess of Sicily . . . but here as elsewhere the Royal family is a mere puppet, the strings being pulled by the lords of the Council, many of whom are men of learning and distinction."[34]

Buffeted by winds, the *Lexington* rounded Cape Horn in late October and crawled northward along the west coast of South America. On each fourth day Sherman, like the other army officers aboard, supervised a quarter of the soldiers as they helped the crew. The other three days he spent reading, playing cards, or sleeping, "this latter being a labor rather than pleasure," Sherman informed Ellen. "He is considered the happiest man who can punish his bed most. I have read all of Washington Irving's works that are aboard, Pickwick, Barnaby Rudge, Shakespeare, everything I could get, and yesterday cast about to determine which I should attempt next—the Bible, History of the Reformation or the Wandering Jew, but have postponed such a task till even a time more urgent than the present."[35]

Over sixty days out from Rio, the *Lexington* reached Chile. For a week the vessel docked at Valparaíso, which, unlike Rio, Sherman found dull and unattractive. Continuing on, the ship had favorable winds for 40 days. But by a mistake the *Lexington* sailed just north of its destination, Monterey. Attempting to come south, it ran into a southern storm, which threw the ship about for a few days. Finally, on January 26, 1847, it dropped anchor in Monterey Bay, concluding a voyage of 198 days from New York.

Landing in California, Sherman found himself amidst a political, rather than military, struggle. To his disappointment, the fighting had ended by the time he, Ord, and Halleck arrived. Most of California was under American control, but two officers, Major John C. Frémont, leading the volunteers, and Brigadier General Stephen W. Kearny, the army commander who was then marching west from New Mexico, claimed to exercise the supreme power. Sherman remembered the younger officers asking one another: "Who the devil is governor of California?" When Kearny finally arrived with two companies of dragoons, even after being roughly handled by the Mexicans at the town of San Pascual, Lieutenant William Chapman of the navy took one look at him and said: "Fellows, the problem is solved. . . . *He* is Governor of California."[36]

As quartermaster and commissary of Company F of the Third Artillery, Sherman supervised the supplying of troops and the disbursing of funds. As he informed Ellen in March 1847,

> We live on beef and bread, but I am putting up a small mill I brought
> from New York to grind some wheat, of which to make *soft* bread and

save our teeth for useful purposes. . . . Just think of my isolation that it takes a year to write and hear an answer with any degree of certainty. . . . Never an hour passes without my thoughts resting on you, and I cannot but reproach myself for having so strongly solicited for active Service—All will yet I hope turn out for the best at least such is my consolation poor though it is.

Every morning in Monterey the chimes of the Catholic church announced Mass. Ord and his brother, Dr. James L. Ord, the assistant surgeon of the *Lexington,* sometimes attended, "producing a most excellent effect as the Californians regard the Americans as all infidels. I went last Sunday but got there too late for Mass."[37]

When Kearny came up to Monterey in March 1847, he brought with him Captain Henry S. Turner, his acting adjutant, and Captain William H. Warner, his topographical engineer. One day Turner and Warner, while visiting Sherman's tent, saw a box full of socks, drawers, and calico shirts. Knowing he would be away a long time, Sherman had laid in a three years' supply. Destitute after the long march from Kansas, the two guests asked if they could have some of the items. When Sherman told them to help themselves, a closeness immediately developed.[38] Except for a period during the Civil War when Turner, then in St. Louis, was so pro-Southern that Northerners shunned him, Sherman thereafter considered Turner his warmest friend, closer even than Van Vliet, Ord, or Phil and Tom Ewing.

Sherman once described Kearny as "a perfect model of the courtly officer and perfect gentleman. . . . He was a great stickler for the exact uniform, neatness of person, and it was said of him that in his long journey from Fort Leavenworth to California on the treeless plains, in New Mexico and the deserts of Arizona, he shaved his face daily, though he tolerated in others the beard and felt hat, the very abominations of the older soldiers of the day." One morning Kearny sent for Sherman and asked for permission to use half of the $28,000 in Sherman's possession to aid the destitute soldiers in Los Angeles. After Sherman cheerfully agreed, Kearny walked him to the door, placed a hand on his shoulder, and said: "Lieut. Sherman I have lent my razors to Capt. Turner—when he is done with them he will send them to you." Sherman answered that he had his own razors. Even though he, like all the Sherman men, possessed tender skin and a wiry beard that made shaving painful, "I shaved it off," Sherman remembered in 1890, "and continued till he left the country the last day of May 1847. Since which time to the present I have never shaved my face. It is a mystery why soldiers *ever* shaved, for the beard is the best possible protection against cold, heat, and dust, but in 1846 all the oldest and best officers, headed by Adjutant General Jones, carried on a fierce war against the beards and felt hats, which however came in with the Mexican War to stay."[39]

Just before leaving for the East, Kearny asked Sherman if he would like to accompany him to Los Angeles to see Frémont, who was still issuing orders and posturing as governor. Along with Colonel John D. Stevenson and two companies of New York Volunteers, they sailed on the *Lexington*. All the way down the officers wondered what Kearny would do to Frémont, with whom Sherman was not impressed. Some thought the usurper would be tried and shot, others that he would be brought back in irons. At Los Angeles, Kearny made clear to Frémont that a brigadier general outranked a major, and Frémont never caused trouble again. Sherman remembered how difficult the situation was for Kearny, who owed his promotion to brigadier to Frémont's father-in-law, Senator Thomas Hart Benton of Missouri.[40]

Colonel Richard B. Mason of the First Dragoons replaced Kearny as governor of California, holding that position until 1849. Liking Sherman, Mason appointed him his adjutant. "Colonel Mason is an excellent man," Sherman confided to Ellen in October 1847, "well suited for his office, a little severe for Civilians, but just and determined." Monterey itself was "full of dirt and fleas—Indeed the filthiness of the town has produced much sickness and carried off many of our soldiers here and one officer of our Company, Lieut [Colville] Minor as clever a young officer as I ever knew. We buried him with the honors of war and have left him in the country far from his family that still thinks him the hearty healthy boy they sent to West Point five years ago."[41]

While Sherman dawdled over supplies and paperwork in California, his comrades from Fort Moultrie were experiencing the gore and glory of combat. Thomas Sherman, Reynolds, Bragg, Thomas, and Judd now possessed the experience that Sherman was sure he would never get. Reynolds was a major, Bill Irvin a colonel of volunteers. From the remoteness of Mexico, Judd sent word that Robert E. Lee of the Engineers was, next to General Winfield Scott, "the most distinguished man of the army." He also sent news of the young ladies of Sullivans Island: "Miss Mary Lamb is engaged to some merchant in Charleston, whom I don't know. . . . Miss Susan Quash had the fever once, just escaped death; Miss Sally's ringlets flow enticingly as ever. Our friend Miss Eliza Toomer is married before now. . . . Miss North has become an elegant and most interesting woman."[42]

If Sherman missed the romance of Moultrie and Mexico, he also missed California's business opportunities. One day he visited his classmate, Captain Joseph L. Folsom, then the quartermaster at Yerba Buena, a town of four hundred people. Folsom was buying lots in the place and induced Halleck, Warner, and several naval officers to invest some money. Sherman, however, "felt actually insulted that he should think me such a fool as to pay money for property in such a horrid place as Yerba Buena." The town later became known as San Francisco.[43]

The Mexican War was ending when in the spring of 1848 two men came to Colonel Mason with some paper holding what they thought was gold. Mason called in Sherman, who took a piece in his teeth and then beat it with an ax and a hatchet. From these unscientific observations Sherman concluded that the specimen was pure metal.[44]

That spring and early summer reports came in of vast discoveries of gold at the fort run by Captain Johann Sutter about forty miles from present-day

Sacramento. Soldiers deserted to join those digging for gold. Sherman heard stories of men earning with their pans fifty, five hundred, even thousands of dollars a day. In Monterey prices soared for mules, horses, tin pans, and anything else that could be used in mining.

One bright note was the first overland mail, brought in by Frémont's famous guide, Kit Carson. Sherman found Carson a small, round-shouldered man, with reddish hair and blue eyes. Carson spoke little and that but hesitantly. Almost alone he had ridden two thousand miles with the mails and would soon ride back.[45]

Drawn to few people, Carson immediately liked the young first lieutenant. The two would meet several times after Sherman became famous, and with great generosity the general tried to educate one of Kit's sons.

In late June and July, Mason, Sherman, and Folsom made a trip to Sutter's Fort and the mines. Cump, back in Monterey, informed John:

> Gold in immense quantities has been discovered. All the *towns* and farms are abandoned, and no body left on the coast but us soldiers. . . . Every thing is high in price, beyond our Reach and not a nigger in California but gets more pay than us officers. Of course we are moving into debt merely to live. I have never been so hard up in my life and really see no chance of extricating myself—All others here in the service of the U.S. are as badly off. Even Col Mason himself has been compelled to assist in cooking his own meals—Merchants are making fortunes for Gold such as I send you can be bought at from 8 to 10 dollars the ounce, and goods command prices 30 times higher than in New York.[46]

In September 1848, four months after the event, word that the Mexican War had ended reached California. Late that month, Sherman and Mason made a second trip to the mines, this time taking Warner along. Mason soon returned to Monterey, but Sherman, Warner, and Warner's clerk set up a general store at Coloma, near the gold mines. Investing $500 each, they each walked off with a profit of $1,500. Warner, meantime, began surveying for Sutter, who paid him $16 a day to set up a town that became Sacramento.

Warner, Ord, and Sherman spent the fall of 1848 camping on the banks of the American River, opposite Sutter's Fort. Capitalizing on the skills he had developed over the fireplaces at West Point, Sherman served as the camp cook. Warner washed the dishes, and Ord looked after the horses.

Before leaving on this second trip, Mason and Sherman had sent to Washington an officer with a sample of California gold and a letter, written principally by Sherman but modified by Mason, describing the strike. Late that December, President Polk announced the discovery in a special message. "The news had gone forth to the whole civilized world that gold in fabulous quantities was to be had for the mere digging," Sherman recalled, "and adventurers came pouring in blindly to seek their fortunes, with out a thought of house or food." Lots in Sacramento sold rapidly. Stockton rose as a trading center. And that "horrid place" Yerba Buena became San Francisco.[47]

— IV —

Back east, the Shermans and Ewings underwent changes that Cump learned about months later. In April 1847 James Sherman, suffering from alcoholism, left Ohio for Fort Des Moines, Iowa, a frontier community of several hundred people. With one thousand dollars, he hoped to enter some kind of business. Unhappy as a printer in Cincinnati, Hoyt Sherman joined James in 1848.[48]

Then on August 1, 1848, Elizabeth Stoddard Sherman died. "She was to our family," John observed, "the connecting link between the Revolutionary period and our times." She had remembered vividly the burning of Connecticut towns by the British and Tories, "the trials and poverty" of the post-Revolutionary period, the early days under the Constitution, and the War of 1812. Now she, and the memories, were gone.

With the passing years John emerged as the brightest and most ambitious of Cump's brothers. Under Polk, Susan Sherman's husband, Thomas W. Bartley, served as the district attorney for Ohio. In 1848, when Zachary Taylor was elected president, John asked Thomas Ewing, like Taylor a Whig, to help him get the position, but Ewing refused, saying John was too young. John had to content himself in December 1848 with his marriage to Margaret Cecelia Stewart, whose father was a leading Mansfield lawyer.[49]

While John was settling down, Hugh Ewing went the other way. To the disappointment of his father and Ellen, Hugh plodded along at West Point. Of the forty-two cadets in his class during his senior year, he ranked fourth from the last in ethics, third from last in both mineralogy and general merit, next to last in artillery, and last in infantry tactics. Worse yet, he became deficient in engineering, and in June 1848 was not permitted to graduate. Thrust out into the world, Hugh gravitated toward the most commonly spoken of way of getting rich. With several friends from Lancaster he left on February 6, 1849, for the gold fields.[50]

Meantime, late in February 1849, Brigadier General Persifer F. Smith, a hero of the Mexican War, replaced Mason as governor of California. Sherman offered to resign from the army, but Smith rejected the application and, because of the young lieutenant's familiarity with the region, appointed him his acting adjutant. Smith thereupon moved his headquarters from Monterey to San Francisco.[51]

Sherman described that winter in San Francisco as "dull" and "hard." "The rains were heavy," he noted, "and the mud fearful. I have seen mules stumble in the street, and drown in the liquid mud!" Food, rooms, and servants were expensive. "Had it not been for the fifteen hundred dollars I had made in the store at Coloma," he remembered, "I could not have lived through the winter."

To supplement their income, Sherman and Ord engaged in surveying. With his profits Sherman bought three lots in Sacramento, which he later sold to a resident of Mansfield.[52]

All the while, both Thomas Ewing and Tom Ewing were trying to help Sherman. After the election of 1848, Taylor nominated the elder Ewing to be his secretary of the interior and the younger to be his private secretary. The father and son made frequent trips to the War Department, extracting from Adjutant General Roger Jones a promise that Sherman's unit, after three years in California, would be sent home within a year. Moving to Washington with her father, Ellen saw Taylor for the first time in May 1849 at the funeral of an Ohio Congressman. "He looks hale & hearty," she informed Cump, "sensible & pleasant. He looks as if he might yet live half a century."[53]

Spending the fall of 1849 in Sacramento, Sherman found there Hugh Ewing and his friends from Lancaster. Persifer Smith, on the other hand, went up to Oregon, promising that on his return he would send Sherman and some other officers home with dispatches. About Christmas time a ship arrived in San Francisco, to which Sherman had returned, with the papers and the orders for Sherman, Ord, and the others.

Before leaving California, Sherman wished to say farewell to Doña Augustias, later the wife of Dr. Ord, and her husband, with whom the officers had boarded in Monterey, and arranged for the steamer *Oregon* to pick him up there. During the visit Sherman agreed to escort two of the Doña's sons to Georgetown College in Washington. To cover their expenses at the school, she gave Sherman a bag of gold dust. On January 2, 1850, the *Oregon* appeared, and Sherman finally headed home.

Passing down the coast, the steamer deposited its passengers in Panama. By mule, boat, and steamer, they crossed the Isthmus. By the end of January, "after a safe and pleasant trip," the passengers were in New York. Sherman took the dispatches to General Scott's office on Ninth Street and then was off to see the families of Uncles Charles and James Hoyt and of Cousin Louisa and William Scott.

The next evening Sherman dined with the family of General Scott, who questioned him "pretty closely" about conditions on the Pacific Coast. Scott startled Sherman by predicting that "our country was on the eve of a terrible civil war." He then entertained his guest with stories of comrades who, while Sherman "had not heard a hostile shot," had taken part in great battles. "Of course," Sherman remembered, "I thought it the last and only chance in my day, and that my career as a soldier was at an end."

With the dispatches, Scott sent Sherman to Washington. There, Sherman found Thomas Ewing and his family in Blair House, on Pennsylvania Avenue directly across from the War Department. Placing the dispatches in the hands of the secretary of war, who seemed uninterested in California, Sherman called on Taylor. He too talked about their army acquaintances. But finding little to do in Washington, Sherman applied for and received a leave of absence of six months.[54] At last he could devote time to his personal life.

— V —

Unlike John, who was rapidly advancing in the legal profession and was prominent enough in politics to serve as secretary of the Whig convention that in 1848 nominated Taylor for president, several members of the family were, by 1850, destitute. After William J. Reese failed in business, he took to drinking, placing his family on the verge of starvation. Early in 1850, Elizabeth Reese noted to John some improvement: "I feel encouraged from the great change in Mr. Reese's habits to hope if he could procure some employ or business, he would give it his whole energies—Since he took the Temperance pledge his whole nature is changed, tho deeply depressed by his circumstances."[55]

But when Cump visited his sister in Philadelphia, he found Reese unwilling to work. Since returning from California, he had given Elizabeth $1,614, all of which Reese squandered. "Poor Elizabeth," Sherman lamented to John. "Starvation is now her lot unless she can find refuge from the Storms of life at Mother's house. She must go west and that soon. . . . Reese still talks of thousands, and tens of thousands and has not for the past year given one cent to support his wife and children." By midyear Elizabeth had followed Cump's advice and moved in with her mother.[56]

Lampson Sherman, meantime, had joined James and Hoyt in Iowa. After the death of his wife, during the summer of 1848, he left the *Cincinnati Gazette* and, with his young son, moved west to start a Whig paper that later evolved into the *Des Moines Register*. "With regard to James," Lamp wrote Cump in July 1850, "I am happy to say a change for the better has taken place since I wrote to you some time ago. He has joined the Sons of Temperance and has remained steady for more than six weeks and I trust will continue to do so." James was working as a butcher.[57]

Amidst this family turmoil, Sherman and Ellen planned to be married. "The lady is a Catholic," Sherman informed his friend, Lieutenant James A. Hardie, "which makes me very anxious to have a friend near me who will appreciate the piety of her character and purity of her motives." As a concession to Ellen, Sherman was getting married in a new uniform, complete with saber and spurs.[58]

Because Sherman was not a Catholic, the wedding, which took place in the Ewing home in Washington on May 1, 1850, could not be celebrated in a church. But two priests officiated, one of them being Charles Ewing's teacher in a Jesuit school in the capital. The three hundred guests included Webster, Clay, Benton, Taylor, and all the members of the cabinet. After the ceremony, the young couple left for Baltimore, Niagara, and Ohio, returning to Washington in early July.[59]

In the middle of July, President Taylor died. The new chief executive, Millard Fillmore, almost immediately changed the makeup of the cabinet. Thomas Ewing left, but his fellow Ohioan and friend, Senator Thomas Corwin, was appointed secretary of the treasury. To fill Corwin's Senate seat the governor of Ohio appointed Ewing, who, having no need for a permanent residence in Washington, leased his house to Corwin and moved back to Lancaster.[60]

While still in Washington, Sherman viewed the Congressional debates attending the Compromise of 1850. "Scarce a day passes in the Senate," he informed Persifer Smith, "without the rights of nullification, secession and dissolution are discussed and what amount of oppression will justify secession—I hope and believe it will come out straight."[61]

To Sherman, the outstanding figure in the debates was Clay, "a noble stag hound assailed from every direction, yet always ready for the conflict." Sherman remembered the dramatic speech of August 1, when Clay vowed to take up arms against his beloved Kentucky if it should rebel against the government: "He was then a very old man, yet he stood erect, threw his head back and looked the very impersonation of an old Soldier. A thrill like electricity then unusual but often felt since, passed through the audience which broke out in loud applause, and it required some minutes of time and the threat of the sergeant at arms to restore order."[62]

In September, as Sherman prepared to return to active duty, his father-in-law pressed General Scott about Sherman's promotion. The pending army bill provided for four captaincies in the Commissary Department. Sherman, Scott promised, would get one of them.[63]

When Sherman was assigned to duty with the Third Artillery at Jefferson Barracks, near St. Louis, he left Ellen, now expecting their first child, with her mother in Lancaster. At his new post he found old acquaintances, including Captain Bragg and Lieutenant Hardie. "Of course my friends inquire why I did not bring you along," Cump informed his wife, "and when I tell them that I did not like to bring you into a strange place, among strangers without first exploring—they think I show a distrust unusual to our class."

From his first days at Jefferson Barracks, Sherman took to St. Louis. Why Ellen's father remained in "that insignificant town of Lancaster" puzzled him, for lawyers with half of Ewing's ability earned between fifteen and twenty thousand dollars a year. Ellen's mother would also love the place. "The large Catholic population, with fine Churches, and well educated priests to her would be particularly pleasing," Cump assured Ellen, "and the annoying troubles about servants she now experiences in Lancaster could not occur here as in all cities there is no difficulty in procuring any class or description of servants."[64]

Early in October, Sherman picked up a St. Louis newspaper and read of his promotion to captain. To the disappointment of Bragg and Hardie, the advance in rank also meant Sherman's transfer to the Sixth Infantry in St. Louis itself. There Sherman served with two officers who would later play roles in his life. Major Don Carlos Buell was the unit's adjutant and Captain Winfield Scott Hancock the regimental quartermaster. To Sherman's delight, Major Stewart Van Vliet soon joined him. With Ellen still in Lancaster, Sherman moved into the Planters' House, just three blocks from his office, where room and board cost thirty dollars a month.[65]

That Christmas, Sherman made the trip down the Mississippi River and then up the Ohio to be with Ellen. "I found all at home well," the captain told Hugh, who, still in California, was nursing a broken leg. "Lancaster is the same dull monotonous place it was ten years ago, and after the life of adventure, though involving hardships and privations, you would not be satisfied to remain a year."[66]

Returning to St. Louis, Sherman heard good news. On January 28, 1851, Ellen had given birth to a girl, named Maria Ewing for her grandmother but ever after called Minnie. Sherman was elated. He anxiously awaited "a description of the baby which," he teased Ellen, "looks like somebody, at least has human shape."[67]

In March, Sherman brought his wife and child to St. Louis. There he moved his family into a rented house on Chouteau Avenue, a little way out of town, where the nights were cooler and cholera not as rampant. "Our house is not very grand and the little furniture we have is not stylish," Ellen informed her mother on April 10, "but we are pleasantly situated and have everything requisite for comfort, and I feel delighted to be at last independent."[68]

In the midst of an involved legal case in St. Louis, Thomas Ewing visited the city—and his beloved Ellen—four times in 1851. The case concerned a Major Amos Stoddard. Around the time of the Louisiana Purchase, Stoddard, who was later killed in the War of 1812, had bought a vast area back of the village of St. Louis. For years after his death his title to the land had been ignored, until his relatives retained a kinsman, Henry Stoddard, the cousin of Sherman's father. He, in turn, hired Ellen's father to aid him, with the promise of a large fee in land. In connection with the Stoddard claim, Thomas Ewing spent four months reading old documents, learning Spanish in the process.[69]

With the successful completion of the case in the summer of 1851, Stoddard and Thomas and Phil Ewing got huge tracts of land as their fees. That September, the auction of a portion of the Stoddard lands brought in $701,600. "A pretty handsome sum," Cump characterized it to John. Henry Stoddard got $150,000 for some of his land, the Ewings "about $60,000."[70]

Surrounded by such wealthy relatives, Sherman, in addition to caring for the Ewing and Stoddard properties, bought for $4,000 four quarter sections of prairie land and twenty acres of wooded land. "I am fully aware of the precarious nature of Land Speculation," he bantered to John, "but you may rely upon it, that I have as yet indulged in none of the extravagant dreams that build on this City. . . . But I do think most favorably of the prospects of St. Louis,—and the future prospects of it are certainly as far as that of any City on this Continent and am willing to risk my small capital on the Chances of this Game."[71]

Meanwhile, in June 1851, Hoyt Sherman visited St. Louis. "Hoyt looks like you in person," Cump related to John, "but resembles Fanny in face." The owner of several buildings and lots, he was heading toward prosperity. Jim was another story. "Jim still drinks—does nothing, is the owner of the log cabin where he now lives—and one third of another."[72]

Early in 1852 Jim's wife threatened to leave him. John informed Cump:

The affair of Jim & Sophia is truly deplorable. It is shameful. He had as good chance to make himself independent in Des Moines as any man ever had. He took with him from here $1000 which he knew he could use as long as he wanted it and by investing it with ordinary prudence ought now be worth $10,000. He has however Hoyt writes spent all his money sold his lots & become a miserable drunkard. What poor Sophia can do or what she had better do God only knows. By all means she ought to go to Lancaster.[73]

The plight of Elizabeth Reese, still separated from her husband, resembled Sophia's. "I have no confidence in any thing for Reese," Cump scoffed to John late in 1851, "unless you can raise two or three hundred thousand dollars for his use. Nothing else will avail him." Unfortunately, Henry Reese, Elizabeth's son, had just been fired from a government job that paid a thousand dollars a year. Unable to learn why, Cump suspected that it involved the handling of money.[74] Twenty years later Henry Reese, then an army major, would be found guilty in a more publicized case involving mismanaged funds.

In September 1852 John Sherman was campaigning for General Scott, the Whig candidate for president, when he received word that his mother, whom he and Cump helped support, was seriously ill. On the twenty-third, before he could reach Mansfield, Mary Sherman died. "This event was wholly unexpected," John noted, "as she seemed, when I left home, to be in the best of health." In a letter to Cump just two days before she died, Mary complained about her home being "appropriated" by Elizabeth and her children, but "she knew she was welcome to more homes than many of her old friends left like herself widowed & poor."[75]

By the end of September Sherman was on his way to New Orleans, where he was appointed commissary. Since the summer, Ellen, expecting her second child, had been with her parents. "I think she has been at Lancaster too much since our marriage," Sherman complained to Tom Ewing, "and it is full time for her to be weaned. Unless New Orleans should be visited by an epidemic, she will not likely leave for two or three years."[76]

On November 17, when Ellen gave birth to a second daughter, the child was baptized Mary Elizabeth, in memory of Mary Sherman.[77] But she would always be known as Lizzie.

3

"I Regret I Ever Left the Army"

— I —

SHERMAN'S LIFE in the 1850s resembled that of numerous other West Point graduates. Like Grant, Bragg, and others, he muddled through good times and bad seeking means to support a growing family. Rapidly he jumped from commissary captain to San Francisco banker, from Kansas farmer and lawyer to Louisiana military schoolmaster. At decade's end Sherman still faced the problem confronting him at its beginning: what to do with the remainder of his life.

Late in the summer of 1852, Sherman heard rumors that something was wrong with army operations in Louisiana. Reaching New Orleans on November 1, he learned what that something was. For the past ten years the army commissaries there had been engaged in nepotism, awarding contracts to companies in which relatives were principals. Sherman's predecessor, Major George G. Waggaman, had dealt with a firm in which his brother was a partner. "I am not at all astonished," Sherman explained to John, "for the Government sends our officers here at entirely inadequate compensation and as it were invite bribery thus—I want to buy 8 or 10000 pounds of sugar, coffee beans or any thing in my line—ask for samples—Oh says the merchant I'll send a sample to your house—the result is bribery." By going to the levee and buying supplies from merchants in the open market, Sherman hoped to end the abuses.

In his letter to John, Sherman showed special concern for two of his sisters. Lonely after the death of her mother, Fanny, the youngest of the Sherman children, began seeing a man named Bowman. "We've got drunkards enough in our family," Cump warned. And Elizabeth was as destitute as ever. "If some one would have the kindness to knock Reese on the head I would be the better pleased."[1]

During his first two weeks in New Orleans, Sherman lived in the St. Louis Hotel. After that, he rented a house on Magazine Street for fifty dollars a month. The day after Christmas, accompanied by the two children, Fanny, who was to spend the winter with them, and a nurse, Ellen left Lancaster, arriving in New Orleans on New Year's night. "Up to this time," Ellen commented to Hugh, "Cump has been housekeeper but the task now becomes mine."[2]

Even before Ellen's arrival, Sherman indicated to Turner, now a prominent banker in St. Louis, his dissatisfaction with his new post. Turner responded:

> I infer from your letter that you are not altogether pleased with N. Orleans; you are much a man of the world, yet may not your present restlessness be ascribed to the fact that you have been transferred from a place where you not only had local interests but many friends, to a strange city where perhaps friendly faces are rarely encountered. And another thing, your mind has been much engrossed of late with property interests, acquiring and improving real estate, the charge of Mr Ewing's large landed interest here may have given you a taste for such business, and the sudden transition to tame Commissary duties has doubtless brought on temporary ennui. Whatever you may determine on, dont think of returning to the line of the Army. Take my word for it, that the duties of a Subaltern in times of peace are wholly incompatible with your intellect or energy.

Turner would soon be on his way to San Francisco to open a branch of his firm, Lucas & Simonds, to be called Lucas, Turner & Co. Needing someone with Sherman's "extraordinary business capacity" out there, Turner offered him "a fair consideration, an interest in the concern," if he would not leave the army but transfer to San Francisco and serve as the bank's business advisor.[3]

In mid-January, en route to San Francisco, Turner stopped in New Orleans and renewed the offer to Sherman, who answered that he could not simultaneously serve the government and a bank. If Turner could arrange for Sherman a six-month leave of absence from the army, the captain might try out the new venture. Before leaving New Orleans, Turner promised Sherman a salary of $4,000 a year plus a share of the profits. Soon after, Turner's partner, James H. Lucas, described by Sherman as "the richest property holder in Saint Louis," arrived in New Orleans and tried to persuade Sherman to join the firm. He admitted that the success of Page, Bacon & Co. in San Francisco had inspired him to open the branch there. He had already lured from that company Benjamin R. Nisbet, its chief cashier.[4]

Enticed, Sherman, whose pay as an army captain was $130 a month, accepted the leave of six months. Disbanding his home, he sent Ellen, Fanny, and the children to Cincinnati in early March on a ship appropriately named the *Tecumseh*, sold his furniture at auction for $293.05, and prepared to leave for the West Coast. "I regret this breaking up," Cump revealed to John, "but I have counted well the chances and must now await the result."[5]

A few days later Sherman left New Orleans on a steamer bound for Nicaragua. In seven days he reached Greytown and with the other passengers crossed to the Pacific, where he and the others boarded the SS *Lewis* for California. But disaster loomed. On April 9, the last morning of the trip, the ship hit a reef about eighteen miles north of San Francisco. Luckily the beach was but a mile away, and by making several trips in the lifeboats the crew conveyed the passengers to safety. "I remained on the wreck till among the last of the passengers," Sherman remembered, "managing to get a can of crackers and some sardines out of the submerged pantry, a thing the rest of the passengers did not have, and then I went quietly ashore in one of the boats."

While the others huddled around fires on the beach, Sherman and a young companion walked inland about three miles. There they came across some men loading a schooner with lumber destined for San Francisco. Early that afternoon Sherman and his friend were aboard the schooner when it headed out toward the city. Approaching San Francisco Bay, Sherman was relaxing atop the lumber when the vessel suddenly overturned. "Satisfied that she could not sink, by reason of her cargo, I was not in the least alarmed," Sherman recorded, "but thought two shipwrecks in one day not a good beginning for a new, peaceful career."[6]

Finally making his way into San Francisco, Sherman found Turner at the boardinghouse of a Mrs. Ross on Clay Street. Occupying the front room upstairs was General Ethan Allen Hitchcock, the mystic, author, philosopher, and soldier whose nephew Henry later served on Sherman's staff during the famous March to the Sea. General Hitchcock now commanded the army in California. Although the rooms were small, Sherman moved in, paying for the privilege $25 a week. To Ellen, he estimated that his monthly expenses would come to $150 a month, more than his salary as a captain. "San Francisco is quite a large city now and is much better regulated than formerly," Cump reported on April 12, "but it wears the appearance of a mushroom of rapid growth & rapid decay." The damp weather in California had already brought on "a pretty hard attack of asthma."[7]

True to his word, Turner had already set up the new bank. For six hundred dollars a month he had rented "an elegant office" on Montgomery Street opposite two giant firms, Page, Bacon and Adams & Company. Numerous other banks, all seemingly prosperous, lined the avenue. The office would cost, Cump estimated to John, $1,200 a month, but, Sherman continued, Turner seemed unconcerned. "The best & most lucrative business is in discounting paper & loans—3 pc a month is the lowest rate of interest & some charge as high as 5 pc or 60 pc a year—This you would suppose is outrageous & is so in fact. Yet we could lend a Million of dollars at that rate & secure it well.—How men can afford to pay such interest I cannot imagine—Yet they do so."[8]

But Sherman quickly realized that Turner had gone back on one of the promises made in New Orleans. The firm was underfunded. Though honorable, Lucas, still in St. Louis, ran everything. A dejected Sherman informed Ellen in May:

> Here I am then a dunce in the midst of a busy prosperous hive of people, having come thousands of miles & then compelled to await the decision of Lucas in St. Louis—I sometimes think I am an out & out fool. Why did I not insist with Turner to draw for all we want & leave

Lucas to provide the means as the contract would compel him to do. I did not however. . . . A feather would now resolve me to embark for New Orleans—swallowing at a gasp all past sacrifices and losses—for I know you understand the whole subject & would not reproach me. What others think is of very little importance.[9]

In July, about to sail for home, Sherman still possessed reservations about the firm. "Lucas letters are written in the best spirit," he told Ellen, "assures us of his unbounded confidence—flatters our management &c &c but does not put up the Cash." Only if Lucas doubled the capital of the bank and promised Sherman one-fourth of the profits till 1860 would he remain. Turner had already assented to these demands. Under them, Sherman would make between $12,000 and $14,000 a year. "Now if we can lay by $6000 a year for 6 yrs we will have $36000 cash to begin with in Saint Louis before any of our children need schools."[10]

Again taking the route via Nicaragua and New Orleans, Sherman headed for Lancaster. Then it was on to St. Louis and the showdown with Lucas. Expecting to be turned down, Sherman asked Lucas to provide $200,000 in cash and a reserve of credit in New York for drafts. Lucas agreed. He also consented to giving Sherman an eighth of the branch's profits, a salary of $5,000 a year, and traveling expenses. "This was so promptly assented to that I was sorry that I had not asked more," Sherman wrote Ellen. He considered the offer "very good news for us," for if he returned to the army he would be sent back to New Orleans, then experiencing a yellow fever epidemic. San Francisco was different. "You will have nothing to endure which delicate ladies have not before done—no sickness to apprehend save sea sickness which is notoriously temporary. . . . Don't get too many things—the less the better—Baggage is bother & expense. The more we save, the sooner will our pile be made and we will be back in a Christian land."[11]

Ellen and her parents found the alternatives—the yellow fever of New Orleans versus the remoteness of San Francisco—appalling. Given the choice, however, Ellen refused to subject her children to disease and picked California. To win over her parents, who had become attached to Minnie, she and her husband agreed to leave the child with them. Everything arranged, Sherman resigned from the army effective September 6, 1853. Thirteen days later, sitting in a New York hotel room waiting to sail into the unknown, Ellen lamented to Hugh: "On the eve of a voyage I have somewhat the feeling that death might awaken in me towards those I leave behind."[12]

The next day, accompanied by Lizzie and Lizzie's nurse, Mary Lynch, Sherman and Ellen began the trip to Nicaragua. "Our ship shows the progress of settlement in California," Sherman informed Hugh, "97 ladies & 50 children." But during the voyage on the Pacific side, three people died, one a recently married young woman. "Cump thought I should witness a burial at sea," Ellen wrote home, "so I went upstairs with him that night and stood by the gangway. The Purser read the Episcopal funeral service—the vessel stopped a moment—I heard a splash in the water, and the affair was over. I never realized so fully before that death is truly the King of terrors. . . . You will believe me when I say I was glad when on October 15, we reached San Francisco."[13]

— II —

In San Francisco, Sherman piled his family into a carriage, which for the extravagant outlay of $8 took them to the Clarendon Hotel, on Stockton Street near Broadway. There for $100 a week, excluding the cost of lights and heat, the family occupied two rooms and received board. After a short time, at Ellen's request, Sherman rented from the son of the English author and traveler Captain Frederick Marryat a small house on Stockton, near Green. Buying Marryat's furniture, the Shermans moved in in early December.

From the beginning, Ellen hated the city and the house. In San Francisco those in want and poverty lived alongside the rich and extravagant. Streets were unpaved. To go shopping Ellen was forced to put on India rubber ankle boots and to wade through mud. She frequently returned home, she told her parents, "with my boots muddy to the top, my stockings muddy above them and my dress—although I raised it considerably—splashed clear to my knees. Mr. Nisbet says that in making New Year's calls last year he left one boot sticking in the mud and was obliged to have the other cut off, his foot was so wet. Yet they call this the 'El Dorado,' the promised land! I would rather live in Old Granny Walker's cabin at home, than here in any style."[14]

Prices were high. An egg cost twenty-five cents, strawberries five dollars a pint. "Cump gives me $75 every Monday to pay the girls' wages, wood, coal, groceries and market," Ellen revealed to her parents, "and yet by Saturday night there is seldom any left—and I am not extravagant."[15]

Sherman, moreover, detested the climate. "I would be foolish to count on a long life," he moaned to Turner, who had returned to St. Louis in November 1853. "Yet I may go on as now, wheezing & coughing, for a long time. . . . San Francisco has a curious climate, and whilst its rain, fogs & winds will doubtless contribute to afflict me with asthma, its coolness & purity may prevent its deleterious consequences."[16]

During the first half of 1854 the construction of two buildings occupied much of Sherman's time. The first was a brick house on Green Street, just beyond Stockton. Stumbling onto the half-built structure in January, Sherman bought it at once. Unlike the house they were renting, the new one had a yard, a side entrance, and an alleyway so that deliveries of coal, wood, and food need no longer be made through the front door. The first floor contained two rooms and a kitchen, the second four large rooms. Each room had a fireplace. The house was "in the best quarter of the City," Sherman reassured Phil in March 1854, "and there is no reason why we should not be content." Sherman's old friend, Major James A. Hardie, a Catholic, visited often. So too did the banker's lawyer, Samuel M. Bowman, and his charming wife. "Within a stone's throw" was the church of Archbishop Joseph S. Alemany, whom Ellen had known as a Dominican father in Somerset and Lancaster. Ellen had no real cause of discontent save Minnie's absence and the distance from home. We ought not to have left Minnie behind, and only did so because your father and mother were anxious for it. I am perfectly satisfied that she is better cared for than if she were with us, but this is now our home, and our entire family should be together. Ellen talks already of going home next Spring, and I shall not oppose, though I am resolved to stay here a long time, and must confess that I do not think Ellen & children should be traveling back & forth, unless some special necessity calls her home, when I will promptly provide her means & escort.[17]

In California, banking was one notch above gold mining as speculation. "We have no incorporated Banks here," Cump advised Phil, "and any individual can hang up his sign & go to work." But money kept rolling in, and Lucas, Turner made profits of $10,000 a month. "We must of course run more risks than prudent people would do, but we risk only the Capital of men who are able to lose the whole amount without ruin."[18]

Needing room for the expanding business, Sherman bought in February 1854 a lot on the corner of Jackson and Montgomery Streets for a new building. Originally estimated at $50,000, the structure cost $93,000 by the time it was finished in midyear. Certain his new bank would make a fortune, Lucas hardly blinked an eye when informed of the increased cost.[19]

That June 8 Ellen gave birth to her first son. "The little fellow has a wonderful appetite," Sherman informed Tom Ewing a week later. Weighing nine and three-quarter pounds, he was "much larger than Minnie or Lizzie was, and is perfectly healthy. We had him baptized as William Ewing Sherman . . . which should have been William Rufus, as he is most decidedly Red. . . . It dont seem that there is any danger of the Sherman or Ewing stock running out, so you must not make that an excuse for diving headlong into the matrimonial state."[20]

But the birth of Willy merely increased Ellen's discontent. "Ellen continues to think California an unfit place for a Christian," Cump complained to Hugh. "It may be for those who can avoid it, fate seems to fix me here, and I cannot help myself. Were Ellen to be more satisfied I should be also, but as it is I see it plain that she must go home next spring, and I doubt much if I ever again attempt to bring my family out. I seem to be doomed to live a vagabond life and might as well submit."

Ellen, meantime, suggested moving across the bay to Oakland, where the winds were not as fierce and Sherman would have room for "flowers, chickens and other rural objects. I have little or no faith in any prolonged existence," Sherman lamented to Turner. " . . . This asthma is so fixed on me and is so severe at times that I care but little how soon it terminates fatally." On a recent trip to Monterey, Sherman, after riding all day, could not sleep and paced outside all night. He returned exhausted. "Nevertheless," he reassured his employer, "I do not permit it to interrupt my occupation. I shall try to fend off this Oakland project unless I find Mrs Sherman's heart set on it when I shall take it under advisement."[21]

Turner responded to these complaints like a major disciplining his errant captain. "You pitch into me like a thousand bricks," Sherman apologized. "Why the deuce can't you let an old soldier growl a little occasionally? It's the safety valve without which we should keep an immense quantity of bad humor cooped up. . . . For the last seven months I have been compelled to sit up more or less each night breathing the smoke of nitre paper and know that this climate will sooner or later kill me dead as a herring."[22]

─── III ───

In the summer of 1854 John Sherman received the Whig nomination for the House of Representatives. Speaking in every community in his district, he denounced the recently passed Kansas-Nebraska Act, sponsored by Senator Stephen A. Douglas of Illinois, which repealed the Missouri Compromise and reopened the question of slavery in the Louisiana Purchase. From the outset Cump, although not disturbed by servitude in the South, was horrified at the thought of slavery in the territories bordering the Missouri River. Still, he hoped his brother would not "be too forward" on this burning issue.[23]

About the time the victorious John was taking his seat in Congress, the air was leaking out of the San Francisco balloon. Real estate declined in value, firms failed, and merchants began to suffer. Coupled with these, Henry Meiggs, the president of a large lumber company, absconded, after forging comptroller's warrants worth a half million dollars. Several banks suffered heavily, but Sherman had required security before lending Meiggs money, and Lucas, Turner lost only about $10,000.[24]

Still, Sherman found himself "infinitely more troubled by my private affairs than by business." Ellen insisted on going home. Sherman wrote Phil:

> I am perfectly aware that this is the worst place in the world for her, but I cannot help it and therefore treat it as beyond remedy. I have no profession or some trade, no physical health to undertake a new life— Whereas here, I can occupy a place of honor and profit, and by prudence & economy have something for the Children. If I break up every year as I have done for the past three or four, it would be folly to expect to benefit my financial affairs. Our expenses the past 18 months have exceeded $15,000. I want Ellen to go home & not to take the children, but to stay until by economy I may either abandon my post, or provide a new & better home. Not to go home now & return in a few months. Taking the children along would be exposing them to too much danger. These are my views & Ellen will not appreciate them. What the result is to be I cannot say. . . . I should like to have some permanent home, but that seems out of the question.[25]

In San Francisco, Ellen faced another problem. In late 1854 the Know-Nothing party, a hotbed of prejudice, nominated a slate for city offices. Realizing one of its nominees was a Catholic, the party's leaders dropped him from the ticket. "And sure enough," Sherman informed Turner, a devout Catholic, "the entire ticket has been elected."

Attacks only strengthened Ellen's faith. "The stronger their prejudice the more I boast of being Irish,—and a thorough Catholic," she wrote her mother; "the more I pride myself upon my descent and thank God for the Faith which the Irish have kept inviolate through so many years of suffering and privation. Nevertheless, while the Know Nothings wage war against us we should not lend dignity to their cause by showing anger. . . . The abuse they utter against the Church only increases our veneration for Her,—blackened but beautiful."[26]

In mid-February 1855, as Ellen prepared to leave for Ohio, word reached San Francisco of the failure of Page, Bacon in St. Louis. At once, anxious depositors stormed the firm's San Francisco branch. On the Saturday the news arrived cash withdrawals amounted to $300,000. The firm's partners, Henry Haight and Frank Page, were ruined. Within a week Adams & Co. also collapsed. Its manager, Isaiah C. Woods, eventually fled to Australia.

Although Lucas, Turner had to pay out $417,000 to nervous depositors, it was able to pull through. "No house in the City has recovered so promptly as we," Sherman bragged to Turner. ". . . Mrs Sherman is the only person not rejoiced at our success, for she says if we had broken I would have gone home— but I'd blow this house to atoms, and squeeze dollars out of brickbats rather than let our affairs pass into the hands of a rascally receiver or a more rascally sheriff."[27]

But the bank run shook San Francisco. Sherman advised General Hitchcock:

> You would hardly recognize this City, so changed is the tone. The Chief Banks broke, & their managers heaped with odium—Haight, Page, Woods and others who strutted the Streets, and sported handsome equipages, are hiding themselves, ashamed to be seen.—Nearly all the rich men here of your day, who counted their hundreds of thousands are now broken down, or reported so. It is comprehended that failures to the amount of millions of dollars must still occur, so that no one is willing to venture.[28]

With the addition of Willy, Sherman found the home on Green Street too small. He therefore exchanged it for a lot on Harrison Street, between Fremont and First, and started building a house that would cost $6,000. Since the house was scheduled to be finished in early April, about the time Ellen was to leave, Sherman arranged to rent it to the Bowmans, who agreed to board Sherman, Lizzie, Willy, Willy's nurse, and Nisbet. He was sure the move would improve his health, for his doctor attributed two recent attacks of asthma to the damp walls of the Green Street house. "That," he told Turner, "will be some amends for my folly in building at this critical time."[29]

On April 7, 1855, the Shermans began the move into the new house. Nine days later Ellen said good-bye to her family and, accompanied by her father's friends William H. Aspinwall and Henry Chauncey, who held the government contract to carry mail from New York to San Francisco, boarded the *Golden Age*, bound for Panama.

But all did not go well, for at two o'clock on the morning of April 29, the twelfth day out, the ship rammed into a coral reef and began taking on water. Fortunately Commodore Watkins, the captain, was on deck at the time. At full speed he directed the ship toward a nearby island, reaching the beach as the engines stopped. Had the *Golden Age* sunk, a thousand lives might have been lost. Rescued by the *John L. Stevens*, the passengers proceeded on to Panama. Crossing the Isthmus by rail, Ellen then sailed up the east coast to New York, reaching it on Sunday morning, May 13.

As Ellen came ashore, Charley, older but still beardless, greeted her. He had been at the University of Virginia, where he was a student, when his father wrote him to meet his sister. For a week and a day he had lounged about New York waiting for her. The night before landing, Ellen dreamed of Lizzie and Willy. She confided to Cump:

> I felt my old desolation returning when I found 'twas only a dream, and I find I have got to nerve myself daily to bear up, or I shall be grieving for them as I grieved for Minnie when I first went to San Francisco. And yet I do not regret having left them. . . . Charley says that Father could not live without Minnie, so we must give her up during his life time. The probability is we will have a large family and it would seem the more selfish to refuse one to Father. Do not ask me to take her away from him—I know you are too kind to insist upon it.[30]

In Lancaster, Ellen found Thomas Ewing confined to his house with rheumatism. She informed her husband:

> I feel that I must devote myself to Father during my visit whatever may be its length and wherever he chooses to go. When I got home and found how much he had suffered how he had been crippled how infirm he continues to be and how he has longed for me I assure you I felt grateful to God for the disposition that urged me, against all obstacles to come. He is determined to keep me as long as possible regrets the children but says that considering your feeling on the subject I did perfectly right in leaving. He feels all the regret for Lizzie that one would for a grown person & says he does not care half so much for seeing Willy. I do not dare to think much of the children and as yet I have so carefully guarded myself as to avoid all grief about them.[31]

Spring rolled into summer, and the longer Ellen stayed in Lancaster the more she dreaded the return to California. Turner, back in St. Louis, had agreed to accompany her in October, but his wife, expecting their thirteenth child, insisted she needed him then. He would go to San Francisco earlier. Ellen commented sarcastically to her husband:

> I have said nothing in reply to that generosity. Mrs. Turner's turn may come to go to Cal. and then she will know what it is to a woman and

to children and she will speak of it in a strain less cool and composed. Beyond the term of your contract no power on earth will induce me to consent to *one year* longer there. We must take now the giving up of children & friends and everything dear but we must not raise our children there. Your health is sufficient grounds for your giving up your contract now if you would only do it but I know there is no hope of that.

Hearing of Turner's decision, Ellen's father said he would send Hugh with her, but Ellen refused to "expose a young man without business to the evil influences of the voyage."[32]

On the day Ellen wrote to Sherman, he was telling her of an incident involving Father Hugh G. Gallagher, the pastor of St. Mary's Cathedral in San Francisco. Coming to the bank, Father Gallagher asked about Ellen "& in joking wanted to know when I proposed to come into the fold—I told him you had Catholicity enough for a very large family, and that my Catholicity was more catholic than his, as mine embraced all Creation, recognizing the Maker as its head and all religions past, present & future as simple tools in the Great accomplishment yet to be. A little too transcendental for Mr. Gallagher."[33]

With Ellen gone, Sherman gathered two or three times a week with friends, including John T. Doyle, the attorney for Adams & Co., to discuss the Crimean War, then taking place in Europe. Doyle would bring the London *Times*, and from its accounts Sherman explained the military maneuvers. During these meetings the participants warmed themselves with a glass of Irish whiskey.[34]

While Ellen was away, several Democratic politicians came to Sherman and, railing against "know-nothingism," offered him their party's nomination for city treasurer. Sherman refused their proposal, even though he could have used the salary of $4,000 a year, "and the office would have chimed in well with my present business." Since the Democrats carried the election, Sherman assumed he would have been elected.[35]

Back in Ohio, Ellen believed she detected anti-Catholicism within the family. Broken in health, William J. Reese had joined Elizabeth and Henry in Mansfield. "I have strong suspicions that they are Know Nothings," she confided to Cump, "and if so they are in favor of admitting free Negroes to the privilege of voting rather than Catholics either foreign or native born. With such a spirit evinced towards my brothers & my children I cannot feel cordial nor would I accept their hospitalities except at your *express* desire were I certain they entertained these views."[36]

Preparing for the trip back to California, Ellen feared the worst. She pleaded to her husband:

Do not distress yourself about me, as I can take pretty good care of myself on the journey and should it be God's will that I should meet death in any form I can with His grace resign myself & meet it calmly. I shall (should my hour come soon) die in the hope that you may give my children a Catholic Mother, if any, and that you may have the gift of faith bestowed upon you. The desire of seeing you a Christian is the hope of my life and in death it will not desert me. Sad would be the remnant of my life should *your* death deprive me of that hope.[37]

Tom Ewing, meanwhile, left the Catholic church. After studying law at Brown University, he became engaged to Ellen Cox, the daughter of a minister, and converted to Presbyterianism. "When once married," Archbishop John B. Purcell of Cincinnati comforted Ellen, "I have no doubt of his being a practical Catholic, as he is already so sound & uncompromising a defender of the Creed of the Cath. Church if assailed in his marriage. . . . Please present to Mr. Sherman my profound respects and affectionate regards. I cannot think of him but as a Catholic who needs a little reflexion—undistracted by business cares—to unite with you in the belief, the practice and the love of the same Religion."[38]

As the archbishop perceived, business woes tormented Sherman. When Turner came out to California, he and Sherman discussed Benjamin Nisbet, who, Cump reminded Ellen, "cannot drink a glass of wine without getting foolish as you well remember, and his manners are not good, whereby he has considerably retarded our business advancement." Sending Nisbet home for a rest, Sherman assumed the cashier's duties in addition to his own, "but of course I am willing to undertake anything to accomplish success in our undertaking."[39]

Ellen returned in late November to a husband certain he "may die at any moment. . . . I can see that all are alarmed," Sherman informed Turner, "Mrs. Sherman very much so." Tormented by asthma, Sherman made out a will and a power of attorney. Even if he survived this winter, he predicted he would never make it through the next. His nights were sleepless, his mind obsessed with worry about business. For Sherman the winter of 1855–1856 was agony.[40]

As his brother suffered, John Sherman emerged as a national figure. In March 1856, he became one of three members of a House committee investigating the undeclared war between antislavery and proslavery forces in Kansas. After taking testimony for two months, John prepared the majority report, which condemned the use of fraud in passing a proslavery constitution.[41]

While John observed lawlessness in Kansas, his brother saw it in San Francisco. On May 14, a Wednesday, a literary gadfly and reformer, James King of William, a designation he chose to distinguish himself from other James Kings, charged in his paper, the *Evening Bulletin*, that James P. Casey, an admitted ballot-box stuffer and the editor of the *Sunday Times*, had been an inmate of Sing Sing Prison in New York. An hour after the issue appeared on the street, an enraged Casey stormed into King's office and demanded an apology. Ordered off the premises, he vowed to kill his defamer. On the street that afternoon, Casey shot King, who collapsed but did not die.

The next day, supposedly peace-loving citizens, fed up with the violence and corruption, organized a Vigilance Committee similar to the one that existed in 1851. On the first day 1,500 people joined. Eventually, according to its head, William T. Coleman, 8,000 men enrolled. On the sixteenth, a Friday, the members of the committee defiantly drilled in the city's streets.[42]

By sheer coincidence, on the Monday before the shooting, Sherman had accepted at the urging of Governor J. Neely Johnson, a Know-Nothing, a major generalship and command of the San Francisco unit of the state militia. Arriving at the bank on Thursday, the fifteenth, he "found everybody intensely excited." Everywhere he heard threats to hang Casey, now in the county jail, and another prisoner, Charles Cora, an Italian gambler who had killed a federal marshal. After consulting with Mayor James Van Ness, Sherman went over to the jail, which he described to Turner as "utterly indefensible . . . a perfect trap in which a small body of men could do nothing." Its rear wall lay flush with the ground, and nearby houses, towering over the jail, offered sharpshooters a haven. Late on Friday, Sherman, Johnson, who had come down from Sacramento, and several others went to the committee's headquarters, where they struck a deal with Coleman. Ten members of the committee would be stationed in the jail to make sure Casey remained there, but they promised to do nothing violent.

Things were quiet until Sunday, when Sherman found the governor and mayor on the roof of the International Hotel, helplessly peering down on a crowd of 5,000 people. Some 2,500 members of the committee, armed with muskets, rifles, and a fieldpiece, took into custody first Casey and then Cora. "San Francisco," Sherman wrote Turner a few minutes later, "is now governed by an irresponsible organization claiming to be armed with absolute power by the people. The government is powerless and at an end."

On Tuesday, May 20, after King died, Sherman correctly predicted that Casey and Cora would be hanged. "Between you and me," he confided to Turner, " 'tis well King is out of the way; if he had recovered, he would have been the veriest tyrant on earth and his paper would have been law. Casey's execution will end the Sunday Times, thus two birds are killed by one stone. Is this the operation of Providence?"[43]

After Casey and Cora were lynched, the Vigilance Committee, from "hired rooms in the very heart of the city," continued to run San Francisco. On May 30, Sherman received a message from Johnson to meet him at Benicia, the headquarters of General John E. Wool, the army commander in California. There Sherman pleaded for weapons with which to arm his militia. After some hesitation, Wool agreed that if Johnson ordered the committee to disband, he would supply the muskets Sherman needed. But after Johnson issued the proclamation, which declared the county of San Francisco to be in a state of insurrection, Wool reversed himself, arguing it was too dangerous to distribute arms.

In protest, Sherman resigned his command. "Thus far the Committee has done no particular harm," Sherman related to Hitchcock in mid-June, "but the fact that such an organization can ride down all opposition and defy the Sheriff, Governor, and all the Constituted authority cannot but exercise a baneful influence upon the future destinies of this Country."[44]

Strangely enough, John, edging closer and closer to abolitionism, sympathized with the hangmen rather than with the hanged. He informed his brother:

I must confess that except as you was personally interested in the contest, my sympathies were all with the Committee. The same class of characters who were so infamous in your City & in election frauds have controlled the cause of "law & order" in Kansas and these committed such calamities with the direct sanction of the authorities that it seemed to me just & right to organize & enforce a higher law. The early movements of the people meet the cordial approval of all good men here.[45]

Sherman disagreed. "There is no doubt we have had a bad administration of law here," he believed, "and more than a fair share of rowdies, but I think the Committee itself no better, and if we are to be governed by the mere opinion of the Committee and not by officers of our own choice, I would prefer at once to have a dictator."[46]

___ IV ___

With interest, Sherman observed the 1856 presidential election, which pitted the Democrat, James Buchanan, who successfully distanced himself from the troubles in Kansas, against the Republican, John C. Frémont, who ran on a platform opposing the further extension of slavery. "I have seen Fremont several times since 1847," Cump informed John, a loyal Republican, "and regard him as a small man out of whom to make a President. If he is qualified, any body may aspire to that office." In California, Frémont's principal backers were the corrupt bankers Joseph C. Palmer and Charles W. Cook. Both had misused state and municipal funds deposited with them.[47]

By October, Thomas Ewing, viewing Frémont as an abolitionist, joined some other former Whigs in endorsing ex-President Millard Fillmore, a third-party candidate. Sherman, too, refused to go along with the Republicans, who in San Francisco had fused with the Vigilance Committee. "I shall vote for Buchanan," Sherman informed Turner, "but if Fremont should be elected I think he should be installed, and tried. I believe, at all events try to believe that our Government ought to be strong enough to endorse the Devil himself for President for four years. . . . For my part I would submit to almost anything—rather than see the United States in danger of Civil War.—Of course a dissolution of the Union cannot be peaceful."[48]

On October 12, a week before Sherman sent this letter, Ellen gave birth to a ten-and-a-half-pound boy. Father Gallagher baptized the infant, Ellen wrote to her parents, "standing under Father's and Minnie's picture." The parents named the child, on whom Ellen was destined to pour out her religious zeal, Thomas Ewing Sherman.[49]

A month later Buchanan was elected, taking California by 53,000 votes to 20,000 for Frémont. "I suppose this will find you back at your seat in Congress," Cump afterwards related to his brother, "reconciled to the defeat of Fremont—over which you would not grieve much if you knew as much of him as I do—I take it that our Government will survive many such elections as in the past and that the solution for the evils of slavery will arise at the proper time."[50]

— V —

Sherman entered the year 1857 dolefully. "In San Francisco," he informed Turner on January 3, "there has not been two thirds of the business of 1853 or 54. . . . San Francisco has been sinking steadily since." Almost daily "our purest and best merchants" were failing. "In my private affairs I am trying my best to economize. I give Mrs Sherman $500 a month and she pays all family expenses—I have sold the horse and when she wants she hires a cab. I of course foot it. She saved the last month and gave me today her check for $250."[51]

Early in January, Turner sent bad news. The partners had decided to close the California house. Sherman answered:

> This took me by surprise, because I always supposed you and Mr Lucas would come out, see for yourselves and then if you saw signs in the future of events such as we have had in the past that you would then come to a determination leaving us to carry it out—The profits of the Past have not been commensurate with our hopes and calculations, for even when we began in 1853 all the world believed that Adams & Co and Page, Bacon & Co were coining money; and this City was supposed to be marching forward at a giant stride toward its sure destination as the Great Pacific City. It is now pretty well demonstrated that we calculated a *little* too fast, that San Francisco though destined at some future time to a high position, has to pass through toil & trouble & misfortune before she attains that end. . . . Still I think the falling off of profits is not the real cause of the suddenness of your determination—You think my life is too precarious to trust. Well I suppose I am not a good judge in my own case but I think that I could if necessary stay till 1860, if by that date you could see your way clear for a successor.[52]

Unfortunately, Sherman was carrying down with him some of his army friends. George Thomas had sent him $2,000 to invest, Bragg $6,000. In 1856, upon receiving a check for over $1,800 from Sherman, Bragg expressed "an obligation I can never forget. But it does not oppress me, Sherman, because I know to whom it is due—It will not be forgotten."

But hard times forced Sherman to sell his friends' property at auction. He disposed of Hitchcock's land at prices so low that, he told Turner, "I am afraid the General will be angry with me." One large lot went for $11,500, another for slightly over $14,000.[53]

By late March, Sherman had no choice but to humble himself before Thomas Ewing. He had accepted an offer from Lucas to establish an office in New York, but what about Ellen and the four children? Sherman informed his father-in-law that he

> may be forced to accept your kind offer of assistance, not in the way of money but to let my family have a home near you till I can again feel able to provide for them wherever I may go. I think Ellen will be

willing to trust me away from her a few years provided I am within reach. She is so persistent in her dislike to this country that I have abandoned all hope of a change and think I had better make any sacrifice now to get away finally, and make no calculation of ever returning.[54]

On the first day of May, Sherman closed the doors of Lucas, Turner. Nineteen days later, with Ellen and the three children—Minnie was still back in Ohio with her grandparents—he boarded the *Sonora* and began the trip to New York. Reaching there on June 13, Sherman accompanied his family to Lancaster and then went on to St. Louis. Shortly after the Fourth of July, Sherman, Lucas, and Turner met in New York and selected an office at 12 Wall Street. On July 21, the new Lucas, Turner opened for business.[55]

Still, the California "venture" haunted Sherman. "My family expenses far exceeded my salary & share of the profits," he revealed to John, "and the consequence is that I am forced to sell the land and property I had bought with my Army savings about St. Louis, the whole of which will be consumed. . . . Even here I cannot guess what the result will be. My opinion here is that Banking is overdone. Every body wants to be a Banker, the consequence being that men of small means offer rates of interest for money and operate to the disadvantage of real capitalists." To his wife Sherman lamented: "Our fate has been cast in a wrong time and I regret I ever left the Army."[56]

4

A Yankee in Rebeldom

— I —

WHEN SHERMAN ARRIVED in New York, he moved into the Metropolitan Hotel, which housed many visitors from St. Louis and the West. But his room, he wrote Turner, was so tiny that the door, if opened, hit the window. He soon moved to a boardinghouse at 100 Prince Street, near Broadway, where a room cost thirteen dollars a week and breakfast two.[1]

Sherman moved into the Prince Street house partly to be near his friend, Major John G. Barnard of the Army Engineers. But he struck up a friendship with a young officer who also roomed there, Lieutenant James B. McPherson. "I was naturally attracted to him," Sherman recalled, "because of his intelligence, his manly bearing; also because he was from Ohio." McPherson had graduated first in what may have been the most remarkable class yet to be trained at West Point, that of 1853. Seventh in the class was another of Sherman's close companions, John McAllister Schofield, a rotund New Yorker who was nicknamed Pud, short for pudding. Farther down in the class was another Ohioan, Philip H. Sheridan, who became, like McPherson, almost a son to the Shermans and was a constant visitor to their home. Ninth from the bottom came John Bell Hood, the Confederate general who later opposed Sherman at Atlanta but who after the war became friends with Sherman and his daughter, Lizzie. During the day Barnard, McPherson, and Sherman went separate ways, but every night they "gossiped about the topics of interest at that day."[2]

Despite these happy evenings, Sherman was tormented in New York, where he feared a repetition of what took place in San Francisco, "the same brilliant opening, the same flattering prospects. Yet I have nothing certain and the California experience has utterly disqualified me for business," he disclosed to Ellen. He also wrote:

I am afraid of my own shadow, and if I was only fit for any thing, I would wipe my hands of this nightmare. . . . I cannot blind my eyes to the fact that I have committed many business mistakes. Worst of all was building for Mr Lucas that Banking House, which by our withdrawal is almost a perfect loss. . . . Of course I dont bother myself about health—If my lungs are actually diseased one winter will fix me off, which to me would be infinitely more satisfactory than struggling with time.[3]

Early in August, Ellen's parents visited New York and reported that Sherman looked well. But Ellen assured him that should he become ill she would leave the children and come east. "I could not endure the trial of being separated from you and you sick. However I trust you may not be soon again troubled with the terrible nightmares that oppressed you during your entire stay in San Francisco."[4]

Late in August the failure of the gigantic Ohio Life and Trust Company shook New York's financial circles. "It seems that I am the Jonah of Banking," Sherman moaned to John. "Wherever I go there is a breakdown—These affairs are Costly to Bankers, as they always more or less lose by the losses of others, and by the rapid depreciation in Collaterals." To repay the debts he had run up for his army friends, Sherman wished to sell to John his properties in and about St. Louis. These consisted of a frame house on a large lot on Morgan Street in the city, twenty acres of land seven miles outside the city, and forty acres located about thirty-six miles east of the Mississippi River. "I do not expect," Sherman wrote Thomas Ewing, "to be able to live on fancy property such as the Morgan St lots." Even though penniless, Sherman proposed that he, John, Taylor, and Hoyt contribute fifty dollars a year to Elizabeth. John agreed to give "if necessary $100," but was not sure Taylor could afford that much.[5]

By the end of September, New York banks and merchants were failing. Sherman informed Ellen:

This condition of things is beyond your or even the comprehension of the wisest, but it is that sad condition of things that has hung like a nightmare over me for four years, and I think I would find myself relieved at attaining the height of your ambition driving a stage or draught at a dollar a day. All about me are paled and excited—I feel natural and at home & tell them to keep cool that we had this condition of things for three consecutive years.

When I cautioned Mr Lucas & Major Turner against the symptoms of this coming event, they laughed at me, and said I had the California scare. Now they have a worse scare than they ever had. . . . Everybody for himself now.[6]

Sherman was in bed on the morning of October 6, when his cousin, James M. Hoyt, came to him with the morning paper, which announced that Lucas's firm in St. Louis had suspended payments. Having no one else to blame, Sherman took out his frustration on Ellen:

You will no doubt be glad at last to have attained your wish to see me out of the Army and out of employment. The matter has hung like a nightmare over me so long that I don't know how to feel. At all events in a few days I will be adrift on the world ready for any thing that may turn up—This is of course a just retribution for my presumption in supposing ourselves qualified for duties which we were not prepared for by careful training.[7]

In mid-October Sherman returned to St. Louis to close out the affairs of his bank. He told Ellen:

Things are as blue as blue can be. You would hardly recognize it as the lively thriving city of 1852. All is dead, dead—and I doubt if I would accept any offer here of business—Turner wants me to settle here and offers me compensation, but I have seen a good deal of Mr Lucas. At one time he thinks himself ruined beyond hope, and when called on to make a small sacrifice, he at once demurs. . . . I ought to have had sense enough to know that I was fit for the Army but nothing else.[8]

Having no other prospects, Sherman agreed to return to San Francisco to close out business there. Informed in late November of her husband's decision, Ellen felt

heart sick & distressed. . . . I am entirely unwilling for you to go out there at all—I dont care what Mr. Lucas has at stake—your life is worth more & you ought not to risk it. But I suppose no opposition of mine can keep you now. For mercy's sake get back before fall or I shall feel tempted to leave the children & go out to you. Please do not mention the army to me again unless you have made up your mind that we are not worth working for.[9]

Just before leaving St. Louis for Lancaster, Sherman was walking along the street when he looked into a face he had not seen since he had left West Point in 1840. Like Sherman, Ulysses S. Grant had fallen upon hard times. In 1854, while serving with the Fourth Infantry in California, he had appeared slightly tipsy at the pay table. His martinet of a commander, Lieutenant Colonel Robert C. Buchanan, thereupon forced him to resign. Broken in spirit, Grant spent the next four years on his wife's farm on Gravois Road outside of St. Louis. Grant and Sherman chatted briefly and then separated, each overwhelmed by financial problems.[10]

In Lancaster, waiting to leave for California, Sherman pressed John for a military appointment. Because of troubles with the Mormons in Utah, Congress was expected to raise four new regiments. Sherman's experience would entitle him to consideration. He had already written to his old commander, General

Persifer Smith. "Keep this to yourself," he advised his brother. "I know that Ellen & Mr Ewing would oppose my attempt."[11]

By the end of January 1858, Sherman was back in San Francisco trying to collect on Lucas's holdings, consisting of $100,000 in real estate and $200,000 in notes, bonds, and mortgages. "The whole town is for sale and there are no buyers," he informed Turner, then reorganizing the St. Louis banking house. He added:

> Leave me out—I wont engage in the business—I am flat broke and utterly disqualified—So is Nisbet. . . . I seem to bring bad luck. . . . Though I tried my best, I see now innumerable errors—I am willing to pay for them to the extent of my means, and assure you on my honor that I reproach no one for the loss of my commission & sacrifice of my time & property. I ought to have known California better than to risk my own & other persons wealth in such a cursed land.[12]

Thomas Ewing tried to rescue his son-in-law—and to keep Ellen and the children nearby. Owning extensive saltworks and coal fields several miles down the Hocking Valley from Lancaster, he proposed that Sherman and Charley Ewing manage them. Sherman told his father-in-law:

> All I now can say is that my wants are simple. . . . I never incurred debt for myself. And hope never to know what it means, but Ellen's wants are artificial & though she professes great willingness to live in a log house, feed chickens & milk cows—I know better. She cant come down to that. . . . If Ellen & the Children are willing to live down Hocking, and you think it proper that I should leave my family there, and can satisfy yourself that I can serve you and them too, I'll hold to my promise to come to Lancaster this Fall, and go to work at Surveying Engineering or whatever you are willing to entrust to my care.[13]

In mid-April, Sherman predicted that he would be in California until September. "I am kept here by no self interest," he wrote Thomas Ewing, "but in consequence of honoring obligations assumed under more prosperous auspices and which would seem to me wrong to disregard now in adversity." For "Brother officers" he had invested $130,000. Of this he had lost $15,000 to $20,000 and felt obligated to "stand some of their loss. All I aim at is to be free this Fall from this fatal scheme, the likes of which has driven to infamy the Head of every Bank, almost, that flourished here as my contemporaries of 1854."[14]

By June, Cump was complaining to Phil that "it will take all my St. Louis property to make me free, and all I aim at is to reach Lancaster in September flat broke. California seems to ruin Everybody that has tried it, and I ought not to attempt to prove an exception."[15]

In early July, having done as much as he could, Sherman left San Francisco for home. Without incident, he reached Lancaster on July 28. Facing him, as so often before, was the problem of how to support his wife and children.[16]

— II —

With Sherman away for such long periods—indeed, his wife wrote him just before he started home, their youngest son "would not know you now were you to step in this moment"—Ellen reared the children with a free hand. She left abundant evidence of her love for each of them, but Tommy drew special attention. Excepting Lizzie, each of the four bore the middle name Ewing. Yet, in September 1857, Ellen informed Sherman: "I have concluded to call the baby 'Ewing' instead of Tom so you will know hereafter who I mean when I speak of Ewing."

On June 15, 1858, Ellen described her plans for the baby: "Ewing will soon win a large share of your heart when you see him. No washerwoman's child gets more fresh air or has more strength & nerve than he and even his own Mother has no stronger will. I flatter myself he will resemble you in intellectual capacity. My great desire is to see him an eloquent Priest some day."[17] Immersed in business woes, Sherman passed over the last comment, for he left no record of discussing it with Ellen.

Throughout August 1858 Sherman remained near Lancaster, figuring out what to do next. On the ninth, fidgeting about, he wrote John of his uncertainty: "Mr Ewing has held out to me an indefinite sort of plan, which I don't fully comprehend, and I doubt if he does, all for the purpose doubtless of keeping Ellen here. . . . I dont want to live in Lancaster and necessity alone will compel me to do it, but having a wife, four children and a body pretty well used up I cannot be as independent in action, as in feeling—or spirit!"

Aggravating it all, Ellen and Elizabeth Reese had for two reasons "declared war to the Knife." First, Elizabeth had "reflected" on Ellen for forcing Sherman to come home when he was "on the high road to wealth & fame." Then came a heated discussion on "a lecturer named Nichols" and "the Catholic question—I do not think Elizabeth intended to offend Ellen, but she did, and this quarrel went a great deal too far—too far to think of repairing & I would not now think of attempting a reconciliation—I suppose too it will spread amongst the other members of our family, and I wish myself back to San Francisco, purgatory, or any where else rather than among a fraternal war, without end—or means of solution." Sherman thought of taking his family to Kansas. "Could I," he asked John, "earn a living there in any known capacity?"[18]

On the same day, Sherman further pursued the Kansas idea. Hugh, recently married to Henrietta Young, the daughter of a wealthy District of Columbia landowner, and Tom Ewing had set up a law practice and real estate firm in Leavenworth, where their father owned property. "The chief object of this letter," Sherman asked Tom, "is to say that if you see any possible chance for me at Leavenworth . . . I could or might assist you in a great deal of out door business, and it may be that my New York, San Francisco & St Louis as well as Army acquaintances could be brought to bear. All I want is a start, and I think I would settle down, never again to budge unless some unexpected Good luck should turn up." About the feud between his wife and his sister, Sherman remarked to Tom: "Ellen would die cheerfully rather than to see any stain or breath of suspicion upon her Religion. . . . At all events now the quarrel is absolute & I would as soon undertake to convert the Mormons as to reconcile the quarrel."[19]

Deciding to visit Leavenworth, which lay on the Missouri River, Sherman stopped first in St. Louis. "Everybody there of my old acquaintance laughed at the idea of my living in Leavenworth," he reported to Ellen from Kansas. "Stewart (Col) offered me the necessary capital & partnership to go into a Wholesale Provision & Grocery business—also said if on my arrival here I did not like the looks of things to write him, and he would guarantee to lend me at once. Offers unsolicited from such men as Col Campbell as would or should satisfy any Broken Officer & Banker." One real estate auctioneer offered to sell out to Sherman. And Sherman's friend Henry L. Patterson, a former land auctioneer, suggested the two become partners. In St. Louis "all patient, prudent, honest men can thrive. . . . It too is a Catholic Community where you feel unannoyed by Protestant prejudices which more or less exist in smaller places."[20]

Arriving in Leavenworth on September 14, Sherman learned that he had crossed paths with Tom, who had returned to Ohio with his wife and was now delivering political speeches. But he found there Ellen's cousin, Hampton Denman, whom he had known in Lancaster and in California. Like the Ewings, the Denmans were politicians, and Hamp, having just been elected mayor of Leavenworth, was busy writing his inaugural address. A stroll about town convinced Sherman of the folly of land speculation. "Every other office is a land or money brokers office," he warned Ellen. " . . . Like *kilkenny* cats they will scoop & trade till nothing but tails are left."[21]

About three miles up the river lay Fort Leavenworth, where Stewart Van Vliet served as quartermaster. Van Vliet was able to offer Sherman two jobs, the first repairing the military road between Leavenworth and Fort Riley, a distance of about 140 miles, and the second auctioning off 200 horses, 200 mules, and sixty wagons for the army. These Sherman eagerly accepted, for they would occupy him for a month, by which time Tom and Hugh would surely return. "You know that in matters of meals, comforts, or what concerns me personally," Cump explained to Ellen, "a tent & Soldiers Ration will suffice—I should not like you to feel at all lowered in the Social scale, & it shall not be.—Nor do I wish to contemplate our Children occupying a lower seat in the Synagogue than we do—and as I know real respectability consists in honorable actions & not in riches—I want to conform to our true position & not spend one cent for pomp—display or vanity."[22]

During the first week of October, when Tom and Hugh finally arrived, they offered Sherman a partnership in their law office. Sherman had read some books, but he knew little about law. Tom, however, agreed to handle the litigation, while Sherman would handle collections, banking, and real estate.

The new firm eventually opened an office on the second floor of a shell of a building on Main Street, between Shawnee and Delaware. Denman ran a land office on the first floor. One day when Kansas's chief justice Samuel Lecompte was in the office, Sherman mentioned that he intended to get a license to practice law. The judge instructed Sherman to ask the clerk of the court for one. When Sherman asked what examination he would have to pass, Lecompte answered, "None at all." He would admit Sherman to the bar because of his general intelligence. "If I turn lawyer it will be bungle bungle from Monday to Sunday," Cump predicted to Ellen, "but if it must be, so be it."[23]

On October 10, after only two days in Leavenworth, Tom was off again, this time to the Republican convention in Topeka, where he hoped to be nominated for chief justice of Kansas. Denman, too, was campaigning, but for the Democratic nomination for governor. "I am disappointed beyond measure that Tom has not come," an anxious Sherman informed Ellen on the twelfth. "Nothing even to assure me he is on the way. . . . If Tom would settle square down to his profession, and let politics alone, I think we could keep pace with this Country, whose progress will not be anything like as fast as Hugh calculates, yet as fast as Ohio, Indiana & Illinois. . . . I am positively certain that Land Speculation in Kansas will prove disastrous to Hugh—and am afraid Tom will be very much troubled by his share in them."[24]

Ellen, meantime, pined for her husband. No longer was she willing to sacrifice herself for her father. She pleaded to Sherman:

> One thing I cannot consent to, and that is to live separated from you any longer. I will wear cheap clothes, put them on the children— eschew society in toto, live far from the church or near it, as I can, do as much of my own work as possible and be more amiable than you have ever known me, if you will only be cheerful & happy. But if you value my health & peace of mind you must not leave me here this winter. I cannot lead this unnatural life any longer suffering anxiety on your account as I do. If your means will permit no better rent a log cabin or its equivalent with two or three beds a rag carpet & a stove and if we can have fuel bread meat & coffee & sugar I shall not despair. I am in bad health and I am unhappy and I beg you to take me with you somewhere.[25]

Even before receiving this letter, Sherman had sent Ellen instructions for coming to Leavenworth. She was to take the railroad to Cincinnati and then come on to St. Louis. While there, Ellen must collect a note for $575. She should also get from Patterson $550 for property he sold for Sherman. "At St Louis you must raise one or both these amounts of money, else we may actually suffer here this winter." From St. Louis, Ellen was to take "the Boats for the Missouri River" and sail to Leavenworth. "Bring one girl servant with low wages but able to do all our work—excepting a part of the Washing," he ordered. "—And bring *all the Children*."[26]

For by this time Sherman was irked at his father-in-law. The elder Ewing had given his daughter two parcels of land near Leavenworth. The first consisted of eight acres about a half mile from the Missouri River on Three Mile Creek, the other eighty lots a mile from the river. On the latter, Ewing insisted that Sherman build a house. "But this addition," Cump told John, "is settled with poor Irish, Butchers &c so as never to be fit for us."

Irritated, Sherman wrote to his father-in-law as he never had before. "I shall insist on all, Minnie included," he said of his plans to unite his family in Leavenworth. "It is full time that she began to regard us as her parents. The propriety of this I know you will agree with perfectly, and therefore I need offer no argument."[27]

But on the night of November 12, Ellen reached Leavenworth without Minnie, who, having lived with her grandparents for four years, seemed more their child than Sherman's. Still, Ellen and the other children received a rousing welcome. "The whistle of the steamboat soon brought Cump and Boyle [Hugh] down to the dock," she related to her mother. "Tom followed almost immediately and I assure you that I felt grateful and happy to see their dear faces beaming with love and pleasure at our arrival."[28]

Ellen brought news of a peace gesture from her father. He had given her an additional two and a quarter acres of land. Cump explained to John:

> If as I progress I find it likely Leavenworth is to become a place of more than ordinary importance I will take property in trade where I can get it but as a general proposition I should had I money to invest lend it at high interest on Bond & mortgage—Interest here is as high as it used to be in California from 2 to 5 percent, and the law enforces any contract for the loan of money. If you have any specie funds I could lend it for you at such rates, but as I know that all persons who borrow at those rates must break up and quit the Country, I should always expect to take the property.[29]

With Ellen Cox Ewing spending the winter with her parents in Lancaster, Cump and Ellen took over Tom Ewing's "pretty place" on the corner of Third and Pottawattamie. Tom stayed and boarded with the Shermans. On New Year's Day the firm for some reason added another partner, Daniel McCook of Ohio, leading Sherman to warn Hugh that "business must swell considerably before we have work for us four."[30]

As 1858 ended, Sherman reported on the railroad fever then engulfing Leavenworth. All proposed routes to the Pacific bypassed the town, but Tom Ewing was being sent to Washington to lobby for a road nonetheless. John, heretofore opposed to a Pacific road as expensive and impractical, answered Cump's pleas for aid by promising now to support it.[31]

Encouraged by his brother's change of heart, Sherman sent him on January 6 a paper entitled "Notes on the Pacific Railroad." It was based, he observed, on talks with all of the important Western explorers, not just army officers but also scouts and mail carriers like Kit Carson. In his paper Sherman narrowed the five projected routes to the West to two. The first, from Council Bluffs through Nebraska, Wyoming, and Utah, and then along the Sacramento River to Benicia, resembled the path later taken by the Union Pacific and the Central Pacific when they completed the first transcontinental railroad. Sherman always considered himself one of the route's founding fathers, for in 1855 he and some partners had invested $10,000 in a railroad that built twenty-two and a half miles of track from Sacramento east to Folsom. Sherman, the vice president of the line, later called it "the real beginning of the Central Pacific, indeed the pioneer of all the Pacific Railroads." The second, and to Sherman the preferable route, led from Leavenworth to Santa Fé and ended at San Francisco.

In this report and in a letter to John, Sherman took issue with former Secretary of War Jefferson Davis, who advocated a southern route that would require buying Mexican territory. In his letter, Cump pleaded:

> I hope you will oppose the purchase from Mexico of any of her frontier States. Sonora is awful, just like the Arizona desert, only more so.—If we have any thing to do with Mexico let it be as a whole—a kind of viceroy to govern under Laws of Congress, with an Army enlisted in the United States.—But don't admit that Mongrel race as Citizens— our standard of Citizenship is low enough without bringing in the Mestizo Indian Negro & Spaniard of Mexico. . . . Of course I would like to be connected with the Great Pacific Road, but were I to look to it, I would starve before it is begun.[32]

The appearance of the report in the *Washington National Intelligencer* on January 18 hardly elated its author. "I did not want John to publish my notes on the Railroad," Sherman confided to Hugh, "but it cant now be helped. My reason is I do not occupy any position warranting the publication."[33]

___ III ___

In February 1859, with the legal business slow, the gold strike at Pikes Peak in the Rockies offered Sherman some hope of profits. The best route to the goldfields, the Old Military Road, passed through Leavenworth and Fort Riley, he informed Thomas Ewing. To supply the migrants with food, Sherman recommended that Ewing convert one hundred acres of his land on the north side of Indian Creek, forty miles from Leavenworth and seven from Topeka, into a farm, over which Ewing's grandnephew, Henry Clark, might be put.[34]

As the trickle of miners going west increased, Sherman convinced both Ewing and himself that he could make money selling corn. The miners were not the only ones in need of it, for on a trip up the Missouri to Council Bluffs early in March, Sherman saw Van Vliet take aboard "two mammoth loads" of empty corn sacks for army use. "Had we begun a month earlier," Sherman mused to Ewing,

> I believe we could have made $5000 easy on this corn business this season. And I yet think by buying and selling we can clear one or two thousand—and be admirably placed for this fall & next winters operations, when we will have a full knowledge of the true character of these Gold discoveries.[35]

Late in March Ellen, expecting her fifth child, left Kansas for the warmth and comfort of the Lancaster house. "I will not attempt to tell you how lonely and badly I felt to see the Emma start taking you and the children back to Ohio," Sherman informed his beloved. "And how I realized the slight hold I have on you and them while Lizzie and Willy seemed glad to go away."[36]

Depressed, Sherman threw himself into the work on the farm. There Clark and Luke, the hired hand, did the heavy work, while Sherman cleaned up the cabin, cooked, acted as a carpenter, and, he later recalled, did "some general supervision of the fencing, plowing, and planting."[37]

Reaching Lancaster, Ellen was heartbroken at the thought of living without her husband. She urged him to take her ten thousand dollars and to "establish yourself in business in St. Louis or Cincinnati or Baltimore, or in any place north of the yellow fever line." She said she would "cheerfully & gladly give it all to you. Pray consider the matter well for I am not partial to Leavenworth. I feel that I shall not live long anywhere & I lack the spirit required in a new place."[38]

Sherman agreed that

> we should not build this year. If I had been reared as a merchant or mechanic I would take your advice & locate in some city, but my education & habits totally disqualify me for this, and it was this knowledge that so disturbed me at San Francisco. I saw that I had abandoned my profession & had nothing to fall back on. I am doomed to be a vagabond, and shall no longer struggle against my fate—As to your money I want it guarded safely, beyond chance of risk so that its income may support you and the children let what fate befall me. I look on myself as a dead cock in the pit, not worthy of further notice, and will take the chances as they come—My best now is Leavenworth, but I don't think we should build till some certain success is demonstrated. . . . I will strive to get your $10,000 invested so as to yield you 1000 a year, & for myself, I can scratch along anyhow—& if necessity compels I can live on a soldiers Ration.[39]

But by mid-May Sherman saw the collapse of his scheme for selling corn. Impoverished miners bought none for themselves and allowed their animals to graze on grass. Convinced he had engineered another failure, Sherman began getting rid of corn at low prices.[40] Would he ever find a way of making a living?

___ IV ___

As a lawyer, Sherman possessed more common sense than ability. He later told of the Irishman who walked into the office in Leavenworth asking for help. Part of his shed extended onto another lot owned by his landlord, who demanded an additional two and a half dollars a month in rent. The Irishman sought relief in court. With Tom Ewing and McCook absent, Sherman was forced to try the case, which he lost. Thereupon Sherman advised his client to carry the shed to another lot, where the landlord could not charge for it.[41]

But the Leavenworth office proved as barren to Sherman as the corn farm. Ewing and McCook were more interested in politics than in law. By the spring of 1859, the free and proslavery parties in Kansas were replaced by the Republicans and Democrats. Like Kansas itself, Sherman's partners split over politics, Tom Ewing being a Republican candidate for the state constitutional convention, and McCook being a Democrat.

In this struggle Sherman sympathized with neither side. And he feared the black man. "The Negros of our Country should remain slaves," he advised John. " . . . If the Republican Party, under the control of its more liberal members, can shape its course, so as to separate itself absolutely from the Abolition Antecedents, and can settle down on some moderate leader like Mr Bates of Missouri I would follow it, but not otherwise. . . . Should Tom be defeated on this issue," he continued, "it will much damage his future political prospects, but I dont know as it will grieve me much, as too much of his time and thought is taken away from his business. . . . Still as a defeat would mortify him very much I cannot but wish him success."[42]

By June 1 Sherman's prospects in Leavenworth had fallen apart. He still had large amounts of corn. Nor could he turn to Van Vliet for help. "They have already made charges against him," Sherman confided to Ellen, "which are perfectly groundless but still enough to make him timid & afraid to deal with friends." Van Vliet stood accused of irregularities in the purchase of supplies for the army. Court had been in session for a week, but Tom had attended only once. "Completely engrossed in politics," he was "called on all the time by dirty politicians to contribute to the Cause, his money time & services. At the moment he is in the Country to make a Speech. . . . My share of the business is at the office. I am not, & never can become competent to go into Court."[43]

When Sherman stored their furniture and moved into a hotel, Ellen showed displeasure:

> What do you propose to do with me next winter & when are we to meet again if you are making nothing now? Can't you come on and rent Father's farm for a year or two? Here we could live on what we would spend for fire wood in Leavenworth. Being in Tom's office is only a wrong. It was instead of a source of profit one of expense last winter & I cannot hope that it will be any better. Tom will *never* practice law or stay a year at a time in Leavenworth—*that* you are convinced of yourself—Why then submit to the provocations which are inseparable from your position there? I hope the republican party will be defeated as I have no sympathy with any thing akin to Abolitionism.[44]

Reared amidst wealth, Ellen found poverty embarrassing. Early in June the priests began accepting donations for the new Catholic church in Lancaster, estimated to cost between $18,000 and $20,000. Thomas Ewing pledged $1,200, his wife $500. Ellen's unmarried younger sister Maria, nicknamed Sis, gave $100, Charley $200, and Philemon $1,000. "Father told *me* not to subscribe anything," Ellen revealed to Sherman, "& I told him I had nothing to give except the will."[45]

After Sherman suggested that it was best the children saw so little of him, Ellen responded bitterly, "They may be left to your *sole* care sooner than you apprehend." She then repeated a previous request: "Should God in his infinite wisdom remove me dear Cump I hope you will not only be with the Children & keep them together but I trust you may give them a good Catholic Mother to assist you in rearing them for heaven."[46]

Repeatedly Ellen urged her husband to join Charley on her father's farm. "You expected me to live cheerfully in Cal.," she argued, "& you think it unkind that I should wish you to live in Lancaster or near it. Of one thing I feel certain that should you come here to live you would be happier than you now imagine." Preferring politics, Tom ignored the law office. "He will never do differently," his sister believed. "You might as well hope for a confirmed drunkard to quit drinking as expect Tom to give up politics entirely."[47]

— V —

Hearing of a vacancy in the army's Paymaster's Department, carrying with it the rank of major, Sherman wrote to his friend Major Don Carlos Buell, the assistant adjutant of the army, about it. Buell knew nothing about the paymastership, but he sent Sherman a Louisiana newspaper and a handbill inviting applications for the superintendency of the state military institute which was to be established outside of Alexandria, Louisiana. Buell believed that Sherman might be appointed to the post, which paid $3,500 a year, for one of the school's founders was General G. Mason Graham, the half brother of Sherman's late commander and friend, Colonel Mason, and the brother of Ellen's former convent teacher.[48]

Desperate for employment, Sherman considered two other projects. He contemplated going out to Salt Lake City and from there driving cattle to California, where he would handle some business for Lucas. Another possibility was a bank in London to be founded by William F. Roelofson of Cincinnati, whose partners included Hugh and Thomas Ewing.[49]

By August 2, 1859, when the Board of Supervisors met to elect a superintendent for the Louisiana Seminary of Learning, it had received numerous applications. Sherman's file, General Graham remembered, consisted only of Buell's recommendation and a letter from Sherman himself, "through the pure modesty of which shone so clearly the intellectual mind, the exalted character and simple honesty of the man, that every member of the board felt its influence." But Sherman's sentence that he had "married a daughter of Mr. Thomas Ewing of Ohio" spurred debate, for some members of the board feared that Ewing was antislavery. In the end, Governor R. C. Wickliffe and State Senator Michael Ryan joined Graham in pushing through the appointment. "All my subsequent connection with the institution, to this day," Graham observed in 1875, "has only served to confirm me in the conviction that in the bargain with Sherman our State and its people got full value received."[50]

Returning to Lancaster, Sherman found Graham's letter telling him of his election. "It is manifest the appointment is offered me at the instance of the family of my old friend Col R. B. Mason," he informed Hugh, "who had an exaggerated notion of my ability." If Sherman had his "own feelings alone to consult," he would go to London, "make a life errand of it, and build up the business from the bottom." But this meant leaving his family. In Louisiana he had "strong friends," including his West Point classmate, former governor Paul O. Hébert, Bragg, Graham, "& others that will sustain me in authority."[51]

In early September, Sherman accepted the Louisiana post, promising to be in Baton Rouge by November 5. Preparing for the job, he visited the Kentucky Military Institute, spending several days consulting with its superintendent, Major Edwin W. Morgan, an 1837 graduate of West Point. He then went to Chicago to talk to Captain George B. McClellan of the Illinois Central Railroad, who a few years back had studied European military education for the army. Already immersed in the details of establishing a college, Sherman hoped to learn the price of each item needed, from textbooks to blackboards, from paper to paint.[52]

On September 5, as Sherman prepared to return to Lancaster before going south, Ellen bore their fifth child. Eleanor Mary Sherman, nicknamed Elly, was truly her father's child. "Every body says did you ever see a child look so much like a grown person as she looks like her Father," Ellen wrote Cump about the month-old infant. When Sis first saw the baby, she shouted: "O! Mercy look at Cump." Charley, too, "exclaimed at the likeness."[53]

Desiring privacy, Ellen moved with her five children into their own home on October 20. "You cannot imagine how nicely we are fixed now how comfortable we are," the tired but happy wife informed her husband. "Father still looks upon it as folly but I have my own opinion of the propriety of the move." Despite her circumstances, Ellen considered herself luckier than Henry Turner's wife, now carrying her fourteenth child. "Poor Mrs. Turner," she commiserated, "—she will certainly have twenty children before she stops."[54]

Late in October, on his way down the Mississippi to Louisiana, Sherman stopped in St. Louis and for once heard good news. In San Francisco, hard times had forced Lucas to take over Sherman's house. Now someone wished to buy it, and Lucas insisted that Sherman take the proceeds, amounting to $5,600. "I propose to place that money with Mrs. Sherman," the grateful man informed Turner, "to place with her Brother Phil," who would lend it "in sums of 1 & 2000, to good farmers" for interest of 10 percent a year. The income would provide Ellen with a nest egg "in case of accident to me."[55]

St. Louis was ablaze with talk of John Brown's raid on the government arsenal at Harpers Ferry, Virginia. "I find Southern men, even men as well informed as Turner, are as big fools as the abolitionists," Sherman wrote home. Many Northerners had denounced Brown, Sherman pointed out. "Yet the extreme Southrons pretend to think that the northern people have nothing to do but steal niggers and preach sedition."[56]

In Louisiana, Sherman went first to Baton Rouge to see the governor. He then headed toward Alexandria, in Rapides Parish, three miles outside of which the academy was to be located. Visiting Governor-elect Thomas O. Moore and Graham, he was especially taken with the latter. "Rather small, exceedingly particular and methodic," Graham was, Sherman told Ellen on Sunday, November 12, "altogether different from his half brother, the General. . . . He was at West Point but did not graduate, but he has an unlimited admiration of the system of discipline and study." Graham, to Ellen's regret an Episcopalian rather than a Catholic, lived on a magnificent estate nine miles from Alexandria and twelve from the Seminary.[57]

Early in his stay in Louisiana, Sherman sent a note to Braxton Bragg, then living on his recently purchased sugar plantation. Bragg answered warmly. He had recommended for the post of superintendent Claudius W. Sears, whom he did not know, solely because Sears had graduated from West Point in 1841. Sherman's election, however, elated him. Graham, who Bragg had met during the Mexican War, was gallant and devoted to the new institution. "You may safely trust to his friendship," Bragg advised.[58]

Moving into one of the rooms of the Seminary, situated on four hundred acres of pineland, Sherman hired four additional carpenters and set them to work constructing mess tables, benches, and blackboards. He boarded with an old black woman who cooked for the Seminary's permanent carpenter, James. "It is very lonely here indeed," Sherman informed Ellen on November 25. "Nobody to talk to but the Carpenters, and sitting here alone in this great big house, away out in the Pine Woods, is not cheerful." Sherman had not as yet received any money, and did not expect to until the legislature met in January.[59]

Writing on November 18, John, soon to be the Republican candidate for Speaker of the House, feared trouble for his brother:

> The recent infamous foray of Old Brown at Harpers Ferry seems to have so excited portions of the South that all from the North are regarded with suspicion and you will not be liked the better for having so bad a Black Republican for a Brother. How unfortunate it is that a People bound together by so many ties & interests should so misunderstand each other. However such differences make up the history of the world from the time of Abraham & Lot to this hour.[60]

In the midst of the Speakership controversy came the revelation that John, along with sixty-seven other Republicans, had endorsed an antislavery work that he had not even read. In *The Impending Crisis of the South*, published in 1857, Hinton R. Helper, a North Carolinian, had attempted to prove that slavery impoverished and degraded poor whites. "If John had not signed for that trifling Book of Helper," Cump lamented to Ellen in mid-December, "he would have been elected, but with that step which I suppose was a thoughtless one, he forfeited all chances of stray Southern [votes] which otherwise he might safely have calculated on."[61]

Knowing the sensitivity of slaveholders, Sherman tried to avoid political discussion. But one evening, at a dinner party at Governor Moore's attended by Bragg, the newly elected head of state public works, state senator Richard Taylor, the son of the former president, Attorney General Hyams, and other local dignitaries, Sherman could not dodge the issue. After the ladies had left the dining room, Sherman noticed buzzing at the other end of the table and detected frequent mention of his name. Moore finally called to him, noting that his brother was the abolitionist candidate for Speaker and that some people believed Sherman should not head a Louisiana college. He asked for Sherman's view of slavery.

Denying that John was an abolitionist, Sherman answered that "the people of Louisiana were hardly responsible for slavery, as they had inherited it." He distinguished between domestic slaves, who were well treated, and field hands, whose "condition" depended upon "the temper and disposition of their masters and overseers." Sherman recommended two changes in the institution. He would forbid breaking up slave families. And he would repeal the law prohibiting an owner from teaching his slaves to read and write, for these talents enriched the life of the slave and made him more valuable. He cited Henry Sampson, a slave whose former owner lived in Rapides Parish. Brought to California by an army officer, Henry was employed in Sherman's bank for $100 a month. After a teller taught him to read and write, his pay jumped to $250 a month. He soon saved enough money to buy his freedom and that of his family and his brother.

After Sherman finished, someone—Sherman thought perhaps the attorney general—slammed his fist down on the table and shouted: "By God, he is right." The debate, marked by "ability and fairness," went on for another hour, but Sherman, having extricated himself from a difficult position, just sat and listened.[62]

Wherever Sherman went, the issue seemed thrust before him. He told Thomas Ewing about Jesse A. Bynum, a former congressman now on the Board of Supervisors. "A little dried up old man," Bynum had "a horror of an Abolitionist. I was told that he was angry at my election, because he thought all from Ohio were real Abolitionists, but today he was unusually polite to me, and told me much of his Congressional experience."[63]

As the Speakership contest droned on—John eventually came within two votes of being elected—Sherman felt the pressure. On December 22, Dr. S. A. Smith, a member of the board and a candidate for the state senate, "pointedly" described to him "the deep, intense feeling which now pervades the South." Sherman answered that he had nothing to do with such questions, but if disunion were "meditated," he would oppose it. If secession occurred, Sherman observed to Ellen, "I would not say what I would do. . . . I know that you in Ohio do not think of the danger of Civil War, but so blind and unreasonable do men become on abstract questions that no one can foresee. Here they discuss all the chances of a Southern Confederacy. For myself I would apprehend nothing, but I would not have you or the children here, should such a movement be actually inaugurated."[64]

—— VI ——

Sherman spent the last weeks of 1859 buying supplies for his academy. He bargained for books and furniture and suggested having uniforms made in New York, whose firms produced better garments at prices cheaper than could be gotten in New Orleans. He also thought it best to emulate the Kentucky system and to forego summer camps until the school had "four classes of well drilled cadets."[65]

Meantime, Thomas Ewing emerged from several meetings with the businessman William F. Roelofson in Cincinnati with a proposal for Sherman. The banking firm would guarantee to employ him in London for two years at an annual salary of $7,500. To show its good faith, it would advance him half a year's salary. "I have talked with Ellen," Ewing informed Sherman just before Christmas. "She is pleased with it."[66]

But Sherman saw in the offer only longer separation from his family. "Were I to go to England on their terms," he wrote his wife, "you would not go, and the only advantage would be that I could gradually save means to work with elsewhere. It is provoking to me to feel that wherever I have been, I am highly esteemed save in Ohio, and were I starving I doubt if I could get the lowest office on a Railroad."[67]

Ellen, on the other hand, favored "trying this London project. I think there is little doubt but sooner or later your post at the College will be rendered uncomfortable to you by reason of the excitement on Slavery which excitement will never be subdued as long as slavery & fanaticism exist—and that will be as long as we live. . . . If you leave down there without any remuneration for your services you cannot feel that they can justly blame you."[68]

The opening of the New Year and of the college coincided. On Monday, January 2, a "bright, cold & clear" day, nineteen of the fifty-nine cadets were on hand. Two days later four more, delayed by the snow and cold of the previous week, straggled in. Sixteen members of this opening class were state appointees. The rest had been selected by the Board of Supervisors. The cadets occupied rooms cluttered from plastering and painting and splattered with tobacco juice left by the carpenters.

The French class began without books, which had yet to arrive from New York. "Some of the Hot bloods talk of Non-intercourse with New York," Cump scoffed to Ellen, "but that is absurd. Every thing but Cotton & Sugar must come from the North."

Of the four other faculty members, Sherman was especially attracted to David F. Boyd, a Virginian who taught ancient languages. Boyd was "about 25 years, and a very clean Gentleman.—Indeed on the whole the Professors are above mediocrity."[69]

Boyd always remembered his first meeting with Sherman. "He received me very kindly," he noted, "and in his characteristic way chatted about everything. He was then, as he ever was, the prince of talkers. I fell in love with him at first sight." Tall but "slightly bent," Sherman was "very striking," possessing hazel eyes and bright red hair, "with a tuft of it behind that would, when he was excited, stick straight out. . . . He believed that the union was supreme and secession treason; I believed the state was supreme and secession a reserved right."[70]

Even as the term began, Sherman was concerned with things other than education. As he told Thomas Ewing on the eighth, he felt tempted by a chance to make $15,000 in two years, & that in London. I could live there cheaply and save in two years 10 or 12,000, which with what Ellen & I have stowed away, would give the position of independence that I have long aimed at & failed to secure. This however is too good a berth to risk. . . . I now handle all the monies, and am absolute master of all the business. We have a Treasurer 20 miles off with Bonds. Whereas I in fact have in my possession all the monies $6000 nearly, and for its safety they have never asked of me a receipt. I cannot therefore mistake the confidence of the Board. Caution must be my plan *now*.[71]

By January's end Sherman had still not heard from Roelofson, but, earning money for the first time in years, he expressed pleasure. "Things seem to settle down as in California," he wrote Ellen, "and I cant go a hundred yards off, without some one coming after the major, the title by which I am known here."[72]

In early February, while contemplating his future, Sherman faced the usual deportment problems presented by teenage cadets. The worst offenders included an acting sergeant who had called another lad a liar, thereby inciting the latter to draw a knife, and two others who complained that Sherman's searches in washstands for tobacco constituted a breach of propriety. "For a day or so the cadets were insubordinate," Cump related to Ellen, "but I soon put a stop to that by getting rid of the five worst, and henceforth I expect no further trouble from that Quarter." If the legislature appropriated for the school $25,000 a year for the next two years and promised to build him "a good house," Sherman preferred "the certainty" of Louisiana to "the doubtful success of the London scheme. . . . Still if Roelofson came, and I see no positive proof of the Legislature acting efficaciously I will tender my resignation & come North in March— It will puzzle them to find a successor, but I must give them time. They can think the matter over now."[73]

Informed by Sherman of the London proposition, Graham immediately wrote to Moore. Sherman's salary must be raised to $5,000 a year, he pleaded. Everyone loved Sherman. Bragg, who had known him for twenty years, praised him lavishly. In Washington last September, Colonel Joseph P. Taylor, Zachary's brother, had said: "if you had hunted the whole army, from one end of it to the other, you could not have found a man in it more admirably suited for the position in every respect than Sherman." Rumor had it that William H. Russell, "the great Utah army contractor," and Beverly Tucker, the American consul at Liverpool, were among the partners in the London venture. In Paris the previous summer, Tucker had warned Professor Francis W. Smith, who taught chemistry at the Seminary, "that if our Sherman & their Sherman was one & the same man, we would not be able to retain him."[74]

On February 11, Roelofson hurriedly visited the Seminary. He found Sherman, substituting for a sick professor, listening to a recitation. For some reason Sherman confessed that he preferred the London proposition, but he added that he would never leave without the concurrence of the board, which had treated him so kindly. At Alexandria, Sherman and Roelofson found General Graham and five other members of the board meeting informally. Faced with Sherman's possible resignation, the six passed resolutions praising Sherman and urging him to stay. In deference to Graham, who begged him to wait ten days to see what the legislature would do, Sherman asked Roelofson to hold off until the twenty-first. "He seemed pleased at our beautiful seminary," Cump confided to his father-in-law the next day, "but regarded it as a kind of exile."[75]

To John, who had finally lost the long Speakership contest, Sherman scoffed at Roelofson's proposal:

> I had heard it before. He wants me North in April & in London in May. They are in a stew about it here—I seem to have filled the measure of their wishes, and they are determined to hold on to me. . . . All the Lancaster folks are bent on having me go to London. . . . I am afraid of those Financial schemes, especially when too many small men are in. The only parties I know in this scheme are not men of wealth experience and high standing—Without these qualities I know it will take a lifetime to inspire Confidence, without which success is impossible.[76]

Hurrying off to Baton Rouge to lobby for his college, Sherman found friends. "Bragg is here," he informed Ellen, "and other acquaintances, and although some look at me rather cross, as being Johns brother, yet on the whole I am treated by all with marked respect. I was never more puzzled. I am very much afraid of that project . . . and yet I feel that you will be banished down here. For me I would as lief be in Mexico as anywhere, indeed I still keep my mind on the Governorship of Guadalajara—Bragg says he will take Oaxaca, so we may be neighbors." Sherman considered London "an old fogy place, out of date and behind times." He "mistrusted" Roelofson, whose "mannerisms were those of an adventurer, & not those of a good business man." Suspicious also was Tom Ewing, now the chief justice of Kansas, who warned Sherman that while visiting Leavenworth Roelofson had left a bad impression.[77]

A telegram from Ellen urging Sherman to take the London post seemingly settled things. Forced by his wife and her family to choose something he did not want, Sherman responded bitterly: "You still prefer London—All prefer London—Again we give up a certainty for an uncertainty—As to your going to London you know well you wont—the alternative is you must remain at Lancaster two years till I can save the means to return and settle in Ohio." Sherman felt "sorry" for Graham, "whose soul was rapt up in the success of this College." To keep him there, Graham had offered to pay the difference "from his own purse—indeed he made such an offer to the Governor, but I would not listen to it. . . . General Graham had almost associated a Providence with us— the deep affection for you by his sister, the confidence in me by his dead brother, united with the accident of my application made him believe it a special Providence—and now he sees that Providence dont control it."[78]

With Graham's permission, Sherman came to Ohio in mid-March, determined to refuse the London post unless he were guaranteed a one-tenth interest in the bank and the promised annual salary of $7,500 for two years. Finding Thomas Ewing in Washington and Roelofson in Europe, he met in Cincinnati with David Gibson, the treasurer of the new firm. Reluctant to make any commitments without his partners, Gibson urged Sherman to wait until Roelofson returned. Finding the excuse he needed, Sherman refused. He would now return to the South.[79]

Back in Louisiana, Sherman unfolded for Hugh his reasons:

Indeed I never did fancy the London scheme. I have always doubted its success—London is an old Town & the English an old People not likely to be caught by new agents or new projects. . . . I am determined to make my own way—and being here will stay, though fully impressed with the belief that it is going to be hard for Ellen. Here she must reconstruct all her ideas—there are no markets, and every thing must come from New Orleans, the Beef & Mutton in winter she would not eat, and chickens & turkeys are rare birds. . . . To tell the truth I would rather be in California, with an old mule, traveling from place to place and fetching up occasionally at Doña Augustias, but I must consider my family. I can provide for them here, as soon as a house is built, but I know & feel the trouble that is in store from the causes I have assigned, and the difficulty of getting to Church.[80]

5

The Insanity of the South—
and of Uncle Charles

— I —

REACHING THE SEMINARY in late March, Sherman found the cadets in their new uniforms "as proud as peacocks." They "hailed my return," Sherman beamed to Graham, "as though I were their grandfather. I had to make them a speech to-night." Happily the legislature had consented to building two houses, one for Sherman and the other for Anthony Vallas, the Hungarian who taught mathematics at the school. Sherman's house, brick and two stories, was to cost $5,000. Sending Ellen a sketch and floor plan of the proposed building, Sherman estimated that from his pay of $300 a month, he needed only $60 to live. If Ellen could limit herself to something near that amount, they could save between $1,200 and $1,500 during the next six months. Setting up house in Louisiana would, he believed, require $2,000.[1]

But politics and the talk of secession occupied more and more of Sherman's thoughts. When in mid-April the Democrats, convened at Charleston to nominate a presidential candidate, could not agree on Stephen A. Douglas of Illinois and split into Northern and Southern factions, Sherman told John that they had

> committed a vital mistake—one from which the Democratic Party cannot recover. I regard it as dead as the Whig Party, though its name may again be seized by some new Combination. . . . Of course, I avoid politics—because it might drive me out, and I might say some thing that would compromise me. . . . I am too dependent now to be foolish— Were I to lose this place, I would have to seek employment in some foreign land—for of course in Ohio I could find no congenial occupation. But I hope the wild demagogues & politicians of this country North & South will not be able to break up this Government—which would first be anarchy, and after who knows.[2]

71

Meantime, Ellen related sad family news. Returning from New York City, Elizabeth Reese, who had patched up her differences with Ellen, reported trouble with Uncle Charles Hoyt. With his first wife, who died in 1831, Uncle Charles had two children—a son, Charles Henry Hoyt, later a career army officer, and a daughter, the elegant Eliza Augusta Hoyt, nicknamed Gussie. But Charles, a prosperous merchant, developed the same illness as his mother, Mary Raymond Hoyt. By 1860 he was in and out of what Ellen called "the Asylum." During one period of derangement, he signed away the property that he held in trust for Gussie and Charles. To regain her inheritance, Gussie had no choice but to sue her father.[3]

Having made up with Elizabeth, Ellen now feuded with her brother Tom and with Dan McCook, both of whom she accused of neglecting her property in Leavenworth. "I will *never* again have any business transaction with Tom," Ellen vowed to Sherman, "for it is seeking the occasion to sin to give him the opportunity of making me angry. . . . When he wants to play the lofty hereafter he must try it with his wife & its my opinion she'll raise him higher than he intends to go."[4]

As the building of his house progressed, Sherman confided to Tom that moving to Louisiana would

> be a trial to Ellen—far, far harder than San Francisco or Leavenworth. . . . I have no doubt one of our first troubles will be that Ellen's servants will all quit, after we have gone into debt to get them here. And then she will have to wait on herself—or "buy a nigger." What will you think of that—our buying niggers—but it is inevitable. Niggers wont work unless they are owned. And white servants are not to be found in this Parish. Everybody owns their own servants. . . . You must be careful in your black Republican speeches not to be down on us too hard, for your own sister may be found by necessity to traffic in Human flesh.[5]

Such a thought horrified Ellen. "I have written," she confided to her father, "that I could not in conscience buy or sell a man and that I consider it a poor investment of money."[6]

Beset by troubles, Sherman looked forward to the end of the school session. In mid-June he was forced to dismiss, against the wishes of the board, two cadets from good families who continually violated the rules. To make a profit, the steward skimped on meals, sometimes withholding the butter and at other times serving no meat. Then, Sherman told Ellen, came Vallas, "a sneaking canting hypocrite—one of those refugee Hungarians who have inflicted our Country. . . . He has made himself so unpopular with the Cadets that they chalk his name all over the walls, insult him in various ways, and even hiss him." Titling himself the "Superintendent Clerk Treasurer," Sherman had "too much to do to do it well. . . . I must gradually shift on other shoulders some of the accounts & writing else I will soon dwindle into a mere scribbler & Book keeper."[7]

By now the presidential campaign was in full swing. Approving a resolution sponsored by Congressman Joshua R. Giddings of Ohio inserting the Declaration of Independence into their platform, the Republicans nominated Abraham Lincoln of Illinois. The Northern Democrats selected Douglas, the Southern Democrats John Breckinridge, and the Constitutional Union party John Bell.

The Ewings drifted all over the election map. "Philemon, Boyle & I think Charley are Douglas men," Ellen reported to her husband. "Father says he would vote for Lincoln had not the party admitted the Giddings clause into their platform. Now that the Know Nothing element has left the party I am for Lincoln in spite of slavery clauses. Aren't you afraid they'll hang me for an abolitionist when I go south?" A week later Ellen added: "At a Lincoln demonstration the other evening Sis & I went out to the gate and waved—so I suppose we are on that side."[8]

In mid-July, when John Sherman came to Lancaster to speak, Ellen "instructed both the boys to hurrah for Lincoln." She hoped to display a flag for the occasion. "Sis is a great Republican & so much in love with John that Cecelia would have good cause for jealousy were her own health bad."[9]

The school term over, Sherman came north early in August. Ohio, with the largest harvest, Thomas Ewing asserted, since the first white settlement, contrasted with Louisiana, where drought had ruined the crops. "If I could transfer the product of this country to Natchitoches," Sherman wrote Boyd, "I would prefer it to all the mines of California. Horses and cattle roll with fat. I hear this is the condition of things in all this region, and God grant it may be one of the many causes to teach men of prejudice and fanaticism of the beautiful relation that should exist between parts of the same country."

Sherman found politics the talk of Ohio. Thomas Ewing revealed that he was consulted before the formation of the Constitutional Union party. He had favored its creation, but felt it should nominate no one and hold itself ready to endorse the most moderate candidate available. John, on the other hand, campaigning in northern Ohio, sounded more and more "radical. I shall see him this summer," Cump informed Boyd, "but can not expect to influence him."[10]

After a week in Lancaster, Sherman went to Washington. Introduced by Buell to Secretary of War John B. Floyd, he requested 145 muskets, which with the 55 in Alexandria would be enough for the expected enrollment at the Seminary. To his surprise, Floyd, a Southerner, acceded to the request, even though Louisiana had already received its allotment of federal weapons. Could Floyd be arming the South?[11]

Sherman went on to New York, where as arranged he met Major Francis W. Smith, the professor of chemistry and commandant of cadets at the Seminary. Scurrying about the city, the two bought and sent south several thousand books, among them 400 on history and geography. Included were the speeches of George Washington, Thomas Jefferson, and Henry Clay, atlases, and volumes on Europe and the Orient.[12]

Back once more in Lancaster, Sherman followed politics closely. He wanted John to break with Senator William H. Seward of New York and Giddings, "the radicals of that party," but, he noted to Boyd, "John laughs at me."

Unopposed in his district, John was campaigning for Republicans in other states. "Everybody says that in case Lincoln be elected he will have a high seat in the synagogue."[13]

With Thomas Ewing and John both "out for Lincoln," Sherman knew that he would be "more 'suspect' than last year" in Louisiana. "Though personally I feel sure of the support and confidence of the Gentlemen who govern the Seminary," he wrote John in October, "yet even they could not justify themselves to the People in keeping me in power if the prejudices I speak of grows, you & Mr Ewing both being as they say *rank* abolitionists, and I maintaining silence & neutrality on a question vital to them." Without success he had applied for a supervisory job with a Cincinnati railroad, solely because Ellen preferred Ohio to Louisiana. "So I shall return to Louisiana—mind my business— Keep quiet, and if Lincoln should be elected and you get a high seat in the synagogue—you must try and get me back where I rightfully belong into the Army—The Inspector Generals Dept. if a vacancy occurs."[14]

—— II ——

The Seminary to which Sherman returned in early October differed from the institution he had left. Now led by Dr. S. A. Smith, the board had decided in Sherman's absence to make the school less military and more academic. Sherman was now earning $4,500 a year, $500 coming from his position as acting treasurer and another $500 from supervising the branch of the state arsenal established at Alexandria at Bragg's suggestion. "These two latter," he warned Thomas Ewing, "may at any time be lopped off."[15]

Sherman was hired to teach engineering and drawing, but the Seminary contained no students advanced enough to take these subjects. Sherman therefore began teaching history and geography. During these classes, he noticed after Lincoln's election that students selected Southern subjects upon which to write and speak. Citing John C. Calhoun, William L. Yancey of Alabama, and other fire-eaters, they considered the defense of slavery and of Southern institutions their highest duty. But, Sherman remembered, during the fateful month of November no one uttered or wrote a word offensive to him.[16]

As South Carolina moved to secede from the Union, the students at the Seminary became unruly. Served a poor supper on the night of November 28, they rioted, smashing dishes and firing pistols. Sherman immediately dismissed five cadets. "I fear the Institution is in danger from causes which arose after I left last summer," he informed Ellen the next day. "The alterations made after I left were wrong in principle, causing Genl Graham to resign, and since then he will take no interest in our affairs. Gov Moore is interested in Politics, same of Dr Smith—So we are left to the charms of the caprices of a panel of Wild Boys. Still, this is a small matter susceptible of remedy, but the secession movement underlays the very safety of everything."[17]

Sherman spent the last day of November in Alexandria with Dr. Smith, who was confident Louisiana would peacefully leave the Union. South Carolina, Georgia, Alabama, and Florida could secede without war, Sherman answered. But the withdrawal of Mississippi, Louisiana, and Arkansas would close the Mississippi River to Northern shipping and "bring war.—For though they now say that Free trade is their policy yet it wont be long before steamboats will be taxed and molested all the way down."[18]

Observing secession from afar, Ellen decided against bringing the children to the South. "Father says there will be no disunion," she informed Cump on December 5, "but you know Father always persists in *believing* what he *hopes*. Philemon says we are to have disunion and a multitude of evils in its train. Philemon quite sympathizes with the South but I do not in the remotest degree. I think the northern democrats are to blame for stirring up this spirit but I have no shadow of sympathy with the South any longer."[19]

In mid-December Sherman met with Dr. Smith and

spoke my mind fully and clearly. . . . I asked to be relieved—But there is no one here to take my place. All are unwilling that Vallas, a hypocritical foreigner who would serve the Devil for his pay, should succeed me. Nor will Dr Smith consent to entrust the monies of the Institution to any of the other Professors. . . . General Graham lays low & says nothing in these times, but I know he is much distressed at the hasty manner in which things are pushed.[20]

Boyd was with Sherman in his room when news arrived that on December 20, 1860, a special convention had voted to take South Carolina out of the Union. Over forty years later Boyd described the scene:

Who knows but my own humble self . . . *how he burst out crying like a child,* and pacing his room in that *nervous way of his,* he turned to me and exclaimed: "Boyd, you people of the *South* dont know *what you are doing!* You think you can tear to pieces this *great Union* without war! But I tell you there will be *blood-shed*—and plenty of it! And *God only knows how it will end.*" And for an hour & more, I sat there listening to him pouring out his great patriotic heart in the agony of grief over *what he then so clearly foresaw.*[21]

The behavior of Buchanan, who had abandoned Major Robert Anderson, the commander of the forts in Charleston harbor, infuriated Sherman. "I regard Buchanans refusal to reinforce Maj Anderson—my old Captain—at my old Fort Moultrie as a pusillanimous act," Sherman wrote John. "He should have been promptly reinforced—3000 men in Forts Moultrie, Sumpter & Johnson with one or two steam frigates would be beyond the danger of attack from South Carolina—and as to exasperating the People—it would have caused less fatal efforts than the pusillanimous abandonment of a brave officer & his Command."[22]

Realizing he must soon leave Louisiana, Sherman was adrift in the sea of uncertainty. He refused to become a "Traitor to Uncle Sam," he told Hugh, but he would "hold on" to his post "to the last minute solely for the pay." Besides, the state legislature owed him $500 for supervising the arsenal, and this money he would not collect until March. Should he leave Louisiana, he would go either to Washington, to seek an army commission, or to St. Louis, where his friends might help him. At the latter place Turner might be angry at him. During the summer Turner, a Virginian, had written Sherman charging Ohioans with "nigger stealing," and Sherman had answered just as sharply. "If the worst comes to the worst," Sherman reassured Ellen, "I will rent your fathers farm and pitch in for bread & butter. We have been too much separated, and I feel deeply at times the absence of you all."[23]

Again being shoved out into the world, Sherman took out his displeasure on Ellen. "I have got pretty near to the end of my rope," he complained to her on January 5, 1861. "I have neither health, strength or purpose to start life anew—Nor can you afford it." In the midst of Sherman's frustration, Ellen had rented "a new house, and begun steps that will result in spending a few more hundred dollars. I wont find fault because I admit that your reasons are good, but it would have been prudent to wait a while. . . . My only hope is that bad as things now look, there may occur some escape, or if dissolution is inevitable that Ohio & Louisiana may belong to the same Confederacy."[24]

Three days later, reading in the papers that Alabama had seized the federal arsenal near Mobile, Sherman predicted to Ellen that the forts at the mouth of the Mississippi would be next. In the face of treason, Sherman had admitted to Dr. Smith "that I hold on simply for pay. This may be an unworthy motive—We need money, and money we must have, and where else to procure it I know not—I cannot unless compelled to come to Lancaster to hang about loose and unemployed—It would be neither a satisfaction to you or to me." With secession imminent, a few of the students at the Seminary were in disorder. "I had a Cadet threaten me yesterday with a loaded pistol, because I detected a Whiskey jug in his Room, & threatened him with dismissal," Sherman told Ellen. "He did not await trial but went off. Although a large majority of the Cadets are good boys, still we have some hard cases."[25]

As Sherman feared, Governor Moore, frightened when the two United States senators from Louisiana warned him that the government planned to reinforce the installations at the mouth of the Mississippi, seized the forts and the arsenal at Baton Rouge, Bragg taking part in the latter action. Caught in the crossfire, Sherman consulted with Dr. Smith, who, Cump told John, "pledged me that in no event should I be asked to compromise my national character." Smith urged Sherman to wait until Louisiana seceded before leaving. To his brother, the beleaguered man revealed:

> I can so ill afford to lose my wages, and hate to hang about Lancaster unemployed, that I yield more than I should. . . . If I leave here I cannot come down to first principles for however willing Ellen may be in theory, yet in practice she must have an army of servants and other comforts that money alone can give. If I leave here I fear I may be forced by necessity to go down to Hocking, or get a farm, and it requires more strength than I possess. . . . If you know the new Secretary of the Treasury and could get for me the offer of the St Louis

Treasury . . . in four years I could reestablish myself there in safety—
Otherwise I fear I am doomed to the Salt wells.[26]

On the sixteenth, the same day that Sherman wrote John, Ellen sent good news. Senator Salmon P. Chase of Ohio was sure to go into Lincoln's cabinet—as it turned out he became secretary of the treasury—paving the way for John's election to the upper house. She added, "John can easily procure you a high position in the Army if you desire it."[27]

When the state authorities sent to Sherman's arsenal 3,300 muskets and 70,000 cartridges taken at Baton Rouge, Sherman notified Moore that he must resign. "Thus I was made the receiver of stolen goods," Sherman later recorded, "and these goods the property of the United States." By now General Graham and the other opponents of disunion "have given up all hope of *stemming* the tide" and wished only for peaceful secession. But, Sherman predicted to Ellen on the twentieth, war was sure to come, for, as he had heard Clay say in 1850, "peaceable secession" was "an absurd impossibility. Much more so is it now, when the commercial interests of the North are so much more influential."[28]

Although Sherman mumbled about his willingness to farm or work at the salt wells, Ellen knew better. Her husband, she insisted on January 29, three days after a special convention voted to pull Louisiana out of the Union, would be satisfied only when he returned to the army. John had already spoken to General Scott about an appointment. Proud that her husband had promptly denounced the rebellion, Ellen called the North "weak because Mr. Buchanan is weak. If Jackson had been in his place the Government would have been strong enough & the rebels weak enough by this time." She found Turner, who had graduated from West Point in 1834, especially despicable. Although he had been

> educated & supported by the Government for years, [he was] ready not only to turn his back on her but to turn the knowledge & the arms she has given him against her. Were I a man in firm health he & I would fight together—not side by side but face to face. . . . A Catholic should be governed somewhat by the fact that the Church has always treated slavery as an evil which should be abolished by wise and moderate means. . . . I used to dislike the Abolitionists but their folly sinks into insignificance when compared with the treason of the South.[29]

On February 16, settling the school accounts, Sherman prepared to leave the Seminary for New Orleans. After a few days he would go to St. Louis. Sherman hoped to reach Lancaster by March 4, the "critical moment" of Lincoln's inauguration. The tormented man reported to Ellen:

> I went up the Bayou last week to visit the Luckettes—Sanfords, Comptons, Grahams and Longs. All however were so full of Northern outrages, wrongs, oppressions &c that it was useless to argue. There seems to be universal regret that I leave. . . . If you really wish me to

settle down in peace you must bear with my impatience and must not misconstrue my motives or denounce so severely my Religious opinions, or what you believe my want of Religious faith. . . . All the Ladies express regret that my departure cuts off all hope of their making your acquaintance. They were prepared to welcome you to this country— But the die is cast, and again I must go forth and when to fetch up will depend on the storms of an unknown sea. I think I would feel more at ease any where rather than Ohio, but I acknowledge the impossibility and impropriety of moving you away.[30]

In New Orleans, Sherman was shocked to find that Colonel Abraham C. Myers, with whom he had served in New Orleans in 1852 and 1853, had left the federal army and accepted that rank in the Confederate army. Myers occupied his old office in the Lafayette Square building. When Sherman asked him if he felt funny about using a desk and papers with "U. S." on them, Myers answered: "No, not at all." Secession was inevitable and would be successful. The Northern and Southern governments would soon be friendly with one another.[31]

At the New Orleans Custom House, Sherman met Beauregard, who, like Sherman but unlike Myers, believed secession would lead to conflict. Beauregard, who later apologized for having allowed a Northerner to educate the two sons he had sent to the Seminary by describing Sherman's term there as "not so very creditable," believed Sherman "felt embarrassed as to his course in the event of war." Sherman acknowledged that the Southern people had been kind to him. Beauregard, a favorite of Confederate President Jefferson Davis, said he would "go with Louisiana 'right or wrong' not that I loved Caesar less but Rome more. We then parted good friends," Beauregard remembered, "to meet again a few months afterwards at Manassas, then at Shiloh, and subsequently in South Carolina."[32] Beauregard might have added that during the Civil War, as Sherman's star grew brighter, his dimmed.

Long afterward, Bragg related how, during Sherman's last night in New Orleans, he wanted to persuade his friend to stay. Bragg had begged Governor Moore to offer Sherman the rank of brigadier general in the new state army, which Bragg commanded. In Sherman's room at the St. Louis Hotel the two sat up nearly all night speculating on what was to come. Bragg saw that Sherman would not accept an offer to stay and with great regret parted from him.[33]

On February 24, Sherman headed up the Mississippi toward St. Louis. Forty years later Boyd, a former colonel in the Confederate army, evaluated this segment of Sherman's life:

I think it was *just then*—in the Pine Woods of La—from 1859 to 1861— that your Father's character loomed up grandest: he turned his back on his best & truest friends, *because he thought we were wrong!* Still, his great living heart never ceased to beat warmly for us of the South. And all thro' that terrible struggle, Genl Sherman had more warm devoted friends in the *Southern* army than any Southern general had![34]

6

Hamlet

— I —

THE YEAR FOLLOWING Sherman's return from the South, where he had headed the Seminary that later became Louisiana State University, was among the most important of his life. The 1850s had been a disastrous decade for Sherman, bringing him financial ruin. The 1860s started out worse. When Louisiana seceded, Sherman left the post he cherished and came north. The trying times continued throughout 1861.

On Saturday, March 2, 1861, Sherman arrived back in Lancaster to welcome and unwelcome news. In the railroad cars coming north he heard John mentioned as Ohio's next senator, filling Chase's seat. But secession was proceeding, and Sherman feared the worst. "Lincoln has an awful task," he wrote John just after the inauguration, "and if he succeeds in avoiding strife and allaying fears, he will be entitled to the admiration of the world." Conflict was sure to come, "and the longer the postponement the more severe must be the application."[1]

At Lancaster, Sherman found a letter from John inviting him to come to Washington to discuss employment prospects. Arriving in the capital on the sixth, he saw "few signs of preparations," though secession was pushing ahead. "Even in the War Department and about the public offices," he later wrote, "there was open, unconcealed talk, amounting to high-treason."

One day John Sherman took his brother, who intended to offer his services to the government, to see Lincoln. They found the president talking to three or four men in a White House room filled with people. When the men left, John walked up, shook hands with the chief executive, took out some papers for some minor appointments, and handed them to the president. Lincoln agreed to appoint those recommended if the positions were not already promised. John then turned toward Cump and said:

"Mr. President, this is my brother, Colonel Sherman, who is just up from Louisiana, he may give you some information you want."

"Ah!" answered Lincoln, "how are they getting along down there?"

"They think they are getting along swimmingly," Sherman said. "They are preparing for war."

"Oh, well," responded the president, "I'll guess we'll manage to keep house."

Infuriated, Sherman, who had resigned his position to protest secession, heard no more of the conversation and always believed it ended there. But according to his brother, Lincoln went on to express the hope that the danger would pass and that the Union would be saved without war, a delusion the president shared with numerous other politicians.

Sherman later recalled:

> I was sadly disappointed, and remember that I broke out on John d——ning the politicians generally, saying, "You have got things in a hell of a fix, and you may get them out as you best can," adding that the country was sleeping on a volcano that might burst forth at any minute, but that I was going to St. Louis to take care of my family, and would have no more to do with it. John begged me to be more patient, but I said I would not; that I had no time to wait, that I was off for St. Louis; and off I went.[2]

Returning to Lancaster, Sherman entertained two prospects—both at St. Louis. He now hoped to get from Lincoln a post in the St. Louis subtreasury. But Frank Blair, whose brother Montgomery was the new postmaster general, objected because Sherman had done nothing for the Republican party in Missouri. "I am the only Northern man who has declared fidelity to the Union in opposition to this anarchical doctrine of State Secession," Cump complained to John, "and yet this is nothing as compared to local partisan service." The second prospect, appointment as president of the St. Louis Rail Road Company, came from Henry Turner, for James Lucas was the company's chief stockholder.[3]

Disgusted and disillusioned, Sherman did not even spare John's feelings. Tom Ewing had recently gone to Washington and asked John for an introduction to Lincoln. But John "put him off, or answered evasively." Tom then requested the same thing of Senator William Pitt Fessenden of Maine, "who promptly took him in his carriage to the President and introduced him so flatteringly that the President gave him absolutely the three leading appointments for Kansas—viz Marshal, Indian agent & some other." Tom, Sherman informed John, might be elected a senator from Kansas, "and if so will come to Washington with a grudge against you." The whole Ewing family, especially Ellen, believed John had "slighted" Cump, for the best John could come up with was the chief clerkship in the War Department, a position Sherman considered

> beneath my deserts, certainly a shock to my pride. . . . I am now with an expensive family actually adrift dependent upon blind chances. My

personal friend Turner may succeed in getting me occupation on a
street Railroad but again he may fail, in which event I will try and get
a Clerkship in some store. It certainly is humiliating to me, who have
filled high posts with honor, credit and success, to be compelled to go
begging for mere manual employment. . . . Now if there be any thing
in St Louis open to your influence I do think you should demand it for
me as a means of mere livelihood till I can recover from the loss I have
sustained in relinquishing my place South. I confess I know of none
such, & that I would starve and see my family want rather than ask
Frank Blair, or any of the Blairs, whom I know to be a selfish and un-
scrupulous set of ——— .[4]

John answered as best he could. He did not even remember Tom asking
to meet Lincoln. Cump must realize that John, now an Ohio senator, had
no power over appointments in St. Louis. How could he possibly get his
brother a job there? He again urged Cump to accept the chief clerkship in the
War Department, a post General Scott and Cump's other friends in Washington believed to be a stepping-stone to high rank in the army. "You seem to
think that the administration overlook your services & high character. I know
this is not so." John had spoken with Chase, Montgomery Blair, and Secretary
of War Simon Cameron, and all had "a high appreciation of your merits—
and you will find will readily and cheerfully accede to you any thing in their
power in a military way. Remember you are known as a military man not as a
civilian."[5]

Certain of the railroad position, Sherman moved his family to St. Louis. On
April 1 he rented a house from Lucas, and on the next day he became president of the line, at a salary of $2,000 a year "and a certain prospect of an in-
crease." A week later, when offered the War Department clerkship, Sherman
refused it, masking his feelings of contempt for the lowly position with an explanation to Montgomery Blair that he had rented a house "and incurred other
obligations" that made it impossible for him to leave St. Louis.[6]

At this time Ellen had some assets, but Sherman was still reeling from his
losses during the 1857 depression. After selling for $10,000 some property that
her father had given her, Ellen had put the money into notes. But Cump was
still in debt. He had already sold 640 acres of land in Illinois, three houses in
St. Louis, and about a dozen lots, "all of which I gave away." Some of this
money went to Braxton Bragg and to Abraham Myers, "who are now high in
power among our Enemies & balance to others whom I will not name. But
now," he informed John, "I own not a foot in St. Louis and only 40 acres in Illinois valued at say $1000."[7]

Sherman's salary with the street railroad would not even begin to meet his
expenses. After an argument, Cump had yielded and allowed Ellen to enroll
Minnie and Lizzie in the Catholic school run by the order that had educated
Ellen, the Sisters of Charity. Willy was attending a school owned by a Catholic widow. "Taking off seven hundred for rent," Ellen estimated to Phil, "it
leaves less than we require for wages schooling &c &c." As it was, the house

they were living in had no shade trees and no yard in which the children could cavort.[8]

That April 12 the Confederates began the bombardment of Fort Sumter. Two days later, John wrote Cump:

> We are on the eve of a terrible war. Every man will have to choose his position. You fortunately have the military education, prominence and character, that will enable you to play a high part in the tragedy. You can't avoid taking such a part. Neutrality and indifference are impossible. . . . For me, I am for a war that will either establish or overthrow the government and will purify the atmosphere of political life. We need such a war, and we have it now.[9]

Frustrated and disappointed, Sherman vowed to let others do the fighting. Frank Blair, the administration's spokesman in Missouri, twice called him to his house, once in the middle of the night, to offer him a brigadier generalship and command of the loyal militia. Because the appointment was in the volunteers and only for three months, Sherman refused it, giving Blair no choice but to appoint instead Captain Nathaniel Lyon, who was destined to be killed in the battle at Wilson's Creek that August.[10]

Self-pity dripping from his pen, Sherman complained to John about his treatment: "You know that Mr. Lincoln said to you and me that he did not think he wanted military men. I was then free, uncommitted and without the means of livelihood, and necessity forced me to seek it here." Ohio had, he wrote,

> always ignored me. When last fall I sought employment on a Rail Road I could not get it. Ohio has always preferred strangers & Foreigners to her Native Born Citizens, and this has always turned me off, when I was really in want. Now she expects me to break a contract for a permanent employment in exchange for a three months service. It may be said that War disturbs all prior engagements. But War existed when I was in Washington. The South had rebelled, had seized Forts, arsenals, and money—had driven out all the faithful servants of our Government, and insulted our national flag in a thousand ways. I resented it by a sacrifice, but that sacrifice was not appreciated, so that the present excitement changes not my attitude at all.[11]

Sherman may have decided not to serve, but he already saw the pattern of the conflict. The early battles might be fought in Virginia and Maryland, "but the Grand operation of the war will be on the Mississippi." Kentucky and Tennessee held "the keys of our present Country," for they would give the South natural boundaries along the Ohio. "If they are hostile," he warned, "I doubt the power of subjugation."

For Missouri, Sherman foresaw bloodshed: "Frank Blair whom I have seen twice is rabid, and would not stop till the whole country is convulsed and Slavery is abolished everywhere. As to Slavery in the abstract, and Slavery in the Territories, I do not particularly take issue—but as to abolishing it in the South or turning loose 4 millions of slaves I would have no hand in it."[12]

From Washington late in April, Tom Ewing described to Sherman the "intense and all pervading . . . fear of an attack." Five thousand enemy troops, less than a day away by rail, could "easily" take the capital. In mid-April his father had seen Lincoln and advised him "if he *had* to draw the sword, not to blow the trumpet first. He blew his trumpet before he had a sword to draw—and now he can't get his sword & is likely to lose his trumpet." Thomas Ewing had come away from the meeting sharing Sherman's belief that Lincoln deluded himself and failed to comprehend the seriousness of the situation.[13]

When Governor William Dennison of Ohio chose George B. McClellan, then the president of the Ohio and Mississippi Railroad, to lead Ohio's troops, Sherman was disappointed, but he called the selection "a most excellent appointment." Neither Lincoln nor Dennison had, he believed, given him "a spark of encouragement. . . . My experience is that no native of Ohio can expect a favor from the state. . . . John thought Dennison would invite me to Ohio," Sherman wrote Tom, "and appoint me to high service in the Volunteers there, but I knew better."[14]

Having left a position in the South because he objected to secession, Sherman was appalled by the daily growth of pro-Confederate sentiment in Missouri. The state permitted slavery, and Governor Claiborne Jackson and many of the leading politicians indicated they would back the South in a war. The hangers-on about the St. Louis hotels "were all more or less rebels," Sherman observed, and the Confederate flag hung from the Southern headquarters at the corner of Fifth and Pine. In Lindell's Grove, at the end of Olive Street, ten thousand pro-Confederates encamped at what they called Camp Jackson. They were led by Daniel M. Frost, a New Yorker who had graduated from West Point with Winfield Scott Hancock in 1844 but had been converted to secessionism.

The opposing sides in St. Louis itched for a fight. The federal arsenal housed five or six companies of troops, led by Lyon. They were augmented by four or five regiments of Home Guards, raised by the German population in support of the Union. Active in the Home Guard movement were Frank Blair and John M. Schofield, whose life for three decades would be intertwined with that of Sherman. Reminiscent of the lawless days through which Sherman had lived in California, newspapers and elected officials, depending on their persuasions, openly discussed attacking and demolishing either the camp or the arsenal.

Disturbed by the growing anarchy, Sherman often visited the arsenal, but he confided in few people. One person to whom he talked almost daily was his friend Colonel John O'Fallon, "a wealthy gentleman who resided above St. Louis." Every business day O'Fallon came to Sherman's office, and hour after hour the two would find the privacy they needed while pacing the pavement outside.[15]

Amidst all this, letters from Tom Ewing, lobbying in Washington, induced Sherman to change his mind about serving in the army. Tom could see why Sherman had declined the offer "to play *sub*" as a War Department clerk, but he believed his brother-in-law was "wrong declining Blairs offer as a matter of policy." The day he received this letter Sherman wrote to the secretary of war offering his services.[16]

During the Civil War few high ranking Northern army officers received commissions or promotions without political sponsors. Early in May, Sherman had three such supporters. Tom Ewing, John Sherman, and Charles Taylor Sherman, who was helping to raise regiments of Ohio volunteers, were all in Washington. On May 7, the day before Sherman dashed off his letter to Cameron, all three went to see Lincoln, who expressed a high opinion of Sherman and, Tom explained to Cump, "said he would *second* your appointment to a high place." John then talked to Cameron, who offered Cump a colonelcy in the regular army and authority to raise a double regiment of 2,200 men. "The promise was unconditional and emphatic," Tom reported, "& applied to the regular army explicitly, John says, & not to the three year levies. We suppose that better than a place as Brigadier Genl in the three years men, but are somewhat in a fog on the subject."

In Washington, Tom and Taylor bumped into newly appointed Brigadier General Irvin McDowell, whom Sherman characterized as "a staff officer too prone to service in a smooth office chair," but who now commanded a large force, including the Eleventh New York Infantry Regiment, nicknamed the Fire Zouaves because its members were Manhattan firemen. With amazement Tom gazed at their bagged red pants, their short jackets, and their skill in drilling. "They would whip any regiment in the City," Tom believed. McDowell talked to the two visitors about appointing Sherman to one of his army's two major generalships or four brigadier generalships. "Now," noted Tom, "we are in doubt whether something better may not be had of those appts. than a Colonelcy in the regular service." Tom had also learned that pride had worked against Sherman. "You would have been apptd Brigadier Genl in Ohio troops if *anybody* had said you would have it—but nobody did."[17]

Meanwhile, in St. Louis, Sherman experienced a slight taste of combat. "Yesterday," he wrote Tom on the eleventh, "I witnessed a scene which has confirmed me more strongly that in Civil strife Militia wont do." When he came home for dinner at three o'clock in the afternoon, "it was manifest something was on foot. The whole town was pouring out to the West," toward Camp Jackson. Rumor had it that the pro-Confederates were now armed with guns and ammunition brought from Baton Rouge—the same weapons whose illegal seizure by Bragg had convinced Sherman to leave the Seminary. Hearing of this, Lyon, "his hair in the wind, his pockets full of papers, wild and irregular," armed his men and marched them to the state encampment. "I knew well enough," Sherman remarked, "that Lyon would not attempt what he could not accomplish. So I staid home quietly to dinner." But Hugh, Charley, and Charley's law partner, John Hunter, rushed out to see the fight. After dinner, while walking the vacant streets, Sherman met men who said that Frost had surrendered. Feeling it was now safe, he grabbed Willy and walked over to the state camp, where he found the stories of surrender to be true. From the spectators came an occasional shout for the Confederacy and for Jefferson Davis. Suddenly scuffles broke out. Then came gunshots. Balls cut branches, and leaves fell from trees. To protect his young nephew, Charley threw himself over Willy, and eventually Sherman carried the boy to safety. In all, about a dozen people were killed, among them a woman and a little girl. "The whole resulted," Sherman told Tom, "from a want of discipline. . . . It was not necessary, but just what I expected, and I blame myself for being there with a child." After the affray, the ever-brave Hugh walked the streets of St. Louis prominently displaying two loaded pistols.[18]

Although Sherman did not know it, another witness to the attack on Camp Jackson was Grant. Blair later contended that while he and Lyon took the Confederate stronghold, Grant and Sherman swore they would have nothing to do with this "damned war." What Sherman did object to was Blair's antislavery view. "I see him daily," Sherman informed Tom Ewing, "and yesterday had a long talk with him. I say the time is not yet come to destroy slavery, but it may be to circumscribe it. We have not in America the number of inhabitants to replace the slaves. Nor have we the national wrath to transport them to other lands. Our Constitution has given the owners certain rights which I should be loath to disturb."[19]

In Washington the lobbying for Sherman continued. On the seventeenth, hearing four brigadier generals were to be appointed, Taylor and Tom hurried over to see Scott, who spoke warmly of Sherman and said that "he would not fail to bear you in mind if he was consulted." But, Tom noted, Scott "seemed offended that he had not been consulted as to the others, & doubtful he would be as to this." Tom and Taylor then saw Secretary of the Interior Caleb B. Smith of Indiana, who said that Sherman's name had come up in the cabinet discussions of appointments and that "he would cordially support you." The next visit was to Attorney General Edward Bates of Missouri, who "expressed himself warmly in your favor." They could not see Chase, but left a memorandum for him.

The chief opposition to giving Sherman a brigadier generalship came from Montgomery Blair. "He spoke of your refusal to accept the Post which they were all anxious to have you fill temporarily, with some bitterness, in cabinet meeting." Because of Blair's stand, Tom sensed that the lobbyists were doomed to failure. Would Sherman, he asked, accept the colonelcy if the brigadier generalship fell through?[20]

Throughout the rest of May, Sherman received assurances from John and Tom that he would be appointed colonel of the Thirteenth Regular Infantry regiment, but he heard nothing from Washington. "I know," he told Thomas Ewing on the twenty-seventh, "the Blairs do not like my refusal to accept the Chief Clerkship of the War Dept. or the leadership of the Dutch militia here. I have made a simple plain tender of my individual services and that is all I will do, and I would not feel slighted if they were ignored." But even before an important battle was fought, Sherman saw that this would be a different kind of war. Hatred of the Yankees was so "intense" in the South that the North would be forced to invade Arkansas, Louisiana, and Mississippi, "where a Regular army with its train of supplies will sustain continued and severe losses."[21] As early as 1861, Sherman foresaw that this war would perhaps be a throwback to the cruel Thirty Years' War of the 1600s or the Seven Years' War of the 1700s.

The suspense ended on May 31, when Sherman's friend, Colonel Schuyler Hamilton, Scott's military secretary, informed him that he was to be appointed to the colonelcy. A week later came a summons from Taylor and Tom: Sherman must come to Washington immediately. Receiving the telegram on a Friday afternoon, Sherman quickly arranged things with his employers and with his pregnant wife. At 5:30 P.M. that same day, he headed east.[22]

___ II ___

As Sherman rode the rails east, his thoughts brought him no joy. With the exception of McClellan, whom Sherman considered a genius, Lincoln's military appointments had, he believed, "afforded Bragg & Davis & Beauregard the liveliest pleasure." Even the newspapers were rising up against the nominations of such mediocre generals as John Frémont and John Pope and of politicians like Nathaniel Banks of Massachusetts and Andrew Reeder of Kansas. "I am afraid they will be playing fast & loose with me," Sherman told Ellen from Pittsburgh, "keeping me dancing attendant on the Secretary, and that I wont stand. This is my second trip, and unless they give me prompt answer I will come back forthwith and consider my patriotic duty fulfilled unless the safety of St. Louis should call all hands to arms."[23]

Just before Sherman left St. Louis, Turner had completed a rapid excursion to Washington, his primary purpose being to get his friend upgraded from colonel to brigadier general. The ideal position for Sherman, Turner believed, was the post of quartermaster general, from which the Virginian Joseph E. Johnston, eventually to be Sherman's archrival, had resigned to join the Confederacy. In Washington, Turner had seen Lincoln and then John Sherman, himself toying with a military career. John was temporarily serving under General Robert Patterson, drilling recruits at Chambersburg, Pennsylvania, and Hagerstown and Williamsport, Maryland, preparing for a possible advance on the federal arsenal at Harpers Ferry, now in Southern hands. "Turner was very much pleased with his interview with you & the President," Cump informed John, "and the only thing which slackened his zeal was some sharp words between him and Montgomery Blair about old General Hitchcock. But on the whole Turner was satisfied from what he saw at Washington that this unhappy war would if possible be confined to the just purpose of maintaining its rightful authority without degenerating into one of angry destruction." Turner understood that either Sherman or Montgomery Meigs, who had been born in Georgia but entered West Point from Pennsylvania, would be appointed quartermaster, but at Pittsburgh Sherman read that the job had gone to "some editor of a Sunday school paper."[24]

Arriving in Washington, Sherman found Taylor still there. That evening they called on Chase, who told them Meigs was the new quartermaster. In a pleasant way Sherman said that Colonel Thomas Swords was better qualified than anyone else, but the position was so important that he was glad to see it filled. "I find Washington less of a camp than I expected," he observed to Ellen, "but the same disagreeable crowd, pressing for contracts and sinecure offices." He had seen his name on a list of colonels in the adjutant general's office, but refused to believe anything until he received orders. "I have settled down into the conviction that I will be all summer engaged in raising a Regt— may be in Ohio, or Missouri—and by Fall must take place on some one of the Lines of Operation."[25]

Finally sworn in as a colonel, Sherman hoped to be able to return to St. Louis to recruit his regiment, which existed only on paper. But Scott insisted that he needed Sherman in Washington, and he dictated an order appointing the new colonel an inspector general with the job of overseeing the training of troops. Realizing that he was not going back to Missouri, Sherman instructed Ellen to pack their belongings and move back to Lancaster.[26] His days as a railroad president were over.

In June 1861 Washington was a hotbed of bluster. Everywhere a listener heard bold talk. Murat Halstead, the editor of the powerful *Cincinnati Commercial,* remembered being with several members of Congress in John Sherman's room one afternoon when a colonel walked in. John introduced the officer as his brother. The congressmen talked on and on about a quick Northern victory over the South. Finally the Colonel spoke up: "The sentiment of the people of Washington is such that they would cut the throats of our wounded on the sidewalk with table knives if our army should meet disaster in this neighborhood." After that, Halstead noted, "There was no more pleasant war talk."[27]

The move east brought back into Sherman's life his West Point classmate George Thomas. Late in June, Cump rode out to see John, then serving as an aide-de-camp to Patterson. Dreams of military glory dancing about in his head, John had come to Harrisburg with some Ohio troops he had raised. There he placed this Sherman Brigade under Patterson's command. Cump was with John when Patterson's lead division began fording the Potomac, northwest of Washington, moving toward Winchester, Virginia. At the head of a brigade was Thomas, waist deep in the Potomac's muddy waters. On the floor of the country tavern at which John was staying, Sherman and Old Tom, as he was called, spread a large map of the United States and on their hands and knees discussed the strategic points in the coming war: Richmond, Vicksburg, Nashville, Knoxville, and Chattanooga. John Sherman always remembered the sight of the two crawling about, accurately predicting the lines of operation of a war that had not yet begun but that would catapult both into glory.[28]

Thomas was a Virginian, but Sherman never doubted his loyalty to the Union. What did bother Sherman the inspector general was the condition of the Northern recruits hovering about Washington. The army was democracy run rampant: poorly armed, untrained, and disobedient. He later recalled: "Their uniforms were as various as the States and cities from which they came; their arms were also of every pattern and calibre; and they were so loaded with overcoats, haversacks, knapsacks, tents, and baggage, that it took from twenty-five to fifty wagons to move the camp of a regiment from one place to another, and some of the camps had bakeries and cooking establishments that would have done credit to Delmonico."[29]

To Ellen, Cump likened the nation to a headless dragon. One branch of government clashed with another, and cabinet members contradicted each other. As head of the army, Scott resented what he believed to be the constant interference of the president, the secretary of war, and Congress, but he could not act without them. Remembering his glory days during the Mexican War, he talked of leading his regulars, his "iron column," into the heart of rebeldom. But he was "very old, very heavy, and very unwieldy" and could not possibly take the field. "My notion," Cump explained to Ellen late in June, "is that Genl Scott wants the Secessionists to attack Washington, but I do not think they will oblige him."[30]

By July 4, 1861, the Confederates had two armies in front of Washington. Beauregard commanded the one at Manassas Junction. His advance guard, Cump remembered, was "almost in sight of Washington." Johnston, the ex-quartermaster, led the other. Patterson was to bottle up Johnston so that in a battle the two Confederate armies could not reinforce one another.[31]

If it was going to be, as the battle cry urged, "on the Richmond," it had to be soon. It was now July, and most of the 20,000 Union troops on the Virginia side of the river and 25,000 in Washington had enlisted for only three months. McDowell was placed in charge of the Army of Northeast Virginia and, preparing for action, organized it into divisions and brigades. Sherman commanded the Third Brigade of General Daniel Tyler's First Division. His force consisted of five units: the Second Wisconsin Infantry Regiment, 700 men; the Sherman battery, 112 men, 110 horses, and six guns; the Thirteenth New York, 700 residents of Rochester; the Sixty-ninth New York, "Irish—1000 strong"; and the Seventy-ninth New York, 900 Scotch Highlanders led by the secretary of war's brother, the gallant Colonel James Cameron.[32]

A more unmilitary-looking brigade probably never existed. The Wisconsin farmers showed up, as Captain Thomas S. Allen noted, in "delapidated gray" uniforms, hardly distinguishable from Confederate gray. Many New Yorkers wore uniforms left over from the War of 1812. Some Highlanders wore kilts. The Sixty-ninth marched with a green flag that had been presented to it for refusing to take part in a parade honoring the British Prince of Wales. Each member of the Sixty-ninth was Irish-born, and each wore scarlet breeches and a red Turkish fez.[33]

Sherman's command was hardly ready for battle. "Green as grass" he called his men. When formed, the brigade existed only on paper. Not until July 11 did the units assemble. Before receiving marching orders, Sherman was able to drill the brigade but three times. Many of the volunteers had never fired a weapon and were almost as afraid of loading their guns as they were of the enemy. Lieutenants, captains, and colonels knew about as much about tactics as the newest recruits. During the first week of training at Fort Corcoran, just south of Washington, Sherman replaced the inexperienced colonel of the Second Wisconsin with the regiment's lieutenant colonel, a West Pointer who soon proved inept. In the midst of the first battle, the lieutenant colonel dismounted and for some reason sent his horse to the rear, rendering himself incapable of leading his men.[34]

Even before any battle, some of the members of the Sixty-ninth, led by that "blathering adventurer and mischief maker," Captain Thomas Francis Meagher, argued that they were no longer in the army. They had enlisted early in April for ninety days but had not been mustered in until a month later. Meagher, "the mouthpiece of a few discontented men," insisted that these enlistments were up at the beginning of July, but Scott ruled that their ninety days began a month later.[35] To both Sherman and Scott, however, the message was clear. Unless a battle was soon fought, the makeshift army would melt away.

On the afternoon of June 29, McDowell presented his plan for attack to Lincoln, his cabinet, and several army officers. It was simple but intelligent. Beauregard, his classmate at West Point, lay between Washington and Richmond, the Confederate capital, with some 22,000 men. Rather than attack the Confederates at Manassas Junction, McDowell proposed to bypass such points, to turn his opponent's left, and to cut the enemy's rail connection with Richmond. This could be done anywhere along the Orange and Alexandria Railroad connecting Manassas and Richmond, but at no place better than Broad Run, about five miles below Manassas. With the railroad cut, Beauregard would have no choice but to backtrack.[36]

The movement was scheduled to begin on July 9, but by then McDowell was still trying to organize his army. Regiments were late in reporting to him, and the chain of command was not even established until the day before the proposed march began. Thus on July 16, a week late, Tyler's division of about 10,000 men left its Potomac camps and headed toward Vienna, Germantown, and Centreville, where the army's five divisions were to meet. Tyler's column consisted of four brigades: Erasmus D. Keyes, Sherman's old Fort Moultrie friend, led the first; Robert C. Schenk, whom Lincoln had appointed a brigadier general for no other reason than he had once been ambassador to Brazil, the second; Sherman the third; and Israel B. Richardson the last. "I think Beauregard will probably fall back tomorrow on Manassas," Sherman wrote his wife as the march began, "and call by R. R. from the neighborhood of Lynchburg all the men he can get, and fight us there, in which case we will have our hands full." Sherman had another sword to "add to his present armory," but he hoped Willy and Tommy would not choose "the military profession. It is too full of blind chances to be worthy of a first rank among callings."[37]

The march to Centreville proved pathetic. One lieutenant of the Second Wisconsin was so heavy he could not march at all. Even though the men carried three days' rations in their haversacks, they frequently stopped to pick blackberries and to loot stores located along the way. Not used to walking in the hot sun, the troops tarried at every stream to fill their canteens. "They were not used to denying themselves much," McDowell later complained. Sherman caught one Wisconsin soldier marching along with a quarter of a fresh mutton across his shoulders. Sherman told the man he would "attend to my case after we whipped the rebels at Bull Run" and confiscated the mutton for his own supper that night. When Sherman sent aides along the column ordering the stragglers to "keep in the ranks" and to "close up," soldiers jeered and yelled back: "Who are you, anyway? Tell Colonel Sherman we will get all the water, pigs and chickens we want." One Highlander captain, dressed in kilts, chased a pig, to taunts of "put on your drawers" and "take off that petticoat." The next morning the captain appeared in his regular uniform.[38]

During the march disillusioned volunteers continued to argue that their enlistments were up. "There was," Sherman told Ellen, "an ugly stampede of 800 Massachusetts men. The Ohio men claim their discharge, and so do others of the three months men. Of these I have the Irish 69th, New York, which will fight."[39]

Along the way a young mounted officer provided Sherman's troops with a colorful diversion. "He wore long, flowing locks, a hat and plume, a la Murat, and was uniformed in a royal purple silk velvet jacket, brilliant with gold trimmings," remembered Allen. The soldiers soon learned that he was a second lieutenant fresh from West Point. His name was George Custer, and he had been sent by Scott with dispatches for McDowell.[40]

Tyler's division became the first to reach Centreville. Elated at finding no enemy, he decided on his own to push ahead, with Richardson's brigade, Sherman's artillery, and some cavalrymen, to Blackburn's Ford. An artillery duel developed, and Richardson found himself trapped. Soon, according to Allen, came the order from "some ignoramus" for Sherman to double time his force to the front in the hot sun. The exhausted troops found no enemy, but stood under a withering artillery fire. "The cannon balls whipped about us on all sides," wrote a member of the Seventy-ninth. "He who had a big, or even a little tree, behind which to shelter himself, was looked upon with envy." The Yankees were able to withdraw, but Sherman always remembered "when for the first time in my life I saw cannonballs strike men and crash through the trees and saplings above and around us, and realized the always sickening confusion as one approaches a fight from the rear." Allen, later a brigadier general, viewed the experience differently, reasoning that "while the sound of big guns was more terrific, the real danger in battle was the whistling 'minnie,' which reached one without note or warning."[41]

On the night of Saturday, July 20, McDowell issued orders for the attack. At 2:20 the next morning Tyler's division, except for Richardson's brigade, was to march to its right along Warrenton Road to the Stone Bridge that crossed Bull Run creek. Under cover of Tyler's movement, Colonel David Hunter, with McDowell's Second Division, and Colonel Samuel P. Heintzelman, with the Third, were to move to the right, cross Bull Run north of the bridge, and turn the enemy's left.

The campaign, as one historian has observed, marked "the twilight of American innocence." It also fortified the Confederate belief that the Yankees were incapable of fighting, a myth Sherman helped dispel the following year at Shiloh. From the beginning things went wrong for the North. Reveille sounded at 2:00 A.M., but the men fumbled about in the dark. The lead brigade, Schenk's, was not ready until 3:00 A.M., and when it moved the troops became enmeshed in the dense woods and thickets. "We never knew where a fence or a tree was located in front of us," observed one marcher, "until we ran slap against it." Many of Schenk's men arrived at the bridge bruised and bloodied.[42]

The lead brigade slowed the entire army. Years later, Sherman remembered "the night-march from Centreville, on the Warrenton road, standing for hours wondering what was meant." Not until about six o'clock did Schenk's men, followed by Sherman's, reach the bridge. Schenk then arranged his troops to the left, or south, of Warrenton Road. Sherman took the right, or north. "Our business," Sherman told Ellen, "was simply to threaten, and give time for Hunter and Heintzelman to make their circuit."[43]

As soon as Hunter crossed Bull Run, he met the enemy. Sherman reported the firing as "brisk." All the while he fearlessly rode up and down his lines, looking for a place where the creek might be forded more safely than at the exposed and narrow bridge. The break came about nine o'clock, when Sherman saw two men ride along a hill across the way. One descended the far bank, crossed Bull Run, and rode toward the Yankees. Waving a gun over his head, he shouted: "You d——d black abolitionists, come on." Some of Sherman's men shot at him, but the colonel was more interested in seeing where he crossed. The rider, the bold Major Roberdeau Wheat of the Louisiana Tigers, had inadvertently done the Yankees a favor.[44]

Shortly after two o'clock Tyler ordered Sherman to cross Bull Run and aid Hunter, who had been engaged since fording the creek. Crossing where Wheat had shown them, Sherman's men came upon some retreating Southern Zouaves. Without orders, Lieutenant Colonel James Haggerty rode out to intercept them, and in full view of the troops a Confederate shot him dead. Arriving at the field of battle, Sherman received orders to pursue the enemy, who were then falling back. Confederate artillery perched on the hills poured in a heavy fire, but Sherman's men kept moving forward.[45]

The most severe engagement developed around Henry Hill, about a half mile southwest of the Stone Bridge. Held by the blue-clad Thirty-third Virginia Infantry, the hill offered the Fire Zouaves not glory but death. Their colonel and lieutenant colonel fell trying to take it, and a withering musket fire cut to shreds the proud regiment and a battalion of marines.[46]

Ordered to take Henry Hill, Sherman made a fundamental error. Inexperienced, he sent one regiment up at a time. First to attack was the Second Wisconsin, whose gray uniforms sometimes confused the Confederates. At one point, however, Allen saw a rebel officer in blue running amidst the members of the regiment urging them to cease firing. The ruse worked, as many Yankees momentarily put down their weapons. Driven back, the Second Wisconsin rallied and went forward again, but a heavy flank fire forced the regiment to retreat in confusion. Its members did not stop till they crossed Warrenton Road, subjected all the way to fire from Northern sharpshooters who mistook the Yankees for Confederates.

Sherman next sent forward the Seventy-ninth New York. The first fire hit them halfway up the hill, but their officers steadied the troops. Then someone spotted an American flag atop the hill. Many members of the regiment stopped firing. Suddenly a terrible volley poured in on the confused Highlanders. They staggered, faltered, and retreated. Among those wounded was Cameron, who was carried to an ambulance dying. Fifteen years later Sherman would make a special trip to the battlefield to show his future nephew by marriage, Secretary of War J. Donald Cameron, the spot where Cameron's uncle had fallen.

The Sixty-ninth fared no better. "The firing was very severe," Sherman reported to his superiors, "and the roar of cannon, musketry and rifles incessant. It was manifest the enemy was here in great force, far superior to us at that point. The Sixty-ninth held the ground for some time, but finally fell back in disorder."[47]

During the assaults Sherman saw for the first time what he had missed in the Mexican War, "the carnage of battle." Men were lying, he observed, "in every conceivable shape, and mangled in a horrible way; but this did not make a particle of impression on me." More frightening were the "horses running about riderless with blood streaming from their nostrils, lying on the ground hitched to guns, gnawing their sides in death." At one point Sherman sat atop his horse on the spot where a few minutes before Confederates, posing as Federals, ripped to pieces the batteries of Captains J. B. Ricketts and Charles Griffin. "Officers and men fell," Allen agreed, "smitten with death and wounds, and horses and caissons went tearing in wild disorder down the hill, breaking and scattering the ascending line of battle."[48]

Within a space of twenty minutes Union spirits plummeted from elation to depression. At three o'clock McDowell rode along Sherman's line, joyously swinging his hat aloft, responding to the cheering soldiers. As he exchanged salutes with Sherman, he was not Sherman's old friend but the victor at Bull Run. Twenty minutes later a different McDowell returned. Outwitting the inept Patterson, Johnston had swung free and brought fresh troops onto the field. McDowell's reappearance signaled defeat. Asked by Sherman for orders, McDowell responded in confusion: "Wait awhile." He left never to return. Such an indifferent answer disgusted Sherman. A few minutes later, when Lieutenant H. B. Jackson of the Second Wisconsin asked what Sherman wanted done with the baggage trains, the frustrated colonel looked him "squarely" in the face and "in a voice that was stern if not savage" said: "I give you no orders at all, sir."[49]

After the vicious fighting on the hill, the Third Brigade retreated in confusion. Seeing a half-moon of cavalry, sabers flashing, emerging from the enemy lines, Sherman and Colonel Michael Corcoran of the Sixty-ninth employed the maneuver taught at West Point. Lesser officers would have stood there and been hacked to pieces, but Sherman and Corcoran rallied what men they could and formed an irregular, hollow square, Sherman riding about in the center. From every side the men braced for the assault. At Sherman's command a powerful volley issued forth from the square, knocking the Confederates out of their saddles. Years later Beauregard marveled at Sherman's "steady and handsome withdrawal" that enabled "many to escape."[50]

Like McDowell, Sherman emerged from the battle disillusioned. He later wrote Ellen:

I was under heavy fire for hours, touched on the knee and shoulder, my horse though the leg, and was every way exposed, and cannot imagine how I escaped except to experience the mortification of retreat, rout, confusion and abandonment by whole regiments. . . . I have read of retreats before, have seen the noise and confusion of crowds of men at fires and shipwrecks, but nothing like this. It was as disgraceful as words can portray, but I doubt if volunteers from any quarter can do better. Each private thinks for himself. If he wants to go for water, he asks leave of no one. If he thinks right, he takes the oats and corn, and even burns the house of his enemy. . . . No curse could be greater than an invasion by a volunteer army. No Goths or Vandals ever had less respect for the lives and property of friends and foes, and henceforth we ought never to hope for any friends in Virginia. McDowell and all the generals tried their best to stop these disorders, but for us to say we commanded that army is no such thing. They did as they pleased.[51]

During the retreat back to Washington, Sherman displayed his anger at the troops. Two days after the battle the men, with no food, no tents, and no blankets, found themselves in a cold rain. Just before noon some Highlanders gathered in a vacant barn. According to the regiment's historian, "I want to go home" was written across every face. Sherman passed by and "in a gruff and unsympathetic tone" asked what the Highlanders were doing. Told they were keeping out of the rain, Sherman ordered them into the woods and advised them to build bush huts. He intended to put his horses in the barn. "True," noted the historian, "the Colonel might have advised us in a more kindly manner—it would have cost him nothing—but the milk of human kindness was rather deficient at that time in the future General-in-Chief of the Army."[52]

One battle was over, but a war still had to be fought. Back at Fort Corcoran, some of the members of the Sixty-ninth, led by Meagher, wanted it fought without them. Their terms of enlistment were up, they argued. One morning Sherman found himself in the middle of a crowd of Sixty-niners, among whom was the Irish captain, who said: "Colonel, I am going to New York today. What can I do for you?" Sherman answered that he did not remember signing a leave for him. His term was up, said the captain, and he was going. He was a lawyer and had neglected his business long enough. Shoving his hand under his overcoat as if he were fumbling for a weapon, Sherman declared: "You are a soldier, and must submit to orders till you are properly discharged. If you attempt to leave without orders, it will be mutiny, and I will shoot you like a dog!"[53]

On the afternoon of July 23 Lincoln and his secretary of state, William H. Seward, rode into camp. With the men gathered around his carriage, Lincoln spoke before each regiment. "Now, boys," he told the Seventy-ninth Highlanders, "keep up a good heart, and all will yet be well." Just as he motioned his driver to go on, one of the men spoke up. "Mr. President," he said, "we don't think Colonel Sherman has treated us very well." He then told Lincoln about the barn incident. "During the recital," remembered the historian of the regiment, Sherman "sat like a statue." Taken by surprise, Lincoln answered:

"Well, boys, I have a great deal of respect for Colonel Sherman, and if he turned you out of the barn I have no doubt it was for some good purpose; I presume you would feel better if you went to work and tried to forget your troubles." With that, the president rode on.[54]

To Sherman the episode illustrated the weakness of a democracy in wartime. "I saw both President Lincoln & Mr Seward," he informed Ellen, "and they are perfectly powerless in this Emergency. They appeal to military men to save the Country from this peril. I know not if it be possible. Newspapers will lay the blame on officers to shield the Men—The People can do no wrong—Vox populi vox Dei."[55]

After Bull Run, Lincoln replaced McDowell with McClellan. Sherman and the other officers at Bull Run were sure they would be next to go. On August 3, Sherman was sitting around with some of them in the lobby of the Arlington House when a young officer came in with a newspaper containing a list of new brigadier generals. On it were Sherman, Heintzelman, Keyes, William B. Franklin, and other colonels who "had shared the common stampede." "By ——— ———, it's all a lie!" warned Heintzelman in his nasal voice. "Every mother's son of you will be cashiered." But the report proved true. Cump was now General Sherman.[56]

As McClellan set up headquarters in Washington, Sherman engaged in the impossible task of turning the volunteers into soldiers. But the volunteers did not want to become soldiers. They desired to go home. On August 14, two hundred of the six hundred members of a Maine regiment under Sherman's command insisted that the president had no right to extend their enlistments, which were up. "They were not violent," Sherman told Ellen, "but simply refused to do Guard or any duty." Sherman disarmed them, placed them under arrest, and consulted with Scott, McClellan, and McDowell. They decided to ship the complainers to the Dry Tortugas in the Gulf of Mexico. Read their sentence, all but sixty-five of the men returned to their unit. The remaining sixty-five were clamped in irons, put on board a man-of-war, and sent off. The following day Sherman similarly exiled thirty-five members of the Thirteenth New York.[57]

Around this time Sherman went to Washington on some business. There for the third time he saw Lincoln and also Scott. With Scott was Major Robert Anderson, the hero of Sumter. He and Sherman exchanged only a "few words," but on Saturday, August 17, Anderson asked Sherman to meet him at Willard's Hotel. There Sherman found him with Senator Andrew Johnson of Tennessee, a Mr. Maynard, and two or three other congressmen from Kentucky and Tennessee. Johnson explained that Anderson was being sent to Kentucky to bolster the Unionists there. Lincoln had agreed that he might take with him three brigadier generals. Anderson had asked for Sherman, Thomas, and Ambrose Burnside of Rhode Island, whom Hugh had known at West Point. "It is a matter of great importance," Sherman informed Ellen, "and upon it may hang the existence of the present Government."[58]

As Sherman remembered it, Lincoln came over to Willard's several days later to discuss the transfers. During the conversation Sherman expressed a desire to remain "in a subordinate capacity." Lincoln promised him this, commenting "that his chief trouble was to find places for the many generals who wanted to be at the head of affairs, to command armies, etc."[59]

At the conference Lincoln expressed reservations about Thomas, whose promotion was being held up because he was a Virginian. "Mr. President," Sherman reassured him, "Old Tom is as loyal as I am, and as a soldier he is superior to all on your list." When Lincoln asked if Sherman would be responsible for Thomas, Sherman replied: "With the greatest pleasure." Thomas received the promotion within a few days.

Sherman decided to tell Thomas the good news himself. Informed by the War Department that his friend was in Maryland, Cump rode out to see him. "Tom, you are a brigadier general," he told his former classmate. "But," added Sherman, "there are some stories about your loyalty. How are you going?"

"Billy," he replied, "I am going South."

"My God, Tom," Sherman exclaimed, "you have put me in an awful position; I have become responsible for your loyalty."

"Give yourself no trouble, Billy; I am going South, but at the head of my men."

Telling the story years after Thomas died, Sherman explained: "And so he did, and no nobler man, no braver, better soldier, and no more courteous gentleman ever lived."[60]

___ III ___

The defeat at Bull Run ushered in one of the most trying periods of Sherman's life. He saw the Northern army as an untrained, disobedient mob. How, moreover, could he fight his Southern friends: Leonidas Polk, Beauregard, Bragg, Boyd, and the former cadets at the Seminary? Like McClellan, whom he so admired, Sherman became haunted by visions of endless lines of Confederate infantry and cavalry mutilating inferior Union forces and gobbling up everything before them. Torn apart by fears, he traveled down the dismal road to depression and hysteria.

After leaving Washington, Sherman spent a few days in Lancaster. At Anderson's order he went on to Indianapolis, where he spoke to Governor Oliver P. Morton, and to Springfield, Illinois, where he saw Governor Richard Yates, imploring them to send reinforcements to Kentucky. Both complained about a shortage of arms and men.

Sherman next went to St. Louis, then commanded by Frémont. At his hotel Sherman was warned that Frémont saw no one. Sherman told Ellen,

> but I started early—got the Sentinel to carry in my card to the Secretary who turned out to be Isaiah C. Woods of California. Of course he hurried out & took me in, and procured me an interview. Fremont was very communicative, and the result I have come to is that he has culled about him men who will swindle the Government and bring disgrace

on us all. Think of Woods, Palmer, & Silvon—the very men who caused the Vigilance Committee of San Francisco, by local and open corruption being now the advisors of Fremont.

In St. Louis, Sherman saw Lucas, Patterson, and Turner. Though Turner denied it, Sherman was sure two of his sons had joined the rebel army. Admiring Turner as a soldier, the state's new governor had offered him command of the militia, but Turner, arguing that he wanted to remain "quiet," had refused it. "I must admit," Sherman conceded, "that Missouri has had a hard time between Lyon, Blair & Fremont."[61] He might have added Turner.

The Kentucky to which Sherman came in mid-September 1861 was vitally important. If the state seceded, the South would have a natural boundary along the Ohio River. As it was, the northern boundary of the Confederacy followed the artificial line that separated Kentucky and Tennessee. For Northern success, Kentucky must be held at all costs.[62]

Like Missouri, Kentucky was a political mess. In August it had voted pro-North by two to one, but its governor, Beriah Magoffin, was pro-Confederate, and its two volunteer armies were feeble. One, stationed at Camp Dick Robinson, twenty-seven miles south of Lexington, between Cincinnati and the Cumberland Gap, was commanded by William Nelson, a Navy lieutenant who wrangled a brigadier generalship in the army. The other was at Jeffersonville, Indiana, across from Louisville. Its commander was Brigadier General Lovell H. Rousseau, a lifelong admirer of Sherman. Meanwhile, the Confederates were gathering one force under Albert Sidney Johnston at Nashville and another under Felix A. Zollicoffer near the Gap.[63]

Confederate troops marched about the state unimpeded. Sidney Johnston advanced to Bowling Green, which he fortified, and then sent General Simon Bolivar Buckner's division toward Louisville. Buckner pushed ahead and destroyed a bridge over a deep stream bearing the regal name of Rolling Fork of Salt Creek, only thirty miles from the city. But for a Unionist who derailed a train along the main railroad track, Buckner might have used the road to menace Louisville itself.[64]

To counteract Buckner, Sherman was sent in mid-September toward the commanding position of Muldraugh's Hill, forty miles outside of Louisville. Taking with him Rousseau's one thousand men plus a thousand Home Guards that were recruited in Louisville, Sherman boarded a train and set out. While the main force proceeded to Muldraugh's Hill, Sherman spent a few days at Lebanon Junction, twenty-six miles from Louisville.[65]

There, a reporter for the *Cincinnati Commercial* found Sherman a bundle of nerves. Pacing up and down in front of the local hotel, "hat pushed down over a thin wiry face united to a sharp, prominent nose," he looked like someone who "had suddenly tumbled out ten minutes too late for the train." His uniform was too small, and his shoulder insignia indicated that "his promotion had outstripped the tailor." In his blunt way Sherman complained about his lack of men. Kentucky was in peril. Where were the troops from Ohio and the other neighboring states that would quickly fall if Kentucky went? As it was, Sherman's troops were a worse looking bunch than he had commanded at Bull Run. They wore, the correspondent noted, the "most extraordinary combinations of colors, farmers in coarse jeans and working clothes, armed with shot guns and rifles, and drilling in squads." Was this the army that would drive the enemy from Kentucky?[66]

Amidst this conflict, Sherman engaged in another war. This one was with newspaper reporters. At Lebanon Junction the correspondent for the *Commercial*, armed with a letter of introduction from Tom Ewing, approached Sherman, who glanced over the note, caring little about its contents. He then warned the reporter to be on the next train for Louisville.

"But, General," urged the journalist, "the people are anxious, and it is not my business to tell anything but the truth of what I see here."

"We don't want the truth told about things here," Sherman answered. ". . . We do not want the enemy any better informed about what is going on here than he is. Make no mistake about that train." Sherman then hitched up his sword, lit a fresh cigar, and continued his walk.[67]

Visions of a vastly superior enemy tortured Sherman. Intelligence reports, varying widely, placed Buckner's force at between 7,000 and 20,000 men, and Sherman was sure he possessed at least 15,000. How could the North resist such a force? At Lebanon Junction the gloomy general called together his leading officers and warned them to expect a battle. He said that "each man must understand that he is to stand and fight down to the stubs."[68]

"All was confusion around him," remembered Brigadier General Richard W. Johnson. Sherman often declared that neither the authorities in Washington nor the people at large had any idea of the vast work necessary to end the rebellion, which was sure to go on for several years.[69]

Late in September, Sherman reached Muldraugh's Hill, where the Louisville and Nashville Railroad ran between the waters of Salt Creek and the Green River. Ellen, her father, and John were all promptly notified of his and the country's impending doom. "They swarm at every point from Washington to Leavenworth," Sherman lamented to Ellen of the Confederates, "at every point superior to us in numbers and equipment, and instead of being wiped out they propose to wipe us out."

After receiving one of Sherman's gloomy letters, Ellen's father left for Columbus, where he hoped to persuade Governor Dennison to dispatch more troops to Kentucky. "I feel so nervous & uneasy," Ellen answered her husband, "that I am fit for nothing. I cannot even write with a steady hand." If Kentucky went, Ohio would be next, and Ellen saw visions of rebels marching through Lancaster. "If we do not send a competent force into Kentucky to drive them out of that state we deserve to have them overrun our own."[70]

On October 8, Anderson, citing "the mental torture of his command," resigned. Being the senior brigadier general, Sherman "had no alternative but to assume command, though much against the grain, and in direct violation of Mr. Lincoln's promise to me."[71]

Without Anderson to lean on, Sherman became more despondent than before. Returning to Louisville, he telegraphed Lincoln that Buckner was at

Bowling Green with over 20,000 Tennesseans, Texans, and Cherokees and with "cars sufficient to move them." Another 6,000 Confederates were at Columbus, Kentucky, just below where the Mississippi and Ohio Rivers met.[72]

Sherman's letters continued to forecast doom. The Southerners, he wrote Ellen on October 12, were massing along the Green River ready to strike at Muldraugh's Hill. Instead of the ten or twenty thousand men he had, he needed fifty or sixty thousand. Before leaving Washington, he had told the War Department that the state needed that many. As it was, his "small force is liable to be overwhelmed—I have purposely excluded all reporters to conceal the weakness of our forces. Yet spies will penetrate as farmers and teamsters and our enemies learn exactly our strength or weakness." Sherman had heard that Cameron and Adjutant General Lorenzo Thomas were on their way to Louisville, but he doubted "if they can do us any material good."[73]

Henry Villard, the correspondent for the *New York Herald*, knew how Sherman hated reporters. But he also knew that every night at nine Sherman went to the local Associated Press office to read the news. Villard made sure he arrived at nine and soon the two, who had met at Bull Run, engaged in long conversations. "He was a great talker," Villard remembered, "and he liked nothing better than to express his mind upon the news as it came. There he sat, smoking a cigar (I hardly ever saw him without one), leaning back in a chair with his thumbs in the armholes of his vest. Or he was pacing up and down the room puffing away with his head bent forward and his arms crossed behind his back." No event escaped Sherman's comment, and Villard considered these sessions "a great treat."

While in Louisville, Villard went on, Sherman visualized the breakup of the Union:

> This dread took such hold of him that, as I was informed by those who were in hourly official intercourse with him, he literally brooded over it day and night. It made him lapse into long, silent moods even outside his headquarters. He lived at the Galt House, occupying rooms on the ground floor. He paced by the hour up and down the corridor leading to them, smoking and obviously absorbed in oppressive thoughts. He did this to such an extent that it was generally noticed and remarked upon by the guests and employees of the hotel. His strange ways led to gossip, and it was soon whispered about that he was suffering from mental depression.[74]

Into this scene came Cameron, fresh from a trip to St. Louis, where he was looking into Frémont's supposed extravagance and arbitrary assumption of power. With his friend James Guthrie, the president of the Louisville and Nashville Railroad, Sherman met Cameron's train at Jeffersonville. Cameron's entourage included Lorenzo Thomas and "six or seven gentlemen who turned out to be newspaper reporters," something Sherman did not then know. Tired from the trip, Cameron wanted to head for Cincinnati and home, but Sherman begged him to come over to Louisville. The secretary asked if all was not well, and Sherman said things were "as bad as bad could be." Cameron then consented to spend a day in Louisville.

The Sherman-Cameron talk took place on October 17 in Sherman's room at the Galt House. Cameron, who was tired and lying on Sherman's bed, first talked about Frémont's expenses, but finally the secretary called: "Now, General Sherman, tell us of your troubles." When Sherman objected to the presence of the strangers, Cameron assured him that they were his friends and could be trusted. Sherman locked the door and proceeded to pour out his heart. Ohio and Indiana soldiers were being sent east. Sidney Johnston would soon invade Kentucky. George Thomas, who had recently taken command of Camp Dick Robinson, and the other Union generals in Kentucky did not have enough arms and men. Johnston could march into Louisville virtually unopposed any time he wished.

All this astonished Cameron. Sherman countered that in Washington Cameron had promised Anderson 40,000 of the best Springfield muskets. Instead of these, Sherman had received 12,000 Belgian muskets that the governors of Pennsylvania and Ohio had rejected. Volunteer colonels refused to use them. Sherman then asked Guthrie if what he had said was true, and Guthrie reaffirmed every word.

During the conversation Sherman took out a large map. He pointed out that McClellan, covering a front of less than a hundred miles, had 100,000 men. Frémont, with the same area, had 60,000. Sherman, with over three hundred miles, had but 18,000. To defend Kentucky he needed 60,000 men at once. To go on the offensive, he would need 200,000. Still on the bed, Cameron threw up his hands and exclaimed: "Great God! Where are they to come from?" Sherman said that many men in the North would enlist if urged. Even now, volunteers were being turned away. The conversation, which Sherman believed to be friendly, lasted all evening. The next morning Cameron, Lorenzo Thomas, and the others left.[75]

At first Sherman thought little about the conversation. To Ellen on October 20, he brushed it off with the brief comment that the secretary "must have been impressed with the perilous situation of our Country." But Sherman still held his fears. "I know as well as I know anything not absolutely certain that the enemy outnumbers us three to one, and I think the Secretary knows it too, but he dare not diminish McClellans forces or those in Missouri and consequently I am left to those States of Ohio & Indiana who have no arms. Should my fears be realized and we be defeated there will then exist no obstacle to the passage of Southern troops to the North and West." Sherman now commanded two principal forces. One was led by General Alexander McD. McCook, the cousin of his former law partner, who had 10,000 Indiana troops "about 50 miles towards Nashville in front of Louisville." George Thomas had another 10,000 men at Camp Dick Robinson, which protected Cincinnati. "At both points there are rumors of an advance by the enemy, and I await with anxiety the result. Should defeat follow it will be most disastrous to us as the whole country will rise against us and scenes of blood will ensue such as History rarely recorded."[76]

On the first day of November, Sherman questioned his own sanity. "Rumors and Reports pour in on me of the overwhelming force collected in front across Green River," he wrote Ellen. " . . . To advance would be madness and to stand still folly. . . . The idea of going down to History with a fame such as threatens me nearly makes me crazy. Indeed I may be so now, and the constant application for passes and little things absorbs all my time." Supplies were arriving "in dribbles just enough to fall into the hands of our Enemies if they know how to take advantage of the situation." The Louisville and Nashville, the only link with the North, was being guarded "by Volunteers who cannot appreciate the true State of the Case, and who are off their Guard & might be surprised and taken any night. This thought alone disturbs my sleep, and I cannot rest. Every night I fear this RR may be broken and 12,000 men left to fight their way back before & behind enemies more ruthless than Indians." Sherman's aide, Captain Frederick E. Prime, who had graduated first in the West Point class of 1850, believed he exaggerated things, but Sherman thought not.[77]

— IV —

Sherman was not the only Civil War general who in 1861 detested journalists. Grant, Joseph E. Johnston, George Thomas, and others viewed them as spies and tried to bar them from their camps. And McDowell, who possessed a speech impediment but never touched even coffee and tea, was hounded by newspaper charges that he had lost at Bull Run because he had been drunk.[78]

Reporters retaliated against generals they disliked with their only weapon: the printed word. In mid-October of 1861 a correspondent of the *Cincinnati Gazette* compared Sherman's manners to those of a Pawnee. When Sherman demanded an apology, the journalist apologized not to him but to the Indians. "He thinks it is business to look scowling and speak gruffly," explained a reporter for the *Cincinnati Commercial*. "He ought to learn better. . . . Aside from business, a more genial gentleman does not exist."[79]

In late 1861 newspapermen tormented Sherman. One of Cameron's friends at the Sherman meeting turned out to be Samuel Wilkeson of the *New York Tribune*. Immediately after the conference he told Villard that Cameron considered Sherman "unbalanced by exaggerated fears as to rebel strength, and that it would not do to leave him in command." Returning east, Wilkeson printed the details of the supposedly confidential interview, embellishing his account with comments about the wild general who deserved to be removed.[80]

Near the breaking point, Sherman asked to be relieved from command, a request that McClellan approved on November 8. Don Carlos Buell replaced Sherman as head of the area embracing Kentucky, whose name was now changed from the Department of the Cumberland to the Department of the Ohio.[81]

Awaiting Buell, Sherman believed every rumor he heard. One day he warned George Thomas that Buckner was supposed to be moving "in force toward Lexington. . . . If it be true that the force at the Gap has been increased, as represented, to 20,000, it would be madness to contend." The next day Sherman warned Old Tom that Sidney Johnston was "making herculean efforts to strike a great blow in Kentucky; that he designs to move from Bowling Green on Lexington, Louisville, and Cincinnati." Johnston had 1,500 wagons, "a large proportion of artillery," and "not far short of 45,000 men." "I am fearful of the worst consequences," Sherman trembled to Anderson, "and will be overwhelmed with ignominy. The President dont seem to comprehend the importance of this case."[82]

Around Washington, Cameron had spread the word about Sherman. On the day Sherman's transfer was announced, the Pennsylvania politician Alexander K. McClure called on Thomas A. Scott, the assistant secretary of war, and asked what it meant. "Sherman's gone in the head," answered Scott. McClure commented "that Scott simply voiced the general belief of those who should have been best informed on the subject."[83]

On that same day a series of events began that showed Sherman to be almost helpless. Captain Prime telegraphed the sad word to Ellen's father: "Send Mrs. Sherman and her youngest boy to Louisville. There is nothing to alarm you but it is necessary to turn Genl Shermans Mind from responsibility now resting upon him."[84]

Ellen's father was not at home, but within two hours of receiving the telegram Ellen started with Philemon, Willy, and Tommy for Louisville, arriving there at three o'clock on the morning of the ninth. The next day she informed John Sherman:

> Knowing insanity to be in the family, and having seen Cump on the verge of it in California I assure you I was tortured by fears, which have been only in part relieved since I got here. . . . Cump's mind has been wrought up to a marked state of anxiety which caused him to request McClellan to make the change. . . . I am puzzled to know what to advise or hope for & I am distressed by his melancholy forebodings. I do not participate in them to any extent, but on the contrary I believe if he could keep in his present command & preserve his health, he would ultimately win laurels inferior to no man's and drive the rebels into the Gulf of Mexico before another year rolls round. . . . He wrote me that he felt almost crazy & I find that he has had little or no food for some time. His mind is certainly in an unhealthy state. . . .
>
> The servant boy who waits on him at table told me this morning that "Gen. Sherman seldom took a meal lately—that sometimes he would eat nothing all day, when he would carry out to him at his office some dinner toward evening." Even this strange servant expressed great sympathy & concern for him without I presume apprehending what we fear.

Prime and the other officers on Sherman's staff also expressed deep concern for him. "He however pays no attention to them or to any one and scarcely answers a question unless it be on the all engrossing subject," Ellen told John. "He thinks the whole country is gone irrevocably & ruin & desolation are at hand—For God's sake do what you can to cheer him & keep him in the position most advantageous to his mind & reputation—If he only had troops enough to gain a victory it would have a good effect on his mind."[85]

Receiving Ellen's letter, John Sherman rushed to Louisville. Philemon took the two boys home on the tenth, but Ellen and John stayed until Buell arrived.[86]

Back in Ohio once more, John sent his brother a strong letter:

I confess my solicitude for matters in Kentucky—Your view was so gloomy that if I could entirely rely upon its correctness it would induce me promptly to go to Washington—But conversations with others—my own observations & the reason of things convinces me that you are not only in error but are laboring under some strange delusion. I am the more convinced of this from your manner and from the disposition of your mind to overestimate difficulties. You have been so harassed with the magnitude of your labors & have allowed yourself so little rest & food that your mind casts a somber shadow upon every thing. This is my conviction confessed to you with the pardon of a Brother. Besides your manner is so abrupt & almost repulsive. This is so unlike your usual manner as to occasion complaint from your warmest friends. Your old acquaintance with men now engaged in a criminal enterprise has impaired your Enlistment. The very fact that such men are opposed to you causing you to overlook the enormity of their crime. They will only be beaten by men who regard them as Rebels—Traitors who have involved their country in war and who as such deserve the punishment of Death.

A few days will be conclusive upon the correctness of your Judgment. If every body else is mistaken a week will disclose—for you will have to admit that if Buckner does not *now* advance it will be because he is not as strong as you supposed. Nothing but your decided statement lowered my faith in our success in Kentucky—and if you are not a true Prophet in one week nothing will prevent me from risking the fortunes & lives of men there for whose safety I feel as high solicitude as I would for my own.[87]

Cump's answer consisted of a rehash of his fears. Recruits were now pouring into Kentucky, but they were untrained. The infantry possessed only the condemned Belgian muskets, and the cavalry had no arms at all. When Sherman bought pistols with which to arm some scouts, the War Department rebuked him for not first getting its permission. The Confederates could at any time overrun the state. He presented a picture of an invincible enemy:

They have delayed for some purpose of their own, but that they design a simultaneous attack on St. Louis, Louisville and Cincinnati I have no doubt. They have the force necessary for a success, and they have the men capable of designing and executing it, Johnston, Buckner & Hardee. . . . Buell is however imbued with the same spirit that prevails in Washington that there are plenty of Union People, South, in Tennessee and Kentucky, and does not share with me in my fear of the People among whom we live.[88]

After Buell took over in Kentucky, Sherman headed west. Reaching St. Louis, he reported to the new commander, General Henry W. Halleck, who sent him to inspect the Union forces in Missouri. Sherman found General Frederick Steele at Sedalia, his troops scattered over a wide area, and General John Pope at Otterville, twenty miles away. Fearing an attack by the Confederate General Sterling Price, Sherman recommended that the Federal forces be consolidated under one command. Disagreeing, Halleck recalled Sherman and ordered him not to move troops about without approval.[89]

In his *Memoirs* Sherman tried to explain away his recall by saying he applied for a leave. Actually Halleck, who was as distressed over his friend's behavior as Ellen and John, suggested the furlough. Not hearing from her husband for ten days, Ellen had gone to St. Louis to see him. There Halleck told her: "You can't work an old horse in the plough all the time. He must be turned out in the barn yard to take a rest. So take your husband home don't let him talk politics or read newspapers for two weeks." As Ellen informed Charley: "I promised to shut him up with the six children which the General concluded would be a very lively not to say severe diversion." Ellen retained "serious fears" about Sherman, "& I still feel somewhat uneasy about him. He has the most gloomy views & apprehensions. I hope the visit home will benefit him."[90]

During the first week Sherman enjoyed his leave. Then on December 9 the *New York Times* reported that "General Sigel is now in command in place of General Sherman, whose disorders have removed him, perhaps permanently, from his command." Two days later Murat Halstead's *Commercial* published a story under the headline "General William T. Sherman Insane." It insisted that while commanding in Kentucky Sherman had telegraphed the War Department three times in one day for permission to abandon the state and retreat across the Ohio into Indiana. The *Commercial* embellished its account with horrible details: Sherman had "frightened the leading Union men of Louisville almost out of their wits"; "the retreat from the Cumberland Gap was one of his mad freaks"; in Missouri "he was a madman," issuing orders "that his subordinates knew to be preposterous and refused to obey."[91]

These articles spurred the Shermans and Ewings into action. Philemon immediately went to Cincinnati to see Halstead, who treated him kindly and on the thirteenth of the month published Philemon's refutation of the charges.[92]

After the appearance of the *Times*'s story, but before reading the *Commercial*'s, John Sherman pursued bigger game. But he emerged from a conference with Lincoln more convinced than ever that his brother's mind was affected. As he wrote Ellen on the fourteenth:

> Last evening I sought & had a long interview about Cump with the President. The conversation was a very free one. It was manifest that the President felt kindly to him and when he went to Kentucky relied upon him more than upon Anderson. All his early movements were

highly extolled. He explained why reinforcements were not sent & how it came about that the rejected muskets were sent from here. Upon the facts stated to me both these things were satisfactorily explained. Then came telegraphic dispatches from Cump that were unaccountable. Letters were received from persons high in the Army & in civil life, as to Cumps extreme depression of spirits, his physical exhaustion. These were unluckily supported by letters & dispatches from him some of which were proven by subsequent events to be extremely erroneous, and all were desponding, complaining, and almost insubordinate. He constantly exaggerated the number & resources of the enemy and looked upon all around him with distrust and suspicion. This condition of affairs was supported by what Cameron & Thomas said, and led to the prompt compliance with his request to be recalled. The President evidenced the kindest feelings for him & suggested that he come here on a visit. I replied that Gen Halleck had only granted a short leave & that Gen S. would leave Lancaster in a day or two. At this he was much surprised and said that Halleck had relieved Cump for 20 days, that he would see Gen McClellan about it.

On the whole I am well convinced that Cump made serious mistakes in Ky. 1st In overrating the enemy & underrating his own force & position—2nd In hasty & inconsiderate demands here and in unreasonable importuning for compliance. 3rd In repelling too positively newspaper reporters & others who have at least the power to create prejudice against him.

. . . Nothing is more transient than such newspaper squibs as you enclose me. If I was in Cump's place I would disregard them—quietly perform his duty wherever sent—and justify the Presidents remark that there was more fighting qualities in Gen. Sherman than in any Brigadier he had appointed. But it is idle for him—for you or any of his friends to overlook the fact that his own fancies create enemies & difficulties where none exist.[93]

Answering John, Ellen blamed her husband's troubles on everyone she could think of. She attributed the harsh newspaper articles to Lorenzo Thomas and General Ormsby M. Mitchel, both of whom hated Cump. Mitchel, the commander around Cincinnati, was supposed to have led an expedition to the Cumberland Gap, but after quarreling with Sherman he went instead to Washington to complain. Ellen also lashed out at George D. Prentice of the *Louisville Journal* for copying the *Commercial*'s story and at McClellan for keeping the trained troops for himself. Finally there was Pope, with whom Sherman had argued in Missouri.

The affair had injured her family:

Nature will paint to your mind & heart what I felt when Tommy came in to us just now to say that a boy had told him that it was published in the paper that "Papa was Crazy."

I cannot persuade Cump to go to Washington. He is feeling terribly about this matter. If there were no kind of insanity hereditary in your family & if his feelings were not already in a marked state I would feel less concern about him but as it is I cannot bear to have him go back to St. Louis haunted by the spectre, dreading the effects of it in any apparent insubordination of officers or men. It will induce & fasten upon him that melancholy insanity to which your family is subject but which is so far removed from what they have represented.[94]

On December 17 Sherman arrived back in St. Louis. "I feel desolate in my room now, without you, dearest Cump," Ellen wrote him. "This time yesterday morning you were here and now I may perhaps never see you again." After her husband left, Ellen had received "a most kind letter" from Halleck, who said "he needed your services badly but he wanted you to stay until you grew stronger as the field duties would be severe. He says you must not give ear to those newspapers. He treats them with the contempt they deserve." While in St. Louis, Sherman must stay away from the Turners. Turner felt lukewarm about the war, but his wife was a secessionist.[95]

While Sherman trained volunteers at Benton Barracks, John and Ellen's father discussed the steps to be taken against Halstead. Even John, after reading the *Commercial*'s attack, favored a suit. By this time both the *Commercial* and the *Journal* conceded they had acted rashly. Apologizing to Ellen, Prentice explained that he was in Washington when his paper copied the "infamous article," an excuse Ellen refused to accept. He did, however, publish a retraction, which the Cincinnati papers copied, and returned $6.37 Ellen had sent him for a subscription, giving it to her free. The *Commercial*, too, was acting more sensibly, but for some reason it was praising Pope to the skies.[96]

None of this satisfied the family lawyers. "The charge of the Commercial is so damnable & injurious," John told Ellen, "that I could not hesitate to take any course that would inflict the highest punishment. Breaking the head of the Editor is a poor way & a law suit is the only alternative. . . . The Commercial has been humiliating Cump in a manner totally inexplicable. Your Father thinks this is one of the rare cases in which a suit is expedient."[97]

Ellen then implored:

So now my dearest Cump, as Father so strongly recommends a suit & John concurs with him in judgment you will not refuse it when you know it be my most earnest wish. Not because I feel so vindictive towards the miserable Editors but because I believe it will be a complete vindication of you & it will enable us to discover who are in the conspiracy against you. Do not let Halleck or anyone else (who is not affected by it & can thus treat it with great indifference) induce you to overlook the request of one who suffers keenly with you & for you.[98]

At year's end Ellen repeated her plea—and again spoke of the malady that afflicted the family:

Father has got home and is unhesitating in the opinion that suit should be brought against these libelers & he says it is important that it should be *instituted immediately.* He says the melancholy and depression to which your family is subject must not be brought up by us & it will be very hard for them to prove that because your Uncle & Grandmother suffered from extreme depression of spirits that *therefore* you were stark mad whilst commanding in Kentucky. Father saw the President & John Sherman saw him after hearing from you & me & he was *most friendly* towards you. Father says *they* will not refer to the family liability to depression so there is no danger of wounding anyone's feelings by that. . . . Father wants to conduct the suit himself—just leave it to him.[99]

But Sherman had no intention of advertising his shame. "Could I live over the past year I think I would do better," he answered Ellen on New Year's Day, "but my former associations with the South have rendered me almost crazy as one by one all links of hope were parted." Like his previous units, those at Benton Barracks consisted of "a mass of men partly organized and badly disciplined, with their thousand & one wants. But this is nothing to the fact that I am here in a subordinate place whilst others occupy posts that I ought to. I cannot claim them for having so signally failed in Kentucky and here I could not demand a higher place."[100]

Perhaps, as Ellen had suggested, if Sherman were in some battle he might redeem himself, regain his confidence, and even drive the enemy into the Gulf of Mexico. Fate would soon partially fulfill Ellen's wish.

7

The Same Game
as at Bull Run

— I —

As 1862 BEGAN, Sherman, then forty-one years old, was a tormented soul looking for direction. "I am so sensible now of my disgrace from having exaggerated the force of our enemy in Kentucky," he wrote John in early January, "that I do think I should have committed suicide were it not for my children. I do not think that I can again be entrusted with a command."[1]

Sherman realized that he had acted shamefully. Both the War Department and Kentucky unionists had asked him to send an expedition, led by George Thomas, through the Cumberland Gap and into East Tennessee. There it would destroy enemy communications and live off the land. Even Buell, when he arrived in Kentucky, commented "that it was all the talk in Washington."

In conjunction with Thomas's movement, the War Department concocted a plan to burn railroad bridges in East Tennessee. At a meeting at Camp Dick Robinson, Sherman gave his approval. Later, Lincoln did, too. Paid in gold, the bridge burners, East Tennessee civilians who favored the Union, began their work, but Sherman, convinced that Thomas needed at least 10,000 men to be successful, never ordered the move. After destroying a half dozen bridges, the Unionists, led by William Carter, the brother of General Samuel P. Carter, were captured and executed. "That the men employed on that occasion somehow suffered death has been the source of my despondency," Sherman told John, "as I may be mainly responsible for it. . . . This horrid Civil War has turned human nature wrong side out. How could I suppose that I would have done any act of such a nature. . . . Also at Louisville I smoked too many segars & drank somewhat because of the nervous anxiety about matters which seemed beyond my control."[2]

During the period of Sherman's obsession, Ellen provided a steadying hand. How, she wrote him on January 8, could he possibly think "you have brought disgrace upon any one? You in whom we all feel so much pride. . . . In giving way to these feelings you may bring on that more serious melancholy that afflicted your Uncle Charles. Do try to drive them away and submitting your will to that of our Good God keep your soul calm and hopeful. We are all in the hands of God & if we have faith in Him & love Him we can have peace of mind under all circumstances." Ellen reported some cheerful news. The *Commercial* now praised Cump's every move. Its correspondent called Sherman at Benton Barracks "a fine appointment as a military man was needed there."[3]

Ever the faithful wife, Ellen decided to plead her husband's case to the president. Writing on January 10, 1862, she described Sherman's predicament that previous fall in Kentucky, with untrained recruits and insufficient arms, explained away his failure to invade East Tennessee, and attributed the newspaper slanders to "conspirators," led by Lorenzo Thomas, who was under suspicion because his daughter had revealed military secrets to her Southern friends. Sherman was now occupying "a subordinate position to Gen. Halleck's department, which seemed an endorsement of the slander." Ellen urged that he be transferred to the East.[4]

The day after writing to Lincoln, Ellen vowed revenge against Sherman's enemies. "John Sherman will attend to your interests in Washington," she comforted her husband, "and as he said to me, attend to those who are hounding you. That traitor Thomas has the police on his track & they have already arrested his daughter. The wicked must eventually be punished. He has not done himself any good by secretly persecuting you for John is his bitter enemy & can do him justice yet."[5]

Two days later came a warning from Ellen about Turner. When Sherman was home, she had extracted from him a promise never again to see the Turners, not

> because they were Secessionists—but *for your own sake*. . . . You could not go into Mrs. Turner's presence without hearing what I would not listen to or bear, and what no Army officer ought to hear without resenting it. It gives your enemies power to injure you & they are on the qui vive for any indiscretion or apparent fault. It has already been hinted in the papers that you are more friendly to Secessionists than to Union people. . . . If Major Turner's prejudices did not blind him, he would perceive that it was an insult rather than a compliment to invite you there to be vilified and ridiculed and held to scorn as we always have been when in his home lately. Mrs. Turner has insulted me grossly many times during our last few visits but regarding her as a monomaniac and for your sake I bore with her. I trust however that you will soon be ordered away from there when this question will no longer vex us.[6]

Obsessed with clearing her husband of the charge of cowardice, Ellen decided on a bold move. Her father had to go to Washington to try a case. Taking along Lizzie, whose weak eyes needed the attention of Eastern physicians, she would accompany her father and plead Sherman's case to government officials. Hugh, now the colonel of the Thirteenth Ohio Volunteers, was stationed nearby, and Ellen could stay as long as she wished with his wife's family. Just yesterday, she informed her husband on the fifteenth, the newspapers had carried welcome news. Lincoln was shipping Cameron off by appointing him minister to Russia. Edwin M. Stanton, a War Democrat, was to be the new secretary of war. "If this be true," Ellen confided, "we will have no difficulty for you as Mr. Stanton is an intimate friend of Father's. . . . No matter what an ignorant populace believe, all intelligent people will *know* that you did well refusing to send those men to destruction through the Cumberland Gap."[7]

Ellen's visit to Washington proved a triumph. On the twenty-ninth of January she and her father saw Lincoln, who revealed that he and Seward had been "strongly impressed in your favor when you were in command of Fort Corcoran" and that he had nominated Sherman for promotion to brigadier general even before the Ohio Congressional delegation had recommended it. She added:

> I asked Mr. Lincoln if he thought you insane when in command at Fort Corcoran. I told him you were no more so now. That I had known you since you were ten years old and you were the same now that you had always been. I told him you had enemies among your fellow Generals, & that the newspaper correspondents were mere tools. That one of the poor miserable wretches had since committed suicide. I told him that Adj. Genl. Thomas and Mr. Cameron were inimical to you & that they had placed you in a false light to him. I represented how you were situated & Buell's advantages &c &c. I told him that I did not come to ask anything but to say a word against those who had conspired against you &c &c in vindication of your name. He seemed very anxious that we should believe that he felt kindly towards you. He and Father are great friends just now. He says John Sherman rather "*turns* up his nose at him, & wont ask him for anything."

After seeing Lincoln, Ellen made the rounds of Washington society. At the home of Secretary Chase she had "a long talk" with Mrs. McDowell. "She has been in an insane asylum she tells me," Ellen wrote Sherman, "but is now completely restored." From her Ellen learned that McDowell was "a warm friend of yours and is very indignant at the slander against you." Mrs. McClellan said the same thing of her husband.

Sherman must rest easy, for he had in Washington three loyal workers to look after his interests: "John Sherman has great influence & so has Tom Ewing. Father will not let an opportunity of serving you slip. A little time will wear away this slander and then you will stand higher than ever."[8]

— II —

Sherman impressed the volunteers who poured into Benton Barracks, but not for ordinary reasons. Getting back to his old self, he was, noted the chronicler of the Fifty-fifth Illinois, "an unassuming individual dressed in plain clothes and wearing a black slouch hat." He seemed the opposite of the regiment's colonel, David Stuart, the eldest son of a partner of the furrier John Jacob Astor. A lawyer who had recently been named in a publicized divorce case, Stuart, according to his men, "walked the deck like a king." The rumors continued that Sherman was crazy, but the men admired "his lack of fuss and feathers." He "bestrode no war horse and bellowed no commands, scarce came up to the ideal standard of romantic volunteers. . . . There was a vigilance, a nervous decisiveness about his movements and speech that was at once felt to the uttermost parts of the enclosure. . . . This same lunatic, William Tecumseh Sherman, the Fifty-fifth followed to the end of the war."[9]

As the days went by, Sherman again grew close to Halleck, whose administrative abilities he admired. One night in Halleck's room at the Planters' House in St. Louis, Sherman and Brigadier General George W. Cullum, Halleck's chief of staff, discussed where the Union army in the West should advance. Talk said it should be down the Mississippi, but the Confederates blocked the river at Columbus, Kentucky, about eighteen miles below Cairo, Illinois, where the Ohio met the Mississippi. Halleck, who had a large map on his table, asked: "Where is the rebel line?" Cullum drew a pencil through Bowling Green, Fort Henry on the Tennessee, Fort Donelson on the Cumberland, and Columbus. Halleck then asked the proper place to break it. Either Sherman or Cullum answered the center. Halleck drew a line perpendicular to the center, and it followed closely the Tennessee River. "That's the true line of operation," he observed. Sherman always credited Halleck with mapping out the campaign that began with Grant's capture of Fort Henry on February 6. After that, Grant invested Donelson and forced its surrender. His line broken, Albert Sidney Johnston abandoned Bowling Green and fell back to and through Nashville, ending up at the rail center of Corinth in northern Mississippi. Thus ended the threat to Ohio and Kentucky.[10]

On February 13, three days before the surrender of Donelson, Halleck, in charge of the army in the Mississippi Valley, ordered Sherman to the supply depot of Paducah, Kentucky, on the Ohio River. Already Sherman and Grant were being drawn together. In his *Personal Memoirs* Grant related how Sherman tried to keep him well supplied, both with the necessities of war and with confidence. A note of encouragement accompanied every shipment sent to Grant. Sherman, Grant's senior in time in grade, made it clear that he was always ready to waive seniority, accept orders, and come to Grant's aid.[11]

Grant had no such relationship with Halleck. Praising Brigadier General Charles F. Smith, Flag Officer Andrew H. Foote, and others, Halleck, within two weeks of Donelson's surrender, accused Grant of resuming "his former bad habits" by leaving his command and going to Nashville without proper authority. Halleck subsequently replaced Grant with Smith. "I think," he wrote the War Department, "Smith will restore order and discipline."[12]

Meanwhile, Sherman remained in Paducah. To an officer of the Fifty-third Ohio, he described the place as "flat as a pancake and wet as a sponge." To Ellen he called it a mass of "mud and dirt." From Paducah, Sherman sent supply boats "in every direction," some for Grant, others for Halleck, Cullum, or

Buell. In addition, with 3,000 men, he threw himself into the task of ministering to the disabled coming from Donelson. Among those caring for the wounded, though she always seemed to just miss seeing Sherman, was Ellen's cousin, the saintly Sister Angela.[13]

Many of the 15,000 or so prisoners taken at Donelson passed through Paducah, and one of these especially interested Sherman. "I had a long interview with Buckner today," he wrote Ellen on February 21. "I used to know him well and he frankly told me of many things which I wanted to know—He was restrained from doing what I knew was his purpose and what he ought to have done . . . by Sidney Johnston."[14]

The capture of Henry and Donelson focused attention on Columbus, Kentucky. On February 25, believing that the Confederates under Beauregard and the bishop-general Leonidas Polk were about to evacuate the city, Sherman urged Halleck to send a force to cut the railroad to the rear, thereby preventing the enemy from carting off its big guns. Several days later Sherman sent some cavalry toward the town. Simultaneously he took 900 men in a steamboat down to Cairo, where they ran into some gunboats preparing to attack Columbus. Arriving at the town, this Union force found the cavalry had already taken it. But the Southerners had escaped. Sherman also noted something that should have stuck in his mind. The enemy's fortifications were "very extensive."[15] He would soon pay dearly for not emulating his friend Beauregard.

Emboldened by the Union victories at Henry and Donelson, Halleck concocted a plan to cut the connection between two principal Tennessee cities, Nashville and Chattanooga. Eventually he broadened the scheme to include the occupation of Corinth, in northern Mississippi, where the Memphis & Charleston and the Mobile and Ohio Railroads intersected. Onto almost fifty transports Smith loaded the Army of the Tennessee, consisting of the divisions led by Generals Stephen A. Hurlbut, John A. McClernand, William H. L. Wallace, Benjamin M. Prentiss, and Sherman. At this time Sherman commanded about 9,000 men, almost all of them from Ohio and Illinois. The convoy moved up the Tennessee toward Savannah, Tennessee, about thirty miles from the Mississippi border.[16]

At Savannah, Smith instructed Sherman to push further south and break the Memphis & Charleston Railroad. Torrential rains and flooding prevented Sherman from successfully completing this task, but on his return he saw Smith, the adjutant during his West Point days, now suffering from a right shin and calf scraped to the bone when he stepped into a small boat. (The leg eventually worsened, leading to Grant's reinstatement as head of the expedition and to Smith's death late in April.) At the meeting, Sherman told Smith about Pittsburg Landing, on the west bank of the Tennessee, nine miles up the river from Savannah. With bluffs seventy feet high, preventing flooding, it was the usual landing spot for Corinth, twenty-three miles away. Smith ordered Sherman and Hurlbut to disembark at the landing and to camp far enough inland to make room for the entire army. Eventually all five divisions settled at the landing. Grant felt secure, for in addition to these troops he could rely on General Lew Wallace, who was at Crump's Landing, across from Savannah, and on Buell's

Army of the Ohio, about 25,000 men, at Nashville. Not oblivious to the danger, the Confederacy rushed troops to Sidney Johnston at Corinth. Five thousand men arrived from New Orleans, Bragg brought 10,000 from Mobile, and Beauregard and Polk came from Columbus.[17]

— III —

During the Civil War no wife was more loyal to a soldier than Ellen was to Sherman, but she sometimes put her church before him. Returning from Washington, she spent a few days in Lancaster and then decided to visit her husband at Benton Barracks. But by the time she got to St. Louis he had left for Paducah. Deciding not to waste the trip, she went to nearby Alton, Illinois, where her brother Charley was serving as a captain in the Thirteenth United States Infantry. What Ellen saw shocked her. Halleck had assigned the regiment, whose colonel he disliked, to guard rebel prisoners taken in Missouri. "The soldiers," Ellen informed John, "have no other quarters, but in the deserted Penitentiary. . . . There is no space anywhere to drill even a company." Even old General Hitchcock had confided to Ellen "that that was *no* place for regulars." At Ellen's insistence Cump had twice asked for the transfer of Charley's unit to his command, but Halleck and his adjutant, Schuyler Hamilton, had ignored the requests.[18]

Returning home, Ellen revealed the purpose of her trip. "By staying so long in Washington," she wrote Charley, "I missed Cump in St. Louis but I do not regret my visit there as I would have gone to see you at any rate. I had intended when I went there to make a decided and urgent effort to get Cump to come into the Church. I felt more disappointed on that account than I can tell you."[19]

Sherman, meanwhile, was laying out Camp Shiloh, near Pittsburg Landing. With his young friend from their Prince Street days in New York, Lieutenant Colonel James B. McPherson, now Grant's military engineer, he rode out ten miles to the front of the landing to a place called Monterey, or Pea Ridge, nearly halfway to Corinth. The two selected the landing for the encampment because the most traveled road from Corinth reached the Tennessee River at that point. In later years Sherman insisted that "General Smith had no idea we should be attacked on that Field." But while surveying the area, Sherman and McPherson heard an ominous report that both ignored. Inhabitants of the area told them "that trains were bringing large masses of men from every direction into Corinth."

Within a few days the encampment was complete. Sherman placed most of his men out front and to the right, around a log meeting house called Shiloh Church, about two and a half miles west of the landing. Prentiss soon took up a position to Sherman's left, and Hurlbut, McClernand, and W. H. L. Wallace formed a line across the rear. Stuart guarded the extreme left, a mile and a quarter from Sherman's other troops.[20]

By April 4 the encampment was completed. Buell would arrive from Nashville any day, Cump told Tom. Grant was still at Savannah, nine miles away, and the army was well fed and well supplied.

On the fourth Sherman had nothing more on his mind than newspaper reporters. "Spies catering to the crassest appetite of our People," he denounced them to Tom Ewing. ". . . I feel loathing towards them. In camp they are fawning synchophants and when your back is turned become libellous or flatterers according to the demand of the Press."[21]

By now the Confederates were on the move. Hearing that Buell was marching with an army of what he believed to be 30,000 men, Johnston and his corps commanders—Bragg, Polk, and William J. Hardee—decided to strike before the Union forces could combine. By noon of April 3 the Confederate army was ready for the march from Corinth to Pittsburg Landing. The Union right rested on Owl Creek, its left on Lick Creek. Both were swollen, preventing Confederate flanking movements but hemming the Northerners between the two streams. Johnston decided that an attack must be frontal. It must also be a surprise. Despite delays, bad roads, and sharp words exchanged by his corps commanders, Johnston had his troops in line to attack on the morning of Sunday, April 6. "I would fight them if they were a million," he said to his bickering assistants. "They can present no greater front between these two creeks than we can, and the more the crowd in there the worse we can make it for them."[22]

The Sherman at Shiloh was a rejuvenated and foolish Sherman who kept telling himself nothing was wrong. Clearly, he was not the Sherman of Louisville, who had ceaselessly warned about enemy attacks. The new Sherman suspected nothing.

A skirmish on April 4 failed to awaken him to the danger. Investigating the mysterious disappearance of six pickets and a lieutenant, Colonel Ralph P. Buckland, commanding Sherman's Fourth Brigade, found a regiment of Confederate cavalry in the woods to his front. It took an entire regiment to drive them off. Sherman himself rode out to the spot, about a mile and a half in front of Shiloh Church, and estimated that a Confederate brigade lay about five miles to his front. But he was unalarmed, and on the fifth wrote Grant: "I have no doubt that nothing will occur more than picket firing. The enemy is saucy, but we got the best of them yesterday, and they will not press our pickets far. I will not be drawn out far unless with certainty of advantage, and I do not apprehend anything like an attack upon our position."[23]

Both Buckland and Major Eldridge G. Ricker of the Fifth Ohio, who investigated the capture of the pickets on the fourth, reported their concern, irritating Sherman. Returning with some prisoners from the First Alabama Cavalry, Buckland rode up to Sherman, who "asked me what I had been doing. His manner indicated he was not pleased." In a memoir Ricker described what happened after his return: "When we got back to the picket-line, we found General Sherman there with infantry and artillery in line of battle, caused by the heavy firing of the enemy on us. General Sherman asked me what was up. I told him I had met and fought the advance-guard of Beauregard's army—that he was advancing on us. General Sherman said it could not be possible. Beauregard was not such a fool as to leave his base of operations and attack us in ours—mere reconnaissance in force." Ricker disgustedly turned and rode off.[24]

But on Saturday, April 5, evidence poured in that the rebels were near. Buckland visited his picket line several times and became convinced that Confederate cavalry filled the woods. That same day Colonel Jesse Appler of the Fifty-third Ohio Infantry informed Sherman that the enemy was approaching. Sherman scoffed, saying the Confederates were no closer than Corinth. The nervous Appler could "take [his] damned regiment back to Ohio." That evening, Sherman estimated to Colonel Jesse Hildebrand of the Seventy-seventh Ohio that the force to his front was small, consisting of two regiments of cavalry, two of infantry, and a battery of artillery.[25]

Captain Charles A. Morton, who as a boy served in Prentiss's Twenty-fifth Missouri and later graduated from West Point, described the unpreparedness for battle. "Keeping vigilance" on the night of April 2, he

> saw the heavens illuminated by the Confederate camp fires. We were astounded at the proximity and apparently great number of the enemy. Our men, visiting the farm houses near by, were warned that they ran great risk of capture, that the Confederate cavalry was scouring the neighborhood. . . . The men who returned to camp on Friday afternoon reported that no detail had relieved them, and that there was no picket whatever on that road between us and the enemy. . . . There was considerable cavalry in the command. Why was it not screening our camp, and even feeling the enemy in his own? Simply ignorance. We had no generals but in rank and authority. . . . The Grant and Sherman of 1864 would have relieved for utter inefficiency generals of no more skill than the Grant and Sherman at Shiloh.
>
> On Saturday afternoon the whole 6th Division, but the camp guard, was reviewed in a field near General Prentiss's headquarters; and the rumor, afterward confirmed, went through the camp that night that a detachment of Confederate cavalry rode up to the edge of the field and witnessed the review. . . . Reflect for one moment upon the profound ignorance of war,—two hostile armies hunting for each other without skirmish line or advance of any kind. . . . Indeed, it was never expected a battle would be fought at Shiloh.

The sudden concentration of forces at and near Shiloh was astounding. On April 5 the Federals numbered 39,830 men, and Buell was but a day or so away. Because of the rapid buildup, officers did not even know the regiments to their right and left. "There was a great variety of small arms and artillery," Morton explained. " . . . Some regiments had never loaded their arms before the battle. The only soldierly quality present was a determination to fight."[26]

At Shiloh, neither Grant nor Sherman nor anyone else realized the extent to which warfare had changed since the campaigns of Scott and Taylor in the Mexican War. By 1861 the advantages of rifled muskets and rifled artillery, which doubled and tripled the effective range of weapons, were recognized, but no one anticipated the intensity of fire. At Bull Run neither side had entrenched. Shiloh was similar, even though Sherman conceded in his memoirs that a single night's work would have made his position impregnable. But, he argued, entrenchments "would have made our raw men timid." Grant tried to explain away the absence of entrenchments by weakly suggesting that the troops "needed discipline and drill more than they did experience with the pick, shovel and axe."[27]

Throughout the week Sherman had scoffed at suggestions he would be attacked. On the morning of Sunday, April 6, he ignored another sign. Hearing occasional shots just beyond his picket line, less than three hundred yards away, Appler, holding Sherman's left, stayed up all night. His pickets, when they came in, reported that a large enemy force was to their front. A member of the Twenty-fifth Missouri reinforced this view. Shot in the arm, he rode up to Appler yelling: "Get into line; the rebels are coming!" Appler sent his quartermaster over to warn Sherman. The quartermaster returned with the message: "General Sherman says you must be badly scared over there."[28]

The unsung hero of Shiloh was Colonel Everett Peabody, the strikingly handsome Massachusetts civil engineer who commanded the Twenty-fifth Missouri. He, too, stayed up all Saturday night while his troops engaged the enemy a mile and a half to his front. By daybreak the wounded were being brought into camp, and Peabody ordered the "long roll," or attack signal. Regiment after regiment followed his troops into battle formation. Like Sherman, Prentiss did not believe the enemy would venture from Corinth. Seeing the troops lined up, he rode up and shouted: "Colonel Peabody, I will hold you personally responsible for bringing on this engagement." Peabody answered that he stood responsible for all his acts. Later, during the battle, the colonel's horse returned riderless. Peabody's men found his body, which was eventually buried in Springfield, Massachusetts, beneath a stone that gave no indication he had saved his army.[29]

At seven o'clock on the morning of Sunday, April 6, Sherman was out exercising a beautiful race mare captured from the rebels a few weeks before. By his side rode his orderly, Thomas D. Holliday, of the Second Illinois Cavalry. The party was in front of Appler's camp when enemy pickets hiding in the bushes lining a small stream fired, killing Holliday. Still Sherman did not suspect a general attack.

An hour later, seeing "the glistening bayonets of heavy masses of infantry" in the woods beyond the stream, Sherman realized the impossible was happening. He rode over to Appler and ordered him at all costs to hold his ground, the left flank of the first line of defense, for it protected one of Sherman's two batteries. Reinforcements for Appler came from McClernand, who responded immediately to Sherman's request for help by sending three regiments. Lining up his force in attacking waves, Sidney Johnston was sending his troops obliquely from Sherman's right to his left, hoping with his 30,000 men to overwhelm Sherman and pass on toward Prentiss and McClernand. Prentiss was soon engaged, and by nine began falling back.[30]

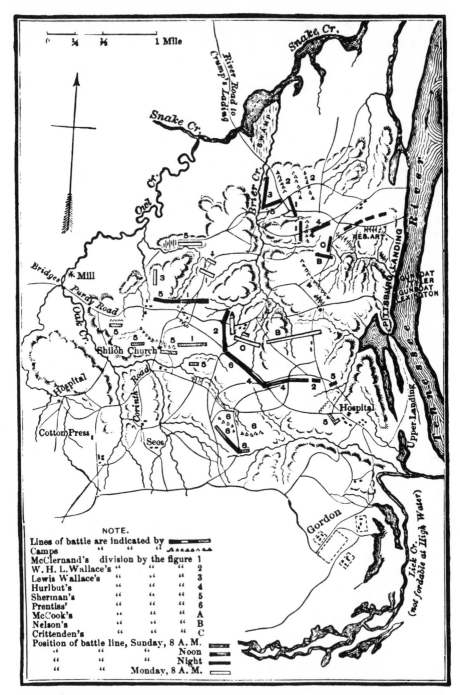

The battle of Shiloh, fought on Sunday, April 6, 1862, and Monday, April 7, 1862. The lines indicate how close the Union troops, camped between two creeks, came to being pushed into the Tennessee River.

Forty years later Sherman's aide, Captain John T. Taylor, described his commander's conduct during the early fighting:

> I am unable to give a word-picture of the awful scene. The precipitate flight of some of our troops at the first fire of the enemy; the bold, brave stand of others; the impetuous charge and counter-charge; the roar of cannon, the shriek of shells, the rattle of musketry, the shrieks of wounded and dying men, filled my very soul with awe, if it were not absolute fear. I confess I felt on more than one occasion during that early morning that I did not want to see a battle fought as much as I had supposed; and I was very indignant at the very unceremonious manner in which the Rebels had begun the fight. But General Sherman's conduct soon instilled in my soul a feeling that it was grand to be there with him.

At one point in the fighting Sherman's horse was shot from under him. Taylor dismounted and gave Sherman his horse. "Well, my boy," Sherman told Taylor, "didn't I promise you all the fighting you could do?" The second horse soon fell. "We caught a battery horse, and the general mounted him, and in less than twenty minutes that horse was struck by a solid shot and instantly killed," Taylor later recalled. "The general was soon mounted on a horse that belonged to some other officer who had evidently been killed or wounded."[31]

By nine o'clock Sherman's position turned hopeless. The two regiments protecting the left flank of the main force, Appler's Fifty-third Ohio and Colonel William Mungen's Fifty-seventh Ohio, had melted away, most of its men disappearing to the rear. Raising the cry "Fall back and save yourselves," Appler led his regiment backwards. With the Fifty-third and Fifty-seventh gone, only the Seventy-seventh Ohio protected Sherman's left—and his headquarters near Shiloh Church.[32]

With Confederates pouring in on his left, Sherman called up the battery of Captain Frederick Behr, meeting it at the intersection of the roads to Corinth and Purdy. As the crews began to unhitch the six guns, advancing Confederates shot and killed Behr. The drivers and gunners fled, abandoning five cannons without a fight. His entire left shattered, Sherman decided to pull back his two right brigades, led by Colonel John A. McDowell and by Buckland, and between 10:00 and 10:30 A.M. they joined McClernand's right.[33]

Clearly, Sherman had made errors before the onslaught, but he thrived in combat. Grant, who had heard the first firing of the battle and reached Pittsburg Landing from Savannah about eight o'clock, commented that although he visited all areas of the field frequently, he "never deemed it important to stay long with Sherman." That day McClernand, who as a Democratic congressman from Illinois had been John Sherman's rival in the Speakership contest of 1860, told Grant "that he profited much by having so able a commander supporting him."[34]

Grant's first visit to Sherman came after ten in the morning. Sherman reported that his men had checked the enemy and were holding their ground. Grant expressed satisfaction, but said that things did not look well with Prentiss on the left. Grant related that on his way up from Savannah he had stopped at Crump's Landing and ordered Lew Wallace to march to Pittsburg Landing and come up on Sherman's right. Thenceforth Sherman and McClernand, expecting Wallace momentarily, knew they had to hold the bridge built over Snake Creek, on their right, for just such a purpose.[35]

In battle Sherman's concentration was complete. Early in the struggle, while he was watching an artillery crew, a minié ball struck the third finger of his right hand, penetrating it to the bone. He drew a handkerchief from his pocket, wrapped it around the wound, and thrust the hand inside the breast of coat. He barely took his eyes away from the fighting.[36]

Sherman later described the battle along his new line in McClernand's camp as "the real fighting," at least for him. The dead and mangled covered the field. At this stage the battle boiled down to a series of fierce, isolated struggles, often fought by unseasoned troops on each side. So many brigade and regimental commanders fell that their replacements had no idea of orders and tactics. Shiloh became a battle of broken regiments, of mass desertions on both sides, and of bloodletting.[37]

Two events on Sunday afternoon illustrated the intensity of emotions during the battle. From the Hornet's Nest, an eroded lane in front of which lay an undergrowth of hickory and oak, Prentiss's men held out until 5:00 P.M., inflicting heavy casualties on the Confederates. "At the front," Morton remembered, "one could walk on the enemy's dead for acres." In desperation, Johnston led a charge against it. He was shot in the leg but ignored his wound and bled to death.[38]

The other incident took place on the extreme left of the Union line, facing Lick Creek. Detached from the remainder of Sherman's division, Stuart's brigade, consisting of the Fifty-fourth and Seventy-first Ohio and the Fifty-fifth Illinois, held the position. But from the beginning Sherman worried about the brigade. Its manpower was thin, and a half-mile gap existed between Stuart's right and Prentiss's left. Sherman and Stuart frequently rode over the ground, and on the Friday before the assault the general gave the colonel written instructions on closing the gap.[39]

Of the units at Shiloh, Stuart's brigade stood most exposed. Warned by a messenger from Prentiss at 7:45 A.M. on Sunday that the Confederates were attacking, Stuart, who possessed enormous courage but no military background, moved the brigade several times trying to find a comfortable position. Like Sherman and the rest, however, he made no effort to entrench, and he left a high bluff nearby for the enemy to occupy.

The first volleys led to chaos. On the Confederate side the Fifty-second Tennessee broke and ran and, with the exception of two companies, took no further part in the battle. Colonel Rodney Mason of the Seventy-first Ohio did the same. Remembered Lieutenant Elijah C. Lawrence of Company B of the Fifty-fifth Illinois:

> As we entered the woods back of our camp, we saw the 71st Ohio making for the rear, on the run; its great colonel (250 lbs. avoirdupois) in

the lead, with his horse at full gallop; and during that day nothing more was seen of them except the Adjutant and seventeen men, who joined B company and did excellent work. Four companies of the 54th Ohio had been sent off to the left and rear to look after some supposed cavalry which they did not find, nor did they find their way back until night, and missed this glorious opportunity of being slaughtered.

At one point the remainder of the brigade, three hundred men of Colonel T. Kilby Smith's Fifty-fourth Ohio and five hundred of Stuart's Fifty-fifth Illinois, bolted and began running to the rear. Riding into the fleeing mob, Stuart, with his "stentorian voice," rallied the men back into line.[40]

From noon until 2:15 P.M. Stuart's eight hundred men huddled on the brow of a hill. Behind them lay a deep ravine. Here occurred one of the most horrible episodes of the war. The Federals would crawl up to the top of the hill, fire without being seen, and then drop back to reload. Badly outnumbered, Stuart's two regiments soon ran out of ammunition and suffered greatly. Of its 800 members, 402 were killed or wounded. "Only the excitement of battle," Lawrence observed, "could sustain a man in the midst of such carnage. As man after man was shot down or mutilated, a feeling of perfect horror came over me at times, and I berated the powers which placed us in such a position and left us alone to our fate. Can it be wondered at when forty-three out of sixty-four of my own company were killed or wounded in that short space of time?"[41]

By four o'clock McClernand and Sherman, still awaiting Wallace's 7,000 men and Buell's Army of the Ohio, decided to pull further back. Indeed, the Confederates pushed the Yankee left to within a quarter of a mile of the landing. Just before dark Grant visited Sherman again, ordering him to be ready to assume the offensive in the morning. Grant said he noticed that at Fort Donelson, when both sides seemed defeated, the one that took the offensive the next day won. He reported that Buell had his army opposite Pittsburg Landing and was starting to ferry his troops across the river.[42]

The accounts of Buell, on the one hand, and his chief subordinates, on the other, vary so greatly that a reader might think they were describing different events. In his battle report Buell insisted that when he arrived at Pittsburg Landing he found huddled along the west bank of the river 4,000 to 5,000 "disorganized and demoralized troops," their number increasing rapidly. The enemy was already shelling the landing, he asserted, when General William Nelson, the first of Buell's generals to arrive, landed with the brigade of Colonel Jacob Ammen. According to Buell, Ammen "immediately posted to meet the attack at that point, and with a battery of artillery which happened to be on the ground and was brought into action, opened fire on the enemy and repulsed him." Buell neglected to mention two important details that Ammen revealed both in his report and in his diary. Grant met Ammen at the landing, and Grant, not Buell, ordered Ammen and the Thirty-sixth Indiana "to support a battery less than a quarter of a mile from the Landing." The battery, as Sherman correctly pointed out, did not just happen to be there. It was one of a half dozen Grant had his chief of staff, Colonel J. D. Webster, assemble, along with the gunboats *Tyler* and *Lexington,* to protect the landing when Stuart and the Federal left gave way.[43]

Buell's subordinates contradicted another of his assertions. Buell insisted that after the divisions of Nelson and of General Thomas L. Crittenden landed, he ordered them to advance, form in front of Sherman's division, and "move forward as soon as it was light." Nelson conceded that all his infantry was not across the river till 9:00 P.M., when on a rainy night it was pitch dark. By 10:30, when Buell and Nelson rode by, Ammen had formed a new line only three hundred yards in advance of his old line. Crittenden, too, reached the landing at 9:00 P.M. By then he estimated the skulkers to be between 6,000 and 10,000. In his battle report, Crittenden recalled: "I was so disgusted that I asked General Buell to permit me to land a regiment and drive them away. I did not wish my troops to come in contact with them." Forcing their way through the mob, Crittenden's men camped at a spot designated by Buell but a half mile from the landing. Far from camping in front of Sherman, Nelson and Crittenden were at least a mile in back of him.[44]

With the soldiers resting as best they could, Sherman decided during the night to urge Grant to withdraw to the east side of the river. Sherman later explained:

> Full of only this idea, I ploughed around in the mud until at last I found him standing backed up against a wet tree, his hat well slouched down and coat well pulled up around his ears, an old time lantern in his hand, the rain pelting on us both, and the inevitable cigar glowing between his teeth, having retired, evidently, for the night. Some wise and sudden instinct impelled me to a more cautious and less impulsive proposition than at first intended, and I opened up with, "Well, Grant, we've had the devil's own day, haven't we?"
>
> "Yes," he said, with a short, sharp puff of the cigar; "lick 'em tomorrow, though."[45]

By daylight on Monday, April 7, the battle was not over, but it had been settled. At Shiloh, Grant and Sherman terribly misjudged the enemy. So too did Charles F. Smith, in bed at Savannah, when Ammen went to see him before departing for Shiloh. He "laughed at me," recorded Ammen, "for thinking a great battle was raging." But by not having won the battle on the first day, the Confederates had lost it. As Morton put it, on Sunday "about dark the head of Buell's army led by a brass band playing merrily patriotic airs marched upon this field of carnage." Lew Wallace also arrived a little after nightfall, and by one in the morning had squeezed his men on Sherman's right along the road to the landing. "From that position," Sherman later told Grant, "Wallace, Sherman and McClernand moved forward at daylight of the 7th meeting little opposition till we regained McClernands camp, and then we waited four long hours for Buells troops to get abreast—When we saw them we pitched in and did not stop till we regained the camps originally occupied."[46]

The two days of fighting produced more casualties than in all previous North American battles combined. Northern killed, wounded, and missing totaled 13,047; Southern casualties numbered 10,699. The North lost fifty generals and regimental commanders, the South forty-four, including Sidney Johnston.[47]

The number of fatalities astounded the survivors. After the fight, the Union army dug a mile of trenches to bury the dead. Officers and reporters who came onto the field three weeks afterwards found bodies still strewn about.[48]

__ IV __

Until their deaths Grant and Sherman were involved in arguments about what happened at Shiloh. In retrospect, part of the difficulty stemmed from the lack of battle reports. It also stemmed from the reports of those who, like Buell, glorified their roles in the battle. In his memoirs, Grant gave his version of the story. But the document he presented to the War Department was sketchy and could hardly be termed a report. Neither Johnston nor the other generals and regimental commanders killed on both sides could submit reports. Ninety-four accounts that might have cleared up numerous points were thus never written.[49]

The battle made Grant and Sherman national figures. It also made famous a reporter, Whitelaw Reid of the *Cincinnati Gazette*. Reid was at Crump's Landing when Grant stopped there to talk to Lew Wallace. Slipping aboard the *Tigress*, he arrived at Pittsburg Landing with Grant. After two days of digging for information, he raced to Cincinnati, where he filed his story, which newspapers throughout the country reprinted.[50]

If true, Reid's story should have led to the instant dismissal of Grant and Sherman. It told of an early morning surprise by the Confederates, of Union officers being bayoneted in their beds and being left "gasping in their agony" for two days, and of a Union army saved by Buell's arrival.

But Reid's story contained numerous errors. He had Prentiss surrendering at 10:00 A.M. rather than holding out until 5:00 P.M. He had Grant taking his time getting to the battlefield, instead of rushing there. And he had Lew Wallace being summoned by Grant after a long delay. Worst of all, he relied or seemed to rely on the statements of Buell and Nelson and on the testimony of members of regiments like the Fifty-third, Fifty-seventh, and Seventy-first Ohio, all of which bolted during the early battle.[51]

In letters to Ellen and to Charles Ewing two weeks after Shiloh, Sherman showed his disgust with Reid's story, already circulating about the country. He wrote Ellen:

> The hue & cry against Grant about surprise is wrong. I was not surprised and I was in advance. Prentiss was not covered by me, and I dont believe he was surprised, although he is now a prisoner & cannot be heard—It is outrageous for the cowardly newsmongers, thus to defame men whose lives are exposed.—The real truth is the private soldiers in battle leave their Ranks, run away and then raise these false issues. The political Leaders dare not lay the blame where it belongs.

They like the Volunteer officers are afraid of the men, but I will speak the truth and I believe still there are honest men enough to believe me.—In the 302 dead, and 1200 wounded of my Division, there was not a bayonet or knife wound, and the story of men being bayoneted in their tent is a pure lie. . . . It is all a lie got up by the cowards who ran to the River & reported we were surprised & all killed. By these false reports they may have *prevented success* coming to us, earlier than it did.[52]

To Charley, Sherman described it as "the same Game that was attempted at Bull Run. Men run away, wont obey their officers, wont listen to threats, remonstrances and prayers of their superiors, but after the danger is passed they raise false issues to cover their infamy." After the battle, Lincoln had asked Halleck who was responsible for "the surprise & dreadful slaughter at Pittsburg Landing." Halleck wired back that "the Confederate officers and soldiers were to blame. . . . So I hope," Sherman commented, "Old Abe will order Beauregard & Bragg to be court martialled for their cruelty in shooting bullets at us in the indiscriminate manner they did."[53]

Years later, Sherman told a story about Reid that sounded more like wishful thinking than reality. "I had him with my army for a while," he remarked, never specifying when or where. "I ordered him shot one day, but got softhearted afterward and revoked the order. I've wished many times since I'd carried it out!"[54]

Another enemy made at Shiloh would torment Grant and Sherman for much of the next year. McClernand, the War Democrat who had represented Lincoln's home district in Congress, was as untalented as he was boastful. "My division," read his report, "as usual has borne or shared in bearing the brunt." McClernand took credit for stemming the Confederate tide "by repeatedly changing front." He also praised his men for killing Johnston. McClernand's battle reports, one of which he addressed directly to the president, contained so many errors that Grant took the unprecedented step of correcting them.[55]

To Ellen and her father, Sherman later denounced McClernand as a coward: "He knows I appreciate him truly and therefore he would ruin me if he could." By five o'clock on Sunday afternoon, April 6, McClernand's division "was a mere squad, and he gave it up as a gone day, when I assured him we could and would hold our ground till night, and night promised strong reinforcements. . . . He knows he showed the white feather at Shiloh, that he hung round like a whipped cow, that his troops reported to me for orders in his presence. Then danger made him complaisant, but when that was past and his self arose, he hated me the more for what I know."[56]

Equally painful to Sherman was the disgrace of Rodney Mason, a member of a prominent family. Although he was the assistant adjutant of Ohio, he was no soldier. As soon as the firing began at Shiloh, he and his men raced toward the landing. Mason later explained to Stuart that he had withdrawn to a line 150 yards back, but Stuart reported that throughout Sunday "I could not find the Seventy-first Ohio Regiment."[57]

In tears, Mason appealed to Grant's good nature. He begged for another chance. Yielding, Grant assigned Mason and his regiment to Fort Donelson and nearby Clarksville, Tennessee. Almost immediately the rejuvenated colonel wrote to a Cincinnati newspaper denouncing Sherman for favoring Illinois officers over those from Ohio. Sherman was responsible for "the stories of the Regiment being disgraced, deprived of its colors &c &c." Told of the letter by Kilby Smith, who commanded the extreme left after Stuart, shot in the shoulder, left the field, Sherman felt the cut deeply. "Col. Mason was a favorite with us all from his social manners," Sherman told Phil, "and you may search in vain in my reports for any unfavorable allusion to him. I knew his Regiment did not stand by their fellows as they should, and I cannot praise them but I spared them censure."

That August at Clarksville Mason's "constitutional weakness overcame him," as Grant put it. He surrendered to a band of guerrillas without firing a shot.[58]

— V —

On the eighth, the day after the battle, Grant sent Sherman with two brigades to see if the Southerners were retreating toward Corinth. About six miles out Sherman spied some tents in a cotton field. Suddenly Nathan Bedford Forrest charged with about 250 Confederate cavalrymen. Forrest's horsemen smashed through Sherman's skirmishers and a regiment of Union infantry. Instantly Sherman, with a supporting brigade, formed a battle line. "The broken infantry and cavalry rallied on this line," Sherman reported to Grant, "and as the enemy's cavalry came to it our cavalry in turn charged and drove them from the field." Sherman escaped by scurrying through mud. At one point Forrest himself pulled up to him. "I am sure," Sherman later commented, "that had he not emptied his pistols as he passed the skirmish line, my career would have ended right there."[59]

As the Confederates retreated from Shiloh, Forrest had been left behind to protect the hospital of surgeon William D. Lyles. The sights in the captured camp sickened Sherman. He once told his comrades:

All who were with me on that 8th of April will recall the scenes of desolation and misery we beheld by the roadside and at the hospital camp of Surgeon Lyles. Wagons hauling in dead men and dumping them on the ground as cordwood, for burial in long trenches, like sardines in a box. Wounded men with mangled legs and arms, and heads half shot away, horrible to behold, and still more of the wounded appealing for water, and for help in any form. If there be any lesson I would impress on the young to-day it would be to warn them against the men who make war necessary; men like Jeff Davis, Yancey and Toombs usually arouse the passions and prejudices of their fellow mortals till war becomes a necessity, whilst they, the real cause, hold back and leave their deluded followers to catch all the blows and buffets of the storm which they had no hand in creating.[60]

On April 12, amid stories of Grant's incompetence, Halleck arrived and again ordered Sherman to cut the Memphis & Charleston. Taking with him one hundred Illinois cavalrymen, under his old California lawyer Major Samuel M. Bowman, a brigade led by Colonel James B. Fry, and two gunboats, the general proceeded up the Tennessee thirty-two miles to Chickasaw Landing. On the thirteenth, Bowman reached the railroad bridge crossing Bear Creek, Alabama, drove away its defenders, and burned the span and five hundred feet of trestles, thereby cutting off the enemy from the Confederate forces to the east. Halleck was delighted with the success of the mission. "So at last I stand redeemed from the vile slanders of the Cincinnati papers," Sherman wrote Ellen of the insanity stories. "I am sometimes amused at the newspaper reporters. They keep shy of me as I have said the first one I catch I will hang as a spy. I now have the lawful right to have a Court Martial, and if I catch one of these Cincinnati newspapermen in my Camp I will have a Court and they will do just as I tell them. It would offer me a real pleasure to hang one or two."[61]

Through it all, Ellen came up with a new villain, neither Jeff Davis nor Bragg nor Beauregard nor Cameron nor Lorenzo Thomas. It was McClellan. Ellen was sure he had plotted against Sherman. In Kentucky, McClellan had deprived Sherman of all the trained men and ignored his communications. He had made Sherman feel "almost crazy." When Ellen was in Washington, McClellan did nothing but attend parties: "Genl. Rosecrans waited there *two weeks* & could not see him and during all that time the correspondents of the New York Herald were seeing him every day & when I was there immediately after he was attending parties constantly. I *know* of three he attended. I hope he will be set aside & cashiered after a while. He is set aside now."[62]

"For mercy's sake," Sherman responded in mid-April, "never speak of McClellan as you write. He ought to have sent me men & officers in Kentucky, but did not, but that he had any malice or intention of wrong I don't believe. I committed a fearful mistake in Kentucky and if I recover it will be a wonderful instance. I have made good progress here, and in time can illustrate the motives that influenced me."[63]

Meanwhile, Charley remained at Alton. Seeking his transfer, Ellen and her father wrote to Stanton, Halleck, and John Sherman, but somebody in Washington, probably Lorenzo Thomas, was holding things up. John could do no good, Ellen told Charley, for "John Sherman & the President are not friendly. John is *ice & salt* to anything that comes near him. Tom says that the old *traitor* Thomas talks of transferring your Regiment to Elmira, N.Y."[64]

By June Ellen was advising Charley to turn to religion for solace. "If Cump had had Catholic faith to console him in his dark & bitter times of last winter I would not have felt very badly on account of them," she wrote. "He told me at the time & he has said since that if I had not been so calm & self possessed he could not have borne them. He himself regretted that he had not Catholic faith."[65]

Amid his brother-in-law's woes, Sherman's life brightened. By the end of April his injury, he told his mother-in-law, was "doing well." The ball had penetrated only to the bone of the third finger, and he was now able to write with the hand. Because the teamsters "had foresight enough" to keep his trunk in the rear, he did not lose it when the Confederates overran his camp. "I thank you kindly for the slippers," he related, "though I think you robbed Mr. Ewing."[66]

More important was Sherman's promotion. Armed with a recommendation from Halleck, John Sherman and Tom Ewing went to see Stanton about it, only to be told that upon reading Grant's report on Shiloh the secretary of war had sent Sherman's name to the president. Lincoln waited only for Halleck's letter. At a meeting with Tom on April 24, the president asked him "to give his compliments to Mrs. Sherman, 'to whom he had taken a great liking.' Tom assured him the liking was reciprocated," Ellen informed her husband, "& told him that I had run up the Republican flag on his nomination &c." Hearing that, Lincoln "rubbed his hands & with much pleasure said 'that's first rate.' Mr. Stanton has expressed for some time both to Tom & John a desire to do you justice. He said the trouble with you was, *you were a General* & those who failed to support you were *not*." Early that May, while in the field, Sherman read in the newspapers of his promotion to major general.[67]

The cautious Halleck saw in Shiloh a lesson. Arriving from St. Louis, he took over a force that included Grant's Army of the Tennessee, Buell's Army of the Ohio, and John Pope's Army of the Mississippi, 100,000 men in all. Against his will, Grant was shoved into the shadows, becoming the second in command with nothing to do.[68]

At the end of April this force began the march from Pittsburg Landing to Corinth, about twenty-three miles. Sherman's division, consisting of three brigades, helped make up the right of the invading force. Following the main road, Halleck was determined not to repeat Grant's mistake. Seven times during the march Sherman's men stopped to construct elaborate entrenchments, for, as one student of military science has put it, Halleck and the War Department viewed the campaign as something resembling "the magnificent strategy of Napoleon at Ulm." Wasting an entire month, the best of the year for accomplishing military ends, the Federal army finally arrived at and occupied the deserted city of Corinth at the end of May. For this campaign Halleck was rewarded. In July he was called to Washington and entrusted with the command of the armies of the United States.[69]

8

Bad Day at Chickasaw

— I —

THE MARCH from Shiloh to Corinth, militarily insignificant, had two important consequences. First, it led to what Sherman considered the most questionable move of the war. An army of 100,000 men made the march. From Corinth this "magnificent" force could have gone anywhere, even to Mobile and Vicksburg, thereby opening up the Mississippi. Sherman always believed that Halleck desired such a movement, but officials in Washington overruled him and broke up his army. Buell was sent toward Chattanooga, and George Thomas was reassigned. Pope went east, McClernand toward Memphis. With his own and Hurlbut's division, Sherman was sent to Chewalla, ten miles west of Corinth, to salvage cars from trains burned and derailed when the Confederates left the area.[1]

The second result was equally significant. Sherman always maintained that he grew close to Grant not at Shiloh but during May 1862. Grant never complained, but those near him knew he was heartbroken by his demotion. Sherman helped ease the pain.[2]

Sherman later termed what happened the turning point of the war. While at Halleck's headquarters one day, he heard that Grant had received a leave of thirty days. Riding over to Grant's camp, Sherman found him packing. Asked why he was leaving, Grant replied: "Sherman, you know. You know that I am in the way here. I have stood it as long as I can, and can endure it no longer." Grant planned to go to St. Louis, where, he admitted, he had "not a bit" of business. Trying to dissuade his friend, Sherman described the newspaper accounts the previous fall that had almost ruined his life. In one version of the story, Sherman then extracted from Grant a promise not to leave without again talking it over with him. In another, Sherman took Grant's letter of resignation, tore it up, and asked Grant to wait at least two weeks.[3]

Sherman summarized the incident to Ellen on June 6:

> The very object of war is to produce results by death and slaughter, but the moment a battle occurs the newspapers make the leader responsible for the death and misery, whether of victory or defeat. If this be pushed much further officers of modesty and merit will keep away, will draw back into obscurity and leave our armies to be led by fools or rash men, such as Ed Baker. Grant had made up his mind to go home, I tried to dissuade him, but so fixed was he in his purpose that I thought his mind was made up and asked for an escort a company of 4th Illinois. But last night I got a note from him saying he would stay. His case is a good illustration of my meaning.[4]

Bivouacked near Chewalla on high, healthy ground, Sherman set his men to work early in June. Chief among his units was his "railroad regiment," the Fifty-second Indiana. Sherman's men found scattered about the area bits and pieces of cars and engines. These trains had been inside Corinth loading supplies on the night of the evacuation, but by mistake the Confederates had burned the Tuscumbia bridge before the cars made it across. The train engineers and guards then hastily dumped whatever they could not carry into the swamps, which, Sherman remembered, "fairly stunk with the putrid flour and fermenting sugar and molasses." Exposed to the hot sun, Sherman "got a touch of malarial fever, which hung on me for a month, and forced me to ride for two days in an ambulance, the only time I ever did such a thing during the war." But by the tenth he had repaired and sent to Corinth seven locomotives, including one his soldiers found "flat on its side in a ditch," about a dozen cars, over two hundred pairs of wheels, and the iron from sixty cars.[5]

During the second half of June and the first half of July, Sherman kept his men busy at various spots in Tennessee and Mississippi. He marched, among other places, to Grand Junction, Tennessee, fifty-two miles east of Memphis, to repair the Memphis & Charleston Railroad. Several times his troops passed through and occupied Holly Springs, the center of all roads to and from northern Mississippi. But Halleck soon concluded that Sherman's efforts were useless, for as soon as Sherman repaired something the Confederates ripped it up again.[6]

In mid-July Sherman learned that Halleck had been called to Washington to replace McClellan as general-in-chief of the Union armies. In the West, Grant would again assume command. Almost immediately, Grant assigned Sherman to Memphis, the post he was vacating. But as much as Sherman liked Grant, he grew despondent at the thought of Halleck's transfer. "The loss of Halleck is almost fatal," he warned John. "We have no one to replace him. Instead of having one head we have five or six, all independent of each other."[7]

— II —

Without the lobbying of Ellen, her father, Tom Ewing, and John Sherman in 1861 and early 1862, Sherman might have ended up roaming the streets of Lancaster looking for a job. But in the spring of 1862 he was known throughout the North as one of the heroes of Shiloh. In November he had sulked away from Kentucky. Now he was confident enough to engage in public feuds.

The object of Sherman's wrath was Lieutenant Governor Benjamin F. Stanton of Ohio. Shocked by the reports of surprise at Shiloh, Stanton published on April 19, 1862, in a Bellefontaine, Ohio, newspaper a denunciation of Grant and the other blundering generals. He also questioned the bravery of the Fifty-fourth and Fifty-seventh Ohio regiments. Shown the article by a friend, Sherman fumed, for Stanton repeated all of Whitelaw Reid's charges.[8]

Trying to capitalize on the number of casualties, Stanton visited Halleck's army with delicacies for the wounded. "He came & went away quick, before danger could possibly arise," Cump reported to Charley. "Such are the men who disgrace Ohio, not men like me who stay in the front Rank. Let them be exposed if Ohio wants to be honored & respected beyond her own limits."[9]

Infuriated, Sherman wrote an answer to Stanton, sending it to Ellen, her father, and Phil for their approval. "The letter cannot be sent *verbatim* to the newspapers," Ellen answered, "for they will not publish it with the slur upon 'Editors & anonymous scribblers.' We will have to strike out *Editors* & leave it 'anonymous & irresponsible scribblers.' "[10]

After Sherman toned down his attack on Stanton, Ellen reported that "Father was very much pleased with it." The evening they received it, Ellen and Phil sent the original to Stanton and copies to the *Cincinnati Commercial,* the (Columbus) *Ohio State Journal,* and the Lancaster paper. Ellen wrote Sherman:

> Philemon ordered one hundred copies of the Commercial to be sent to me & when it comes Father says I must send it to the Editors in every direction. I intend to write to the Editors at Bellefontaine & request the publication in their papers. I will send it North South East & West—to Des Moines—Fort Dodge, St. Louis, Louisville—Indianapolis, Mansfield all the Eastern Cities & to all my particular friends—also to California & even to the Editors in the most obscure villages in the State. I am so glad to see you bid them defiance. But you ought to be a little circumspect in your denunciation & not too sweeping & too general. Many of the Editors & their correspondents are true friends of yours and admire you and you ought not in common politeness to repulse them all without distinction. The correspondent at Shiloh of the St. Louis Republican wrote of all the officers there but of you in particular in the most noble manner denouncing the general abuse & its authors. The same of the Louisville Journal. I believe however that the correspondent of that paper held out the idea of a surprise whilst praising you to the skies.[11]

While taking care of her husband, Ellen also looked out for Charley and Hugh. The day after Shiloh, Halleck promised Sherman that he would relieve Charley's unit with a detachment from Pope's army, but he went back on his word. Charley was more qualified, according to Ellen, than Dan McCook "& so many hundreds of others who now command regiments," but he remained in "a jail which was considered too foul for convicts." Hugh, a colonel in the East, also desired to be transferred to Cump.[12]

In a strange letter to her husband, Ellen showed the strain of bearing these burdens. Rachel Ewing Sherman, born on July 5, 1861, was approaching her first birthday when her mother wrote: "The baby is the loveliest child you ever saw and very smart. She is our idol. She is too sweet to live here long & I pray from my heart that God may take her to Heaven in her loveliness & purity that her eternity may be secure & that we may have one at least of our little flock constantly interceding for us before the throne & in the presence of the Lamb that was slain for our redemption."[13]

___ III ___

Arriving in Memphis on July 21, 1862, Sherman found a dead city. Stores, schools, and churches were closed. The inhabitants were, Sherman was convinced, "all more or less in sympathy with our enemies." Sherman reopened these places. With the Mississippi in Union hands from Memphis north, trade quickly revived.[14]

Sherman restored the city's mayor to office, but he saw in the Confederate abandonment of Memphis a plot. He informed Ellen early in August:

> I have been here two weeks, and still flows on the *current* of people asking me all sorts of questions—for in me is *centered* all the Government there is here. No sooner had our troops got to Memphis before flocked in all sorts of merchants with guns, pistols, salt bacon and the very things which command high prices and these things were being sold and carried into the Interior. I have no doubt the surrender of Memphis was made knowing that our People for the sake of a little profit would supply them the very things they stood so much in need of. I have stopped all this and expect to be universally abused by the Northern merchants. Also the town was full of Jews & speculators buying cotton for gold silver & treasury notes, the very thing the Confederates wanted, money. I am satisfied the army got enough money & supplies from this Quarter to last a year.[15]

Sherman acted quickly to close the leak that allowed hard money and supplies to be carried south. He permitted the sale of cotton only through a complicated system, with the money being held for a time by his quartermaster. Sherman further prohibited the purchase of cotton with gold, silver, or treasury notes, for these inevitably ended up in the Confederate treasury and were used to buy arms in the British colonies. Salt, used to cure bacon and beef, was as valuable as gunpowder and was scarce in the South. Sherman banned its shipment out of the city.[16]

But Sherman's rules proved faulty. No passes were needed to enter and to leave Memphis, leaving enforcement in the hands of the pickets guarding the five main roads in and out of the city. These young, inexperienced soldiers frequently yielded to temptation and accepted bribes. "The consequence," noted a reporter for the *Cincinnati Commercial*, "is that the whole Confederacy is in a fair way to be supplied with salt through what may be termed the Memphis sieve."[17]

Sherman's policies in Memphis would have appalled Ellen, for they tended to encourage prostitution and drinking. To support a new police force intended to keep order, Sherman allowed the mayor and aldermen to levy a $5 tax on hacks and a $2 tax on dogs. But he would not permit a $50 tax on every house suspected of being a brothel, thus allowing such places to flourish.

Under Sherman, the number of grog shops also increased. Since drinking places were taxed $25 a month, the civil government encouraged their establishment. Nowhere in Sherman's Memphis, observed a reporter, was a person more than ten feet from one. Inebriated soldiers were everywhere. When stopped for being drunk, they merely took their apprehenders out for a drink. The gin sold in most places was cut with turpentine, the wine with camphene. For this "refined and devilish species of torture," concluded the reporter, "we must thank General Sherman, whose ingenuity is certainly only equaled by his versatility."[18]

During these relatively peaceful days, cotton speculation abounded. About the time of Sherman's cotton order, the *Commercial* observed that army officers conducted much of it. Buying cotton cheaply, they used army transportation to carry it to the river, where it could be shipped north and sold at exorbitant prices.[19]

Among those reportedly involved in the trade was Grant's father, Jesse R. Grant. Colonel Robert C. Murphy, who was cashiered from the Eighth Wisconsin Infantry after surrendering Union garrisons at Iuka and Holly Springs, both in Mississippi, to attacking Confederates, once told Joseph B. McCullagh of the *Commercial* that, on Grant's order, many of his men were too busy hauling and guarding Jesse's cotton to fight. Incensed by the report, Grant had a bitter argument with McCullagh next time they met.[20]

Sherman continued to lash out at greedy Northern merchants. "Cincinnati furnishes more contraband goods than Charleston," he wrote Ellen late in August, "and has done more to prolong the war than the State of South Carolina. Not a merchant there but would sell salt, bacon, powder and lead, if they can make money by it."[21]

Agreeing with Sherman's earlier comment to Ellen, numerous observers blamed Jews. "The army is followed by hordes of Jews," commented the correspondent for the *Commercial*, "who pick up the precious cotton by all means legitimate and illegitimate in their power. They are perfect vultures." Albert D. Richardson of the *New York Tribune* seconded this view: "Glancing at the guests who crowded the dining-hall of the Gayoso, one might have believed that the lost tribes of Israel were gathering there for the Millennium. Many of them were engaged in contraband traffic, supplying the Rebels with food, and even ammunition."[22]

In mid-August the authorities in Washington countermanded Sherman's currency order and allowed the free trading of cotton and other goods. Sherman asked John:

What are the lives of our soldiers to the profits of the merchants? . . .
My full belief is we must colonize the country de nova beginning with
Kentucky & Tennessee, and should remove four millions of our people at once South of the Ohio River taking the farms and plantations
of Rebels. I deplore the War as much as ever, but if a thing has to be
done let the means be adequate. . . . Although our Army is this far
South we cannot stir from our Garrisons. Our men are killed or captured within sight of our lines.[23]

When this letter appeared in the *New York Tribune* shortly after Sherman's
death in 1891, a statement in it intrigued newspapermen. "I have one man under sentence of death for smuggling arms across the lines," Sherman commented, "and I hope Mr. Lincoln will approve it." Sherman was referring to
M. A. Miller, a former Confederate captain of engineers, who in 1891 was living on a farm in Henrico County, near Richmond. "Mr. Lincoln did approve the
sentence of death," Miller told the *New York Times,* "but I am still here while he
and Gen. Sherman have gone to join Lee and Jackson and other good soldiers."

For a month Miller had been smuggling arms to the Confederates "with no
serious difficulties." But one afternoon in July 1862, he was transporting two
boxes of officer's swords across a river when a picket boat came along. Miller
jumped onto the gunwale of his vessel trying to sink it, but the skiff was too
heavy and would not dip. He was arrested, taken to the Memphis military
prison, tried, and sentenced to be shot on the next Friday. He escaped by in-
ducing a guard, who did not know the gravity of his crime, to let him go home
to see a sick child. While at home, he went upstairs, jumped out of a window,
and fled to the Confederate lines.[24]

For someone who had practiced law, Sherman possessed primitive ideas
about justice, as he showed in the case of Colonel Thomas Worthington of the
Forty-sixth Ohio. The son of an early governor or Ohio and a graduate of the
West Point class of 1827, Worthington, according to Sherman, thought he knew
more about war than all of the generals combined. Early in the summer of 1862
he issued a pamphlet charging that Sherman was surprised at Shiloh. This, observed Colonel Walter Q. Gresham of the Fifty-third Indiana, was what Sherman wanted, for he was now able to arrest Worthington and try him for insubordination. Thrown in were accusations of drunkenness.

Sherman preferred the charges against Worthington. He also named the
court that tried him. It included Gresham, later a federal judge and President
Grover Cleveland's secretary of state. At the beginning of the trial Worthington's attorney objected to Sherman's dual role. *"I was the only member of the court
to sustain the objection,"* noted Gresham; "it seemed to me then, and has ever
since, contrary to our institutions to allow the accuser to name the court to try
the accused. Other members of the court were lawyers by profession and must
have known better than to vote to override the challenge." Sherman testified
at the trial, which resulted in Worthington being dropped from the army rolls
as of October 1, 1862. In 1867 President Andrew Johnson modified the verdict
and granted Worthington an honorable discharge.

Gresham and his wife always maintained that Sherman tried to cover up this sorry episode. The published *Official Records* of the war ignored it. With the exception of Gresham's, the biographies and autobiographies of the officers involved did the same.[25]

In dealing with Memphis's newspaper editors, Sherman displayed better sense. At the beginning of the war the city possessed two newspapers, both pro-Southern. The *Memphis Appeal* was so outspoken that its editors moved out of the city and published it from a boxcar so the Yankees could not shut it down. The other paper was the *Argus*, owned by D. A. Brower, later the editor of the *Little Rock Gazette*, and H. L. Priddy. Remembered Priddy:

> Brower and I had to simulate a degree of loyalty, but whenever we got a chance we cheered the stars and bars.
>
> Gen. Sherman gave us considerable latitude, but we finally went too far, and he called us down. He did it in a gentlemanly, sociable way, however, that didn't wound our feelings. He galloped up to the office one day at noon, threw the bridle rein of his big black stallion to an orderly, and strode into the editorial room. A crowd of citizens gathered on the other side of the street and mourned for the fate of the newspaper and the editors. I think they had an idea that Sherman was going to amputate our heads and all the forms, but he didn't. He sat down and, resting his feet on the table, said: "Boys (we were both youngsters), I have been ordered to suppress your paper, but I don't like to do that. I just dropped in to warn you not to be so free with your pencils. If you don't ease up, you'll get in trouble."
>
> We promised to reform, and as the General seemed so pleasant and friendly, I asked him if he couldn't do something to increase the circulation of currency. There was no small change, and we had to use soda-water checks issued by a confectioner named Lane. We dropped soda-water checks in the contribution box at church, paid for straight whisky with them, and received them for money. If Lane closed his shop, the checks would have been worthless.
>
> Gen. Sherman comprehended the situation and quick as a flash said: "You need a medium of exchange that has an intrinsic value. Cotton is king here. Make cotton your currency. It is worth $1 a pound. Make packages containing eight ounces represent 50 cents, four ounces 25 cents, and so on. Cotton is the wealth of the South right now. Turn it into money." "But the money drawers would not hold such bulky currency," said I. "Make 'em larger," said the General, and with that he strode off. As he mounted his horse and galloped away he shook his whip at Brower and me and shouted: "You boys had better be careful what you write or I will be down on you."[26]

Meanwhile, Sherman wrestled with the slavery question. Two Confiscation Acts, passed in August 1861 and July 1862, freed slaves employed against the United States or owned by those supporting the rebellion. By late August Sherman had taken 1,600 black men from their masters. A thousand were working on a fort overlooking the Mississippi, about 200 on the levee, and 300 or 400 as teamsters and cooks. Women also came into Sherman's lines, but the general could find no use for them. Few planters came to his headquarters seeking the return of slaves, but mistresses, used to the comforts of the plantation, constantly pestered him to return runaways.[27]

In charge of the black laborers was Captain William L. B. Jenney, Sherman's chief engineer, who employed them at $10 a month and rations. With the material from some houses taken down to clear the site for the fortifications, the Negroes built a community in a broad ravine on the river bank, just south of the fort. Called Happy Valley, it soon had four thousand inhabitants. Desirous of setting up some sort of government for the village, Jenney asked about and was told everywhere that Tom Alexander was the man to govern the place. Jenney sent for him and was so impressed he immediately put him in charge. "Remember," Jenney instructed Alexander to tell the other slaves, "no work, no pay."

Tom Alexander made Happy Valley a model village. Using the old and feeble men during the day and volunteers at night, he established a police force. Each morning all the men not at work cleaned the community. One morning, while riding through the place, Jenney came upon "a very pleasant young white woman." She was there to teach school, and Alexander had the men build a house for her. Before and after hours she instructed the men who worked on the fortifications. During the day she held classes for the women.

Only one thing bothered Alexander. His wife and children were still on a plantation about fifteen miles outside of town. One day Alexander followed a cavalry unit headed out that way. At the plantation the master, when he saw Tom's earnestness, allowed him to take his family home with him. "Captain Jenney," Alexander told the officer, as he presented to him a double-barreled shotgun he had taken from the plantation, "you should have seen that house this beautiful Sunday morning, just full of flowers. Every one came to give us congratulations and everyone brought flowers. I tell you, that village today is Happy Valley sure enough."[28]

But even John believed Sherman was too wishy-washy on the subject of slavery. People in the North were becoming converted to the idea of emancipation. Generals like John C. Frémont and Benjamin F. Butler were popular, John pointed out, while Buell, Thomas, and McClellan were not. "It is not for military merit," he wrote, "for most persons concede the inferiority in many respects of the officers first named, but it is because these officers agree with & act upon the popular idea that we must treat these rebels as bitter enemies to be subdued—conquered—by confiscation—by the employment of their slaves—by terror—energy—audacity—rather than by conciliation." He urged his brother to "show no favor or even toleration to rebels."[29]

Answering John, Cump thought

> you are wrong in saying that Negroes are free & entitled to be treated accordingly by simple declaration of Congress. . . . Not one Nigger in

ten wants to run off. There are 25000 in 20 miles of Memphis—All could escape & would receive protection here, but we have only about 2000 of whom full half are hanging about camps as officers servants. Some place some system of labor must be devised in connection with these slaves else the whole scheme fails.[30]

— IV —

With her husband in Memphis, Ellen busied herself with her favorite pastime: the advancement of her family. During the summer of 1862 Tom and Charley both looked to the future. Giving up his plans to make a fortune on the transcontinental railroad, Tom returned to Kansas and began raising an army regiment. At the same time Ellen went to Columbus to see Governor David Tod and "to make one *last* effort to get poor Charley into the Vol. Service. I tell you Cump," she advised, "I can never feel satisfied whilst he is kept at that ignominious post. It is a humiliation too deep to be borne by a young fellow as full of ardor & ambition as he was."[31]

A week later Ellen reported some success. Charley was now a mustering officer in Springfield, Illinois, "heartily rejoiced to get away from Alton on any terms." But he still longed to be with his brother-in-law. Ellen's cousin, Sister Angela, after nursing the sick in Memphis, was being sent to the Academy of Notre Dame, in South Bend, Indiana. The school had "a fine new building . . . with baths & every modern comfort." Philemon, as religious as his sister, sent his children to school there, and Ellen was preparing to enroll Minnie and Willy. Meantime, Hugh Boyle Ewing, commanding a regiment under Sherman's friend General Ambrose E. Burnside in the East, was in heavy fighting. Fortunately, he was well.[32]

Responding to the pleas of Ellen and her father, Sherman sent north, to Major General Horatio G. Wright, a regiment to escort back to Memphis Charley's unit, the Thirteenth United States Infantry. "They kept both—That was dishonest & unfair," Sherman complained to Ellen, "and I have so written to Wright at Cincinnati. They see an awful danger at Cincinnati, but they dont think of us who are far in the advance. The next time they want one of my Regiments I'll insist they send me another first." The matter dragged on until early December, when Sherman reported the arrival of the Thirteenth Infantry and Charley.[33]

With Hugh and Charley in the army and Tom about to enter it, Ellen and her father turned toward helping Philemon. Thomas Ewing intended to go to Washington to speak to Lincoln about having Phil appointed Sherman's judge advocate. Cump endorsed the plan, for he now wasted six hours a day reviewing the proceedings of trials and the like. "I am very anxious to have you press Philemon's appointment & to get him assigned to Cump if possible," Ellen told her father after McClellan's pyrrhic victory at Antietam, where Union forces stopped Robert E. Lee's advance into Maryland but let his army escape. "I think you can accomplish it through Stanton & Halleck. I cannot think much of the President's heart or judgment now that he persists in sustaining that horrible opiate McClellan." If this did not work, Ellen suggested, her father could ask Tod to appoint Phil a major. Sherman could then ask for him as his judge advocate.[34]

Capping the activities at home was a resumption of the feud between Ellen and Elizabeth. Now they argued about Mary Hoyt Sherman's house in Mansfield, into which Ellen desired to move. No one was more entitled to the home than Sherman. "You remember that for years I supplied mother with ready money," Cump reminded Ellen. "I never kept an account of it as it was freely given. Every time I went home I overhauled her books & accounts paid all her bills and left her insured." Elizabeth was too poor to help, and Taylor contributed only "wood, potatoes fruit &c. all of which he got as fee or from his own property." Even though knowing Ellen wanted the house, Elizabeth allowed an Episcopalian minister to move into it. "Elizabeth presented it to him," Ellen charged. "I don't want you to write Elizabeth again. I shall feel truly hurt if you do."[35]

— V —

One evening in early November, Ellen, visiting Memphis, was sitting around talking to her husband and several subordinates in a parlor. Suddenly General Morgan L. Smith, Kilby Smith, Stuart, and others entered. After going through a ceremony, they presented Sherman with a sword. Stuart and Sherman then delivered "touching" speeches. "All the newspaper compliments in the world," Ellen told her father, "would have failed to gratify Cump half as much as this evidence of attachment & confidence on the part of his tried and valued officers." Sherman had recommended Stuart and Buckland for promotion, but, Ellen believed, his letters would have "little weight whilst McClellan's blighting influence stands behind the throne."[36]

At this time Union forces in the West were still scattered about. Sherman was at Memphis, Hurlbut at Jackson, Mississippi, and General Charles S. Hamilton at Corinth. General William S. Rosecrans commanded the Army of the Cumberland, while Halleck directed operations from Washington.[37]

Like a cork in a bottle, Vicksburg, overlooking a hairpin bend, blocked Northern control of the Mississippi River. From the city the Confederates were able to fire down upon Union ships headed south. On November 2, with Halleck's approval, Grant, with 30,000 men, began his first southward drive to gain control of the city. Opposing him with about an equal number of troops was Lieutenant General John C. Pemberton. James B. McPherson, now a major general, commanded Grant's left wing, Hamilton the center, and Sherman, at Memphis, the right. Entrenched on a line behind the Tallahatchie River, below Holly Springs, Pemberton had fortified Grand Junction and Holly Springs, both on the Mississippi Central Railroad. Grant captured these towns, but he became disheartened, partially because the road carrying his supplies needed constant repairs and partially because he read in newspapers that Lincoln was ready to appoint McClernand to, as Grant put it, "a separate and independent command within mine, to operate against Vicksburg by way of the Mississippi River."[38]

Still, on the fifteenth, Grant telegraphed Sherman to meet him at Columbus, Kentucky. There Grant explained that he wanted Sherman to start from Memphis, move along the Mississippi Central, and join him on the Tallahatchie, eighteen miles south of Holly Springs and about seventy from Memphis. Leaving Memphis on November 26 with three small divisions totaling 18,000 men, Sherman reached the river on December 2 at a town named Wyatte, to find that Pemberton, Earl Van Dorn, and the other Confederates had withdrawn toward Grenada. The Southerners had burned the bridge at Wyatte, but Sherman had brought boats with which to cross his infantry and cavalry. Two miles beyond the river he found two long lines of entrenchments, both abandoned. Sending his cavalry ahead to join Grant, then pressing the rear of the retreating enemy, Sherman returned to Wyatte to build a new bridge.[39]

The construction of the bridge presaged the days of total war. To get material the Union troops tore down the houses comprising the village. While the work was going on, Sherman lived in the large timber home of an old farmer. In the evenings after dinner, while sitting before the fire in the big chimney smoking their pipes, the members of Sherman's staff amused themselves by calling Sherman's attention to the ceiling and roof timbers, ideal for the bridge. "General," the old farmer pleaded, "you certainly would not take down your own quarters and sleep out on the lawn in the rain,—you will all die of colds." To this Sherman answered: "That bridge must be built if it takes the last house in the town." When Sherman was leaving, many of the residents came to him and demanded vouchers for the value of their homes. "Call upon the Southern Confederacy," Sherman answered. "You let them burn the old bridge and I was forced to use your houses, in exchange for which I give you the bridge. Take good care of it; do not force me to build another." The destruction of the town was so complete that on military maps the name "Wyatte" became "Wyatte Bridge."[40]

Endless rain made the Mississippi roads practically impassable. With the cavalry and artillery almost sinking out of sight in the mud, the troops, emulating the calls on the river, frequently yelled out "By the mark twain" and "No bottom." But Sherman noted the richness of the land through which he passed. "We find plenty of corn, fodder, cattle, hogs, sheep, &c.," he wrote John, "so that our enemies have not been starving."[41]

With the expedition bogged down in mud, Grant heard news that made him recoil. McClernand's expedition down the Mississippi to Vicksburg was inevitable. Grant desired, as he put it in his *Personal Memoirs*, to have a "competent commander in charge," rather than the political general, McClernand. Calling Sherman, then at College Hill, ten miles away, to a meeting at Oxford, Mississippi, Grant mapped out his plan to head off McClernand. He would keep Pemberton busy around Grenada and move toward the rear of Vicksburg. Meantime, Sherman would take the four divisions led by Brigadier Generals Morgan Smith, Andrew J. Smith, George W. Morgan, and Frederick Steele down the Mississippi to the Yazoo River. He would go up the Yazoo and attempt to capture Vicksburg from the front. "I confess," Sherman later recorded in his *Memoirs*, "at the moment I did not dream that General McClernand, or anyone else, was scheming for the mere honor of capturing Vicksburg."[42]

By noon of December 12, Sherman was back in Memphis, having returned with Morgan Smith's 7,000 men as his escort. "I also brought in the Regulars & my 20 lb Parrotts," Sherman wrote Ellen. "I took Charley from his horse and he footed it in manfully 75 miles in 3½ days. He is here in fine feather and delighted with his first bloodless campaign."

To Ellen, Sherman noted how Memphis had changed:

Today I worshipped in Cavalry and Mr White preached a *real good* Union sermon. Four months ago he omitted the prayer for Jeff Davis out of naked respect for our presence. The streets are lively, the Theatre crowded and really the Town looks prosperous. Cotton comes in freely and trade thrives. I don't believe a real secessionist now wants to recall the past. If I can take Vicksburg and accomplish the same there and finally being up in Louisiana, I feel that I can make that state admit that "Union is a Necessity"—This is all my ambition and I hope I will be permitted to stick to the Mississippi.[43]

Ellen responded sarcastically:

Your attendance at White's Church was noticed in the paper. I suppose E. Reese is exulting that you go to Episcopal Church instead of Catholic. . . . Did you know that Burnside was a Catholic? He came into the Church & received the Sacraments just before starting on his expedition last winter. . . . Father writes that Secretary Stanton told him you were "by far the best General we have—administrative & in the field"—So do not provoke me again by putting yourself below Mc-·Clellan.[44]

Sherman's first problem was to find ships for his 31,000 men. Luckily, in St. Louis, the army possessed a remarkable quartermaster, Lewis B. Parsons. On December 11, 1862, Parsons received a telegram from Grant requesting transportation for Sherman's army, including cavalry, artillery, infantry, and animals, to be at Memphis on the eighteenth. At the time, only eight suitable vessels were docked in St. Louis. Winter was approaching, and fuel was scarce. General Robert Allen, the supervising quartermaster, thought the order impossible to fill, and immediately telegraphed so to Grant. But by seizing coal transports and boats on various western rivers, Parsons accumulated over seventy ships. On the desired date he had them at Memphis, 450 miles from St. Louis. Within forty-eight hours the troops, with the exception of Steele's 11,000 men, who were picked up at Helena on the twenty-fifth, embarked.[45]

While the ships were being loaded, Sherman met for the first time his naval escort, Admiral David Dixon Porter. Fresh from a meeting with the plain-looking and plain-spoken Grant, Porter sent word that he would call at Sherman's headquarters. Thinking Sherman would dress regally, Porter wore his finest clothes. Sherman, on the other hand, had heard that Porter disliked dressing up, so he kept on his working clothes. Each was surprised by the appearance of the other. Porter was immediately taken with Sherman's naturalness and with the swiftness with which he gave orders. "I though myself lucky," he noted, "to have two such generals as Grant and Sherman to cooperate with."[46]

Although the expedition, led by Porter in his flagship *Black Hawk*, left Memphis on the twentieth, two days after Grant's proposed date, it reached the mouth of the Yazoo on Christmas, as scheduled. Sherman and Porter decided that the best point of debarkation lay twelve miles up, at the Johnson plantation, on the bank toward Vicksburg.[47]

The army landed on the triangular alluvial plain about twelve miles long and four or five wide. Flowing westward into the Mississippi, which it met nine or ten miles above Vicksburg, the Yazoo constituted the northern boundary of the triangle. The Mississippi, bearing strongly eastward at the bend above Vicksburg, was the southern border. Chickasaw Bayou, a deep, sluggish stream meandering from the Yazoo to the bend in the Mississippi, constituted the shortest and eastern side of the triangle. Parallel to and just beyond Chickasaw Bayou ran a range of hills that started at Haines Bluff, six or seven miles up the Yazoo from Chickasaw, and ran down to Vicksburg.[48]

Answering the complaints of Steele and of Brigadier General Frank Blair Jr., who led a brigade in Steele's division, Sherman later revealed that geography plus Confederate preparations determined the landing site. Several naval officers had been up the Yazoo the previous year and found Snyder's Bluff, the high ground before Haines Bluff, filled with heavy guns, earth forts, and rifle pits. The Yazoo itself was obstructed by a raft and torpedoes, one of which had sunk the gunboat *Cairo*. All agreed that the landing must be lower down, at the Johnson plantation, even if Haines Bluff was to be the point of attack.[49]

Sherman's movement, like that of the British in the Revolutionary War that ended with the defeat at Saratoga, was supposed to be part of a three-pronged attack. But General Nathaniel Banks, who was supposed to come up from New Orleans, never moved. Grant, too, failed Sherman. On December 20, General Earl Van Dorn's Confederate cavalry attacked Grant's supply depot at Holly Springs. Carrying turpentine in their canteens, they used it to burn Grant's ammunition and guns, 1,800 bales of cotton, forty-two railroad cars, and two locomotives. Grant now did not even try to bottle up Pemberton, who used the railroad to reinforce Vicksburg.[50]

Momentarily expecting Grant and Banks, Sherman decided to make feints at Haines Bluff and at Vicksburg itself. But the real attack was to come at the head of Chickasaw Bayou on the morning of the twenty-ninth. Sherman ordered Morgan, reinforced by two of Steele's brigades, thirteen regiments in all, to cross the bayou and advance to the hills, a distance of about three-fifths of a mile. The assault was to be made over ground directly in front of Blair, commanding Steele's first brigade, and Colonel John F. DeCourcy, commanding Morgan's third. Supporting DeCourcy was Steele's third brigade, led by Brigadier General John M. Thayer, later the governor of Nebraska.

These officers were a varied group. Blair, Sherman's old St. Louis acquaintance, was handsome and brave. He was also a politician, and was often more concerned with his public than with his military career. Violating Sherman's orders, he carried with him a reporter from the *Missouri Republican* so that its readers might be informed of his every move.

Morgan was also a politician, but he possessed none of Blair's bravery. An Ohio Democrat who later served two terms in Congress, he had seen service with Scott in the Mexican War. In 1866, when Morgan was a congressman, Sherman wrote Ellen of him: "He would not fight at Chickasaw and lost me a battle otherwise won."

DeCourcy was the Rodney Mason of Chickasaw. A soldier of fortune who had served in the British army, he demanded more of others than of himself. A strict disciplinarian, he required soldiers on guard to walk for hours carrying knapsack, overcoat, blankets, and haversack. "The slightest infractions of discipline, little irregularities committed in entire innocence," noted the historian of the Forty-second Ohio, "were punished by the most degrading penalties. A favorite device of the austere Colonel was to have the men whose muskets were found spotted with rust, loaded with rails and marched up and down in front of headquarters during the evening."[51]

The attack on Chickasaw Bluffs ushered in a controversy similar to, but less publicized than, that about Shiloh. Years later, in an article for *Century* magazine that became part of the *Battles and Leaders* series, Morgan presented a callous Sherman unconcerned about sending men to certain death. To protests that an attack was suicide, Sherman, safe in his headquarters, supposedly answered: "Tell Morgan to give the signal for the assault; that we will lose 5000 before we take Vicksburg, and may as well lose them here as anywhere else."[52]

About noon on the twenty-ninth the battle of Chickasaw began. Under a deadly fire DeCourcy and Thayer squeezed their men over a narrow corduroy bridge. At the same time Blair's brigade, crossing a bayou to the left, offered less of a target to enemy riflemen as they struggled through mud, water, and abatis to dry land. Blair and Thayer then drove the enemy from its first line of rifle pits and pushed to a road that lay along the base of a hill. Assaulting the enemy's second line, the Federals encountered a heavy fire from rifle pits and batteries. The Northern column, Sherman reported, "faltered, and finally fell back to the point of starting." The Northern killed and wounded were over a thousand.[53]

At first the Blair family blamed Sherman for the slaughter. "Sherman behaved in the most incompetent manner," Blair's wife informed her father-in-law from St. Louis. " . . . Even the Germans, officers & men alike believe it was his deliberate intention to sacrifice Frank." Colonel Francis Hassendubel of the Seventeenth Missouri "*refused* positively to storm the place Frank attacked telling Sherman it would take ten thousand men to take the position & he would not attempt it with 2800. Sherman covered himself with a blanket & remained on foot which does not surprise me at all as all those who knew him here knew him to be cowardly."[54]

But the story of Chickasaw was the failure of Morgan, DeCourcy, and Steele to follow orders. Sherman had planned an attack by thirteen regiments—four led by Blair, four by DeCourcy, and five by Thayer. But DeCourcy and his four regiments refused to advance beyond the first line of rifle pits. Both Blair and Thayer came back from the battle complaining that DeCourcy had deserted them. During the assault on the second line of pits, moreover, Steele and Morgan diverted to the right four of Thayer's regiments, leaving Thayer only the Fourth Iowa, led by the brave Colonel James A. Williamson. The Federal attack, which advanced to the foot of the enemy's last line of works, was thus carried by only five of the thirteen regiments, one of Thayer's and four of Blair's.[55]

The most telling analysis of Chickasaw came, shortly after Sherman's death, from Thayer. He remembered that when passing the first line of enemy rifle pits, he noticed Union soldiers entering them and wondered what they were doing. Thayer and Williamson then advanced to the second line, which ran near the bluffs. Stationing the Fourth Iowa parallel to the enemy pits for an assault, he ordered Williamson to wait while he brought up his other four regiments.

> When I turned back, to my dismay and horror, I found only the Fourth Iowa Infantry had followed me. No other regiment was to be seen. It was awful—a repetition of Balaklava, although mine was infantry and Earl Cardigan's force was cavalry.
>
> My first thought was of those troops that I had seen in the rifle-pits, and I said to Colonel Williamson: "Hold your ground, if possible, while I go back and get those troops up to support you."
>
> I returned to the place where I had seen them and found General Blair, in a very earnest and excited conversation with an officer who, I was informed, was DeCourcy. He was urging DeCourcy to get his men forward, having anticipated my intentions. I joined in the conversation, but to no purpose. I then started to return to where the Fourth Infantry was and met Colonel Williamson bringing his regiment. He had less than five hundred men in the morning; one hundred and fifty-two were killed and wounded in less than thirty minutes, and to have remained would have been a murderous sacrifice of his men; for two lines of rifle pits along the height and several batteries were bearing upon his regiment, as they had been bearing upon us as we marched forward to the assault. In leading the assault I had marched side by side with Colonel Williamson at the head of his regiment. On getting back to the field where I had left them I saw General Steele, and in no very respectful language demanded to know why he had taken the four regiments away from me without my knowledge. . . . Steele replied that after I had moved forward across the bayou General Morgan came to him and directed him to turn Colonel Abbott, with the Thirtieth Iowa, which had followed the Fourth Iowa in accordance with my orders. Abbott, knowing Steele to be my superior officer,

obeyed the order instead of carrying out my order, and before crossing the bayou, turned away to the right. . . . The other regiments did the same. Each commander, except Colonel Abbott, complying with my order to follow the preceding regiment. The four regiments were thus parted from me, and I was left to proceed with the Fourth Iowa, which was only a half regiment.

My regret always has been that I did not prefer charges against Morgan and Steele, for between them they were responsible for one of the most terrible blunders which has ever occurred in military affairs. There was a conflict between them as to which ranked the other, and General Sherman had placed Morgan in command of the assault to be made that day.

DeCourcy's men were staying in the rifle-pits when Blair's brigade and my Fourth Iowa were moving toward that most horrible assault. They never went beyond the line of rifle-pits which hugged the bayou. . . .

At Balaklava the Earl of Cardigan was ordered to charge with his six hundred men the whole Russian army. I was ordered to take the Chickasaw Bluffs and to lead my command as the assaulting column when I had three thousand five hundred men; but when I got into the field directly in front of the enemy's batteries and rifle-pits, I found myself with less than five hundred men. The other four regiments were nearly full, having been in the field but a short time. It was worse than a blunder. It was a crime, a terrible crime, and the responsibility for that crime rests upon Morgan and Steele.

General Morgan wrote to me a couple of years ago asking me for a statement on my part in that terrible affair. I gave him a partial statement, which he found anything but agreeable, and I have never heard anything further from him.[56]

In their official reports, all written within a week of the battle, Morgan, Steele, Thayer, and Williamson agreed that a gross error had stranded Thayer and Williamson while assaulting the second line of enemy pits. "I could not account for it," Thayer wrote on December 31, 1862. "I had supposed that five regiments were following me." Steele blamed Morgan, and Morgan merely called the incident a "mistake." In the horrible thirty minutes Williamson's Fourth Iowa stood exposed and alone "under a fire which," Williamson reported, "cannot be described," 112 of its 480 men were killed or wounded. Thayer also mentioned the regiments that skulked: "I ordered and begged them, but without effect, to come forward and support my regiment, which was now warmly engaged."[57]

Prevented by fog from making a combined land and naval attack further up the river at Haines Bluff and hearing that McClernand was at the mouth of the Yazoo ready to assume command, Sherman, late in the afternoon of December 31, decided to withdraw. He ordered his troops to march to the river, where Parsons was to embark them as rapidly as possible. At the time the transports were scattered for miles, either looking for fuel or serving as hospitals, but

Parsons rounded them up and the army sailed away before eight o'clock the next morning. "Of the work of such a night," Parsons observed, "no one can have any proper conception who was not on the ground, or is not intimately familiar with similar military movements; and I question if a like speedy and safe embarkation of so large an army, in the face of a victorious enemy, was ever effected, under any command."[58]

The man who met Sherman on the morning of January 2, 1863, was the ultimate politician. Having represented Lincoln's district in Congress for ten years, McClernand had poured into the president's ear stories of western farmers who demanded the opening of the Mississippi, down which they sent their goods. With the aid of Senators Orville H. Browning and Lyman Trumbull of Illinois and over the objection of Halleck, he convinced Lincoln that he was the warrior to open up the river.[59]

Knowing McClernand from Shiloh, Sherman despised him. "He was and is the meanest man we ever had in the west," Sherman observed, "with a mean, gnawing ambition, ready to destroy everybody who could cross his path. He would not give me an order to renew the attack on his arrival, but was ever ready to throw on me the blame of failure." McClernand had spent the fall in Illinois, Ellen joined in to John, "electioneering for the Senate." When his chances evaporated, he concocted the Mississippi River expedition. He proceeded to marry his sister-in-law and took the bridal party with him to Memphis. Ellen considered it shameful to "supercede Cump who has not given himself one days rest & who refused to be carried from his post at the road side last summer when dangerously ill—so dangerously they thought he would die." "Lincoln," Ellen observed to Cump about McClernand's appointment, "ought to be impeached as an imbecile for that very act."[60]

McClernand was a classic example of someone who took himself more seriously than the world took him. In Springfield, Porter revealed, he had failed to recruit "a single soldier. . . . He couldn't even get a transport to bring him down the river, but had to take passage in one of the old rams, half officered and manned." During the trip from Memphis to the Yazoo, McClernand was seasick.

Long before McClernand arrived, Sherman and Porter discussed redeeming themselves with an expedition to Fort Hindman, or Arkansas Post, the Confederate installation guarding the Arkansas River. At first such a modest project did not interest McClernand, who spoke about " 'sweeping to the sea'—how," Sherman commented, "he had no more idea than a baby." But at a meeting on board the *Black Hawk* McClernand, with Sherman "looking daggers at him," suddenly suggested the plan as his own. "If you let me have three gun boats," McClernand said, "I will go and take the place." As Porter told the story:

> Now Genl McClernand had about as much idea of what a gunboat was or could do as the man in the moon. He did not know the difference between an iron-clad and a "tin-clad." He had heard that gun boats had taken Fort Henry and that was all he knew about them. I said to

him "I'll tell you what I will do General McClernand. If General Sherman goes in command of the troops, I will go myself in command of a proper force, and will insure the capture of the post." McClernand winced under this, and Sherman quietly walked off into the after cabin. He beckoned me to come there while McClernand was apparently deeply engaged in studying out a chart making believe he was interested in order to conceal his temper.

Sherman said to me, "Admiral, how could you make such a remark to McClernand? He hates me already and you have made him an enemy for life." "I don't care," said I, "he shall not treat you rudely in my cabin, and I was glad of the opportunity of letting him know my sentiments."[61]

Compared with the assault of December 29, Arkansas Post was a simple task. Up to this time Sherman's force had been known as the Right Wing of Grant's Thirteenth Army Corps. McClernand renamed it the Army of the Mississippi—after the river he was going to reopen—and divided it into two corps, the first commanded by his fellow Democrat, Morgan, the other by Sherman.

Heading back up the Mississippi, the expedition reached the mouth of the White River on January 8. Going up the White a short way, the boats then entered the "cut-off" for the Arkansas. Early on the morning of the tenth the Union soldiers disembarked about four miles below Fort Hindman. At first Sherman thought he could circle around and attack the fort from the rear, but this route contained a swamp and a bayou. McClernand, therefore, called Sherman back and sent him along the river bank to the front of the fort. Sherman's men marched to within a half mile of Hindman, then bore off to the right. During the bright, moonlit night of the tenth they built a line of fortifications. At about ten o'clock in the evening Sherman and his staff spread their blankets on the ground near a big cypress tree and prepared to sleep.

No one had eaten anything since leaving the boat, so Captain John T. Taylor, Sherman's aide, decided to surprise the general. He mounted his horse, groped his way back to the boat, found the driver of their mess wagon, and ordered him to hitch up. About one in the morning Taylor returned to camp with the wagon. Told what his aide had done, Sherman said: "Well, sir, you ought not to have done so; no one else has had anything to eat since we have, and we can stand it if the troops can. Captain, send that wagon back to the boat."[62]

The Federal assault began at 10:30 the next morning. From about one o'clock on, Porter's gunboats inflicted heavy damage from the front. By this time Captain Jacob T. Foster of the First Wisconsin Battery, who had been sent with six guns in a roundabout way to a position a mile and a half above the fort, from which he could cut off possible reinforcements from Little Rock, began bombarding the post from the rear. Caught in this cross fire, the Confederates surrendered at about 4:15. At a cost of 129 killed and 831 wounded the Union forces took 5,000 prisoners, seventeen cannons, 1,500 animals, and large amounts of small arms and ammunition. After dismantling the fort, the expedition returned to Milliken's Bend on the twenty-first to await Grant.[63]

For a month after the defeat at Chickasaw, Sherman remained despondent. Among his troops, the story circulated that his insanity had returned. Already, he told John on January 17, he was being charged with the defeat at Chickasaw, while McClernand was being hailed as the conqueror of Arkansas Post: "I led the columns, gave all orders, and entered the place when he came along and managed the prisoners & captured property. . . . But I know enough of the gnawing desire for fame & notoriety that consumes him and doubt if my name will appear in his Record save to fill some common place blank."[64]

By the end of January, Sherman was in camp near Vicksburg, decrying Grant's failure to follow up the Arkansas Post victory. Fearing that Banks might have come up the river and might be trapped below Vicksburg, Grant had hurried downstream and was not even in camp. Sherman wrote Ellen:

> It was simply absurd to supercede me by McClernand, but Mr Lincoln knows I am not anxious to command, and he knows McClernand is and must gratify him. He will get his fill before he is done. He sent his Chief of Cavalry Colonel [Warren] Stewart out on some errand yesterday and he was killed. McClernand is now sick in bed, and what is doing is left to me as usual. I know one fact well, that when danger is present, or important steps are necessary Sherman is invariably called for, but in unloading steamboats repairing roads &c &c I get provoking short orders to do this and so.

Sherman concluded with an ominous prophecy: "Vicksburg is very strong & it will be only by a dreadful sacrifice we can get a footing & then the Battle."[65]

9

Vicksburg and Sherman's First March

SHERMAN'S FAILURE at Chickasaw had aggravated the Union problem. How could a strengthened Vicksburg, standing on a bluff two hundred feet above the Mississippi, be taken? After the capture of Arkansas Post, McClernand had proposed pushing further up the Arkansas River to Little Rock, but Grant, who resented the Illinois politician as much as Sherman did, directed him to join Sherman at Young's Point, Louisiana, directly opposite Vicksburg.

The previous summer Major General Benjamin F. Butler, commanding New Orleans, had come up with a scheme that caught Lincoln's attention. Why not dig a canal across a loop in the river opposite Vicksburg? Using "Butler's ditch," the theory ran, Union troops and supplies might be safely transported below Vicksburg, rendering the city "an inland town."[1]

After riding over the muddy terrain for the first time, Sherman derided the canal as "no bigger than a plantation ditch." Both of its ends rested in calm water that did not so much as ripple, let alone flow. Nor were the Confederates asleep. From Vicksburg south a dozen miles to Warrenton, also on the east bank of the river, they placed heavy guns that could reach much of the canal. Forcing his men to go out with shovels into the mud to widen the canal by nine feet was to Sherman "a pure waste of human labor." "I have never seen men work more grudgingly," he informed McClernand, "and I have endeavored to stimulate them by all means." A week after starting on the project, Sherman told Ellen: "Our men are working on the Canal, but mostly make a levee to prevent the Canal overflowing the ground of our Camps. If the River rises 8 feet more it will be all over this Country except levees and we would have to take to trees."[2]

Early in February Sherman complained that heavy rains continued to hamper the project. "The River is rising," he wrote to Ellen, "and soon we shall be afloat—it takes all our men to keep off the Mississippi—Vicksburg remains opposite laughing at our condition. Our Canal is full of water but no sign of the Mississippi choosing it for its new bed." Sixty miles above Vicksburg, at Lake Providence, McPherson's men had begun "a more valuable plan." Passing through rivers and bayous, Lake Providence emptied into the Mississippi a hundred and seventy miles below Vicksburg. The army hoped to widen and deepen the waterways. "If successful," Sherman noted, "boats will be able to go to New Orleans without approaching Vicksburg or Port Hudson."[3]

One day, while his officers were discussing the stupidity of their project, Sherman received an order from McClernand to "immediately blow up the bottom of the canal. It is important," McClernand commanded, "that this be done to-night, as tomorrow it may be too late." With "a roguish twinkle" in his eye, Sherman handed the order to Captain Jenney, indicating that he had no idea what it meant. Meeting McClernand a few minutes later, Jenney politely asked him what he wanted. McClernand flew into his usual rage, saying: "You can dig a hole, can't you? You can put powder into it, can't you? You can touch it off, can't you? Well, then, won't it blow up?" Jenney learned that a steamboat captain had told McClernand that the bottom of the canal consisted of sand and clay that would wash away and deepen if exploded. "I rode away," Jenney later remarked, "and a suppressed 'Damn' was all the blowing up it received that night."[4]

The fiasco ended in early March. Heavy rains flooded the canal and the levee, submerging most of the peninsula and forcing Kilby Smith's men onto a strip of land ten feet wide at the top, "the Mississippi on one hand, an impassable swamp on the other." Smith and the other officers took refuge on a steamboat.[5]

Murat Halstead, for one, called for the removal of the army commanders. "There never was a more thoroughly disgusted, disheartened, demoralized army than this is," the editor wrote Chase on February 19, "and all because it is under such men as Grant and Sherman. . . . How is it that Grant, who was behind at Fort Henry, drunk at Donelson, surprised and whipped at Shiloh, and driven back from Oxford, Miss., is still in command? . . . Our noble army of the Mississippi is being wasted by the foolish, drunken, stupid Grant. He can't organize or control or fight an army."[6]

If Sherman disliked newspapermen before Chickasaw, he detested them after it. The first reports of the battle, appearing in the *Missouri Republican*, depicted Blair as the Union hero and Sherman as the villain. Unfortunately for Sherman, the account was widely reprinted and set the tone for other stories.[7]

Sherman had ample reasons for suspecting Blair. He had banned journalists from the expedition, only to find that the Missouri general had taken with him for, Cump told John, "self-glorification" several reporters, including the correspondent of the *New York Herald*, Thomas W. Knox, who showed his gratitude by publishing an account, identified as coming from Blair's flagship, highly favorable to his benefactor. For some reason Knox also believed that De-

Courcy and his brigade deserved "especial honor." Questioned in front of Kilby Smith, Major Charles McMillen, Sherman's medical director, and Major John H. Hammond, Sherman's assistant adjutant, "the scoundrel," as Smith labeled him, admitted "not only that his article was false, and malicious, and based upon false information received from parties interested in defaming General Sherman and his command, but that he renewed the old story of his insanity for the purpose of gratifying private revenge."[8]

Infuriated, Sherman dashed off to Blair twenty-two questions about Knox's relationship to the Missourian. Blair responded to Sherman's satisfaction, arguing that he did and said nothing to influence Knox against Sherman. "I could hardly believe," Sherman retorted in turn on February 2, "that a white man could be so false as this fellow Knox." The reporter had bragged about publishing falsehoods. He had, moreover, revealed military secrets. The Confederates in Vicksburg could now approximate to within one thousand men the size of the Federal force opposite them. "I do know," Sherman continued, "that the day will come when every officer will demand the execution of this class of spies; and without further hesitation I declare that if I am forced to look to the New York Herald as my law and master instead of the constituted authorities of the United States my military career is at an end."[9]

Disregarding the advice of Admiral Porter, who tried to calm him down, Sherman arrested Knox and made plans to try him. At the same time, in letters to Ellen and to John, he vowed to resign from the army. "I think I can establish his character," Cump told Ellen of Knox, "and if the President has not nerve to back the officers who are fighting his battles, but yields to the clamor of the Press, I can slide out and let the Press do his fighting. . . . I cannot allow a newspaper Reporter to come into my Camp, against orders, and tell me to my face that I must tell him the Truth else he will publish Falsehood."[10]

To John, Sherman wrote similarly:

> I am still resolved to quit and seek retirement. I only wait the favorable opportunity. I have done my share and suffered enough from the enemies of our Govt North & South and have a right to look to myself and family before all the good name I carried into the Volunteer service is gone. If I wait much longer I will be unable to earn a livelihood. St. Louis will be my choice or I may go to California.
>
> The Press has now killed McClellan—Buell, FitzJohn Porter, Sumner, Franklin, and Burnside. Add my name and I am not ashamed of the Association. If the Press can govern the Country let them fight the Battles.[11]

Sherman's letter shocked John. In the past year Cump had fought back from oblivion to prominence. Charley was now with him. So too was Hugh, who led one of Sherman's brigades. John told Cump:

> I have taken a sincere pride in all you have done & have heartily sustained you. Do you wish to humiliate me—& not only me but Halleck Stanton (the Secy of War who is truly your friend) Mr. Ewing. We are

the only members of our family now in a condition to aid the others by kindly influence. Must this be given up? And all because scoundrels libel you and men are envious. Great God I wish you had been libeled as much as I have been & got used to it. . . . You will live to serve your country when "Old Abe" will be consigned to infamy as a fool & baboon. . . . It is a fearful disposition of Providence, or the folly of party leaders that he is President while our Country is passing through this violence. But we must make the best of it. If we save our political institutions it will be because of their inherent strength.[12]

As Ellen saw it, leaving the army constituted surrender:

Nothing that you are capable of doing could cause me deep mortification except your resignation at this time. . . . Do you not see that you would thus be giving your enemies—the correspondents—the triumph they wish. *They will then have written you down.* . . . I do not like to see you put yourself in the category with McClellan, Porter & others—why not put in Fremont? Porter was cashiered by as good a court as Tom Worthington had & McClellan is in my estimation a traitor & I have not taken my opinion from the papers for they have been disgusting absolutely loathsome in their sickening adulation of a man who has never been within range of the enemy's balls—& never means to be.[13]

Instead of resigning, Sherman threw himself into the Knox case. On February 5, 1863, he convened a court-martial board that Thayer headed and that included McClernand. Knox was accused of revealing information to the enemy, of being a spy, and of disobeying Sherman's order barring reporters from the Chickasaw expedition. During the trial Sherman testified against Knox, while Steele and Blair testified for him. On the evening of February 18 the court acquitted Knox of the first two charges, but it found him technically guilty of disobeying Sherman's instructions. He was to be expelled from the lines of the Army of the Tennessee and ordered not to return.

The matter did not end there. At the urging of Albert D. Richardson of the *New York Tribune* and of James M. Winchell of the *New York Times,* Lincoln agreed on March 20 to revoke the banishment if Grant concurred, something Grant refused to do without Sherman's consent. "Come with sword or musket in your hand," Sherman advised the reporter who desired to return, "prepared to share with us our fate in sunshine and storm . . . and I will welcome you as a brother and associate; but come as you now do . . . as the representative of the press, which you yourself say makes so slight a difference between truth and falsehood, and my answer is, Never."[14]

The affair disgusted Sherman. After its conclusion, he wrote John:

Knox is simply nobody, but he represents the Press, and as such expects to rule the Country. Mr Lincoln pulled hither & thither by every shade of policy—trimming his sails to every puff of wind has done what? Actually endorsed the opinion that to disobey the orders of the

War Dept—the orders of a Major Genl in command of 30,000 men—
and to publish a tissue of falsehood, is a "technical offense." If he thus
sustains his officers, they have little to rest upon to meet a popular
Rebellion.

    . . . McClernand has his batch of toadies which the army understands
and who would sign the death warrant of his son for a newspaper
puff—Knox was Thayers eulogist—and his recommendation was a
matter of course, but the idea of Mr Lincoln yielding was infernal.[15]

John saw in this misadventure a deeper meaning:

How fervently I wish Lincoln was out of the way—any body would do
better. I was among the first of his political friends to acknowledge how
fearfully we were mistaken in him. He has not a single quality befit-
ting his place. I could name a thousand evidences of this but that Knox
affair is one. He is unstable as water—afraid of a child & yet sometimes
stubborn as a mule. I shall never cease to regret the part I took in his
election and am willing to pay a heavy penance for this sin. This error
I fear will be a fatal one as he is unfit to control events and it is fearful to think what may come during his time.[16]

—— II ——

The first three months of the Vicksburg campaign constituted a study in frustration. The attempts to divert the Mississippi and to find passages through the
clogged rivers and lakes failed. So, too, did an expedition devised by Porter and
Grant in mid-March. With five ironclad gunboats and three tugs, the admiral
planned to go up the Yazoo to Steele's Bayou, opposite the Johnson plantation,
Sherman's landing spot during the Chickasaw assault. After traversing a series
of waterways, Porter hoped to reenter the Yazoo on solid ground far above
Haines Bluff. Detecting the move, the Confederates felled trees, stopped the
gunboats, and killed or wounded almost all the Yankees who showed themselves. The enemy was in the process of blocking Porter's retreat with trees
when Sherman received his plea for help, written on tissue paper and delivered
by a black man who hid the note in his tobacco. Sherman got the message at
nine o'clock on the evening of March 19. By midnight he had loaded three
small regiments on a transport. Reaching firm ground, the men debarked and
marched through mud and heavy rain to rescue Porter.[17]

    Returning to camp, Sherman found himself drawn into politics. Thanks to
the lobbying of his father, Hugh was promoted to brigadier general in March.
And, early in April, the Senate approved Tom Ewing's appointment as a
brigadier, even though his father believed he had not earned such high rank.
But it rejected Stuart, who had been involved in a notorious divorce case.
"Great reason," Ellen told Sherman, "because an innocent man had been accused of committing adultery that he should therefore be rejected as General,
after his faithful services to his country." Sherman found it hard to believe that

Stuart, who must now resign, could be rejected by a Senate that had promoted such scandalous lovers as Generals Daniel Sickles and Philip Kearny.[18]

Stuart's resignation created a problem, for he had taken over the division of Morgan L. Smith, who had been seriously wounded at Chickasaw. Ellen wasted no time selecting his successor. "Should Col. Stuart be gone," she urged Cump, "I hope you will be able to put Boyle in command of the Division. Charley would then be under his brother under his brother-in-law—Most agreeable to him."[19]

But fate—and Congress—deemed otherwise. While rejecting Stuart, the senators dared not do the same to Blair, who was promoted to major general. "Morgan Smith would rather have the Devil take over his Division than Frank Blair," Sherman informed his wife, "and though Frank Blair seems very fair and friendly I feel certain he will oust me & have my place in six months. I dont care much and as soon as he calls for the place I will give it him." To John, Sherman commented that Blair "dont pretend to know much of the military but keeps well posted in Politics. I am afraid of that Class of men."[20]

Amidst all this, Sherman and Ellen discussed other disturbing news. "Hugh got to drinking," the general wrote home on April 10, "but I took steps that have proven effective and I trust may endure forever."

"I am deeply distressed & anxious about Boyle," Ellen answered. Alcohol had, after all, plagued her brother since his West Point days. "I will not intimate to any one what you told me but I must implore you Cump to lose no time—not an hour—in correcting the matter and thoroughly too. *It will not do* & you must be *stern* & *severe* if necessary. I pray most earnestly that your efforts have been effectual even before this."[21]

To make matters worse, Sherman heard that an unwelcome visitor was on his way from Washington. Following Lincoln's issuance on New Year's Day of the Emancipation Proclamation, Lorenzo Thomas was "coming here about nigger Regiments. I'll hold my tongue, and if he says nigger to me, I'll show him my morning Reports, ask him to inspect my Brigades or Battalions, or ask him to sing the Star Spangled Banner and go back whence he came. When he wants my official opinions again he must ask his questions in writing and take Californical answers."[22]

— III —

Frustrated by the failure of the canal and by the blocked waterways, Grant decided on something revolutionary. He would march his Army of the Tennessee down the Louisiana side of the river from Milliken's Bend, just north of where the Yazoo emptied into the Mississippi, as far south as he could, which turned out to be Perkins Plantation, a magnificent estate well below Vicksburg. Grant would then run his transports past Vicksburg's batteries, cross his men to the Mississippi side on them, and attack the city from the rear. During this movement, McClernand's Thirteenth Corps was to occupy the right, McPherson's Seventeenth the center, and Sherman's Fifteenth the left.[23]

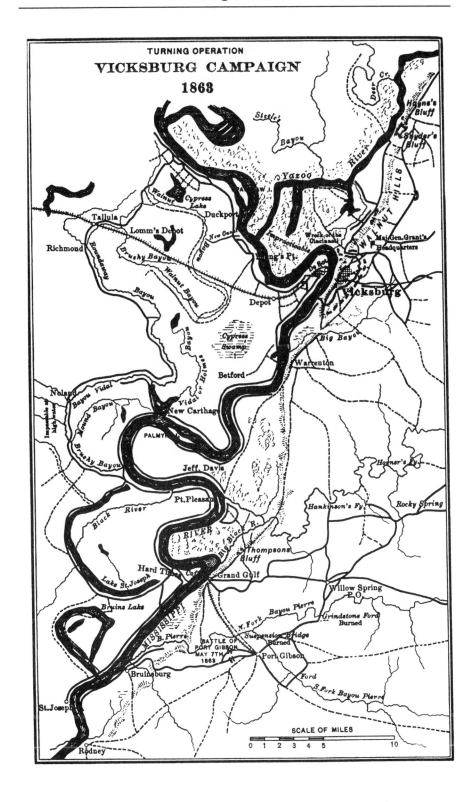

TURNING OPERATION

VICKSBURG CAMPAIGN
1863

From the beginning Sherman considered the scheme wild. "The only true plan," he informed Ellen, "was the one we started with," the three-pronged attack that had failed in December. "It is my opinion that we shall never take Vicksburg by operations by river alone." Early in April, after a consultation with Blair, McPherson, Grant, Assistant Secretary of War Charles A. Dana, and others, Sherman dashed off a letter to Grant's adjutant, Colonel John A. Rawlins, expressing his reservations. But once put into effect, as Sherman often said, he did his best to ensure the success of the plan.[24]

The first step was to get the transports south of Vicksburg. At ten o'clock on the night of April 19, Porter, in his flagship *Benton,* led five other ironclad gunboats, three transports, and ten tugs down the Mississippi toward that mighty fortress. In his memoirs Sherman described what happened:

> Anticipating a scene, I had four yawl-boats hauled across the swamp, to the reach of the river below Vicksburg, and manned them with soldiers, ready to pick up any of the disabled wrecks as they floated by. I was out in the stream when the fleet passed Vicksburg, and the scene was truly sublime. As soon as the rebel gunners detected the Benton, which was in the lead, they opened on her, and on the others in succession with shot and shell; houses on the Vicksburg side and on the opposite shore were set on fire, which lighted up the whole river; and the roar of cannon, the bursting of shells, and finally the burning of the Henry Clay, drifting with the current, made up a picture of the terrible not often seen. Each gunboat returned the fire as she passed the town, while the transports hugged the opposite shore.[25]

On the night of the twenty-second, with Sherman standing on the Louisiana side urging them on, six more transports passed the batteries. All were badly cut up, but only the *Tigress* sank, though its cargo was saved. The successful five joined the other ships at the Perkins plantation, and on the twenty-fourth Grant established his headquarters there.[26]

Grant had taken an enormous risk and won, for without the gunboats and transports the troops could not be ferried across the river. Still, Sherman had no faith in the project. The fleet was bottled up between enemy points, Vicksburg above and Port Hudson below. On the twenty-sixth, Sherman warned John:

> They are in a fatal trap. They must escape below Port Hudson or be burned. They cannot operate against Vicksburg any better below than above the city. Vicksburg can alone be taken by a powerful army moving inland in cooperation with the Gunboats & a floating force in the River, the plan we made at Oxford in December last—but clamor, newspaper clamor unnerves & unmans every American and makes him helpless. . . . I say we are further from taking Vicksburg today than we were the day I was repulsed. . . . I dont believe in the starvation cry, for wherever we penetrate the Land we find plenty of Cattle & Corn. I have met many Vicksburg officers & soldiers under flags of truce, they are fat, healthy and as well clad as we are.[27]

Sherman shuddered to think what would happen if Grant failed. "Even Grant is cowed & afraid of the newspapers," he informed Ellen. What if McClernand should be placed in command?

> He is the impersonation of My Demon Spirit. Not a shred of respect for truth, when falsehood is easier manufactured & fitted to his purpose—an overtowering ambition and utter ignorance of the first principles of war. I have in my possession his orders to do certain things which he would be ashamed of now—he knows I saw him cow at Shiloh—he knows he blundered in ignorance at the Post & came to me—beseechingly Sherman what shall we do now? And yet no sooner is the tempest past and the power in hand—his star is to be brightened and none so used to abuse—none so patient under it as Sherman—and therefore Glory at Sherman's expense—The day will come when they will know that Sherman has about as much feeling as is proper, and though he may bottle it up when it does come out somebody will feel it,—indeed McClernand was at the bottom of all the stories of mismanagement, of want of medicines, supplies &c—fault finding during the period he was not in command. My opinion is that this whole plan of attack on Vicksburg will fail, must fail, and the fault will be on us of course, but Grant will be the front—his recall leaves McClernand next—I would simply get a leave & stay away.[28]

But Grant was stronger and wiser than Sherman imagined. The commander proposed to land on the Mississippi side at Grand Gulf, near the mouth of the Big Black River, fifty miles below Vicksburg. While McClernand and McPherson crossed with their corps, Grant hoped to divert the attention of General John C. Pemberton, in charge of the Confederate forces in Vicksburg, with two other movements. He sent Colonel Benjamin H. Grierson with 1,800 cavalrymen on a raid that eventually covered from La Grange, Tennessee, to Baton Rouge. And on the twenty-eighth he asked Sherman to go back up the Yazoo, land his force there, and feign an attack at Haines Bluff, near the scene of the repulse the previous December. "I do not give this as an order," Grant said, "for the papers will call it another failure of Sherman to capture Haines Bluff."

When Sherman read this letter, Jenney heard him say: "Does General Grant think I care what the newspapers say?" Sherman then jumped into a boat and rowed to Porter's flagship to discuss the expedition. The planning over, Sherman embarked part of Blair's division and with Porter, two ironclads, four small gunboats, and ten transports sailed back up the Yazoo. The men were landed, marched back and forth, reloaded onto transports, and landed and marched in several other places to make it look as though reinforcements were constantly arriving. Told by the commander at Haines Bluff that the real attack was there, Pemberton diverted troops from Grand Gulf to help out.[29]

While at Haines Bluff, Sherman received a message from Grant ordering him to Grand Gulf. He was to cross the river and proceed toward Jackson, the capital of Mississippi, taking with him 120 wagons already loaded with food and ammunition, enough to supply Grant's army of 43,000 men and 10,000 horses for five days. Sherman immediately instructed his two other division commanders, Steele and General James M. Tuttle, to meet him at Grand Gulf and began marching his men southward. Reaching Grand Gulf on May 6, his units crossed the Mississippi that night and the next day.[30]

With McPherson's corps and McClernand's corps still ahead of him, Sherman pushed his troops on, overtaking Grant on the evening of the twelfth. That night word arrived that McPherson had defeated two brigades of the enemy at Raymond, which guarded the rear of Jackson. The Confederates had retreated into the capital. General Joseph E. Johnston was expected momentarily to assume command of the Southern forces there. With McPherson taking the left-hand road and Sherman the right, the troops marched through torrential rains and reached Jackson on the fourteenth to find, after some minor fighting, that Johnston had retreated through the town and headed north. At a conference in a hotel facing the statehouse, Grant revealed that he had intercepted some messages from Pemberton to Johnston about the two linking up. The Federals and Confederates could each count on something near 45,000 men, but the Southerners were separated, whereas Grant's army was together and ready to strike at either segment of the enemy force. Grant ordered McPherson to rejoin McClernand, while Sherman remained in Jackson for a day destroying anything of military value.[31]

Sherman spent May 15 carrying out Grant's wishes. He wrecked railroads in every direction. Then came the arsenal, the government foundry, and a cotton factory. But in his report Sherman mentioned the destruction "by mischievous soldiers" of two establishments not "justified by the rules of war." A Catholic church was set afire. And the Confederate Hotel, formerly named the United States Hotel, was destroyed by some officers and men who, after being captured at Shiloh, were refused supper there because the owners would not accept Northern greenbacks. "Many acts of pillage occurred that I regret," Sherman apologized to Grant, "arising from the effect of some bad rum found concealed in the stores of the town."[32]

The next day, while marching toward Bolton, eighteen miles west of Jackson, Sherman met a member of Grant's staff, who told him of a battle that day. Hoping to join Johnston, Pemberton had come out of Vicksburg, crossed the Big Black River, and entrenched on a ridge called Champion's Hill. Reinforced by General Alvin P. Hovey of the Thirteenth Corps, McPherson engaged the foe for almost seven hours, four of them hard fighting. Several times Grant sent orders to McClernand, reinforced by Blair, to push forward and attack, but McClernand never moved. "It was a matter of wonder," observed General Isaac H. Elliott of the Thirty-third Illinois Infantry, "that Grant did not relieve McClernand then and there." Champion's Hill, McPherson's finest hour, ended all thought of a Southern linkup. Pemberton withdrew into Vicksburg. Pulling their troops in, the Confederates even abandoned Haines Bluff and the scenes of Sherman's December disaster.[33]

Sherman now marched his men rapidly toward Vicksburg. Just beyond Bolton, he was drinking water at a well when he spied a book on the ground.

Handed it, he saw it was a copy of the Constitution. Its title page bore the name Jefferson Davis. From a Negro, Sherman learned that the place was indeed the plantation of the Confederate president, whose brother, Joseph, lived with a niece nearby.

Pushing on to the Big Black River, Sherman found Blair there. After burning all the bridges across the river, some Confederates had entrenched on the other side. When Sherman found out that Blair had ordered Captain Charles Ewing to take some men, cross the river atop artillery horses, and drive off the enemy, he countermanded the order. Creeping down to the river bank, he hid behind a corncrib and directed artillery fire into the Confederate trenches. A lieutenant and ten men soon scrambled out and surrendered. By night Blair's troops had built a pontoon bridge spanning the obstacle.[34]

Once over the river, Sherman marched his men to within two miles of Vicksburg's forts. Grant directed him to the right, where his troops would occupy the northern segment of the semicircle surrounding the city. McPherson occupied the center of the line, and McClernand, reaching toward Warrenton, the left. By 8:00 o'clock on the morning of the nineteenth Sherman's right rested on the Mississippi above the city, the Union fleets at the mouth of the Yazoo and at Young's Point plainly visible. "Nothing separated us from the enemy," Sherman reported, "but a space of about 400 yards of very difficult ground cut up by almost impractical ravines, and his line of entrenchments." On high, dry ground, the foe surrounded, Grant had achieved what one military analyst called "an amazing success, the greatest of Grant's life, and from a purely strategical point of view one of the greatest in military history."[35]

Counting on the demoralization of the enemy, Grant ordered a general assault for 2:00 P.M. on May 19. Charley's unit, the Thirteenth Regulars, reached the works first and planted its colors on the exterior slope, but the Federals were driven back, a third of the men being killed or wounded. Despite losing a portion of a finger, Charley saved the colors. Hugh, too, was under heavy fire. Sherman came away from the assault complaining to Ellen that McClernand "did *not* press his attack as he should."[36]

Grant decided to try again. At ten o'clock on the morning of the twenty-second every battery in the Army of the Tennessee began firing at Vicksburg. Then, instead of concentrating on specific points, Grant committed the blunder of attacking all along the line, three and a half miles long. From trenches and from forts built along the crests of slopes, the Confederates returned what Sherman called "a staggering fire."[37]

About noon, Grant realized that Vicksburg could not be taken by assault. Leaving his horse in a valley, he walked to Sherman's front. Sitting on the grass, the two generals were talking over the events of the day when an orderly came up and delivered a message from McClernand. Mistaking some advanced picket posts for enemy lines, McClernand said he had taken portions of two Confederate forts and that "the stars and stripes are floating over them." He asked for reinforcements and begged for another general assault so his troops would not be overwhelmed. Major Julius Pitzman, Sherman's other engineer and aide, who was present, remembered that neither general believed McClernand, but since McClernand was second in command Grant felt obliged to comply with the request. Before he left, however, Grant told Sherman: "If we are not successful we will have to proceed with a regular siege and you better have Pitzman go to work on your front." After this third attack failed, Sherman confided to Ellen: "McPherson is a noble fellow, but McClernand is a dirty dog."[38]

Dashing off a letter to Governor Richard Yates of Illinois, McClernand blamed the fiasco on others. He had asked for reinforcements, but had received none. Rumor had it that his rashness was responsible for casualties to other army corps. This was false. He had led the way from Milliken's Bend to Vicksburg. He welcomed an investigation to determine the truth.[39]

On the twenty-fifth all of the Federal dead and some of the wounded remained on the battlefield, festering in the broiling Mississippi sun. Pemberton set aside two and a half hours for a truce. During that time Colonel Samuel H. Lockett, the chief engineer of the Vicksburg defenses, was near Jackson Road trying to observe as much as he could of the Union formations when an orderly told him that General Sherman wished to speak to him. When they met, Sherman gave him some letters that had been entrusted to him by Northern friends of some of those in Vicksburg. For a short time the two officers joked about Sherman being a postman. The general then invited Lockett to sit with him on a nearby log, where each praised the engineering work of the opposing army. Lockett found Sherman so captivating that he could not fulfill his main task, the observation of the Union forces.[40]

With the failures of May 19 and May 22, Grant turned to a siege. By June 5 he had two hundred and twenty guns booming at Vicksburg, which was protected by eighty-nine different earthworks. The Union force, close to 70,000 men by mid-June, also entrenched. The troops constructed an intricate system of trenches, with steps for riflemen, who protected their heads with sandbags or heavy green logs. Sherman and McPherson, being engineers, supervised their own operations. McClernand, on the other hand, knew nothing about such things, and he left them to a lieutenant who had graduated from West Point in 1861. On June 11, Sherman complained to Ellen that McClernand was still further back from the enemy "than where I began the first day."

The Federal lines advanced about thirty feet a night, when it was safest to dig. The opposing forces eventually came to within thirty feet of each other. Men in one trench could throw grenades and clods of dirt at the other, but no one dared to raise his head to fire a shot. At night the pickets usually talked over the situation and agreed not to shoot at each other without warning. To ease the boredom the combatants often discussed various topics: the origins of the war, Lincoln's Emancipation Proclamation freeing the slaves in those portions of the Confederacy not in Union hands, Grant's campaign, and the like.

The men traded Southern tobacco for Northern dried coffee grounds and exchanged newspapers. Every morning Sherman and many of his troops read the *Vicksburg Citizen* of the day before. As the siege went on, the journal was printed on brown wrapping paper or on the back of cheap, straw-colored wallpaper. Editorials extolled the mule meat the residents were eating, praised the women killed in the bombardment, and spoke of Vicksburg's will to survive. "On the narrow belt of neutral ground between the two lines," remembered one regimental historian, "the officers of both armies met, West Point classmates in blue and gray chatted over school-boy reminiscences, and agreed that it was a monstrous pity for two such armies of the same race to be cutting each other's throats."[41]

The end for McClernand came amidst the digging and the booming artillery. On May 30, 1863, in the wake of the disastrous defeats, McClernand issued to his troops an order praising their performance at Champion's Hill and telling them that if the other two corps had done their duty Vicksburg would now be in Union hands. Violating regulations, McClernand sent the foolish document to various newspapers. Blair read it in the *Memphis Evening Bulletin* of June 13 and fumed. If Sherman and McPherson did not take steps to remove McClernand, Blair, who had been instrumental in getting Frémont out of Missouri, would. Both generals complied with the request, writing long letters to Grant. Sherman denounced McClernand's statement as "a catalogue of nonsense . . . an effusion of vain glory and hypocrisy. . . . It substantially accuses General McPherson and myself, with disobeying the orders of General Grant in not assaulting on the 19th and 22d of May, and allowing on the latter day the enemy to mass his forces against the 13th Army Corps alone." On May 19 McClernand was the one who refused to attack. His recent order was a rare instance of a general congratulating his troops on their defeat. In his letter the usually even-tempered McPherson alluded to an oft-told story about McClernand, who once said in a speech in Illinois: "Some men were born to one walk in life, and some to another. Thank God, I was born a warrior insensible to fear." Countered McPherson: "Though 'born a Warrior,' as he himself stated, he has evidently forgotten one of the most essential qualities, viz: that elevated, refined sense of honor, which, while guarding his own rights with zealous care, at all times, renders justice to others." On the eighteenth Grant removed McClernand, replacing him with Sherman's close friend, Major General Edward O. C. Ord.[42]

McClernand may have gone, but Sherman still feared and hated him. "He swears vengeance against me," Sherman informed Ellen on June 21, "to whom he attributes his downfall. All such vain and selfish men are as much enemies to Good Govt as the Rebels and I would kill them with quite as much gusto."[43]

The day after Sherman wrote this letter, Grant received word that Johnston, with 28,000 men and 2,500 cavalry, was crossing the Big Black River on his way to Vicksburg. To meet him, Grant sent Sherman to Bear Creek, thirty miles from Vicksburg, with five divisions. At the railroad bridge crossing the Big Black and at Haines Bluff, a distance of eight miles, Sherman set up entrenchments, supported by artillery. "Joe Johnston will give me little time to combine after he moves," Sherman warned Ellen. "He may approach from the North, North East or East, all of which routes I am watching closely, and it will be exceedingly difficult to judge from signs the Real point from the feints. Their Cavalry is so much better than ours that in all quick movements they have a decided advantage."

Charles A. Dana, the assistant secretary of war, several times visited Sherman at Bear Creek and "always came away enthusiastic over his qualities as a soldier. His amazing activity and vigilance pervaded his entire force." In addition to the railroad crossing and Haines Bluff, Sherman occupied the commanding spots, set up rifle pits at strategic points, and guarded every possible place to cross the Big Black. "By his rapid movements, also, and by widely deploying on all the ridges and open headlands," Dana remembered, "Sherman produced the impression that his forces were ten times as numerous as they really were."[44]

Inspired by the success of Grierson, Sherman sent two of his divisions on raids into the interior. On the twenty-sixth Blair led his men northeast for sixty or seventy miles through the country between the Yazoo and the Big Black. Destroying whatever food and forage he could locate, Blair made it impossible for Johnston to march an army through that region unless carrying supplies. Finding that Johnston did not come, Brigadier General Peter J. Osterhaus, guarding the bridge over the Big Black, crossed the river and destroyed whatever he could not carry away. In general, the days spent between the two rivers afforded Sherman's troops a pleasant interlude. They set up healthy camps, ate well, and washed from their clothes the red earth ground into them while in Vicksburg's trenches.[45]

Meantime, at the outskirts of the beleaguered city, Grant prepared for an assault on July 6. Seeing the preparations, Pemberton, weakened by the siege, asked for terms on July 3. The surrender took place the next day. By noon, when Jenney first rode through the city, it "seemed filled with a gigantic picnic; thousands of little parties were seated here and there on the ground, the 'Yanks' playing the host." Jenney heard one Confederate say: "You outgeneraled us, you did. 'Twas General Starvation that outflanked us." On the morning of July 9 Port Hudson fell to General Nathaniel P. Banks, and on the sixteenth the steamboat *Imperial* landed in New Orleans, having made the trip undisturbed from St. Louis.[46]

—— IV ——

To John, Sherman explained why for him July Fourth was not a day of rest:

> When our army lay around about Vicksburg digging trenches and slowly camping on the doomed City rumor from every quarter told that General Johnston, the same that opposed Patterson at Winchester two years ago, was gathering a vast army to relieve Vicksburg, that Jeff Davis had said must be held at all hazard. Grant was uneasy and I was called from my trenches and ordered to see to it.[47]

To drive Johnston out of Mississippi, Sherman was given Ord's Thirteenth Corps and his own Fifteenth. He was also allowed to keep the two divisions of General John G. Parke's Ninth Corps that had been assigned to him in mid-June. In all, the Expeditionary Army, as it was called, contained 30,000 men.

"For near two months," Sherman informed Ellen as he started from the Big Black River for Jackson, "I have spent in my clothes ready to jump to the saddle, for I have been close upon an enemy since we crossed the Mississippi."[48]

The campaign to Jackson, Sherman's first march, was among the most difficult and unusual of the Civil War. Heading again toward the Mississippi capital, the Federals moved in three columns. Captain F. H. Mason of the Forty-second Ohio described the "terrible suffering. The atmosphere was like an oven." Retreating toward Jackson, Johnston hoped to make the country impassable for another army. His men dumped kerosene into cisterns and removed the handles of water pumps. They drove mules, horses, and dogs into the ponds and streams, shot them, and left the carcasses to fester. The water, described a Pennsylvania captain, became "covered with a nasty revolting green scum full an inch thick and as stringy as toasted cheese."

Water, Mason wrote, became

> practically unobtainable. The men almost perished from heat and thirst. Scores were prostrated by sunstroke in a single day. The men filled their canteens from muddy, stagnant pools, green and poisonous with slime and filth, and this water, drank by the heated and perspiring men, induced nausea and serious digestive difficulties. It was not known precisely where Johnston had gone, and each of the three columns, marching toward a powerful enemy, was not only obliged to march by daylight, but to proceed with the greatest caution. The troops were therefore kept tramping over the dusty roads through the long, broiling days, and angry complaints were heard against what was mistaken for the careless cruelty of the commander.

Infuriated, explained Lieutenant Seth Alonzo Ranlett, the adjutant of the Thirty-sixth Massachusetts, by Johnston's disregard of "the rules of honorable warfare," the army, "from the commanding general down to the private soldier," vowed to destroy everything it passed.

Ord's column moved over Champion's Hill. The soil on the rocky hill was thin, and the bodies of horses and men killed six weeks before were coming out of their shallow graves. The sight was horrible.[49]

On the march the army lived largely on green corn, then coming into season. The men placed the corn, husk and all, on a fire kindled between two rails. When the husks burned off, the corn, cooked by the steam, was done. The men and animals so stripped a field that if it was worth a million dollars before they came, estimated one regimental historian, "it was not worth one thousand dollars" afterward.[50]

Early on the morning of the ninth some of the soldiers again came to Brierfield, the plantation of Joe Davis. The mansion, located at the head of a magnificent lawn, was aflame, set afire by stragglers. Later, in the attic of an old log house owned by Joe Davis, Hugh Ewing's troops discovered Jeff Davis's private library, containing his books, mementos, and letters. Tossing everything onto a huge pile on the floor, the soldiers trampled over priceless items while selecting souvenirs. One soldier came away with a gold-headed cane President

Franklin Pierce presented to Davis when he was secretary of war. Sherman tried to sort the papers that were left, but he gave up and sent them to Grant.

Some of Jeff Davis's animals ended up in strange places. The members of the Thirty-fifth Massachusetts gave one of his cows to Ben: Perley Poore, the Washington correspondent of the *Boston Journal.* And during the final stages of the war Grant rode one of Davis's horses.[51]

By the tenth Sherman's force had driven Johnston back into Jackson, the juncture of the Vicksburg and Meridian and Mississippi Central Railroads. Sherman then began an investment similar to that of Grant at Vicksburg. Vicksburg lay against the east bank of the Mississippi, Jackson against the west bank of the Pearl River. Sherman sent Parke's Ninth Corps to the left, above the town, his own Fifteenth Corps to the center, and Ord's Thirteenth Corps to the right, below the town. Eventually Ord's flank was to rest on the river, while Parke's would come to within two miles of it. Closing his lines, Sherman began punishing Jackson from every direction. On the twelfth and thirteenth the Federals lobbed 3,000 shells into the city.[52]

On the twelfth the worst mishap of the siege occurred. Crossing an open field far in advance of the line, General Jacob G. Lauman's division of Ord's corps ran into a deadly flank fire from Southern troops. Within twenty minutes the Third Iowa lost 114 of its 241 members. In all, Lauman lost 475 men. "My remembrance is that the opinion in the army there," observed Ranlett, "was that General Ord was responsible and that Lauman was the scapegoat." Not about to reprimand his lifelong friend, Sherman kept Ord and sent Lauman back to Vicksburg.[53]

That day brought news of the fall of Port Hudson and of Lee's retreat from Gettysburg. "The cheering along the lines was deafening," Ranlett remembered, "and the drooping spirits of all were roused by the glorious tidings."[54]

By the fifteenth Sherman, taking part in his second siege, was losing patience. At the very moment of glory he had been ordered away from Vicksburg. To Ellen, he rambled:

> When desperate schemes are in contemplation or pursuit after Battle Sherman is called for. He don't mind abuse, has no political aspirations, and moves with celerity—Therefore I am the man for any and every emergency. . . . This is a beautiful country, handsome dwellings and plantations, but the Negros are gone, houses vacant field of corn open to cattle, and our Army has consumed or is consuming all the cattle hogs sheep chickens turkeys and vegetables Everything. . . . I am pledged to a 30 years war without asking anything and only two years are passed.[55]

Facing annihilation, Johnston retreated across the Pearl on the night of the sixteenth. By the eighteenth Sherman had taken 500 prisoners and all of Johnston's heavy guns. By July 21 he was able to tell Grant: "We have desolated this land for 30 miles." North and south of the city the Yankees had ripped up the railroads. Cavalry units on missions of destruction rode as far as Brookhaven, fifty-three miles to the south.[56]

Jackson suffered greatly. A little after six o'clock on the morning of July 17, 1863, the Fifty-first Pennsylvania Infantry regiment, taunting the Western troops, became the first Federal unit to enter the city. Planting its colors in front of the state capitol, the regiment stacked arms in the street. Its members then dashed off looking for the comforts denied them on the march. Having smoked weeds, ground coffee, tea, paper, and almost everything else that would burn, the soldiers immediately broke into the tobacco warehouses. Then came the whiskey, grocery, clothing, and drug shops. They entered private homes and carried off money, jewelry, and other valuables. Pianos, furniture, and china were smashed. Hogsheads of sugar were rolled into the street and split open. By noon some members of the regiment were parading around in women's clothing. Sherman and several other generals passed them and laughed. Only the brigade commander, Brigadier General Edward Ferrero, feigned anger, but he soon gave in and smiled.[57]

Chaplain M. D. Gage of the Twelfth Indiana Infantry described the plundering and what it portended:

> The furniture which adorned the costly mansions was scattered through our camps, where it was left on our return to Vicksburg. Parlor carpets were removed to give an air of comfort to the tents, and the massive mirrors, that could not be removed, were shivered into ten-thousand fragments. All this was unauthorized, but almost unavoidable in a large army. Not only in the city, but throughout the surrounding country, the scene of desolation prevailed. The wealth of this lovely Capital and the fertile region in which it nestled, as a bright gem, was made the sport of flames, or appropriated by the army. . . . For a distance of fifteen miles on every side, the country was scoured by persevering foragers, and all available supplies for the army were gathered in. This was necessary to subsist the troops, and to impoverish the enemy; and was but the introduction of a system which Sherman's army subsequently carried into full operation in Alabama, Georgia, and South Carolina.[58]

After rendering the city and countryside a shambles, Sherman undertook to feed the inhabitants. With Grant's permission he supplied eight hundred destitute women and children with two hundred barrels of flour and a hundred of salt pork. In exchange for a Confederate promise not to return to the land west of the Pearl, Sherman even proposed setting up "a kind of trading depot" at the Big Black railroad bridge, where people might exchange produce, clothing, and supplies. Grant rejected the notion as being beyond the scope of army operations.[59]

On July 20 the troops started back toward Vicksburg. The dust and polluted ponds remained, but this time the route carried the lucky ones through an area filled with luscious peaches, huge watermelons, figs, nutmegs, and cantaloupes. The men filled their haversacks, blouse sleeves, and handkerchiefs with the delicacies. Five days later the expedition recrossed the Big Black and went into camp. On July 28 Sherman submitted to Grant his report. He praised his men but noted "too great a tendency to plunder and pillage."[60]

Awaiting Cump was a letter from John relating the news from the East, where no generals comparable to Grant or Sherman had emerged. General Joseph Hooker was discredited after being defeated in early May at Chancellorsville, "just when he thought he had Lee in his power." And General George G. Meade had briefly tasted glory. As Vicksburg was falling, he had stopped Lee's advance northward at Gettysburg and "was at once a Hero." But Meade, John continued, had "allowed Lee to escape him & all his popular honors are lost. . . . Poor Lincoln, after suffering with the pains of martyrdom will leave the Executive chair with the reputation of an honest clown. He has certainly assumed much power not conferred upon him by the Constitution."[61]

But at his camp on the Big Black, Sherman for the first time since December found things quiet. In the shadow of the Union victories at Gettysburg, Vicksburg, and Port Hudson, he had completed his first march.[62]

10

Willy, Chattanooga, and Knoxville

— I —

ULYSSES S. GRANT believed that the end of the Vicksburg-Jackson campaign should lead to the beginning of another enterprise. Now promoted to the rank of major general in the regular army, he proposed to strike at Mobile. With Mobile captured the Federals could then act out one of two scenarios. First, they might operate against Bragg's rear. Thus threatened, Bragg would draw men from Chattanooga, which the Yankees might then capture. Or, from Mobile, the Northerners might move into and devastate Georgia, the breadbasket of Lee's army.[1]

As wise as he was capable, Admiral Porter entertained similar notions. He next foresaw, he revealed to Sherman,

> the battle of Atlanta, which will correspond somewhat with the battle of Armageddon foretold in the Scriptures. If we ever get the Rebels south of that range of mountains which separates North Carolina from Tennessee, and stand where a man can touch the boundaries of North Carolina, South Carolina and Georgia, with the richest market behind us in the country, the Rebellion will go up like old Mallory's Ram fleet, but I fear not till then.[2]

Seldom receptive to imaginative schemes, Halleck rejected these notions. Instead, he dispersed Grant's grand army, sending segments of it every which way—to Louisville, to Natchez, and to Missouri.[3]

During this lull, Sherman rested. His troops, he told John, had been "on the jump" for the past seven months. "We have cleared the Valley, and have a right to some relaxation." Sherman furloughed large numbers of men. The remainder lounged about clean, comfortable camps on the west side of the Big Black.[4]

With time on his hands, Cump invited Ellen to visit with some of the children. Ellen's mother, who had undergone two operations, was now better, freeing Ellen. "We are all so crazy to go, except the two little ones," Ellen answered, "that we cannot wait. . . . The thought of going down to you has spread a sunshine over everything—All have gone to bed to dream happy dreams & my heart is full of joy—God grant that nothing may occur to mar the happiness we anticipate."[5]

Taking Minnie, Lizzie, Willy, and Tommy with her, Ellen, escorted down the Mississippi to Vicksburg by Grant's principal staff officer, General John A. Rawlins, arrived at Sherman's camp on the evening of August 15. There she heard that Congress had made her husband and McPherson, now commanding Vicksburg, brigadier generals in the regular army, Cump's promotion to date from the day Vicksburg fell. In camp she and Cump moved into two large hospital tents. Minnie and Lizzie occupied a smaller tent next to their parents, and Willy and Tommy slept several tents off with Charley.[6]

While in Mississippi, Ellen and the children entertained themselves in various ways. Never an athlete, Ellen's chief pleasure consisted of visiting Mrs. Julia Grant at the lovely house in Vicksburg where she was spending the summer with her husband and four children. Lizzie and Tommy rode about in their mother's carriage. Minnie, whom her father described as "really a beautiful woman . . . though only in her 13th year," loved to accompany her father on horseback. So, too, did Willy, who rode Sherman's favorite horse, Old Sam. A large, half-thoroughbred bay, Sam possessed strength and speed. He was also fearless. Noise never annoyed him, and in battle he just kept on eating. Once, when shot through the neck, he ignored the wound. "But," Sherman later wrote, "what endeared the horse most to me and my family was, that he was the favorite of my son Willy in our Camp on Big Black, who used to ride him almost daily and attend me in the drills and reviews of that summer." Sherman felt that Willy was safe riding Sam, for no matter where they wandered Sam would always bring him back for supper.

Adapting to army life, Willy became the pet of Sherman's troops. He learned the manual of arms and was made an honorary sergeant by the troops of the Thirteenth Regular.[7]

But the carefree days soon ended. The previous year, on October 30, 1862, Rosecrans had replaced Buell, who had failed in a campaign that should have led to the Federal capture of Chattanooga, in command of what was now called the Army of the Cumberland. Now, in September, Rosecrans faced Bragg at Chattanooga. Deceived by a Federal feint to his right, Bragg withdrew from the city, and on September 9 Rosecrans entered it. Thinking Bragg was retreating, Rosecrans pursued him with scattered forces. At Chickamauga on the nineteenth and twentieth, Bragg turned on the Yankees and defeated them. Rosecrans's army was saved from destruction only by the gallant stand of George Thomas, thereafter extolled as "the Rock of Chickamauga." Rosecrans was driven back into Chattanooga, where his army faced starvation. While these battles took place, Grant was in bed, suffering excruciating pain after being thrown from a horse while visiting Banks in New Orleans.[8]

Sherman got his first intimation of these developments on September 22, when he received an order from Grant to ship one of his divisions to Vicksburg, en route to Chattanooga. Sherman immediately sent off his First Division, led by General Peter J. Osterhaus. The next day Sherman was summoned to Vicksburg, where Grant showed him "the alarming dispatches from Halleck." Grant had decided to send Sherman with two of his other divisions to Chattanooga and instructed him to get ready. On the twenty-fifth Sherman returned to his camp and started his divisions moving.

Halleck had ordered that Sherman and his corps, 20,000 men in all, move eastward from Memphis repairing the Memphis & Charleston Railroad as they marched. Sherman therefore took passage for himself and his family on the steamer *Atlantic*, bound from Vicksburg to Memphis. When the boat was ready to leave, Sherman noticed that Willy was missing. An officer of the Thirteenth Infantry found him at McPherson's house, carrying a double-barreled shotgun. "I joked him about carrying away captured property," Sherman remembered.[9]

Both Ellen and Minnie came on board ill. Ellen suffered from one of her severe headaches, Minnie from a high fever. But Willy, too, was ill. As the boat passed Young's Point, Sherman showed his family the location of his old camp. For the first time he saw that something was wrong with Willy, who on questioning admitted he was sick. Ordinarily Ellen would have noticed such a thing right away. She later wrote Cump:

> There were so many persons on the boat & I was so engrossed with Minnie & in so much pain myself that I did not give him the attention he ought to have had. . . . I tried to persuade him to eat some dinner & when he staid so long at the water closet I sent for him & tried to persuade him to go to bed. I remember looking over at him as he sat on a chair in the cabin, in the course of the afternoon & remarking the bright red in his dear cheek & thinking how it contrasted with the pure white. Oh! if I had only gone to him then & used some tender persuasion to get him to bed.[10]

Dr. E. O. F. Rorer, the surgeon of the Fifty-fifth Illinois, happened to be on board the ship, and when he examined Willy he found traces of typhoid fever. As the steamer plodded on in low water, Rorer told Sherman that he feared for Willy's life. Memphis contained needed medicines and skilled physicians with whom the doctor might consult.

The *Atlantic* finally reached Memphis on October 2. Willy was carried to the Gayoso. Rorer called in the most experienced physician in the city, but the child sank rapidly. At one point he was alone with Father Carrier, the French priest whom, with Cump's consent, Ellen had sent down to serve Catholic soldiers in Hugh's division. "Willy then told me in very few words," the priest remembered, "that he was willing to die if it was the will of God *but that it pained* him to leave his father & mother." Father Carrier tried "to soothe his feelings" and "told him that it was not certain he would die." Grieving for the child, he comforted Willy with the thought: "If God wishes to call you to him—now—

do not grieve for he will carry you to heaven & *there* you will meet your good Mother & Father again."[11]

The day after reaching Memphis, Willy died. His body was placed in a metal casket and escorted to the steamboat *Grey Eagle* by members of the Thirteenth Infantry. Charley accompanied his grieving sister and the children back to Lancaster, where Willy was buried, Cump lamented to Ellen, "in that low damp place where I used to trap the quail. It seems to me a dream and I still think of him as a baby, toddling over the San Francisco hills, and clinging to me. I must not think of him so much & yet I cannot help it."[12]

Dead at the age of nine, Willy had been a younger version of Sherman. Alone of Sherman's children, he displayed an affection for the military. Of all the children, he took the greatest pride in his father's achievements. "He was my 'Alter Ego,'" Sherman informed Ellen, "and tis I must mourn in silence not you."[13]

Amid his grief, Sherman dashed off a letter to Tommy. "You are now our only Boy," he wrote his sensitive son, "and must take Poor Willy's place, to take care of your sisters, and to fill my place when I too am gone. I have promised that whenever you meet a Soldier who knew Willy that you will give him half you have. Give him all if in want, and work hard to gain knowledge & health which will when you are a man, insure you all you need in this world."[14] But could Tommy, so different from Willy, ever be the family's hope for the future?

—— II ——

A mourning Sherman threw himself into his army duties. Rosecrans's entrapment panicked the War Department. In addition to Sherman, Hooker and two corps—the Eleventh, led by the pious, one-armed Oliver O. Howard of Maine, and the Twelfth, commanded by Henry W. Slocum of Brooklyn—were detached from the Army of the Potomac, put on trains, and shipped west. Exactly one week later these 27,000 troops reached Bridgeport and Stevenson, Alabama, ready for duty.[15]

For Sherman and his men the first leg of the rescue journey was the trip from Memphis to Corinth. Because the railroads were occupied carrying supplies, the troops were forced to march. But on Sunday, October 11, Sherman was able to get room on a train for himself and his staff. Hugh sat by his side. Perched on the roof, guarding the occupants of the cars, was a battalion of the Thirteenth Infantry.

The ride almost ended in tragedy. At noon, as the train pulled into Collierville, Tennessee, twenty-four miles east of Memphis, Confederate General James R. Chalmers, with 2,500 cavalrymen and eight pieces of artillery, swooped down on the town, guarded only by Colonel D. C. Anthony and the 240 men of the Sixty-sixth Indiana. Chalmers immediately sent his adjutant to demand the capitulation of the train and the town. "Anthony referred the demand for surrender to me," Sherman related to Ellen, "and my answer was no." The attack began at once and lasted for almost four hours. "For some minutes the enemy held our train *which was shielded by a Brick depot.*" Then, for some reason, Chalmers rode off. "Among the plunder they took was Charleys sword," Sherman noted. An enemy soldier also got away with a large cake a resident of Memphis had baked for Jenney. Sherman himself lost his rambunctious mare Dolly. "I have the satisfaction to know," he informed Ellen, "she will break the neck of the first Guerrilla that fires a pistol from her back." Though without Dolly, Sherman was sending Sam to Lancaster for a rest. "We must take care of that horse for Willy's sake, but we need nothing to remind us of him." In the ensuing campaigns Sherman rode his favorite bay Duke, who had a white star on his forehead and a white left hind foot.[16]

The next night, after repairs to the locomotive, which had been hit by artillery fire, Sherman's party pulled into Corinth. There he heard a rumor, confirmed on the sixteenth, that Grant was to be put in command of a new Military Division of the Mississippi, combining the Armies of the Ohio, the Cumberland, and the Tennessee. This, Sherman told Ellen, was "the same idea I foreshadowed in my days of depression and insult."

Sherman remembered Corinth well:

> I have stood by Grant in his days of sorrow. Not six miles from here he sat in his tent almost weeping at the accumulated charges against him by such villains as Stanton of Ohio, Wade & others. He had made up his mind to leave for good—I begged him, and he yielded. I could see his good points & his weak points better than I could my own, and he now feels that I stood by him in his days of dejection and he is my sworn friend. Corinth brings back to me the memory of these events & bids me heed my own counsels to others.[17]

Obeying Halleck's order to repair the Memphis & Charleston, Sherman spread his men out and advanced slowly. On the nineteenth he reached Iuka, twenty miles east of Corinth. Six days later he learned that he was now commander of the Army of the Tennessee. Sherman immediately placed McPherson, with the Seventeenth Corps, in charge of Mississippi and Major General Stephen A. Hurlbut, with the Sixteenth Corps, in charge of West Tennessee. Blair took over the Fifteenth Corps.

Sherman explained these moves to Ellen from Iuka:

> The change in Command is radical. I dont pretend to understand all the merits of Rosecrans position. I know that He & Grant had sharp words & feelings over at Corinth & here a year ago, and that Grant does not like him—beside Rosecrans has all along had a set of flunkeys about him pouring out the oil of flattery that was sickening to all true men. In my judgment there is no surer index of weakness & meanness than the Common disposition to exaggerate little Skirmishes into Grand Battles. I have ordered the Press in Memphis to dry up, & never again publish such stuff as followed the Collierville matter.[18]

Still lame and in severe pain, Grant, too, was struggling toward Chattanooga. From Nashville he took a train to Bridgeport, where he shared a tent with Howard. He had to be lifted into the saddle for the forty-five-mile ride to Chattanooga. Almost without escort, Howard remembered, he rode through territory filled with enemy sharpshooters and cavalry, "across swollen streams, through deep mud, and along roads that were already deemed too wretched and too dangerous for the wagons." At times soldiers had to carry him in their arms. But Grant stuck it out and reached Chattanooga on the evening of October 23.[19]

Four days afterward Sherman was seated on the porch of a house in Iuka when a dirty, oddly dressed stranger approached. He announced himself as Corporal Pike, and he had a telegram from Grant. General George Crook had sent him from Huntsville, Alabama, with it in a canoe. Pike had paddled down the Tennessee River and over Muscle Shoals, being fired at by enemy guerrillas the whole way. He had made it to Tuscumbia, Alabama, which, luckily, Blair had just captured. Blair sent him on to Sherman. The message ordered Sherman to stop work on the railroad, to cross the Tennessee, and to proceed "with all possible dispatch toward Bridgeport."[20]

Sherman immediately gathered together his available divisions, but in his eagerness to help he committed a cardinal mistake. Fearful that if he left his wagons the enemy might get them, he took them along. With the exception of Brigadier General John E. Smith's division, which had been detached from McPherson for the expedition, each of Sherman's divisions, loaded down with baggage, crawled along. After crossing the Tennessee at Eastport, Sherman marched his men to Florence, Alabama, and then along the Tennessee to Rogersville, where the Elk River emptied into the Tennessee. Finding the Elk "swollen and impassable without making a large bridge 200 feet long," Sherman proceeded northeast to Fayetteville, Tennessee, where his men were able to cross using a stone bridge. Sherman's force now split, Blair, with Osterhaus's and Morgan Smith's divisions, turning south, "thereby," Sherman told Ellen, "avoiding the mountain on the other Road." Sherman, with two other divisions, moved directly into the mountains, coming out six miles above Bridgeport, Alabama, arriving after dark on November 13. He left his scattered army, which was about three days behind, to catch up. That night Sherman shared the tent of Lieutenant Colonel William G. Le Duc, Howard's quartermaster. When the colonel had been Sherman's classmate at How's School in 1836, he was just "plain Bill Duke."[21]

Sherman had good news for Ellen. Charley, now a lieutenant colonel in the Fifteenth Corps, was with Blair. So, too, was Hugh, who "has the leading Division and has done well—He has not tasted a drop since his return, and if he could contemplate himself now, and after a days drinking he would never touch a drop."[22]

A mourning Sherman entered Bridgeport. "I cannot banish from my mind Poor Willy," he told Ellen, "but I can begin to think of him as he was a good boy, whose loss to us is terrible but for him it may be well as he has escaped the long toils & vexations of life. He knows how we loved him and if he sees us now, he knows how we mourn his absence."[23]

Summoned by Grant, Sherman took a steamboat from Bridgeport up the river to Kelly's Ferry. There one of Grant's horses awaited him, and he rode the remaining eight miles into Chattanooga.[24]

At army headquarters on the evening of the fourteenth Grant, Thomas, and several other officers were, Howard recorded, "sitting together" when Sherman "came bounding in after his usual buoyant manner." Grant, "whose bearing towards Sherman differed from that with other officers, being free, affectionate, and good humored, greeted him most cordially. Immediately after the 'How are you, Sherman?' and the reply, 'Thank you, as well as can be expected,' he extended to him the ever welcome cigar. This Sherman proceeded to light, but without stopping his ready flow of hearty words, and not even pausing to sit down."

Grant offered Sherman "the chair of *honor*," a rocker with a high back. When Sherman retorted that Grant deserved it, Grant spoke about giving "proper respect to age" and Sherman accepted it.

Grant, Sherman, and Thomas then got down to the proposed campaign. The discussion resembled more a conversation than the formal meetings Howard had seen in the East. Sherman, who Grant said was accustomed "to 'bone' his campaigns, i.e., study them hard from morning till night," even while on horseback, spoke rapidly but thoughtfully. Thomas, who knew the area better than anyone else, furnished the specifics. Grant listened carefully "and now and then made a pointed remark." To Howard, the scene resembled a courtroom: "Thomas was like the solid judge, confident and fixed in his knowledge of the law; Sherman, like the brilliant advocate; and Grant, rendering his verdict like an intelligent jury."[25]

The next morning Grant, Thomas, Sherman, and several others walked out to Fort Wood, part of the Chattanooga defenses. It offered a panoramic view of the scene. The line of Confederate trenches, tents, and sentinels, from Lookout Mountain on the south to Tunnel Hill on the north, induced Sherman to remark: "Why, General Grant, you are besieged." Grant acknowledged that he was. He explained that Thomas's mules and horses were so starved they could not haul guns. The men were so hungry that they often stole the few grains of corn allotted to animals. Bragg had sent General James Longstreet, with 17,000 men, east toward Knoxville, where the Confederates hoped to trap the force of General Ambrose Burnside. Not realizing that the detachment of Longstreet weakened Bragg immeasurably, Grant hoped that a Federal assault would force Bragg to recall Longstreet. But, Grant continued, Sherman and Hooker must begin the attack, for their troops were fresher and stronger than those of the Army of the Cumberland.[26]

Within the Federal lines the men were busy building pontoon boats for a bridge. Taking over an abandoned sawmill, Brigadier General William F. ("Baldy") Smith, the Army of the Cumberland's chief engineer, had cut stacks of wood for the boats. His plan was to surprise the Confederates by utilizing the bend in the Tennessee River opposite Bragg's mountain entrenchments. From Bridgeport Sherman's army would pass through the valley of

Lookout Mountain and cross the western spur of the river at Brown's Ferry, almost opposite the northern end of Missionary Ridge. Moving east, it would cross the eastern spur over a pontoon bridge to be laid in secrecy at night. The crossing would take place three miles south of where the Tennessee met Chickamauga Creek. Sherman would then be in a position to attack Bragg's right, which rested on the Chickamauga at Tunnel Hill.

At first glance the plan seemed far-fetched. On November 8, still hovering about the western camps, Dana described it as such to Stanton. But on the sixteenth, as Sherman looked over the terrain, he turned to Smith and said: "Baldy, it can be done!"[27]

In his report and in his *Memoirs,* Sherman described how he rushed back to muster his men for the Tunnel Hill campaign. Missing the last steamboat at Kelly's Ferry, he commandeered a rough boat manned by four soldiers, occasionally taking a turn at the oars.[28]

But, as might be expected, he never mentioned that among the reasons for his failure to meet the date decided upon was his hasty planning. His divisions were coming every which way. After crossing the Tennessee at Bridgeport, Hugh Ewing was detoured to Trenton, Georgia, southwest of Chattanooga, to give Bragg the impression he was trying to turn, as Rosecrans had tried, the Confederate left. Osterhaus and Morgan Smith were struggling with the badly cut-up road to Brown's Ferry. Fortunately for Sherman, his men met only token resistance, for as he admitted in his *Memoirs* they were "strung all the way back to Bridgeport."[29]

Colonel James Harrison Wilson, who hated Sherman and intrigued with his enemies, later argued that Sherman should have taken his men to Cairo by steamboat and from there by rail to Louisville, Nashville, and Bridgeport. Even Henry Villard, who admired Sherman, believed he had committed a serious mistake by allowing his divisions to cart along baggage. "General Grant was greatly surprised when he learned of the blunder," Villard observed, "but generously assumed the responsibility for it, though Sherman deserved the direct blame."[30]

On the afternoon of the twentieth Sherman reached Hooker's headquarters, four miles from Chattanooga. Awaiting him was an order from Grant to attack the next day. But Sherman's troops were in such disarray that he requested a postponement. John E. Smith alone had arrived and was in position. Hugh Ewing was still mired at Trenton, and the other two divisions were struggling, Sherman wrote Grant, "along the terrible road from Shell Mound to Chattanooga." On the twenty-first Morgan Smith's division crossed over at Brown's Ferry. Hugh Ewing's followed on the twenty-third. After that, the Brown's Ferry bridge was so badly splintered by trees the Confederates had thrown into the river that Osterhaus dared not use it. Accordingly, Sherman decided to undertake the movement against Bragg's right with the three divisions that had crossed, reinforced by General Jefferson C. Davis's division of Thomas's army. Osterhaus's unit, in turn, was lent to Hooker for the assault on Lookout Mountain.[31]

As Sherman's divisions, all from the West, approached the troops of the Army of the Potomac, the taunting began. "We volunteered our condolence," observed the historian of the Fifty-fifth Illinois, "because they could no longer draw from the quartermaster rye straw for their beds and Day & Martin's blacking for their brogans. . . . We said to each other, with simulated admiration, 'What elegant corpses they'll make in those good clothes!' " The Easterners, in return, scoffed at the "dusty and dirty, ragged and shoeless" hillbillies.

The Westerners noticed that each Eastern corps possessed an insignia. Howard's Eleventh bore a crescent, Slocum's Twelfth a star. Other corps had as badges shields, crosses, and clover leaves. The story circulated about Chattanooga that an Army of the Potomac man asked one of Sherman's Irish veterans what his badge was. The Irishman slapped his cartridge box and answered: "Badge is it? Why forty rounds here to be shure, besides twenty in me pocket." Later, when the brave, mustachioed soldier-politician John A. Logan took over the Fifteenth Corps, he heard the tale and adopted as his insignia a cartridge box with forty rounds.[32]

The three-day battle opened on Monday, November 23, but, contrary to plans, Sherman's men did not fire the first shot. Grant ordered Thomas, holding the line opposite Missionary Ridge, to determine Bragg's strength and learn if the Confederates were withdrawing. In full view of the enemy, Thomas's 25,000 men feigned, as Howard put it, "a gay parade" and at 2:00 P.M. attacked and took Orchard Knob in the center of the Confederate line.[33]

On that day Sherman at last had his divisions in position. Under cover of hills, General Giles A. Smith's brigade proceeded to the point about a mile up Chickamauga Creek at which the 116 pontoon boats destined to become the bridge across the Tennessee were hidden. At about eleven at night four oarsmen and twenty-five men entered each boat and the expedition, led by the Eighth Missouri and the Fifty-fifth Illinois, started. The long line of pontoons floated noiselessly down the narrow creek, then entered the Tennessee, swollen by heavy rains. Hugging the west shore, which was the farthest from the enemy, the boats came alongside enemy pickets. Just below the first picket post, the men in the first boat veered over to the east bank. Its twenty-five soldiers quietly sprang ashore and captured the guards. Subsequent boats did the same, until all the outposts were taken.

Guided by a lantern on the west shore three miles below the mouth of the Chickamauga, the boats disgorged their human cargoes on the eastern bank. With their entrenching tools, the soldiers immediately threw up earthworks. As fast as the boats were unloaded, the oarsmen rowed for the opposite shore, where other troops of the Fifteenth Corps waited to be ferried across. Before daylight, the divisions of Morgan Smith and of John Smith, 8,000 men in all, were in line and facing the enemy.

Now the engineers went to work. Baldy Smith personally directed the building of two pontoon bridges, the main one across the eastern spur of the Tennessee and a smaller one across the Chickamauga, near its mouth, where the 8th Missouri and 116th Illinois had been left to guard Sherman's left flank. Within seven hours these were completed. "I have never beheld any work done so quietly, so well," Sherman reported about the bridge across the Tennessee, "and I doubt if the history of war can show a bridge of that extent (viz, 1350 feet) laid down so noiselessly and well in so short a time. I attribute it to the genius and intelligence of General William F. Smith."[34]

By noon of November 24, aided also by the little steamer *Dunbar,* operated by Wilson, three of Sherman's four divisions were across the Tennessee, and the fourth, Jeff Davis's, was crossing on the completed bridge. An hour later, in a light drizzle and low clouds that concealed the movement, the corps advanced toward Bragg's right, the northern end of Missionary Ridge. The object was Tunnel Hill, through which the tracks of the East Tennessee & Georgia Railroad passed, defended by only two to three hundred members of Confederate General Patrick R. Cleburne's famed division. Meeting slight resistance, Sherman's men took two high points that on maps appeared to be part of the continuous crest called Missionary Ridge, but which he now saw were separated from it by a deep valley and a steep hill covered with woods. Fearing Tunnel Hill was heavily fortified, Sherman stopped after taking the two hills.

By halting Sherman lost the advantage of surprise. His operation now became one of entrenchment and direct attack. A master at sieging and flanking, as he showed at Jackson and would later show in Georgia, Sherman, in common with every other Civil War general, possessed no special skill in frontal assaults, even when, as at Tunnel Hill, his force outnumbered the enemy.[35]

Just after Grant died, Sherman and Baldy Smith argued about what happened at Missionary Ridge. With clarity and forcefulness, Smith insisted that Grant had diverged from Smith's original design and possessed no battle plan at all. Sherman countered that Grant always was flexible. "In my experience," Sherman wrote, "Grant never had a rigid, cast iron plan to be adhered to, but acted at each moment according to the state of facts. . . . I was ordered to keep up a 'noisy' battle to induce Bragg to weaken his centre, which he did, and which General Grant had anticipated." After digesting these vague assertions, Smith answered: "I was very sorry to get your letter . . . or rather I was sorry on getting it, to read its contents."[36]

The fighting brought mixed results. On the twenty-fourth Hooker, with two divisions and a brigade, drove in Bragg's southern flank in the struggle on Lookout Mountain that Brigadier General Montgomery C. Meigs, the quartermaster of the Federal army, who watched it, labeled "the battle above the clouds." Sherman was not as successful. Though reinforced by Howard's corps of the Army of the Potomac and Jeff Davis's and Absalom Baird's divisions of the Army of the Cumberland, he made no progress. Leading the charge up the hill on the twenty-fifth were two brigades of Hugh Ewing's division. That of Brigadier General John M. Corse came to within eighty yards of the Confederates before falling back. Corse himself was wounded and carried off the field.[37]

Major General Carl Schurz, the German refugee who led a division in Howard's corps, remembered meeting Sherman for the first time in the midst of Ewing's attempt to take Tunnel Hill. Sherman was sitting on a stone fence watching the men struggle up the slope under heavy fire when Schurz came over. He asked Schurz to sit next to him, and the two were soon engaged in "lively conversation." Sherman was, Schurz recollected, "in an unhappy frame of mind," using "language of astonishing vivacity." He attributed his failure to the big ravine, not shown on any map, that separated the two captured hills from the tunnel. Sherman knew he had failed, for instead of ordering Schurz's division to support Ewing, he spoke vaguely about keeping it in reserve.[38]

In their battle summaries, and indeed throughout their lives, Grant and Sherman explained away Sherman's failure as best they could. "Column after column of the enemy was streaming towards me," Sherman declared. Urging that Thomas begin his assault, Sherman observed: "I know our attack had drawn vast masses of the enemy to our flank and felt sure of the result." Grant wrote similarly: "From the position I occupied, I could see column after column of Bragg's forces moving against Sherman."[39]

In reality, the episode only demonstrated the futility, with rare exceptions, of frontal attacks in the Civil War. During the battle, Cleburne's division, which had been ordered to Nashville but been recalled after the Union capture of Orchard Knob, received assistance from only two other brigades and two regiments. Yet Sherman, with four divisions and the three regiments of Howard's corps, could not budge the Confederates and suffered, including prisoners, thirteen hundred casualties.[40]

One of the exceptions occurred immediately. At about 2:30 P.M. on the twenty-fifth, watching Sherman's repulse, Grant walked over to General Thomas J. Wood, who led a division of the Army of the Cumberland. He noted that Sherman was "having a hard time" and suggested that if Wood and General Philip H. Sheridan advanced to the rifle pits at the base of Missionary Ridge, Bragg might draw troops from his right to strengthen the center. Wood responded that if Grant ordered the move, he would try it. Grant then spoke to Thomas and General Gordon Granger, who gave the order to four divisions. Grant instructed Wood to halt after capturing the first line of pits, an order Wood transmitted to his subordinates. But after reaching the designated spot, the troops, realizing the rifle pits afforded them no protection against the artillery and sharpshooters on the ridge, bounded over them and without orders continued to the top of the hill. "In fifty minutes from the time the movement was commenced from Orchard Knob," Wood recorded, "the first flags were seen flying on the crest of the Ridge."[41]

During the charge, made by eighty-nine regiments at six different points, Grant sent a message to Wood asking whether he had ordered it. If so, Wood "had gone beyond the pale of his orders, and that possibly dire consequences might flow from this disobedience."[42]

But in their autobiographies and histories, Grant, Sherman, and Grant's chronicler, Adam Badeau, insisted that the battle had followed some design of Grant. According to this version, Sherman's attack against Tunnel Hill was made to induce Bragg to weaken his center. Grant could then send the Army of the Cumberland to the top of Missionary Ridge. "The whole plan succeeded admirably," Sherman boasted in his *Memoirs*. When Baldy Smith later asked whether, as reported in Badeau's history of Grant, Sherman had spread this fantastic version of events, Sherman evasively answered: "Questions such as you propound me do not admit of a categorical answer."[43]

Wood left for posterity his opinion of such accounts:

This statement of General Grant is absolutely refuted by the anger displayed by him (which display was witnessed by many living men, and has been publicly attested by several responsible witnesses) when he saw my division commence the assault of Missionary Ridge, accompanied by the breathing out of threatenings and slaughter, against myself especially if the assault failed. General Grant's statement in his memoirs on this point is further refuted by the fact that, from the division commanders down to the humblest private in the two divisions most conspicuous in the assault, no man has ever yet been found who does not say the orders received peremptorily ordered him to halt at the base of the Ridge. If General Grant intended the assault of the crest of the Ridge to follow immediately on the heels of the initial success, with simply a halt for re-formation and without further orders, he certainly kept that intention severely to himself.[44]

Charles D. Brigham of the *New York Tribune,* who stood on Orchard Knob with Grant and Thomas during the battle, reported that the charge up the ridge completely surprised Grant. "Well," the imperturbable Thomas said, "let them go. It's all right!" "If it doesn't turn out right," Grant answered, "some one will suffer."[45]

At Missionary Ridge the troops knew more than the generals. "That night," observed Colonel Samuel H. Hurst of the Seventy-third Ohio, "our hardtack and coffee were better than a prince's feast, and our earthy bed was a couch for kings."[46]

— III —

About midnight of the twenty-fifth Sherman sent Morgan Smith to the tunnel. Smith found only the dead and wounded, the enemy having slipped away in the dark. Early the next morning Sherman, pursuing Bragg, crossed his men over the pontoon bridge spanning the Chickamauga. The soldiers then marched over ten miles of muddy roads to Chickamauga Station on the Charleston railroad. There they found burning immense piles of corn, beans, and army stores, gathered, Sherman thought, "for the famous invasion of Kentucky." But the troops also found unburnt corn, with which they made corn cakes, and forage for their horses.

On the next day, November 27, in a soaking rain, the expedition entered Georgia. It destroyed mills and shops in Graysville and marched toward Ringgold, where Hooker, also in pursuit, had caught up to Bragg's rear. But just beyond Ringgold, Cleburne's men turned on Hooker and severely mauled the Yankees. The smoke of battle told Sherman's troops something was going on there.[47]

On November 30, Sherman had just reached Charleston, Tennessee, about thirty miles northeast of Chattanooga, when Wilson rode up with a message from Grant. Longstreet was besieging Knoxville. Ambrose Burnside, with 12,000 men, estimated that his supplies would last only until December 3. Grant had sent Granger with two divisions toward Knoxville along the road following the Tennessee, but Granger was moving slowly "and with reluctance." Taking whatever men he needed—which turned out to be Hugh Ewing's and Morgan Smith's divisions of the Fifteenth Corps and Howard's Eleventh Corps—Sherman was to march the eighty-four miles to relieve Burnside.[48]

Sherman's expedition to Knoxville was the reverse of the one to Jackson the previous summer. This time hunger and bitter cold, not polluted waterholes and heat, were the chief enemies. The men, already absent from camp a week, had left with but two days' rations. They carried no change of clothing and only one blanket or coat each. The officers had only a rubber blanket that could be used as bedding. Noted the historian of the Fifty-fifth Illinois Infantry:

> The weather was severely cold, ice forming nightly over the pools in the muddy roads, sometimes nearly an inch in thickness, and all suffered greatly from want of clothing. . . . Soldiers disposed to be scrupulous about personal cleanliness could often be seen at night washing their shirts in the creek and drying them before the camp-fire. The rations were almost exclusively corn-meal and such meat, fresh or salt, as our foragers brought in. We had but one wagon for all uses, and were forced to rely exclusively upon the neighboring country for subsistence. One day the regiment feasted upon newly cured hams, turkeys, fresh mutton and beef; the next, perhaps, it had little but corn-meal. Large quantities of excellent sorghum molasses were found. Every mill we passed was set in motion to grind grain. . . . Poultry of every kind abounded; but gobbling and quack and cackle speedily hushed in the land, and the army left of the abundance only bones and feathers behind.[49]

In two columns roughly five miles apart, the Yankees marched through the fertile valley of East Tennessee, a stronghold of Unionism. Men who had hidden for months in the pine woods to escape Confederate conscription now came forward. Clothed in homespun garments, they were openly defiant of Jefferson Davis and loyal to the Union. When an officer of the Seventy-third Ohio asked a resident where all the young men were, the older man proudly responded: "Twenty thousand of them from East Tennessee are in your army, sir." With bands playing, Howard's shivering men passed through one loyal town after another. "Our march," Hurst remembered, "was an almost unbroken ovation."[50]

Schurz left one picture of Sherman on the march. One cold morning he "noticed a rather decent-looking house" with smoke coming out of its chimney and two orderlies in the front yard holding saddled horses. Entering, Schurz found Sherman and Davis, whose chief claim to fame was that on September 29, 1862, he had shot and killed the obnoxious General William Nelson after a quarrel in the Galt House in Louisville, toasting their feet before a crackling wood fire. A few minutes later Howard, "the Christian soldier," entered.

Sherman greeted him: "Glad to see you, Howard! Sit down by the fire! Damned cold this morning." With that Sherman winked to Davis with his left eye and smiled. Davis, probably the army's champion curser, thereupon began talking about some obscure subject, throwing in a profusion of "damns." Howard made several attempts to change the subject, but, encouraged by Sherman's winks and remarks, Davis continued on. Finally Howard got up and left, and Sherman and Davis broke out in laughter. When Schurz said something about Howard's suffering, Sherman answered: "Well, the Christian soldier business is all right in its place. But he needn't put on airs when we are among ourselves."[51]

Sherman found it impossible to reach Knoxville by December 3, but he sent ahead a small brigade of cavalry, which arrived on that night, to let Burnside know help was near. Learning of Sherman's force from a captured messenger, Longstreet dawdled for a while, hoping to lure Sherman further away from Grant. With the relief expedition at Maryville, thirteen miles south of Knoxville, Longstreet withdrew during a chilly rain on the night of the fourth and fled up the valley of the Holston River toward Virginia.[52]

Taking with him only Granger's two divisions, Sherman rode into Knoxville on the sixth. He immediately saw, as he recorded in his *Memoirs,* a large pen with fine cattle. Burnside and his staff lived in a mansion. Burnside explained to Sherman that his men were pursuing Longstreet. With Granger's help, he was sure he could push the Confederates out of East Tennessee. But Granger growled about leaving Knoxville to chase Longstreet, creating such a bad impression that Sherman vowed never to take him on another campaign.[53]

In his *Memoirs,* Sherman spoke of sitting down with Burnside to a sumptuous meal of roast turkey at an elegantly set table. He could not help blurting out that he had thought "they were starving." Burnside fumbled through some explanation about receiving bacon, beef, and cornmeal from the Unionists on the south side of the river. "Had I known of this," Sherman commented, "I should not have hurried my men so fast; but until I reached Knoxville I thought our troops were actually in danger of starvation."

Grant considered this among the most objectionable statements in Sherman's *Memoirs.* The moment Longstreet abandoned the siege of Knoxville, he pointed out to Sherman, supplies flowed in from every direction. To honor Sherman, who had made the march with troops cold and tired, Burnside had borrowed plates and napkins from one house, preserves and sweetmeats from another, and set a lavish table. "Burnside was really more destitute of the means to keep up armed resistance to the enemy from scarcity of ammunition," Grant noted, "than from scarcity of provisions."[54]

Marching back to Chattanooga, Sherman's army resembled Washington's at Valley Forge. Having had only one shirt during the expedition, the men were in rags. Shoes were full of holes. A quarter of the men, having no shoes at all, wrapped their feet in rags or fresh rawhide. Within Howard's corps three hundred men organized a barefoot battalion. Almost the entire army came back with "graybacks," a term sometimes used for Confederate soldiers but in this case for camp vermin.[55]

___ IV ___

The battles of Chattanooga and Knoxville were over, but the struggle for fame and glory continued. Sherman still did not envision Grant as a great leader. "Dont allow yourself to be drawn into a league against Halleck," he warned John after returning to Lancaster from Knoxville. "He has more capacity than any man in our Army. Grant has qualities that Halleck does not possess but not such as would qualify him to command the whole Army. The war has not yet developed Halleck's equal as a General in Chief."[56]

Hooker went even further. Basking in the sunshine of the victory above the clouds, he dispatched to Chase a long letter criticizing his colleagues. Sherman's performance at Tunnel Hill he characterized as

> a disaster. Sherman is an active, energetic officer, but in my judgment is as infirm as Burnside. He will never be successful. Please remember what I tell you. It was natural for Grant to feel partial to his old companion and do all possible to enhance their renown; nevertheless you will appreciate my nervousness in being placed in a situation in which this partiality was manifest wholly at my expense.[57]

Meigs's comments bothered Sherman and Ellen even more than Hooker's. After watching the battle for Missionary Ridge from Orchard Knob, Meigs described to Secretary of War Stanton the defeat of the Army of the Tennessee and the magnificent charge of the Army of the Cumberland. Stanton had published the letter as, Cump complained to John, "semi-official. Meigs apologized to me for using Thomas's name instead of mine throughout, which he charged to a copyist, but made no amends for the repulse."[58]

Ellen proposed to correct the situation. She wanted John to get from Stanton a copy of Sherman's campaign report, which she would give

> to the world. The Army of the Tennessee, or rather the 15th Army Corps marched from Memphis to Chattanooga—*passed* the Army of the Cumberland & *took the post of honor and of danger* on the extreme left, bore the heaviest of the enemies fire & had the enemy massed against them for *four* hours before the Army of the Cumberland advanced to make the preconcerted attack on the centre which had been left comparatively easy by the action of the 15th Corps. After an *unfaltering* struggle in which they were entirely victorious they started in pursuit after which they were turned about & marched without blankets & many of them without shoes to Knoxville where they arrived in time, only in consequence of the fact that they were well disciplined, brave and thorough soldiers and *under skillful generals*. The weather during their march to & from Knoxville was quite severe and without blankets they kept warm at night only by *standing* around camp fires which we would consider a fatigue & which to them must have been a poor rest after the long days' marches. The way was tracked with blood from their cut & bruised feet. They tore down towns to build bridges &

overcame obstacles which were keeping Gordon Granger back & would have prevented him (although first ordered) from raising the siege of Knoxville. . . . But a grateful Congress recognizes the services & returns thanks to Thomas & Burnside & Hooker & their armies, overlooking the men on whom they relied & whom the records will *prove* to have lost more heavily than any of them.[59]

The lack of recognition irked Sherman, too. He noticed, he informed John,

that Resolutions of thanks have been introduced in Congress to Hooker and his Army, and Thomas & his Army, but not one word of Sherman & the Army of the Tennessee. Now it is known to all the Army, that the best fighting in Hookers Army was done by one of my Divisions viz Osterhaus the 1st Division 15th Corps, which could not join me because a Bridge across the Tennessee at Browns Ferry was broken, and which I volunteered to leave with Hooker rather than delay the impending Battle—The Army of the Tennessee marched rapidly from Memphis to Chattanooga, crossed the Tennessee and began the Battle. We had the initiative & most important point of that Battle, and afterward without rest or preparation, in consequence of the slow & dilatory movement of a part of the Army of the Cumberland I was required with the Army of the Tennessee to march 130 miles further shoeless to relieve Knoxville. All these things are known officially to the War Dept and if thanks are voted to the rest & the Army of the Tennessee left out I must construe it as personal and quit. I want the Army of the Tennessee to have its share of official recognition but for myself I ask nothing. . . . The truth is General Thomas a particular friend of mine did not go outside the entrenchments of Chattanooga at the time of Battle or after. I was with my men *all* the time. And I repeat one Division of my troops did Hookers best fighting. . . .

I want a pretext to get rest, and if this injustice be done the Army of the Tennessee, because I led it, I will quickly avail myself of the opportunity to seek rest in another quarter of the world.[60]

Possessing powerful friends, Sherman in February 1864 got his congressional vote of thanks. In his *Memoirs* he placed the resolution immediately after his official report, the inference being that the second developed naturally from the first.[61]

More importantly, the recent campaigns and marches, coupled with the loss of Willy, had hardened Sherman. To Major Roswell M. Sawyer, who was the assistant adjutant in northern Alabama, he explained his views on the last day of January 1864. Previous wars, he noted, were of two kinds. Some had been fought between armies, not people. During the Napoleonic wars, for example, French farmers had been free to sell supplies to both sides. In the late seventeenth century, on the other hand, the English had driven Irish farmers from their lands and replaced them with Scottish immigrants. Sherman intended to follow this latter example. Those Southern civilians who "remain in their houses and keep to their accustomed business" would not be touched. "But if any one comes out into the public streets and creates disorder, he or she should be punished, restrained, or banished, either to the rear or front as the officer in command adjudges." Those who preached "eternal war" would lose everything. "I know thousands and millions of good people who at simple notice would come to North Alabama and accept the elegant houses and plantations there." Southerners must yield. "All the powers of earth cannot restore to them their slaves any more than their dead grandfathers. Next year their lands will be taken, for in war we can take them, and rightfully, too, and in another year they may beg in vain for their lives. . . . To the petulant and persistent secessionists, why, death is mercy, and the quicker he or she is disposed of the better." Sherman urged Sawyer to read this letter to "some of the better people" of Alabama "so as to prepare them for my coming."[62]

11

Commander
of the Armies

— I —

IF THE CIVIL WAR had ended with the Chattanooga-Knoxville campaign, Sherman would have emerged from it with a reputation as an energetic, reliable officer, but as nothing more. With the exception of the siege of Jackson, which he designed and carried out, he had shown bravery but only traces of the organizational ability he later demonstrated. Nor had he been particularly distinguished in battle. Indeed, of all the Union commanders, only Grant and perhaps Thomas would have been worth studying—Thomas because of Chickamauga and Grant because of his campaign to the rear of Vicksburg.

With Chattanooga in Union hands, Grant began thinking about his next campaign. Just before Christmas of 1863 he called to his headquarters at Nashville many of his leading generals, including Sherman, Sheridan, Logan, and Brigadier General Grenville M. Dodge, who, with part of the Sixteenth Corps, was repairing the railroad from Decatur to Nashville. At the time, Grant believed that the next campaign would be where Longstreet still lingered, up the valley of East Tennessee and into Virginia.

Sherman, on the other hand, dreamed of a campaign to release the soldiers still guarding the Mississippi River from Confederate infantry and cavalry. To Grant at Nashville, he suggested a dual movement. From Vicksburg he would strike out toward the east and Meridian. Simultaneously, Banks would leave New Orleans and go up the Red River to Shreveport, a move Sherman characterized as "my favorite scheme." Grant agreed to the proposal.[1]

The Nashville conference was not all work. On their arrival Grant took Sherman, Rawlins, Dodge, and others, still dressed in work clothes, to see the military governor of Tennessee, Andrew Johnson, who lived in a fine new house. After a brief conversation, Johnson began a tirade against the Confederates. Screaming that "No rebel need hope for mercy from me," he brought his fist down on the piano with such force that the impact resounded throughout the house. "We left," Dodge related, "all of us rather disgusted, as his tirade was uncalled for, and while I was in command of Middle Tennessee I hardly ever put my hand on a rebel, taking his stock or forage, but Johnson tried to stop it and protect him."

That night Sherman suggested they go to the theater. Sitting in the front row of the balcony, the officers saw a butchered version of *Hamlet*. Sherman got so excited that several times he said: "Dodge, that is no way to play Hamlet!" Dodge warned him not to talk so loud or some of the boys would notice them. During Hamlet's soliloquy over Yorick's skull, a soldier yelled out: "Say pard, what is it, Yank or Reb?" The house in an uproar, Grant suggested that they leave. "We left," Dodge commented, "and no one knew that the two great soldiers of the age had been listening."[2]

The most disagreeable episode occurred at a dinner given by Granger, the commander at Nashville. Granger's mother or mother-in-law kept pounding away at Sherman for the pillaging and "stealing" done by his men on the march to Knoxville. After putting up with it for a time, Sherman turned on her and said: "Madam, my soldiers have to subsist even if the whole country must be ruined to maintain them. There are two armies here; one is in rebellion against the Union, the other is fighting for the Union—if either must starve to death, I propose it shall not be the army that is loyal. There is nothing too good for the soldiers who wear the blue." After a pause, he uttered words that he would repeat in September 1864 in a letter to the mayor of Atlanta: "War is cruelty. There is no use trying to reform it; the crueler it is, the sooner it will be over." According to Dodge, the response "put a cold douche on the dinner and no effort of any of us could relieve the strain. The lady said no more, for it was a great rebuke."[3]

— II —

Having been in the field for over a year, Sherman asked for and received a leave to spend the Christmas holidays with his family. Returning to Lancaster, he found himself a celebrity. One afternoon neighbors came over to the Ewing house to pay him homage. People crowded around him, and young girls, always his favorites, stared at him.[4]

At this point in the war Sherman felt satisfied with his achievements. "Today," he wrote John, "I can do more with Admiral Porter or the Generals out west than any General officer out west except Grant, and with him I am as a second self. On this score you can see Dana, who was with me at Knoxville. I would on no account come east and will so far as I can control it hold fast to the Mississippi."[5]

On New Year's Day Sherman left Lancaster with Minnie, who was going with him to Cincinnati on her way to the convent school she attended. At Morrow they missed their connection. Several days later, Sherman wrote home:

The night was bitter cold, but my time was so short that I had to get to Cincinnati that night. Learning that a train would come along at 1:45 I concluded to sit up, so along with some of the passengers we went to the tavern where we got supper & played cards till the time for starting. I laid Minnie on a sofa and covered her up with coats & shawls, and we sat up and kept the room warm—She slept a while, but I had to rouse her at 1:45—The train came & we got to the Burnett House at 4 AM, the worst hour of the 24—All in bed, house cold, and a room reserved for General & Mrs Sherman. We tried to get a fire started, and to keep warm Minnie & I slept together. Bright & early we were up & met many at Breakfast, and all day People called.[6]

Leaving Minnie made Sherman blue. To Ellen, he wrote:

I ought to be well schooled now at parting, but really I felt bad to leave Minnie alone in that dark house. Almost as bad as when Lizzie clung to me for life in the School at Mrs King's Old House. I confess myself amazed at the calm & easy manner of Minnie at all times, unabashed, almost too much so for her years. And yet she seems loving and kind. To me she acts somewhat like Willie with that simple confidence that is very captivating. She will make a beautiful woman, and we cannot be too careful of her in her next three years.[7]

From Cincinnati, Sherman proceeded by rail to Cairo. In gunboats supplied by Porter, he spent the next two weeks surveying enemy guerrilla activity along the icebound Mississippi. Landing at Memphis, commanded by General Stephen A. Hurlbut, and at Vicksburg, commanded by McPherson, he explained that he wished them to accompany him on his expedition. Taking 20,000 men, he expected to leave Vicksburg early in February. His objective was to destroy Meridian's warehouses and repair shops and to wreck the two railroads, the Mobile & Ohio and the Vicksburg & Charleston, that intersected at the town. Sherman also hoped to safeguard the Mississippi River by making it impossible for the enemy to survive east of Jackson. After wrecking Meridian, Sherman told Halleck, he might move toward Selma, Montgomery, or even Shreveport.[8]

At Memphis, Sherman also met with Brigadier General William Sooy Smith, the cavalry chief of the Military Division of the Mississippi, who was to lead 7,000 men during the raid. Smith was to leave Collierville, twenty-four miles east of Memphis, on or before February 1 and head straight for Meridian, a distance of 250 miles, where he was to meet Sherman about February 10. Sherman warned Smith about General Nathan Bedford Forrest, who would be in the area with no more than 4,000 Confederate cavalry and would unquestionably attack Smith. Smith must "overwhelm" and "utterly destroy" Forrest.[9]

Preparing for the expedition, Sherman remained at Memphis, whose citizens on January 25 tendered him a dinner at the Gayoso. At the affair Sherman gave two speeches. In the first, to the general audience, he blamed Louisiana's secession on "foreigners." The two United States senators, John Slidell, a New Yorker, and Judah P. Benjamin, "a Jew, born in Havana," had engineered the state's seizure of federal forts and mints. And the man who had shipped 4,800 Federal rifles to Sherman at Alexandria was a Pole. Bragg was a North Carolinian, Governor Moore "the same." Only Sherman's friend Beauregard was a native of Louisiana.

After the festivities, Sherman's friends pressed him into delivering another talk. In it Sherman praised his two favorite soldiers, Halleck and Grant. "I spoke of your indomitable industry," Sherman told Halleck. He recalled how, while off stormy Cape Horn aboard "the Old Lexington" in 1846, Sherman, Ord, and their friends played cards. But Halleck strapped himself to his berth and spent the time "boning harder than you ever did at West Point." Halleck knew his "profession" better than Lincoln, Chase, and Seward combined. As for Grant, Sherman praised "his simple courage in his cause" and "his utter absence of vainglory and selfish pride."[10]

The speeches over, the expedition, consisting of 21,000 men and four divisions, two in Hurlbut's Sixteenth Corps and two in McPherson's Seventeenth, preceded by a light force of cavalry, began the trek east on February 3. Marching in two columns the Federals passed over the Big Black River and onto familiar territory. Hurlbut's men trudged through Joe Davis's plantation, McPherson's through Champion's Hill. Each column encountered Confederate cavalry, which resisted the Union advance for about twenty miles.[11]

On February 6 the Federals entered Jackson, now a rubble heap. But this did not satisfy those in McPherson's corps who, as prisoners of war, had been abused in Jackson. They began torching the city's remaining buildings. The destruction shocked many Union soldiers, one of whom remembered seeing a black boy fingering the keys of a piano that some Federals had tossed into the gutter.[12]

Moving east toward Meridian in perfect weather, the Northerners found a country abounding in cattle, hogs, sweet potatoes, and corn. But, with rare exceptions, each town suffered the same fate: almost total destruction. "The once pretty village of Brandon," twelve miles east of Jackson, was burned. So too were Hillsboro, the county seat containing all the court records, and Decatur, further east. When the 124th Illinois reached Decatur, it was, recorded the unit's chaplain, "but little better . . . than a pile of smoking ruin."[13]

As the Federals approached, the Confederate force under Lieutenant General Leonidas Polk, the bishop-general, abandoned Meridian, moving eastward into Alabama. Polk eventually fell back across the Tombigbee River. Entering Meridian on the fifteenth, Sherman found the enemy's camp "well stocked with Shoes Clothing & Ammunition of Cincinnati and Philadelphia Manufacture. This greed after gain," he later complained to John, "encourages the South to believe what our Army already knows that our People are so avaricious that they would sell our lives for a small profit." He did not want his brother Hoyt, who was thinking of speculating in cotton, to engage in such a "dirty business—Until he is drafted let him cultivate potatoes & vegetables to feed his family."[14]

Sherman spent five days wrecking Meridian. Hurlbut's men destroyed sixty miles of railroad, McPherson's fifty-five. "Meridian," Sherman informed his superiors, "with its depots, store-houses, arsenal, hospitals, offices, hotels, and cantonments no longer exists."[15]

A private in Sherman's army left a picture of unbridled destruction:

Soon after our arrival at Meridian, a soldier was seen to deliberately set fire to an occupied residence, and when the family took refuge in another house, he followed and wantonly applied the torch to that. Upon being arrested he gave as a reason for what he had done that some time before he had been a prisoner in rebel hands, and in being transferred had stopped at Meridian. While waiting transportation at the depot, this woman, whose house he had burnt, stepped up to him without provocation or cause, and deliberately spit in his face, and he had sworn he would be revenged. All who witnessed the burning buildings can testify that he kept his word, and it is almost useless to add that he was not punished.[16]

When Sherman left Meridian on the twentieth, he still had heard "nothing whatever of General Smith." In his *Memoirs,* published in 1875, Sherman wrote so hostile an account of this failure that Smith protested. "You seem to think," Sherman responded with a venom uncharacteristic of him, "that I should not have written 'my memoirs,' but 'yours.' "[17]

Twenty years after Sherman's death, Smith, still bitter, gave Dodge his version of the episode. At their Memphis meeting Sherman had told him to leave Collierville on the first of February, taking with him 7,000 men divided into four brigades, one of which, led by Colonel George E. Waring Jr., was then a hundred miles away. Smith, not knowing Waring and fearing he might be late, asked Sherman if he should go without him. "No, no," Sherman answered, "if you do you will be too weak and they'll lick you." Smith then asked if it were necessary to reach Meridian at the appointed time. Again Sherman said "No." Any movement beyond Meridian, say to Mobile, would depend on Smith's arrival, but at the moment Sherman planned to stop at Meridian.[18]

Because Waring was delayed by ice storms, Smith did not leave Collierville until February 11. His columns soon made up half the delay with forced marches. They crossed the Tallahatchie River and advanced against token opposition. With ease Smith pushed southeast toward West Point, Mississippi, a hundred miles above Meridian. His men totally destroyed Redland, Okolona, and Egypt Station. Only two houses were left standing in Egypt, located in one of the most fertile and beautiful prairies in the world. The town of Aberdeen, however, received different treatment. Entering it, General Benjamin H. Grierson called on the mayor and his family. He then entertained the ladies present by playing on the piano a few Southern airs, finishing his concert with "The Star-Spangled Banner."[19]

On February 20, when his cavalry reached the outskirts of West Point, Smith ran into trouble. A mile north of the town his men met and drove back an enemy brigade. But his scouts insisted that the Southerners, with between six and seven thousand men, blocked his front, right, and left. Coupled with this, he received, as he noted, "exaggerated reports" that Forrest was soon to be reinforced by General Stephen D. Lee. Sure he was riding into a trap, Smith decided on February 21 to withdraw.

Sherman had warned Smith that a retreat would enable the enemy cavalry to mass. As it turned out, Smith was forced to fight the pursuing Confederates all the way back to the Tallahatchie. In one Confederate charge Forrest's brother, Colonel Jeffrey E. Forrest, lost his life.[20]

Meantime, six thousand refugees, five thousand of them black, followed Sherman's army back to Vicksburg. Some of the slaves marched all the way from Meridian, the men "loaded down like pack mules," the women carrying feather beds on their heads and heavy bundles in their arms. Others were in wagons drawn by animals. The chaplain of the 124th Illinois called it "the most remarkable hegira of negroes the southwest had ever known."[21]

For Sherman the most haunting part of the Meridian trip came near its end. Crossing the Big Black, the general saw the ruins of his old camp. He rode, Sherman told Ellen, "on that familiar Road, where but a few Months ago Willy ran to me his whole heart beaming in his face—All came back as a flash, and I could hardly realize that I should never see him again. . . . Though dead he is still our Willy and we can love him as God only knows how we loved him."[22]

On the day Sherman returned to Vicksburg, he wrote Ellen of his disgust with Sooy Smith:

> Had the Cavalry reached its destination at the time fixed we should have captured Polks army, but as it was it was driven defeated across the Tombigbee. . . . Somehow our Cavalry is not good. The Secesh with poor mean horses make 40 & 50 miles a day, whereas our fat & costly horses wont average 10. In every march I have ever made our Infantry beats the Cavalry & I am ashamed of them.[23]

Immediately after reaching Vicksburg, Sherman headed for New Orleans, where he was to confer with Porter and the Federal commander in Louisiana, General Banks, about the Red River expedition. On the way he stopped at Natchez on a mission of mercy. David F. Boyd, now a captain in the Confederate engineers, had been captured near Alexandria, the site of the old academy. Fearful of being incarcerated for a long period in a Federal prison, Boyd begged Sherman to engineer his exchange. "I never saw a man evince more gratitude," Sherman informed Ellen after arranging things. Sherman introduced Boyd to everyone and laughed when Boyd resented his comment to Porter: "Admiral Porter, this is Mr. Boyd; he thinks he is a Confederate captain, but he is in reality my old professor of languages." "He told me all about the people up river," Sherman added, "and said they talked about me a great deal, some with marked respect and others with bitter hatred." The Confederates had chiseled out the motto over the door of the school: " 'By the liberality of the General Government of the United States. The Union, Esto perpetua.' The fools!"[24]

Sherman's stay in New Orleans involved more pleasure than business. "I was there but two days," he confided to Ellen, "one of which I was 8 hours at table, breakfasting out & dining out." He met there his old friend from California, General Charles P. Stone, now married "to a Creole Blonde." Also there was his Fort Moultrie companion, General Thomas W. Sherman, "with his one leg," having lost the other at Port Hudson. "Mrs. Banks was there and is a smart Yankee woman."[25]

With Porter and Banks, Sherman worked out the details of the Red River scheme. For it he would loan Banks ten thousand men, under Brigadier General Andrew J. Smith, who had led a division on the Meridian expedition. But Sherman distrusted Banks, who, having been a major general longer, outranked even Grant. Banks was spending most of his time preparing for the inauguration of a civil government in Louisiana. In Lafayette Square, Sherman saw scaffolds for the fireworks and benches for the audience. Banks implored him to stay over March 4 to participate in the ceremonies, which would include the playing of the "Anvil Chorus" by the bands in Banks's army, the ringing of church bells, and the firing of cannons by electricity. Believing such nonsense to be out of place in wartime, Sherman left.[26]

Returning to Memphis, Sherman was not hopeful. "I think we can whip them in Alabama and it may be in Georgia," he told Ellen of the Confederates, "but the Devils seem to have a determination that cannot but be admired. No amount of poverty or adversity seems to shake their faith—nigger gone—wealth & luxury gone, money worthless, starvation in view within a period of two or three years—are Causes enough to make the bravest tremble, yet I see no signs of let up."[27]

At the moment Ellen refused to offer her usual encouragement. She and her father followed Sherman's campaign in the newspapers, but she was preoccupied with her mother, who died after a painful illness. On the day Sherman left Meridian, Archbishop Purcell sang the Requiem Mass. Charley, Tom, and Hugh were home, but Hugh was angry because Sherman refused to recommend him for promotion. "The fact of his having once or twice indulged in too much liquor," Ellen scolded Sherman about Hugh, "cannot be urged as a reason, when Grant has been in the same condition quite as often and when it is well known that Hugh has never any more failed in duty than Grant. He and his men have been *foremost* in the march, in assaults & in pursuits yet men who *will not face a storm of bullets* have had recommendations for Maj Genl from you & Genl Grant. Mr. S. Smith for one."[28]

—— III ——

When Sherman, traveling north, was between Vicksburg and Memphis, Captain Adam Badeau of Grant's staff came on board his ship, the *Westmoreland*, with a letter from Grant. Dated March 4, it announced that Grant would soon be promoted to the newly revived rank of lieutenant general. Grant praised Sherman and McPherson "as the men to whom, above all others, I feel indebted for whatever I have had of success." In answer, Sherman warned his friend not to set up headquarters in Washington, the hotbed of intrigue. In June 1862 Sherman had advised Halleck not to go to Washington, and he now offered Grant similar counsel.[29]

Called east to accept his promotion and to meet Lincoln, Grant always remembered an incident that occurred there. On March 10, the day after receiving the promotion, he went out to visit the commander of the Army of the Potomac, General George G. Meade, whom he had known slightly in the Mexican War. During their talk Meade suggested that Grant might want to replace him. He especially mentioned Sherman and implored Grant to make any changes he desired. Meade said he would willingly serve wherever placed. Grant then assured Meade that he had no intention of removing him. Sherman was needed in the West. "This incident," Grant commented, "gave me even a more favorable opinion of Meade than did his great victory at Gettysburg the July before."[30]

Returning to the West, Grant called his generals together at Nashville on March 18. Sherman, Sheridan, Rawlins, Granger, and Dodge, who left the fullest account of the meeting, were among those present; McPherson, John A. Logan (who had taken over the Fifteenth Corps), and Blair were away. Grant announced that he was to command all of the armies. Sherman would replace him as head of the Military Division of the Mississippi, and McPherson would lead the Army of the Tennessee.

At least one general, James F. Rusling, was "certain" Thomas felt "aggrieved" by Grant's choice of Sherman. Thomas commanded the Army of the Cumberland, which was much larger than Sherman's Army of the Tennessee. But loyal soldier that he was, he said nothing and did what was asked of him.

Grant spoke of the Army of the Potomac, relating how well equipped and well fed it was. When Sherman asked Grant about some of the officers in the East whom they both knew, Grant answered that several of them had scoffed to him: "You have not yet met Bobby Lee."

Laying down the plans for the coming campaign, Grant expected all of the Union armies—Sherman would be pitted against Joe Johnston, who had succeeded Bragg—to move on May 1 and to stay with the enemy until one side or another was destroyed. "I expect you to move against Johnston," Grant ordered Sherman, "and to keep him busy and keep him from sending any of his army to aid Lee, and if he sends any of his force to aid Johnston, I will send you two men to his one." Dodge remembered that during the ensuing campaign, Sherman often said: "We must press Johnston so that under no circumstances can they detach a Corps or any part of their command to reinforce Lee."

Grant wanted to take east with him many of his generals, but Sherman objected so strenuously that Grant yielded and took only Sheridan. That afternoon Grant left for Washington. Sherman accompanied him to Cincinnati, where in a room at the Burnett House they spent the night poring over maps and coming to a general understanding of what was to take place.[31]

Sherman's command embraced four armies. General Frederick Steele headed the Department of the Arkansas. But, taking part in the raid to Shreveport, he and his army were soon transferred to the Military Division of the Gulf, embracing New Orleans.

The three other armies were to participate in the coming campaign. Sherman's favorite, McPherson, that dignified, cheerful, courteous Prince of Soldiers, led the Army of the Tennessee, which included Sherman's old favorite, the Fifteenth Corps. Thomas commanded the largest unit, the Army of the Cumberland, then at Chattanooga. John M. Schofield, at Knoxville, was in charge of the smallest unit, the Army of the Ohio.[32]

At Chattanooga at the end of the month, Sherman and his three commanders decided on the organization of their forces. Howard's Eleventh and Slocum's Twelfth Corps were consolidated and given to Hooker, Sherman's enemy since their days together in California in the late 1840s. Howard would replace Granger, whom Sherman disliked after his performance on the Knoxville march, and go along as head of the Fourth Corps. But Slocum, because of his interest in black troops, would not. He would replace McPherson at Vicksburg, which had numerous Negro regiments.[33]

The massacre on April 12 at Fort Pillow, on the Mississippi forty miles above Memphis, convinced Sherman to leave colored troops behind. At that place Forrest's men killed a large segment of the garrison, both black and white, when, instead of surrendering, they raced down to the river hoping to be rescued by a gunboat. Cump explained to John about the black troops:

> Of course, Forrest & all Southerners will kill them and their white officers. We all knew that, and should not expose small detachments— We were using them in moderation and in connection with whites as fast as the demands of service justified, but it was made a Policy, and all had to bend to it—then it became the means by which Massachusetts and other States could dodge their share. They raised the cry that a negro man was as good to stop a Rebel bullet as a White Man. But is it the only use you can put a soldier to to stop a bullet? I thought a soldier was to be an active machine, a fighter. Dirt or cotton will stop a bullet better than a mans body. We ought not to engraft a doubtful element in any army *now*, it is too critical a period.[34]

Hugh and Charley also presented problems. After fighting with Sherman from Vicksburg to Knoxville, Hugh again pressed for a major generalship. But Sherman had no vacancies. He had twelve brigadiers commanding divisions, all of whom thought they merited promotions. Charley's case was different. "Tell him plainly," Sherman instructed Hugh, "to warrant my full favor he must stop gambling & show that he saves money for a rainy day." Charley eventually agreed to accompany his brother-in-law, who appointed him McPherson's assistant inspector general.[35]

Although deprived of 20,000 men, half by Banks's failure on the Red River and the other half by furloughs in the Seventeenth Corps of McPherson's army, Sherman still possessed a huge force. By early April, Schofield had 12,000 infantry and 5,000 cavalry; Thomas had 40,000 infantry and 5,000 cavalry; and McPherson led 20,000 infantry and 5,000 cavalry. "Combined," Sherman revealed to Ellen, "it is a big army and a good one, and it will take a strong opposition to stop once in motion."[36]

Thomas had an extensive network of spies, who kept the Federals well informed. Johnston was at Dalton, Georgia, thirty miles from Chattanooga, with about 50,000 men. With reinforcements, principally troops from Mississippi, his force would probably approach 60,000. Preparing for a defensive war, the Southern general was entrenching wherever possible.[37]

Sherman's principal supply network consisted of three railroads that connected to form a line from Louisville, his prime base, to Atlanta. The Louisville & Nashville, covering 190 miles, was the first, and the Nashville & Chattanooga, 151 miles long, the second. The third railroad, the Western & Atlantic, whose track Sherman planned to follow, connected Chattanooga and Atlanta, a distance of 138 miles. In addition, Sherman was able to use the Memphis & Charleston and the Nashville & Decatur to shuttle empty cars between Nashville and Chattanooga, thereby easing the burden on the main road.[38]

Feeding and supplying the army became a monumental task. In the old days a military axiom dictated that an army could not operate more than a hundred miles from its base. Supplied by wagons pulled by mules, the soldiers and teams would eat up the contents in twenty-five days, or twelve and a half out and twelve and a half in. "Rosecrans," Sherman pointed out, "nearly starved an army at Chattanooga with a haul of some 60 or 70 miles from Bridgeport and Stevenson by way of Waldrens Ridge."

The railroad changed all that. Unlike mules, locomotives did not eat hay and corn. One locomotive could haul 160,000 pounds. Since a man ate three pounds a day, one trainload would feed 50,000 soldiers. An animal consumed fifteen pounds a day. To sustain and supply an army of 100,000 men and 35,000 animals, 130 cars, carrying ten tons each, must get through every day. Expecting to lose two trains a week to accidents and to the enemy, Sherman estimated that to ensure that his army got what it needed he must have on hand 100 locomotives and 1,000 cars.[39]

In response to Sherman's complaints that supplies were not accumulating fast enough, Lincoln and Stanton authorized him on April 2 "to take military possession of the railroads within your command." Reserving the railroads for supplies, he issued on April 6 an order banning civilian passengers—even the sister-in-law of Fanny Sherman Moulton—and goods. To keep civilians off the line, Sherman even suggested the death penalty for conductors who accepted "a cent" in fares. As he related to John,

> I make the Soldiers march, & yet I am bored to death by men & women to go to Chattanooga and Knoxville. Of course I deny all, even Mrs Lenet, sister to Moulton, who wanted to see her husband. A parcel of preachers came with a positive demand . . . under some promise of Sec of War. They were denied and persisted in a written application. I endorsed "Certainly not." The road is wanted purely for military freight. 200 pounds of powder or oats are worth more to the U. S. than that amount of bottled piety. . . . I will not be behind hand when the Grand beginning is announced. I can tell you nothing more. I hope Grant will be equally retentive. He ought not to trust even Mr Lin-

coln, and as to a Member of Congress I hope Grant will make it a death penalty for one to go south of the Potomac.[40]

Sherman's team now accumulated materials rapidly. From Louisville Brigadier General Robert Allen, who had helped round up the boats Sherman needed for the Chickasaw expedition, shipped goods and cars to Lieutenant Colonel James L. Donaldson, the chief quartermaster at Nashville, and to John B. Anderson, the superintendent of railroads there. Then it was on to Chattanooga, where Lieutenant Colonel Langdon C. Easton handled things. By the end of April between 130 and 190 cars filled with supplies were arriving in Nashville each day, and on the twentieth Quartermaster General Montgomery C. Meigs reported to Sherman that Nashville contained enough grain to feed 50,000 animals until New Year's Day and enough rations to feed 200,000 men for four months.[41]

In late April, Sherman inaugurated an even stricter policy. No more food would be distributed to the Unionists in East Tennessee. In one month alone, Sherman informed Meigs, Thomas had issued 230,000 rations to civilians. "I would rather have these rations in our wharehouses at Chattanooga and Ringgold." Questioned about the decision by Lincoln, Sherman answered that the railroad could not serve both civilians and the army. "One or the other must quit," he insisted, "and the army don't intend to unless Joe Johnston makes us."[42]

Just before leaving Nashville for Chattanooga, Sherman warned Donaldson that he must keep supplies coming. General Rusling heard him say: "I am going to move on Joe Johnston the day General Grant telegraphs me he is going to hit Bobby Lee; and if you don't have my army supplied and keep it supplied we'll eat up your mules, sir—eat your mules up!"[43]

After several postponements, Grant selected May 5 as the starting date for the campaign. On April 28, Sherman telegraphed Halleck that he would be ready. That day he left Nashville for Chattanooga. By the twenty-ninth Thomas, with 45,000 men, was in position. Schofield, with 13,000 troops, would be ready by May 2. And McPherson, with 20,000 men, was marching toward Chattanooga. All of Sherman's cavalry was heading toward Dalton.[44]

On May 4, Thomas was at Ringgold, about fifteen miles inside of Georgia, Schofield was on his left, near Red Clay, and McPherson was at Chattanooga, ready to advance. That day, Sherman wrote what he suspected might be his last letter to Ellen:

> I sent Minnie & Lizzie Bouquets collected on our Battle Field of last November, and if any ill fate attends me in this, they will remember me by that. The weather is beautiful, and the Army is in fine condition. . . . Charley has not yet reported to me. Tomorrow I will be off & may not write for some time, but the telegraph will announce the result of our first steps. My love to the children, & let what fate befall us, believe me always true to you & mindful of your true affection.[45]

General William Tecumseh Sherman at a West Point reunion in 1877. (Courtesy of Special Collections, United States Military Academy Library)

Ellen Ewing Sherman. Painting by G. P. A. Healy. (Courtesy of the National Gallery of Art)

John Sherman as secretary of the treasury in 1879. Painting by D. Huntington for the New York State Chamber of Commerce. (Courtesy of Special Collections, U.S.M.A. Library)

This painting of Ulysses S. Grant by Paul Louvrier overlooks the main reading room of the West Point Library. (Courtesy of Special Collections, U.S.M.A. Library)

Siege of Vicksburg. Sherman's sharpshooters in the rifle pits. From *Frank Leslie's Illustrated*. (Courtesy of Special Collections, U.S.M.A. Library)

Sherman's troops at Vicksburg attack the Confederates with hand grenades on June 13, 1863. The opposing lines were twenty feet apart. From *Frank Leslie's Illustrated*. (Courtesy of Special Collections, U.S.M.A. Library)

Sherman at the height of his fame. Charcoal drawing by
George I. Parrish Jr. (From the author's collection)

Sherman's great Confederate rival, General Joseph E. Johnston. During the presidency of Grover Cleveland, Sherman helped get him a federal job. (Courtesy of Special Collections, U.S.M.A. Library)

Sherman's classmate and longtime friend, General George H. Thomas. (Courtesy of Special Collections, U.S.M.A. Library)

Confederate General John B. Hood, who became friendly with the Shermans after the war. (Courtesy of Special Collections, U.S.M.A. Library)

"Engagement at Snake Creek Gap," at the beginning of the Atlanta campaign. Sketch by Theodore R. Davis, who accompanied Sherman's troops, for *Harper's Weekly*, June 4, 1864. (Courtesy of Special Collections, U.S.M.A. Library)

Sherman's troops at Kennesaw Mountain, June 22, 1864. The mountain is four miles in length and some four hundred feet high. From *Frank Leslie's Illustrated*. (Courtesy of Special Collections, U.S.M.A. Library)

Civilians moving south from Atlanta during Sherman's bombardment of the city. This sketch by D. R. Brown appeared in *Harper's Weekly* on October 15, 1864. (Courtesy of Special Collections, U.S.M.A. Library)

General Oliver Otis Howard, who led one wing of Sherman's army on the great march. (Courtesy of the Library of Congress)

General Henry W. Slocum, who led the other wing of Sherman's army on the great march. (Courtesy of the National Archives)

General Sherman and his staff in a large Confederate fort west of Atlanta, October 1864. Sherman is facing left with his arm on the cannon. Kennesaw Mountain is in the distance. Photo by Sherman's official photographer, George N. Barnard. (From the Orlando M. Poe Collection, Special Collections, U.S.M.A. Library)

Sherman's men occupying a Confederate fort looking south after the fall of Atlanta. Photo by George N. Barnard. (From the Orlando M. Poe Collection, Special Collections, U.S.M.A. Library)

Sherman's Bummers foraging in South Carolina. From *Frank Leslie's Illustrated.* The artist reported that on this plantation, owned by a leading Confederate named Fitzgerald, the Federals confiscated $70,000 in gold and silver and a large cache of the finest Madeira wine. (Courtesy of Special Collections, U.S.M.A. Library)

Thomas Ewing Sherman, who broke his father's heart when he decided to become a
Jesuit. In 1858 and 1865 his mother, who insisted she had nothing to do with Tom's
decision, wrote Sherman of her desire that Tom become a priest. Sherman disinherited
Tom but later tore up the will. (Courtesy of Special Collections, U.S.M.A. Library)

The Sherman statue by Augustus Saint-Gaudens was unveiled in New York on Memorial Day of 1903. Made of bronze, the statue, like its granite base, is gilded. It now stands on Fifth Avenue at the beginning of Central Park. The model for the head of Victory was the general's beautiful niece, Elizabeth Sherman Cameron, whom Henry Adams loved for twenty-five years. (Courtesy of Special Collections, U.S.M.A. Library)

12

"We Must Kill Those Three Hundred Thousand"

— I —

GENERAL WINFIELD SCOTT once offered advice to Grant, Sherman, and any other Northern generals who would listen. "Beware of Lee advancing," he warned, "and watch Johnston on the retreat. You may whip Johnston at a stand; but the devil himself would be defeated in the attempt to whip him retreating." Johnston excelled, Southern newspapers hopefully suggested in early May of 1864, at drawing an enemy from his position and then pouncing upon him.[1]

For the Union forces the campaign began on the morning of May 7, when Thomas moved on Tunnel Hill, the next town down the railroad line from Ringgold. He found it practically undefended. Tunnel Hill offered a panoramic view. From it Sherman could see a mountain range, Rocky Face, which Howard, commanding the Fourth Corps of Thomas's army, thought resembled the Palisades that ran along the Hudson River in steepness and appearance. A gap called Buzzard's Roost cut the mountain in two and opened the way to Dalton, three miles beyond. Through it passed a road, a small stream, and the Western & Atlantic Railroad. Sherman avoided a direct attack on Buzzard's Roost, for Johnston had made a fortress of it.[2]

Shortly after Sherman had taken over the Division of the Mississippi, he went to Chattanooga to discuss matters with Thomas. At the meeting Thomas, who knew the geography of the area better than anyone else, suggested a plan to overwhelm Johnston at the start of the campaign. McPherson and Schofield would draw Johnston's attention by feigning a direct assault on Buzzard's Roost. Thomas, meanwhile, would "throw my whole force through Snake Creek Gap," ten miles south and west of Dalton and five northeast of Resaca, the next stop on the railroad line. Knowing Snake Creek Gap to be unguarded, Thomas intended to place his force between Dalton and Resaca, thereby blocking John-ston's rear. The only path open to the enemy would be to the east, through "difficult country." If Johnston attacked, Thomas was sure to repulse him. Sherman rejected the plan, arguing that he wanted to use the Army of the Cumberland as the reserve for his other two armies.[3]

But Sherman adopted a modified version of the scheme. On the May morning that Dodge, commanding the Sixteenth Corps of the Army of the Tennessee, reported, Sherman ordered McPherson to send him that night to Ship's Gap, in the first range of mountains leading into Snake Creek Gap. "Why, General," McPherson pointed out, "that is thirty miles away." "No mat-ter," Sherman responded, "let him try it." Dodge asked for a guide, and McPherson promised to send one if he could find one. Sherman handed Dodge a map with the road and Ship's Gap marked. About midnight of the next night, May 8, one of Dodge's brigades reached the summit of Ship's Gap and passed through Snake Creek Gap before the Confederates discovered that Union troops were behind them.[4]

In instructions to McPherson, dated May 5, 1864, Sherman made clear his desire. "I want you to move . . . to Snake Gap, secure it and from it make a bold attack on the enemy's flank or his railroad at any point between Tilton and Resaca," a distance of seven miles. He added:

> . . . I hope the enemy will fight at Dalton, in which case he can have
> no force there that can interfere with you. But, should his policy be to
> fall back along his railroad, you will hit him in the flank. Do not fail in
> that event to make the most of the opportunity by the most vigorous
> attack possible, as it may save us what we have most reason to appre-
> hend—a slow pursuit, in which he gains strength as we lose it. In ei-
> ther event you may be sure the forces north of you will prevent his
> turning on you alone.

To both Thomas and Schofield, who were to keep Johnston occupied at Dal-ton, Sherman noted that McPherson was to go through Snake Creek Gap, break the railroad if possible, and strike Johnston's flank if he found the Confederates retreating.[5]

At six o'clock on the morning of May 9 Dodge, with two divisions, headed toward the Rome crossroads in Sugar Valley, there to await further orders. Reaching the crossroads after a minor cavalry battle in which the Confederates were routed, Dodge, receiving assurance that General John A. Logan's Fif-teenth Corps was behind him, was ordered forward to the road connecting Cal-houn and Dalton, one mile west of Resaca. After capturing a small enemy force at Bald Hill, three quarters of a mile west of Resaca, Dodge notified McPher-son, who soon arrived and, Dodge remembered, "directed me to send a few mounted men up the Dalton road to reconnoiter the country and find an ap-proach to the railroad in that direction." Eighteen cavalrymen, "all I had left," took off, striking the railroad about two miles south of Tilton. Finding the area patrolled by enemy cavalry, the Federals succeeded in cutting the telegraph wires and in burning a wood station. They reported back to Dodge at dark.[6]

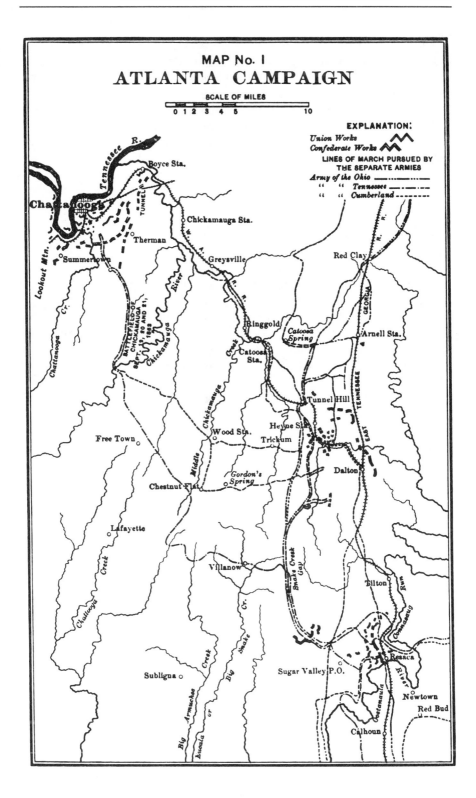

MAP No. I

ATLANTA CAMPAIGN

SCALE OF MILES

EXPLANATION:

Union Works
Confederate Works

LINES OF MARCH PURSUED BY
THE SEPARATE ARMIES

Army of the Ohio
"   "   Tennessee
"   "   Cumberland

A movement late in the afternoon by Dodge's Fourth Division also failed to reach the railroad. Viewing through a spyglass the Confederate works in Resaca, defended by 4,000 men, McPherson concluded that an attack on the town would have enabled Johnston to cut him off from the rest of Sherman's army "as you cut off the end of a piece of tape with a pair of shears." Between 5:00 and 6:00 P.M. he ordered his entire force back toward the gap.[7]

Waiting anxiously for word from McPherson, Sherman conjured up images of complete victory. At seven o'clock the next morning he wrote Halleck that he believed "McPherson has destroyed Resaca." If so, he would "swing round through Snake Creek Gap and interpose" between Johnston and Georgia. But by that evening Sherman knew that McPherson "did not break the road." Following instructions, McPherson had drawn back "to the debouches of the gorge. . . . I must feign on Buzzard Roost, but pass through Snake Creek Gap, and place myself between Johnston and Resaca, when we will have to fight it out. I am making the preliminary move. . . . I will be in no hurry."[8]

As time went on and Sherman mulled over the events of May 9, the more the disappointed general exaggerated his instructions to McPherson. "Had McPherson fallen on Resaca with the violence I had ordered," Sherman wrote John the next month, "Johnston's army would have retreated eastward losing all his Artillery & wagons. Since that time I have had no alternative but to press his Rear." And in his campaign report that September, two months after McPherson had been killed, Sherman said of the episode: "I was somewhat disappointed at the result." As Captain Henry Stone, who served on Thomas's staff during the campaign, later observed: "Disappointment is a mild word to apply to the feeling he showed when he learned of the failure of his cherished scheme. If he had said, 'I was extremely angry, and almost determined to relieve McPherson of his command,' his statement would have been nearer the truth."[9]

For two days, May 10 and 11, Sherman corresponded much but did little. Finally, on the twelfth, he began moving his forces around Dalton to Snake Creek Gap. That night, warned by the concentration of Federals at the Gap, Johnston evacuated Dalton, taking with him everything of value.

By the thirteenth the two armies faced each other before Resaca. Standing behind four miles of entrenchments, General Leonidas Polk held the Confederate left, General William J. Hardee the center, and General John B. Hood the right. Sherman arranged his forces in a semicircle opposite the enemy. McPherson, occupying the Union right, faced Polk, Thomas opposed Hardee, and Schofield, on Thomas's left, confronted Hood. Howard, commanding Thomas's Fourth Corps, took up a position on the extreme left.

Skirmishing began the next morning. Sherman and Thomas then rode along the line, inspecting it, parking ambulances, and placing batteries. Early in the day a mix-up developed on the Union left. General John M. Palmer's Fourteenth Corps found itself crowded between Hooker's Twentieth and Schofield's Twenty-third. As the Federals advanced, the troops of General Absalom Baird, commanding Palmer's Third Division, interspersed with those of General Henry M. Judah, commanding Schofield's Second Division. At eleven o'clock, when General Jacob D. Cox, on the extreme left, began attacking the Confederate works, Judah insisted on following, even though his men and Baird's were mixed up. Ignoring Baird's pleas for time, Judah sent forward both divisions before Baird had time to notify his brigade commanders of the attack. Not knowing what was ahead, the divisions descended the almost vertical slope of a ridge and emerged into an open valley plainly visible to the Confederates. Those who reached a creek got stuck in its miry banks and were driven back. Four days later Sherman relieved Judah of his command.[10]

Heavy fighting took place in the center of the line. Two divisions of Hood's corps emerged from the Confederate works, swung to the left, and attacked the troops of General David M. Stanley, commanding Howard's First Division. Stanley's line wavered, and the regiments on the left dropped back in confusion and disorder. Informed by Howard of the battle, Thomas, with Sherman standing at his side, sent over General Alpheus S. Williams's First Division of Hooker's corps. "Into the deadly breach, over the bodies of the fallen," reported Captain Joseph W. Miller of the *Cincinnati Commercial*, "came on the double-quick" Colonel James S. Robinson's brigade. It "advanced to the assault with desperate determination to drive back the solid columns of the enemy, and save the army from disaster. . . . A nation's thanks are due Joe Hooker, and may it never forget Robinson's brave brigade, whose gallantry to-night is on every tongue."[11]

The battle continued on Sunday, May 15. But on that day General Thomas W. Sweeny, the one-armed Irishman who led a division of Dodge's corps, was able, after an unsuccessful attempt the previous night, to cross the Oostenaula River at Lay's Ferry and, after sharp fighting, was able to protect the laying of a pontoon bridge. His communications threatened, Johnston abandoned Resaca and that night crossed to the south side of the Oostenaula.[12]

Even this early, Schofield remembered, rivalries developed within the Union army. During the early fighting Cox took a hill that offered a view of the enemy's works. Schofield, Cox's commander, immediately rode over to tell Sherman. A score of generals, including Sherman, Thomas, and Hooker, came back with Schofield, for they wanted to see the fortifications McPherson had feared to attack. The group on the hill was so large that it soon attracted the attention of Confederate sharpshooters and cannoneers. The enemy fire became so heavy that all the generals, except Sherman and Hooker, dashed for cover. Neither of these brave peacocks would give the other the satisfaction of moving first. The two strutted and pranced, seeming a foot taller than they actually were. Finally, as if following some signal, they slowly walked off together toward their horses and safety.[13]

—— II ——

As the armies moved south of the Oostenaula, the topography changed dramatically. The mountains around Chattanooga gave way to sandy, hilly soil. The armies entered an area with large houses, luxuriant farms, and magnificent trees. The cultivated fields overflowed with corn, wheat, and cotton. "The people have most all gone away—frightened away by rebel lies," Howard informed his wife. "Our men however are apt to pillage & destroy unless restrained."[14]

But the key to the campaign remained the railroad. Each mile Sherman marched into Georgia weakened his army. At Dalton and subsequent spots, Sherman was forced to leave garrisons to protect his lifeline. Only freight cars were allowed south of Chattanooga. Field and staff officers, with their possessions, traveled on top of these cars. Enlisted men, lieutenants, and captains were detained at Chattanooga. There a captain was assigned a lieutenant and fifty soldiers belonging to different regiments. He drew rations and equipment for these men. Then he was given one wagon and up to five hundred head of cattle, which he had to deliver to Sherman's chief commissary. The field and staff officers considered the top of freight cars, with its locomotive smoke, dust, and even rain, a luxury compared with driving cattle.

These herds left a path of destruction across Georgia. Their crops and houses trampled, families suffered greatly. Along with the wounded, they were often gathered up, put in the empty boxcars heading north, and shipped to Nashville. From there, in one of the cruelties of the Civil War, the Union quartermaster exiled them farther north, away from the railroad line. One officer found Paducah, Kentucky, along the Ohio River, filled with Georgians. Many of the towns north of Paducah were so saturated with refugees that the residents would not permit any more to come ashore.[15]

Johnston retreated along the Western & Atlantic, Sherman following. On the eighteenth Sherman's troops were at Adairsville, sixteen miles south of Resaca, where they destroyed the Georgia state arsenal. "If we can bring Johnston to battle this side of the Etowah, we must do it," Sherman advised Schofield, "even at the hazard of beginning battle with but part of our forces."[16]

Northern generals were sure that the Confederates planned to assault them before they reached the Etowah. If Johnston struck Hooker and Schofield while the Yankees were between Kingston and Cassville, just north of the river, Sherman would have found it difficult to send aid through the broken and rough terrain that formed a plateau. In his battle report, Johnston explained why the attack never took place. On the night of the nineteenth Polk and Hood argued that "Federal artillery would render their position untenable the next day, and urged me to abandon the ground immediately and cross the Etowah." Hardee, "whose position I thought weakest," disagreed and was sure he could hold his ground. But Johnston, facing opposition from two of his three corps commanders, "crossed the Etowah on the 20th, a step which I have regretted ever since."[17]

At this point Sherman decided to rest his army, now at Cassville and at Kingston, directly west of it. But Sherman had no rest. Howard left a picture of him sitting for hours by a window in his headquarters in Kingston, "drumming with his pencil upon the window sill." Occasionally he would transfer his thoughts to paper. When a church bell clanged, Sherman thought some of his soldiers were playing pranks. For interrupting him, he ordered them arrested. The transgressor turned out to be Howard's friend, Reverend E. P. Smith, of the United States Christian Commission, who was announcing Sunday services. The minister was hauled before Sherman, who, when told it was the Sabbath, said: "Sunday, Sunday! Didn't know it was Sunday; let him go." That morning the church was filled with Union soldiers.[18]

Writing Stanton from Kingston on May 23, Sherman was full of self-praise. In previous dispatches, he contended, he had underestimated his conquests "in prisoners, guns, muskets, and material." If Grant could "sustain the confidence, the esprit, the pluck of his army," engaged in bitter fighting as it approached Cold Harbor, Virginia, "he will do more good than to capture Richmond or any strategic advantage."

When Dana read the letter to Meade, the general's eyes bulged an inch and his voice sounded, according to his aide, Colonel Theodore Lyman, "like cutting an iron bar with a handsaw" as he replied: "Sir! I consider that dispatch an insult to the army I command and to me personally. The Army of the Potomac does not require General Grant's inspiration or anybody else's inspiration to make it fight!" All day and at dinner he described the Western troops as "an armed rabble." Even Grant had said that he had never seen such fighting as was taking place in Virginia.[19]

Meanwhile, Sherman extended his right and occupied Rome, where his men destroyed Confederate supplies and several factories used to make weapons. A little west of Rome, the Federals captured some large cotton mills that manufactured cloth for the Confederate army. "The mills were burned," remembered the colonel of the Twentieth Connecticut, "and some six hundred female operatives were sent north within our lines."[20]

Leaving Cassville, Johnston crossed the Etowah and moved ten miles south to Allatoona. Similar to Buzzard's Roost and Snake Creek Gap, it was, Sherman informed John, "a space of the Mountains making one of those formidable passes, which gives an army on the defensive so much advantage." Fortunately, Sherman knew the region well. In 1844, when helping Inspector General Churchill take testimony on the Florida War claims of Georgia volunteers, he had ridden over the area between the Etowah and Kennesaw Mountain. Recalling that Allatoona Pass was impenetrable, he decided to march his army west of the railroad and then to meet the Western & Atlantic again at Marietta, below Allatoona.[21]

On the night of the twenty-fourth, after marching in the rain over "mere cowpaths," much of the army camped at Burnt Hickory, which Stone called "as desolate, rocky, dreary, and forbidding a resting-place as ever sheltered an army." Sherman moved his army toward Dallas, eight miles south of Burnt Hickory and almost equidistant between Marietta to the east and the Chattahoochee River to the south. But Johnston had rushed his men, and on the evening of the twenty-fourth Hardee, holding the Confederate left, was just east of Dallas, Hood, on the right, was at New Hope Church, four miles northeast of Dallas, while Polk held the center, closer to Hood than to Hardee. "The whole of Johnston's army was admirably chosen for defense," noted Cox, being placed behind a series of ridges fronted by valleys.[22]

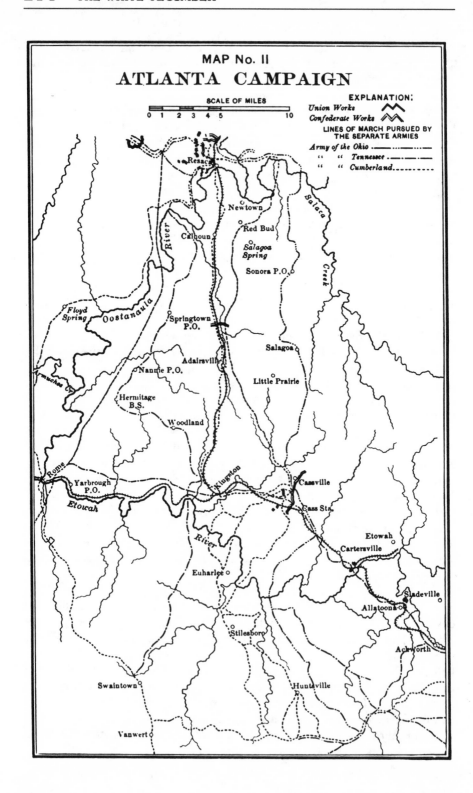

MAP No. II

ATLANTA CAMPAIGN

SCALE OF MILES

EXPLANATION:

Union Works
Confederate Works

LINES OF MARCH PURSUED BY
THE SEPARATE ARMIES

Army of the Ohio ....
"   "   Tennessee ....
"   "   Cumberland..........................

Unaware of the disposition of the Confederate forces, General John W. Geary found his division, Hooker's Second, facing on May 25 strong opposition. A prisoner brought the shocking news that Geary, his men deployed in woods so thick that, Stone remembered, "one could not see the length of a company," was facing Johnston's whole army. Adding to the danger, Geary's division was six or seven miles from any other unit of the Army of the Cumberland. "Almost in a whisper," Thomas ordered Stone "to ride back to Howard fast as I could and hurry up the Fourth Corps." Hearing increasing firing as he rode out of sight, Stone feared "that I should next hear of General Thomas as an inmate of Libby Prison."

Stone's journey proved eventful. At 2:20 P.M. he found Howard, some six or seven miles to the rear. Stone "never saw men moving so slowly; but Howard assured me he could not march faster without using them up." Heading back, Stone met Williams near Pumpkinvine Creek bridge, three miles from Geary's position. Told of the situation, Williams, "like the gallant soldier he was," rushed his men forward. Soon after, Stone stumbled upon Sherman, who, like the Sherman at Shiloh, seemed annoyed by the affair. "Let Williams go in anywhere as soon as he gets up," Sherman told Stone. "I don't see what they are waiting for in front now. There haven't been twenty rebels there today."[23]

At a little after 5:00 P.M. Hooker had his men lined up, and the battle began. "It would be impossible to conceive of a more appalling, terrifying, if not fatal, rain of lead and iron than this one, which our line met at New Hope Church," wrote Edward R. Brown of the Twenty-seventh Indiana. The intensity of the battle, fought until dark in the rain, led the soldiers to call the place "The Hornet's Nest" and "Hell Hole."[24]

After the battle, Sherman commiserated little with Hooker, whom he criticized for waiting until all three of his divisions had arrived before attacking. To McPherson that night, Sherman still questioned whether the Federals had faced Johnston's whole army. "We are in dense woods," he noted, "and see but little, but infer the enemy is behind hastily-constructed log barriers. . . . I don't believe there is anything more than Hood's corps, but still Johnston may have his whole army, and we should act on that hypothesis."[25]

Sherman's main attempt at flanking the enemy came on May 27. At ten that morning Howard was to "wheel" to the right, advance his left southward, and approach and turn the Confederate flank. Marching about, Howard could not find the Confederate flank. Finally, at Pickett's Mill, two miles northeast of New Hope Church, he ordered an attack. Charging "in steady throngs" to "within a few paces of our men," reported Confederate General Patrick R. Cleburne, the Federals shouted: "Ah! damn you, we have caught you without your logs now." Awaiting them "with calm determination," the Southerners "slaughtered them with deliberate aim." Confederate officers said they had never seen such carnage.[26]

At Dallas on the twenty-eighth more fighting developed. Believing the Yankees were pulling back, Johnston ordered Hardee to determine the Northerners' strength east of Dallas. If, as Johnston suspected, the Federals—principally Logan's corps—were weak, General William B. Bate's division was to attack. Bate's plan was to send a brigade against the enemy. Should it meet little opposition, four cannon shots would advise his three other brigades to charge. At 3:45 the first Confederate assault met with savage resistance. No cannon shots were fired, but two of Bate's three remaining brigades charged anyway, with tragic results. At Pickett's Mill the North sustained heavy losses. At Dallas it was the South's turn. "The scales," Howard observed, "were thus evenly balanced."[27]

McPherson's army now faced the problem of withdrawing from Dallas and of moving, as Sherman had ordered, toward the railroad at Marietta, thus getting below the mountains in front of Marietta. Several times on May 29 and 30 he attempted to withdraw, but each time, Sherman told Schofield and Thomas, "he was assaulted and felt compelled to resume his breast-works. It is utterly impossible that our enemy can hold all his line in strength, and we must work to the left."[28]

After riding over the ground, Sherman began moving the Army of the Tennessee to the left one division at a time. By June 1 McPherson was finally able to reach New Hope Church. Schofield and Hooker also "shifted to the extreme left," and on June 2 advanced two miles in heavy rain and thunderstorms. By June 5 McPherson was at Acworth, five miles below Allatoona and ten below the Etowah. "I expect the enemy to fight us at Ken[n]esaw Mountain, near Marietta," Sherman informed Halleck, "but I will not run head on his fortifications. An examination of his abandoned lines here show an immense line of works, all of which I have turned with less loss to ourselves than we have inflicted on him."[29] Sherman neglected to mention that the campaign to avoid the mountains and reach the railroad at Marietta had failed.

—— III ——

Brown noted that from June first on three things seemed to occur regularly. One was constant cannonading and picket firing. The second was "a deluge of rain." Finally, at least once or twice a day the regiment moved either to the front or to the flank, digging new entrenchments wherever it settled.[30]

Unlike late May, when they were bogged down, Sherman's men were able to move relatively swiftly. On June 4 Colonel Edward M. McCook's cavalry entered Acworth, driving from the town the last fifteen Confederates. The next day McPherson reached the railroad at Acworth, a village of twenty or thirty houses. Johnston retreated down the line to "the hills," Sherman told Halleck on June 11, "embracing" Lost Mountain, Pine Mountain, and Kennesaw. "The Etowah bridge is done and a construction train has been to our very camp. Supplies will now be accumulated in Allatoona Pass, or brought right up to our lines. One of my chief objectives being to give full employment to Johnston, it makes but little difference where he is, so he is not on this way to Virginia."[31]

From Acworth, Sherman dashed off to John his analysis of the campaign:

My long and single Line of Railroad to my Rear, of limited Capacity is the delicate point of my game, as also that fact that all of Georgia except the cleared bottoms, is densely wooded with few Roads, and at any point an enterprising enemy can in a few hours with axes & spades make across our path formidable works, whilst his sharpshooters & spies & servants in the guise of peaceable farmers can hang round us and kill our wagoners, messengers & carriers. It is a Big Indian War. Still thus far I have won five strong positions, advanced a hundred miles & am in possession of a large wheat growing region and all the Iron mines and works of Georgia. Johnstons army is still at my front and can fight or fall back as he pleases.—The future is uncertain but I will do all that is possible.[32]

On June 10 Sherman began moving again. Reinforced by the 9,000 men of Blair's Seventeenth Corps, McPherson, on the left, was to try to follow the rail-road from Acworth to Marietta. Thomas, in the center, was to "strike" the northern end of Kennesaw, the southernmost of the three mountains. Schofield, on the right, was to determine "the enemy's strength about Lost Mountain," the westernmost range. In heavy rain only McPherson made progress, reaching Big Shanty, the next station down from Acworth. From Big Shanty on the morn-ing of the eleventh, Sherman was able to see the strong Confederate fortifica-tions on Kennesaw and Pine Mountains. Late that night Captain John C. Van Duzer of Thomas's staff telegraphed to Washington: "Impression is prevalent that Johnston will fight here."[33]

Sherman was warming himself before a fire in an old house on the twelfth when he received a dispatch from Phil telling of the birth the day before of a baby boy. Sherman confessed to Ellen,

> It took me somewhat by surprise, but was not altogether unexpected. Well, I am glad you are over the terrible labor and hope that it is the last you will have to endure. Of course, I am pleased to know the sex of the child, as he must succeed to the place left vacant by Willy, though I fear we will never again be able to lavish on any one the love we bore for him. . . . I agree with you that we should retain Willys name vacant for his Memory, and that though dead to the world he yet lives fresh in our memories.

A few days later Ellen named the child, whom her husband would never see, Charles Celestine Sherman.[34]

With the army bogged down in rain and in "an interminable wilderness," Howard witnessed a touching scene. In a clearing he came upon a small, win-dowless cabin occupied by a mother and "six very pretty children." The woman and her son had planted a couple of acres of corn and wheat, but the soldiers and their animals had trampled everything. The woman cried to Howard that her husband was in the Southern army, but she and the little ones had not brought on the war. "Oh," Howard wrote to his wife, "how much misery & suf-fering grows out of this rebellion. Would God it might have an end."[35]

On the fourteenth, as the weather cleared, one of the most discussed inci-dents of the campaign occurred. Johnston, Polk, and Hardee rode over to view the enemy's position from the top of Pine Mountain. Walking about only 600 years from the Union lines, the three were in full view of Howard and his officers. Suddenly Sherman rode up. "How saucy they are," he said and ordered a nearby battery to fire at the group. Sherman then rode off to inspect another part of the line.

Noticing the gunners preparing to fire, Johnston warned his companions to scatter. Most of them ran, but Polk, stout and dignified, walked slowly. His biographer asserted that he strolled over to the edge of the hill to see the enemy better. A cannon shot crashed through his chest, killing him instantly. Kneeling beside Polk, Hardee wept: "this has been a dear visit . . . little did I think this morning that I should be called upon to witness this." Johnston joined in: "I would rather anything than this."

Howard learned of Polk's death later that day. Union signal officers, having broken the Confederate flag code, intercepted a message: "Why don't you send me an ambulance for General Polk's body?" "What Sherman and I noticed and remarked upon more than any gathering of men," Howard later wrote, "were the little tents which were pitched in plain sight on our side of the hill-crest. It seemed to us unusually defiant. After our cannon firing, the hostile tents disappeared."[36]

Determining who killed Polk constitutes an exercise in frustration. In 1932 Lloyd Lewis, in his biography of Sherman, credited the kill to Captain Hubert Dilger, a Prussian artillerist serving in the Fourteenth Corps. Dressed in buckskin breeches, he presented a romantic picture as he ordered his battery to fire by clapping his hands.[37]

Several others, including General Stanley, Captain Stone, Captain Alexis Cope of the Fifteenth Ohio, and some historians, believed the shot came from guns commanded by Captain Peter Simonson of the Fifth Indiana Battery. Simonson himself was killed by a Confederate sharpshooter two days after Polk. But as in the case of Dilger, those who attributed the shot to Simonson submitted neither proof nor details.[38]

Next came General Walter Q. Gresham, who led Blair's Fourth Division. In a letter to his wife, Gresham, who later served as President Chester A. Arthur's postmaster general and President Grover Cleveland's secretary of state, offered his candidate, Captain Edward Spear Jr.:

> Others claim the honor but there is no doubt about Spear's guns doing the work for prisoners that we captured the day of the charge pointed out to me just where Polk was killed which is immediately in my old front—Genl McPherson & Genl Sherman both say my Dro [Detachment of Regulars] has the honor of killing the rebel Bishop & General.[39]

Brown best analyzed these claims. He wrote:

> At least a dozen batteries, and more than a hundred gunners, claim the distinction of firing the fatal shot. Infantry regiments innumerable claim it was fired by the battery they were supporting, and probably

half the soldiers in Sherman's army claim they saw it fired. The latter claim would be hard to disprove, as the shot was fired in open day light and the mountain was visible to a large part of the army. The fact, as Sherman states it, is that this shot was one of a hundred or more, fired by several batteries in volleys. So it would be impossible, or almost so, to tell by what battery the shot was fired, much less who sighted the gun.[40]

Again rain set in, leading to an episode the Third Wisconsin long relished. Sherman was with the regiment near Pine Mountain when firing broke out in a ravine about a half mile away. Unrecognizable in his waterproof clothing, he ordered a lieutenant in the quartermaster department to ride over and find out what was going on. The adjutant of the Third Wisconsin recorded what happened:

> The lieutenant not liking such exposure said: "Excuse me, sir, I am a non-combatant" (with the accent on the bat). "A what, sir, a what, sir," growled Sherman, "a non-combat-ant? I did not know I had such a thing in my army. What is your name, sir?" By this time the quartermaster saw who he was talking to, and with apologies hurried off to get the information desired.[41]

For Sherman, the next few days were grim. Early in the morning of June 15 Thomas's men found Pine Mountain abandoned. Believing Johnston had fallen back everywhere, Sherman ordered an advance, which met with resistance. After inspecting the line, Sherman informed Halleck at 9:00 P.M. on June 16 that he was "now inclined to feign on both flanks and assault the center. . . . If, by assaulting, I can break his line, I see no reason why it would not produce a decisive effect." At nine the next night Sherman reported that Johnston "had abandoned Lost Mountain and some six miles of as good field-works as I ever saw. . . . My right now threatens his railroad to Atlanta. I worked hard to-day to get over to that road, but the troops seem timid in these dense forests of stumbling on a hidden breast-work."[42]

Rains continued on June 18 and Sherman spent part of the day writing to Grant a letter that tried to "explain" why "our movement has been slower than you calculated." Sherman's first stab at the Confederates, at Resaca, "was really fine," but McPherson "was a little over cautious" and enabled Johnston to escape. Still, McPherson "has done very well." Schofield, too, with a small force, "has done as well as I could ask." Seldom an admirer of Northern cavalrymen, Sherman went on to criticize his two chief officers, General Kenner Garrard and General George Stoneman. The first was "over-cautious," the second "lazy. . . . Each has had fine chances of cutting in but were easily checked by the appearance of an enemy."

Sherman saved his main criticism for Thomas and the Army of the Cumberland, which thus far had borne the brunt of the fighting. This army was "awful slow. A fresh furrow in a plowed field will stop the whole column and all begin to entrench. I have again and again tried to impress on Thomas that we must assail and not defend; we are the offensive, and yet it seems the whole Army of the Cumberland is so habituated to be on the defensive that, from its commander down to the lowest private, I cannot get it out of their heads." Sherman "came out without tents and ordered all to do likewise, yet Thomas has a headquarters camp on the style of Halleck at Corinth." Thomas "promised to send it all back, but the truth is everybody there is allowed to do as he pleases, and they still think and act as though the railroad and all its facilities were theirs."

Mulling the campaign over, Sherman concluded that Thomas's slowness had "cost me the loss of two splendid opportunities which never recur in war." The first was at New Hope Church—Sherman erroneously called it Dallas—when Hooker took four hours to get ready, enabling Johnston "to throw up works to cover the head of his column." The other occurred just yesterday, after the Federals "broke" one of Johnston's lines. A fast movement would have enabled the Northerners to reach the railroad near Marietta, thus getting behind Kennesaw. "I ordered Thomas to move at daylight, and when I got to the point at 9:30, I found Stanley and [Thomas J.] Wood quarreling which should not lead. I'm afraid I swore, and said what I should not, but I got them started." The army failed to reach the railroad back of Marietta, but Sherman assured Grant that he held "all the high and commanding ground" except Kennesaw, "which I can turn."[43]

To describe this letter, as one historian does, as "a craven and dishonest attempt to forestall censure from Grant for having failed to achieve decisive results in Georgia by putting the blame on others" is to misunderstand Sherman. Nor is it reasonable to deduce from one letter that Sherman had been "reduced to an emotional condition akin to the one that had afflicted him in Kentucky and Missouri in the autumn of 1861."[44]

In his letter, Sherman conceded that no army could "keep up with my thoughts and wishes." Impulsive and often short-sighted, Sherman the soldier achieved his lasting accomplishments not in battles but through marches and maneuvers. After the war, newspapermen such as Joseph B. McCullagh of the *Cincinnati Commercial* and the *St. Louis Globe-Democrat* often joked, with some accuracy, that it was impossible to find a battle Sherman had won. In his reports, his letters, and later in his *Memoirs*, Sherman was guilty of exaggerations and distortions. But if anything, the letter to Grant indicated not Sherman's insanity but his vanity and his frustration at being bogged down. It also demonstrated his impulsiveness—when writing he usually just dashed off whatever came to mind. Schofield, his friend for thirty years, considered this quality his greatest weakness.[45]

___ IV ___

By June 20 Hooker feared that his corps, consisting of the divisions of Williams, Geary, and Daniel Butterfield, had fought so hard that it would soon collapse. "He only wonders that there is a man alive in it," his adjutant wrote of Geary's unit, "and Butterfield's division is in the same condition; Williams' but very little better."[46]

Nonetheless, on June 22 Sherman ordered Hooker to advance toward Marietta from a position to the west of the town. Schofield, occupying the extreme right, protected Hooker's right. At Kolb's Farm, at the road connecting Powder Springs and Marietta, Hood attacked. Federal losses were slight, but Hood's casualties totaled 1,500.[47]

Strangely enough, the Union victory worsened the enmity between Sherman and Hooker, which went back to the days when both served on the staff of General Persifer Smith. While in California, Hooker had gambled heavily, speculated in land, and refused to pay debts incurred in the cordwood business. Several times he ended up in court. One story had it that he borrowed money from Halleck and Sherman and never repaid it.

There were other things. Late in 1863, in a long letter to his friend, Secretary of the Treasury Salmon P. Chase, Hooker scoffed that during the Chattanooga campaign Sherman, after four fruitless assaults, had withdrawn "with losses more severe than those experienced by that officer in his attack on Vicksburg, the 28th and 29th of December 1862. . . . Sherman is an active, energetic officer, but in judgment is as infirm as Burnside. He will never be successful. Please remember what I tell you." During the Atlanta campaign Hooker so openly criticized Sherman's timidity that Butterfield warned him: "You must be guarded."[48]

Having been in battle after battle, Hooker was jittery at Kolb's Farm. At four in the afternoon, a half hour before Hood began his main assault, Hooker informed Thomas that Confederate "prisoners represent that the whole rebel army lies between my immediate front and Marietta, and that they are marching in this direction." Dismissing Hooker's complaint that his line was too thin and needed reinforcing, Thomas answered: "Your line is no weaker than General Howard's, and he has maintained himself against all attacks up to the present time." At midnight of that day Hooker in effect conceded Thomas had been right when he informed his superior: "The conduct of the troops throughout the day was sublime."[49]

Sherman soon entered the picture. In the afternoon of June 22, while standing on a hill in front of Thomas's center, he signaled Hooker: "How are you getting along? Near what house are you?" The answer, although sent at 5:30 P.M., did not reach Sherman until 9:30: "We have repulsed two heavy attacks and feel confident, our only apprehension being from our extreme right flank. Three entire corps are in front of us." Notifying Thomas of the messages, Sherman recalled that at 5:30 he was but two miles from the Kolb house. He had heard "some cannonading," but had "no idea" Hooker was being attacked. To both Hooker and Thomas, Sherman expressed doubt that the Twentieth faced three corps. That would be Johnston's entire army. Especially puzzling was Hooker's comment about his right flank, for in written instructions, for which Schofield had signed that morning, Sherman had ordered Schofield to protect Hooker's right.[50]

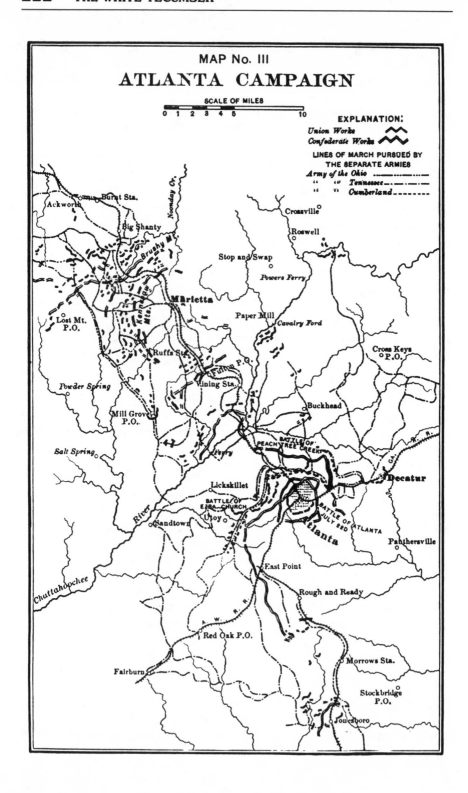

MAP No. III

ATLANTA CAMPAIGN

SCALE OF MILES

0 1 2 3 4 5   10

EXPLANATION:

Union Works

Confederate Works

LINES OF MARCH PURSUED BY
THE SEPARATE ARMIES

Army of the Ohio ....
   "   "   Tennessee ....
   "   "   Cumberland ....

Thomas, too, was puzzled. Responding to Sherman at ten that evening, he gave no details of the battle because he obviously knew as little about it as Sherman. He had, he told Sherman, believed earlier in the day that Hooker "was stampeded" when he had complained about the thinness of his line, but Thomas now conceded that the enemy might have thrown against Hooker "as much of his force as he could possibly spare." To be safe, Thomas had sent Howard to support Hooker. Schofield, moreover, had told Thomas "in person" that he had followed Sherman's orders about protecting the right. Thomas's last sentence exuded confidence: "The enemy cannot possibly send an ovewhelming force against Hooker without exposing his weakness to McPherson."[51]

Riding over to Kolb's Farm the next day, Sherman was severe, directing at Hooker three complaints. Hooker, Sherman charged, had violated propriety by sending his response of 5:30 to Sherman himself, even though Hooker was answering a message from Sherman. Sherman next argued that Hooker's comment about the extreme right insulted Schofield, even though Schofield never thought so and remained friendly with Hooker. Finally, Sherman took issue with Hooker's assertion that he faced Johnston's three corps. In his *Memoirs* Sherman insisted that "I reproved him more gently than the occasion demanded." But Hooker's biographer displayed more accuracy when he commented: "This was sorry treatment of the man who so far had carried the brunt of Sherman's fighting."[52]

— V —

As the days slipped by, Sherman, his army bogged down, jumped from one idea to another. "I have nothing new to report," he informed Halleck on the evening of June 25. Still looking beyond Kennesaw to Marietta, Sherman hoped to "stretch" Johnston's line "until he weakens it and then break through." The following day Sherman wrote Ellen: "My Lines are ten miles long, and every change necessitates a large amount of work. Still we are now all ready and I *must* attack direct or turn the position. Both will be attended with loss and difficulty—but one or the other must be attempted."[53]

By this time Sherman had already decided to attack. "An army to be efficient," he explained in his campaign report, "must not settle down to a single mode of offense, but must be prepared to execute any plan which promises success. I wanted, therefore, for the moral effect to make a successful assault against the enemy behind his breast-works, and resolved to attempt it at that point where success would give the largest fruits of victory."[54]

Sherman's order of June 24 called for all three of his armies to attack. But after inspecting the enemy works to Schofield's front, Sherman decided to send the Twenty-third Corps on a diversion along the Union right flank. Riding with Thomas along the front lines trying to find a spot to assault, Stone remembered their frustration. Searching for half a day, riding at times almost into enemy pickets, Thomas found nothing, settling for a place simply because the Union and Confederate lines were close. "The whole army," Stone recalled, "was in a fever of anxiety, dread and hope."[55]

Taking place on the hottest day of June, the attack, as Stone pointed out, brought only "death" and "utter failure." Northern casualties numbered 2,600, Southern but 522. "It is a wonder," commented Howard, "our loss was not greater." Seven brigade and regimental commanders and a chief of artillery were killed. Four regimental commanders were wounded. Among the dead was Howard's young friend, Brigadier General Charles G. Harker, whom he compared to McPherson in ability and personality. Harker had been a cadet at West Point when Howard taught there.[56]

Wounded at Kennesaw was twenty-eight-year-old Colonel Daniel McCook, Sherman's former law partner in Kansas. Shot in the right breast just below the collarbone while leading a charge, he was carried off the field and taken to his home in Steubenville, Ohio. On July 16 he received a message from Sherman telling him of his promotion to brigadier general. "The promotion is too late now," McCook responded. "Return my compliments, saying 'I decline the honor.'" The next day he died. He was buried in Cincinnati, eventually joined by his father, who was killed leading militia against the Confederate raider John Hunt Morgan, and four brothers, all of whom died in battle.[57]

Learning of McCook's death, Ellen wrote Cump:

> Poor Dan McCook is gone. I am very very sorry and feel truly sad about it, particularly as I fear whilst serving his country he forgot his God. . . . What is time & what is earthly glory to poor Dan McCook now? And our Willy—how differently he now views these things from his home in heaven. May his prayers be your shield & guard until we all join him to be separated no more.[58]

While the main attack on Kennesaw brought no benefits, the diversion by Schofield along the Union right flank paid enormous dividends. At 4:00 A.M. on the twenty-seventh Cox, with Schofield's Third Division, maneuvered about the enemy's left. Well to the southwest of Kennesaw and Marietta, he drove the enemy down Sandtown Road and crossed Olley's Creek. At noon, reporting in person to Schofield, he said that he had advanced to the crest of the ridge overlooking the valley of Nickajack Creek, which meandered parallel to and west of the railroad before emptying into the Chattahoochee River. From this point Cox clearly saw Johnston's works. He believed that, if reinforced by General Milo S. Hascall's Second Division, he could threaten the enemy's left rear. Late in the afternoon, Schofield signaled Cox: "Make your position very strong. I regard it as the key to the next movement."[59]

Within the next few days Sherman strengthened his right. On July 1 Schofield's corps, reinforced by a division from Hooker, pushed to within five miles of the Chattahoochee. At 4:00 A.M. on the next morning the energetic General Morgan L. Smith of Logan's corps crossed his men from the left to the right of the Union line, and at 7:30 A.M. Schofield was able to report: "Smith's division is here."[60]

During the night of July 2 Johnston's army abandoned Kennesaw and withdrew through Marietta, ripping up a mile of track as it went. Sherman's army was in pursuit, Thomas following the railroad and McPherson moving along the Sandtown Road toward the mouth of Nickajack Creek. "Whether the enemy will halt this side of Chattahoochee or not," Sherman informed Halleck on the morning of the third, "will soon be known." By evening, however, Sherman had convinced himself that Johnston would cross the river as rapidly as possible.[61]

The Fourth of July proved Sherman to be wrong. The Federals pressed the Confederates to a line of works at Smyrna Camp Ground, six miles below Marietta. When Howard, with whom Sherman was visiting, warned that the enemy was strongly entrenched at the edge of a thick woods, Sherman responded: "Nonsense, Howard, he is laughing at you. You ought to move straight ahead. Johnston's main force must be across the river." After fighting broke out, Sherman conceded: "Howard, you were right."[62]

By the fifth the Confederates were gone, having withdrawn to a commanding line of entrenchments almost six miles long along the north bank of the Chattahoochee, a deep, rapid stream passable in the main only over bridges. By the next day the Union left extended up the river to the mill town of Roswell, which Garrard's cavalry captured, the right downstream to the mouth of Sweetwater Creek. From his headquarters at Vining Station, directly opposite Johnston's fortifications, Sherman could peer down on the enemy and on Atlanta, nine miles away.[63]

Having learned his lesson at Kennesaw, Sherman again decided to get behind Johnston. On the eighth Schofield was able to cross the river and set up two pontoon bridges between Johnston's northernmost entrenchments and Roswell, but the Federals needed a bridge at Roswell.[64]

At the river Dodge's Sixteenth Corps, with the rest of McPherson's army, occupied the extreme right. Sherman rode over to Dodge's headquarters, took out his map, and asked Dodge, perhaps the greatest railroad builder of his day, how long it would take to construct a bridge at Roswell, about thirty miles away. Believing he would have to go into the woods to get timber, Dodge estimated a week. An hour later McPherson ordered him to Roswell. There Garrard had found some wool and cotton mills, whose owner proclaimed his neutrality by flying over his house a French flag. Garrard had burned most of the mills. With Sherman's permission to "destroy all Georgia" if needed to make the bridge "good and strong," Dodge took apart whatever still stood and used the beams. The Sixteenth Corps arrived on Monday. By Wednesday the bridge, 710 feet long and wide enough to accommodate armies going in both directions, was finished. Informed by Lieutenant Edward Jonas of Dodge's staff that the structure was ready, Sherman laughed, believing the report to be a joke. Assured by Jonas it was true, Sherman called it an astonishing piece of work.[65]

Because the mills made fabrics for Confederate shirts, Sherman instructed Garrard to arrest its workers, four hundred young women. Each of Garrard's cavalrymen carried a woman, and her children if she wished, on his horse twelve miles to Marietta. From there Sherman sent them on trains toward

Indiana, for, he told Halleck, "they are as much governed by the rules of war as if in the ranks." In 1906 Colonel William D. Pickett, Hardee's inspector general, still boiled over the incident. He denounced the burning of the factories as "unnecessary and wanton destruction of private property; but when it was emphasized by the gathering together of the operatives, composed largely of women and children, shipping them to Louisville, Ky., and turning them loose in a large city, these acts will forever be a stain upon the character of the Federal commander."[66]

—— VI ——

Johnston again retreated. On the night of the ninth he withdrew to the south side of the Chattahoochee. Just after the war, when they became friends, Johnston revealed to Sherman that the crossing of the river by the Federals greatly demoralized him, convincing him, Sherman later told his engineer, Captain Orlando M. Poe, "that I had the Army & ability to do pretty much what I wanted."[67]

Some units crossed the Chattahoochee over pontoon bridges. Others eventually crossed at Roswell. Still others, such as the Eighty-first Ohio, "preceded by a brass band, discoursing music all the sweeter for being on the water," waded across. With trees to protect them from the burning rays of the sun, a river in which to swim, and numerous springs of sparkling water nearby, the troops found the banks of the river the most peaceful place they had yet seen in Georgia.

During the stay along the Chattahoochee the Northern and Southern troops arranged an informal truce. Rebels bathed in the river alongside Yankees. Indeed, the story circulated that Sherman, while bathing nude in the river, was approached by a teamster who did not know him and asked, "Water is cold, eh?" "Not very, sir," Sherman answered with utmost civility.

On shore the Confederates mingled freely with the Federals, exchanging tobacco for coffee. "Warm-hearted, full of fun, ready to give or take a joke, never harsh or ill-tempered," observed the historian of the 150th New York Infantry of the Southerners, "in all—except uniforms—they seemed one with ourselves."[68]

In seven weeks Sherman's army had marched from Chattanooga to within a half dozen miles of Atlanta. But the campaign was more innovative technically than tactically. To protect the railroad, the army's salvation, Captain William E. Merrill, Thomas's chief engineer, developed the octagonal two-story blockhouse. Allowing soldiers to see in all directions, it proved so effective that in August and September 1864, when General Joseph E. Wheeler took his Confederate cavalry from Atlanta to Nashville and then to the Tennessee River, he was able to destroy only one small railroad bridge.

Innovations also helped Sherman's army cross natural obstacles. Merrill invented the hinged canvas pontoon bridge. Built in Nashville, it could be folded, carried in an army wagon, and used for crossing streams. "In lightness and mobility," Merrill told Sherman, "I think it has no superior." Sherman's railroad bridges were equally unique. Composed of interchangeable parts, they could be pieced together in hours. "The rapidity with which Sherman spanned rivers and chasms," observed one regimental historian, "not only dumbfounded the rebels, but astonished his own men."

Merrill bragged, too, about his method of acquainting the army commanders with the terrain. Each day he sent observers to see what was ahead. Through a "fac-simile photo-printing process" that used tissue paper and sunlight, Merrill then printed and distributed negative image maps (white lines on black background) containing the latest information. Never before had an army gone to such lengths to overcome its ignorance of geography.[69]

While Sherman watered himself and his horse in the Chattahoochee, tragedy struck at home. "Poor James is dead," John wrote of their eldest brother. Fanny Sherman's husband, Charles W. Moulton, who practiced law in Cincinnati, had employed him "upon his solemn & repeated pledge to me that he would not drink—This he frequently did—& had spells of Delirium before he died—and died in the effort to break off his habit." Ellen, sick since the birth of the baby, dragged herself out of bed to attend the funeral.

In his letter, John discussed the Republican presidential ticket, nominated that June, of Lincoln and Andrew Johnson:

> As for Lincoln & politics there is absolute indifference. No one seems to think or care for the political canvass. No meetings are held and no speeches are made. Every one holds himself uncommitted as far as possible waiting for events. Heretofore at this season of the Presidential year, we have had excitement without limit. Now there is nothing. If the Democratic leaders had a particle of patriotism or sense they would beat us easily. . . . The conviction is general that Lincoln has not the energy, dignity or character to either conduct the war or to make Peace. . . . A popular ticket would be Grant & Sherman—You have been associated together in the popular mind & could easily be elected. I know that such an event would be repulsive to you and I do not for your sake desire it, but only allude to popular opinion.[70]

On the morning of July 17 the last of Sherman's army, Palmer's and Hookers' corps, crossed the Chattahoochee. Sherman now divided his army into two wings, the right consisting of these two corps plus a division of Howard's, the left including McPherson's troops augmented by Schofield and Howard's two other divisions. At two o'clock on the afternoon of the eighteenth, Logan's men reached the Georgia Railroad near Stone Mountain, fourteen miles east of Atlanta, and by evening had ripped up five miles of track. That night Sherman slept at Sam House's, a large plantation from which everybody but "a sick negro" had fled. The plantation lay eleven miles from Atlanta.[71]

Throughout the campaign Dodge kept two spies in Atlanta with instructions to report only to him, and then only in great emergencies. Early on the morning of July 19 one of them, a member of the Second Iowa Infantry, came out with the Atlanta paper. It contained the order, dated the seventeenth, relieving Johnston and placing Hood in command of the Confederate army. Johnston had been removed even though, with a weak cavalry that was actually a quarter of the 10,000 troopers listed, he had lost but 10,000 men to Sherman's 20,000. Knowing the importance of this news, Dodge rode over to Schofield, with whom Sherman was marching that day. Sherman asked Schofield, Hood's classmate at West Point, what they could now expect. "This means a fight," Schofield answered. "Hood will attack you within twenty-four hours." Sherman then sat down on a tree stump by the roadside and issued orders calling McPherson in from Stone Mountain and closing his force around Thomas.[72]

This prediction proved accurate. Hood ordered two of his three corps, those of Hardee and General Alexander P. Stewart, the latter commanding Polk's old unit, to attack the Federals at Peachtree Creek, which, Hood explained in his campaign report, emptied into the Chattahoochee near the Western & Atlantic crossing and formed a "considerable obstacle to the passage of an army. . . . Feeling it impossible to hold Atlanta without giving battle, I determined to strike the enemy while attempting to cross this stream."

The attack, from right to left, was intended to drive the Federals into a pocket south of Peachtree Creek. It was to begin at one o'clock on July 20. But that morning General Joseph Wheeler of the Confederate cavalry observed McPherson's and Schofield's troops advancing unopposed from Decatur toward Atlanta. To cover the Decatur Road, Hood decided to move his army to the right, a half mile or so. The movement, replete with frequent stops, ate up three hours.[73]

Finally, at 4:00 P.M., the Confederate attack fell heavily on units of the Army of the Cumberland. Hardee assaulted General John Newton's division of Howard's corps, which had already crossed the creek and had set up a rail barricade, and Stewart the three divisions of Hooker's corps, then in open ground. Also involved was a brigade of Palmer's Fourteenth Corps, making a total of four divisions and one brigade that repulsed the attack of two Confederate corps. Hood blamed the delays—and the defeat—on Hardee, who in turn used much of his report on the battle to defend himself.[74]

Spending the day with Schofield and Howard, Sherman did not even know a battle was going on until Thomas signaled the message to him at 6:15 P.M. During the twentieth, McPherson, east of Atlanta, had moved cautiously, fearing the bulk of the enemy force was to his front. At 8:45 P.M. he realized his mistake and reported to Sherman: "I do not think there has been much of anything but cavalry in front of us on the left." That day McPherson might well have advanced to the outskirts of Atlanta.[75]

The next morning, when Sherman and Thomas came to look over the battlefield, Hooker spoke with pride of the fight put up by his men, pointing to his losses, close to 1,700 killed, wounded, and missing. Implying that there had been mass desertions, Sherman callously answered: "Oh, most of 'em will be back in a day or two." Hearing that, Lieutenant Colonel Charles H. Asmussen, Hooker's assistant inspector general, "almost beside himself with rage," begged

Stone "to give him a pistol that he might shoot the condemned son of a female dog who cast such a slur on brave men."[76]

Hood was not through assaulting. During the night of the twentieth he learned from Wheeler that McPherson's left flank stood exposed, "standing out in the air" near the Georgia Railroad between Decatur and Atlanta. In and around Decatur, which lay east of Atlanta, Wheeler found large numbers of enemy wagons. Hood planned to send Hardee around McPherson's left and rear. Meantime, Stewart and General Benjamin F. Cheatham, in command of Hood's former corps, were, along with General Gustavus W. Smith and the Georgia militia, to cover Atlanta's defenses.[77]

Sherman first interpreted the withdrawal of Stewart and Cheatham as a sign that the Confederates were abandoning Atlanta. Indeed, during the night Schofield, Howard, Palmer, and Hooker all reported that the enemy had abandoned its works and was retreating. Stone remembered Colonel Charley Ewing riding into Thomas's camp at sunrise of the twenty-second, swinging his cap wildly, and, without saluting or dismounting, yelling: "The rebels have gone. March right through Atlanta and go into camp on the other side." With that, he rode off. But by 11:00 A.M., as a stream of artillery shells emerged from Atlanta, Sherman realized he was mistaken. He ordered McPherson and Schofield to bring up their guns and "open a converging fire." Sherman also planned to send Dodge's corps to destroy the Georgia Railroad beyond Decatur, further isolating Hood.[78]

Noticing the Confederates strengthening their works around Atlanta, McPherson feared another attack from Hood. Riding over to see Sherman, he argued that the greatest danger to his army lay along its left flank, to which he desired to send all of the Sixteenth Corps but one brigade. Believing McPherson to be overcautious, Sherman nonetheless agreed to the request. McPherson conceded that if Hood attacked it would be by one o'clock. If no engagement occurred by then, he would send at least one division of Dodge's corps to rip up railroads. According to Sherman's report, McPherson left "near noon."[79]

As early as 8:00 A.M. of the twenty-second McPherson had taken steps to strengthen his left, then guarded by Blair's Seventeenth Corps. He ordered Dodge to move Sweeny's division from the right to the extreme left, where it would mass to Blair's left. A brigade of General John W. Fuller's Fourth Division was to come up on Sweeny's right, covering the gap between Sweeny and Blair. Sweeny moved promptly, and by noon his men had bivouacked to Blair's left, at an angle of about forty-five degrees. Fuller was not yet in position and was awaiting further orders when about noon he wisely placed Lieutenant Seth M. Laird and the Fourteenth Ohio Battery on a nearby hill.

Here Dodge and Fuller, who were lunching together, disagreed. Dodge said that about noon—Fuller insisted "it was near 1 o'clock"—shooting began. Sweeny's skirmishers immediately reported that the enemy was in the timber to the rear of the Seventeenth Corps. Perceiving the Confederates were attacking in force, Fuller immediately ordered troops into position on the right of Sweeny, closing some of the gap between Sweeny and Blair. His units "hotly engaged," Dodge sent a staff officer to General Giles A. Smith, who led the division of the Seventeenth Corps directly to Fuller's right, hoping he could close the rest of the gap, but the messenger found Smith, too, under heavy attack.[80]

McPherson was lunching with Blair and Logan when he heard shots. With some members of his staff he immediately rode off in the direction of the firing. Watching from a "commanding position on Dodge's right," McPherson marveled at "the sweeping deadly fire from Fuller's and Sweeny's Divisions, and the guns of the 14th Ohio Battery fairly mowed great swaths in the advancing columns." According to Lieutenant Colonel William E. Strong of his staff, "General McPherson's admiration for the steadiness and determined bravery of the 16th Corps was unbounded." About the time Dodge's men repulsed a second attack, McPherson sent Strong with two messages: he was to ask Blair "the condition of affairs along his line" and was to tell Giles Smith to hold his position, for McPherson would send troops to occupy the gap between Fuller and Smith.[81]

Sherman believed that McPherson was alone during much of what followed. An orderly, Private A. J. Thompson of the Fourth Ohio, who made a career out of talking and writing about McPherson's death, was nowhere near him. "His account," Sherman commented of Thompson in 1881, "has been printed again and again with variations, slight, depending on the quantity and quality of his last drink."[82]

Major Charles E. Putnam, then on the staff of Giles Smith, was positive he was the last Federal to speak to McPherson. Early in the morning of July 22 he was two miles in front of the Northern pickets when he saw a cloud of dust rising from Atlanta. Believing the Confederates were either evacuating the city or preparing for an attack on the Union left flank, he reported what he had seen to Smith. After trying but failing to find Blair, Putnam came upon McPherson, on whose staff he had served after the fall of Vicksburg. McPherson was alone. Together the two watched in admiration as Dodge's men repulsed the enemy. "I then dashed into the woods," Putnam wrote Dodge in 1910, "and shortly after entering the same, there was a slight angle in the road and I turned to look over my shoulder to see if he was following me, and I saw him not three hundred feet away. I escaped, but we all know the fate of poor McPherson."[83]

Riding into the gap, McPherson came upon some members of the Fifth Confederate Regiment, commanded by Captain Richard Beard. "I could have touched him with my sword," Beard later wrote. "Not a word was spoken. I threw up my sword to him as a signal to surrender. He checked his horse slightly, raised his hat as if he were saluting a lady, wheeled his horse's head to the right, and dashed off to the rear in a full gallop." Private Robert F. Coleman then fired at McPherson, bringing him down.[84]

A short time later Private George Reynolds of the Fifteenth Iowa, himself wounded in the arm, came upon McPherson, alone but still alive. Reynolds immediately recognized him and asked if he wanted anything, but McPherson was unable to reply. Ignoring his own wound, Reynolds gave McPherson water and stayed with him until he died, about forty-five minutes later. After McPherson had died, several rebel officers came up and asked McPherson's rank. Told who he was, they seemed surprised. They took his papers and his pocket watch but nothing else. Two other Confederates soon came along. They threatened to take Reynolds, who appealed that he wanted to guard the body and was himself wounded. After they left, Reynolds went for help. For his bravery he received the Seventeenth Corps's Gold Medal of Honor.[85]

McPherson's body was borne back to Sherman's headquarters at Howard House in an ambulance. Carried inside, it was placed on a door ripped from its hinges and was examined by a physician. Schofield remembered how Sherman "manifested deep feeling when the body was brought to the Howard House. I recollect well his remark to the effect that the whole of rebeldom could not atone for the sacrifice of one such life."[86]

The news fell hard on McPherson's fiancée, Emily Hoffman of Baltimore. In June, Sherman had written her explaining that he needed McPherson. Emily must postpone their wedding. After McPherson's death, Sherman again wrote to her, trying to console her. But she could not be comforted. For a year she stayed in her room. Finally emerging, she lived a cloistered life and never married.[87]

Connecting the fallen man with Willy, Ellen grieved more for McPherson than for Dan McCook or Jim Sherman:

> He is associated in my mind with dear Willy because of our visits to his house which was the last house that Willy ever was in—his table was the last at which he sat. . . . The last morning we were at Gen'l McPherson's I asked dear Willy, when brushing him up a little if he had said his prayers the night before & he said he had forgotten because his head ached badly. I then said well try and remember them every night Willy. . . . He answered so sweetly & so from pity I will try Mama never to forget them again. And when I brushed his hair I said now don't you feel satisfied with your hair Willy when you find it so much like Papa—he said yes with one of his proud smiles—I said "I always told you I loved red hair the best & that your hair was the prettiest in my eyes of any." He went out of the room so happy but he soon returned to it to lie on the floor with his head on a pillow. He ate nothing that morning nor after that. How could I have been insensible to his danger so long. I hate myself when I think of it and it grieves me to death to think what I might have done had I been more keen sighted & more anxious.[88]

With Logan, the senior officer, temporarily in command of the Army of the Tennessee, the fighting continued. At one point Brigadier General Charles R. Woods, commanding Logan's First Division, hastily rode up and reported to Sherman and Schofield that the enemy had driven his men back and isolated them from the rest of their corps. Schofield described what happened next:

> When that break was made in the line immediately to the left of mine,
> I had a rare opportunity of witnessing Sherman's splendid combat as a

simple soldier, the occasion for which occurs so rarely to the general-in-chief of a great army. Sherman at once sent for *all my* artillery, which responded to his call at a full gallop. He led the batteries in person to some high open ground *in front of our line*, near the Howard House, placed them in position and directed their fire, which from that advanced position enfiladed the parapets from which our troops had been driven and which the enemy then occupied. With the aid of that terrible "raking fire," the division of Union troops very easily and very quickly regained the entrenchments they had lost.[89]

The fighting, which continued until dark, was among the fiercest of the campaign. Union casualties, including missing, totaled 3,722. Confederate losses, from Cheatham's corps, which Hood ordered forward when he believed he had victory in hand, and from Hardee's, totaled about 7,500. Watching much of the battle with Sherman and Schofield, Howard remembered the intensity with which Sherman viewed it. "I had never till then seen Sherman with such a look on his face," he noted. "His eyes flashed. He did not speak. He only watched the front. There appeared not only in his face, but in his whole pose, a concentrated fierceness." Sherman had sent Cox with two brigades over toward Dodge, and Schofield had positioned several batteries to help. But when Schofield suggested that he assault Cheatham's flank and that Thomas be placed between the attackers and the defenders of Atlanta, Sherman, his face more relaxed, answered: "Let the Army of the Tennessee fight it out!"[90]

The selection of McPherson's permanent successor raised difficulties. On the day after McPherson's death, Thomas met with Sherman and objected to Logan. The previous spring Logan had quarreled with Thomas, whose guards had refused to let Logan's officers use the railroad to and from Nashville. Without consulting Thomas, Logan had complained directly to Sherman. Thomas also resented statements by Logan's officers that they had been sent to Chattanooga to rescue the Army of the Cumberland.

Thomas suggested that Sherman let Lincoln name the commander, but Sherman replied that he would do it. The two quickly passed over Hooker, by far the most qualified for the post, and settled on Howard, whose conduct at Chattanooga and during the privation of the march to Knoxville had impressed Sherman.[91]

During a march after the battle of the twenty-second, Dodge noticed Sherman at a log house. Logan was sitting on the porch. Dodge said of Logan:

> He hardly recognized me as I walked in, and I saw a great change in him. I asked General Sherman what the change in commanders meant—why Logan was not left in command. . . . Logan could hear every word that was said between Sherman and myself. Sherman did not feel at liberty to say anything in explanation of this change. He simply put me off very firmly but nicely as he could, and spoke highly of General Howard, who had been given the command. I went away

from the place without any satisfaction, and when I met Logan on the outside I expressed to him my regrets, and I said to him: "There is something here that none of us understand." Logan said: "It makes no difference; it will all come right in the end."[92]

Logan remained with Sherman, but Hooker did not. Learning Howard, who had served under him at Chancellorsville, was to be appointed his superior, he wrote Thomas asking to be relieved "from an army in which rank and service are ignored." One story circulated that Lincoln had telegraphed Sherman imploring him to give the Army of the Tennessee to Hooker. Sherman supposedly responded that he preferred Howard. After Lincoln again urged Hooker, Sherman offered to resign. Lincoln then dropped the matter.[93]

Arriving in the North, Hooker unleashed a bitter assault upon Howard, Sherman, and Halleck. "I inclose you a specimen of what he publishes in Northern papers wherever he goes," Halleck later wrote Sherman. Dictated by Hooker, the stories were written by "such worthies" as Daniel Butterfield and George Wilkes, the owner of the newspaper *Wilkes' Spirit of the Times*.[94]

Sherman and Hooker remained bitter enemies. "Hooker got mad," Sherman told Ellen, "because he was not appointed to the command and has gone North. This ought to damn him, showing that he is selfish, & not patriotic. He was not suited to the Command." To his temporary successor and friend, Pap Williams, Hooker called Sherman "a fool or a knave. I think the latter, and I know that he is crazy. . . . This matter is not over. It will have a long tail to it." After the war, when Sherman's California lawyer and wartime biographer, Samuel M. Bowman, met with Hooker and assured him that Sherman had no personal quarrel with him, Fighting Joe replied: "No sir! No sir! It was envy— he knew that whenever I rode by there the soldiers' hats went up, and he knew they despised him."[95]

During the turmoil over McPherson's successor, the Union army was still. Then, on the morning of July 27, Sherman ordered Howard to transfer the Army of the Tennessee from its position on the left of the Union line. Howard was to take his men along a road just beyond a wooded ridge and head for a point on the Lick Skillet Road. The move would place Howard outside of Hood's left flank and enable him to cut Hood's railroad. Skeptical, even though Sherman kept insisting that Hood would not "trouble me," Howard deployed his divisions one at a time, enabling each to protect the flank of the preceding one. But this process took time, and not until 11:00 A.M. on July 28 were all three corps in position for the march. Dodge, holding the left, and Blair, in the center, faced Atlanta from the west, about two miles from the center of the city. Blair's right approached a crossroads about a quarter of a mile above a Methodist meeting house called Ezra Church. Logan placed one of his divisions almost directly in back of the church, and his other two almost at right angles to the Seventeenth and almost parallel to the road.[96]

As some shots rang out, Howard remarked to Sherman, who had rejoined him, that he thought a battle would soon take place. Sherman repeated that he did not think so. Fortunately, Logan agreed with Howard. He halted his men, and Howard had them pile logs and fence rails to their front for protection. Saying that he still disagreed with Howard, Sherman rode off, leaving a grateful Howard "to conduct my first battle alone."[97]

The struggle filled the rest of the day. About 11:30 in the morning Morgan L. Smith's division, trying to take a nearby hill on the right of Logan's line, met strong resistance. Soon after, Confederates, commanded by Howard's West Point classmate General Stephen D. Lee, appeared all along Logan's front. His men huddled along the crest of the ridge. Logan, alone and on foot, ran along the line, "an almost exultant expression lighting up his dark face" as he encouraged his troops: "Hold them! steady, boys, we've got them now." The first attack repulsed, the men continued to pile to their front "anything which can stop a bullet." During the interlude between charges, reinforcements arrived from the two other corps. The most notable additions were two regiments from Blair armed with repeating rifles. They were sent to bolster the right flank, around which some enemy skirmishers had already pushed. After a second charge had been repulsed, Howard, riding along the line, shouted to the men of the Fifty-fifth Illinois: "Well, boys, I thought I had seen fighting before; but I never saw anything like this." Darkness ended the battle. Union losses totaled 632, Confederate about 3,000.[98]

After Ezra Church, Sherman's army bogged down. Hood's line, extending for fifteen miles around Atlanta and manned in part by Georgia militia, was so hidden by the contour of the land that Union commanders could not detect its weak spots. In the interim, Sherman hoped cavalry raids would weaken the enemy. His three cavalry divisions, led by Stoneman, Garrard, and Brigadier General Edward M. McCook, Dan's cousin, were to leave separately, rip up railroads south of Atlanta, and then unite and move on Macon, 131 miles away. At Stoneman's urging Sherman agreed to let the entire force, numbering 8,500 men, ride on to Andersonville, to free the 23,000 Union prisoners there. Unfortunately, the three cavalry units never came together. Each was beaten. Stoneman advanced to the Ocmulgee River bordering Macon and shelled the town. For some reason he then retreated. Fumbling about, he believed himself trapped by a superior force and with 500 men surrendered. He remained a prisoner till exchanged late in September. Only Garrard's division succeeded in getting back in decent shape. For two or three weeks small groups of cavalrymen straggled back to camp. "It was," observed Captain Stone, "the most disastrous adventure of the campaign."[99]

Sherman was furious. "I have already lost Stoneman & near 2000 cavalry in attempting to rescue the prisoners at Macon," he fumed to Ellen. "I get one hundred letters a day almost asking me to effect the exchange or release of these prisoners. It is not in my power." In 1867, when Granger and Stoneman were mentioned for promotion, Sherman opposed both. "The former is a Constitutional growler & shirk—never does anything he can help," Cump informed John, "& Stoneman though at times a good man is weak and gets bewildered. I have nothing to say for them."[100]

___ VII ___

From August 4 to August 15, Sherman's infantry remained stationary. During the lull two thoughts occupied Sherman: how to threaten Hood in Atlanta, about which he spoke little, and race, about which he wrote much.

Busy fighting a war, Sherman had no stomach for the politics of race relations. Early in the summer of 1864, Congress approved a law allowing each state to recruit Southern Negroes and to deduct the number enlisted from the state's draft quota. Massachusetts immediately commissioned John A. Spooner a lieutenant colonel and authorized him to raise a regiment in Georgia. Sherman scoffed at the idea. No one could find recruits in that state, he warned Spooner, "for I assure you I have not seen an able-bodied man, black or white, there, fit for a soldier, who was not in this army or the one opposed to it." For several reasons the general disliked the new law: "Civilian agents about an army are a nuisance. . . . The duty of citizens to fight for their country is too sacred a one to be peddled off by buying up the refuse of other states. . . . The negro is in a transition state, and is not the equal of the white man. . . . These are some of my peculiar notions, but I assure you they are shared by a large proportion of our fighting men."[101]

On August 6, when Sherman wrote to Ellen about black soldiers, he was in an ugly mood. His army was bogged down, and on that very day Palmer had resigned because Sherman had asked him to take orders from Schofield, his junior in time in grade. He complained to her:

> Agents are coming to me from Massachusetts, Rhode Island and Ohio to recruit Negros as fast as they can catch them to count as soldiers. I remonstrated to Mr Lincoln in the strongest terms but he answered it was the Law and I had to submit. Niggers wont work now, and half my army are driving wagons, loading and unloading cars, and doing work which the very Negros we have captured might do, whilst these same niggers are soldiers on paper, but I can't get any—The fact is modern Philanthropy will convert our oldest & best soldiers into laborers whilst the nigger parades & remains in some remote & safe place. It is an insult to our Race to count them as a part of the quota.

After newspapers, without his permission, published his letter to Spooner, Sherman lashed out at abolitionists:

> I don't see why we cant have some sense about Negros, as well as about horses, mules, iron, copper &c—but say nigger in the U. S. and . . . the whole country goes crazy. I never thought my Negro letter would get into the papers, but since it has I lay low—
> I like niggers well enough as niggers, but when fools & idiots try & make niggers better than ourselves I have an opinion.[102]

As Sherman fumed, his troops lived behind a strong line of entrenchments, sometimes within three hundred yards of the enemy. About once a week each regiment went to the rear for a day and a night of rest. Most of the men tried to keep as clean as they could under the circumstances, but an incorrigible might be dragged to a nearby stream and scrubbed. The more he resisted, the harder the scrubbing.[103]

During the hot days and cool nights, picket duty was the most disagreeable chore a soldier performed. Many of the pickets stood in pits or holes that permitted them to see the enemy without being exposed. Cramped and uncomfortable, a soldier performed such service for twenty-four hours, beginning at 2:00 A.M. A few yards away stood an enemy picket, just as uncomfortable, and the two often arranged a truce.[104]

Two insects made life in the trenches unbearable. The grayback, or camp vermin, was always present. So, too, was the house fly, which thrived in Georgia and made sleep impossible. Trying to eliminate this pest, a half dozen or more men each contributed a spoonful of sugar, which was sprinkled in a circle on the trench floor. The powder from a few cartridges was then placed over the sugar. When flies swarmed to get the sugar, the soldiers ignited the powder and burned them. This device, however, hardly dented Georgia's fly population.[105]

The food served the soldiers was ample but dull. "Most of the time we had full rations of the three essentials, hardtack, bacon and coffee," remembered Lieutenant Colonel Wilbur F. Hinman of the Sixty-fifth Ohio, "but the daily bill of fare became painfully monotonous. There was no possible chance to do any foraging, and the soldiers would have given a week's pay for a supply of vegetables."

Sometimes cattle arrived from Chattanooga, but by now they found little to graze on along the way. Consequently, they were more bones than meat. The men, as they picked on the lean bones, said that the commissary officers killed each night only those cattle they knew could not survive the next day.

The soldiers were also fed desiccated vegetables, which came in slabs about a foot square and an inch thick. Hinman described them as "a mixture containing pretty nearly everything known to the vegetable kingdom." The juice had been squeezed out, enabling what was left to last indefinitely. With desiccated vegetables the soldiers made soup, a cubic inch of the first yielding a quart of the second.

The Sanitary Commission, the Civil War equivalent of the Red Cross, tried to supply fresh vegetables, such as onions and carrots. Most of what it sent was sidetracked and never reached the front. Onions, used to combat scurvy, were the most welcome treat. Eaten raw, they reached Sherman's men three or four times, a bushel being allotted to a regiment. "The soldiers," noted Hinman, "would gladly have devoured thousands of bushels if they could have had them."[106]

Sherman ate no better than his troops. General James F. Rusling, who visited him during the siege, consumed a dinner of hardtack, bacon, sweet potatoes, and black coffee, served on a table made by a camp carpenter from a clothing box. Sherman's chairs consisted of "rickety camp stools and United States cracker boxes."

After dinner, Sherman produced a handful of cigars and smoked incessantly as he gave orders and dictated letters and telegrams. He talked about everything but his future plans. Thomas, Schofield, and Howard came in and consulted with him. "It was easy to see," commented Rusling, "that he held them all in high esteem and regard, as they did him. They were a fine sight to see—all great soldiers—but Sherman easily dominated them all. His keen intelligence, incisive speech, prompt decision, and determined will readily made him chief everywhere."[107]

The Civil War was among the last conflicts to combine brutality and gentility. An example occurred two days after the battle at Kennesaw. With the bodies of the dead decaying in the heat, Northerners and Southerners declared a truce to enable burial parties to do their work. The officers and men on both sides mingled with each other, swapping stories, newspapers, and Northern coffee for Southern tobacco.[108]

The August stalemate brought a similar gesture. One beautiful Sunday evening, amid the quiet, a Northern band just behind the fortifications struck up "The Star-Spangled Banner." The Yankees cheered. A Confederate band answered with "The Bonnie Blue Flag." The Southerners went wild. For an hour the bands played alternately: "Hail Columbia" and "Dixie"; "Red, White and Blue" and "My Maryland"; "John Brown's Body" and "Ole Virginny." Then followed some sentimental tunes: "Annie Laurie," "Sewannee River," "The Girl I Left Behind Me," "Old Kentucky Home," and "Home, Sweet Home." During this interlude the war no longer existed.[109]

___ VIII ___

Stalled before Atlanta, Sherman decided that he could not bomb the city into submission. On the morning of August 13 he wrote Halleck that he had decided on another tactic. From the east he had already pressed the enemy to East Point, just below Atlanta. But, he told Halleck, terrain that lent itself to natural defenses made it impossible to push further south, where he might cut the road to Macon. Sherman had issued orders for a different plan. He intended to leave one corps—the Twentieth—to guard the Chattahoochee bridge. With the other 60,000 men, "reduced to fighting trim," he hoped "to make a circuit of devastation around the town," covering fifteen or twenty miles. Before starting, Sherman wanted to replace Palmer as commander of the Fourteenth Corps with the energetic Hoosier, Jeff C. Davis, whom Sherman considered "the best officer in that corps." Realizing the dangers of his plan, Sherman concluded: "If I should ever be cut off from my base look out for me about Saint Mark's, Fla., or Savannah, Ga."[110]

The army commanders once more turned to cavalry raids. On August 10 Hood sent Wheeler, with a cavalry force estimated at 6,000, behind Sherman's lines. From Allatoona, Resaca, Dalton, and other points to the rear, Union officers described Wheeler's damage to the Western & Atlantic, which he tore up at several spots before crossing into Tennessee and raiding to near Nashville. After a march of 600 miles, Wheeler returned on September 10, "wearing out all his horses," Stone related, "and gaining nothing of the least value to the Confederacy."[111]

While Wheeler was gone, the Union cavalry general Judson Kilpatrick conducted a raid around Atlanta that, Kilpatrick promised, would enable him to break the railroad to Macon. Leaving on August 18, Kilpatrick rode around Atlanta. Returning four days later, he assured Thomas that he had torn up four miles of railroad track between Rough and Ready and Jonesboro, south of Atlanta, and ten miles at other places. He had, he bragged, brought in seventy prisoners, horses, wagons, and guns. In reality, he had ripped up but a half mile of track, which the Confederates quickly repaired. On the very day Kilpatrick returned, Logan's signal officer reported the arrival in Atlanta of a train consisting of eleven cars.[112]

Kilpatrick's failure convinced Sherman that he must move to the south and southeast and cut Hood's communications. On the night of August 25 the Twentieth, commanded from the twenty-seventh on by General Henry W. Slocum, moved out of the lines and withdrew to the Chattahoochee. The rest of Thomas's army moved to the right. On the night of the twenty-sixth, Howard's army did the same. Like a giant wheel—the Army of the Tennessee holding the right, the Army of the Cumberland the left, the Army of the Ohio the pivot—the Federals swung around. On August 28, a clear, warm Sunday, Howard reached the Atlanta & West Point Railroad near Fairburn, southwest of Atlanta, and the Army of the Cumberland reached Red Oak, several miles northeast of Fairburn. Here, instead of continuing the movement, Sherman spent a day and a half ripping up track. Not until August 30 did the army push eastward toward the Macon railroad.[113]

At first Hood, not knowing where Sherman was, interpreted the move away from Atlanta as a withdrawal. The people of the city rejoiced. Not until 6:00 P.M. on the evening of August 28, when he ordered first Hardee's and then Lee's corps to Jonesboro, did Hood realize what the Federals were doing. Even then, according to Hardee, Hood believed that only two Northern corps were headed for Jonesboro.[114]

The last day of the month brought heavy fighting. Covering twelve miles on August 30, Howard's men pushed to within a mile of Jonesboro. Ordered by Hood to drive the Yankees back across the Flint River, just to their rear, Hardee arrived at Jonesboro before daylight on August 31, but to his dismay Lee's troops straggled in, the last three brigades not reaching him until 1:30 in the afternoon. When he realized the attack would have to be held off until afternoon, Hardee urged Hood to come to Jonesboro to direct it himself, but Hood ignored him. The assault, launched heavily against Logan's corps, was a failure from the start. On the Confederate left Cleburne, leading Hardee's corps, attacked first, hoping to turn the enemy's right flank. Lee, on the right, was to follow up when he heard Cleburn's full fire. Mistaking Cleburne's skirmishers for the main attack, Lee advanced prematurely. As he announced in his battle report, his men lacked "that spirit and inflexible determination that would insure success. . . .

The attack was a feeble one and a failure, with a loss to my corps of about 1,300 men in killed and wounded."[115]

At 6:00 P.M. on August 31, even before learning the results of the battle of Jonesboro, Hood had ordered Lee back to defend Atlanta. An hour later Thomas suggested a plan for trapping Hardee. While Howard held the enemy at Jonesboro, Thomas would throw his army across the railroad at Lovejoy's Station, below Jonesboro. This would block Hardee and cut off Hood's line of retreat to Macon. Sherman rejected the proposal. He had already ordered Schofield and Stanley, with Thomas's Fourth Army Corps, to move down the railroad, breaking it until they reached Davis, working up from Jonesboro. He proposed to go as far south as Griffin, fifty miles below Atlanta, wrecking the rails. On the last day of August, Sherman made clear what he considered to be his chief mission. "I don't believe," he wrote Thomas, "anybody recognizes how important it is now to destroy this railroad."[116]

On September 1 the work went on. At 4:00 A.M. Stanley had his parties moving down the track, and around 10:30 they came to the point where Baird had ripped up but three hundred yards of road, "and that," according to Stanley's chief of staff, "poorly." At noon Stanley reached Morrow's Station, four miles from Jonesboro. Belatedly, Sherman saw an opportunity to trap the Confederates in Jonesboro. But here the Union intelligence broke down, possibly because of the absence of Dodge, who had been shot in the forehead on August 19 and had gone north to recover. Dodge's two spies in Atlanta were known only to himself, and without access to them neither Sherman, nor Thomas, nor Kilpatrick knew who was where. During September 1 Thomas was sure all three Confederate corps occupied Jonesboro. After talking to "a citizen," Kilpatrick placed the number at two, Lee's and Hardee's, and, for whatever reason, Sherman agreed with Kilpatrick.[117]

Sherman always blamed Stanley, who came up late, for the failure to trap Hardee in Jonesboro. "But," Stone insisted, "the delay was wholly due to his own reiterated persistence in destroying the railroad instead of attacking the enemy." That night, in messages to his commanders, Sherman repeated his intention to follow the Confederates to Griffin. "Whenever the opportunity offers to break the railroad without much risk," he instructed Kilpatrick, "do so."[118]

During the early hours of September 2, Sherman could not sleep. At 2:00 A.M. he heard "heavy firing and saw a large fire in the direction of Atlanta," about fifteen miles away. Sherman walked to the house of a nearby farmer, who listened and said the noise sounded like a battle. At four Sherman heard other explosions. Was the enemy blowing up ammunition, or had Slocum advanced from the Chattahoochee and engaged in battle?

What Sherman heard was the destruction by Hood of five locomotives and eighty-one boxcars, twenty-eight filled with explosives and rifles. These supplies were supposed to have been shipped to Griffin or Macon the night before, but they had not been. On the morning of September 2 Sherman found that Hardee had slipped out of Jonesboro. Retreating south, Hardee's troops occupied a strong line of works a mile in front of Lovejoy's Station. At 5:30 P.M.

Stanley attacked, and his men took some of the works before being driven back with heavy losses.[119]

Early in the morning of September 3, while near Lovejoy's Station, twenty-three miles south of Atlanta, Sherman received the welcome news. Hood had blown up "his magazines" in Atlanta and left on the same night. Slocum, Sherman informed Halleck, was now in the city. "So Atlanta is ours, and fairly won. I shall not push much further on this raid, but in a day or so will move to Atlanta and give my men some rest." On the fourth Hood made it to Lovejoy's. Sherman had taken Atlanta, but the Confederate army was once more united.[120]

In a long letter to Halleck, Sherman analyzed the campaign. To his friend, who had rescued him in 1861 from the "perfect 'slough of despond'" into which he had fallen, he confessed he owed "all I now enjoy of fame. . . . I ought to have reaped larger fruits of victory. . . . My part was skillful and well executed." As for his generals, Thomas was "slow, but as true as steel; Schofield is also slow and leaves too much to others; Howard is a Christian, elegant gentleman, and conscientious soldier. In him I made no mistake. Hooker was a fool. Had he staid a couple of weeks he could have marched into Atlanta and claimed all the honors."[121]

Halleck answered by praising Sherman's campaign as "the most brilliant of the war." Its "results," however, were "less striking and less complete than those of General Grant at Vicksburg." Hooker had "made a mistake in leaving before the capture of Atlanta. I understand that when he was here he said that you would fail, your army was discouraged and dissatisfied, &c." In newspaper articles Hooker was blaming Halleck for his troubles at both Chancellorsville and Atlanta. "The funny part of the business is that I had nothing whatever to do with his being relieved on either occasion. . . . His animosity arises from another source. He is aware that I know something about his character and conduct in California and fearing that I may use that information against him, he seeks to ward off its effect by making it appear that I am his personal enemy, am jealous of him, &c. I know of no other reason for his hostility to me." Halleck characterized Thomas, of whom he was extremely fond, as "a noble old war horse. It is true that he is slow, but he is always sure."[122]

To Ellen, Sherman emphasized his achievements. He had beaten Hood

> on the strategy and fighting, and if my troops had only been as smart as my old Tennessee army I could have bagged all of Hardees Corps at Jonesboro. Still on the whole the Campaign is the best, cleanest and most satisfactory of the war. I have received the most fulsome praise of all from the President down, but I fear the world will jump to the wrong conclusion that because I am in Atlanta the work is done. Far from it. We must *Kill* those three hundred thousand I have told you of so often, and the further they run the harder for us to get them.[123]

13

"A Scene I Pray My Eyes May Never See Again"

— I —

IN TRIUMPH the band of the Thirty-third Massachusetts Infantry, Sherman's favorite, led Slocum's entrance into Atlanta, marching down the streets playing patriotic songs. Hailing the Northerners as deliverers sent by God, Negroes lined the streets. "We found more Union sentiment in Atlanta," recorded the historian of the Third Wisconsin, "than anywhere else in the South." Despite the havoc caused by two months of Federal bombardment, women brought out buckets of water, about the only thing they could spare, for the thirsty soldiers. Before leaving, Hood's army had stripped much of the city, saying the Yankees would steal anything of value anyway.[1]

The correspondent of the *Cincinnati Commercial* found in Atlanta much ruin. "Grant walked *into* Vicksburg," he observed, "McClellan walked *around* Richmond, but Sherman is walking *upon* Atlanta."[2]

Determined to make Atlanta "a pure military garrison," Sherman barred sutlers and traders from entering the city. He also ordered all the civilians out of it. In Memphis, Vicksburg, Natchez, and New Orleans, all captured from the enemy, he had seen divisions of troops bogged down caring for civilians. Such a thing, he vowed, was not going to happen in Atlanta, whose citizens he could not possibly feed. Residents were free to go either north to Chattanooga or south to a neutral camp at Rough and Ready, the next railroad station below Atlanta. They could take any property they could transport. As wagons loaded with civilians, dogs, cats, furniture, and pianos left the city, Sherman wrote Halleck: "If the people raise a howl against my barbarity and cruelty, I will answer that war is war, and not popularity-seeking. If they want peace, they and their relatives must stop the war."[3]

Howl the people did. Southern newspapers denounced Sherman as a "leader of highwaymen," "the chief among savages," and the "foremost villain in the world." In the North, the *Dayton* (Ohio) *Empire* said that compared with Sherman, General Benjamin F. Butler, the beast of New Orleans, "becomes a high-toned and most gallant gentleman." Exchanging letters with the Union commander, Hood called Sherman's order unprecedented. Sherman desired "to place over us an inferior race," whom Southerners had "raised from barbarism to its present position. . . . Better die a thousand deaths than submit to live under you or your Government and your negro allies!"[4]

But almost as soon as the Federals entered Atlanta, commerce revived. "Several bakeries were opened and did a brisk business," noted the historian of the 150th New York Infantry, "asking a dollar for a medium-sized loaf of bread, and the same for a pie with a crust like shoe leather." To their joy, the Union soldiers found immense quantities of tobacco. On the day before the city fell, a plug of tobacco sold in the Federal camp for a dollar, cigars for fifteen cents each. After its capture, a plug of tobacco cost five cents, cigars twenty-five cents for a hundred.[5]

Meanwhile, petty struggles raged within Sherman's beloved Army of the Tennessee. Their terms of service over, many of its soldiers went home to reenlist. All three corps commanders were gone, too. Blair and Logan left to take care of politics. And in mid-August, Dodge had been shot in the forehead while peering at the enemy's works. First believed to be dying, he was now recovering. His temporary replacement was his friend, Brigadier General Thomas E. G. Ransom, the beloved twenty-nine-year-old Vermonter whom the troops called McPherson Number Two.[6]

A week after entering Atlanta, Ransom asked Howard about the changes to be made in the Army of the Tennessee. Howard believed a new campaign would begin soon, for Grant had "ordered Sherman to push the enemy and keep him in our front by all means." This would disappoint the troops, who wanted a rest.

Howard was thinking of eliminating a corps and of sending Blair to the Mississippi River to organize a new Seventeenth Corps there, Ransom informed Dodge. He added:

> [Howard] also said that he would have to consult with Blair about this change, as he "would not have a difficulty with the Blair family for the world."—You see therefore that in all probability Blair's and Logan's interests will be looked out for probably at your expense. . . . Between you and I general, Howard has shown great weakness in this last movement, and he will not do. He will soon become a tool to be led and controlled by stronger men.[7]

After speaking to both Sherman and Howard, another of Dodge's friends came to similar conclusions. Colonel George E. Spencer had once headed Dodge's secret service and now commanded the First Alabama Cavalry. With Dodge's financial help, he would serve two terms as a United States senator from Alabama during Reconstruction.

Spencer came away from his conversations convinced that Sherman and Howard preferred Dodge but feared Logan and Blair. In a letter to Dodge, he wrote:

Howard owned that this was the case. He said he had issued once the order for Blair to go to Memphis and that Blair refused. He also said John A. Logan was a very troublesome man and made him feel uneasy, and that he believed he would endeavor to get him superseded at Washington. I told him that I thought that would be the case.

. . . Logan has left nothing undone that would injure you. This I know from a dozen different sources, even down to orderlies. He has our old orderlies, and they see and hear many things and told me what they know.

. . . Howard has no nerve and is a granny, and Sherman—I am at a loss to know what to think of him. I was never treated as cordially and friendly in my life. He inquired particularly about you and hoped you would return and you would not object to what was done, &c, &c. . . . I was puzzled by him, and hardly know what to think.[8]

Luckily for Sherman, the Confederates were squabbling as much as the Federals. At Macon on September 22, 1864, Jefferson Davis warned Sherman that his doom was at hand. Like Napoleon in Russia, the Yankee general had overextended himself. "Sherman can not keep up his long line of communication, and must retreat. Soon or later he must, and when that day comes the fate that befell the army of the French Empire in its retreat from Moscow will be re-enacted. Our cavalry and our people will harass and destroy his army, as did the Cossacks that of Napoleon, and the Yankee General, like him, will escape with only a bodyguard."

Davis went on to denounce Governor Joseph E. Brown, who had accused the Confederate president of abandoning Georgia to the invaders. "Shame upon such falsehood," Davis responded. "Where could the author have been when . . . Polk and when Stephen D. Lee were sent to her assistance? Miserable man. The man who uttered this was a scoundrel."

Hoping to take advantage of this split within the Confederate ranks, Sherman invited Brown, Confederate vice president Alexander H. Stephens, and Senator Herschel Johnson to Atlanta for a conference. Saying that neither he nor Sherman possessed the authority to make peace, Brown refused the invitation. But he withdrew the Georgia militia from Hood's control, arguing its members were needed to harvest the sorghum crop.[9]

By September 26 Sherman had shipped south 446 families, containing 705 adults, 867 children, and seventy-nine servants. "We have tried three years of conciliation and kindness without any reciprocation," Halleck wrote Sherman on the twenty-eighth, endorsing this policy. "On the contrary, those thus treated have acted as spies and guerrillas in our rear and within our lines. . . . We have fed this class of people long enough. Let them go with their husbands and fathers in the rebel ranks, and if they won't go we must send them to their friends and natural protectors."[10]

For the close to five thousand civilians who remained in Atlanta and for his troops, Sherman tried to make life bearable. At his suggestion the band of the Thirty-third Massachusetts gave a series of concerts in the theater. Nor did Sherman neglect the theater, his great love. For seventeen nights a company consisting of Atlantans and members of the Third Wisconsin put on plays. These events brought in $8,000, much of it going to charity.[11]

Sherman loved to tell how, after the fall of Atlanta, he closed a shop with a big sign that had been opened by an agent of the Indiana Sanitary Commission. The agent protested to Stanton, who asked Sherman for an explanation. Said Sherman:

> . . . I told him I hadn't any *Indiana army* down there, but a U. S. Army—that I had already authorized two Sanitary Agents, one of the U. S. & one of the Western San Com,—and that I wasn't going to have any man come there to make distinctions among my men. . . . I wouldn't have one man nursed because he was from Indiana & his best neighbor left to long & pine for what he couldn't get because he was from Ohio. And that was the last I ever heard from Mr. Sect Stanton about State Sanitary Agents.[12]

With her husband in one spot for the first time in months, Ellen was able to send him news from home. Having enrolled Minnie and Lizzie in Saint Mary's Academy, which her cousin, Sister Angela, supervised in South Bend, Indiana, Ellen desired to leave her father and move there. "He little appreciates," she wrote Cump from South Bend, "that the great attraction to my heart to this place is Willy's grave. All the attention & compliments which your fame have won for me are nothing to the pleasure of seeing a flower bloom on that."[13]

Ellen and her father agreed about one thing. Tom Ewing, who commanded Federal forces in Missouri, was about to resign. If Cump would send a strong recommendation for Charley, now Sherman's inspector general, to Lancaster, Tom and Ellen's father would see to it that Charley became a brigadier general. Ellen went on to complain that Charley seldom wrote home. Would Sherman mention that to him?[14]

Sherman rejected the suggestion that Charley be promoted. Charley had commanded in battle neither a regiment nor a brigade. Until he had, he could expect nothing. "I cannot," Sherman argued, "do a wrong act because he is my brother. You know that. There has been too much of this during the war, and the consequence is two-thirds of the Brigadiers are at home. But he need not be uneasy. The war will last all his life and he will have ample chances to become Lt Genl if he has the industry."[15]

— II —

In Macon, Jefferson Davis had boasted that his armies would drive the Yankees from Georgia, perhaps even chasing them across the Ohio River. Reading the speech in Northern newspapers, Sherman surmised that the Southerners would soon move. He guessed right, for on September 26 Forrest, attacking Sherman's communications, captured Elk Ridge, Tennessee, about fifteen miles north of Pulaski. In the process, Forrest destroyed part of the Central Southern Railroad, which connected Nashville and Decatur, Alabama. To meet this danger in Middle Tennessee, Sherman sent Thomas to Chattanooga.[16]

Evading Sherman, Hood, with between 35,000 and 40,000 men, moved north, hoping to sever the Yankee communications. The Confederate army marched easily to the Chattahoochee, placing Hood where he had been two months before. Having lost track of the enemy, Sherman vowed, in a message to Grant on October 1, to assault Hood if he moved against the railroad. If, however, Hood continued on to Tennessee, Sherman would let Thomas take care of him. But Sherman now saw one thing clearly: "We cannot remain on the defensive." He proposed "to destroy Atlanta, and then march across Georgia to Savannah, or Charleston, breaking roads and doing irreparable damage."[17]

Learning that Hood's design was the railroad, Sherman left Slocum to protect Atlanta and set out after the Confederates. On the third and fourth of October his force crossed the Chattahoochee, and on the fifth the army reached Kennesaw and Marietta, north of which Hood destroyed the telegraph. Sherman rightly suspected that the enemy was heading toward Allatoona Pass, the cut in the mountains that contained a warehouse with a million rations of bread and a herd of nine thousand cattle. By flag, he signaled over the heads of the enemy from Vining's Station to Kennesaw and finally to Rome. The message ordered General John M. Corse, at Rome, to rush to Allatoona, thirty-five miles away. Allatoona was thinly defended, by 905 men under Lieutenant Colonel John E. Tourtellotte of the Fourth Minnesota.

From Kennesaw, Sherman could see the enemy campfires at Dallas, to the west. Smoke along the railroad from Big Shanty to Allatoona, a full fifteen miles, indicated that Hood was at work. Hoping to place Cox and the Twenty-third Corps between Hood's army at Dallas and the detachment attacking Allatoona, Sherman sent Cox due west. He was to burn houses and brush along the way to indicate his progress. The remainder of the army Sherman sent straight for Allatoona, eighteen miles to the northwest.

From the signal station, a small shanty that was dark inside but housed a telescope that extended outside, Sherman and the signal officer peered toward Allatoona, looking for a message. Sherman was about to give up when the signal officer picked up a flag waving the letters "C," "R," "S," "E," "H," "E," "R"— short for "Corse is here."

Receiving Sherman's message on the fourth, Corse had telegraphed to Kingston for cars to transport his men. Two trains, one of twenty cars and another of ten, were immediately dispatched toward him. The smaller train, however, hit a portion of spread track and derailed. But by 8:00 P.M., an hour after the twenty cars arrived, Corse had loaded 1,054 men into them. At 1:00 A.M. on the fifth, his men reached Allatoona.

The enemy, under General Samuel G. French, who had graduated in the same West Point class as Grant, numbered between four and five thousand men. By 8:00 A.M. of the fifth, French surrounded the Federals. He then addressed a message to the opposing commander, giving him five minutes to surrender and "avoid a needless effusion of blood." Corse answered "that we are prepared for the 'needless effusion of blood' whenever it is agreeable to you."[18]

Soon after the Confederate assault began, the Northerners were forced back into two small redoubts laid out on either side of the track by Colonel Orlando M. Poe the previous June. On the eastern side the Yankees were able to turn back the enemy with the aid of a 10-pound Rodman cannon dragged into position by hand. The men in the western redoubt, some armed with Henry repeating rifles, which contained a sixteen-shot magazine, withstood four Southern attacks. In the heavy fighting on the west only two field officers escaped being killed or wounded. Tourtellotte was shot in the hip, Corse grazed across the face and ear. About 1:30 P.M. the battle ended. In his report, Corse put the Federal casualties at 707, the Confederate at 231 dead and 411 wounded.[19]

Years later, when Corse was postmaster of Boston and Tourtellotte was Sherman's aide, the revivalists Dwight L. Moody and Ira Sankey made famous a song entitled "Hold the Fort, for I Am Coming," supposedly a message from Sherman to Corse. But Sherman denied using these words. He did, however, attest to the message Corse had sent him after being wounded: "I am short a cheek-bone and an ear, but am able to whip all h——l yet."[20]

Arriving at Allatoona on October 9, Sherman had no idea where Hood had gone. Corse, back at Rome, sent Spencer's First Alabama Cavalry and a regiment of mounted Illinois infantry to scout about, and they reported the enemy to be south of Rome. But Hood's raid convinced Sherman it was folly to stay put and try to protect his supply line. That evening, he wrote Grant:

> I propose we break up the railroad from Chattanooga, and strike out with wagons for Milledgeville, Millen, and Savannah. Until we can repopulate Georgia, it is useless to occupy it, but the utter destruction of its roads, houses and people will cripple their military resources. By attempting to hold the roads we will lose 1,000 men monthly, and will gain no result. I can make the march, and make Georgia howl! We have on hand over 8,000 cattle and 3,000,000 of bread, but no corn; but we can forage in the interior of the State.[21]

Hood continued to attack the railroad. In mid-October he ripped up seven miles of track around Big Shanty and thirty-one between Dalton and Resaca, threatening both towns. He then retreated to the south. Sherman pursued him a short distance before letting him go.[22]

Sherman made no secret of his frustration. To his generals one day he remarked: "Johnston being a sensible man I could generally divine his movements, but as Hood is not, I can tell nothing at all about them." Another time he said: "Damn Hood! If he will go to the Ohio River I'll give him rations!" And when Hood was reported to have reached Decatur, Sherman declared: "Let him go North. My business is down South!" Letting out his anger, Sherman warned Colonel W. W. Wright, who estimated that it would take four days for his crews to replace the burnt railroad bridge over the Oostenaula: "Sir, I give you forty-eight hours or a position in the front ranks."[23]

Upon receiving Sherman's request that he be allowed to destroy the railroad and Atlanta and then march east, Grant telegraphed to Lincoln his opposition to so risky a venture. His chief of staff, John A. Rawlins, thought the plan so foolish that he made a special trip to Washington to present his objections. Halleck characterized Sherman's proposal as madness, and predicted Sherman's ruin to Senator Charles Sumner of Massachusetts. After sleeping on it, however, Grant had faith in his friend and changed his mind. Still, Grant's initial opposition disturbed Lincoln and Stanton, both of whom feared that "a misstep by General Sherman might be fatal to his army."[24]

On October 16, while Sherman was at Ship's Gap, the spot in the first range of mountains below Chattanooga at which Dodge had opened the Atlanta campaign, he received a cipher dispatch from Halleck authorizing him to march across Georgia to the sea. The decoded message said that a northern fleet would await him on the coast at "Horse-i-bar Sound." The message puzzled Sherman. Did Grant and Halleck prefer that he march to Savannah or Mobile? After much contemplation, Sherman and his staff concluded that the cipher referred to Ossabaw Sound, about twenty miles below Savannah.[25]

On the nineteenth, Sherman advised Halleck that he was still convinced that Hood "will concoct more mischief. We must not be on the defensive, and I now consider myself authorized to execute my plan to destroy the railroad from Chattanooga to Atlanta, including the latter city (modified by Grant from Dalton, &c), strike out into the heart of Georgia, and make for Charleston, Savannah, or the mouth of the Appalachicola."

Marching to the sea was innovative enough, but to Halleck Sherman expounded another novel idea:

> I must have alternatives, else, being confined to one route, the enemy might so oppose that delay and want would trouble me, but, having alternatives, I can take so eccentric a course that no general can guess at my objective. Therefore, when you hear I am off have lookouts at Morris Island, S. C., Ossabaw Sound, Ga., Pensacola and Mobile Bays. I will turn up somewhere and believe I can take Macon and Milledgeville, Augusta and Savannah, Ga., and wind up with closing the neck back of Charleston so that they will starve out. This movement is not purely military or strategic, but it will illustrate the vulnerability of the South. They don't know what war means, but when the rich planters of Oconee and Savannah see their fences and corn and hogs and sheep vanish before their eyes they will have something more than a mean opinion of the "Yanks." Even now our poor mules laugh at the fine corn-fields, and our soldiers riot on chestnuts, sweet potatoes, pigs, chickens, &c. The poor people come to me and beg as for their lives, but my answer is, "Your friends have broken our railroads, which supplied us bountifully, and you cannot suppose our soldiers will suffer when there is abundance within reach."[26]

In late October, while at Gaylesville, Alabama, directly across the state border from Rome, Sherman mulled over his plans. Swinging out toward Decatur, Hood would undoubtedly march north to Huntsville and into Tennessee. Sherman would send Thomas with a force large enough to defeat Hood and then go his own way. He told Ellen:

> I am about to order the abolishment of all Headquarters except those of Doctors and Teamsters. Hood can march all round me and laugh, whilst I drag along with a Wagon train. This Wagon train in the end will defeat me. Soldiers get along well enough, but we are borne down with Generals, Headquarters and Staffs. I might be a hundred miles from here on my journey were it not for the excuse of wagons and artillery, but I am sending it back.[27]

At this time Ellen faced her own problems. The baby, whom her husband had never seen, had caught a cold. "Instead of getting better," Ellen revealed, "it is worse and I have the most serious apprehensions that he will never recover altho I do not think him in very immediate danger. He is sick enough to die in a week should he continue to grow worse. . . . It may be that Willy has prayed for him to come to him, and that God intends to take him too in innocence and purity. If so he is to be envied and not pitied, but we would all be grieved to lose our little pet."[28]

—— III ——

For half a century old soldiers argued about who originally suggested the March to the Sea. One observer credited the idea to General Ambrose E. Burnside. On September 30, 1863, while in Knoxville, he suggested that to relieve the enemy pressure on Rosecrans, the War Department allow him to lead an expedition to Dalton, Rome, Atlanta, and "thence to some point on the coast. . . . It is proposed to take no trains," he informed Halleck, "but to live upon the country and the supplies at the enemy's depots, destroying such as we do not use." Halleck answered coldly: "Distant expeditions into Georgia are not now contemplated."[29]

In 1894, General John S. Fullerton, who kept a celebrated diary of the Atlanta campaign, claimed the honor for his hero, General George H. Thomas, who early in September of 1864 purportedly asked Sherman to permit him to move rapidly to Andersonville, where he would free 30,000 Union prisoners. From there he desired to march to the seacoast. Sherman, meantime, would go after Hood. According to Fullerton, the audacity of the plan startled Sherman. As late as September 28, 1864, Fullerton pointed out, Sherman informed Grant that he thought it "better to hold on to Atlanta and strengthen my rear" than to march anywhere.[30]

Grant, too, had his advocates, including Henry Van Ness Boynton of the *Cincinnati Gazette*. But as late as November 1, 1864, Grant asked whether Sherman did "not think it advisable now that Hood has gone so far North to entirely settle him before starting on your proposed campaign. . . . If you can see the chance of destroying Hoods army attend to that first & make your move secondary." The next day, after Sherman answered that Thomas could take care of Hood, Grant responded: "Go on as you propose."[31]

Sherman denied the claims of these generals, but he acknowledged that others before him suggested a march:

> Montgomery Blair in Washington was the first person I heard speak of Marching to the Sea. He wanted five thousand men in 1861, before the battle of Bull Run, to be armed with broomsticks with which he proposed to march from Kentucky to Mobile. I believe he changed his mind afterwards. So in 1862 every soldier of Gen. Buell's fifty thousand not only conceived the idea, but absolutely undertook it. Every officer of the Army of the Cumberland, before the XX Corps joined it, "conceived the idea" of "cutting their way to the sea," and it was common talk around the campfires of the West.[32]

Sherman decided that if permitted to march he would divide his army into two wings of two corps each. But to his embarrassment, two of his four corps commanders, Blair and Logan, were away. "Blair only reached me by a scratch," Sherman later commented, "for surely within one or two days of his arrival at Kingston I cut the Railroad and wires behind me to prevent the very thing *recorded by Grant,* that orders were contemplated in Washington to forbid my making the March to the Sea, which at that date was construed extrahazardous." Logan never did arrive for the march.[33]

Spencer, who was to lead a brigade of Sherman's cavalry, knew how troublesome the two politician-generals were. On November 1, he reported to Dodge:

> I had a long talk with General Sherman about you yesterday. He denies any attempt on his part to, in any measure, take a command from you, and says he would prefer you to either Blair or Logan, but three columns in the Army of the Tennessee was too small, etc. Blair and Logan, he says, have a political power and that it is useless to fight, that Blair was soreheaded because he was not given the army, and that was the reason I accused him of injustice and underrating you; all of which he denied.
>
> I have found out the secret of managing him; it is to complain of bad treatment and injustice on his part. He can stand anything but that, but I don't think he is governed by rules of justice, but by whims and he cannot stand a person that will stand up and insist upon his rights. Blair he pronounces an unmitigated nuisance. Logan is a bitter enemy of yours,—why I cannot imagine. If you were here now, you would have the 15th Corps, as Logan is not here and unless he gets here in the next two days, he will not be here in time. . . .
>
> I have gotten along well with Corse, and he is a friend of yours, but he is intensely selfish and is looking out for number one.[34]

Meanwhile, the presidential election was at hand. To Sherman's chagrin, McClellan, the Democratic candidate, who had ignored him during the dark days of his "madness" in Kentucky, now wrote him twice asking for help. When, on September 20, the *New York Herald* published a story attributing to Sherman the comment that McClellan would get "ninety-nine out of every hundred" votes in the army, Sherman denied saying so. Having lived in Ohio, California, Missouri, Louisiana, and Kansas, he was a permanent resident of no state and could not vote. Both he and Grant were, he confessed to Halleck, "deficient" in the "principles of history" and were "mere actors in a grand drama. . . . Show this letter to the President, except this conclusion: Damn the mischievous newspapers."[35]

Both Cump and John ended up supporting Lincoln only because they feared McClellan's election would bring disunion. "I know he dislikes me," John confided to his brother about Lincoln, "& I believe in his mind has no friendship for you. He is a singular man. It is hard that we should tread through this difficult & dangerous ordeal as a Nation with such a head, but if we do so successfully it will demonstrate the strength of our Government."[36]

Sherman's last letter to Ellen before leaving for the sea was an ode to two fallen souls. The first was Willy:

> To see his full eye dilate & brighten when he heard that his Papa was a Great General, would be to me now more grateful than the Clamor of the Millions. Why I cannot tell I do not think that Tommy or any- one else would feel in me one bit of the pride that Willy did. He seemed to know me better than anyone else, and realized the truth that if I labored it was for him. He knew or seemed to know that all I had was his, whether of money or property or fame. I may be in error, but with him died in me all real ambition and what has come to me since is unsought, unsolicited.

The second was Ransom. "Yesterday," Sherman continued, "I had Willy's death brought before me in painful reality." Ransom, "one of our youngest & best generals, McPhersons favorite, and who shared with us all the Mississippi Campaigns took sick on this march, and neglected himself till too late." On the road to Rome, Sherman saw him being carried "on a litter on the shoulders of men." His face bore "that look I can never forget—the same that Willy had for two days before he died." The doctors said that Ransom might recover, but Sherman knew better. Carried into a nearby house, Ransom died a few hours later.[37]

On November 6, Sherman sent Grant a long farewell message. "I felt com- pelled to do what is usually a mistake in war," he admitted, "divide my forces, send a part back into Tennessee, retaining the balance here." He had already dispatched Stanley, with 17,000 men, and Schofield, with 10,000, to Nashville. This gave Thomas two full corps of infantry, 5,000 cavalry, and 10,000 dis- mounted cavalry with which to bottle up Hood and Beauregard, the latter now directing Confederate movements in the West. Hood was at Florence, Alabama, quiet enough, but "that devil Forrest" had emerged from nowhere to capture two gunboats and five transports on the Tennessee River, at once depressing Sherman and exciting his admiration. Sherman had already exiled to the rear his "sick and wounded and worthless, and all the vast amount of stores accumulated by our army in the advance." In a few days his troops would be paid, Lincoln would be reelected, and he would leave Atlanta.

Three possible routes were open to him. Sherman might move southeast to Macon and then east to Augusta, reaching the sea at Charleston or Savannah. From either of these he could march north to reinforce Grant in Virginia. The "second and easiest route would be due south." Sherman could free the prisoners at Andersonville and destroy 400,000 bales of cotton, but this route would take him away from Grant. The third direction was southwest. It would enable Sherman to join with General E. R. S. Canby in the reduction of Mobile and to destroy "my old enemy Beauregard." Even now Sherman could not tell Grant which of the three paths he would take. "I will not attempt to send couriers back," he concluded, "but trust to the Richmond papers to keep you well advised."[38]

By the eleventh, with Lincoln reelected, Sherman had decided to head toward Macon. He had, he informed Halleck, burned everything of value in Rome. He intended to do the same in Atlanta "and to start on the 16th on the projected grand raid. All appearances still indicate that Beauregard has got back to his old hole at Corinth, and I hope he will enjoy it. My army prefers to enjoy the fresh sweet-potato fields of the Ocmulgee."[39]

As much as Sherman complained about journalists, he was responsible for the biggest newspaper blunder of his life. On November 9 the *Indianapolis Journal* published a brief account of Sherman's plans. The next day the *New York Times* elaborated on the article. Its story was, Grant told Stanton, "the most contraband news I have seen published during the war. The Times lays out Sherman's programme exactly and gives his strength. It is impossible to keep these papers from reaching the enemy, and no doubt by to-morrow they will be making the best arrangements they can to meet this move."[40]

Stanton blamed Sherman for the disclosures:

They come from Sherman's army, and generally from his own officers, and there is reason to believe he has not been very guarded in his own talk. I saw today, in a paymaster's letter to another officer, his plans as stated by himself. Yesterday I was told full details given by a member of his staff to a friend in Washington. Matters not spoken of aloud in the Department are bruited by officers coming from Sherman's army in every Western printing office and street. If he cannot keep from telling his plans to paymasters, and his staff are permitted to send them broadcast over the land, the Department cannot prevent their publication.[41]

Grant moved at once to stop the reports. Following his orders, General Alfred H. Terry of the Army of the Potomac was able to confiscate all copies of the controversial newspapers before they reached the South. The *Journal* had admitted getting its information from officers in Chattanooga. Grant vowed to send the culprits to the Dry Tortugas as punishment, but Major General Alvin P. Hovey in Indianapolis was unable to find out who they were.[42]

— IV —

Before leaving Atlanta, Sherman organized his infantry force of 55,000 men into two wings. Howard led the right wing, consisting of the Fifteenth Corps, headed by the Prussian, Major General Peter J. Osterhaus, and the Seventeenth Corps, led by Blair. Slocum commanded the left wing, which consisted of Jeff C. Davis's Fourteenth Corps and Alpheus Williams's Twentieth. Kilpatrick led the cavalry, 5,000 strong. Sherman also took along 1,800 artillerymen and sixty-five guns. His train consisted of 2,500 wagons, each pulled by six mules, divided equally among the four corps. For the sick, who turned out to be few, he had 600 ambulances, each drawn by two horses. The number of horses in the caravan, including those of the cavalry and the officers, totaled about 24,000. Confident he could feed the animals along the way, Sherman carried forage for only three days.[43]

On November 15, most of the army was moved out of Atlanta. Poe and his engineers then went to work. Wrecking the railroad to Chattanooga constituted the Civil War version of Hernando Cortés destroying his ships so his men could not turn back when he marched against the Aztecs in Mexico. Now, in a day and a night, Atlanta was turned into a Carthage. Poe destroyed the car shed, the depots, the rolling mills, the machine shops, the foundries, and the arsenals. All of the city's hotels except the Gate City fell before the flames. So, too, did between four and five thousand homes. "The crowning act of all their wickedness and villainy," General W. P. Howard of the Georgia militia reported to Governor Brown five weeks after Sherman left, "was committed by our ungodly foe in removing the dead from the vaults in the cemetery, and robbing the coffins of the silver name plates and tippings, and depositing their own dead in the vaults."

In Atlanta, the evening of the fifteenth brought no darkness. Colonel Adin B. Underwood, of the Thirty-third Massachusetts, remembered:

> As the band was playing in the theatre that night, the flaming red light from the approaching fire, which flooded the building, the roar of the flames and the noises of the intermittent explosions, added scenic effects which were not down in the bills, and will never be forgotten. And when later in the night it serenaded Sherman and played in the light of the flames "John Brown's soul goes marching on," the members must have appeared to the crest fallen chivalry like so many Neros fiddling with delight at the burning of Rome.[44]

On the morning of the sixteenth the soldiers, each carrying a knapsack with from three to five days' rations, a half of a shelter tent, and forty rounds, began marching. To cover as wide a path as possible and to convey the impression that the Federal army was threatening both Macon and Augusta, Sherman assigned to each of his corps a different route. Osterhaus's men occupied the right, Blair's the right center, Davis's the left center, and Williams's the left.[45]

During the first day Sherman traveled with the 104th Illinois of Davis's corps, which headed toward Stone Mountain. An officer of the regiment remembered:

> We had three views of him, as all will recollect, first sitting on the porch of a log cabin, the humble abode of a Georgia "cracker," where we had halted to rest, a cigar in his mouth, while beside him sat one of the female "poor white trash," puffing away at her corn-cob pipe. We soon after passed by with as straight faces as possible and about noon halted for dinner. The General and Staff passed us, and as we moved on after dinner we saw him sitting on the door steps of another cabin eating his crackers and meat with his fingers. The third time we saw him sitting in the passageway between the two ends of a cabin, a dozen or two negroes standing around and staring at him in wonder and awe.[46]

On the second day out the food gatherers went to work. On November 9, in his field order to his commanders, Sherman encouraged his army to "forage liberally on the country during the march." The foragers were soon dubbed "bummers," a word brought west, Sherman believed, by Hooker's Twentieth Corps. In New York bummers were firemen who at election time sat around the engine house on their "bums" waiting for politicians to buy their votes. But, Sherman insisted, his bummers "were not stragglers in an offensive sense. . . . They were ahead, and on both flanks, serving admirably the purpose of Advance Guards and flankers."[47]

Each day, the commander of a brigade selected about fifty men for foraging. Leaving on foot early in the morning, they scoured the countryside for miles. They ransacked plantations and houses and confiscated horses, mules, carriages, wagons, carts, and other means of transportation. These the foragers loaded with hams, bacon, turkeys, chickens, corn, sweet potatoes, molasses, pickles, and anything else edible. They also drove in cows, sheep, and hogs. The bummers took it all to a point a few miles ahead of the marching column. When the troops reached them, they turned over their supplies to the commissary department and rejoined their units. Early in the journey the foragers were extremely successful. On the second night out the Third Wisconsin feasted on a supper of beefsteak, port steak, sweet potatoes, and honey.

Foraging had its dangers. The men detailed were encouraged to keep together, for they often ran into bands of enemy cavalry and infantry. Some foragers were captured and hanged. Others had their throats cut. Still others were forced to join the Confederate army. "Some of the foraging parties," Sherman reported, "had engagements with the enemy which would, in ordinary times, rank as respectable battles."[48]

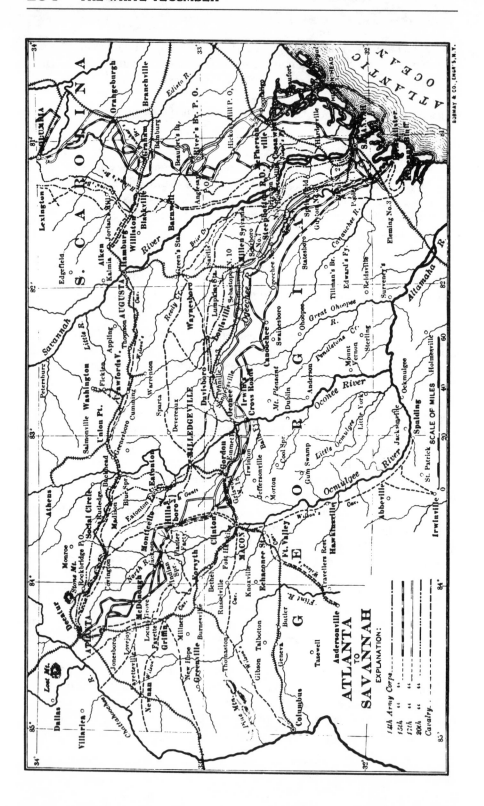

Among his men, Sherman gained a reputation for winking at abuses. He once told the band of the Thirty-third Massachusetts that his army was destroying a million and a half dollars of supplies a day. He had no intention of interfering with this work. Underwood related:

> Almost the first day out, Sherman met a soldier who had been out foraging on his own hook, and had a ham on his musket, a jug of sorghum molasses under his arm, and a big piece of honey in his hand from which he was eating. "Forage liberally on the country," the soldier dryly said for Sherman's benefit, quoting from his general order issued just before the start. The General tried to be stern but laughed inwardly.[49]

Once, some members of the Third Wisconsin found a barrel of molasses. They were rolling it to camp when Sherman came along. For a moment the general and the men stared at each other. Then Sherman took an ax, knocked in the head of the barrel, dipped his finger into the syrup, and tasted it. He told the men to help themselves, but in an orderly way. He did not want the syrup wasted and wanted as many men as possible to enjoy a canteenful.[50]

A day or two later Sherman was riding alone and with his coat off when he came upon a soldier "covered with plunder." When Sherman threatened him with arrest, the soldier began cursing, using words like "damn" and "hell." Back and forth they argued, until Sherman identified himself and demanded to know to whom he was speaking. Swinging chickens in his hands, the culprit answered: "Oh, hell, General, I am Abner F. Dean, *Chaplain* of the 112th Massachusetts." Without bothering to salute, the clergyman picked up whatever he had dropped and walked away.[51]

To stop the foraging by stragglers and others not authorized, Sherman issued Special Field Order Number 120, but he felt helpless to enforce it. On November 19, Sherman and his judge advocate, Major Henry Hitchcock, the nephew of General Hitchcock, passed soldiers grabbing pigs, chickens, and cattle. An elderly woman ran out of a nearby house and asked Sherman to stop the men. The general said he could not do it. That night, before the campfire, he said to Hitchcock: "I'll have to harden my heart to these things. That poor woman today—how could I help her? There's no help for it. The soldiers will take all she has. Jeff Davis is responsible for all this."

Both Jeff C. Davis and Slocum condemned the wanton destruction. Davis told Hitchcock that most soldiers believed Sherman wanted them to burn and pillage houses. "I am bound to say," Hitchcock wrote to his wife, "I think Sherman lacking in enforcing discipline. Brilliant and daring, fertile, rapid and terrible, he does not seem to me *to carry out things in this respect.*" At Kingston, Charley Ewing had confided to Hitchcock that his brother-in-law's great weakness was his inability to have his *"orders carried clean out."* Hitchcock did not know whether to attribute this fault to Sherman's "natural energy" or to his "necessary preoccupation with large matters."[52]

When Jeff C. Davis, a Hoosier long suspected of proslavery sentiments, threatened to shoot those who unnecessarily torched houses, Chaplain John

J. Hight of the Fifty-eighth Indiana condemned him. "The order contained some slanders on the command," the chaplain wrote. "It berated our people after the manner of the rebel papers."[53]

The foragers brought in so many fine gamecocks that cockfighting became a common sport. The successful birds were named "Billy Sherman," "Johnny Logan," "Pap Williams," and the like. The unsuccessful ones, labeled "Beauregard," "Hood," and "Hardee," ended up in the stewpan.[54]

Sherman's troops were as efficient in wrecking railroads as they were in foraging. For this purpose Poe developed a cant hook that was placed on each end of track. As many men as possible got hold of the handles and twisted in opposite directions. The result was a section of track that became useless unless brought to a machine shop and reshaped. Another method was to ignite a pile of railroad ties. The center of the rail was placed on the fire. The men would then wrap the red-hot center around a tree or a telegraph pole. Just as chimneys of burned houses became known as Sherman's Monuments, twisted rails became known as Sherman's Doughnuts, Sherman's Corkscrews, and Sherman's Hairpins. At every milepost along a railroad, the soldiers tried to bend softened rails into the letters U.S., prominently displaying them on inclined surfaces.[55]

Almost from the first day out, thousands of slaves, using every conceivable means of transportation, joined the marching columns. "Wherever Sherman rode," wrote Underwood, "they crowded about him shouting and praying with a touching eloquence. They evidently regarded him as the great deliverer." Some saw the approach of the army as a chance to reunite families separated by slavery. The chaplain of the Seventy-eighth Ohio heard one woman plead to be taken to Savannah, where she might join her husband and children, from whom she had been sold several years before. Another woman had heard that her son, whom she had not seen for four years, was in Macon. Never believing that blacks were the equals of whites, Sherman nonetheless spent hours talking to the refugees, trying to dissuade all but the able-bodied men, whom the army could use, from accompanying him. His policy, however, was never to turn back those who followed his army.[56]

The handsomest of the women slaves were pampered by the soldiers. Captain David P. Conyngham of the *New York Herald* reported that young women sometimes dressed in the fine clothes picked up at plantations. They stowed away by day in baggage wagons, "feasted at the servants' mess at night," and, briefly at least, "led luxurious lives."[57]

Early in the march, at the towns of Conyers and Covington, the invaders were also attracted to the young white women. "The ladies, at some of the houses, are represented as intelligent, beautiful, and rebellious," observed Chaplain Hight. "A pretty traitor is no better than an ugly one—male or female. Many of the officers are boiling over with sympathy for these pretty female rebels, but I have none and have a great contempt for all officers who have."

On the second day out, Hight noted the first case of attempted rape. "Rumor says that one of the soldiers was shot by a woman whom he was attempting to outrage," he wrote. "May such villains die the same death."[58]

General Judson W. Bishop of the Second Minnesota recalled a different kind of incident that took place as the troops were leaving Covington. On the veranda of a comfortable farmhouse several ladies sat watching the soldiers, one of whom noticed traces of recently dug-up ground. Eagerly the soldiers began digging at the spot. After a few minutes they uncovered a pine box. According to Bishop,

> The ladies, too, seemed to be excited and anxious about it—perhaps their money or their silver spoons were in peril. The box being carefully uncovered the top was pried off and there exposed to view were the remains of a spaniel dog, rebuking his disturbers with an odoriferous protest that reached their consciences by the most direct route. The lid was replaced, the pit refilled and the earth and sod carefully replaced and dressed over ready for the next brigade. Now the lady of the house graciously remarked that poor Fido was not resting in peace very much that day; this was the fourth time he had been resurrected since morning.[59]

Meanwhile, Howard's infantry and Kilpatrick's cavalry feigned an attack on Macon. Kilpatrick's men actually penetrated the town's defenses but were pushed back. On November 22, led by General P. J. Phillips, who some of his troops swore had been drinking that day, 3,700 Georgia militiamen, mostly old men and boys, attacked Howard's veterans, many armed with the deadly Spencer repeating rifles. The Confederate force then fell back into Macon, which Howard had no intention of assaulting.[60]

While the right wing pushed on past Macon, Sherman's left wing approached the state capital, Milledgeville, a town of some 2,500 people about a hundred miles southeast of Atlanta. The night of November 21 was so cold that water froze in the soldiers' canteens. Huddled around fires, Slocum's troops could not sleep. Many were half-shod, for they had started out with poor shoes and had thrown away their new ones rather than break them in on a long march.

Seeking shelter from the cold on the twenty-second, Sherman was directed into a log cabin. Finding Poe and some others before a fire in one room, he looked about and saw a small box marked "Howell Cobb." Sherman then realized he was at the plantation of Cobb, the secretary of the treasury under Buchanan and now the head of the Georgia militia. He sent word back to Davis to spare nothing. That night many of the regiments camped on the plantation. The troops burned Cobb's fences to keep warm and ate or burned a huge mound of peanuts, about a thousand bushels.[61]

On the morning of November 23 a brigade of the Twentieth Corps, its band playing "Marching Along," entered Milledgeville. As the head of the column approached the state capitol, the band changed to "Yankee Doodle." From doors and windows the white residents of the town looked on silently. At the capitol the keeper came out, opened the gates to the park surrounding the building, and gave the keys to Colonel William Hawley, who was appointed commander of the city. As the flag of one of the regiments was hoisted atop the capitol, the band struck up "The Star-Spangled Banner." The Third Wisconsin was to guard the town, but it arrived too late to stop the pillaging of the capitol building. "Relic hunters ransacked everything," noted Underwood, "and carried away, before the provost guard arrived, books, archives, minerals, fossils and millions of State bonds and unsigned Georgia State money." Some of the men used paper money to cook coffee. Others played poker with it.

Ever in search of romance, the Federals also used the money to ingratiate themselves with the hundreds of girls who worked the looms of a large cotton factory in town. Learning the girls had not been paid for months, the soldiers, according to the adjutant of the Third Wisconsin, "trudged back to the state treasury, got a bushel of the 'money' and took it to the factory giving the girls $800 or $1000 apiece, making them very happy—for a short time."[62]

In his *Memoirs*, Sherman made much of the comments in the newspapers he found at Milledgeville. Beauregard, former United States senator Benjamin Hill, and the leaders of the state legislature, including Underwood's school chum, Julian Hartridge, implored Georgians to "Arise for the defense of your native soil!" and "destroy the enemy by retarding his march." These comments seemed to shock Sherman, who just before beginning the march had written: "I am going into the very bowels of the Confederacy and propose leaving a trail that will be recognized fifty years hence."[63]

After urging his fellow Georgians to stand fast against the invaders, Brown, taking along a cow, a supply of cabbage, and all but the heaviest pieces of furniture, abandoned the governor's mansion and fled east by train. Many members of the state legislature, in session the day before the Federals entered the town, did the same. Slocum set up headquarters in the Milledgeville Hotel, and Sherman moved into the governor's mansion. Spreading out his blankets, Sherman slept on the floor.[64]

In Milledgeville, the capitol and private homes were spared. But the penitentiary, most of whose 150 prisoners had been released by Brown under promise that they would join the Confederate army, was burned without orders. Sherman did authorize the destruction of the depot and the arsenal. The latter, a brick building, contained cutlasses and pikes kept, the Northerners said, to put down a possible slave insurrection. The magazine, also made of brick, housed large quantities of ammunition. Reverend George S. Bradley, the chaplain of the Twenty-second Wisconsin, saw six wagons being used to cart this ammunition to the nearby Oconee River, into which it was dumped.[65]

During the one-day stay a group of colonels, fortified by brandy and bourbon, assembled in the chamber of the state Senate and held a mock session of the legislature. Opening with a drink, the delegates named a Committee on Federal Relations, one of whose members was Colonel Charles Ewing, who had rejoined Sherman in early November. The committee drew up a resolution denouncing secession and authorizing Sherman's army to return Georgia to the union. As the cry "the Yanks are coming" rang out, the session broke up. "It was the talk of the army for days," noted Edwin E. Bryant of the Third Wisconsin, "and Gen. Sherman 'enjoyed the joke' as heartily as the rest."[66]

On the twenty-fourth, Thanksgiving Day, the march resumed. After menacing Macon, Howard, with the right wing, moved toward Swainsboro and Savannah, destroying track as he went. The left wing bore southeast, striking the railroad connecting Macon and Savannah below Sandersville. Wearing a slouched black hat and a black cloak with a collar so high it hid half of his face, Sherman, buried in thought and looking neither to the right or left, rode with the Twentieth Corps. Often the men would ask, in voices loud enough for him to hear, whether "Uncle Billy knows where he is going?" Uncle Billy never answered.[67]

Averaging ten miles a day, Slocum's column moved relentlessly toward the Confederate stockade at Camp Lawton, five miles above Millen. Completed only a month or so earlier, Lawton housed at its peak over 10,000 Yankee prisoners. As his troops approached the prison, Sherman sent Kilpatrick to try to break the railroad to Savannah, over which the prisoners might be sent. But before Kilpatrick was able to reach them, the prisoners were shipped to Savannah, and from there to other prison camps.[68]

Entering the compound on December 4, the Federal troops grew sick at what they saw. Carved out of an unbroken forest, the stockade was constructed of pine logs twenty-two feet long and fifteen inches in diameter, the logs being set six feet into the ground. Inside, the low fence signified the "dead line," beyond which no Yankee could venture without fear of being shot. Like Massachusetts under the Puritans, Camp Lawton contained stocks for the punishment of inmates.

Some prisoners lived in crude huts. Many lived without any covering, exposed to frost, rain, sun, and dew. Seeking protection, these men dug out of the earth what were called "gopher holes." "And there, also," remembered Underwood, "was the village of graves, nine hundred of them, for the one month's occupation by the brave Federal soldiers under the tender mercies of the sons of the Huguenots." Predicted Chaplain Thomas M. Stevenson of the Seventy-eighth Ohio: "God will certainly visit the authors of this crime with his terrible lightning."[69]

Because of such camps, the Yankees shot all canines. "Wherever our army has passed," observed Stevenson, "everything in the shape of a dog has been killed. The soldiers and officers are determined that no flying fugitives, white men or negroes, shall be followed by track-hounds that come within reach of the powder and ball."[70]

In retaliation for what they saw at Camp Lawton, Sherman's men burned the depot at Millen. Then Sherman's columns pivoted, turned aside from Augusta, where Bragg was awaiting them, and went to the right, down the peninsula formed by the Ogeechee and Savannah Rivers. Having left the Georgia of corn and cotton, of chicken and turkeys, of hams and sorghum, the Federals were now in the "piney woods," a sixty-mile tract of huge trees. "The men seemed as pygmies beside those massive pines," observed Bryant, "running up tall, straight, their branches so high, a lumberman's paradise."[71]

Tired of chickens and turkeys, the troops longed for the Promised Land of the coast. "Their mouths fairly watered, day by day," commented Underwood, "as they thought of oysters cooked in all styles of the art—stewed, fried and roasted on the half-shell. They counted the days for these luxuries and for a smell of the salt sea."[72]

Nearing Savannah, General Jeff C. Davis played the leading role in a series of heartless episodes. On December 3 Davis's Fourteenth Corps, followed by a large number of blacks, reached Buck Head Creek, a deep, swampy stream about forty feet wide. The Confederates had burned the bridge over the creek, but the men of the Fifty-eighth Indiana soon laid pontoons. Within the Fourteenth Corps, observed Hight, a fellow Hoosier, Davis had a reputation as "a military tyrant, without one spark of humanity in his make-up. He was an ardent pro-slavery man before he entered the army, and has not changed his views since." After marching his troops over the creek, Davis ordered the bridge taken up, abandoning the Negroes who were following his army on the other side. "The scene made an impression on my mind that will never be forgotten," Hight wrote. Among the slaves the cry arose that Wheeler's cavalry was coming. Panic-stricken, many plunged into the water and tried to swim across. "Some were drowned," Hight remembered, "how many is not known."[73]

On December 9, at Ebenezer Creek, a swollen stream about 170 feet wide and 8 or 10 feet deep, Davis repeated the order. On the pretense that enemy soldiers might be to the front, guards prevented between five and six hundred slaves from using the pontoon bridge. To a gathering of Civil War veterans, Colonel Charles D. Kerr of the Sixteenth Illinois Cavalry described what happened:

> My regiment was in the rear of everything in the Fourteenth Corps that day. As soon as we were over the creek, orders were given to the engineers to take up the pontoons, and not let a negro cross. The order was obeyed to the letter. I sat upon my horse then and witnessed a scene the like of which I pray my eyes may never see again.
>
> Already the shots from Wheeler's carbines were beginning to tell upon the dense mass upon the farther shore. Rushing to the water's brink, they raised their heads and implored from the corps commander the protection they had been promised. Sherman was many miles away, the prayer was in vain, and with cries of anguish and despair, men, women, and children rushed by hundreds into the turbid stream, and many were drowned before our eyes. From what we learned afterwards of those who remained upon the land, their fate at the hands of Wheeler's troops was scarcely to be preferred. I speak of what I saw with my own eyes, and no writer who was not upon the ground can gloss the matter over for me. . . . It was unjustifiable and perfidious, and across the stretch of twenty years my soul burns with indignation to-night as I recall it.

Kerr obviously aimed his remark about a "writer who was not upon the ground" at Sherman, who in his autobiography callously explained away Davis's cruelty by arguing that the slaves abandoned at Ebenezer Creek had fallen asleep.[74]

On December 8, Sherman was involved in a different kind of episode. His army was moving easily, covering fifteen miles a day, being harassed intermittently by the Confederate division led by General Lafayette McLaws. As they approached the seacoast, the Federals found themselves in the swamps, amidst the rice plantations of the Savannah River. For a week the soldiers, the Negroes, the horses, and the mules subsisted on unhulled rice, each soldier being allotted a gill a day. "We pounded (or hulled) rice in mess pans with the butts of our guns," remembered a member of the 104th Illinois. "However, not being able to get all the hulls off, when eating the rice some of it scratched all the way down." Worse yet, the Yankees, who had begun the march amidst plenty, were reduced to cooking and making coffee with swamp water.[75]

Riding along, Sherman came upon a group of men standing around a handsome young lieutenant of the First Alabama Cavalry named Tupper. Before withdrawing, some Confederates had placed torpedoes in the road, which were set to detonate when walked on. Tupper was helping scrape the dirt off one when he stepped back and exploded another. Hitchcock described the "poor fellow's leg" as "horribly torn and mutilated, raw and bloody end of bone and torn muscles, etc., where torn off. Piece of shell had also run up leg *inside*, along the bone, and came out near knee, shattering bone. Leg was soon afterwards amputated above knee—hope he'll recover but doubtful. . . . But this is Southern 'chivalry'—as their lying newspapers probably illustrate 'Southern honor'!"

Sherman called it "not war, but murder" and immediately ordered some prisoners with picks and shovels to dig out the remaining torpedoes. "They begged hard," Sherman recollected, "but I reiterated the order, and could hardly help laughing at their stepping so gingerly along the road, where it was supposed sunken torpedoes might explode at each step." The prisoners found seven of the deadly instruments without incident. "Had I not done so promptly," Sherman later said of his decision, "many a good man would have been killed or lacerated along the hundreds of miles we had still to travel before reaching the end of our journey."[76]

That night Sherman arrived at Pooler's Station, eight miles from Savannah. During the next two days his entire army reached the city's defenses and invested them, the Fourteenth Corps on the extreme left, touching the Savannah River, the Twentieth Corps next to it, then the Seventeenth Corps, and finally the Fifteenth on the extreme right. While reconnoitering the railroad leading into Savannah, Sherman noticed some rebel artillerymen about eight hundred yards off preparing to fire. He warned the officers about him to scatter, saw a white puff of smoke, and then "caught sight of the ball as it rose in its flight." Someone called to a Negro crossing the track, but before the man understood the danger, the ball, a 32-pounder, struck the ground and on the first bounce caught him under the right jaw, tearing off his head and "scattering blood and brains about." A soldier covered the body with an overcoat, and Sherman's party scrambled away.[77]

Sherman decided not to attack Savannah, where Hardee commanded the Confederates, but "to open communications with our fleet, supposed to be waiting for us with supplies and clothing in Ossabaw Sound," where the Ogeechee River met the Atlantic Ocean, twenty or so miles south of Savannah. Overlooking the spot was Fort McAllister, guarded by twenty-three cannons, a mortar, and about 250 men, commanded by Major George W. Anderson. Some nights before Howard had sent his intrepid scout, Captain William Duncan, past the fort in a canoe to inform Admiral John Dahlgren that Sherman had emerged from the interior of Georgia. While Slocum pressed the siege of Savannah, Sherman sent Howard's engineers and a division of men to rebuild King's Bridge, which traversed the Ogeechee fourteen and a half miles southwest of Savannah and afforded access to McAllister. At dawn on the thirteenth General William B. Hazen, commanding the Second Division of the Fifteenth Corps, crossed the completed bridge and advanced toward the fort. Sherman, meanwhile, rode ten miles down the left bank of the river to the rice plantation of a Mr. Cheeves, where Howard had placed a signal station that overlooked the lower portion of the river.[78]

Joined by his aide, Captain Joseph C. Audenreid, Poe, and Charley Ewing, Sherman stood atop the roof of a shed attached to Cheeves's rice mill. At about 2:00 P.M., Hazen, who was about to attack, signaled back to find out if Sherman was watching. Assured he was, Hazen finished his preparations. Suddenly, through his glasses, Sherman saw a faint puff of smoke advancing along the river. It grew bolder and bolder until a smokestack became visible. One of Dahlgren's steamers had made it to the river and was coming up it. After a while, officers on the vessel signaled with a flag: "Who are you?" The answer came back swiftly: "General Sherman."[79]

With but an hour's daylight left, Hazen's men emerged from the woods in front of the fort, pressed forward to the outer works, and with regimental colors flying entered them. Advancing to the main works, the head of the column disappeared. Fearing disaster, Sherman put down his glasses. He could not bear to watch. But Charley Ewing was sure the men had disappeared into lower ground. Within a few moments the Federals reappeared. In another minute they reached the parapet. The victory, however, was costly. The Unionists lost 24 killed and 110 wounded, compared with 14 killed and 21 wounded for the Confederates.[80]

After the fall of the fort, Sherman and Howard went down the river on a small boat, manned by a crew of volunteer officers, to the house in which Hazen had set up headquarters. Battling the tide for four hours, the rowers reached the house with hands blistered and arms weary. That evening Anderson joined the Union generals for supper. As the Confederate major described it, Sherman "looked like a game rooster with all his feathers ruffled and seemed to be in a very bad humor." Noticing Sherman's anger, Hazen stepped on Anderson's foot to warn him of the coming storm. "Do you condone the use of torpedoes in civilized warfare?" Sherman barked. "It's inhuman. It's barbarous. And this is your Southern Chivalry."

Later, the Federal officers walked over to McAllister, about a mile away. "Inside the fort lay the dead as they had fallen," Sherman lamented, "and they could hardly be distinguished from their living comrades, sleeping soundly side by side in the pale moonlight." In a yawl Sherman and Howard proceeded about six miles down the river to the mouth of the Ogeechee, where they found the vessel they had seen, the *Dandelion*. From its commander they learned that Dahlgren was aboard his flagship, the *Harvest Moon*, in Wassaw Sound, seven or eight miles to the north. General John G. Foster was in command of the department, with headquarters at Hilton Head, on the ocean just over the South Carolina line. Sherman also found out that Grant was at Petersburg, Virginia, having made no progress against Lee. Returning to Hazen's headquarters, Sherman shared Hazen's blanket and soon fell asleep on the floor.[81]

In the middle of the night the general was awakened by one of Foster's officers. Foster, on a steamer several miles down the river, wanted to see Sherman. Suffering from a Mexican War wound, he could not make the trip up. Could Sherman come to him? At the meeting Foster told Sherman that he had failed to break the railroad connecting Charleston with Savannah, even though he had a division of men. He did, however, have at Port Royal, just above Hilton Head, abundant supplies of clothing, coffee, sugar, and hardtack, all of which Sherman needed.[82]

Capturing Fort McAllister opened a supply path to Sherman's army. Foster forwarded from Port Royal 600,000 rations. And Sherman's army received its first mail. Arriving with it on the fourteenth, Colonel Absalom H. Markland had also brought to Sherman greetings from Lincoln. One division mailman noted that "it took a six-mule army wagon loaded to the big canvass cover" to carry his share of the letters. The soldiers now learned which states had voted for Lincoln and of the attempt by Confederates to bring the war home to the North by burning down buildings in New York City.[83]

On the evening of the next day, December 15, Colonel Maxwell V. Woodhull, an aide of Howard's, was sitting alone before a campfire when an officer and his orderly rode up. The officer identified himself as Colonel Orville Babcock of Grant's staff. He asked for Sherman, who was staying with Howard but was so fatigued by the activities of the past forty-eight hours that he had retired early. Woodhull went inside the tent in which Sherman was sleeping, awakened him, and told him of the visitor. Babcock carried a letter from Grant, dated December 6, in which Grant suggested that Sherman leave his cavalry and artillery on the coast and by sea bring his infantry to Virginia, where it was needed against Lee.

After a short time, Sherman emerged from the tent alone and came over to the fire. "He was," remembered Woodhull, "deep in thought, and utterly oblivious to his surroundings." Not bothering to dress, Sherman had thrown his overcoat, loosely buttoned, over his gray drawers and gray stockings. Despite the chill, he wore no boots. Lost in thought, he stood brushing ashes over one foot with the other. Finally he turned and went back into the tent to continue his conversation with Babcock.[84]

The suggestion that he abandon Savannah, whose capture was imminent, and sail north bothered Sherman enormously. Woodhull always believed that in front of that fire Sherman's ideas crystallized, for the next day he suggested to Grant that, after capturing Savannah, he "instantly march to Columbia, South Carolina, thence to Raleigh, and thence to report to you. But this would consume, it may be, six weeks' time after the fall of Savannah; whereas, by sea, I can probably reach you with my men and arms before the middle of January."[85]

On the sixteenth, when Sherman wrote his first letter home, he was in high spirits. He crowed to Ellen:

> I have no doubt you heard of my safe arrival on the coast. The fact is I never doubted the fact but the Southern Blatherskites have been bragging of all manner of things but have done nothing. . . . We have destroyed nearly two hundred miles of railroad and are not yet done. . . . I can now starve out Savannah unless events call my army to Virginia. . . . I do not apprehend any army attempt to relieve Savannah except Lee's, and if he gives up Richmond it will be the best piece of strategy ever made, to make him let go there.[86]

Concentrating on Savannah, Sherman sent Charley Ewing with a flag of truce to demand the surrender of the city. Although surrounded on all sides but the east, which contained a plank road leading to South Carolina, Hardee rejected the demand. While Sherman went to Hilton Head to confer with Foster about blocking off that route, Hardee's army crossed the Savannah River over a pontoon bridge and escaped. He took with him his light artillery and destroyed an ironclad ram and the navy yard but left his heavy guns, stores, cotton, railway cars, and steamboats. On the morning of December 21, a division of the Twentieth Corps marched into Savannah.

The next day Sherman entered the city. Finding nothing else suitable, he accepted the offer of Charles Green, a British cotton merchant, to use his home as a headquarters. Decorated with mahogany, walnut, and gold, furnished with costly furniture and rare works of art, and filled with exotic plants and tropical fruit trees, the house was a far cry from what Sherman was used to. On that same day Sherman telegraphed Lincoln, presenting "as a Christmas-gift the city of Savannah, with one hundred and fifty heavy guns and plenty of ammunition, also about twenty-five thousand bales of cotton."[87]

The band of the Thirty-third Massachusetts had led the march into Atlanta in early September and had spent Thanksgiving in the capital of Georgia. On Christmas Day, Sherman, fulfilling a promise, brought the musicians to Savannah. In Pulaski Square, before an audience including thousands of blacks, the band played "Yankee Doodle," "The Star-Spangled Banner," and "Dixie." "There was such a mass," remembered Underwood, "that Sherman, reluctantly, had to order the square cleared, finally."[88] Sherman's favorite band had serenaded from Atlanta to the sea.

14

"Gone to Join Willy"

— I —

ON DECEMBER 3, before Sherman emerged from the interior of Georgia, the London *Times* marveled at the events of the past six months. "Since the great Duke of Marlborough turned his back on the Dutch," the paper commented, "and plunged heroically into Germany to fight the famous battle of Blenheim, military history has recorded no stranger marvel than the mysterious expedition of General Sherman on an unknown route against an undiscoverable enemy." Six months before, Sherman had left Chattanooga. Through flanking movements, he "found himself in August before the defenses of Atlanta." He had captured the city. But by attacking Sherman's communications, Hood had made Atlanta as untenable to Sherman as Sherman had made it to Hood. With much of his army Sherman then turned away from Hood. Like Marlborough in 1704, he had marched into mystery.[1]

Grant, for one, thought the march to Savannah entitled Sherman to a reward. Writing to his father, Jesse R. Grant, on December 20, he praised Sherman as "one of the greatest, purest, and best of men. He is poor and always will be." Grant, who according to his father had already received $80,000 in gifts from grateful Northerners, suggested that Ohioans establish a fund to buy Mrs. Sherman a furnished house in Cincinnati. To such a worthy cause the commander, no longer the impoverished wood peddler, pledged $500. His chief quartermaster, General Rufus Ingalls, offered $250 more. Led by John D. Caldwell of Cincinnati, the Ohio testimonial committee raised $10,000 in gold, which it gave to the Shermans in March.[2]

From Savannah on December 24, Sherman thanked Grant for changing the request that he sail with his army to Virginia. He had thought through his plans "so long and so well, that they appear as clear as daylight." He had deceived the enemy into believing that his next objective would be either Augusta or

Charleston. He intended to ignore both, to occupy Columbia and Camden, and to head toward Wilmington and the Charleston & Wilmington Railroad. "Charleston," he informed Grant, "is now a mere desolated wreck, and is hardly worth the time it would take to starve it out." From Wilmington he would move on Raleigh. "The game is then up with Lee, unless he comes out of Richmond, avoids you, and fights me; in which event, I should reckon on your being on his heels."[3]

That same day Sherman warned Halleck about what his troops might do in South Carolina. "I almost tremble at her fate, but feel that she deserves all that seems in store for her. . . . I look upon Columbia as quite as bad as Charleston, and I doubt if we shall spare the public buildings as we did at Milledgeville."[4]

On Christmas Day, Sherman sent greetings to Thomas. "Had any misfortune befallen you I should have reproached myself for taking away so large a proportion of the army and leaving you too weak to cope with Hood," he wrote. "But as events have turned out my judgment has been sustained; but I am none the less thankful to you, and to Schofield, and to all for the very complete manner in which you have used up Hood." Sherman hoped Thomas would be able to march into Alabama and do there what he had done in Georgia.

Savannah brought back to Sherman the days when he and Thomas were stationed in nearby Fort Moultrie:

> Here I am now in a magnificent house, close by the old barracks around which cluster so many of our old memories of Rankin, and Ridgely, and Fraser and others. But the old families that we used to know are nearly all gone or dead. I will not stay here long, however, but push Northwards as the season advances.
>
> The old line oaks are as beautiful as ever, and whilst you are freezing to death in Tennessee we are basking in a warm sun, and I fear I did you personal injustice in leaving you behind whilst I made my winter excursion. But next time I will stay at home and let you go it.[5]

A city of about 20,000 people, Savannah was indeed lovely. Rows of trees graced Bay Street, its central thoroughfare. Many intersections contained small parks adorned with willow-leaf trees. Magnolias shaded private homes, and shrubs and flowers bloomed the year round. The center of town contained a monument of Count Casimir Pulaski, the Pole killed on October 9, 1779, during the American attempt to retake the city from the British. Just beyond the city lay plantations, surrounded by oaks with branches as thick as the trunks of trees in the North.[6]

The streets of Savannah soon became Yankee thoroughfares. In early January, Hight observed:

> The soldiers are generally ragged and dirty, as they have not drawn a supply of clothing since the campaign began; and, besides that, they have been doomed to sit over smoky, pitch pine fires. The officers are, many of them, "dressed to kill." The stars of the 20th Corps prevail in

numbers and pomposity. The little fellows from "down East" go strutting up and down the street, pregnant with their own importance and superiority. What a pity there are not more women to smile approvingly upon them. Oh, for the perfume of cambric handkerchiefs.[7]

One continuous oyster bed, the waters around Savannah yielded a delectable treasure. On New Year's Day of 1865 the soldiers of the Sixteenth Illinois Cavalry enjoyed a meal consisting of oyster soup, oysters on the half shell, roast goose, fried oysters, roasted oysters, rice, raisins, and coffee with condensed milk. "A little top-heavy as to oysters," Colonel Kerr related, "but we don't complain."[8]

For a week Sherman savored the fruits of his triumphal march. Like an eager tourist, he visited the Pulaski House, the hotel where Lieutenant Sherman had stayed two decades before. In a letter to Ellen, he described his quarters at Green's home as "an elegant chamber. . . . My bed room has a bath and dressing room attached which look out of proportion to my poor baggage." His old friends—the Goodwins, Teffts, Cuylers, Habershams, and Laws—were "all gone or in poverty, and yet the girls remain, bright and haughty and proud as ever. There seems no end but utter annihilation that will satisfy their hate of the 'sneaking Yankee' and 'ruthless invader.' "

The leading citizens of Savannah, including Mayor Richard D. Arnold, came to him to pay their respects. Some of them took part in a peace meeting, "*without suggestion from us*," Hitchcock wrote home. " . . . But the greatest indoor feature of our residence in Savannah has been the General's new-found colored friends, who have come by hundreds, I was going to say, to see 'Mr. Sherman.' " On the morning Sherman entered the city, he climbed the roof of a warehouse to visit a signal station. When he came down, a crowd of former slaves had gathered to shake his hand. He spent most of several days talking to blacks. Hitchcock described the scene:

> He has always had them shown in at once, stopping a dispatch or letter or a conversation to greet them in a off-hand—though not undignified way—"Well, boys,—come to see Mr. Sherman, have you? Well I'm Mr. Sherman—glad to see you"—and shaking hands with them all in a manner highly disgusting, I dare say, to a "refined Southern gentleman." The Gen'l gives them all good advice—briefly & to the point, telling them they are free now, have no master nor mistress to *support*, & must be industrious & well-behaved &c.[9]

On December 30, 1864, the steamer *Fulton* arrived at Hilton Head with mail, recent newspapers, and for Sherman word of a tragedy. Opening letters from Thomas Ewing, from Hugh, and from John, Sherman read of the death of his baby son on December 4. From the *New York Herald* of December 22, he learned that little Charles had been buried in South Bend, next to Willy. For Ellen, losing this second son had been indeed trying. She told her aunt:

> His agony was appalling. He wrestled with death like a strong man struck down suddenly in the prime of life. I believe he saw heaven

before his last great struggle for such a piercing unearthly gaze I never beheld as he cast upwards just before his movement forth. . . . Mother's superstitions are generally regarded as idle but I always had a strong presentment that Charley would not live. I felt that Willy would pray to have him taken early to heaven.[10]

Ellen understood that her husband could not mourn for the baby. "Willy's death was indeed a more terrible blow," she conceded to John. "It has not embittered life, but it has rendered it in a measure tasteless to both his father & myself. Even Cump's last letter to me written before he started for Savannah was one long lament for his lost boy—his 'Alter ego'—his idol. He says 'with Willy died in me all real ambition.' "[11]

Sherman responded as Ellen predicted. On the last day of 1864, he wrote:

The last letter I got from you at Kingston made me fear for our baby, but I hoped the little fellow would *weather* the ailment, but it seems he too is lost to us, and gone to join Willy, for he was but a mere ideal, whereas Willy was incorporated with us, and seemed to be designed to perpetuate our memories. But amid the Sum of death and desolation through which I daily pass I cannot but become callous to death. It is so common, so familiar that it no longer impresses me as of old. You on the contrary surrounded alone by life & youth cannot take things so philosophically but are stayed by the Religious faith of a better and brighter life elsewhere. I should like to have seen the baby of which all spoke so well, but I seemed doomed to pass my life away so that even my children will be strangers.

. . . After having participated in driving the Confederacy down the Mississippi, I have again cut it in twain, and have planned & executed a Campaign which Judges pronounce will be famous among the grand deeds of the World. I can hardly realize it for really it was easy . . . ; but here I am in the proud city of Savannah, with an elegant mansion at my command, surrounded by a confident, brave and victorious army that looks to me as its head—Negros & whites flock to me and gaze at me as some wonderful being, and letters from Great men pour in with words of flattery and praise, but still I do more than ever crave for peace and quiet, and would gladly drop all these and gather you and my little ones in some quiet place where I could be at ease.[12]

From St. Mary's Academy in South Bend, which Elly and Rachel were attending, Ellen returned in late December to a subject upon which she had dwelt even before her marriage:

My greatest comfort would be to know that you my dear husband were blessed with the faith which sanctified your children—that you believed in Jesus Christ through whom they were redeemed. Why can you not make your great works meritorious by offering them to God and doing them in His honor? If you do this you will perhaps be rewarded with faith & receive for your labors an imperishable crown in the kingdom of God where our dear ones await us. If you die without the faith you leave us miserable the rest of our lives with a weight of sorrow upon the heart which no worldly influence can dissipate. Why then not ask it of God? . . . The members of the Sherman family would be glad to see you a Catholic because they fear to see you die without any faith. How you can live since Willy died, without the faith I cannot conceive & from my heart I pity you for my own sufferings since his death have been more than I could have borne without its consolations.[13]

As before, Sherman ignored the suggestion.

Amid the grief of losing two sons, Ellen began carving out the future for her remaining son. She was enrolling Tommy, whom she described as "very backward for eight years old," in Notre Dame Academy, which Willy had attended. "I am anxious that he should be a missionary Priest and join the Paulist Fathers," Ellen revealed to Sherman. "Of course he will decide for himself but I hope he may be called to that glorious life."[14]

Ellen's comments began a brief struggle for Tommy's soul. "I am glad Tommy is now finally established at school," the general answered. "I will risk his being a Priest—Of course I should regret such a choice and ask that no influence be lent to produce that result—Let him have a fair manly education, and his own instincts will lead him right—I dont care how strict he may be in Religion, but dont want him a Priest, but he is too young for even the thought."[15]

Upset, Sherman wrote Tommy about his future: "When I was a boy I was not as smart as you, and you can take your own time learning as fast as you please and when you get old enough can choose for yourself whether to be a Soldier, a Lawyer, Doctor or Farmer. . . . I dont want you to be a Soldier or a Priest but a good useful man."[16]

During this debate, Ellen continued to push for Charley's promotion. Several times she asked John to press the matter with the president, even though she knew "that you are not very partial to Mr. Lincoln. . . . I am expecting other letters of recommendation and as my brother Tom is going on to Washington at the time of his resignation I have concluded to wait and get him to press Charley's appointment then." From her husband, early in January, she demanded a letter of recommendation: "I do not intend to take no for an answer but feel that you owe it to him as otherwise his relationship would be a disadvantage to him. He is better than Jno A. Logan & see what position he holds."[17]

In deference to Ellen and to her father, then in Washington arguing cases before the Supreme Court, Sherman sent Charley there with dispatches for the War Department. But he could not recommend Charley's promotion. He explained his position to Ellen: "To make him a Brigadier at the expense of Colonels who have commanded Brigades in half a dozen battles and for two & three years would be a gross injustice to the latter which I cannot commit. . . . To be a General and not to command is a farce. . . . If you let Charley alone he will be content, for he knows the truth."[18]

Despite their differences, Charley always revered Sherman. Hugh, however, did not, for he was convinced his brother-in-law had mistreated him. In January 1863 Hugh had been in Louisville with a brigade of troops, "on my way to join my old friend and commander General Rosecrans," when he heard of Sherman's defeat at Chickasaw. He immediately telegraphed the War Department and got his orders changed. He joined Sherman and, despite his drinking, capably led a division of the Fifteenth Corps at Jackson, Missionary Ridge, and Knoxville.

A quarrel with Logan induced Hugh to leave the Army of the Tennessee. When Logan countermanded one of his orders, Hugh showed him the regulations justifying it. Early in April 1864 Hugh was transferred to Louisville. But this post led nowhere, and Hugh now wanted to rejoin Sherman. "I cannot give him a command here," Sherman explained to Ellen, "without displacing such men as Mower, Corse, Wood, Hazen and others that have filled their parts to my entire satisfaction." Before the Atlanta campaign, Sherman had called Hugh to Nashville and "offered him the command of his old Division which he declined and if he now finds himself out he should not blame me but himself."

Sherman had no room for Hugh, but Thomas might need him in Tennessee. Accordingly, Sherman sent Hugh a letter to be shown to Thomas. But, Hugh complained, the letter contained "praise so faint and dubious, that self interest, as well as self respect, prevents the use of it—I have therefore taken the liberty before forwarding the letter to erase from it all relating to myself." Sherman had thoughtlessly said that Hugh had been "relieved" from service with the Army of the Tennessee because of "some trouble with Logan" and had not given him "due credit for my services under you. . . . I need not say to you that this letter is not meant to prompt official favor."[19] Hugh would take a long time before forgiving Sherman.

—— II ——

"It seems impossible," Sherman revealed to Ellen in early January, "for us to go anywhere without being where I have been before." From 1840 to 1846 he had traveled over much of Florida, Alabama, Georgia, and South Carolina. The past year had taken him back to many of these places, "and every bit of knowledge then acquired is returned, tenfold." In moments alone he thought of hunting with Jim Poyas and Mr. Quash, and of riding "by moonlight to save daytime."[20]

By early January, Sherman's plans for the ensuing campaign were fixed. On the second General Barnard, now Grant's chief engineer, brought a letter authorizing the march northward into the Carolinas. Sherman could follow any route he deemed advisable, but Grant hoped he would be able to emerge near the rear of Petersburg or, failing that, at one of the seaports in North Carolina held by the Federals.[21]

On the last day of 1864, Captain K. R. Breese of Porter's fleet arrived with the news that General Benjamin F. Butler, the beast of New Orleans, had botched the Union attack on Fort Fisher, which guarded Wilmington, one of Sherman's targets in North Carolina. In an obvious slap at Grant, Butler had boasted that he would take the fort without wasting Northern lives. His plan, if it can be called that, consisted of igniting a steamer loaded with powder near Fisher. The explosion, Grant later recorded, had "no more effect on the fort, or anything else on land, than the bursting of a boiler anywhere on the Atlantic Ocean would have done." Even after Porter's ships hammered the fort, Butler, calling the place impregnable, withdrew without fighting. Grant then dismissed Butler, who returned to his home in Lowell, Massachusetts, and began delivering speeches justifying his conduct.

Breeze brought from Porter a request that Sherman send one of his divisions to capture the fort. Sherman was overjoyed at hearing from his good friend, but he was planning his own campaign. He could not get bogged down in someone else's. He was awaiting supplies of coffee, sugar, and hardtack before setting out.[22]

After General Terry captured Fort Fisher on January 15, Grant's friends were elated. "I never saw Gen Butler," Cump wrote John, "but cannot deny that I look on his downfall as the addition of 20,000 men to Grants army. The trouble with such men is they wont fight themselves, but keep their commands out.—Terrys success simply fulfills Grants calculation, and stamps Butlers pretension about shedding blood uselessly as poltroonery & knavery."[23]

Waiting for supplies, Sherman had no work for his army. This meant inspections and parades. On January 7, while roaming about Bay Street, Chaplain Hight stumbled across Sherman and his generals waiting to review the Fifteenth Corps. Sherman wore an "old fashioned, 'sideboard' shirt collar, the only one, I suppose, in the Army of Georgia. It looks very odd and out of place." His gloves were "dingy and old," his hat "sorry looking, and destitute of ornament. When he saw the boys coming he twitched himself this way and that, tugged at his collar, pulled at his coat and made sundry adjustments of his apparel, by way of preparation for the coming ordeal. But he failed to make any improvement in his appearance. He returned the salutations of the Division, Brigade and Regimental commanders with a gentle wave of the hand, which seemed to say, 'All hail—Avaunt!' "[24]

Then, on January 11, the secretary of war, accompanied by Simeon Draper of New York, Montgomery Meigs, General Edward D. Townsend, the adjutant general of the army, and other officials, arrived in Savannah. Stanton immediately put Draper in charge of the 31,000 bales of captured cotton in the city. He also ordered the obliteration of all marks, numbers, and figures on the bales, something Sherman considered peculiar, for the secretary thereby destroyed all records of ownership. Later on, Savannah planters filed claims against the government for three times the number of bales confiscated.[25]

The next day Stanton, standing atop a porch in the center of town, reviewed Kilpatrick's cavalry. Small and natty, Kilpatrick rode past wearing "brand new canary gauntlets," a yellow sash that "looked like it was just out of the shop," and sky blue pants decorated down the leg with gold cord that, halfway below the knees, separated into two seams. After the parade, the soldiers cheered thrice for Stanton, for Lincoln, and for Sherman.[26]

The cotton and the parades were sideshows, for Stanton's chief interest in Savannah was Sherman and race relations. On December 30, 1864, Halleck, without mentioning Jeff C. Davis, warned Sherman about "a certain class, having now great influence with the President . . . who are decidedly disposed to make a point against you—I mean in regard to 'Inevitable Sambo.' They say that you have manifested an almost *criminal* dislike to the negro, and that you are not willing to carry out the wishes of the Government in regard to him, but repulse him with contempt." These critics argued that Sherman might have brought with him into Savannah 50,000 slaves and opened "a road by which as many more could have escaped from their masters; but that instead of this you drove them from your ranks, prevented them from following you by cutting the bridges in your rear, and thus caused the massacre of large numbers by Wheeler's cavalry." Halleck considered it "of the greatest importance to open outlets by which the slaves can escape into our lines. . . . Could not such escaped slaves find, at least, a partial supply of food in the rice fields about Savannah, and occupation in the rice and cotton fields on the coast?"[27]

Three days later Chase, now the chief justice of the Supreme Court, wrote Sherman about using blacks in the army. He noted:

> You are understood to be opposed to their employment as soldiers, and to regard them as a set of pariahs, almost without rights. In your first report after opening communications with Gen. Foster you spoke of the necessity of ridding your camp of the surplus negroes, mules &c. I do not remember the exact words, but I do remember the report. I felt that an expression classing men with cattle found place in a paper which cannot fail to be historical.
>
> . . . For myself, indeed, I freely say that I see no reason why all citizens may not vote subject only to such restrictions as are applicable to all irrespective of color.[28]

On the twelfth of January, Stanton brought up the question. Angered by the massacre at Ebenezer Creek, Major James A. Connolly of Davis's corps had written to his congressman a letter of protest, the substance of which found its way into the *New York Tribune*. Asking for an explanation, Stanton showed the newspaper article to Sherman. "I had heard such a rumor," the general innocently proclaimed in his *Memoirs*. Called in, Davis said that he took up the bridge because he needed it elsewhere. He harbored, he argued, no bias against the freedmen.[29] Neither Stanton nor Sherman realized that Davis's action was part of a pattern, for he had stranded the fleeing slaves at both Buck Head Creek and Ebenezer Creek.

That night, Stanton and Sherman met with twenty black leaders. When Stanton asked them how they could best take care of themselves, their spokesman, Garrison Frazier, a former slave who had saved a thousand dollars in gold and silver, bought freedom for himself and his wife, and become an ordained Baptist minister, answered that his people needed land. After twelve such questions, Stanton intimated that he wished to ask them something about Sherman, who left the room. Stanton then asked what the black leaders thought of the general. Frazier responded that before Sherman's arrival they looked upon him as a servant of God. Some of those present had called upon Sherman immediately after his arrival, "and it is probable he would not meet the Secretary with more courtesy than he met us." They considered him "a friend and a gentleman." With justifiable pride, Stanton later told Henry Ward Beecher, the Brooklyn minister who became a close friend of the Sherman family, that this conversation constituted the first instance in American history of a high government official conferring with a "poor debased people to ask them what they wanted for themselves."[30]

At Savannah, Stanton came up with the idea of settling freed families on the abandoned plantations in the Sea Islands off South Carolina and Georgia and along the country bordering the St. Johns River in Florida. Sherman wrote the draft of Special Field Order Number 15, dated January 16, 1865, and Stanton revised it. Under it, each family was to be allotted up to forty acres of "tillable ground." This, as the historian Eric Foner has pointed out, plus Sherman's authorization of the use of army mules by the settlers, led to the origin of the phrase "forty acres and a mule" when referring to what the freedmen might get or expect from the government.[31]

In the order, Sherman specified that African Americans could be recruited into the army only in accord with the rules set by Congress and the president. Sherman aimed this provision at the "ravenous state agents from Hilton Head who enticed and carried away our servants" and the blacks who made up Sherman's pioneer corps, which had done great service during the March to the Sea. "Repeal that mischievous act of sending agents to get recruits," Cump growled to John shortly after Stanton departed.[32]

Soon after putting his order into effect, Sherman sent along to his old friend from Missouri, General Rufus Saxton, who was in charge of settling the refugees at Beaufort, South Carolina, seven thousand of the fifteen thousand freedmen who had followed him to Savannah. "Many of them are from far up in Georgia," he reported, "and a long, weary, and sorrowful tramp they have had. Many of them, with little children, have not brought a thing with them, and have most miserable covering. Bales of clothing can be disposed of among them."[33]

After his discussions with Stanton, Sherman finally answered Halleck's Sambo letter. He and the secretary had "talked over all matters freely, and I deeply regret that I am threatened with that curse to all peace and comfort—popularity." Sherman knew "enough of 'the people' to feel that a single mistake made by some of my subordinates will tumble down my fame into infamy. But the nigger? Why, in God's name, can't sensible men let him alone? . . . Of course that cock-and-bull story of my turning back negroes that Wheeler might kill them is all humbug. I turned nobody back." At Ebenezer Creek, Jeff C. Davis did abandon "certain plantation slaves—old men, women and children . . . not because he wanted to leave them, but because he wanted his bridge. He and Slocum both tell me that they don't believe Wheeler killed one of them."

Sherman compared the race issue to a pendulum:

> The southrons pulled Sambo's pendulum so far over that the danger is it will on its return jump off its pivot. There are certain people who will find fault, and they can always get the pretext; but, thank God, I am not running for an office, and am not concerned because the rising generations will believe that I burned 500 niggers at one pop in Atlanta, or any such nonsense. I profess to be the best kind of a friend to Sambo, and think that on such a question Sambo should be consulted.
>
> They gather round me in crowds, and I can't find out whether I am Moses or Aaron, or which of the prophets; but surely I am rated as one of the congregation, and it is hard to tell in what sense I am most appreciated by Sambo—in saving him from his master, or the new master that threatens him with a new species of slavery. I mean State recruiting agents. Poor negro—Lo, the poor Indian! Of course, sensible men understand such humbug, but some power must be invested in our Government to check these wild oscillations of public opinion.[34]

While in Savannah, Stanton confided to Sherman that he was suffering a great deal of pain and had come south to escape the bickering and turmoil in Washington. State governors quarreled incessantly with the War Department about their draft quotas, and the government verged on financial chaos. The price of everything had risen sharply, and Stanton appealed to Sherman as a soldier and patriot to help things by speedily ending the war.[35]

Sherman had his own Washington problems. Charley Ewing returned to Savannah with word that some congressmen wanted to promote Sherman to lieutenant general, making him Grant's equal. Cump urged John to scotch such efforts: "In military titles I have now the Maximum, and it makes no difference whether that be Maj Genl. or Marshal." To Grant he wrote that he did not desire promotion:

> It would be mischievous, for there are enough rascals who would try to sow differences between us, whereas you and I now are in perfect understanding. I would rather have you in command than anybody else, for you are fair, honest, and have at heart the same purpose that should animate all. I should emphatically decline any commission calculated to bring us into rivalry, and I ask you to advise all your friends in Congress to this effect, especially Mr. Washburne. . . . The flurry attending my recent success will soon blow over, and give place to new developments.[36]

By the time Stanton left Savannah, Sherman was ready to "dive again beneath the surface to turn up again in some mysterious place." He intended, he informed Ellen, to "feign on Augusta and Charleston, avoid both and make for Columbia, Fayetteville and Newbern, N. C. Don't breathe, for the walls have ears, and fore knowledge published by some mischievous fool might cost many lives."[37]

About to start, Sherman entertained no sympathy for the state that he believed had started the war. In Savannah, when Mrs. Elliott, whose family Lieutenant Sherman frequently visited when she was a young girl in Charleston, expressed a desire to return to South Carolina, Sherman said: "You will be going, madam, out of the frying pan into the fire. My army is composed of some of the most lawless ruffians upon earth. Here in Georgia, I can with difficulty control them, but when I enter South Carolina I shall neither be able nor desirous to do so. You have heard of the horrors of war; wait until my army gets into South Carolina and you will see the reality."[38]

Sherman wrote similarly to Ellen. He complained about the "rain, rain, and all the Country under water." But in the Carolinas a rainy January usually meant a pleasant February. "It is the Rare month," he recalled, "the month of out door sports and in door grand times, and I am about to offer them a season of unusual liveliness which should be a full compensation for the hospitalities of bygone periods."[39]

On January 21, Sherman left Savannah aboard a steamer bound for Beaufort, which Howard had earlier occupied. Two days later, after stopping at Hilton Head to see Foster, he arrived there. Slocum's wing, meanwhile, began crossing into South Carolina at Sister's Ferry, forty miles above Savannah, where the Savannah River, swollen by rain, was three miles wide. The weather was so bad that Sherman realized he could not begin the second phase of the march until February 1. To deceive the enemy into believing he was preparing to attack Charleston, now defended by Hardee, he proceeded with some aides to Pocotaligo, twenty-five miles inland, along the railroad to Charleston.[40]

Preparing to leave Pocotaligo, Sherman was confident but wary. His army now faced a danger from Lee, who might at any time decide to abandon Richmond and move south to meet the invaders. "I must risk Hood," Sherman warned Grant on the twenty-ninth, "& trust you to hold Lee, or be on his heels if he comes south."

Grant's last letter to Sherman, which he was sure would not arrive before the march began, thanked his friend for saying he would decline a promotion. He added: "No one would be more pleased at your advancement than I, and if you should be placed in my position and I put subordinate it would not change our personal relations in the least. I would make the same exertions to support you that you have ever done to support me, and would do all in my power to make our cause win."[41]

15

The Carolinas

— I —

DURING THE CIVIL WAR, Sherman made five marches. The first, from Vicksburg to Jackson in July 1863, resembled hell: thirsty soldiers tramping in the broiling sun, finding pool after pool polluted by the carcasses of animals slaughtered by Johnston's men. The second, to Knoxville in freezing weather, was without preparation. Despite Sooy Smith's retreat, the Meridian expedition of February 1864 had been pleasurable and had given Sherman the experience necessary for his March to the Sea. The journey through South Carolina, the lower portion of which consisted of icy swamps, constituted the fifth.

As in the March to the Sea, Sherman divided his army into two wings. Howard commanded the right wing, consisting of Logan's and Blair's corps, and Slocum headed the left, made up of Jeff C. Davis's and Williams's corps, plus Corse's division and Kilpatrick's cavalry. As before, Sherman's force totaled 60,000 men.[1]

Opposed to Sherman were what he called "scattered and inconsiderable forces" for which he had "a species of contempt." In overall command was Beauregard. Wheeler commanded a division of cavalry, reduced by losses to the size of a brigade. General Wade Hampton, for whom Sherman developed a deep hatred, had been dispatched to his native state from Lee's army with two small divisions "to punish us for our insolent attempt to invade the glorious State of South Carolina." Sherman knew that these forces "could hardly delay us an hour." Wheeler, Hampton, and Hardee, who had gone north from Savannah toward Charleston with about 10,000 troops, had a combined force that Sherman estimated at 15,000. What Sherman called the "broken fragments of Hood's army which escaped from Tennessee," about 25,000 men, was being rushed across Georgia to Augusta to try to block Sherman's advance.[2]

But Sherman's persistent fear, shared by his entire army, was that Lee might decide to abandon Richmond, march south, meet Sherman head-on, and destroy the force that was more used to pillaging than fighting. If Lee retreated with but a few hours start, he could, by burning bridges and destroying railroads, slow up Grant and confront Sherman before help arrived. Indeed, that fall Sherman had thought for a long time before deciding that he could spare Cox, now in charge of the Twenty-third Corps, which he sent to aid Thomas in Tennessee. Sherman would have preferred to have taken into the Carolinas 70,000 men instead of 60,000.[3]

On February 1, Howard's army started up the Salkehatchie River. Blair's corps was to cross at Rivers Bridge, about forty-five miles above Beaufort, and Logan's at a bridge further up. On the third, both corps were still on the southern bank of the river, swollen from the rains. On the opposite bank were some Confederate defenses that Howard called "the strongest I ever saw."

General Manning F. Force, who led a division in Blair's corps, described the rivers in South Carolina as masses of "tangled swamps, miles across, dense with trees, vines and thickets, and meandering through them the many channels of icy water." Joseph E. Johnston's engineers had pronounced it "absolutely impossible for an army to march across the lower portion of the state in winter." Handed such a report, Johnston, who had been given command of the Confederate army in the Carolinas that February, assumed Sherman would not even try such a thing.

At Rivers Bridge, General Joseph A. Mower and General Giles Smith led their divisions through three miles of underbrush and freezing water up to their shoulders. They then assaulted and routed the Confederate brigade on the other side. In this attack, Colonel Wager Swayne of the Forty-third Ohio, later a prominent New York corporation lawyer and the brother of a Supreme Court justice, lost a leg. He was sent back to Pocotaligo.[4]

Meanwhile, Sherman's left wing, far to Howard's south, marched through the flooded lowlands, some units struggling to complete two miles a day. A reporter for the *New York Herald* found General Williams, who commanded the Twentieth Corps, nestled in the bend of a tree, his blanket wrapped around his corpulent body. His aides occupied the branches above him. To make itself more comfortable, the corps dismantled every building in the village of Hardeeville.[5]

Leaving Georgia, Sherman had given Slocum advice. "Don't forget," Lieutenant Joseph B. Foraker of Slocum's staff heard him say, "that when you have crossed the Savannah River you will be in South Carolina. You need not be so careful there about private property as we have been. The more of it you destroy the better it will be. The people of South Carolina should be made to feel the war, for they brought it on and are responsible more than anybody else for our presence here. Now is the time to punish them."[6]

Confederate atrocities added to the resentment against the mother of secession. To stop the Northerners, the Southerners had placed torpedoes in the road. One tore off the leg of a sergeant from the Seventy-ninth Pennsylvania.

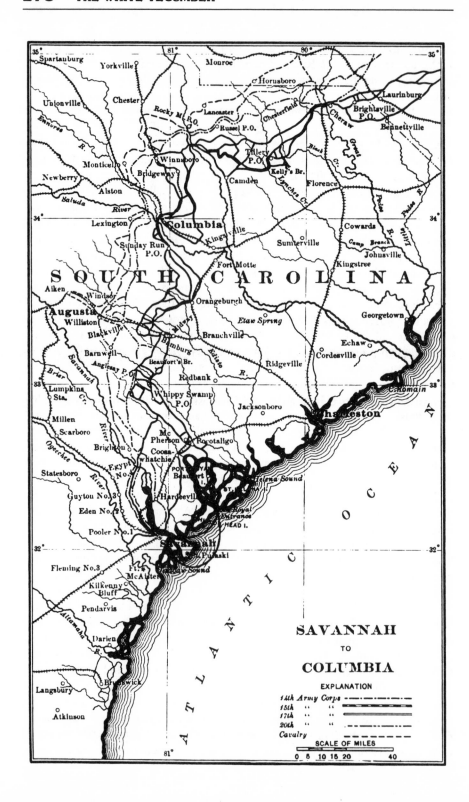

SAVANNAH

TO

COLUMBIA

EXPLANATION

14th Army Corps
15th   "   "
17th   "   "
20th   "   "
Cavalry

SCALE OF MILES

0   5   10 15 20   40

At about the same time, Slocum's men found the bodies of three Union soldiers who had been shot and buried by Wheeler's cavalry.

In retaliation, Kilpatrick's and Slocum's men left a trail of torched towns. By the time Foraker reached the first two villages, Robertsville and Lawtonville, each containing 600 to 800 people, they were ashes. "There was not a house left in either place, only a lot of naked chimneys, and many of them had been thrown down." Sherman joked that Kilpatrick's cavalry had changed the name of Barnwell to Burnwell. Once, when Kilpatrick asked how he was to let Sherman know where he was, Sherman reportedly answered: "Oh, just burn a bridge or something and make a smoke, as the Indians do on the plains." Trying to save their homes, many inhabitants hung out white flags, but the troops ignored these and invariably burned any houses they passed. As Underwood lamented, "South Carolina's punishment had begun."[7]

Wheeler tried to negotiate an end to the burning. At Grahams he left untouched 300 bales of cotton, valued at a quarter of a million dollars. He also sent to Howard a note promising he would cease burning cotton if the Yankees stopped torching houses. "I hope you will burn all cotton," Sherman responded, "and save us the trouble. We don't want it; and it has proven a curse to our country. All you don't burn I will." Sherman had issued orders not to disturb "private houses, occupied by peaceful families." Naively he asserted: "I think my orders are obeyed."[8]

Amidst the destruction, Howard encountered good fortune. Near Midway, almost halfway between Augusta and Charleston, he was astride his horse deploying two divisions to meet what he thought was a nearby enemy force when he saw someone coming down the road. The rider, on a white horse with rope halter and rope stirrups, was a bummer. He wore a swallow-tailed coat and a silk hat. Approaching Howard, he shouted: "Hurry up, General, we've got the railroad." A group of foragers had captured it without a fight. Joined by Williams's corps, Howard's men spent two days ripping up thirty miles of rails, "so that," Underwood noted, "nobody but a junk dealer would have any further use for them."[9]

On the eleventh the entire army, lying around Blackville, again began moving, crossing the south fork of the Edisto River. It, too, ran through a swamp, whose waters were covered with a crust of ice a quarter of an inch thick. "It seemed at every step," remembered Underwood, "as if a knife was cutting the flesh; everybody screamed with the pain, and the chorus of shouts was so funny that everybody had to laugh in turn. Many men were used up by that swamp." Those brave enough to wash in the nearby brooks ended up picking icicles out of their hair.[10]

Howard's men proceeded to Orangeburg, just a half mile below the north fork of the Edisto and forty-five miles southeast of Columbia. There, some buildings in the center of town burned down. Both Sherman and Howard attributed the torching not to their troops but to "a Jew merchant," who, angry because the Confederate commander had destroyed a large supply of his cotton, burned down his own store. The fire spread to adjacent establishments.[11]

Even the most sensitive officers did not shed a tear at the destruction of the homes that during the Revolutionary War had sheltered such generals as Nathanael Greene and Lord Cornwallis. One day, however, Lieutenant Frank H. Putney of the Twelfth Wisconsin was riding with another officer when he noticed an untouched plantation between Midway and Orangeburg. As they approached it, a middle-aged man came out and asked for a guard. Putney answered that he had none to give. Pointing to a one-story frame building near his house, the stranger identified it as his library. He wanted to know who was in command and where he could be found. Intrigued, Putney asked the man his name. With a bow the stranger answered: "William Gilmore Simms, sir." Putney then told him of the joy reading his works "had brought me in my far away Wisconsin home." When the main column approached, Putney told the story to Charley Ewing, who placed guards on the plantation. But Ewing explained that Simms would have to ask the same favor of every brigade that passed. Woodlands, Simms's estate, escaped destruction at the hands of the Federals, but several months later Simms's servant, Isaac, got angry and burned it down. Simms's friend, the poet Paul Hamilton Hayne, afterward maintained that Sherman had ordered the torching of the library, a baseless charge that two historians have accepted without question.[12]

By the fifteenth General Charles R. Woods, who led Logan's First Division, was across the Little Congaree River, a half dozen or so miles below Columbia. Sending his men through a cyprus swamp to his left, he captured a newly built Confederate fort and advanced to the west bank of the Congaree. That night, as the Federals lay on the ground resting, Confederate artillery shelled their camps, something Sherman denounced as an attempt to kill "a few miserable soldiers, rolled up in their blankets asleep." Contrary to "civilized warfare," this act, which caused the deaths of one officer and several men, could only provoke "retaliation."[13]

In their memoirs Howard and Sherman tried to convey the impression that Federal artillery retaliated but little for the Confederate shelling. Sherman, in fact, insisted that he found Captain Francis De Gress firing his 20-pound Parrotts into Columbia and instructed him only to send a few shells near the railroad depot, where Negroes were taking corn and meal, and to fire three shells at the new statehouse, then being built by an Italian engineer. But in his admirable study of Sherman and Columbia, Marion B. Lucas estimated that Sherman's artillery fired at least 325 rounds into and near Columbia. Professor Lucas concluded that the shelling "resulted not from an overzealous General Sherman, but from the bad judgment of Beauregard and Hampton in not declaring the city to be open when they knew it could not be defended."[14]

On the next day, February 16, Sherman issued Special Field Order Number 26. It placed Howard in command of Columbia and authorized him to destroy public buildings, railroads, and manufacturing shops but to "spare libraries, asylums and private dwellings." That day, Howard began replacing the burnt bridge across the Saluda and Broad Rivers, which met at Columbia to form the Congaree.[15]

Learning that Sherman had sent Slocum and Kilpatrick toward Winns-boro, twenty-six miles to the Confederate rear, Hampton, fearing he would be trapped between the forks of the Congaree and Catawba Rivers, abandoned Columbia. Between 8:00 A.M. and 9:00 A.M. on the morning of the seventeenth, Mayor Thomas Jefferson Goodwyn and three aldermen rode out in a carriage displaying a flag of truce, determined to surrender the city to the first general they met. They settled instead for Colonel George A. Stone, the commander of Woods's Third Brigade. But confusion reigned, for, Stone observed in his battle report, after Goodwyn surrendered unconditionally, a battalion of cavalry attacked Stone's troops. Instructing a corporal and three privates to shoot the mayor and aldermen if one soldier was killed or wounded, Stone took forty men and some skirmishers and drove the enemy off.[16]

Later that morning Sherman and Howard were sitting on a log watching a pontoon bridge being layed when a courier brought a message from Stone say-ing that the mayor had surrendered Columbia. This same messenger also gave Sherman a note in pencil from Sister Baptista Lynch, the mother superior of the Ursuline convent in Columbia. A family acquaintance, she had been Min-nie's teacher in the convent at Reading, near Cincinnati. She now asked for pro-tection. Sherman handed the note to Charley Ewing "and told him to go to this lady and assure her that we had no intention to do them or anybody undue violence in Columbia; that our stay would be short, as we were bound for Rich-mond. . . . At that moment," Sherman wrote years later, "I did not consider Columbia as of any more importance than the hundreds of small towns of Geor-gia and Carolina through which we had passed."[17]

Between two and three o'clock in the afternoon Sherman, Howard, Logan, and their staffs, followed by the Fifteenth Corps, rode into Columbia. It seemed to Sherman as if the entire population, white and black, lined the thorough-fares. "I saw half a dozen piles of cotton *on fire* in the Streets," Cump told John in 1866, "one large pile near the market house where the great conflagration began, which fire our soldiers were putting out as I rode by it."

Sherman explained that Hampton had set these blazes. "I saw Wade Hamptons cotton order printed in a Columbia paper, but kept no copy, as it was notorious, for he openly declared that Yankee footsteps should not pollute his threshold and he commanded every thing like corn fodder &c to be burnt lest we should get it." Mayor Goodwyn had "complained to me of the cotton burn-ing order of Wade Hampton."[18]

In Columbia the Confederate foolishness equaled the Yankee lawlessness. Only three and a half hours before Union forces entered the city, and after much of the cotton was blazing, Hampton finally realized his mistake and re-scinded his order. The Confederates, moreover, burned the depot, which was filled with provisions. Hearing the building was about to be torched, women ran into it to help themselves to supplies. Suddenly gunpowder exploded. "It was brutal," recorded a member of the Fourth Minnesota after helping a woman whose hands and face were "burned to a crisp," "to burn and destroy food needed by the people of the city that they professed to befriend and more brutal still to blow up a building when the lives of women and children were exposed to death thereby."[19]

When they first met, Goodwyn complained to Sherman about something else. Blockade runners had brought into the coastal communities of South Carolina huge amounts of liquor. Believing Sherman was heading toward them, the residents of these cities had sent this liquor to Columbia for safekeeping. Goodwyn had implored Hampton and Beauregard to remove or destroy it before they left, but they considered it private property and refused. "Who ever heard," Sherman told the Reverend J. Toomer Porter, an Episcopal minister from Columbia who became Howard's friend, "of an evacuated city being left a depot of liquor for an army to occupy. I found one hundred and twenty casks of whisky in one cellar."[20]

Having worked all night and marched into Columbia without breakfast, many of the members of Stone's brigade, drinking from buckets of whiskey brought out to them, Howard observed, by "traders and negroes," were soon drunk. By three o'clock in the afternoon, when the Fourth Minnesota, bands playing and colors flying, marched into town amidst a gusting wind from the northwest, conditions portended tragedy. "In marching through," recorded the regiment's historian, "we saw a good many drunken soldiers and drunken negroes. Had to pass long ranks of cotton bales on fire, which was so hot we could scarce march past them on the sidewalk."[21]

Goodwyn had arranged for Sherman to stay at the home of Blanton Duncan, who had the contract for printing Confederate money and had fled with Hampton. Located six or seven blocks in back of the partially constructed new statehouse, the home was big and comfortable. Toward evening, Sherman was resting when Goodwyn came and informed him that a lady he had known as a lieutenant at Fort Moultrie wished to see him. The woman turned out to be the sister of James Poyas, with whom he used to hunt. She told how when she heard a Sherman was leading the Union army she was not sure whether it was T. W. Sherman or W. T. Sherman. She had kept the Federals from pillaging her house by showing them Sherman's signature in a book he had given the family years before. Before leaving Columbia, Sherman sent her a large supply of rice and one hundred pounds of ham. That same evening Sherman visited Harriet H. Simons, the wife of the brother of his old friend James Simons of Charleston. He sent her a half barrel of hams and a supply of rice.[22]

Twice that early evening Sherman comforted Columbians. On the way back to Duncan's house, he told Goodwyn: "Go home, and rest assured that your city will be as safe in my hands as if you had control of it." He added, however, that he was compelled to burn some of the public buildings. Between six and seven o'clock he similarly remarked to Reverend Porter: "You must know a great many ladies. Go around and tell them to go to bed quietly; they will not be disturbed any more than if my army was one hundred miles off."[23]

Tired from his walk over much of Columbia that late afternoon, Sherman was resting on one of Duncan's beds when, soon after dark, he noticed bright light shining on the walls. He sent a member of his staff to investigate. The officer returned with word that a block of buildings opposite the burning cotton was also ablaze. Woods and his men were there, but wind was spreading the fire.

At eleven o'clock Sherman, accompanied by his adjutant, Major Lewis M. Dayton, walked to the Simons home and from there saw the inferno. He advised the ladies to take their valuables and move to the Duncan house, and even provided wagons for their baggage. When Mr. and Mrs. Simons returned to their house the next day, they found they were among the lucky ones. Their home stood untouched.[24]

As the fire spread, a second brigade of the Fifteenth Corps was brought into the center of town to fight the fires, but its members soon became as drunk as Stone's men. Finally, General John M. Oliver's disciplined veterans, the Third Brigade of Hazen's Second Division, were sent in. "They arrested all the men on the street," reported one of Howard's officers, "and very frequently had to use force, and many men would not be arrested, and were shot. *Forty* of our men were killed in this way, many were wounded, and several dead drunk men were burned to death."[25]

Writing to Sherman on February 21, General Woods blamed the fire, which began in the western portion of the city, on "villains," including local prisoners who had been freed that day. "The town itself was full of drunken negroes and the vilest vagabond soldiers, the veriest scum of the entire army being collected in the streets." Given the "gale that was sweeping over the place, the absence of any proper water power, and the fact that the city was filled with both citizens and soldiers who were in no ways disposed to have the scene closed, it was an almost impossibility to arrest the flames." Woods accurately estimated that "about one third of the city was destroyed."[26]

The conflagration overwhelmed observers. Chaplain Thomas M. Stevenson of the Seventy-eighth Ohio noted:

> The next morning when riding through the ruins of the city all was quiet and still as death; broken furniture and charred fragments covered the streets, and burnt walls stood black, shattered and lonely. I could not restrain the dropping tear of pain and regret. In the parks and in the suburbs of the city, women were sitting and guarding a few things saved and carried there by the arm of some kind hearted soldier. Major Mills, of the Seventy-eighth, carried upon his horse women and children outside the burning part of the city, until nearly morning.
>
> The next day soldiers seemed not cheerful; their hearts went back in sympathy with the suffering people. All condemned and regretted the city had been burnt, but whom to blame they scarcely knew.[27]

Professor Lucas has dismissed many of the commonly heard charges against the Northern troops. Eyewitness accounts of soldiers spreading the fire were, he concluded, "notoriously small in number." After studying the affidavits given by those at the scene, he found only four reports of soldiers cutting hoses and destroying fire apparatus. Numerous people, on the other hand, applauded the bravery of the Federals who helped fight the fire.

Most importantly, the fire led to psychological warfare, even though it was not called that. Despite their blunders, neither Sherman and Howard nor Beauregard and Hampton wished to destroy a third of Columbia. Like other South Carolinians, Columbians had vowed to fight to the end. They did not. "Long before Columbia was captured," Professor Lucas observed, "Columbians had given up."[28]

For the next half century the residents of Columbia conducted a campaign to show not that they had surrendered but that they had been burnt out of their homes by a savage Yankee commander leading an army of savages. Hampton never admitted that, amid burning cotton and exploding depots, he had abandoned his people. He found it better to denounce Sherman's brutality. Sherman, in turn, conceded nothing and admitted nothing.

The burning of the Ursuline convent and school stands as an example of distortion. The convent, located one block north of the spot where the fire began, soon became endangered. By eleven in the evening, when the nuns led the young girls out of the convent, sparks and burning timbers had made holes in their dresses and veils.[29]

Sister Baptista Lynch talked only of the kindness of Sherman and of Charley Ewing, whom Sherman sent to the convent with Major J. W. Comyn because both were Catholics. She spoke of fleeing from the burning convent with her students and of spending the night in the church yard. "On the following morning General Sherman made us a visit, expressed his regret at the burning of our convent, disclaimed the act, attributing it to the intoxication of his soldiers, and told me to choose any house in town for a convent and it should be ours." With Sherman's consent, she selected the Methodist Female College, but she also wished to save the beautiful old home of General John S. Preston, the brother-in-law of Hampton, for both men had been kind to her when the convent was established and anti-Catholic feeling ran high. "That is where General Logan holds his headquarters," Ewing told her, "and orders have already been given, I know, to burn it on to-morrow morning; but if you say you will take it for a convent, I will speak to the General and the order will be countermanded." Several nuns and pupils were then sent to occupy the Preston house. True to his word, Ewing induced Sherman to change the order.[30]

But for decades it was fashionable to thrash the Yankees. In a memoir, Madame Sophie Sosnowski, who ran a Columbia boarding school for girls, "the loveliest flowers that could adorn a nation," insisted that Irish soldiers had told her Sherman would not allow them to enter the city. "And this as the men assured us, was *to prevent them from protecting Roman Catholic property.*" William Gilmore Simms later repeated this charge.[31]

Twenty years after the burning, Sara Aldrich, whose parents owned a plantation in Barnwell called "The Oaks," added to the legend. One of the students sent to the Preston home, she was still appalled because Logan's officers had left wineglasses and cigar butts around. Someone had even desecrated a statue of Eve by clothing it with a coat and cap and by painting on it a moustache, which the girl rubbed off. As Sara saw it, Sherman, while talking to Sister Baptista, was consumed with guilt: "No wonder the man's eyes shifted and sought the ground; no wonder he nervously bit his moustache and tried to hurry through the interview he knew he had to bear, and yet would have avoided."[32] The girl never bothered to explain who or what forced Sherman "to bear" the interview.

Unlike Sara, Sister Baptista displayed the kindest feelings for Sherman. On May 15, 1865, she wrote him that her order was seeking $100,000 from the government with which to buy the Methodist Female College. Could Sherman help? "When I assure you that we have been ever since your visit 'like the birds in Noah's Ark' occupying the upper story of this College, without comfort, convenience—on a superabundance of sympathy from some of our separated brethren, you will understand our great anxiety to get a suitable building entirely to ourselves, where we can observe our Rule & reopen our Academy."

The Sister ended by praising Sherman and by sending her regards to Minnie:

> Allow me General to take this opportunity of thanking you for the kind & prompt attention shown us by your Officers, especially Col. Charles Ewing, & Captain Comyn, which I readily understand would not have been given without your concurrence & in gratitude for which, we have offered our daily mementos—
>   With kind remembrances to our former little pupil from her Convent friends.[33]

In 1875 the *Louisville Courier-Journal* made the most drastic charge against Sherman. It called him a "hyena" and a "vindictive tiger" who had ordered and supervised the burning of the convent. The article went on: "When the lurid glare of the flames shot high into the heavens, and whilst Sherman was sitting upon his horse in front watching them with grim, demonic satisfaction, the lady superioress collected the inmates who had fled from the burning monastery, marched them to the front, and there, with uplifted hands, in which was held a cross, pronounced and called upon heaven to pronounce a curse upon him."

Infuriated, Ellen answered the article. Sherman, she insisted, had instructed her brother and Comyn, both Catholics, to help the nuns and their students. "They executed the orders with zeal and great kindness, and under continued instructions from General Sherman they assigned to them a goodly share of commissary stores and attended to their wants until the army left the place." To accuse Sister Baptista "of deliberately calling down a curse upon a man" was "to slander a Religious."[34]

In 1887 Sherman, tired of being pilloried every few years as the destroyer of Columbia, finally pushed aside the issue. The Sisters of Charity had just bought the Preston house. He offered them advice:

> I hope they will use it to teach charity of opinion on earth, as it will be in Heaven. Too much has been written and published about Columbia, S. C. It was and is a played-out old town, not of as much importance to the world as Denver, Cheyenne, San Francisco or Tacoma, yet

people talk of it merely as a diversion, and the next time our Army has occasion to go there, there will be no further occasion to discuss its utter elimination from history.[35]

— II —

On February 20, Howard's right wing left Columbia and marched north. Two days later it joined the left wing, which had arrived the previous evening at Winnsboro, in the beautiful, rich country north of the state capital. Upon entering the town, the men of Williams's Twentieth Corps had found fires set by the advance guard and foragers of the Fourteenth Corps. "Only the timely arrival of the troops and the personal efforts of the Generals, saved the place," reported Underwood. Slocum, Williams, General John W. Geary, and General Henry A. Barnum "burned their whiskers and scorched their clothes, trying to put out the fire." Winnsboro, the home of wealthy planters, was full of refugees from Vicksburg, Nashville, Atlanta, Savannah, and Charleston, who had fled there never expecting the Union army to advance that far.[36]

Feigning a movement to Charlotte, North Carolina, to which Beauregard had sent all his detachments, including a corps of Hood's old army, Sherman's entire force made a great right wheel and headed east. Sherman's right wing approached Camden, the scene in 1780 of a noted Revolutionary War battle. The men entered the city completely soaked, but found there to warm them a large supply of whisky and bottled wine, some dated 1832.[37]

The destruction of Columbia had soured many of the Yankees on burning houses. Instead, they stole. "Soldiers were everywhere, pillaging," Hight wrote on the twenty-first. "Our men are robbing all the houses as we pass along. Not so many houses are burned as formerly, for all are tiring of the work."[38]

On the twenty-third, Sherman visited the camp of the Fifty-eighth Indiana. Sitting around the fire, he informed the soldiers that on February 17, the day Columbia had burned, the Confederates had abandoned Charleston. He knew, he said, the Charlestonians "couldn't stand when you boys were coming up here." Taking some Carolina beans, he told the men: "You can make money by cooking them an hour and a half." He agreed with the soldiers that they did not measure up to Yankee beans. "But we must forage off the country, even if the supplies are not so good."[39]

The next few days brought an inhuman series of murders and threats. On the second day after retreating from Columbia, Confederate general James Chesnut stopped at a farmhouse inhabited by a family he called the M's. The father was away, but the mother and "a very handsome girl" were home. Chesnut suggested "to the mother the propriety of sending her out of the track of both armies. The girl answered quickly, 'I will stay with my mother.' "

That night some of Wheeler's men came into Chesnut's camp and told a horrible tale. They had passed the house of the M's, "the mother raving of what had been done." She had been bound and forced to witness the rape and murder of her daughter by seven Northerners who had just left. Wheeler's men overtook them, cut their throats, and marked upon their breasts: "These were the Seven."[40]

As Kilpatrick complained to Wheeler, other atrocities followed. On February 21 a Yankee lieutenant, a sergeant, and seven men were "inhumanly and cowardly murdered" after being disarmed. That same day nine cavalrymen were found murdered, "five in a barn-yard, three in an open field, and one in the road. Two had their throats cut from ear to ear." Kilpatrick threatened to retaliate by shooting eighteen of his prisoners, but he relented after Wheeler, answering immediately, insisted he knew nothing of the killings.[41]

Forty years later, one Confederate veteran unashamedly attributed these murders to a squad of scouts under the command of two lieutenants of the Fifty-first Alabama Cavalry. "One of these ex-lieutenants opens the monthly meetings of our Camp with prayer," he revealed, "and the other was until recently president of a female college in Alabama. I have never been able to get details from these scouts, for they are averse to talking about it."[42]

On the twenty-fourth, Sherman entered the fray. He complained to Hampton that some of his men had been murdered after being captured, their bodies labeled "Death to all Foragers." He cited the atrocities of February 21 and the discovery by Slocum of twenty-one soldiers, throats cut, in a ravine. Sherman had ordered some Confederate prisoners "to be disposed of in like manner. . . . Of course," he continued, "you cannot question my right to 'forage on the country.' It is a right as old as history. . . . I have no doubt this is the occasion of much misbehavior on the part of our men, but I cannot permit an enemy to judge or punish with wholesale murder."[43]

Hampton answered sharply. For every Confederate soldier Sherman "murdered," he vowed to execute two Yankees, "giving in all cases preference to any officers who may be in my hands." The "thieves whom you designate as foragers" invariably burned the homes of those they had just robbed. "To check this inhuman system," Hampton had ordered his men "to shoot down" all incendiaries:

> You fired into the city of Columbia without a word of warning, after its surrender by the mayor, who demanded protection to private property; you laid the whole city in ashes, leaving amidst its ruins thousands of old men and helpless women and children, who are likely to perish of starvation and exposure. Your line of march can be traced by the lurid light of burning houses; and in more than one household there is an agony far more bitter than that of death. The Indian scalped his victim regardless of age or sex, but with all his barbarity he always respected the persons of his female captives. Your soldiers, more savage than the Indian, insult those whose natural protectors are absent.[44]

On February 28, the day after Hampton wrote his letter, the last murder of a Union forager took place. The victim, a member of the Thirtieth Illinois, was found with his skull bashed in. Upon his body lay a card with the warning to foragers. Through his adjutant, Colonel Cornelius Cadle Jr., Blair ordered

General Force to retaliate by shooting one of the two hundred prisoners he had taken.

On March 2, thirteen miles from Cheraw, South Carolina, Force carried out the order. The privates, separated from the commissioned and noncommissioned officers, drew slips from a hat. One had a cross on it. About halfway through the process a private from North Carolina threw up his hands and shouted, "I have it." Over six feet in height and about thirty-five years old, he was, Cadle observed, "a typical poor white." Chaplain Stevenson remembered him as "a good old grey haired man, the father of nine children, and a subject of the cruel system of conscription."

Fifteen minutes later the Confederate, guilty only of bad luck, was shot to death by a detail from the regiment whose forager had been clubbed. He was buried where he fell. Within the hour, under a flag of truce, Sherman notified Hampton of the shooting. "Upon the march the next day," Cadle recalled, "the commanding officer of the 30th Illinois told me that the order signed by me had been posted on the man's head-board. I expressed my opinion of this in quite forcible language, and for several days acted with much care to prevent falling into the hands of the enemy, lest the order that I signed might decorate *my* grave."[45]

___ III ___

On March 3, on the way to Cheraw, just below the border of North and South Carolina, Sherman came to a fork in the road. Seeing a Negro, he asked him where the right branch led. "Him lead to Cheraw, master," the former slave said. Told Cheraw was eight to ten miles away, Sherman inquired if any guerrillas were about. "Oh! no, master," came the answer, "dey is gone two days ago; you could have played cards on der coat-tails, dey was in sich a hurry!"[46]

Rumor spread through the Fourteenth Corps, with which Sherman marched, that 30,000 Confederates defended Cheraw and that Lee had said Sherman must be stopped there. According to the story, Sherman, as the army approached the town, sent Logan a message asking him to halt so that the Twentieth Corps, which had not yet had the honor of capturing an important point during this phase of the campaign, might occupy the town. "I have halted my corps," Logan replied by messenger, "but my bummers took Cheraw yesterday."[47]

Arriving in Cheraw, a pleasant old town on the Great Pee Dee River, a couple of hours later, Sherman stayed with Blair in a large house owned by a blockade runner, whose family remained in the home. Howard had already placed his pontoon bridge over the river, a deep, navigable stream, and Mower's division was across. The Cape Fear River in North Carolina remained the sole natural obstacle in the advance toward Goldsboro.[48]

At noon on the afternoon of March 3, Blair invited Sherman to lunch. During the meal Blair served some Madeira from bottles covered with dust and cobwebs. Sherman kept asking where Blair got the wine, but Blair kept evading the question. Blair afterward sent Sherman "a case containing a dozen bottles of the finest madeira I ever tasted." Blair had found eight wagonloads of the stuff, which had been sent to Cheraw from Charleston for safety by some old, aristocratic families. Blair thoughtfully distributed small quantities of the drink to the troops.

After lunch Blair asked Sherman if he needed some saddle blankets or a rug for his tent. Taking Sherman to a space under the stairway, he pointed to a pile of carpets that had also arrived from Charleston for safekeeping. Sherman later sent over an orderly, who staggered back loaded with carpets.[49]

The Federals found in Cheraw a huge amount of arms and ammunition. The prizes included two dozen cannons, mostly 20-pound Parrotts, two thousand muskets, and 3,600 barrels—twenty tons or so—of gunpowder. Through the carelessness of a soldier, several tons of gunpowder exploded, killing some men, destroying several buildings, and breaking glass for miles around.[50]

An incident in Cheraw added to Sherman's hatred of reporters. Several years after the march he was at a reception when a friend asked if he would like to meet Horace Greeley, the editor of the *New York Tribune.* "No, sir!" snapped Sherman. "If I could have caught Mr. Greeley during the war I would have hung him." At Cheraw, Sherman found in a room occupied by Hardee a copy of the *Tribune,* which was widely circulated in the South. At a time when the Confederates expected Sherman to attack either Charlotte or Raleigh, the paper revealed that Sherman's supply fleet was headed for Morehead City, North Carolina, the depot for Goldsboro. "This item of newspaper news," Sherman contended, "cost me a fight which I had hoped to avoid."[51]

On the fifth the Seventeenth Corps left Cheraw and headed toward Fayetteville, North Carolina. As during the Jackson campaign and the drive toward Atlanta, Sherman again faced Joe Johnston—that wily opponent, Sherman learned at Cheraw, having been placed in command of Confederate forces in the Carolinas.

As he moved, Slocum was particularly interested in locating the line separating the Carolinas. One day, spying a middle-aged man standing in front of a log house watching the army pass, Slocum approached and said that the stranger must be a Union man. "No," he answered, "I am not a Union man." Slocum then said he must be a secessionist. "No, I am not a secessionist either." Asked what he was, the man responded: "I am a Rebel." Slocum turned to his staff and commented: "We have crossed the line."[52]

Entering North Carolina, Logan's Fifteenth Corps found the going trying. A little after noon on March 9, heavy rains turned the terrain into "a quicksand swamp. . . . It was the worst day and night the command ever saw in the service," lamented the historian of the Ninety-third Illinois. Wagons and ambulances sank up to their axles. "The mules laid down in the sand, in utter despair. Think of that! Mules in despair!" They were finally unhitched and led across the swamp. Using ropes, the men spent all day and night pulling the wagons through sixty rods of wet sand. "General Logan was there nearly all night, tugging at the ropes like a trojan, covered with mud from head to feet, and shouting: 'Hee, o'hee!' Everybody else was there, too, doing the same thing, in the same condition, and shouting the same shout, all together."[53]

For Kilpatrick, the morning of March 10 proved memorable. On the evening of the ninth, advancing toward Fayetteville, his men ran into the rear of Hardee's retreating column. From prisoners Kilpatrick learned that Hampton, also heading for Fayetteville, was to his rear. Planning to trap Hampton, he divided his force, posting one brigade at a hamlet called Solemn Grove, another three miles to the north, and a third three miles to the southeast. That night Kilpatrick stayed at a house where the roads to all three intersected. Even with the enemy lurking about, Kilpatrick took his pleasures seriously. Although small and far from handsome, the general, known for his amorous adventures, had with him a beautiful young lady.

Toward morning, Kilpatrick became restless. He got up, stepped out onto the porch, and was standing in his nightshirt when several men dressed in Federal uniforms rode up and asked for Kilpatrick's headquarters. "Something in the tone of voice, perhaps, aroused my suspicion," Kilpatrick related, "and I promptly replied, 'Down the road about half a mile,' and away they went." While Kilpatrick was following them with his eyes, Cobb's Legion of the cavalry division of Confederate General Matthew C. Butler came roaring toward him. Having captured Kilpatrick's rear pickets, the horsemen approached undetected until some of Kilpatrick's three hundred prisoners recognized them and bellowed the Rebel yell. In his nightshirt and drawers Kilpatrick ran around the corner of the house toward a swamp. He was fortunate enough to catch a stray horse and ride off bareback.[54]

Hearing the wild scene, Kilpatrick's companion emerged from the house. She was Marie Boozer, the reigning queen of Columbia, whom General Preston admired as "the most beautiful piece of flesh and blood my eyes ever beheld." Seeing she was in danger, a Confederate cavalryman gallantly dismounted and carried her to a drainage ditch, where she was able to crouch out of danger.[55]

Meanwhile, Kilpatrick rallied a few men and began to fight. Others joined him. Before long they charged. By the time General John G. Mitchell's brigade of the Fourteenth Corps arrived, the Confederates had scrambled away.[56]

Although the Southerners claimed to have taken 350 prisoners, Kilpatrick came out of the fight much better than he might have initially expected. But for decades Confederates argued about what happened to Kilpatrick's personal items. Some lucky Southerner, possibly Wheeler, ended up with his decorated pistols and holsters. A Confederate who had been a prisoner rode off with his large black horse. Another Southerner soon appeared atop Kilpatrick's favorite, a spotted saddle horse. The soldier, so the story went, gave the animal to Wheeler, who after the war graciously returned it to Kilpatrick.[57]

— IV —

On Saturday, March 11, Union forces entered Fayetteville, North Carolina, located on high ground along the west bank of the Cape Fear River. The city, evacuated by Hardee as the Federals approached, was 95 miles from Wilmington and 130 miles from the ocean. Sherman made his headquarters at the Federal arsenal that the Confederates had taken over in 1861. Before leaving, Sherman's men destroyed that and other government buildings and machinery and equipment of value to the enemy.[58]

After six weeks of roaming about, Sherman and his army again emerged to the world. A few days earlier, Sherman had sent scouts by different routes to inform General Terry, who had taken Wilmington, of his approach to Fayetteville. Shortly after noon on Sunday, March 12, the gunboat *J. McB. Davidson* came chugging up the river. Terry had sent it with messages for Sherman, who ordered it to start the return trip that evening at six. On it, with dispatches for Grant and Lincoln, he sent Captain Samuel H. M. Byers, a former Confederate prisoner to whom Sherman had taken a fancy at Columbia after reading his poem, "Sherman's March to the Sea." The verse, soon set to music, had been smuggled through enemy lines in the artificial leg of an exchanged prisoner.[59]

Sherman also sent to the coast many of those who had accompanied his army from Columbia. These included Marie Boozer, her mother, Mrs. Amelia Fenster, a Union sympathizer, and her younger sister, whose beauty rivaled Marie's. After leaving Sherman's army, Marie went to New York, where she married a wealthy businessman. Rumor had it that her other husbands included Brigham Young, to whom she was "sealed" in a Mormon ceremony and with whom she supposedly lived in Salt Lake City until some army troops rescued her.[60]

For Sherman and his troops, reaching Fayetteville was exhilarating. "The effect was electric," the general remembered, "and no one can realize the feeling unless, like us, he has been for months cut off from all communication with friends, and compelled to listen to the croakings and prognostications of open enemies." A second steamer brought some newspapers. Captain Eli J. Sherlock of the 100th Indiana got hold of a copy of the *New York Tribune* and read it aloud to a large group of soldiers eager to hear news of the outside world. After he was through, a soldier from the Seventeenth Corps offered him a $1,000 bill in Confederate money for the paper. Sherlock refused the offer.[61]

As Byers was about to leave for the coast, Sherman accompanied him to the riverbank. "Don't say much about how we are doing here," Sherman advised, putting his arm around Byers, one of sixteen survivors out of eighty men captured during a charge at Missionary Ridge. "Don't tell them in the North we are cutting any great swath here. Just say we are taking care of whatever is getting in front of us."

Arriving at the little log cabin that served as Grant's headquarters at City Point, Virginia, Byers delivered his message to Grant. While he was doing so, Ord entered the room.

"Look here," said Grant. "Look here, Ord, at the news from Sherman. He has beaten even the swamps of the Carolinas."

"I am so glad," replied Ord, rattling his spurs. "I am so glad. I was getting a little uneasy."

"I not a bit," Grant countered. "I knew Sherman. I knew my man. I knew my man."[62]

Resting at Fayetteville, Sherman thought of "my special antagonist," Johnston, who "would not be misled by feints and false reports, and would somehow compel me to exercise more caution than I had hitherto done." He had, he wrote Ellen, stripped the countryside so bare that it could not support Johnston's army. But he was up against a foe far shrewder than Beauregard, Hampton, or Hardee.

Sherman estimated Johnston's force at 37,000 infantry and 8,000 cavalry. Of these, Hardee's 10,000 men and the cavalry were to Sherman's front. The remainder was assembling near Raleigh, the North Carolina capital. "I can whip Jos. Johnston," Sherman bragged to Terry, "provided he does not catch one of my corps in flank, and I will see that the army marches hence to Goldsboro in compact form."[63]

Contrary to what he told Terry, Sherman again split his force. On the thirteenth and fourteenth his soldiers marched out of Fayetteville and crossed the Cape Fear River over two pontoon bridges. Kilpatrick's cavalry, in advance of four divisions of the left wing, was then sent to make a feint on Raleigh. Meanwhile, Howard's eight divisions, reinforced by two of Slocum's, headed northeast toward the army's real objective, Goldsboro, where Sherman hoped to link up with Terry and Schofield's Army of the Ohio. In late afternoon on the fifteenth, Kilpatrick encountered strong opposition. His command dismounted, threw up a barricade of poles, rails, and logs, and sent a message back to the infantry for help.

That day, which was filled with thunderstorms and lightning, Brigadier General William Hawley's brigade of the Twentieth Corps tramped eleven miles up the east bank of the Cape Fear River, much of it over an old plank road. In early evening the command encamped at the graveyard of Bluff Church. Some of the men had eaten supper, others were preparing it or lying on the flat tombstones, when a messenger rushed into camp. Kilpatrick, five miles away, needed help. In two minutes the brigade was back on the road.

Marching in blackness, without torches that might give away their position, the men tramped in knee-deep mud that sucked off shoes. "Some stumbled and lost their guns," remembered the adjutant of the Third Wisconsin, "and were thankful that they were not trampled under by the on-moving column and buried alive." At midnight the brigade reached Kilpatrick.

Retreating from Fayetteville, Hardee had halted on a narrow neck of land between the Cape Fear and Black Rivers. Johnston hoped Hardee could there block the Federal advance until he could bring up his entire force. His aim was to destroy Slocum's wing of the divided army.[64]

At 3:00 A.M. on the sixteenth Hawley ordered an advance. His brigade, "encased in an armor of mud," pushed ahead a mile, then met strong resistance and halted. The Yankees had stumbled into the battle of Averasboro.

Sherman, Slocum, Kilpatrick, and Brigadier General Nathaniel J. Jackson, the commander of the First Division of the Twentieth Corps, came up and congregated in front of the Thirteenth New Jersey to discuss the situation.

"General Kilpatrick," Sherman said matter-of-factly. "I want you to move your cavalry to the left and develop the enemy's line."

The cavalryman looked at Sherman and asked: "How do you propose that I shall do it?"

"Move your men to the left and engage the enemy," Sherman answered. "Develop their line—make a damn big time—you know how to do it, you know how to do it."

As confused as before Sherman offered his explanation, Kilpatrick departed.[65]

Williams's entire corps was eventually moved up, but in sporadic fighting it advanced only three miles. By five o'clock the enemy occupied a line of works across the road to Averasboro. The Federals then took a position within a hundred yards of the enemy. Now the sharpshooters went to work. Any move brought on a volley. A sergeant of the Third Wisconsin inadvertently exposed his leg, "and in an instant it was knocked off by a cannon ball."[66]

By the next day, the morning of St. Patrick's Day, Hardee was gone. He now placed his force so that he could move toward either Goldsboro or Raleigh, depending on which way Sherman went.

During the surprise battle the Federals lost 12 officers and 65 men. The wounded numbered 477. All came from Williams's Twentieth Corps. Sherman called it "a serious loss, because every wounded man had to be carried in an ambulance."

The Southerners left on the field 108 dead and 68 wounded men. While visiting the house in which surgeons were caring for the wounded Confederates, Sherman saw "arms and legs lying around loose, in the yard and on the porch." In a room a pale, handsome young man whose left arm had been amputated close to the shoulder heard Sherman's name and asked if he were the general. The young man introduced himself as Captain Macbeth, the head of a battery that had been captured. He remembered when young Sherman used to visit his house in Charleston. Indeed, the Macbeths had been the first of "our old Charleston friends" for whom Sherman had searched when he reached Savannah. Sherman asked about his family and arranged for him to send a letter to his mother. Sherman later saw him in St. Louis, where Macbeth worked as a clerk for an insurance company.[67]

The most famous Confederate prisoner might well have been wary of the Ides of March. Seeking shelter on that rainy March 15, Sherman was sitting in a cooper's shop when a tall, slender prisoner was ushered in. Sherman, the embodiment of carelessness and poor taste in dress, remembered the prisoner's nattiness: "the most approved rebel uniform, with high jack-boots beautifully stitched." His name was Colonel Albert Rhett. He was the son of the secessionist Charleston editor Robert Barnwell Rhett, and he was disgusted because Kilpatrick's scouts had captured him behind his own lines. Adding to the indignity, Rhett, who for years had commanded the artillery at Fort Sumter, was taking part in his first engagement since the Confederate abandonment of Charleston.

Engaging in the grand illusion of a camaraderie between opposing officers, Sherman invited Rhett to dinner, much to the annoyance of Hitchcock. Opinionated and arrogant, Rhett at dinner denounced Jefferson Davis as a "fool" and criticized the Southern leaders for allowing Sherman to march through Georgia without a great battle. Sherman might have been stopped, he believed, even though it would have cost 30,000 to 40,000 men. When Sherman said the South did not have 30,000 men to lose, Rhett countered that with one cavalry regiment to enforce the conscription law, he could raise 100,000 men in a month or "they may chop my head off—I'll make that bargain. . . . Why, I've shot twelve men myself in the last six weeks and not long ago I took a pack of dogs and went into the swamps and in three days I caught twenty-eight men with them."

What amused Sherman mortified Hitchcock. He characterized Rhett as a "devil in human shape, who is but a type of his class, and whose polished manners and easy assurance made only more hideous to me the utterly heartless and selfish ambition and pride of class which gave tone to his whole discourse. . . . Do you wonder that I say this class must be *blotted out?*—The class of which Rhett, Jeff Davis, Toombs, and the like are types?"[68]

While not punishing Rhett the way Hitchcock wanted, the Federals added to his difficulties. During the battle of Averasboro, Sherman was on his horse when a man approached him walking without shoes or coat, his head bandaged with a handkerchief. He was the intrepid cavalryman Captain William Duncan, who had been captured at Fayetteville while scouting for Howard. As Wade Hampton watched, the Confederates had taken his hat, coat, and shoes. When Duncan appealed to Hampton as one officer to another, Hampton cursed him. In retaliation, Kilpatrick made Rhett walk the rest of the way to Goldsboro. The story even circulated that Kilpatrick confiscated Rhett's fancy boots, but the cavalryman later returned them because none of his officers possessed "feet delicate enough to wear them."[69]

— V —

From Averasboro, Sherman's left wing turned east, Jeff C. Davis's corps leading the way. Until the morning of March 19 Sherman stayed with this wing. He planned then to join Howard, to the right, whose units were creeping closer and closer to where he believed Terry and Schofield would be. But while doing so, Howard was widening the gap between himself and Slocum.

At this point Sherman's conduct resembled his behavior before the battle of Shiloh. The heavy rains had stopped, and the morning of the nineteenth was balmy and springlike. Fruit trees were beginning to bloom. At 7:00 A.M. Brigadier General William P. Carlin's First Division of the Fourteenth Corps started forward. As Sherman, Slocum, and Davis approached the point where Sherman must turn off, they heard firing. Davis remarked that the firing seemed heavy, but Sherman replied: "No, Jeff, there is nothing there but [Colonel George G.] Dibrell's cavalry. Brush them out of the way. Good morning; I'll meet you to-morrow morning at Cox's Bridge." He turned to the right and rode off.[70]

By ten o'clock Carlin's advanced units were at the intersection of the road to Goldsboro. The spot was two miles below the little village of Bentonville. Suddenly the Federals faced breastworks thrown across the road. About noon, Carlin's lead brigade attacked, slowly pushing the Southerners back a mile through a forest and across a field. A devastating Confederate rifle fire then greeted the Yankees, forcing them in disarray back across the field and into the forest. Carlin called up the rest of his division and dug in.[71]

In early afternoon Slocum and Davis were in a wooded area talking when a sickly looking young man in Confederate gray ran out of the enemy lines. Brought before Slocum, the man identified himself as a Union soldier who had been captured and, to avoid being sent to a prison, had joined the enemy army. He said that Johnston's entire army, 30,000 men—5,000 more than Slocum possessed—lay entrenched up ahead. Johnston's plan, described by Colonel Charles S. Sheldon of the Eighteenth Missouri as Napoleonic, was to crush Slocum's wing of Sherman's divided force before Howard could aid it and then to go after Howard. As they talked, Major William G. Tracy, one of Slocum's aides, rode up and recognized the man as John T. Williams, with whom he had enlisted at Syracuse, New York. Further confirmation of Williams's story came from Colonel Henry G. Litchfield of Davis's staff, who, after inspecting the lines, reported to Slocum: "Well, general, I find a great deal more than Dibrell's cavalry. I find infantry intrenched along our whole front, and enough of them to give us all the amusement we want for the rest of the day."[72]

The shock and thrill of battle ensued. Carlin's men failed to stop the Confederate assault on the Union left. As Davis tried to rally his men, Slocum sent out two messengers. General Alexander C. McClurg, Davis's chief of staff, went back to Williams, whose Twentieth Corps was four or five miles to the rear, conveying the order to advance as rapidly as possible. And to Sherman, Slocum sent Foraker, the youngest member of his staff. Sherman always remembered his first picture of Foraker, a "knight errant with steel cutlass" and red spurs, riding up to him covered with mud. Even then Sherman marked Foraker, who became governor of Ohio and a United States senator, for high office. Slocum's departing words warned Foraker: "Ride well to the right so as to keep clear of the enemy's left flank, and don't spare the horse-flesh." When a staff officer suggested that Slocum's advance divisions charge the enemy, for the force ahead could hardly be as powerful as described, the general wisely replied: "I can afford to be charged with being dilatory or over cautious, but I cannot afford the responsibility of having my command crushed and captured as another command was at Ball's Bluff."[73]

McClurg easily found General Williams, who, splendid officer that he was, was only a mile back, riding ahead of his corps, surveying the land. Receiving the order, Williams rode back to his troops and hurried them forward. By 2:30 two brigades of his First Division, Brigadier General William Hawley's Second and Brigadier General James S. Robinson's Third, arrived on the field. About 4:00 P.M. Brigadier General William Cogswell came into line with a brigade of Williams's Third Division. Samuel Toombs of the Thirteenth New Jersey described the scene: "Our works were about quarter done when the firing became furious; the troops of the Fourteenth Corps were forced back and the vast field was soon covered with men, horses, artillery, caissons, &c., which brought vividly to our minds a similar scene at the Battle of Chancellorsville in Virginia." But here the Federal line firmed and held.

A lull ensued. "It was," observed Toombs, "that great stillness we had often before noticed which precedes the breaking out of a storm." The Confederates soon surged forward. "They were permitted to come within close range when we poured a volley into them with counter shouts which threw them into great confusion." Thus the day passed. Night came, and with it calm.[74]

Miles away, Foraker reached Sherman, camped on a road on a sloping hillside, as darkness approached. Sherman's staff was nearby, and about twenty yards up the hillside Logan rested on a blanket. Sherman saw Foraker approaching, walked to him, and read Slocum's message. As if awakened from a "deep reverie," he called for Logan, who immediately jumped up. Even before Logan reached him, Sherman ordered him to send Hazen, whose division was closest to the left wing, to Slocum.[75]

On the morning of the twentieth the cautious Johnston did not resume the assault. To succeed at this point he would have had to place his whole army between Sherman's two wings, something he was not reckless enough to try. Northern reinforcements came in the entire day. Hazen's men arrived at daylight. So, too, did two of Slocum's brigades that had been guarding the wagon trains. By early afternoon Logan's entire corps and two divisions of Blair's Seventeenth Corps also arrived.

When first attacking Slocum, Johnston's army was astride the road to Goldsboro and faced directly west. Its line formed a "V," the angle resting on the road from Averasboro to Goldsboro, the flanks resting on the winding banks of Mill Creek. Slocum's wing faced the enemy line on the left, Howard's the one on the right. The armies were in place, but for what? The day brought only skirmishing.[76]

Tuesday, March 21, was a windy, rainy, disagreeable day. All that day Mower, who commanded Blair's First Division, had waited to reconnoiter the woods to his right. At 2:00 P.M. the rain slackened, and he decided to lead his troops forward. "In we went," reported Sheldon. "In our front the marsh was so deep and such a tangle of vines that all the mounted officers were speedily on foot, and the intrenching tools thrown away." At three o'clock the division reached open ground. The men began racing madly across a jagged ravine and up a hill populated by Southern artillery. Stunned by this sudden success, Mower halted his command within sight of the Mill Creek bridge, Johnston's sole avenue of escape. Realizing that Johnston's entire army could be trapped here, he sent messengers back to Blair urging that Sherman attack all along the line.

Johnston tried to stave off disaster with his cavalry. Wheeler's horsemen charged against and around Mower's left, Hampton against the right. The Federals retreated down the hill into the jagged ravine, and to the edge of the swamp. Throughout this attack, the brave Mower was more the tiger than the lamb. Cursing Hampton's "roystering, cheering, and defiant" cavalrymen, he shook his fist in the air, raised himself high on his horse, and shouted to an aide: "God, man, wouldn't you like to wade in there with a saber!"[77]

When Howard learned of Mower's appeal for support, he ordered Blair's whole corps to his aid. He also instructed Logan to advance and seize the rifle pits to his front. But as Mower began to move again, Sherman ordered him back. He also recalled Blair. Not receiving Sherman's command, Howard saw Blair withdrawing and began arguing with him. Blair told him: "The withdrawal is by Sherman's order!" Explaining his failure to exploit Mower's advantage, Sherman later admitted: "I think I made a mistake there, and should rapidly have followed Mower's lead with the whole of the right wing, which would have brought on a general battle, and it could not have resulted otherwise than successfully to us, by reason of our vastly superior numbers."[78]

Perhaps Schofield best guessed what went through Sherman's mind at this point. Sherman possessed "unusual intellectual activity and great confidence in his deliberative natural judgment." But he was also nervous and impulsive. This, Schofield insisted, "made him unduly distrustful of his own judgment in emergencies when under great responsibility. . . . For this reason Sherman's capacity as a tactician was not by any means equal to that as a strategist."[79]

By the next day Johnston had retreated north toward Smithfield and Raleigh. At Bentonville, Sherman's losses totaled 1,604, Johnston's 2,343. "My recollection of the battles of Averasboro and Bentonville," Colonel Kerr of the Sixteenth Illinois Cavalry later lamented, "is saddened by the thought of the many brave men of my regiment who fell there, so near the end of the war."[80]

— VI —

The army that Sherman led across the Neuse River—where, at Cox's Bridge, it met Terry with two divisions of the Tenth Corps—and toward Goldsboro looked like no other. Marching along the river, the Third Wisconsin passed a regiment of black troops. Having marched "in black mud" and washed without soap "in swamp water," the white soldiers, "smeared from head to foot with the pitch of North Carolina pine," looked blacker than the blacks. "We uns is whiter dan you uns, for a fac," joshed the colored soldiers.[81]

Sherman's soldiers entered Goldsboro, a town of 2,500 people, with banners floating proudly in the breeze and bands blaring out the music of the Union. There Sherman found Schofield with the Twenty-third Corps. The return to simple pleasures thrilled the troops. Within a few days the men received new clothing and new shoes. Their old clothes, infested with lice, were either burned or buried. Preparations were made to pay the troops for the last six months, and quartermasters brought in rations. "What epicures then!" remembered Adjutant Bryant of the Third Wisconsin. "To sit down and eat from a cracker box a nice, clean 'hardtack,' with no pitch or swamp muck on it; to have coffee with brown sugar sweetening, and some bacon or delicious side-pork as salty as the sea!" Camps were laid out and the routine of army life resumed.[82]

Proud of his men, Sherman decided to parade them before the other generals. Schofield, Cox, and Blair stood with him as the Seventeenth Corps began marching by. "The men were in motley garb," Force remembered, "bare feet, tattered coats, felt hats, beaver, straw hats—every known style of head covering was seen." Kerr believed that "probably in all the wars of the world there never was seen so bizarre and comical a sight as the leading regiment of this column which commenced that review. Nearly every soldier had some token of the march on his bayonet from a pig to a potato."

As the men passed, Blair looked at them and said: "See those poor fellows with bare legs."

"Splendid legs!" Sherman answered. "Splendid legs! I would give both mine for any one of them."

The parade was the shortest on record. After one or two regiments passed the reviewing officers, it simply dissolved.[83]

Two divergent events captured the spirit of the army at Goldsboro. The first, a letter from Sherman to his friend William M. McPherson of St. Louis, showed that Sherman retained his old racial beliefs:

> I have always thought we mixed up too many little side issues in this war. We should make a single plain issue & fight it out. The Extreme Radicals North & South have long since dodged, *shirked* the dangers of this war & left the Moderates to blow each others brains out. I again repeat I make up my opinions from facts & reasoning, and not to suit any body but myself. If people don't like my opinions, it makes little difference as I don't solicit their opinions or votes. . . .
>
> I see my name occasionally alluded to in conversation with some popular office. You may tell *all* that I would rather serve 4 years in the Sing Sing Penitentiary than in Washington & believe I could come out a better man. If that aint emphatic enough use stronger expressions and I will endorse them. Let those who love niggers better than whites follow me, and we will see who loves his Country best—A nigger as such is a most excellent fellow, but he is not fit to marry, to associate, or vote with me, or mine.[84]

Exactly one week later a member of the Twelfth New York Cavalry was punished for raping an old woman in Goldsboro. A brigade of armed men formed three sides of a square, in the center of which was dug an open grave. The prisoner approached, following four men carrying a coffin. The man was conducted to the grave. Two chaplains knelt and prayed. The prisoner's hands were tied behind him and his eyes were bandaged. He knelt beside his coffin. From a dozen paces a guard of twelve men fired. The prisoner fell forward. Observed a member of the 113th Ohio: "I do not desire to witness another scene like this."[85]

16

"I Will Take a Regiment of My Old Division and Clear Them All Out"

— I —

JUST BEFORE their triumphant army entered Goldsboro, Sherman, Slocum, Davis, Blair, Logan, Williams, and some of the division commanders gathered at Slocum's headquarters for a celebration. The campaigns that had brought the army from Chattanooga across Georgia and through the Carolinas were ending. Everyone congratulated Sherman and spoke, Joseph B. Foraker remembered, "in most glowing terms of the place he would hold in history." When either Logan or Blair said these campaigns would make the commander the next president of the United States, Sherman answered that he had no desire for political office. Popularity was, he argued, fleeting, for the American temperament was as fickle as the French, who loved to exalt one day and tear down the next. Sherman said that he made these remarks from experience. After the battle of Shiloh, rumors of drunkenness had almost ruined Grant. Similarly, in Kentucky, the insanity stories had come near destroying Sherman. Sherman might be popular at the moment, but might not be by election day. He seemed to sense that he was heading for trouble.[1]

The linkup with Schofield and Terry gave Sherman 90,000 men, a force so powerful that the danger of Lee abandoning Richmond and coming south to engage him disappeared. But in Goldsboro, Sherman received a letter from Grant. Dated March 16, it troubled him greatly. Unlike Sherman, Thomas, "slow beyond excuse," had ignored Grant's orders to be ready to move from Knoxville, where he had accumulated "a large amount of supplies," to the border of Virginia. Although skillful on defense, Old Tom was incapable of conducting a campaign. "He never can make one there or elsewhere," Grant confided to Sherman.

Grant was convinced that Sherman was "entirely safe against anything the enemy can do. Lee may evacuate Richmond and he can not get there with force enough to touch you." But Grant closed with a bombshell: "My notion is that you should get Raleigh as soon as possible and hold the rail-road from there back. . . . From this point all N. C. roads can be made useless to the enemy without keeping up communication with the rear."[2]

As Sherman continually told Schofield, he desired to move not toward Raleigh but into Virginia, toward Lee. "United with Schofield," Sherman later confided to the Chicago artist George P. A. Healy, "I was not afraid to meet Lee & Johnston united in an open field. I proposed to march straight for Burkeville. That would have shut off all supplies to Richmond—compelling Lee to leave—force him to attack me, avoiding Grant." Disturbed by Grant's suggestion, Sherman, while collecting supplies for his next move, decided to visit Grant at City Point, Virginia.[3]

Leaving Schofield in command in North Carolina, Sherman, with a couple of staff officers, left Goldsboro on the evening of March 25. At Morehead City the party boarded the captured blockade runner *Russia,* which reached Fortress Monroe on the morning of the twenty-seventh. From there Sherman telegraphed John to meet him at City Point. Sherman proceeded up the James River, reaching his destination that afternoon. He found Grant in the comfortable hut the commander and his family occupied on the bank of the river, overlooking the wharf. "This," Sherman observed, "was about 3 PM."

Julia Dent Grant remembered Sherman entering the cabin and beginning to converse with her husband. Grant suddenly looked up, saw his wife writing letters, and asked Sherman if he thought it safe to let Mrs. Grant hear them. Sherman turned to Mrs. Grant and asked her where the Tombigbee River was. Mrs. Grant did not know. Sherman next asked the location of the Chattahoochee River. Again Julia Grant did not know. Returning to her husband, Sherman then said: "Oh, yes, Grant, I think we may trust her."

Talking for roughly an hour, Grant and Sherman ironed out their differences. Sherman volunteered to march his army north to help Grant, but Grant replied: "No, I can manage everything myself. You hold Joe Johnston just where he is. I do not want him around here." Sherman would need until April 10 to resupply his army. On that day, the two generals decided, he would begin a new march, to Burkeville, Virginia, via Raleigh.[4]

After the discussion, Grant said the two must go and see Lincoln, who was aboard the steamer *River Queen* at the dock. In 1868, Sherman recalled:

> We walked down, went on board her, sent our names to him & followed to the After Cabin, where he alone received us, with marked "impressment." I had not seen him since 1861, when I was with the Army of the Potomac, when I had seen him several times. At first he looked haggard & careworn. I understood he had come down the Bay from Washington to escape the cares and harassments of political life.—As we engaged in conversation he warmed up and looked more like himself—we did not sit at a table, nor do I recall having any maps

or papers.—We merely sat at our ease, in such chairs as happened to be there.

Grant began by describing affairs for Lincoln. At that moment General Philip Sheridan was crossing from the north to the south side of the James River, hoping eventually to break the sole railroad open to Lee. Cutting it would force Lee to fight, run, or surrender. Sherman recalled:

Mr. Lincoln seemed very quiet, and at the same time anxious, he repeated several times that he was perfectly satisfied to leave the whole thing to us.

Once or twice, he addressed his conversation to me, in a pleasant jocular strain, laughing heartily at the stories he had heard of the Bummers, of turkeys, &c and our high state of living. He laughed at my former troubles with the Sanitary Commission & Christian Commission & told an apt illustration of the confusion their super philanthropy had sometimes occasioned. We sat less than one hour & excused ourselves. We then went up to Grant's quarters, where Mrs. Grant was. After some conversation Mrs. Grant said to her husband—Mr. Grant did you see Mrs. Lincoln.—No said Grant. I did not ask for her. Sherman did you. I said no. I did not know she was aboard. Well said Mrs. G. you are a pretty pair. Now, you have got your foot in it.[5]

The next day Grant and Sherman returned to the *River Queen*, "partly to correct the blunder of the day before." Mrs. Lincoln was sick and could not see them, but a second conversation with Lincoln ensued. Both generals believed that one more battle would be necessary to end the war. Lincoln hoped not and several times said that enough blood had been shed. He repeatedly asked if Schofield could handle things while Sherman was away. Sherman assured him Schofield could. Later, Sherman asked what should be done with Jefferson Davis and the other Confederate leaders when the war ended, and the president implied that Davis ought to "escape the country" but he could not say so openly. About noon of March 28 Sherman and Grant parted with Lincoln at the gangway of the *River Queen*. Sherman never saw the president again.[6]

At Grant's suggestion several of the eastern generals, including Meade and Sheridan, came to see Sherman. Lyman, Meade's aide, remembered Sherman as "a very remarkable-looking man, such as could not be grown out of America—the concentrated quintessence of Yankeedom." The general was tall, spare, and sinewy,

with a very long neck, and a big head at the end of same. . . . All his features express determination, particularly the mouth, which is wide and straight, with lips that shut tightly together. He is a very homely man, with a regular nest of wrinkles in his face, which play and twist as he eagerly talks on each subject; but his expression is pleasant and kindly. But he believes in hard war. I heard him say: "Columbia!— pretty much all burned; and burned good!"

Lyman described Sheridan as "scarce five feet high, with his sun-browned face and sailor air." Sherman appealed strongly for Sheridan's services, against which the cavalryman, who wanted to remain with Grant, protested. While Sheridan was still in bed on the morning of the twenty-eighth, Sherman came in and again implored him to join his army, but Sheridan was adamant.[7]

Accompanied by John and by the son of Secretary Stanton, Sherman returned to Goldsboro in high spirits. "I think Mr Lincoln would say amen if I had robbed & appropriated the contents of a Bank," he told Thomas Ewing. And to Ellen he commented: "Indeed officers from every quarter want to join my 'Great Army.' Grant is the same enthusiastic friend. Mr Lincoln at City Point was lavish in his good wishes and since Mr Stanton visited me at Savannah he too has become the warmest possible friend. . . . Oh, that Willy could hear and see—his proud little heart would swell to overflowing."[8]

Early in April, Sherman reorganized his army, making several significant changes. Slocum's left wing became the Army of Georgia. Sherman now shoved out the good-natured, amiable, capable Pap Williams as head of the Twentieth Corps, replacing him with Mower. Howard's wing once again became the Army of the Tennessee. And Sherman formally added to his command Schofield's Army of the Ohio, whose two corps were under Terry and General Jacob D. Cox, both admirers of Sherman.

While reorganizing the army, Sherman attended to the interests of the Ewing family, but with varying results. With Tom having resigned from the army, Charley received the promotion to brigadier general and was assigned to command a brigade in Blair's corps. Hugh, now at New Bern, North Carolina, awaiting orders, was less fortunate. To Ellen, Sherman explained:

> It is utterly impossible for me now to amend the fatal mistake Hugh made in quarreling with Logan & giving up his Division in North Alabama. I offered to restore him before we started for Nashville but he emphatically declined in spite of my earnest advice, and now I cannot & will not displace a Junior, who has worked and fought as my Division Commanders have done from Chattanooga to this place. I want you to be of my mind on this point because I fear that Hugh thinks I can & will not give him a Division. Tis not so without a breach of decency. A cry would properly go up if I were now to displace Woods, or Hazen or Corse, or any of my 13 Division Commanders to give position to Hugh. Had he come with me from Nashville he would long since have been a Major General, with a command & history of which he would have been proud. Whereas now he is one of those Senior Brigadier Generals that Army Commanders perfectly dread. They will not accept a Brigade, the legitimate command of a Brig Genl, but insist on a Division which is the legitimate command of a Maj Genl. All the young Maj Genls now with me are younger men than Hugh, but the Services & Battles of the last year have carried them over him, not from any fault of his, but as a just reward for their own zeal & labor.—

Charley has now a Brigade and if too is not too impatient to be Commander in Chief, may in due season be a Major Genl also.[9]

During the early days of April, important news reached Sherman. On the sixth he learned of the fall of Richmond and Petersburg. The leaders of the Confederate government were fleeing south toward Danville, Grant's army in pursuit. Believing that Lee would try to unite his army with Johnston's, then at Smithfield, between Goldsboro and Raleigh, Sherman prepared to attack before Lee reached there. Then on the eighth Sherman received a cipher dispatch from Grant describing Lee's army as "demoralized" and down to 20,000 men. Trying to cut Lee off, Grant would move toward Burkeville and Danville, near the Carolina line. "If you can possibly do so," he urged, "push on from where you are and let us see if we can finish the job with Lee's and Johnston's Armies. . . . Rebel Armies now are the only strategic points to strike at."

Sherman answered immediately: "It is to our interest to let Lee & Johnston come together, just as a billiard player would nurse the balls when he had them in a nice place. I am delighted and amazed at the result of your move to the South of Petersburg, and Lee has lost in one day the Reputation of three years, and you have established a reputation for perseverance and pluck that would make Wellington jump out of his Coffin."[10]

On the tenth, as his army was about to move, Sherman made to Ellen a dire prediction: "It looks like the end of the war approaching, but dont think so—Jeff Davis will sacrifice every man in the South & even his wife & child before he will give up his pride—He & at least 100,000 men in the South must die or be banished before we can think of Peace. I know them like a Book. They cant help it any more than Indians can their wild nature but still it is a truth as disagreeable as many others in Nature."[11]

A few hours later, Sherman's army marched toward Raleigh, fifty miles to the northwest. In intense heat the skirmishing began six miles out of Goldsboro, but the column kept advancing. At 10:00 A.M. on the eleventh, Slocum's men reached Smithfield, finding it abandoned. They spent the rest of the day rebuilding a destroyed bridge over the Neuse River.

That night, Sherman received a message from Grant at Appomattox. Lee had surrendered on the ninth. On the morning of the twelfth staff officers told the troops the news. Adjutant Bryant described the scene: " 'You are the man we've been looking for, for four years,' cried the joyous soldiers. They cheered and cheered. Then they yelled and hugged one another; and the word went through the lines, 'We must push Jo. Johnston now.' " As regiments came along, band after band halted in the Smithfield square and, Hitchcock remembered, "made the little old town echo with music as beautiful as it was patriotic."[12]

Crossing the river, Sherman pushed on toward Raleigh. Shortly before he reached it, a train, bearing a flag of truce "to which," Sherman observed, "they were not entitled," passed unharmed through Hampton's and then Kilpatrick's cavalry. The train carried three former North Carolina governors—David L. Swain, William A. Graham, and Thomas Bragg. They brought a letter from

Governor Zebulon Vance, asking for protection for the citizens of Raleigh. They spoke with Sherman, ate a good dinner, and that night stayed in the tents. Swain, whom Hitchcock's mother knew as a child, slept in Hitchcock's bed. The next morning, when Hitchcock accompanied Sherman to see them off, Swain came over to him and said: "Good bye, Major—*we* are not enemies, I hope." At 7:30 on the thirteenth, when the Federals entered Raleigh in a heavy rain, they found the envoys there, but Vance, fearing arrest, had fled with everything, including his furniture. They also found that Wheeler's cavalry had plundered the city before evacuating it.[13]

On entering Raleigh, Sherman sent his cavalry in the rain to Durham Station, twenty-five miles up the railroad. From there Kilpatrick reported on the morning of the fourteenth that under a flag of truce a package had arrived for Sherman. It contained a letter from Johnston calling for an end to "the further effusion of blood" and for a truce terminating "the existing war." Sherman replied that he was "fully empowered" to negotiate an agreement ending hostilities. "I will add that I really desire to save the people of North Carolina the damage they would sustain by the march of this army through the central or western parts of the State."[14]

At 9:30 A.M. on the next day, Sherman telegraphed a hopeful message to Grant and Stanton. He was sending copies of his correspondence with Johnston. "I will accept the same terms as Genl Grant gave Lee and be careful not to complicate any points of civil policy." He had seen in Raleigh numerous important men, all of whom agreed that the war was over and that the Constitution and laws of the United States must be obeyed. "This great fact once admitted all the details are easy arranged."[15]

In 1868, reviewing these events for his friend, Professor John W. Draper of New York University, Sherman revealed that while waiting for further word from Johnston two thoughts occupied him. The first was the fear of guerrilla warfare. Without some kind of agreement Johnston might retreat through Hillsborough, Greensboro, and Charlotte. Breaking up his army, he could take refuge in the mountains of South Carolina and Georgia, from Spartanburg to Athens, and resist indefinitely, doing to the Yankees what the Spaniards did to Napoleon early in the century and what the Indians were now doing in the West. Howard, Slocum, Logan, and Blair, the latter three skillful politicians as well as able soldiers, dreaded the prospect of "chasing" Johnston's army and urged Sherman to procure his surrender "on any terms." The second notion reflected Sherman's deep-seated belief that he was a soldier, not a politician. Any terms decided upon he would jot down "as carelessly and hastily as I do this letter, in the firm belief that they would never see light, other than after the Cabinet had looked at them, remodeled them and sent me specific 'orders.' "[16]

Kilpatrick handled the arrangements for the meeting, which was to take place somewhere between Sherman's advanced guard at Durham and Johnston's rear guard at Hillsborough. At eight o'clock on the morning of April 17, just as Sherman was about to enter a railroad car taking him to Durham, the telegraph operator, whose office was upstairs in the depot, ran down and told the general that he was receiving a message Sherman should see. Sherman held the train for nearly half an hour, and the operator returned with the telegram written out. From Stanton, it announced that Lincoln had been assassinated and that an attempt had been made on the lives of Secretary of State Seward and his son. Sherman asked the operator not to reveal its contents to anyone and left for the meeting. The train started out. At Morris's Station, Logan came aboard and told Sherman that he hoped some kind of peace could be arranged, for he and his troops dreaded the thought of a long march to Charlotte, 175 miles away.[17]

At Durham, Kilpatrick joined Sherman. Preceded by a single soldier carrying a flag of truce and a company of soldiers acting as a guard, the generals rode forward to meet Johnston. About five miles up the road, two men carrying flags of truce in opposite directions met. Word was passed back to Sherman, who rode up and greeted Johnston, whom he had never seen. With Johnston was Hampton, "whom I scarcely noticed because I had contempt for him and tried to show it." Sherman disliked Hampton "because, whilst he professed to be a model gentleman and soldier he had personally struck with his sword, and abused in foul language several prisoners who fell into his hands at Fayetteville. So much so that I did not address one word to him, though to all other Confederate officers, I endeavored to be frank, cordial and even jocular."

Together Johnston and Sherman rode to a single-story frame house the Confederates had just passed. A Mr. Bennett and his wife were in the home, but left when asked. In a room containing two beds and a table, the two generals faced each other. First, they chatted briefly about mutual acquaintances. Then Sherman said he had just received bad news, "the worst in my judgment, that had happened for a long time, especially damaging to his cause." He showed Johnston the dispatch about Lincoln. "The perspiration came in heavy blots on his high forehead as he was reading, and he made many ejaculations, such as 'Great God!' 'Terrible!' &c. &c. . . . He declaimed against it in terms harsher than I did, and I believed him sincere. I still believe he was sincere."

The conferees then turned to business. Johnston said that every life now lost was murder. His cause was gone. He asked nothing for himself, but wanted to know what to tell his soldiers. Johnston suggested that the surrender be universal, that it be applied to all Confederate soldiers, ending the war throughout the country. He believed that Davis would issue such an order and that his men would obey it. The generals agreed that if this could be done now, the Southern troops could raise a crop of corn and potatoes in 1865, thereby avoiding starvation and its twin associates, crime and disorder. Sherman repeatedly offered the terms Grant gave Lee, but Johnston said he wanted conditions that might be acceptable to Confederate armies in Texas, Louisiana, Georgia, and Alabama.

After talking for three hours, Johnston asked for a postponement of several days, which Sherman construed as an attempt to find Davis, then a fugitive, and to get written orders. Sherman agreed to a delay of one day. They would meet at the same place at noon the next day.[18]

Returning to Raleigh, Sherman issued an order informing his troops of Lincoln's death. That night and the next morning he consulted with Schofield, Slocum, Howard, Logan, and Blair. He later recollected:

All advised me to agree to some terms, for they all dreaded the long and harassing march in pursuit of a dissolving and fleeing army—a march that might carry us back again over the thousand miles that we had just accomplished. . . . We discussed all the probabilities, among which was whether, if Johnston made a point of it, I should assent to the escape from the country of Jeff. Davis and his fugitive cabinet; and some of my general officers, either Logan or Blair, insisted that, if asked for, we should even provide a vessel to carry them to Nassau from Charleston.[19]

The next day, April 18, Sherman and Johnston met again. The Confederate then informed the Federal that John C. Breckinridge, who had been vice president during the Buchanan administration and was now the Confederate secretary of war, was nearby, and he thought Breckinridge's presence might be helpful. When Sherman objected, Johnston said that Breckinridge was also a major general in the Confederate army, and Sherman agreed to let Breckinridge attend in that capacity. With great emotion, Sherman remembered, Johnston appealed to him as one old army officer to another and by reason of Sherman's long residence in the South "to help *him*, and help them in their terrible strait." Sherman recalled how at that moment the idea flashed through his brain that the distinction between Union and non-Union men in the South was gone. It was "the difference between tweedle-dum and tweedle-dee." No one was then talking about Negro suffrage. Congress had imposed on the South an ironclad oath of loyalty. An old soldier who trusted other old soldiers, Sherman "believed that we could use for our purposes the best men of the South, who were in the Confederate Army."[20]

If anything, Sherman was guilty of naïveté. He stepped to the table and rapidly wrote out the terms he was willing to send to the new president, Andrew Johnson. Possessing a fertile mind, Sherman many times said that he never revised anything, government reports excepted. In an almost illegible handwriting, the words flowed from his pen. This time, venturing into the field out of which he had vowed to stay, his impulsiveness betrayed him.

Wittingly or unwittingly, Sherman waded into the turbulent waters of Reconstruction. His memorandum contained seven parts. After agreeing to a truce, the Confederate troops would keep their weapons until surrendering them at their state capitals. As foolish as the retention of arms might seem, Sherman's third and fifth provisions were worse. According to these, the president would recognize the existing Southern state governments and permit Confederates to vote after the former rebels took the oath of allegiance to the federal Constitution. In effect, Sherman's proposals would restore the seceded states, still controlled by the Confederate leaders, to their former positions in the Union.[21]

Carrying the signed agreement to Raleigh, Sherman was ecstatic. If the authorities in Washington agreed, he wrote to Ellen, "this cruel war will be over. I can hardly realize it, but I can see no slip. The terms are all on our side. If approved I can soon complete the details, leave Schofield here and march my army for the Potomac, there to be mustered out and paid."[22]

That night, as Hitchcock left for Washington with the truce, Sherman's generals gathered at his headquarters to discuss its terms. Slocum, later a congressman from Brooklyn, heard only praise for it. Returning to his headquarters at midnight, Slocum found his temporary chief of staff, the astute Carl Schurz, waiting up to learn Sherman's terms to Johnston. Of all the generals, Schurz alone "expressed regret and predicted just what subsequently happened." Years later Schurz described his feelings:

> I was very much distressed not as if there could have been any doubt as to the final outcome, but on account of General Sherman. With all his companions in arms, I esteemed him very highly, and cherished a genuine affection for him. And now, to think that, at the very close of his splendid career in the war for the Union, he should by one inconsiderate act bring upon himself the censure of the government and of the country was sad indeed. And this one inconsiderate act was so foreign to what had been, and were again to be, his natural tendencies.[23]

At 4:00 P.M. on April 21, Hitchcock arrived in Washington with the agreement. Carefully going over the document before submitting it to Johnson and Stanton, Grant saw immediately, as he wrote Sherman, "that it could not possibly be approved." At a hastily called cabinet meeting at eight that evening, Grant read aloud the messages. Those present united in condemning Sherman's interference in political matters. Stanton and Attorney General James Speed, who professed friendship for Sherman, led the attack. "Stanton came charged with specific objections," noted Secretary of the Navy Gideon Welles, "four in number, counting them off on his fingers. Some of his argument was apt and well, some of it not in good taste nor precisely pertinent." Welles later remembered that he and the others were willing to go along with the condemnation of Sherman because at this time Stanton had convinced them he had evidence linking Jefferson Davis to the assassination of Lincoln and the attempts on the lives of the cabinet members. "Strange stories were told us and it was under these representations, to which we then gave credit, that we were less inclined to justify Sherman."

Grant volunteered and received permission from Stanton and Johnson to go to Raleigh. He was to convey the word that warfare was to resume. He was also to show Sherman a message from Lincoln to Grant, dated March 3, 1865, prohibiting Grant from conferring with Lee on anything but military matters. Finally, Grant was to replace the disgraced Sherman. "After the cabinet meeting last night," Stanton informed General John A. Dix of New York on the following day, "General Grant started for North Carolina to direct operations against Johnston's army."[24]

But Grant entertained no desire to supersede his loyal friend. Arriving unannounced with Hitchcock, after a voyage during which he was seasick, at 6:00 A.M. on April 24, he did not even broach the subject to Sherman. Far from being distressed or insulted, Sherman took the rejection of his memorandum matter-of-factly. He immediately informed Johnston that the agreement had been voided in Washington and took steps to negotiate another one. On April 25 he wrote a friendly letter to Stanton:

> I admit my folly in embracing in a military convention any civil matters, but unfortunately such is the nature of our situation that they seem inextricably united, and I understood from you at Savannah that the financial state of the country demanded military success, and would warrant a little bending to policy. When I had my conference with General Johnston I had the public examples before me of General Grant's terms to Lee's army and General Weitzel's invitation to the Virginia Legislature to assemble. I still believe the Government of the United States has made a mistake, but that is none of my business.[25]

Sherman and Johnston again met at Bennett's house on the twenty-sixth. This time their convention followed that between Grant and Lee. The next day Grant took the original copy of the agreement and headed back to Washington. Thinking the matter settled, Sherman prepared to visit Savannah.[26]

But on the twenty-eighth, just before Sherman left to go south, the *New York Times* of April 24 arrived. It contained the full text of Stanton's letter to Dix, announcing to the world what Sherman considered confidential: the rejection of the peace proposal. The letter implied that Sherman had knowingly violated Lincoln's instructions of March 3, about which Sherman knew nothing. Completely misshaping a letter from Halleck, Stanton implied that Sherman had been bought off by the Confederates. Now in command of the Army of the James and of those parts of North Carolina that Sherman's men did not occupy, Halleck had warned that "Jeff Davis and his partners" were headed south with a large amount of specie. Rumor had it that Davis intended to bribe Sherman or some other general and escape with "this gold plunder." Halleck concluded his message with a sentence that Stanton, connecting Sherman and Davis, left out: "Would it not be well to put Sherman and all other commanding generals on their guard in this respect?"

Stanton thought he saw other evidence that Sherman was involved in a plot to let Davis escape. Sherman had, he charged, ordered George Stoneman, then on a cavalry raid, to withdraw from Salisbury, North Carolina, opening "the way for Davis to escape to Mexico or Europe with his plunder, which is reported to be very large." General Cox later used choice words to describe Stanton's confusion: "Only complete ignorance of the actual military situation could account for so erroneous a statement." In reality, Stoneman had struck Salisbury on April 13 and then headed northwest toward his base in East Tennessee. He had reached Statesville, forty miles away, when Sherman, hearing that Davis was fleeing, immediately recalled him. "By turning towards me," Sherman explained to Grant of Stoneman, "he was approaching Davis, and, had he joined me as ordered, I would have had a mounted force greatly needed for Davis's capture, and for other purposes."[27]

Accompanying this article were Stanton's reasons, now expanded to nine, for disapproving of Sherman's terms to Johnston. Broad and imaginative, they asserted that Sherman and Johnston "knew that General Sherman had no authority to enter into any such agreement"; that their pact acknowledged "the rebel government"; that it would enable the Confederate states to reestablish slavery; that it might pave the way for payment of the Confederate debt; that it would put into jeopardy the new government of West Virginia; that it would abolish the Confiscation laws, which had dealt a bitter blow to slavery; that Sherman had given the Confederates terms Lincoln had "deliberately, repeatedly, and solemnly" rejected; and that "it formed no basis of true and lasting peace."[28]

In his reminiscences, published in 1900, Cox uncovered another example of Stanton's manipulations. At 9:00 A.M. on April 24, after reaching Raleigh and conferring with Sherman, Grant had sent Stanton a long telegram explaining Sherman's behavior. But in a cabinet meeting Stanton, implying that Sherman was engaged in some nefarious plot, read only the first and third sentences of the long message. Published in the *New York Times* on April 26, 1865, as part of a letter from Stanton to Dix, the excerpt created the impression that against Sherman's will Grant had informed Johnston the truce was void.

Grant's entire telegram conveyed no such idea and explained Sherman's thinking when negotiating with Johnston:

> I reached here this morning and delivered to Gen. Sherman the reply to his negociations [sic] with Johnston. He was not surprised but rather expected this rejection. Word was immediately sent to Johnston terminating the truce, and information that civil matters could not be entertained in any convention between Army commanders.
>
> Gen. Sherman has been guided in his negociations [sic] with Johnston entirely by what he thought was precedents authorized by the President. He had before him the terms given by me to Lee's Army and the call of the rebel legislature of Va. authorized by Weitzel, as he supposed with the sanction of the President and myself. At the time of the agreement Sherman did not know of the withdrawal of authority for the meeting of that legislature. The moment he learned through the papers that authority for the meeting of the Va. legislature had been withdrawn he communicated the fact to Johnston as having bearing on the negociations [sic] had.

Three hours later Stanton replied caustically: "Your dispatch received. The arrangement between Sherman & Johnston meets universal disapprobation. No one of any class or shade of opinion approves it. I have not known as much surprise and discontent at anything that has happened during the war. . . . The hope of the country is that you may repair the misfortune occasioned by Sherman's negotiations."[29]

Stanton's motive in all this was easy to fathom. In Washington, stories had spread that Sherman, immensely popular, was the new darling of the Conservative Democrats, who might try to put him in the White House in 1868. Knowing only the garbled story Stanton had told, Senator Zachariah Chandler of Michigan blurted out to President Johnson and Montgomery Blair that Sherman "was the coming man of the Copperheads & this blunder had come out just at the right time to destroy him." In disgust Blair left the room. "I think father never managed anything so well," Stanton's son bragged of the campaign against Sherman. "Had there been any delay a powerful opposition might have been organized, and all might have been lost."[30]

Sherman's response to Stanton's accusations was something, Schurz observed, "I shall never forget." At the governor's mansion in Raleigh, a musty old pile of bricks nicknamed "The Palace," Sherman had assembled a dozen or so of his generals in a large room stripped of furniture by the fleeing governor. All were upset at the unexpected turn of events. The generals were quiet.

> But Sherman was not mute. He paced up and down the room like a caged lion, and, without addressing anybody in particular, unbosomed himself with an eloquence of furious invective which for a while made us all stare. He lashed the Secretary of War as a mean, scheming, vindictive politician, who made it his business to rob military men of the credit earned by exposing their lives in the service of their country. He berated the people who blamed him for what he had done as a mass of fools, not worth fighting for, who did not know a thing was well done. He railed at the press, which had altogether too much freedom; which had become an engine of villification; which should be bridled by severe laws, so that the fellows who wielded too loose a pen might be put behind bars—and so on, and so on. A foreigner unacquainted with the American character and American ways, hearing this wild outburst, might have believed that here was the beginning of a mutiny of a victorious general against his government. But we who knew Sherman to be one of the most loyal souls in America, were troubled by it only because we feared that by a similar volcanic eruption in public he might seriously compromise his character before the people.[31]

Never one to hide his feelings, Sherman dispatched a long letter to Grant. His rank and past services entitled him, he argued, to something better than Stanton leaking news of cabinet meetings to the *New York Times*. He had never seen Lincoln's order of March 3. Nor did Stanton "or any human being ever convey to me its substance." Sherman was further infuriated by Stanton's charge that he had let Davis escape: "Even now I don't know that Mr. Stanton wants Davis caught."

The editor of the *Times* had implied that Sherman was insubordinate. "I have never in my life questioned or disobeyed an order," Sherman argued, "though many and many a time have I risked my life, health, and reputation in obeying orders, or even hints to execute plans and purposes, not to my liking." To withhold from him "the plans and policy of Government" and then to expect him to negotiate an armistice was "unfair." Surely Sherman's service in bringing an army of 70,000 men "in magnificent condition across a country hitherto deemed impassable," and in placing "it just where it was wanted on the day appointed," answered charges that he was "insubordinate, and wanting in common sense." His service also entitled him to be consulted before a document such as Stanton's was released to the "dogs of the press. . . . As Mr. Stanton's most singular paper has been published, I demand that this also be made public, though I am in no manner responsible to the press, but to the law, and my proper authorities."[32]

The most regrettable aspect of the controversy was that it ended the long association between Sherman and Halleck. First drawn to each other as young officers going "around the Horn" to California in mid-1846, Sherman and Halleck had remained close friends. "I confess I owe you all I now enjoy of fame," Sherman had written when given his commission as a major general in the regular army, "for I had allowed myself in 1861 to sink into a perfect 'slough of despond.' "[33]

Just after Lincoln's death, Halleck warned Sherman of an assassin "sworn to murder you. His name is said to be Clark." Slender, with a low forehead and dark, sunken eyes, he was "a Texan by birth, and has a very determined look." "He had better be in a hurry," Sherman answered, "or he will be too late." Refusing to "believe that even Mr. Davis was privy to the diabolical plot," Sherman blamed instead "a set of young men of the South who are very devils."[34]

A week later, on April 26, swept along by Stanton, Halleck informed Meade, Sheridan, and General Horatio G. Wright that they were to disregard Sherman's truce with Johnston and, indeed, all orders from Sherman. "The bankers here," Halleck warned Stanton from Richmond, "have information today that Jeff. Davis' specie is moving south from Goldsborough in wagons as fast as possible." Halleck suggested that through George Thomas orders be sent to General James Harrison Wilson, then on a cavalry raid through Georgia and Alabama, to "obey no orders from Sherman," the inference being that Sherman had sold himself to "the rebel chiefs," whose "plunder" was "estimated here at from six to thirteen millions." When Sherman opened his copy of the *New York Times* for April 28, he saw Halleck's letter, leaked to the press by Stanton, reprinted in full, along with the paper's observations that "Sherman's brain is seriously affected."[35]

An article in the London *Times* of April 5, before Lincoln's assassination, fed Stanton's fires. Arriving in the United States late in the month, the piece by an unknown author traced Sherman's affinity for the South and warned that Sherman's politics were "more in harmony with those of General Lee than those of President Lincoln." Of all the American generals, the story asserted, Sherman most closely resembled Oliver Cromwell and might try to grab power, just as Cromwell had done in England two centuries earlier. "Vain, eager, enthusiastic, fanatical, at times gloomy and reticent, at others impulsive and talkative, by some regarded as half mad when the fit is on him," Sherman possessed the stuff of "which great and mysterious actors in history are often made." In "the Armageddon now approaching," he would side with the South. In a meeting, Stanton brought this damaging article to the attention of President Johnson and the cabinet.[36]

Over the years Sherman convinced himself that his peace proposals had followed Lincoln's suggestions, a dubious proposition at best. But comments by two of his officers, both almost as deeply wounded by the episode as he, illustrated what Stanton and Halleck had done to Sherman. The first, Foraker, noted that "one issue of the *New York Herald* that reached us at Raleigh was so offensive that General Slocum ordered it gathered up and destroyed." And on April 28 Cox, later the governor of Ohio and a cabinet member, recorded in his diary:

> Some of the Northern papers are very bitter on Sherman for the terms first offered by him, and it is manifest from the dispatches sent by the Secretary of War to New York to be published there, that the new administration is willing to give Sherman a hard hit. He made a great mistake in offering to Johnston the terms he did, but he has done the country such service that the administration owed it to him to keep the thing from the public and to come kindly to an understanding with him, instead of seeming to seek the opportunity to pitch upon him as if it desired to humble him.[37]

—— II ——

On Saturday, April 30, 1865, Sherman started not north but south toward Savannah and Charleston, supposedly, Cox noted, "to inspect that part of his command but really to avoid visiting Washington." While reviewing Wilson's cavalry in Georgia, Sherman exhibited great generosity, ordering the issuance of corn, meal, and flour to the grateful people of Savannah and Atlanta. He left it for Schofield and Cox to accept Johnston's surrender.

That Monday, May 2, Cox and Schofield, accompanied by the 104th Ohio and an excellent brass band and drum corps, took a train westward from Raleigh to meet General Johnston. At Hillsborough, slightly beyond Durham, Hardee got on. The commandant of cadets at West Point just before the war and the author of a widely used manual on tactics, he proved, despite the death of his young son at Bentonville, to be an entertaining and charming companion. Laughing, he told Cox and Schofield that during the first year of the war he was one of those "hot Southerners" who believed one rebel "could whip three Yankees." That notion was soon knocked out of his head. Hardee's view of events paralleled Sherman's. Both were convinced that politicians had dragged their sections into war and then stepped back to watch the soldiers slaughter one another. "The politicians," Hardee charged, "would never give up till the army was gone."

At Greensboro, Cox and Schofield were escorted to Johnston's headquarters. Johnston apologized for the slovenliness of his camp, saying that discipline was difficult to maintain in an army about to disband. After taking care of the details of the surrender, Johnston, at first stiff and formal, warmed up and spoke freely. In the highest terms he praised the persistence of the Union army and the ability of Sherman. "Indeed," he said with a smile, "Hardee here reported the Salkehatchie Swamps as absolutely impassable; but when I heard that Sherman had not only started, but was marching through those very swamps at the rate of thirteen miles a day, making corduroy road every foot of the way, I made up my mind there had been no such army since the days of Julius Caesar." Hardee admitted the inaccuracy of his report, but added he would still have believed such a march impossible if Sherman had not done it.[38]

Meanwhile, Sherman's family, reading Stanton's attacks, closed ranks behind the general. On April 26, Ellen wrote:

> You know me well enough to know that I never would agree in any such policy as that towards perjured traitors as many of them are being deserters from the Regular Army of the United States. . . . I know that you could not allow your army to be in the slightest degree imperilled by this armistice and however much I differ from you I honor and respect you for the heart that could prompt such terms to men who have cost us individually one keen great pang which death will alone assuage—the loss of Willy.[39]

Then, on May 1, 1865, Tom Ewing, soon to be the attorney for three of the accused assassins of Lincoln, wrote Cump from Washington. Sending along all the newspaper clippings he could find on the peace negotiations, especially those in Eastern papers, "which are semi official and unofficial," Tom attributed the worst of them to Stanton, who intentionally conveyed the impression "that he had good reason to believe you would disobey the orders of your Government." To reinforce this belief, "he deliberately brought before the President & Cabinet the 'Armageddon' letter to the London Times, and caused the fact that the Cabinet considered it to be telegraphed hence over the Country." Stanton's organ, the *Washington Republican*, "published that letter, & openly suggested that you were in conspiracy with Johnston, Lee & Davis—and the New York Times did not fall much short of it in reckless comment on it. Both these papers changed the word 'Lincoln' where it last occurs in that letter for 'Johnson', so as to give point to the infamous suggestion for conspiracy, & show that the writer knew of the intended assassination of Mr. Lincoln, and that it was in the plans of the Conspirators!"

Tom urged Sherman to write to the adjutant general hurling back Stanton's "infamous charges. . . . Whatever it might cost, were I you I would not submit to this great wrong: nor suffer my hands to be tied by red tape, while the Thugs of the administration were assassinating me." The *Cincinnati Commercial* and the *New York Tribune* had already "condemned Stanton & Halleck, and ridiculed the Armageddon cabinet consultation. The Commercial has defended, generally, the armistice and the Tribune but faintly objected to it. There is an almost universal feeling of indignation, manifest in the press & everywhere else, at the conduct of the Government towards you—And a calm, dignified and severe denunciation of that conduct from you, will meet with a hearty & general approval."[40]

On May 3, two days after Tom sent his letter, Sherman, aboard the steamer *Russia,* passed the ruins of Forts Moultrie and Sumter and arrived in Charleston. Walking the familiar streets, he saw desolation. Sherman searched for his old friends, but with the exception of a portion of the family of Mrs. Pettigrew, they were either gone or dead.[41]

Reaching Morehead City on the night of May 4, Sherman found in port the revenue cutter *Wayanda,* carrying Chief Justice Chase, his daughter Janet, Whitelaw Reid, and a few others to New Orleans, where they intended to study the efficacy of giving the vote to southern blacks. For three days storms kept the *Russia* and *Wayanda* anchored in Beaufort Harbor, and during these days Chase and Sherman talked frequently. Janet Chase Hoyt later remembered how, first seeing her father, Sherman grabbed his arm and showed him a table-ful of newspapers critical of his peace proposals. "If Mr. Lincoln had lived," she recalled Sherman saying, "I should never have been insulted in this fashion! We neither of us are the kind to kick an enemy after he is conquered." Sher-man raved on and on, his face "red with indignation as he strode up and down the cabin like an enraged lion, stopping now and then to pound the table as he emphasized some point, and then resuming his hurried walk again." Suddenly realizing there were other members of the party, Sherman turned to Janet and said: "Why, child, I forgot you, let me see what I can get for you." But Chase and his party had to leave.

At Morehead City, Sherman explained to Chase why he opposed giving the vote to loyal blacks. It would, he argued, "revive the war and spread its field of operations. Why not therefore trust to the slower and not less sure means of statesmanship? Why not imitate the example of England in allowing causes to work out their gradual solution instead of imitating the French whose Political Revolutions have been bloody and have actually retarded the development of Political Freedom."[42]

Ready to leave for Virginia, where he would meet his troops, Sherman sent Halleck a harsh telegram: "After your dispatch to Mr. Stanton of Apl 26 I can-not have any friendly intercourse with you. I will come to City Point tomorrow, and march with my troops and I prefer we should not meet."[43]

Sailing toward Virginia, Sherman boiled. "A breach must be made between Grant and Sherman, or certain cliques in Washington, who have a nice thing, are gone up," he confided to Ellen. "I am glad Grant came to Raleigh, for he saw at a glance the whole thing and went away more than satisfied. But heaven and earth will be moved to kill us. Lincolns assassination was not plotted in Richmond, but near his Elbow."[44]

Arriving at Old Point Comfort, Virginia, Sherman met a dispatch from Hal-leck inviting him to stay with him in Richmond. Sherman refused. Then, at his camp near Richmond, Sherman found waiting a telegram from Halleck. "You have not had during this war, nor have you now a warmer friend and admirer than myself," Halleck began. If Halleck had used offensive language, he re-gretted it. He then hinted at the pressure Stanton had placed upon him: "If fully aware of the circumstances under which I acted, I am certain you would not attribute to me any improper motives." Halleck wished to continue as Sher-man's "personal friend" but left the matter with Sherman.[45]

After a sleepless night spent mulling over recent events, Sherman found he could not forgive Halleck. "When you advised me of the assassin Clark being on my track," he answered, "I little dreamed he would turn up in the direction and guise he did, but thank God I have become so blase to the dangers to life and reputation by the many vicissitudes of this cruel war, which some people are resolved shall never be over, that nothing surprises me." Sherman intended to march his army through Richmond. Halleck would do well to stay away, for many of Sherman's men were incensed "by what the world adjudges an insult to at least an honest commander. If loss of life or violence result from this you must attribute it to the true cause—a public insult to a brother officer when he was far away on public service, perfectly innocent of the malignant purpose and design."[46]

Sherman's revenge came on May 10. Halleck ordered Jeff C. Davis to parade his troops before him. Cump bragged to Ellen:

> I forbade it. Tomorrow I march through Richmond with Colors flying & drums beating as a matter of Right and not by Halleck's favor and no notice will be taken of him personally or officially. I dare him to oppose my march—He will think twice before he again undertakes to stand between me and my subordinates. Unless Grant interposes from his yielding & good nature I shall get some equally good opportunity to insult Stanton. They will find that Sherman who was not scared by the Crest of Lookout, the Ravines of Kennesaw, and long and trackless forests of the South is not to be *intimidated by the howlings of a set of sneaks who were hid away so long as danger was rampant,* but now shriek with very courage. *I will take a Regiment of my old Division & clear them all out.*

Stanton opposed him because Sherman did not favor Negro suffrage. The freedmen did not want to vote, Sherman insisted to Ellen. They wanted "to work and enjoy property and they are no friends of the Negro who seek to complicate him with new prejudices."[47]

On that same day, having just submitted his report of the Carolina campaign, in which he severely criticized Halleck and Stanton, Sherman dispatched to Grant a letter equally rash. Enclosing a copy of his note to Halleck, he vowed to

> treat Mr Stanton with like scorn & contempt unless you have reasons otherwise, for I regard my military career as ended save & except so far as necessary to put my Army in your hands. . . . No amount of retraction or pusillanimous excusing will do. Mr Stanton must publicly confess himself a common libeller or—but I wont threaten. . . . He seeks your life and reputation as well as mine. . . . He wants the *vast* patronage of the Military governorships of the South, and the votes of the Free Negro . . . for political Capital, and whoever stands in his way must die. Read Hallecks letter and see how pitiful he is become. Keep *above* such influences, or you will also be a victim—See in my case how soon all past services are ignored & forgotten. Excuse this letter. Burn it, but heed my friendly counsel.[48]

Frustrated, Halleck next issued an order forbidding Howard's men from entering Richmond. From outside the city the Western troops could see ex-Confederate soldiers coming and going freely, but when they attempted to visit the city, Halleck's guards stopped them at the pontoon bridge. Unwilling to submit, some of Sherman's men gathered at the bridge, overwhelmed the guards, and shoved their way into Richmond.[49]

Writing to Logan, who, with Howard suddenly called to Washington by Stanton, now commanded the right wing, Sherman saw Halleck's move as "a part of a grand game to insult us—us who marched 1,000 miles through a hostile country in mid-winter to help them. . . . If such be the welcome the East gives to the West, we can but let them make war and fight it out themselves. I know where is a land and people that will not treat us thus—the West, the Valley of the Mississippi, the heart and soul and future strength of America, and I for one will go there."[50]

On May 11 and 12 Sherman marched his great army across the pontoon bridge over the James River at the south end of Richmond. Ignoring Halleck's headquarters, the caravan advanced as before in two columns. Slocum's left wing proceeded to Hanover Court House, where Patrick Henry had made his speech asking for liberty or death. The right wing took the more direct route, toward Fredericksburg.[51]

As his men passed through some of the fields where the Army of the Potomac had engaged Lee's Army of Northern Virginia, Sherman shifted from corps to corps to view the battlegrounds. At Spotsylvania Court House, the site of a fierce struggle the year before, the troops of the Twentieth Corps saw the zigzagging earthworks, the trees riddled with shot, and the thousands of unburied skeletons bleaching under the blaze of the Southern sun. The remains of over 800 bodies lay in one pine grove of a few acres, said to be where, on May 12, 1864, Hancock's corps had charged the Confederate works and nearly crushed Lee. Passing through the Wilderness, where two mighty armies clashed in a forest eight miles wide, the Twentieth halted at Chancellorsville. Then part of the Eleventh and Twelfth Corps, its men had fought there on Sunday, May 3, 1863, when Lee and Stonewall Jackson had outgeneraled Hooker. The sad scenes remained: the bones of dead horse and dead rider decaying together; the knapsacks, now moldy, placed in piles along Plank Road before the charge by Union soldiers who did not live to reclaim them; the ground where the Eleventh Corps swung out and, rear and flank unprotected, was surprised by the Confederates. While the troops were visiting familiar spots, Sherman was seen walking, hands behind him, to and fro on the ridge near Chancellorsville House, shaken by the scenes of slaughter, now thankfully ended.[52]

As Sherman's army passed through insignificant towns that had been immortalized by the suffering inflicted there, Ellen saw signs that Stanton wanted peace. She informed Cump on the seventeenth:

> I assure you, we are truly charmed to find that you have had so good an opportunity of returning the insult of that base man Halleck. This being public and the army participating makes it equal to his insult and is perfectly satisfactory to your friends everywhere. We have not felt so much pleased with anything since the fall of Savannah—since "Sher-

man marched down to the Sea." . . . Father is very anxious to see you. He thinks Stanton & the President will lose no means to destroy you if you lay yourself liable to or compromise yourself in any way towards Stanton as he is a *Superior Officer* &c. . . . Two days after Stanton fulminated that astounding falsehood I *telegraphed you* through him stating "Father & I highly approved your memorandum" &c &c. Stanton replied that he would forward the dispatch without delay & signed himself very truly my friend. . . . He evidently wishes to conciliate. . . . I would rather have seen that defiant parade through Richmond than anything else since the war began. Father says Stanton can be impeached on his falsehoods accompanying your memorandum.[53]

On the nineteenth Sherman reached Alexandria, where he pitched camp. The next day he visited Grant, Johnson, and the cabinet. With outstretched arms the president welcomed him warmly: "Genl Sherman, I am *very* glad to see you—*very* glad to see you,—*and I mean what I say.*" Johnson assured Sherman that he knew nothing of Stanton's articles until he had seen them in the newspapers and that Stanton had not shown them to him or to the cabinet before they were published. Nearly all of the cabinet members told the general the same thing. But Stanton said nothing to Sherman. Yet, a few days later, Sherman bragged to Hitchcock that Stanton was already "backing down" and "had sent half a dozen people to him to try & make it up."[54]

That day Sherman learned of a grand parade to be held the next week, during which the president and the cabinet would review the eastern and western armies. On the twenty-second, the day before the review began, Sherman testified on his peace proposals before the Congressional Committee on the Conduct of the War. As described by Stanton's most recent biographers, who completely ignored the secretary's repeated acts of duplicity against Sherman, "cocky Tecumseh," saying his terms conformed to Lincoln's, answered questions "in a curtly defiant manner." In reality, Sherman's words, when later printed with the documents he submitted, covered thirty-two pages. Even Stanton's biographers conceded that Sherman was forced to testify amid rumors that he planned to take over the government.[55]

The Grand Review began on the twenty-third, when Meade's army paraded from the Capitol to Pennsylvania Avenue and the reviewing stand in front of the White House. As the troops reached the stand, general officers took places on it and stood until the entire army passed.

That evening General Sherman's four corps, the same force Stanton feared might enter Washington and overthrow the government, silently moved from their camp and bivouacked in the streets and suburbs near Capitol Hill. At nine o'clock the next morning, on a bright, hot day, Sherman's 53,000 infantrymen, who within eleven months had tramped from Chattanooga to Atlanta, then to Savannah, and finally to Washington, awaited the signal to start this briefer march.[56]

Several days before the review, Sherman had called Howard to the office of General Townsend, the adjutant general of the army. Wanting to make amends to Logan, he asked Howard, who was about to become head of the

Freedmen's Bureau, to relinquish command of the right wing so that Logan could lead it in the parade. Howard protested that he had commanded that wing since its formation, and Sherman replied: "I know it, but it will be everything to Logan to have this opportunity." Then Sherman said gently: "Howard, you are a Christian, and won't mind such a sacrifice." Howard answered: "Surely, if you put it on that ground, I submit." During the parade, whenever Howard, thinking those lining the streets wanted to cheer Sherman, began to draw slightly toward the rear, Sherman instantly called him forward and insisted they ride side by side.[57]

Marching down Washington's streets, Sherman's army was easily recognized as the flower of the New World. On a superb dapple gray stallion Logan, "as swarthy as an Indian and as statuesque," followed Sherman and Howard, leading the two corps of the Army of the Tennessee. Hazen, "compact and martial," commanded the first of these, the Fifteenth Corps. Next came Blair, "tall and masterful," with the Seventeenth Corps, its badge an arrow.

Slocum, "slender and dignified," led the Army of Georgia. The Twentieth Corps, with Mower, came first. Composed of the old Eleventh and Twelfth Corps, which had fought in the East at the Second Battle of Bull Run, with Hooker at Chancellorsville, and with Meade at Gettysburg, it had been formed by Hooker and sent to Lookout Mountain. The final corps was Jeff C. Davis's Fourteenth, which had been with Sherman since the bitterly cold days of the march to relieve Burnside at Knoxville. "The magnificent physique of the men at once elicits the admiration of all," noted a reporter for the *New York Times*; "tall, erect, broad-shouldered, stalwart men, the peasantry of the West—the best material in the whole world for armies." At Shiloh such men had dispelled the Southern boast that Yankees could not fight.

Each brigade that passed was preceded by the only black soldiers that Sherman tolerated and admired. His battalion of black pioneers had performed nobly from Chattanooga to Goldsboro. Parading in the garments worn on the plantation, they carried the shovel and the ax and marched with "an even front, sturdy step and lofty air."[58]

The most novel feature of the great parade was the "Bummer Brigade." This was led by two tall black soldiers, their feet almost touching the ground, on tiny mules. Then came a caravan of packhorses and mules. Some were loaded with the pets of soldiers: chickens, dogs, coons, goats, and roosters. Others bore pots, pans, and kettles.[59]

As Sherman rode past the headquarters of the Washington army, he waved his hat at a bandaged figure in the window. The walking corpse in return saluted him. William H. Seward, who had been wounded in the assassination attempt on the night Lincoln was killed, had not seen Sherman since the visit to Fort Corcoran in 1861. General Christopher Columbus Augur, in charge of the defenses in Washington, had made Seward comfortable and furnished him with a good position to see the military display.[60]

At the reviewing stand a controversial episode occurred. Hitchcock left the best description of what happened:

I dare say the N. Y. papers of this morning contain by letter—for it was not sent, probably not allowed to go, by telegraph—an account of Sherman's giving Stanton the cut *on the stand* on Penn. Av. where the President &c &c were sitting to see our Army pass. When the Genl, riding in advance of his Army, with his staff &c, had passed the stand, we all dismounted & marched up into the stand where the Genl went up to the President, saluted and shook hands, & was welcomed by the various dignitaries around the Prest. Stanton was sitting next to the Pres. on his right, & among others advanced & offered to shake hands with Sherman, but the latter *cut* him entirely. . . . The incident was plainly seen by many even across the Avenue with their opera glasses.[61]

Writing anonymously in the *Washington Chronicle* of May 15, John Sherman, Stanton's next door neighbor, applauded his brother's action. Stanton "*must expect open defiance and insult,*" John warned, "*and neither his person nor his rank can shield him.*" Even though Stanton's son and the secretary's assistant, Dana, denied the snubbing ever took place, the pro-Stanton *New York Times* conceded that Sherman "took the occasion of a grand review . . . to refuse the hand of Mr. Stanton, when tendered to him, in friendly greeting. Even if Gen. Sherman had sustained all the wrongs he seems to think have been inflicted on him," the paper answered John, "he ought to know better than to seek redress in so childish and absurd a manner."[62]

Sherman, however, was pleased with his studied insult. He bragged to Schofield of the parade:

It came off in magnificent style. . . . Stanton offered to shake hands with me in the presence of the President but I declined, and passed him to shake with Grant. . . . Halleck tries to throw off on Stanton and Stanton on Halleck, and many men wanted me to be patient under the affliction for the sake of patriotism but I will not, the matter being more than official, a personal insult, and I have resented it, and shall continue to do so. No man I dont care who he is shall insult me publicly or arraign my motives. Mr Johnson has been more than kind to me, and the howl against me narrowed down to Halleck & Stanton, and I have partially repaid both.

Sherman reiterated his belief that black suffrage was a bad idea: "I have reason to believe Mr Johnson is not going as far as Mr Chase in infusing Negro vote on the Southern or any states. I never heard a Negro ask for that and I think it would be his ruin. I believe it would result in riot & violence at all the polls North & South."[63] Two days after Sherman wrote these words, Johnson issued his proclamation allowing, as Sherman had, the old Southern leaders to come back into power.

Some of Sherman's soldiers, especially, Grant told Sherman, "when a little in liquor," reflected Sherman's attitude toward Stanton. At Willard's on May 26 many of the officers were "drinking and discussing violently the conduct of Mr.

Stanton." They "occasionally would jump on the counter and give three groans for Mr. Stanton, then get down and take another drink."[64]

Despite his bitterness, Sherman soon made up with Stanton, with whom he worked on numerous occasions. In 1868 Stanton even implored the general to accept an appointment as secretary of war. But the squabble with Halleck never ended. In June, Halleck submitted to Stanton a long defense of his actions, insisting again "that I was innocent of any intended offense." Reading the long account in the newspapers, Sherman wrote Tom Ewing: "If his answer was published in contrast with his original telegram to Stanton he could see how inconsistent is his reasoning, but I will leave the subject where it is and believe he and Stanton both will think a second time before attacking me." Soon sent to California, Halleck never again saw Sherman.[65]

17

"Whatever We Do Here Causes Death"

— I —

ACCOMPANIED BY Ellen and their son Tommy, who had come east for the Grand Review, Sherman left Washington in the beginning of June and headed toward New York and the East Twenty-third Street mansion of William Scott, the widower of his lovely cousin, Louisa Hoyt Scott. For days crowds eager to see the great general stood outside the house. Rosecrans, Dix, Wager Swayne, Stewart Van Vliet, and Sherman's distant cousin, the noted lawyer William M. Evarts, all visited him. Wherever Sherman went, people gathered around his carriage, eventually forcing him to surrender all hope of going anywhere during the day.[1]

With Van Vliet, Baldy Smith, Ellen, and Tommy, dressed in the uniform of a corporal in the Thirteenth Infantry, Sherman left the city and sailed up the Hudson toward West Point. At Cozzen's Hotel, near the academy, he stopped to greet General Scott and then proceeded to his destination, where examinations were being held. Captain Charles King, a cadet at the time, remembered Winfield Scott as "the most pompous and ponderous of our generals and Sherman the least so." Wandering aimlessly around the academy, accompanied by his adjutant, Colonel Lewis M. Dayton, Sherman was "offhand, easy-going, democratic." In "rapid, nervous speech," he struck up conversations with cadets, telling them how things were done in his day. He was informal and approachable. "Everybody who had a suitable house and table invited him to dinner," King recalled, "but he never knew where he was going—nor cared." To invitations he replied: "Ask Dayton. I'm just browsing around." But Sherman and General Scott shared one trait. Each never missed the opportunity to kiss a pretty woman.[2]

After trips to Lancaster, Chicago, and Cincinnati, Sherman was in Louisville on a hot Fourth of July bidding adieu to the veterans of the Twentieth

Corps, soon to be mustered out. From the summit of a hill he spoke in a low, resonant voice to the troops gathered below about "the heroic dead," about the "broken and disabled," and finally about those fortunate enough to have survived without injury. He admitted that when the Twentieth Corps had first come to him, he had no faith in eastern troops. But Resaca, New Hope Church, and Peachtree Creek had changed his mind, and he afterward relied on the Twentieth as much as he did the Fifteenth. He counseled his soldiers to equal in civil life their wartime accomplishments and gave them "his blessing and farewell."[3]

For army officers, peace brought a mad dash for position. Sherman once told his friend General Régis de Trobriand that while the wartime army contained six hundred colonels, the peacetime force had but twenty-five. President Johnson divided the country into five military divisions, one for each of the major generals in the regular army. With headquarters in his beloved St. Louis, Sherman was placed in charge of the area between the Mississippi River and the Rockies.[4]

Sherman's command included sixty-six former generals, all reverting to ranks of colonel and below. Such old-time army officers as Canby, David Hunter, and Thomas W. Sherman were reduced to colonels. David Stanley and Kenner Garrard became majors. And Kilpatrick, James Harrison Wilson, Gordon Granger, Anson McCook, and Jeff C. Davis, on paper at least, were captains.[5]

Even while setting up his new office, Sherman felt the wrath of Stanton. The secretary had sent the general to St. Louis as a form of exile, not knowing Sherman had lived there and had many friends there. The secretary, Cump told Ellen, "would drop me like a hot potato if possible. Stanton is as vindictive as old satan and is so industrious and has the business of his office so complicated that Mr Johnson fears to break with him, and Grant is not equal to him in energy of thought and therefore will be kept back. Stanton still holds the reins and I must be careful of him."[6]

Stanton aimed his guns at John, whose Senate term was to end early in 1866. "It is apparent that I am to have a fierce contest for reelection," John informed his brother in late July. "In W[ashington] I found that the patronage of the War Dept was used unscrupulously against me. I cannot afford now to be beaten although the office if secured is of little value."[7]

Sherman was "sorry you feel uneasy about the election. Of course you should gain the next election if possible, but during that term should wean yourself of the place. Washington has ruined more men than it has made. Politics in our Country is fast becoming a specialty & is becoming as exclusive and vindictive as the English Lords. . . . Were I in your place I would gradually look to a more independent life."[8]

When Stanton arbitrarily ordered away one of Sherman's aides, the general was sure the Secretary "would be glad to kill me." Stanton was, he wrote to Tom Ewing, "on a par with Jeff Davis and other traitors who set up their ipso dixit for law. . . . The law never contemplated a Sec of War to give orders to the personnel of the Army. Nobody ever did so before but Jeff Davis, as Sec of War and that was but the prelude to his great treason by ordering the Rebellion of half our Country. I would make an issue of this case, but am not ready yet."[9]

John hoped his brother would ignore Stanton: "The tables will be turned some day & he will be the most hounded as he is now the most hated man in America."[10]

— II —

After the Civil War, Northern businessmen often aided the returning heroes. New Yorkers raised $105,000 for Grant, part of which he used to buy a house in Washington. Sherman received help from two sources. The Sherman Testimonial Fund of Ohio, which Grant had helped form in December 1864, raised $9,696.10, with which Sherman bought $15,000 worth of interest-bearing bonds.[11]

The second gift was more sizable. Congress allowed Halleck to draw $225 a month for quarters in California, but it allotted Sherman in St. Louis only $48. That August, Sherman's St. Louis friends gave him $30,000 for a house. Sherman thereupon bought a home on high ground along Garrison Avenue. "Street cars pass the front door," he informed John, "and I will keep a carriage." Sherman's furniture soon arrived, and on September 22 the family moved into its first home together since 1861.[12]

Preparing to leave Lancaster for St. Louis, Ellen bemoaned her fate as

the wife of a hero for I am stared at and become the subject of invidious & "odious comparisons" no doubt. Of course, every good looking young fashionable thinks it a pity so distinguished a man could not have her for his wife instead of the worn down old woman before her— Youth flies and its roses leave the wife whilst the husband is acquiring a name, another commentary upon human vanity. Fame and triumph have no keen relish to me now for with every indication of them arise the thoughts of Willy in death's cold embrace and the hope that when these things have passed we may join him speedily in his present abode. I always knew that Cump must succeed if health were spared him & I therefore feel no particular elation at his present success although the country seems wild with joy.[13]

Having her family together failed to console Ellen. "Poor Cump had no idea that he was inviting Willy to meet his death when he wrote for us to come there," she recalled to her cousin late in 1865 of her Vicksburg trip. She added:

It has been said in many places (& printed too) that I went down against the General's judgment & without his knowledge. I had no intention of going until I received his letter telling me *when to start* & to take *all* the children. God, who is my witness, knows that I endured the fatigues & discomforts of the journey down more for the sake of giving pleasure to the children (Willie & Minnie particularly) & to their Father than with any anticipation of pleasure myself. Being deeply interested in the soldiers & my heart so tenderly alive to the risks which my husband & brothers had seen & were yet to brave, I could not fail to both feel & express much joy at the prospect of seeing them in camp and doing all in my power towards their enjoyment during their season of rest. The horrors of that journey home—the sufferings—the agony—the death, the desolation of heart with which I awoke to renewed sorrow each morning on my way from Memphis up was more than I ever could describe and more than I could bear, without the faith & grace which supported but could not cheer me.[14]

Commanding the army on the plains, Sherman's chief concern became the transcontinental railroad, the Union Pacific, construction of which began about the time he reached St. Louis. In July the company's engine Number One, the *Major General Sherman,* arrived at Omaha, the road's starting point. That October, Sherman, with his aides sitting atop the cars shooting at wild partridges, rode out in a train pulled by the engine to celebrate the completion of the first sixteen miles of track, from Omaha to Papillon. Orator after orator spoke of the determination to finish the road, which had yet to pass through two thousand miles of plains, mountains, and deserts inhabited by Sioux, Cheyennes, and Arapahos. Sherman, on the other hand, recalled losing $10,000 on the road of which he had been vice president in 1855 and 1856. The construction of twenty-two and a half miles of track from Sacramento east to Folsom had also brought forth boastful oratory. At that time Sherman's friend Edward Baker had painted magnificent word pictures of the union of East and West "by bands of iron." Like many others, Baker had ignored the sectional turmoil that would soon "swallow up half a million of the brightest and best youth of the land," including himself, for he was killed in October 1861 at Ball's Bluff.[15]

In late 1865, John Sherman was still fighting for his political life. Stanton, a Radical who believed in Negro suffrage and a strong Reconstruction policy, had shoved forward as John's rival General Robert C. Schenk. Having just returned from Arkansas, where, after talking "freely with whites & Blacks," he remained a firm believer in Johnson's plan of allowing the South back into the Union with few restrictions, Sherman scoffed at Schenk as a military man. "When did he hear a shot," he wrote John of Schenk, "but that he made good time for the Potomac. During the real death struggles of the War, he was a kind of Constable of Baltimore squabbling with feeble gossips & old women, which well enough in its way, had about as much military merit, as guarding prisoners on Johnsons Island. . . . If I can learn that Stanton uses his quarrel with me against you, I will make his ears tingle with something he will like as little as the shouts that went up when I declined to recognize him personally at the Grand Review."[16]

When the Ohio legislature reelected John, Cump was elated. But the episode reinforced his old belief. "You know that I have always expressed a strong aversion to politics," he confided to Colonel Willard Warner, formerly an aide but now a member of the Ohio legislature, "and you will believe me sincere when I repeat that I feel more so now than ever, & all the talk of using me for such purposes is in express violation of my often repeated & emphatic wishes. I will never be a candidate for civil office."[17]

Early in 1866, Sherman's relations with Hugh Ewing reached a low point. Unemployed, Hugh was irked at Sherman for not recommending him for one of Ohio's three colonelcies in the regular army. The Union army had one thousand generals, Sherman revealed to his father-in-law, two hundred of whom looked to him "as their only friend and champion." Of these he had endorsed only fifteen. Sherman had already recommended for the Ohio colonelcies more than three men, each of whom was better qualified than Hugh.

Extremely irritated, Hugh had visited Goldsboro within site of Sherman's headquarters, but he had not bothered to call on him. At Tom Ewing's house in mid-February Sherman met Hugh and offered him his hand, but there the reconciliation ended. Hugh was still hurt because Sherman, in the recommendation to Thomas, had described him as a fine drill officer. "He construed that as my judgment of him altogether," Sherman explained to Charley, "whereas I suppose I used it as appropriate to what Thomas would specifically need, but if his friendship of me was so shallow as to be determined by a forced construction of a hastily written letter, I will make no effort to regain it. . . . So the case stands. Tom urges you out—and Hugh in—making the service a convenience. I am more accustomed to have the service the Principle, & the individual Secondary."[18]

In February 1866, when Johnston vetoed a Freedmen's Bureau Bill, Sherman applauded. Two Radicals, Senator Charles Sumner of Massachusetts and Representative Thaddeus Stevens of Pennsylvania, "were resolved to make an issue," Sherman told Thomas Ewing, "and no concession on the part of the President could have satisfied their extreme wishes. . . . The Republican Party was drifting so headlong to the opposite extreme that Mr. Johnson had no alternative but to assent to a new Revolution, or to separate himself from them."[19]

Amid these other troubles, Sherman faced financial problems. The taxes on his new home were so high that he regretted not selecting a smaller house. Moreover, he confided to Edward Ord, a Catholic, sending his children to religious instead of to public schools, "which are free and for which all are taxed," was a great expense for someone on a major general's salary.[20]

Already Grant was playing the game that would lead to his financial downfall. "Grant comes here as often as asked," Colonel Bowman informed Sherman from New York in March. "He brings his staff—accepts presents from anybody and all the time wears the same imperturbable countenance! Grant is not afraid of the people, is not afraid of himself, he floats along in the crowd naturally—and is really a good fellow. But the best of all is everybody takes his excellences for granted and he is at no trouble to prove them. Happy man!"[21]

General Daniel Butterfield, who had raised the $105,000 for Grant, volunteered to do the same for Sherman. But after thinking it over, Sherman refused the offer. "How you are to get along in the high position you hold," Butterfield argued, "educate & provide for your children &c on your pay in these times is a mystery to me."[22]

Financial relief came that July, when Congress created for Grant a new rank, General of the Army. At Grant's suggestion Sherman was appointed and confirmed as a lieutenant general, doubling his pay. "I wont use words to express my personal thanks to you," Sherman wrote Grant upon reading the news, "but await a fitting time to prove it by acts. The fact that so firm a friendship & mutual confidence exist between us is often referred to as the Great Cause of our success. At all events I do attach a vital importance to it and will continue my efforts to fulfill any thing you may desire."[23]

___ III ___

The spring of 1866 brought renewed interest in the transcontinental railroad. In charge of determining the Union Pacific's route, Grenville M. Dodge sent his surveyors out, and by mid-May the road had completed eighty miles of track. Officials promised to finish two hundred before year's end. Sherman vowed to inspect every thirty miles of road as it was completed and bet Major Luther S. Bent, the company's general ticket agent, a basket of champagne that he would do so. But that would have meant riding to the end of the line every month. After a few trips, Sherman gave in and wrote Dodge, "I am ready to pay my bet." In New York, just before he died, Sherman remarked to Dodge that if he could get Bent to come east, he would give him the champagne.[24]

That spring the army created the Department of the Platte, with headquarters at Omaha, to protect the railroad workers. By July, Dodge was already screaming to Sherman about Indians molesting his work parties. The road was being surveyed and built north of the Platte River in Nebraska, but all of the army posts and stagecoach stations were south of it, affording the crews slight protection.[25]

Moping about St. Louis bored Sherman. That summer a hundred thousand Americans were expected to push west, up the Arkansas, the Smoky Hill, the Platte, and the Missouri Rivers, in search of the Promised Economic Land. Some were lured by mineral discoveries, others by the free land offered by the Homestead Act of 1862. Many succumbed to wanderlust.

With John and three aides, Sherman set out in mid-August on a tour of the West. When he began his trip, the Union Pacific's Eastern Division, which would connect Kansas City with the main railroad line, had been built to Manhattan, Kansas, and was but a month from Fort Riley. Awakening with the energy of a hibernating bear, the main line had stretched from Omaha to Fort Kearney, 194 miles. Near Kearney, Cump and John descended from the train and climbed aboard a Dougherty ambulance, a four-wheel carriage with leather cushions and seats that could be converted into beds. "John Sherman and I are in the leading ambulance," Sherman explained to Ellen about the trip toward Fort Laramie, in the southeast corner of Wyoming Territory. "Driver and his sack of corn & blankets in front—our valises & blankets behind, and John & I are seated on hay in the bottom leaning back against the valises. We travel from daylight to about 10 AM and lay 4 hours for grass, when we continue so as to make our journey of 35 miles a day. . . . I have a full thousand miles yet to travel, through a country where small bands of Indians are prowling more to steal than to kill."[26]

Reaching Laramie, a ragbag of a post with buildings scattered every which way, Sherman found the talk "all about the Black Hills about 600 miles off *yet*, where the whites think there are heaps of Gold, and the Indians say is the only place left for them to hunt." Up to this time about thirty travelers had been killed, but Sherman was sure that individuals, not tribes, had done the evil work. "It is one of those irresistible conflicts," he informed Ellen, "that will end only in one way. One or the other must be exterminated and as Grant says our tail is longest and the poor Indian in the End must go under."[27]

From Laramie the brothers pushed on toward Denver, then but six years old. Finding it safe to travel, they dismissed their escort halfway there and arrived on September 10. Spending three days in the town, punctuated by a series of tiring dinners and balls, the Shermans left on the thirteenth and headed for Fort Garland, at the head of the Rio Grande.[28]

In Colorado Sherman came across, for the first time since the Atlanta campaign, General Rusling, who was inspecting the West for the quartermaster general's office. Joining "outfits," as Rusling put it, the two parties journeyed together for a month, along and through the Rocky Mountains. "Camping out at night by some quiet lake or foaming torrent," the travelers built high campfires from the fallen cedars and pines. Ceaselessly Sherman talked and smoked. Stretching out on a blanket before a fire, cigar clenched alternately between his teeth and his fingers, he "often talked half the night away." One moment, Rusling revealed, he would discuss his famous comrades—Grant, Thomas, McPherson, Sheridan—the next his noted opponents—Lee, Johnston, Hood. Or he would go on and on about Alexander the Great, Caesar, Cromwell, Washington, Napoleon, and Wellington. Tireless, Sherman was usually the last to fall asleep and the first to awaken.[29]

As the party moved south, Sherman met pleas for aid. At the mining community of Colorado City, now Colorado Springs, the townspeople, led by the Reverend William Howbert, begged for army protection. "General Sherman received the appeal with utter indifference," noted Howbert's son, "and replied that he thought we were unnecessarily alarmed, since there were no hostile Indians in the region." Sherman sarcastically remarked that it would be very profitable for the community if it could have troops located nearby, to whom farmers might sell grain and other products at high prices. "With this remark he dismissed the committee."[30]

Pushing on, Sherman and Rusling in mid-September traveled through a pass "rough enough to creek every bone in the body" and arrived at Fort Garland, a series of one-story, whitewashed adobe buildings located in a basin surrounded by mountains 15,000 feet high. In a region, Cump wrote Ellen, inhabited "by a mixed breed of Mexicans and Indians," the fort was in territory acquired by the United States during the Mexican War.

In command of the fort, with three companies of New Mexico Volunteers, was Sherman's old friend from California days, Kit Carson. "Kit has a New

Mexican wife and six children as wild as deer," Sherman divulged to Ellen. "He succeeded in getting them in over to see me for a few seconds, but they soon escaped and I have not seen them since. . . . Kit is a good fellow but getting old—He now talks about settling down."

Having come more than four hundred miles without soldiers, Sherman felt completely safe. "We have had several of the Big Chiefs of the *Utes* here who have the same old story and wind up begging for flour and sugar," he reported to Ellen. "All the game is gone, and the Indians must soon follow, and it is hard to say what we are to do with the Country."[31]

As Rusling pointed out, Sherman enjoyed the days and nights with Carson "as a schoolboy let loose." He asked a thousand questions, laughed incessantly, and seldom seemed happier. "Meanwhile he smoked constantly, and kept up that everlasting long stride of his up and down the floor or ground, with his hands deep in his trousers pockets, as if he would never weary."[32]

Leaving Garland with a buffalo robe, a beaver skin, and a letter, gifts from Carson to Tommy, Sherman and John were back in Denver on October 10. There John, who missed a month of campaigning and felt he must return to Ohio, left by coach for Fort Riley. Following the Smoky Hill River, Sherman arrived at Ellsworth, Kansas, ninety-five miles west of Riley, on the twelfth, talking along the way with the Kiowas, Cheyennes, and Arapahos. Approaching the fort, Sherman found herds of buffalo. "We killed 11 in all," he told John. "I killed two." From Fort Riley, Sherman rode back to St. Louis in the railroad cars.

In St. Louis, Sherman found a message from the president. He was needed in Washington.[33]

— IV —

On the twenty-fifth of October, Sherman arrived in Washington to find a political and diplomatic muddle. During the American Civil War, the French emperor, Napoleon III, had sponsored a puppet government in Mexico, led by Archduke Maximilian of Austria. From Johnson, Sherman learned that the president desired to send Grant and the new American minister, Lewis D. Campbell, to find and talk to President Benito Juárez, then hiding pending the withdrawal of the French. But Grant, believing Johnson considered him too favorable to the Radicals and wanted to ship him off to get rid of him, refused to go. During his conversation with Johnson, Sherman, sensing some kind of plot, said very little, asking only why Johnson believed the United States would be more welcome in Mexico than the French. "I have no doubt there is some plan to get Grant out of the way," Cump wrote Ellen, "& to get me here, but I will be a party to no such move. . . . I dont want the extreme Radicals to govern this Country & I did and do wish Mr Johnson success in general terms— but I am opposed to Mexico in all its phases—and to any intermeddling with other people." Sherman reported to Ellen another sad note. Johnson had allied with General George W. Morgan, now a Democratic congressman from Ohio, "who would not fight at Chickasaw & lost me a battle otherwise won."[34]

To extricate Grant from his peculiar predicament, Sherman volunteered to join Campbell, John's rival for the House Speakership in 1860. But from the beginning the trip proved a fiasco. Sherman confided to Ellen:

> Campbell is quite an inferior man, though according to his own report he used to be the Whig leader in the House of Representatives. He drank so much the first two days out (in confidence) that I spoke to him and got from him a promise of abstinence till we reached Mexico. I put it in the form of a mutual pledge, so that I cannot now take my usual nooning. But it makes no difference to me, and I would have been ashamed to meet French & Spanish officers with a Drunken Minister as our National Representative. I dont know why our Govt will select such men to represent us in such delicate missions.[35]

Few things in Sherman's life failed so completely as the Mexican mission. After fruitlessly searching for Juárez, Sherman decided to come home, leaving Campbell to follow. On the return trip he stopped at New Orleans, where Philip Sheridan insisted Sherman stay with him. "He has a beautiful place," Sherman told Grant, "and lives most comfortably, to the envy of all the marriageable girls of his acquaintance." In New Orleans several of Sherman's old generals, including David Stuart, Mower, and Morgan Smith, visited him. So, too, did Bragg, impoverished and unemployed; Richard Taylor; and Taylor's brother-in-law, Colonel William W. S. Bliss. But Hood, Longstreet, and Beauregard did not call. Coming up from New Orleans by rail, Sherman passed through Jackson, Mississippi, which his army had twice devastated, Granada, Grand Junction, and Jackson, Tennessee. Each railroad station bore the scars of Yankee visits: lonesome chimneys, twisted rails, and pieces of destroyed locomotives. "At first," Sherman confided to Grant from St. Louis, "I thought it imprudent to risk the trip lest some one might say or do something not agreeable, but wishing to get here so as to spend some of the Holiday with the children I concluded to risk it and am glad I did so. I saw any number of ex-Rebels all the way, and saw or heard nothing that was at all disagreeable. . . . A great many people called to see me, and it was hard to realize that only two years ago we were such bitter enemies."[36]

Reaching New Orleans after Sherman left, Campbell worsened a bad situation by drinking in public. As a friend wrote Sherman: "At the Metairie Jockey Club Ball—a gathering as you know of the very elite of the City—at a party at Genl Sheridans on Tuesday evening last, and again last night at a party given on the Iron Clad vessels here, has this occurred, until gentlemen speak to me in the street about it, and our National name and character are disgraced." Even the arrival in New Orleans of Campbell's daughter failed to stop his spree. "When I measure the caliber of such men," Sherman complained to Thomas Ewing of Campbell, "I am sometimes amazed that our Govt should entrust delicate business to them. I would not trust him in charge of a picket Guard."[37]

Sherman arrived in St. Louis in time for the birth, on January 9, 1867, of his last child, Philemon Tecumseh Sherman, who throughout his long and fruitful life bore his father's nickname. "Cump is very much pleased with his boy," Ellen related to her father, "and well he may be for the child is large & strong & healthy and exactly like him. The Doctor says had the child been less strong he could not have saved him and as it was two minutes longer & he would have perished beyond recall—He did not breathe for some time after his birth."[38]

Despite the joy of having another son, the great heartache of Sherman's life remained. "Aren't you haunted by the thousands of Ghosts that flit about those deep & tangled Ravines that make up Vicksburg?" Sherman asked Ord, who had been with him on the march to Jackson and now commanded the military district embracing Arkansas and Mississippi. "With all the discomforts of our ugly winters here, I prefer them to the jungles & miasma of yr latitude but hope you will all come out alive & well. It was Vicksburg that cost me my Willy, and I cannot but feel that it must be an unpleasant spot in my memory."[39]

As men of influence, Sherman and John looked after their relatives, their efforts being rewarded during the first three months of 1867. The brothers used their connections to secure the appointment of their cousin, Charles H. Hoyt, as a major and army quartermaster. Henry Reese, Elizabeth's son, became a major and army paymaster. After the appointment, Sherman heard stories that Henry had been involved in the defalcation of funds, but Henry's explanation satisfied his benefactors and they let the appointment stand, a decision they eventually regretted. John was also able to push through the confirmation of their brother Lampson as collector of revenue in Des Moines.

The choicest plums went to Hugh Ewing and to Charles Taylor Sherman. Nominated by Johnson to be minister to the Hague, Hugh stood in danger of being rejected by the Senate until John took hold of things. "In Hugh's case," John confided to Cump, "I felt an interest chiefly on Tom's account and I no doubt saved him." Taylor's appointment as federal judge for the Northern District of Ohio presented a different problem. Johnson had no particular reason for nominating him to a lifetime position and did so as a favor to the general. "In regard to C. T. S.," Bowman, who had just published a book on Sherman's wartime experiences, informed his idol, "I desire you to know, and never forget, that much is due in that matter to Kilby Smith (who is a power in Washington and) who put his soul into it and by a hundred devices contributed to the desired result."[40]

Away from Washington, where in the House of Representatives Butler and Logan were among those pushing for the impeachment of Johnson, Sherman occupied himself with army affairs. In March 1867, after Congress passed a bill dividing the South into five military districts, Johnson offered to send Sherman to New Orleans, but Sherman refused, partially because he did not wish to displace Sheridan, whom he and Ellen loved deeply, and partially because he knew the position would drag him into politics. Remaining in St. Louis, Sherman split his department into three segments. Terry commanded the army along the upper Missouri, Augur the one along the Platte, and Hancock the one on the southern plains. Sherman saw in the railroad the solution to the Indian problem. Once the road reached the Black Hills and the Smoky Hill, he predicted to Dodge, "we can act so energetically that both Sioux and Cheyennes must die, or submit to our dictation."[41]

Convinced that his generals could handle any emergency, Sherman made plans to tour Europe. Howard's favorite, Captain William Duncan, now had an office on Wall Street and planned to rent a steamer in June and sail for the Mediterranean. He offered Sherman "a State Room & two passages *free.*" The general decided to take Minnie along and spend four months visiting Marseilles, Genoa, Rome, Paris, Amsterdam, Vienna, Turkey, Egypt, and Spain. Grant agreed to allow his friend to go on half pay, but Seward was not as generous. He insisted the mission be diplomatic. "So," Sherman told Ord, "instead of a quiet, pleasant trip I expect to be bedeviled from the time we reach Gibraltar till we come out—and worse yet to be put to an expense I cannot afford."[42]

The clamor created by the builders of the Pacific railroad forced Sherman to postpone his tour. Indians had attacked work parties along the Platte. "A few scattered cases of this kind become exaggerated," Sherman scoffed to Ord, "till war is regarded as sure to come, but I am not convinced of it and may by my presence prevent or modify it, so I have concluded to stay and try my hand. . . . What with Indians, Rebs, & Negros we are not destined to share the Peace that was promised us after the war."[43]

On July 20, 1867, Congress created a peace commission to deal with the Indians. With typical frankness Sherman, one of its members, characterized his colleagues to John. His neighbor, Senator John B. Henderson, a Missouri Democrat, was "the best & most thoughtful man on the Commission." The reformer John B. Sanborn "does very well." Commissioner of Indian Affairs Nathaniel G. Taylor "is a good hearted man but a perfect stereotyped edition of the old Indian policy." Sherman considered Terry "a first rate officer," but the old Indian fighter, General William S. Harney, was "of no account." Finally, Sherman called Samuel F. Tappan of Massachusetts, whom he would eventually admire greatly, "a mere nothing. At first, a decided majority was against the Military & favoring the civil policy, but Henderson and Sanborn now vote with me."[44]

At North Platte, Nebraska, on September 19 the commission convened to discuss things with a dozen Cheyenne, Oglala Sioux, and Brulé Sioux chiefs. The night before the meeting, Sherman informed Ellen, "the Indians got on a big drunk and are not now in condition to have their talk. . . . Indians are funny things to do business with, and the more I see of them the more satisfied I am that no amount of sentimentality will save them the doom in store for them."[45]

The council met in two large wigwams combined into one—the chiefs, including Spotted Tail, Man-Afraid-of-His-Horse, Pawnee Killer, Big Mouth, Crazy Elk, and Swift Bear, sitting on one side, the commissioners on the other. Several chiefs explained that the railroad was "the cause of great trouble. The country where we live is overrun by whites. All our game is gone." If the building stopped and the Indians received ammunition with which to kill game, all would be well.

Sherman responded with none of the kindness he had shown the defeated Joe Johnston. He warned:

> We build iron roads, and you cannot stop the locomotive any more than you can stop the sun or moon, and you must submit, and do the best you can, and if any of you want to travel east to see the wealth and power of the whites you can do so, and we will pay your expenses. . . . This Commission is not only a Peace Commission, but it is a War Commission also. We will be kind to you if you keep the peace, but if you won't listen to reason, we are ordered to make war upon you in a different manner from what we have done before.

Henry M. Stanley, the correspondent for the *New York Herald*, remembered how this rough talk shook the chiefs. Man-That-Walks-under-the-Ground, an Oglala Sioux, answered poignantly: "I am a red-skinned man. I am poor. You are rich. When you come to our villages we always share with you. Where is the living I am to get? What am I to do? This day I ramble with nowhere to go."

Leaders of proud people, the chiefs had been forced to listen to speeches like Sherman's and to beg for powder and ball. Thoroughly disgusted, Pawnee Killer, a Cheyenne, left the meeting, donned fiery red paint, and stormed away. Three or four other chiefs followed him.

The next day the commissioners agreed to supply the Indians with ammunition for hunting buffalo. But, Stanley mused, whether Pawnee Killer and the Cheyennes would keep the peace was "rather dubious."[46]

— V —

Meanwhile, fate had drawn Grant into the controversy between Johnson and Congress. To protect Stanton, a Radical, Congress had passed in March 1867 the Tenure of Office Act, which forbade the removal of those approved by the Senate without that body's consent. In August, Johnson tried to force Stanton out, but the secretary refused to resign. Johnson thereupon transferred Stanton's duties to Grant. "All the romance of feeling that men in high places are above personal considerations and act only from motives of pure patriotism, and for the general good of the public, has been destroyed," Grant confided to Sherman in mid-September. "An inside view proves too truly much the reverse. I am afraid to say on paper all I fear and apprehend but I assure you that were you present there is no one who I would more fully unburden myself to than yourself, or whose advice I would prize more highly."[47]

Called to Washington by President Johnson, Sherman arrived at 6:00 A.M. on the morning of October 6. He was at Grant's house before the general was downstairs for breakfast. Walking to Grant's office, the two discussed the situation. After talking to Johnson and to Thomas Ewing's old friend and law partner, Attorney General Henry Stanbery, Sherman told Ellen: "The President dont comprehend Grant, and tho' there is no breach it is manifest there is not a cordial understanding."[48]

Grant's greatest concern was who would be the new secretary of war. Sherman informed Ellen's father:

> If a successor is to be appointed he would prefer me, and would dislike of all things McClernand, or Frank Blair. The former is a mean envious and impracticable man, that caused him and me more real trouble than any volunteer General we had to deal with. Blair is a good fellow socially, but not to be trusted in many matters. Were he charged with the claims growing out of the war, he would in a month make precedents that would swamp the Treasury. Neither of these names was mentioned to me at Washington or I would have spoken of them to the President.

Sherman did mention to Johnson "a moderate Republican of fine military Record, a finished scholar and one who would have blocked the game of Stanton beyond hope of disturbance," but Johnson did not even ask the person's name.[49]

The trouble extended into January 1868. During that month Sherman stayed in Washington revising with Sheridan and Augur the army regulations. The generals convened in a room next to the office of the secretary of war, and Grant, the acting secretary, and later Stanton frequently dropped in to chat.

On Saturday, January 11, with the Senate about to vote on the propriety of Stanton's removal, Grant came in and said he had been reading the Tenure of Office Act. If the Senate disapproved of Stanton's removal and Grant held on to the office, he would be subject to a fine of $10,000 and a prison term of five years. Grant was determined to tell the president that he intended to vacate the position. For an hour that day Johnson pleaded with Grant, promising to pay any fine and serve any sentence in Grant's place. The general remained adamant.[50]

Grant and Sherman spent that Sunday together. The result was a plan to have Johnson nominate General Cox, now the governor of Ohio, as secretary of war. A moderate, Cox would be satisfactory to both sides. On Monday, January 13, Sherman went to the White House and broached the idea to Johnson, "but there must be something behind the scenes," Sherman speculated to Ellen, "for he gave me no encouragement." Both Stanton and Johnson were "strong, stubborn willful men, that would embroil the world, rather than yield their point. Your father agreed with me perfectly, but Tom is out & out Democratic now, and would precipitate trouble with the Republicans. The fact is this matter will damage all politicians. It is a double edged sword that cuts both ways." On that very day the Senate voted to restore Stanton to the War Department.[51]

On the fourteenth, the Washington *National Intelligencer* carried what Sherman described as "a violent attack on General Grant which seemed inspired by the President and cabinet." That day, Grant and Sherman had a long talk with Johnson, who was calm and friendly. But reports had it that when Grant yielded his office to Stanton, Johnson had cursed and kicked about the White House chairs. At a cabinet meeting Johnson questioned Grant like an inquisitor, demanding "Yes" or "No" answers to a series of questions. When in Washington soon after, Stewart Van Vliet learned "that Grant at that Cabinet meeting was very confused & lost his head."[52]

When Sherman got to the War Department on the fifteenth, he confided to Ellen, Stanton sent for him. Viewing himself as the consummate politician, the secretary told Sherman

> how much he respected me and admired me, etc, etc, all very loving, and I told him simply that I shall not recall the past, but wanted the Army to be kept out of politics, etc, etc. I thought he would ask my opinion of his present status, but he did not. I should have advised him to resign. I deem it wrong to hold a cabinet office, when he knows the President dont want him, and the President will not give any orders to the army through him.[53]

In late January, after considering Tom Ewing and his father for appointment as secretary of war, Johnson offered the post to Sherman for six months. Sherman refused it. "I wish you as far as possible to keep clear of political complications," Thomas Ewing wisely advised his son-in-law. Offering similar counsel to Sherman, Grant toyed with the idea of urging Stanton to resign, but he soon concluded that to do so would "incur his further displeasure; and, therefore, did not directly suggest it to him. . . . I would advise that you say nothing to Mr. Stanton on the subject unless he asks your advice. It will do no good, and may embarrass you."[54]

At January's end Sherman left Washington "to escape the political storm I saw coming." But in mid-February Johnson concocted another scheme aimed at drawing Sherman to the nation's capital. "After I thought the danger which I have avoided so long had passed," Sherman wrote Thomas Ewing, "it has come upon me like an avalanche." Johnson nominated Sherman for brevet general, a meaningless rank, and ordered him to Washington to command the new Military Division of the Atlantic. "Now it is notorious this is a device to have me there. . . . He never heeds any adviser," Sherman complained of Johnson. "He attempts to govern after he has lost the means to govern. He is like a General fighting without an army—he is like Lear raving at the wild storm, bareheaded and helpless. And now he counts me to go with him into the Wilderness." Luckily, Johnson did not push the plan and allowed Sherman to remain in St. Louis.[55]

Testing the Tenure of Office Act, Johnson appointed General Lorenzo Thomas ad interim secretary of war. Stanton immediately ordered Thomas, his longtime friend, arrested. For Thomas, Sherman possessed no sympathy. He observed to Thomas Ewing:

> At the beginning of the war, he came near being arrested because of his leaning to slavery, and because his daughter in her correspondence with her friends south revealed secrets she heard from her father, then

Adj Genl—Later he turned so "Black" that he revealed a conversation with me had in Louisville by Secretary Cameron, under the express injunction of secrecy,—and still later he came down to Vicksburg and in an address to my troops he spoke of his power from President Lincoln to remove any officer who did not cooperate with him in raising Negro troops, a threat which every body who heard him interpreted as directed against me. I dont care at all, but I cannot form an alliance with such men as against my old comrade in arms.[56]

Following Stanbery's advice, Johnson sent to the Senate papers nominating Thomas Ewing as secretary of war. "I will support him," John informed Cump of the nomination, "but it is idle. It is too late. Mr E. might have been confirmed before the recent complications. Thomas is a fool & has involved the President far more than he probably designed." Pointing to the Thomas appointment, the House began impeachment proceedings against Johnson.[57]

After a lengthy trial, during which Tom Ewing worked with Evarts in planning the president's defense, the Senate acquitted Johnson. But the affair soured Sherman more on politics. In the midst of the trial, Ellen reported that her husband now believed Spotted Tail would make the best candidate for president in 1868.[58]

___ VI ___

During the spring of 1868, Sherman turned to the work of the Indian commission. The railroad, finished past Cheyenne, was now heading toward the Great Salt Lake. Although called east to testify on April 14 at Johnson's impeachment trial, Sherman was back at Fort Laramie by month's end. There the commissioners concluded a treaty with the Sioux, who agreed to move to reservations but retained the right to hunt along the railroad as long as buffalo roamed there. Viewing this concession skeptically, Sherman advised Sheridan: "Until the buffaloes & consequent[ly] Indians are out from between the Roads we will have collisions & trouble."[59]

From Fort Laramie, Sherman and Tappan headed through familiar country. In a Dougherty they rode 95 miles to Cheyenne. Then "in a regular coach" they traveled 105 miles to Denver, which Cump and John had visited in 1866. Sherman now found the town "even duller, by reason that the Rail Road carried travel past, and no body comes here unless on business pertaining to Colorado. . . . I am of course held responsible by the Frontier people for not rushing to war because of occasional depredations some of which have undoubtedly been committed by white men. Yet as I don't ask their votes I can stand their personal abuse."[60]

From Denver the two commissioners headed for Fort Sumner in eastern New Mexico, where for three days they conferred with the leaders of the Navajos. These Indians had formerly lived in "the vast region between New Mexico and Colorado," but wars with Mexicans, who stole their children and sold them into peonage, and with white intruders had reduced their number to 7,200. During the Civil War the army had moved the Navajos east to a reservation on the Pecos called Bosque Redondo, or round forest, because it contained a small supply of wood, since used up. The nearest timber was now a hundred miles away.

On May 28, the first day of the conference, Sherman asked about the poverty of the Indians. They had no farms and herds. He wanted to know why. Chief Barboncito answered that God had once given his tribe the choicest land, between four mountains and four rivers. The Navajos grew the whitest corn and owned the finest horses and sheep. But the government moved the Navajos from their haven and transported them to a desert. Each year the Indians planted seed, but it did not grow two feet high. Their sheep and horses died. Those Navajos who were once wealthy now had nothing and slept on gunnysacks. The chiefs were impoverished. The first two years worms destroyed their corn crop. The third year a hailstorm ruined it. "It seemed that whatever we do here causes death. Some working at the acequias take sick and die, others die with the hoe in their hands; they go in the river to their waists and suddenly disappear. Others have been struck and torn to pieces by lightning. A rattlesnake bite here kills us. . . . When one of our big men die, the cries of the women causes the tears to roll down on to my moustache." The chief asked that his people be allowed to return to their home near the Sierra Chuska, the mountain of rain, west of the Rio Grande in northwestern New Mexico. Deeply moved by Barboncito's words, Sherman even consented to allow the Navajos to go outside their reservation to hunt and trade. He promised to help return the Navajo children taken by Mexicans.

On May 30 Sherman and the chiefs sealed their agreement with a treaty. "We have never found any person heretofore who told us what you now have," Chief Gañado Mucho told Sherman as the conference ended, "and when we return to our own country we will return you our best thanks."[61]

During his stay in the Southwest, Sherman displayed more compassion for the Navajos than for the other residents of the area. As he informed Ellen:

> Santa Fe is the oldest town in the United States except St Augustine, but the People with a few exceptions are *greasers* of the commonest sort, and their houses gardens &c are about as they were when Moses was a baby—houses of adobe, no floors, no windows—the interior common to dogs, cats, bugs & fleas. No cultivator but by irrigation and that on the smallest scale—At a mile distance the town or city looks like an old abandoned Brick yard—The territory is the poorest land in the United States except Arizona and the people are so dependent on the profit resulting from the occupation by the Army that any one that attempts economy is their enemy—I am so regarded, but it is an outrage on us as a people, that we have to banish a large part of the Army here.[62]

While Sherman was in New Mexico, Kit Carson and his wife both died. During his stay with Carson in 1866, Sherman had asked what the scout was doing about the education of his children. Sherman said that Notre Dame, the Catholic college in South Bend, Indiana, had presented him with a scholarship covering tuition for twenty years, and he promised to reserve it for one of Carson's children. In the summer of 1868 Kit's eldest son, William, came east. Sherman sent him to Notre Dame and paid $450 annually for the boy's board and books, but after two or three years the president of the college conceded he could not make a student of young Carson. Sherman later tried to get William an army commission at Fort Leavenworth, but the boy failed to pass the Board of Examiners.[63]

___ VII ___

Rushing back east to attend the wedding on June 20 of his beautiful niece Mary, the daughter of Taylor, to the dashing, ambitious Colonel Nelson A. Miles, Sherman found the country awash in presidential politics. The Republicans had nominated Grant for president, the Democrats Governor Horatio Seymour of New York, whom Sherman privately labeled "a pure Copperhead during the War." To balance the ticket, the Democrats selected for vice president Frank Blair, who scoffed that in 1861 Grant and Sherman had watched while he and Lyon had taken Camp Jackson. At the time, both war heroes had vowed to have nothing to do with the "damned war."[64]

When Dodge urged Sherman to come out for Grant, Sherman refused. Everyone knew, Sherman explained to Grant, that he was a personal friend of the candidate. His endorsement would therefore amount to nothing. Moreover, if Grant were elected, Sherman would undoubtedly be put in charge of the army. He did not want to make it seem as if he were endorsing Grant for personal gain. "John Sherman will of course support you enthusiastically both on personal and party grounds," Sherman added. "The Ewings seem to have interested themselves so much with the President that I can't answer for them."[65]

Three weeks after Sherman sent this letter, Thomas Ewing paid a physical price for the strains of his involvement in Johnson's defense. Suffering a series of hemorrhages, he aged, Ellen told her husband on July 17, ten years within a few days. "He has had no return & can now ride out but he is pale & thin & stooped & aged," she observed. *"He seems to cling to life."*[66]

But even as Ellen wrote, Sherman was on his way to the end of the Union Pacific's track to meet Grant. For two weeks the two traveled together over the West. The most noteworthy event took place late in July at Laramie, where Grant, Sheridan, Harney, Sherman, and several other generals met Dodge, Thomas C. Durant, the vice president of the Union Pacific, and Sidney Dillon, the railroad's managing director of construction. By altering the route proposed by the surveyors, Durant and Dillon had tried to force Dodge into leaving the company. But at Laramie, Grant and Sherman insisted that Dodge must stay with the line and that his surveys were accurate and must be followed. In the face of such opposition, Durant backed down. Dodge then took Grant, Sherman, Sheridan, and some of the others to his home in Council Bluffs for a vacation. On the way, Dodge predicted that the road would connect with the Central Pacific, building east from Sacramento, by the next April or May. Sherman expressed doubt, but when Dodge said it could be done Sherman conceded that Dodge had met every statement he had thus far made, and he would, Dodge remembered, "give up his judgment for mine."[67]

In August, Sherman faced more Indian troubles. In Kansas, the Cheyennes and Arapahos "broke out again." Sending Sheridan against them, Sherman, who three months before had been to the Navajos the Great Parent, now took the opposite turn. "My solution is that war is popular with them," he told Ellen of the Indians, "and they only look at it from the stand point wherein it is easier to starve than work. Probably in the end it will be better to kill them all off." To John, Sherman wrote similarly: "We must not let up this time, but keep it going till they are killed or humbled. I will do my best to keep it within bounds as to men & money."[68]

Such a policy shocked Tappan. "I would certainly object to being hung for Wilkes Booth's crime simply because I am of the same race," he argued to Sherman. "For the same reason I object to the punishment of the innocent for the acts of the guilty which is not a fair and honorable way of doing. And whatever code, whether it be that of a soldier or civilian, that establishes such a rule, I must denounce if all the world calls me crazy—a fool—a woman or what not."

Tappan recalled that at the conference with the Navajos, Barboncito had thrown his arm around Sherman and expressed his gratitude. "With an eloquence surpassing all art," the chief had said: *Do this for my people and we will look up to you as our father and as our mother—it seems to us now that you are a God.* Those words struck Tappan "as the highest compliment ever paid to a soldier." Sherman must deal as fairly with the Cheyennes: "Consider the many provocations they have had, how we have deceived them so often and that they are human."[69]

If events in the summer of 1868 convinced Sherman that some Indians must be exterminated, those in the early fall brought the beginnings of a break with Grant. Making speeches daily for the Republican candidate, John urged his brother to attend a great soldiers and sailors convention for Grant in Philadelphia on October 1. "They are exceedingly anxious for you if only to appear & review the soldiers," John explained. "It will show your interest in the matter without requiring you to say one word about politics or the election." But Sherman refused, arguing that his presence would constitute an endorsement of Grant. Nor, during the campaign, would he consent to publish a letter complimenting his friend, even though Sheridan and other generals did so.[70]

Grant's election in November created a problem for Sherman. When Grant became president, Sherman undoubtedly would succeed him as commander of the army. He "would consider it a mean thing" should Congress abolish the rank of general because Grant was leaving it. He informed John:

> In any European Government, it would have been an absurdity that I commanding a hundred thousand men in Battle, in more than one Campaign when the very existence of the nation was at stake should

have the simple rank of Major Genl, a rank universally assigned to and actually held in my own Army by every Division Commander of 5,000 men, and with pay less than is received by the secretary of the British Commander in Chief, viz less than £1000 in Gold. During the whole war I lived as plain as a Lieutenant, without tent even, and with a single servant to cook paid by myself leaving for my family so little that they were in debt at the close of the war. . . .

Now if I go to Washington, no matter what my pay I will not exceed it a cent, but of course I should not be stinted measly. Grant has lived beyond his salary, but had more than $100,000 donated by his friends in New York. I declined an effort on the part of Gen Butterfield to attempt the same for me, because it would have left me under a kind of obligation to favor him, as Grant has actually done. He has been kept in New York since the war closed to the detriment of other officers who had superior claims.[71]

In mid-December Sherman and Grant attended a large gathering of veterans in Chicago. There, "at one or two stolen interviews," the president-elect revealed that he intended to nominate Sherman for the rank of general. Grant added that for the time being he would retain Schofield, who had been appointed secretary of war by Johnson that June.

Grant agreed to satisfy Sherman on another sensitive point. At least three secretaries of war had jumped over the heads of generals and issued orders directly to subordinates. John C. Calhoun had so abused General Andrew Jackson during the Florida campaign of 1817. Later, Jefferson Davis's repeated use of the practice induced General Scott to move his headquarters to New York, away from Davis. Finally, Stanton had summarily ordered away one of Sherman's aides. In Chicago, Sherman secured from Grant a promise not to allow such a thing to happen again.

Picking Sherman's successor proved more of a problem than selecting Grant's. The president-elect favored Sheridan, who eventually received the promotion to lieutenant general and was placed in command of the Department of the Missouri. Hancock, Meade, and Thomas, all major generals in the regular army, believed they had claims to the position, especially Thomas. But Old Tom refused to complain to Grant about the selection and ended up succeeding Halleck as commander of the forces along the Pacific.[72]

The thought of returning to Washington, with its politics and its expenses, panicked Sherman. One day, Ellen related to her father, when Cump was "on the rampage" about taxes, he wrote to his lawyer in California offering for sale a piece of property he had bought for Lizzie. Immediately, the lawyer sold the property for $2,000. Ellen first heard of the deal when she dropped in at Sherman's office one day and saw the deed on the table, ready for her to sign. Sherman believed he would need the money to live in Washington.

A group of New Yorkers, including Hamilton Fish, Peter Cooper, and William H. Aspinwall, who from 1849 to 1857 had run a line of steamers in California, came to Sherman's rescue. Raising $65,000, they proposed to buy

Grant's house at 205 I Street, complete with carpets, chairs, and much of the furniture, and present it to Sherman as a gift. "I do not feel certain of anything until I get it," Ellen confided to Thomas Ewing, "but this would be a great thing for us. Cump had begun to growl fearfully about expenses and had indulged in various absurd and provoking assertions as to our future—how we would have to live on bread & water and entertain company and other such vagaries that wise men are prone to indulge in. I think it will all turn out right in the end."[73]

On a cold, rainy March 4, Sherman and Ellen were in Washington for Grant's inaugural. During the next two days Grant nominated Sherman to the rank of general and through Schofield issued the order prohibiting the secretary of war from jumping over the head of the commanding general. But by month's end Grant replaced Schofield with John A. Rawlins, and under the influence of the new secretary and of Logan, who sought revenge on Sherman, he suddenly changed his mind and rescinded the order. On March 29, Sherman complained to Schofield:

> There was no conflict, no case, no cause for the change here. I was at the Presidents on Thursday night, and just as I was taking my leave, he said, "I guess we have got to revoke that order of Schofields"—I inquired which one and he explained. I told him that he himself had dictated the order—that he had been of that mind for a long time, and that he had so told me at Chicago—&c &c. The next morning Friday I wrote him a note begging him to delay a while till he could think further, but after the Cabinet meeting I went up to Rawlins Room to talk about some discharges he had ordered, on the application of Butler and Senator Williams, without one reason or Cause assigned, when he shew me the draft of the order which I read carefully, and asked the modification of one or two words, but he said it had been passed on in Cabinet & must stand. We then had a general discussion of the effect which I insisted would ultimately defeat me, in the Universal army wish that every branch of the Army should have one head, and one common duty & interest; but he insisted the change was forced on them by political considerations, that Butler, Logan &c contended your order took from the Secretary duties and powers devolved on him by Law, and that it changed the Civil nature of the Department of War. I said I would cheerfully conform to any decision they arrived at, but that I thought a wrong had been done me by not thinking of that beforehand.
>
> . . . I would like you to show this to Sheridan and keep it for the future, as my version of this matter, but to be used only for your own deliberation and use.[74]

18

At War with Grant

Social LIFE IN WASHINGTON, as distinct from the political, was hardly the horror Sherman had envisioned. Grant's house at 205 I Street Northwest, into which the family moved, was on a block that constituted an oasis in a run-down neighborhood. One of a row of red brick houses built in 1857 and 1858 for Senator Stephen A. Douglas of Illinois and Vice President John C. Breckinridge, it was a mile from the War Department, to which Sherman commuted on a "bob-tailed," a one-horse streetcar.

The children rapidly adjusted to the new city. Minnie became the co-mistress of the house and one of the belles of Washington society. With the exception of young Cump, her brothers and sisters attended school. Lizzie, quiet and ever devoted to her parents, commuted to the school at Georgetown Visitation Convent, where Elly and Rachel boarded. For five days a week Tom was at Georgetown, studying at the college run by the Jesuits.[1]

During the early days of the Grant administration, the Sherman family found itself caught up in the whirligig of White House dinners and dances. At these Julia Grant was lively and animated, talking to other women about the theater, fashions, and even gossip. The president usually stood about, Minnie remembered, "perfectly silent." At one party the young ladies bet whether any of them could entice Grant into a conversation. All of them failed, until late in the evening one of the girls was seen discussing something with the president. They were talking about Grant's favorite subject, horses and races. Among the amused witnesses to the wager was General Thomas, "who was himself a reticent quiet gentleman and appreciated the difficulty of the undertaking."[2]

The Sherman house was a popular gathering place. Sheridan was the most frequent and most welcome guest. "We had known him so long and so well," Minnie observed, "he felt quite at home with us." Calling at the Sherman home one afternoon, Sheridan learned that Ellen, objecting to such frivolity, would not allow Minnie to attend a dance that evening. On the back of his calling card Sheridan, a Catholic, appealed to Ellen, promising "to say his prayers, go to church, and be very good if she would let Miss Minnie go." Under such pressure, Ellen yielded. At one dance Minnie complained that Sheridan, who was short, never danced with her. "Why really, Miss Minnie," Sheridan answered, "I feel like a basket hung on your arm."[3]

Young Cump always remembered his first meeting with Sheridan. The great soldier was downstairs in the parlor sitting on a high chair when Lizzie came for her brother, warning him not to stare at the general's swinging legs. From the moment he entered the room Cump did nothing but that. Sheridan finally asked for another high chair, and the two sat next to each other swinging their legs in unison. "And ever after, whenever I met him, General Sheridan recalled that incident."[4]

When in Washington, Indian chiefs frequently visited Sherman, whom they called "Walk-a-heap." On one occasion Sherman gave a chief a box of cigars, but on the way out the Indian, through an interpreter, offered to exchange the cigars for Minnie. When his proposal was refused, the chief left with a growl. Young Cump recalled some Sioux who, when introduced to him, kept running their hands through his flaming red hair. "Thereafter," he wrote, "I differed from nearly all the other boys of my generation in having no desire to go West to fight Indians."[5]

— II —

In late 1869 and early 1870 three men close to Sherman died. After a long battle with consumption, Rawlins died on September 6. For a while Sherman took on the duties of secretary of war, but eventually Grant asked him to suggest candidates, preferably from the West, from a list of volunteer generals. Of these, Sherman preferred Dodge. But because of Dodge's connection with the Union Pacific, with which, even though the railroad was completed in May 1869, the secretary of war must deal extensively, Grant ruled him out. He chose instead another Iowan, General William W. Belknap, who had fought at Vicksburg and Atlanta and was now the collector of internal revenue at Keokuk. A dramatic speech at the Chicago veterans convention had thrust Belknap before Grant and led to his selection.[6]

The second death occurred on October 4, 1869, in Norwalk. Uncle Charles Hoyt had been kind to the Shermans as early as 1830, when he helped raise money for his widowed sister Mary and her children. At one time he amassed considerable wealth. But he spent the last decade of his life in and out of a mental asylum. "Uncle Charles was too old to ever hope for a change," Cump lamented to John, "and it would have been better for his family had he died ten years ago. I have had assurances that he was perfectly calm & easy save when talking of money, and then he was wild & speculative, drawing checks on Banks, & purchasing Gold with about as much sense as the bulls & bears of New York." John's response was equally gloomy: "He had many good qualities, but his visionary recklessness dissipated his Fortune & led to his insanity. The latter is Hereditary in our branch of the Hoyt family."[7]

For Sherman, an especially harsh blow came in March 1870. Against his will, for both he and his wife were from the East, George Thomas had been sent by Grant to command the army along the Pacific Coast. Rightly, Thomas suspected that Grant disliked him.

But Grant was not Thomas's chief enemy. Since the campaign that had crushed Hood, Thomas and Schofield had argued about who deserved the most credit. Then, on March 12, 1870, a letter signed "One who fought at Nashville" appeared in the *New York Tribune* attacking Thomas's role in the campaign. Thomas and his staff were sure it came from Schofield. At a banquet given in Thomas's honor by Halleck, the former commander along the Pacific, came further evidence of Schofield's treachery. Halleck related that just before Nashville, Grant, disgusted with Thomas's inactivity, had issued an order transferring command of his army to someone else. News of Thomas's victory at the battle forced Grant to rescind the order. Prodded by Thomas, Halleck admitted that the man scheduled to succeed him was Schofield. Working things over in his mind, Thomas also remembered a comment Sherman had once made. At Atlanta, Sherman had given Schofield the choice of either marching with him to Savannah or of aiding Thomas in Tennessee. Even though campaigning with Sherman offered greater opportunity for glory, Schofield chose Tennessee. All this added up to a plot by Schofield to replace Thomas.

Brooding, Thomas decided to write his own account of the Nashville campaign. But on March 28, his answer unfinished, he suddenly felt a throbbing in his temple. That day he died. Grant remembered Sherman coming into the White House and saying with deep emotion: "I'm afraid Old Tom is gone."[8] The issue, however, did not perish with Thomas, for his defenders would seek revenge for the slights of Grant, of Schofield—and of Sherman.

While Thomas was in the West, Logan, now a congressman from Illinois, was busy in the East. Seeking revenge on Sherman and on West Point in general, he introduced a bill to lower Sherman's pay and allowances from $18,000 to $12,000, to reduce the number of officers in the army, and to abolish the ranks of general and lieutenant general with the deaths of Sherman and Sheridan. He did not, however, strike at the number of aides allotted to high officers, for such a rule might have affected Grant.[9]

In speech after speech Logan continued his attack. One day it was career officers; the next, the military academy; on the third, the killing of Indian women by soldiers. "Had I not been here," Sherman informed Augur from Washington, "I am sure Logan would have hit the Regular Army and West Point a fatal blow. He will persevere and may yet succeed, but I know & feel the sense of the Country is against him, although no one in the House feels disposed to stand up against his vehement invective and bold assertions. His notion is hostility to West Point influence and he will never pardon me for selecting Howard before him, to succeed McPherson."[10]

Caught in the crossfire of an ambitious secretary of war who, with Grant's blessing, continually bypassed the general of the army in issuing orders and of a Congress that as of January 1, 1871, lowered Porter's pay $200, Admiral David Farragut's and Sheridan's $500 each, and Sherman's $1,500, the general desired to return to St. Louis. The problem, he revealed to Ord, was "the elephant of a House bought of Grant at the extravagant cost of $65,000." Unable now to afford the taxes and expenses that went with such a large home, he had tried but failed to sell it for $50,000. If forced to remain in Washington, he planned to convert the house into two. He would live in one and rent the other. After Grant insisted that he needed his general in Washington, Sherman followed the latter course. When the house was finished, the Sherman family occupied the new 207 I Street and rented 205 to General Giles A. Smith, now Grant's second assistant postmaster general.[11]

On top of it all, Sherman considered a failure the Radical program of Reconstruction, which granted the freedmen the right to vote. In August 1870, he complained to John:

> Our Country is bound to be governed by its meanest people, and soon no honorable man will be tolerated. The extension of the franchise dont elevate the ignorant, but pulls down the educated. Still there is no escape, and we must go through the whole series of worms—minors, convicts &c heretofore excluded until we reach the reductio ad absurdum—But Grant says he wants me to remain in Washington and I suppose I must for seven years, till I can retire under the 30 years Clause, unless meantime that door of escape is also cut off.[12]

John also found himself at war with the president. "I do not know what has got into Grant," he complained to his brother in October 1870. Since 1861 John, Ohio's most prominent Republican, had supported Grant. "Yet I have no more influence in bestowing office in Ohio than Vallandigham or Pendleton," both Peace Democrats during the war. Grant had turned the state's patronage over to his soon-to-be secretary of the interior, Columbus Delano, "a broken down, defeated Whig politician when I entered Congress. He ran for every high office in the State—Governor, Senator &c but could never secure popular support." Yet "every personal friend I had in office has been turned out on one pretext or another and all offices have been filled with his partisans. . . . I have made up my mind that if Gen Grant yields to this I will contest it in the Senate, and if beaten there will either resign or make an open contest with the administration. Indeed I feel like resigning at any rate."[13]

Sadly, Cump responded that President Grant was not the same man General Grant had been. He was under the influence of Logan, Butler, Senator Simon Cameron of Pennsylvania, and Senator Zachariah Chandler of Michigan, "men who care no more for him and who would gladly sacrifice him." Friends everywhere asked Sherman what had caused the change in Grant and "hold me responsible for not telling him the exact truth. I have ventured to do so more than once, but without success, and henceforth I shall not thrust my advice where it is not needed. I saw him yesterday, and he seems to be unconscious that he is losing the confidence of some of the best men of our Country."

The meddlesome Cameron was responsible for Delano's appointment. He "instigated Grant to break with General Cox," his first secretary of the interior. Cump further explained:

> [Cox] was in my judgment the most honest & outspoken member of the Cabinet, and about the only one in that body that could talk strongly and rationally. I know from him that the President "went back" on him in certain matters that had been agreed on between them, just as he went back on me when I was doing just what he asked me to do, before he was installed as President & *after*. . . . As his friend I would like to show him your letter that he may see that by yielding to the importunates about him, he is risking his now modest, and sincere friends.[14]

John, however, wanted his remarks to remain confidential. He answered:

> I have no doubt that your opinion of Grant is a correct one—that he is honest, sincere and strait-forward. Yet he is easily influenced by adroit men who will flatter or humor him. His renomination for a second term is a foregone necessity even if it leads to defeat. You care but little which party is uppermost, but I have been so long connected with the Republican party that I feel the deepest interest in its success and shall as heretofore stand by it and Gen Grant who now represents it unless absolutely snubbed and ignored. Even then I prefer to stand out of the way rather than promote feuds and dissensions in our ranks.[15]

___ III ___

In March 1871 Sherman planned a brief escape from Washington. He decided to visit Louisiana, Texas, and Fort Sill in the Indian territory. "If the Comanches should get me," he joshed to Schofield, now in command of the Division of the Pacific, "it will be a source of regret that my death will do none of you good, for the Grateful Country has provided that my vacancy shall not be filled, and I feel that Congress would be made happy at the economy produced by my demise."[16]

On his way to Texas, Sherman stopped in Baton Rouge, the current home of his old military school, "whose professors and students somehow regard me as yet connected with them. The Institution," he proudly told Ellen, "has had a hard time, but has borne itself well and now bids fair to become one of the best if not the best University in the Country." In an obvious move to help the school, Sherman arranged to have the army's main post located near it.[17]

In New Orleans, Sherman delivered before the American Union Club a brief speech that caused a sensation. Decrying the recent Ku Klux Klan Act, which authorized the president to use troops to abolish terrorism in the South, Sherman argued that Northern reports of Southern outrages were exaggerated. He opposed the use of the army in Reconstruction and insisted that if his terms to Joseph Johnston had been followed Reconstruction would have settled itself.[18]

Publishing extracts of the speech, Democratic newspapers in New Orleans, Knoxville, Goldsboro, and Montgomery urged Sherman to run against Grant in 1872. In the North, the *New York Herald,* through much of May, said the same thing. From the Comanche reservation at Fort Sill on May 25, 1871, Sherman sent the *Herald* a letter with an oft-quoted phrase:

> Now as to politics. I think all my personal friends know my deep-seated antipathy to the subject: yet, as you seem not to understand me, I hereby state, and mean all that I say, that I NEVER HAVE BEEN AND NEVER WILL BE A CANDIDATE FOR PRESIDENT; THAT, IF NOMINATED BY EITHER PARTY, I SHOULD PEREMPTORILY DECLINE: AND EVEN IF UNANIMOUSLY ELECTED, I SHOULD DECLINE TO SERVE.
>
> If you can find language stronger to convey this meaning, you are at liberty to use it.[19]

Accompanied by Inspector General Randolph B. Marcy, Sherman arrived at San Antonio, Texas, on April 28, 1871. There he prepared for a trip of 800 miles through Indian country. Following a line of military installations, the party reached Fort McKavett, 172 miles northwest of San Antonio, and then moved on to Fort Concho, 54 miles north of McKavett. To some soldiers service in these outposts resembled banishment, but not to Sherman. "I confess that in this wild roving about," he wrote Ellen from Fort Concho, "camping by the side of some stream, with pickets out to give alarm if necessary, & mules picketed close in there is a charm that cannot be described or reasoned about."

From Concho, Sherman traveled 150 miles to Fort Griffin, then 60 miles more to Fort Richardson, reaching there on May 17 without having seen an Indian. At Richardson the settlers complained to Sherman and the post commander, Colonel Ranald S. Mackenzie, of raids, two mothers begging the general to find their children, whom Indians had carried off.

On the second night at Richardson, a teamster staggered in with a horrible story. Twenty miles west of the fort, on the road over which Sherman had just traveled, a hundred braves had surprised a caravan of ten wagons, killing seven teamsters and capturing the wagons and forty-one mules. Five teamsters escaped by running into the nearby woods.

Sherman was at Fort Sill, in the Wichita Mountains, 123 miles from Richardson, when on May 27 a group of Kiowa chiefs came in for their rations. While there, one of them, Satanta, boasted that he had led the attack on the teamsters, reciting the details of the episode down to the number of mules captured. "If any other Indian comes here and claims the honor of leading the party," Satanta said, "he will be lying to you, for I did it myself."[20]

Sherman immediately ordered General Benjamin H. Grierson, the commander of the fort, to arrest Satanta, Satank, and Big Tree, "three as influential and bad Indians as ever infested any land." Standing on Grierson's porch, the two generals began discussing the episode with several chiefs. Sherman explained to his son Tommy:

> All were offering any number of mules & horses, if I would overlook this case, and let Satanta go, but I would make not the least concession. Whilst this talk was in progress, another noted Chief—Lone Wolf, rode up, hitched his horse, came on to the porch, with two Carbines and a bow, which he handed to several Indians, and some say he cocked his Carbine, but this I did not see—but I did see Stumbling Bear string his bow and pull out an arrow. The guards in the front of the house cocked their guns and aimed them; but we were all mixed up with the Indians, and to have fired at them, some of us would have been hit. . . .
>
> As Satanta lost three warriors killed and three wounded, and as one warrior has been killed here, he says the account is even, and therefore I ought to be satisfied. I answered him that it was a cowardly act for a hundred professed Warriors to attack a dozen Citizen Teamsters, and that all his hundred in time would be hung up like dogs as he would be. He begged me to take him out now & shoot him, but I told him he should hang in Texas. This they dread terribly.[21]

On the way to Texas, Satank managed to slip out of his manacles but was killed attempting to escape. Satanta and Big Tree, however, became the first Indians convicted in a civil court, a decision reversed in 1873. Until his death in 1873 Big Tree remained free. But Satanta, returned to prison in Texas after being charged with breaking parole, grew despondent and in 1878 killed himself. In 1963, following a Kiowa ceremony that ensured Satanta a happy journey to Oklahoma, his bones were buried at the Fort Sill post cemetery.[22]

Returning to Washington, Sherman reentered the political whirlpool. He confided to Thomas Ewing:

> I feel every day the growing jealousy of Genl Grant & his Cabinet, who think I do not blow their trumpet loud enough. This is not my task or my office, and I am resolved not to have my latter tour of life poisoned by political Factions. I will not be used by either party, and will consequently be kicked by both. . . . The same causes which made Jefferson Davis as Secretary of War push aside Genl Scott, will reproduce the same or similar result with me, and I may be lucky enough to anticipate the event. In St. Louis I would be more at ease and less a subject of envy & jealousy to the rising youth, who aspire to the civil honors and control of the Country.[23]

Running for reelection, John Sherman found his troubles continuing. In July 1871, he informed Cump:

> I never rec'd a courtesy or kindness from Grant, & never expect to. I have been his supporter since Shiloh—but owe him nothing. He will be renominated & I hope elected—so will I & it is better for the coun-

try that in our relative positions we are independent of each other. I hope you & he will preserve your ancient cordiality, for though he seems willing to strip your office of its power yet I have no doubt he feels as warm an attachment to you as given his temperament he can to any one.[24]

That October, Thomas Ewing died. Exactly two years before he had fainted while reading a brief before the Supreme Court. Remaining at the Capitol all night, he gained strength and recovered.

In 1871 there was no recovery. For several weeks a sharp, mysterious pain tortured the old statesman, and on October 26, two months shy of age eighty-two, he died.

To satisfy possibly himself but surely Ellen and Philemon, his most devout children, he was received into the Catholic church on the last day of his life by Archbishop John B. Purcell and Father Dominic Young, who years before had baptized young Cump in the Ewing parlor. Archbishop Purcell presided at the Solemn Requiem Mass at St. Mary's church in Lancaster.[25]

Thomas Ewing's death caught Sherman in the midst of preparations for his long-desired European tour. In August, while dining in Washington with Belknap and Admiral James Alden, the latter announced that he had been promoted to rear admiral and placed in charge of the European squadron, then near Nice, France. He intended to leave soon on the frigate *Wabash* and invited Sherman, who had never been to Europe, to join him. Sherman jumped at the chance and took along Colonel Joseph C. Audenreid and, at Grant's request, the president's son Fred, a second lieutenant of cavalry stationed in Colorado.[26]

Putting to sea on November 17, the *Wabash* reached the Madeira Islands on December 5 and landed in Cádiz, Spain, built on the Atlantic Ocean a thousand years before Christ by the Phoenicians. "From Cadiz sailed all or nearly all the expeditions which colonized America," Sherman informed Ellen, "and the little harbor of Pelos from which Columbus sailed is but a few miles up the coast."[27]

At Gibraltar Sherman's party left the *Wabash*. Passing through Córdoba, a town much as it was a thousand years before, the general arrived in early January at Madrid. That city, he wrote home, was

> about the size of Baltimore. . . . I wish you would write to Phil & tell him I have carefully sought for a portrait of Christopher Columbus in Cadiz, Sevilla, Grenada & now in Madrid, and I assure you he is unknown.—The bookstores in Logan or Lancaster contain more books & engravings for sale than the whole of Spain.—Mark Twains descriptions are perfect—You can see thousands of saints, sculptured and pictured, but no poor mortal who has done some act of historical merit like Columbus.—He & Cortes & Pizzaro are unknown in their origin—while saints by the million are as cheap as dirt.[28]

If the works of art in Madrid surprised Sherman, those in Rome shocked him. Romans told of the time Michelangelo became angry "at some man who attempted even a fig leaf in the Cistine Chapel of the Vatican, probably the painting of greatest perfection in the world. In every house here," Sherman confided to Ellen, "in the stairway niches, on chandeliers, and over the mantles are figures mostly female, as naked as Eve before the fall. . . . Though they are very beautiful & graceful, I will not venture to invest in any of them, for I know [in] spite of their sanction by the Pope himself in his chapel at the Vatican, you would consign them to the garret, or some worse place."[29]

To Henry Turner, a devout Catholic, Sherman displayed his cynicism toward religion:

> I have seen the Pope and saw plenty of Cardinals with their purple caps kiss his hands and his foot, and when he approached us bowing low, on being informed that I was the illustrious General Sherman and my Aide was the equally famous American soldier Audenreid, he stopped and entered in a most friendly conversation with us, and invited us to accompany him in his round to the visitors of the morning, many of whom were American ladies of my acquaintance, full of rosaries and tokens for this old man's blessings; and when the Pope was through he turned and blessed us. He seems a good old man, but not likely to thrive in these utilitarian times.[30]

During his conversation with Sherman, Pius IX asked about Fred, then ill, who the pope knew to be in Rome. Pius hoped the president's son would not leave without visiting him. The next day Fred went to the Vatican, returning with a load of presents the pope had given him for his friends at home.[31]

Disappointed because Alden's fleet could not meet him at Naples early in March 1872, Sherman made his own arrangements and continued on to Cairo. There he stayed with General Charles P. Stone, formerly of the American army but now the adjutant general to the viceroy. But writing to Tommy from Cairo, Sherman only briefly mentioned the Nile and the Suez Canal. Instead, fearing that Tommy, now fifteen, might become as lost to him as Willy was, he dwelt on schooling and religion. Even now, Sherman feared the influence of the Georgetown priests on his son. He was

> not satisfied that Georgetown is a College with Professors skilled in teaching modern sciences that [in] spite of all opposition are remodeling the world, but your mama thinks Religion is so important that every thing else must give place to it, and now that you are big enough to think for yourself, you must direct your mind to the acquisition of one class of knowledge or the other. . . . Your Religion is good enough and I would not shake your Faith in it so long as you leave to others a free choice according to their moral sense, and their means of judgment. It may be that the Creator designed that all people should have the same general Faith, but somehow though his power & goodness are unlimited he has freely left all to choose.[32]

Leaving Egypt after a pleasant visit with the khedive in his palace four miles outside of Cairo, Sherman and his party moved on to Constantinople.

There, Sherman told Turner from Russia, the "Sultan of Turkey treated us as Royal Guests, and sent us hither in his own splendid steam yacht 'Sultanieh' as large as the 'Golden Gate' of California." Then it was on to Moscow and an audience with Tsar Alexander II.[33]

After being treated royally in Italy, Turkey, and Russia, Sherman was snubbed in Germany. There the emperor and prime minister were still smarting because Grant had allowed the French to buy $14 million worth of arms during the recent Franco-Prussian War. Arriving unexpectedly in Berlin in the middle of the night, Sherman had to try three or four hotels before finding accommodations. From Potsdam the emperor sent Sherman such a lukewarm message—he had "nothing against" meeting the general—that Sherman declined to see him and left Berlin disgusted.[34]

Sherman found government officials in Vienna more sociable. The Austrian emperor, speaking French to Audenreid, animatedly discussed the United States. At one point Sherman remarked to him "that I had been surprised to find the lively interest which the officers, especially the war minister, Baron Kuhn, took in our war history, and that it was a national compliment." During dinner at the palace the general noticed that when the men started on their cigars, the prime minister's wife took out a large Havana and smoked it with relish.

One evening the Americans went to the *Volksgarten*. There, Sherman reported,

> we heard Strauss's band, and saw Strauss, who looked like a wild musician, waving his arms to the music, and occasionally seizing his violin and torturing it for a few minutes. I saw the model of band-masters— one who grows and thrives in spite of fun and ridicule. The custom of the Germans of going to these cheap open-air concerts must be, on the whole, healthful, socially and morally, for everybody bears testimony to the utter absence of drunkenness and rowdyism. And yet the whole community seems, for pleasure and recreation, to rush for beer.[35]

From July 6 to July 29, Sherman and Audenreid stayed at the Grand Hotel in Paris. Fred Grant left for home, but on the fourteenth Tommy arrived to replace him. In France, Sherman met the leading political figures and at a breakfast given by the American ambassador renewed acquaintances with Henry M. Stanley, the journalist who had recently found in the deep of Africa the medical missionary David Livingstone.

But since the deathbed conversion of Thomas Ewing, religion seemed more than ever to push Sherman and Ellen apart. Early in July she implored him to visit the Catholic archbishop when he reached England. Sherman answered that

> the moment I go to see him, and not make the rounds of the Archbishop of Westminster, York &c &c, it will be whispered & printed that the American General is a Catholic, and I will be judged accordingly— A few days ago one of the best informed Americans I know spoke of something & said of course you are looking at it as a Catholic, must see

it different &c. I answered he was in error. I was not a Catholic, and from the nature of my mental organization could not be, but that my family were, and I did not or could not shake their faith &c &c probably that he dont care to see me, but that you do. In that view I may seek an interview but if it is followed by any public announcement, I must counteract it, by a similar publicity.[36]

Of Ellen's brothers, Tom took religion lightly, but Philemon and Hugh matched her in devoutness. Phil's eldest daughter, Mary Agnes Ewing, was already Sister Mary Agnes of the Holy Cross. Word that Hugh's daughter Alice had entered a convent hardly surprised Sherman, "for all her education has tended to that one conclusion." Minnie was too fun-loving and vivacious for a cloistered life, and Lizzie was too devoted ever to leave her parents, but Sherman immediately feared for Elly and Rachel, who were still young enough to be molded by their mother. "I certainly do not wish them to follow their cousin into a convent," Sherman wrote Ellen from Scotland, "but to grow up qualified to make good wives." He would "be much rejoiced," moreover, if Tom followed "his lineage" into law.[37] Events would justify Sherman's concern for his children.

— IV —

Arriving in New York on September 15, Sherman learned that his nephew, Major Henry Reese, had been arrested in Louisville. An army paymaster, he was accused of using public funds for private purposes. To cover payroll checks drawn on accounts from which he had taken money, he deposited checks from his cousin, Alfred Hoyt, and from a Brooklyn bank. "These to a disbursing officer under Treasury Law," Cump told John, "constitute a felony, a Penitentiary offense, and we have now in prison several officers for the identical thing." A military court found Reese guilty. He was reprimanded and suspended from duty for four months. In December, however, Grant, who had just been reelected, remitted the latter part of the sentence.[38]

Grant's second inaugural, in March 1873, took place on a day that began fair and warm but turned snowy and cold. The West Point corps of cadets found itself caught in the changing weather without overcoats. After the ceremony, Ellen noticed the cadets shivering in the street in front of her house, waiting for Sherman to arrive. She invited the entire corps into her basement, which contained three large rooms, a hallway, and a kitchen, and conjured up a brew of hot water and rum. With the assistance of the cook and some servants, she proceeded to take the chill out of the cadets. "My father, who arrived later," young Cump remembered, "was not told until the Corps had departed, and then damned the whole proceeding."[39]

The spring of 1873 brought troubles with the Modoc Indians. Numbering between 400 and 800 people, the Modocs claimed the land, commanded by General Canby, along the California-Oregon border. Led by their chief, Captain Jack, they resisted being placed on reservations. Moved onto one, they wandered off it and onto the region along the Lost River, thereby bringing complaints from their white neighbors. Grant pursued a peace policy, which the Indians seemed one day to relish and the next to mock. Nonetheless, in April 1873, talks began between the Modocs and a peace commission.

Within the tribe a war faction ridiculed Jack's supposed weakness. Canby, the argument ran, was squeezing the tribe into less and less land. Humiliated by the militants, Jack acceded to their demand to kill the commissioners. Warned of Jack's intentions by his interpreter's wife, an Indian, Canby scoffed. But on Good Friday, April 11, in the midst of a conference, Jack drew a pistol and shot Canby in the face, killing him. "Any measure of severity to the savages will be sustained," Sherman telegraphed to Schofield, Canby's commander in the Northwest.

Three days after Canby's death, Sherman named as his successor Colonel Jefferson C. Davis of the Twenty-third Indiana, the same Jeff Davis who twice on the march to Savannah had taken up pontoon bridges and abandoned fleeing slaves to the tender mercies of Wheeler's cavalry. Characterizing his soldiers as "cowardly beef eaters," Davis relentlessly pursued the Modocs, apprehending Jack on June 3. "Davis should have killed every Modoc before taking him if possible," Sherman advised Sheridan after the capture; "then there would have been no complications."

But no complications developed. Convicted by a panel of officers, Jack and three other Modocs were hanged that October. Their heads were shipped to the Army Medical Museum in Washington.[40]

By 1874 the army haters were at it again. In April, Congress approved Logan's bill cutting the number of enlisted men to 25,000. Instead of eliminating units, the new law reduced the size of each company. "In the present organization there are . . . in all 430 companies," Sherman explained to his companion at Shiloh, General Stephen A. Hurlbut, currently a congressman from Illinois. "Now dividing 20,000 by 430, you have for each company 46 men. Make the usual allowance for 'sick,' 'in confinement,' 'extra duty,' &c, and I ask any man how he would like to be posted in the Indian country with such a company." Logan, moreover, had slipped into his bill a provision reducing Sherman's staff from six to three. Sherman argued that he could do without any aides. Indeed, he reminded Hurlbut, he had none at Shiloh. "But this reduction of my staff looks personal, invidious and mean."[41]

The leader of a disemboweled army, Sherman finally received permission to transfer his headquarters to St. Louis. Despite a promise "to give the subject his personal attention," Grant had ignored Sherman's pleas and continued to allow Belknap to issue orders directly to quartermasters, physicians, and even sergeants. Sherman told Ord:

> To pretend to command an army thus is a farce. To remain here as a kind of apologist for the Line of the Army is beneath the dignity of my office & character, and though willing to make as much personal sacrifice as any body I cannot endure this longer—I will go to St Louis this fall, and if I pass into a nobody I will at least maintain my own self re-

spect—As to playing courtier by taking Fred Grant on my staff, I wont—I took him to Europe, and got no thanks for it.—Fred is good enough, but there are officers on my own staff of more merit & claim on my personal kindness.[42]

Toward Grant, Sherman displayed bitterness. "Had he told me in 1869 that my office was to be a sinecure," he complained to William Conant Church of the *Army and Navy Journal*, "I surely would not have come to Washington at all to be laughed at by the War Department Clerks, the meanest of which has more official influence than I have. . . . I never treated a corporal thus." Sherman suspected that Grant "had enticed me to Washington to rid himself of a house in a bad neighborhood, at an exorbitant price. Although this was designed by my friends as a favor, it has proven an elephant of the largest proportions, tying me down here, by actual poverty—and he has never said one word of sympathy or explanation. . . . It is humiliating to be used as a tool."[43]

Luckily Sherman was able to sell the house. Half of the payment was in notes, the rest in property on E Street, which he was then able to exchange for a house in Côte Brilliante, a suburb of St. Louis. Only one event delayed the move from Washington, Minnie's marriage on October 1 to Lieutenant Thomas W. Fitch of the United States Navy. After the Roman Catholic ceremony, performed by Archbishop Purcell in St. Aloysius Church and attended by Grant, the members of the cabinet, and everybody who was anybody in Washington, the Shermans held an elaborate reception at 207 I Street. The main dinner course included Maryland terrapin, salmon, duck, chicken, ham, tongue, and oysters.[44]

Following the wedding, the family returned to its house in St. Louis. "St. Louis is very smoky & dirty," Sherman reported to his son Tom, just beginning his studies at Yale, "bears the same relation to Washington which a foundry does to a parlor—but the one is producing and self maintaining, whereas the other is dependent on luxury, & will collapse like the French Noblesse of 1789, on the first Grand Crash—which is not very remote."[45]

19

Of Lizzie and Tom

— I —

SHERMAN'S YOUNGEST SON remembered St. Louis in 1874 as "being horribly dirty." The smoke from soft coal kept the air "dark and sooty." The streets, poorly paved, were "limestone dust in the dry weather and splashy mud in wet." The bath and drinking water was muddy, and many areas of the city were "squalid and wretched. I pronounced it the worst city in the country, which my mother qualified with the opinion that it had the nicest people in the country."[1]

The Shermans moved back to the home at 912 Garrison Avenue in a sparsely developed neighborhood. A sturdy, two-story red brick house, it contained six rooms on the bottom floor and six bedrooms on the second. In marked contrast to this dwelling were the stable and carriage house, both wooden, old, and dilapidated.[2]

During the stay in St. Louis, Sherman developed a routine. He ate a large American breakfast at eight and had a sandwich and cup of coffee in his office at 12:30. Dinner, served between 6:00 and 6:30, was more than ample, but Sherman usually left the table before dessert, unless that course consisted of boiled apple dumplings, plum or fig pudding, or sponge cake. "In my estimation," wrote young Cump, "our food then was the best ever. We had old colored mammy cooks, versed in the arts of Louisiana cookery, supplemented by my mother's expert guidance in a liberal use of quite a variety of wines, brandy and rum for sauces." Sherman regularly consumed two daily bracers of bourbon and water, one of which he termed his "nooning."

To Ellen's relief, Lizzie took over management of the household, one of her chief functions being to see that her father, who seldom threw clothes away, looked presentable. Sherman accepted the disposal of his suits and linen, "but he complained bitterly when his oldest, shabbiest and most comfortable hats and shoes disappeared. However, no one ever succeeded in 'putting over' a silk hat on him."[3]

The Shermans entertained fewer guests in St. Louis, but former army officers passing through town stopped with them. David F. Boyd visited for several days. So too did John B. Hood, "tall, full bearded and handsome with a sad face." He had become friendly with Sherman during the visit to New Orleans in April 1871 that led to the southern and northern editorials imploring Sherman to run against Grant. When the life insurance company of which he was president collapsed, he came to St. Louis to see Sherman about selling his Civil War papers to the War Department, which argued they belonged to the government, anyway. Hood was so taken with Lizzie that he left the papers with her. Lizzie later turned them over to Senator Randall Gibson of Louisiana, who handled the sale to the government.[4]

—— II ——

During his adult life Sherman read constantly. On the march to Savannah he consumed the novels of Sir Walter Scott. When he came home from the war, he read to his children every night. In St. Louis, he introduced his youngest son to Shakespeare's tragedies and histories, to the novels of Scott, Charles Dickens, and William M. Thackeray, to the stories of Bret Harte and Mark Twain, to poetry, and to military and historical works.[5]

Away from the distractions of Washington, Sherman spent much of his time on a literary project he had begun in 1872. During his European tour George Bancroft, the famous historian who was Grant's minister to Germany, urged Sherman to collect his reminiscences and to write his memoirs, else future generations would "embrace & perpetuate wrong facts and reasons." Following Bancroft's suggestion, Sherman began working on the book. By January 1875 he had completed the first volume and was well along with the second. D. Appleton and Company agreed to publish the reminiscences and to pay Sherman forty cents for each two-volume set sold. "It may involve me in some controversies," Sherman predicted to his son Tom, "but these I can avoid by absolute silence."[6]

Appearing in early May of 1875, the *Memoirs* sold 10,000 copies within three weeks. In line with Bancroft's suggestion, the general added much to the history of battles and events. Many of the incidents and observations remain unmatched in Civil War literature: the apprehensions of Colonel Sherman when approaching from the rear his first battle, Bull Run; the fear shared by participants at Shiloh; the joy of the western troops upon learning of Lee's surrender.

But few figures, principally Johnston and Sherman himself, emerged from the two volumes untarnished. As Sherman explained to John:

> Of course, I could not tell the truth without treading on somebody's toes and I have no intention to be disturbed by any amount of criticism. I tried to deal in praise or censure as little as possible, only to ac-

count for my own conduct. Logan did not make the March to Sea at all, but was in Illinois making speeches and he was peculiarly obnoxious to Thomas. Hooker left us when we were up against Atlanta and reported at Cincinnati & Washington that I had run up against a rock & the Country should be prepared for a disaster from that quarter.

And Stanton's aim was to ruin Sherman at the height of his popularity.[7]

At least one of those assailed in the *Memoirs* took the matter lightly. Joseph Hooker published a letter in the *New York Times* criticizing the book, but Henry Slocum, his subordinate at Chancellorsville, found him only mildly annoyed at Sherman. Hooker, in fact, approved of Sherman's criticism of Stanton. He showed Slocum a letter, dated October 14, 1864, from George Wilkes, the editor of the newspaper *Spirit of the Times*. In it Wilkes told of an interview he had with Stanton, who bragged that he had placed Hooker in charge of Ohio, where "he can not only build up himself," Slocum told Sherman, "but can undermine you. There is not a doubt but that the letter is a truthful statement of the interview." "I have always believed that Stanton came to Savannah in December 1864 somehow to damage me," Sherman confided to John, "on the theory that I was not a compliant tool. . . . Stanton found he could not catch me on the Negro question and put it off till the last chance of the war, when he had to or abandon the design."[8]

Sherman's enemies within the Grant administration inspired the bitterest attacks on the *Memoirs*. The conspirators included Belknap and two of Grant's former aides, General Horace Porter, now with the Pullman Company, and Colonel Orville E. Babcock, Grant's secretary. The three supplied material to the egotistical James Harrison Wilson and to Baldy Smith for magazine articles critical of Sherman. They also whispered into Grant's ear against the book. "Genl Grant told me in the presence of Senator Conkling," Sherman wrote to Orlando Poe, "that before the *reading* of my Book he was *hurt*, but on a careful perusal he found nothing he could *correct*, but he might have advised certain omissions for 'policy sake.' But he added, I wish when you were about it you had punctured another bubble, the 'battle above the Clouds' which he proceeded to do himself."[9]

Belknap and Babcock, both soon to be involved in scandals, sponsored the most vicious of Sherman's denigrators. Henry Van Ness Boynton had been born in Massachusetts in 1835 and was graduated from the Kentucky Military Institute. Mustered out as a breveted brigadier general after being wounded at Missionary Ridge, he became in December 1864 the Washington correspondent of the *Cincinnati Gazette*, a newspaper consistently critical of Sherman. Even John Sherman, who went out of his way to court reporters, labeled Boynton "a professional libeler."[10]

Late in 1875 Boynton's answer to Sherman appeared. Entitled *Sherman's Historical Raid*, his book announced on its title page that it was "based upon" the records of the "war office," an admission that Belknap had fostered its writing. In twenty chapters Boynton attacked every aspect of Sherman's war record and concluded by denouncing Sherman for attempting to usurp the powers of the secretary of war and the "staff corps."

The Sherman who emerged from Boynton's pages was self-centered and unjust to his distinguished companions. He tried to steal Grant's glory, loaded his failures onto Thomas and McPherson, insulted Hooker, Logan, and Blair, and slandered Stanton. He was responsible for the surprise at Shiloh, for the debacles at Chickasaw Bayou and Kennesaw, for the timidness at Resaca, and indeed for every mishap that befell the western army.[11]

The backward glance of history reveals serious defects in Sherman's *Memoirs*, but it also shows that Boynton did not know of them. Sherman's chief fault was not that he blamed others for his mistakes but that he glossed over or ignored events damaging to himself: his breakdown in 1861; the endless lobbying on his behalf by Ellen, John, Thomas Ewing, and Tom Ewing; the squabbles within the family; Halleck's selflessness in saving Sherman time after time, only to be spurned because of a fortnight of weakness; the impulsiveness and family history of mental illness that led Sherman to mistrust his own judgment. These constituted as much a part of Sherman's story as Shiloh and Bentonville.

Boynton, moreover, ignored Sherman's unique military accomplishments. He would have had to search deep into history to find parallels to the march without water to Jackson in July 1863; to the extraordinary chess game played by Johnston and Sherman from Resaca to the Chattahoochee; and to the winter campaign through the swamps of South Carolina, where each morning the soldiers of the greatest army since Julius Caesar's picked the icicles out of their hair.

Of all Boynton's charges, the accusation that he had betrayed Thomas cut Sherman most deeply. Sherman told General C. H. Grosvenor:

> To me it seems simply ridiculous that General Boynton should arraign me for stripping General Thomas of his well earned Fame—he who in life never had a kind word for General Thomas whereas I have been his intimate friend and eulogist for forty years (since 1836). . . . Because I simply recorded what was notorious, what is admitted by his *warmest* and *best* friends,—that he was slow, deliberate and almost passive in the face of exasperating danger, but true as steel when the worst came. Some men who before were silent now become his defenders as *against* me. Pooh upon such hypocrites![12]

Three lawyers came to Sherman's defense. Late in 1875 Charles W. Moulton of Cincinnati, Fanny's husband, published a short book dissecting Boynton's argument chapter by chapter. Meanwhile, Hitchcock, now practicing law in St. Louis, and Bowman, doing the same in Baltimore, went over the *Memoirs* with an eye to revising them. But the two could not decide what to change. "If we can't agree," Sherman explained to Bowman, "I don't see how the general public will."[13]

But for years Boynton's attacks haunted Sherman. "I know he was paid $600 Govt. money and supplied with hired clerks to copy extracts of official reports, emasculated to suit their purposes," Sherman wrote John in 1886. "Babcock was the main spirit, and his motive was to prevent my influence in cutting the wings of the Staff Corps in Washington who are inimical to the Real Army which does the work, with which Grant and I were in full sympathy."[14]

Two of Sherman's enemies soon disappeared from the scene. In December 1875 Babcock was indicted for being a part of the Whiskey Ring, which defrauded the government out of the tax on liquor. Only the president's intervention saved him from conviction. The next March Belknap was impeached for selling trading posts in the Indian territory. To avoid a trial, he resigned. Sherman commiserated to John:

> I feel sorry for Belknap. I dont think him naturally dishonest, but how could he live on $8,000 a year in the style that you all believed? I am glad that explosion has come—for he acted towards me without frankness & meanly—gradually usurping all the power which had been exercised by Genl Grant—leaving me almost the subject of ridicule; and he took advantage of the publication of my Memoirs to create the impression that I had belittled Genls Thomas, McPherson & my old comrades in arms, a thing that is not in the Book—He used that scamp Boynton to rake among the records for scraps to antagonize with my positive aspirations. The whirlwind that is now let loose in Washington will do good. . . . I think I see the dawn of better times.[15]

To Admiral Porter, Sherman hinted at misdeeds by the president. "All this time I am sorry for Grant," the general noted from St. Louis, "for while he supposed he was using others dexterously, they were using him. Barring his selfishness I do not believe he would connive at wrong, yet here those who knew him best before the war make no comment & express the opinion that he has deliberately salted away a fortune. I almost hope so, for poverty will be terrible for him to struggle with again."[16]

Three days after Belknap resigned, Grant choose his replacement, Judge Alphonso Taft of Ohio. "We have a new Secretary of War," Sherman informed Tom, like Taft's son, William Howard, a student at Yale. Taft "has the reputation of being a sterling honest judge—but doubtless as innocent of all knowledge touching our army, as a baby. . . . The parasites that fattened Belknap now flitter around the new Secretary, but I think he will have perception enough to see through their motives."[17]

Summoned to Washington in late March, Sherman encountered a surprise. Unlike Belknap, Taft acceded to Sherman's request that the general command the army. In return, Sherman agreed to do what he vowed he would never do: return to Washington. "I have been perfectly vindicated by events in my controversy with Belknap," he rejoiced to Tom, "and nearly every body is most complimentary of the Memoirs—Indeed never before have I stood higher in public estimation, but the exalted are *always* the target for envy and malice. In that I must be cautious. No young man ever had a better start than you, and you shall have every possible assistance till you can be self maintaining."[18]

In mid-April Sherman reopened his office at the War Department. While Ellen and the family remained in St. Louis, he moved into the Ebbitt House in Washington. Then, in mid-May, Grant decided to make Taft his attorney general. As the new secretary of war, the president selected J. Donald Cameron, the son of old Simon Cameron. "I dont like the change," Sherman complained to Ellen. "Judge Taft is a man of sense, and sees the whole question at once, but if the new Secretary be a chip off the old block, he will dispense his personal favors, not from any sense of right, and as a reward for good service, but to oblige his Pennsylvania friends."[19]

Only in the case of Samuel Tappan was Sherman ever more wrong about anyone. A tall, pale, sickly widower, Cameron early assured the general that "he would trust to me all military matters—reserving to himself the political. Of course," Cump informed Ellen, "as yet he does not see how intimately they are associated."[20]

From the outset Cameron, who during the war had run the family business, was attracted to the famous general. Two days after being sworn in, he went with Sherman to Bull Run to see the spot where his uncle, Colonel James Cameron of the Seventy-ninth New York Highlanders, had fallen while serving under Sherman.

That September the secretary, accompanied by his grown daughters, Lida and Virginia, whom Sherman found completely captivating, and the Shermans—the general, Ellen, Elly, Tom, and young Cump—took the Kansas Pacific and the Union Pacific across the continent. Young Cump remembered being awakened one morning by his father and being led to the back platform of the train. Sherman pointed to a herd of buffalo that he said would be the last they would ever see. The boy looked but noticed only "a large black moving blur, beneath a cloud of dust." The most memorable episode of the trip was a visit to Salt Lake City, where Apostle George Cannon showed the party around. Sherman always admired Brigham Young and the Mormons for making the desert bloom and thought "plural marriage" no worse than "tandem polygamy," as he called divorce and remarriage.

Through Sherman and John, Cameron met their niece, Elizabeth Bancroft Sherman, the youngest of Taylor's four daughters. The talk of Washington when she later stayed with the general at the Ebbitt for several months, Lizzie was tall and thin, with a blond complexion, luxurious brown hair, and light blue eyes. Although twenty-six years her senior, Cameron fell hopelessly in love with Lizzie, still in her teens and two years younger than Cameron's oldest daughter.[21] The Shermans and Camerons, bitter enemies since the early days of the war, were about to join hands.

Meanwhile, with Grant's term ending, Ellen reported

> a growing impression that the Republican party will want you as their Presidential candidate. I beg you will not allow yourself to be beguiled into it. The newspaper abuse which would be heaped upon you & me & each & every child we have would be intolerable to you & they would drag the dead from their graves to villify them & what is more

you could not be elected by reason of your family being Catholic. . . .
I beg you to resist all allurements to *this terrible* step—Let politicians
enter the arena—they belong to the animal tribe & can bear the brutal combat & *you cannot.*

Sherman answered reassuringly: "You need never fear that I will ever be
infested with the poison of Presidential aspiration." He left such desires to her
cousin, James G. Blaine, and to others "trained in that school of scandal and
abuse."[22]

Lonesome without his family, Sherman asked Ellen in mid-June to move
to Washington, where they would stay until he retired in six years. "Your letter
of Sunday was a regular bomb shell," she replied. "I was stunned and incapac-
itated for more than twelve hours & not until now could I think or feel on the
subject." If the family moved, Fitch, who with Minnie and their baby must stay
in St. Louis to attend to his wire business, would take over the house on Garrison Avenue. But Ellen lashed out at Grant and his wife:

I am unwilling to go into a new house of our own in Washington with
the mean patched worn damaged dirty old furniture Mrs. Grant defrauded you into paying her enormously for—It is here now—let it remain here—and if we are to live temporarily in Washington let us rent
or board in order to be unencumbered when we leave. Something may
happen within six years to make it desirable for us to return here. The
set of parlor furniture which I bought in New York during your absence
in Europe & the dining room chairs which I bought at the same time
with my piano & some other articles of my own are all worth taking—
The rest of the furniture (Grant's) I had reupholstered & it is now
dingy again & the dining room table & clock sideboard were broken
& damaged in every way when they were made over to us—the table
has always required propping—the glass in sideboard was sullied &
worn & the clock broken & all the veneering broken off it as well as
off the hat rack bed steads & every other piece of furniture in the
house.

   The carpets had been patched in hundreds of places parlor carpets
& all besides being worn in spots—two of them I threw out when we
went into the house for they were too dirty for me & too worn to be
worth cleaning being thread-bare. . . . This would have been dear
when we took it had we given $5000 for it but $25000!!![23]

___ III ___

In mid-July of 1876, just three weeks after George A. Custer died at the Little
Bighorn at the hands of the Sioux, led by Crazy Horse and Sitting Bull, Sherman noticed in the *New York Herald* a letter about himself. Written by the abolitionist Wendell Phillips, whom he had never met, it charged "to me certain
absurd declarations about exterminating all the Indians." Phillips did not spec-

ify, the general complained to his friend Samuel Tappan, like Phillips a resident of Massachusetts, which newspapers contained his supposed statements. Sherman recalled how he and Tappan gave back to the Navajos, without killing a single one, their original territory. They had also assigned reservations in the Indian territory west of the Arkansas to the Kiowas, Comanches, Arapahos, and Cheyennes, who used to roam from the Platte to the Rio Grande. And they settled, under the care of army generals, the Snakes in Wyoming and the Sioux north of Nebraska. Incompetent civilian agents, not the army, had brought on the recent Indian wars. "During all this time I did not 'exterminate' an Indian, or think of such a thing." Phillips's "assault on me in the New York Herald is simply infamous and unwarranted."[24]

A week later, writing to Miles, blocking Sitting Bull's escape route along the Yellowstone River in Montana, Sherman seemed to contradict what he had argued to Tappan:

> We have for years known that there were certain Sioux that would have to be subjugated before any attempt could be made to domesticate them. Had the Govt allowed us the Military to keep control after 1869, this matter would have been settled, but the good people of New England would insist that we were a blood thirsty race of men—and that Christian ministers alone could be trusted—The result is as we know—I surely have never underrated the trouble or numbers, and have sent every officer & man that Sheridan, Terry or Crook has called for. . . . Meantime however those Sioux must be terribly punished. If Crook and Terry can kill a thousand or more, I will expect that the Montana people will push their settlements & lines of travel down the Yellowstone, and from that quarter, rather than from the Missouri I look for an amelioration of your Region of the Yellowstone.[25]

To Lizzie's sister, Mary Sherman Miles, Sherman wrote similarly: "I am well pleased with the situation of affairs and hoped these Indians will be so severely handled that war on such a scale will never again recur. Dont feel mercy, and I will try to send you the earliest notice of any thing essential. But the New York Herald seems to get news quite as early as we do and you better read it daily."[26]

Almost against his will, Sherman looked, in the fall of 1876, at the presidential race between the Republican, Governor Rutherford B. Hayes of Ohio, and the Democrat, Governor Samuel J. Tilden of New York. Sherman favored the Republican but did not fear the Democrat. "Tilden has the wisdom of the serpent," he confided to Miles, "not such a character as I like *at all*, but he is no fool, and must see that in this Land Freedom and Law must be supreme, and he cannot ignore the existence in spirit and in fact of the armies of 1864–5."[27]

When three states reported two sets of election returns, neither Hayes nor Tilden was declared elected. As Congress met to straighten out the mess, Sherman foresaw "a war of words if not a war of blows. Better to be," he comforted Miles, "among the Indians, than among the politicians."[28]

Meanwhile, Tom finished his course at the Sheffield Scientific School at Yale. At the commencement in June 1876 the college conferred on Sherman a doctor of laws degree. That fall Tom moved back to St. Louis, where he enrolled at the Washington University Law School. In October, with his Blackstone under his arm, Tom went down to Hitchcock's office and began his clerkship. "I am sure that if Tom goes on as now," Sherman predicted to Ellen, "he will in two years enter on a Career not only brilliant but successful in a business sense. My business friends there will be his, and they are among the best in the West. I know you are more concerned as to his Moral & Religious status—but the other is equally important."[29]

As inauguration day approached, Hayes, staying with John Sherman in Washington, presumed he would be elected and began piecing together a cabinet. "From what has transpired I think John will be Secretary of the Treasury," Sherman wrote home, "and Evarts Sec. of State—I have not the remotest hint as to the new Secretary of War—Logans friends are here from Illinois pressing his claims, and he may be the successful one—He professes great regard for me, but will make things uncomfortable very soon."[30]

Declared the victor, Hayes made George W. McCrary of Iowa his secretary of war. "Our duty is simple and plain," Sherman informed Schofield, now in command of West Point, "to sustain the constituted authorities. We have a President whose whole character is embraced in the expression of a 'Gentleman and Scholar'—surrounded by a family and influences of the most refined nature—We have for Secretary of War, a man comparatively young, who is universally regarded as a strong lawyer, and rising man—all of these express themselves kindly & respectful of our Calling."[31]

But between the Democrats, who desired to cut further the size of the army, and office seekers, Sherman again found the capital unbearable. "To live in Washington is simple torture," he groaned to Miles, "day & night besieged by women begging for office. . . . I do honestly believe you are better off on the Yellowstone than we are here."[32]

Taking along Tom, now twenty-one, and his aides, Colonels Poe and John M. Bacon, Sherman escaped from Washington by spending the summer of 1877 inspecting army installations in the Far West. Don Cameron, whose beloved Lizzie was visiting her sister, Mary Miles, had hoped to join them, but politics intervened. After Grant left office, Simon Cameron resigned from the Senate and engineered Don's election as his successor. The son could not possibly go away for four months. He did, however, entrust to Sherman a package for Lizzie. "We found Genl & Mrs Miles occupying a good log house with a flat dirt roof," Sherman informed the new senator from Miles's camp along the Tongue River in southern Montana, "but really most comfortable considering the surroundings. I also found Miss Lizzie remarkably well, somewhat sunburnt but none the worse looking therefore. I have delivered into her hands the parcel you committed to my charge without having seen the contents." Miles, who had recently defeated 15,000 Sioux, had about three hundred prisoners in his camp. The rest of the tribe had either been sent south or had accompanied Sitting Bull into Canada.[33]

For years Lieutenant Hugh L. Scott, later the army's chief of staff, remained amused by an incident involving Tom, who knew nothing about Indian customs. Visiting a camp of the Northern Cheyennes during a medicine ceremony, Tom persisted in trying to enter the skin lodge, an act that would "break" the medicine going on inside. He finally realized he was doing something wrong when White Bear, a chief with a great scar across his face, brandished a knife a yard long.[34]

By steamer Sherman and Tom, accompanied by General Terry, ascended the Bighorn River to the mouth of the Little Bighorn and then started up the Yellowstone River. After conferring with Sheridan, they proceeded by land two hundred miles to Fort Ellis. Passing near towns bearing familiar names—Terry and Miles City, Montana, and Sheridan, Wyoming—Sherman and Tom traveled south seventy-five miles by wagon and another seventy-five by pack mules to Yellowstone National Park and then headed west.[35]

In mid-September the party emerged onto Walla Walla in Washington Territory, after a journey from Missoula of 360 miles "through mountains & forests with Roads," Sherman bragged to Ellen, "that Tom will remember long after I am gone. Our health is robust in the extreme, and Tom can now eat hard bread & bacon, and thinks boiled cabbage a great luxury. . . . I think this trip fills the measure of his expectations, and he really regretted to part with our mules yesterday. They have always proven true & faithful, carrying us over roads that would have discouraged any horse." After a steamboat trip to Portland and a stagecoach ride to California, Sherman hoped to arrive in St. Louis by October 15, so that Tom would not miss any law classes.[36]

Sherman returned to Washington and trouble. The Democrats, controlling the House of Representatives and its Military Affairs Committee, vowed to reduce the army to 17,000 men. "I was before the Committee," Sherman scoffed to Miles, "and appealed to them in the interests of our troops on the Frontier, but I might as well have appealed to a Council of Coyotes."[37]

— IV —

In January 1878 Sherman, living at the Ebbitt House, entertained four attractive ladies. Ellen and Elly came in from St. Louis, Lizzie Sherman, "as fresh & beautiful as ever," as Sherman described her to Miles, from Cleveland, and Ada Moulton, Fanny's daughter, from Cincinnati. "Proud of my two nieces," Sherman escorted them to receptions and balls.[38] It was one of the happiest interludes of his life.

The toast of Washington, Lizzie Sherman set her wedding date at May 14. But on the last day of March, Sherman dined at the home of Don Cameron. After the meal, Sherman told Lizzie, Cameron "invited me into his private office and said he was made very uneasy & unhappy by the terms of a letter he had received from you." Cameron had informed his betrothed that he must attend a political convention in Harrisburg on May 15 and asked that their wedding be pushed up. To this request Lizzie replied coldly, hinting at a postponement until fall. Pushing his niece toward marriage, Sherman wrote to her:

Now you know that Mr Cameron, not unlike yourself, is of a most san-
guine nature, and thinks & feels much faster & stronger than words,
so I infer that you were in pain & irritable from your sprained ankle.
Or like most women thought the Pennsylvania convention small matter compared with the wedding—He asked me to write to you which
I now do with my usual bluntness & awkwardness. I believe you are
fully competent to decide all questions for yourself; but once engaged
I advise an early & speedy fulfillment, the sooner the better. I vote for
the earliest date.[39]

The wedding, attended by a thousand guests, including the general, John,
Tom Sherman, and Elly Sherman, took place in Cleveland on May 9. The bride
was twenty, the groom, a widower with six children, one the age of his young
wife, five days shy of forty-five. "Elizabeth was so beautiful," recalled a friend.
"I can see her now, standing between tall General Sherman and short General
Philip Sheridan as she cut the wedding cake."[40]

Four days later Ellen and the children attended Tom's graduation from law
school. But instead of beginning for Sherman a period of satisfaction and pride,
Tom's graduation ushered in his greatest disappointment since the death of
Willy. On May 20, without warning, Tom wrote his father that he never intended to devote his life to law because he had "chosen another profession, in
one word I desire to become a priest—a Catholic priest." If he had told his
father four years ago, he explained, Sherman would have said that he had been
influenced by his teachers at Georgetown. But the years at Yale had only increased his desire to join the Jesuits. "In justice to myself however I must say
just this one thing; that if you were a Catholic, instead of being chagrined, disappointed and pained at the step I am going to take, you would be proud,
happy and contented in it." Tom had informed his mother of his decision a
week ago, and she had given her "consent and approval."

Washington gossip connected Lizzie's wedding and Tom's decision. The
young man was smitten with his cousin, the story said, and when he lost her
to Cameron, in a marriage into which her family had pushed her, Tom turned
to religion. Indeed, Tom could never have fit into Lizzie's world. Ravishingly
tempting, she tolerated rather than loved Cameron, describing their first
physical experience as virtually a rape. More in her orbit were writers and artists
like the historian Henry Adams, who adored her for twenty-five years but who
was too vain and self-pitying ever to win her, the novelist Edith Wharton, and,
even though she like Adams detested Jews, the brilliant art expert Bernard
Berenson.[41]

Heartbroken by Tom, Sherman warned Ellen that he "may be driven to ex-
tremes." But Ellen pleaded her innocence. She had not, she insisted, influenced Tom:

> I have not dared to meddle with anything so sacred as between his soul
> & his God. I have known nothing of it until his decision was made. He
> never gave me even a hint of it until Sunday the 12th inst, when he
> told me all. . . . We would freely offer our son's life in battle for his

country—In his belief he is offering his life in a higher holier cause & for the country which has no bounds that he and *others* may gain inheritance there and shall we thwart him or deprecate what he holds highest?[42]

Ellen may have satisfied herself that she had no hand in Tom's decision, but she could hardly convince anyone who has read her correspondence. Over the years she twice suggested the idea to Sherman. On June 15, 1858, when Tom was twenty months old, she told her husband: "I flatter myself he will resemble you in intellectual capacity. My great desire is to see him an eloquent Priest some day." And on January 4, 1865, when her husband was in Savannah, Ellen related how, when she "left Tommy at the college" in South Bend, the boy, then eight, promised to "study hard and endeavor to become what you wish him to be. I am anxious that he should be a missionary Priest and join the Paulist Fathers. Of course he will decide for himself but I hope he may be called to that glorious life."[43] If Ellen twice wrote such things to her husband, one can only imagine how many times she whispered such sentiments into her son's ear.

Tom's decision ate away at Sherman. At first he yielded to Ellen's pleas and told only his closest relatives: Charley Ewing, Tom Ewing, now a Democratic congressman from Ohio and a leading advocate of cheap money, John Sherman, and Don Cameron. But Sherman was not one to keep things to himself. He sent a series of long letters to his dearest friends, explaining his misfortune and grasping, as he wrote Henry Turner on May 27,

> for sympathy if not help. . . . I have never thrown a single obstacle in his way to practice the Religion of his Mother, and do not now question his perfect right as to himself of being as ardent a Catholic as his own conscience and judgment approve, but I do oppose most vehemently his purpose to abandon—to desert me now, and to enlist in a Church which claims his soul, his mind and his person. I can hardly endure the thought. I cannot turn against him, but I do against that Church, which has poisoned his young mind, wound its tentacles around his heart and weaned him from his Father. . . . Death—suicide on his part could have been borne, but deliberately to abandon us all, and shut himself up in a Catholic Cloister as the slave of Religion, his very existence instead of being a support will be an enduring nightmare—worse than this even I will be haunted with the dread of the same fate being prepared for my only other boy.[44]

The Sherman who wrote to Schofield the next day was tormented:

> I have warned Bishop [Patrick John] Ryan of St. Louis, that if the Catholic Church or papers boast of their achievements, of having captured the Son of General Sherman, that General Sherman will himself denounce them with all the vehemence of his nature, and with all the force of his personal & official character, for having perverted the nature of a noble son, not for his Eternal welfare but for their worldly

purpose. Though they take him from me, they shall not carry with him my silent assent—but my open curse.[45]

To Charley Ewing, whom Ellen was pushing forward for appointment by Hayes as governor of Utah, Sherman stressed the most puzzling portion of the story:

Not one word, look, or gesture but seemed in accord with my plans; with his knowledge I had made a most favorable business engagement with Hitchcock—Even at Cleveland he did not tell me, but soon after his return to St Louis he wrote positively and firmly—I remonstrated with all the force I could, almost to bitterness,—but today has come an answer which is irrevocable, saying he has engaged his passage—This whole matter has come on me so sudden that I am not myself & yet must go on with a leaden heart. . . . Not only am I not a Catholic, but an enemy so bitter that written words can convey no meaning.[46]

Tom Ewing's son, Tom Ewing III, then fifteen, remembered going down to Sherman's office to pick up a map when Sherman began telling him about Tom. "I had never seen on any person's face an expression of quite so intense feeling," young Tom noted a half century later; "it was so intense that it frightened me so I could make no response. . . . When he saw that I would say nothing he turned with a sharp gesture and sat down at his desk and I left the room."[47]

At the urging of John Sherman, Tom Ewing, and Charley, all of whom opposed his becoming a priest, Tom agreed to go to Washington to see them and his father. "I got home yesterday," Sherman told Elly on June 4, "and found Tom and Rachel at the Ebbitt. Tom was still of the same mind, but somewhat shaken by the pressure from his uncles—all of whom feel as I do only not so keenly—They had not built up a lifelong fabric to topple to the ground as mine did." Tom and his father spoke for hours. "I tried coaxing, persuasion, threats, demands," Sherman informed Samuel Byers, "every thing, almost abusing myself before my own son. . . . All he could answer is that it was a 'vocation' from Heaven—I thought in my heart it was a vocation from Hell." At that time the Democrats in Congress had cut off Sherman's allowance for horses and fuel and had reduced his allowance for quarters from $250 a month to $125. "Indeed for some days I felt I was between two millstones, the Country insulting me in my profession, and the Church taking my son, whom I had educated at great Cost, for this very emergency," Sherman told Byers. Father and son agreed that Sherman would write to John Cardinal McCloskey of New York, the first American cardinal, who would decide whether Tom should sail for England and a Jesuit monastery.[48]

Meeting with the cardinal at Mt. St. Vincent in New York, Tom presented Sherman's letter. In it the general described Ellen as "absolutely more Catholic than the Pope" and pleaded with Cardinal McCloskey to dissuade Tom from becoming a priest. "This of course," observed John Cardinal Farley, his secretary at the time, "his eminence could scarcely do, after hearing the young man's story." With the cardinal's approval and a message of encouragement—"a ray of light on a dark day"—from his Uncle Philemon, Tom sailed for England on June 5. On that day, Sherman lamented to Schofield:

> I infer he is now on the ocean, and shall mourn him as lost to me forever. I will endeavor to check my feelings which now run high & angry against the Catholic Church, which has in my opinion insidiously decoyed into her muster the son whom I had for twenty years trained for another purpose. I know that we often err in this regard—but my case seems peculiar, and I fear its effect on me, regarding my other children. If the Catholic Church appropriates them as fast they reach maturity, what interest can I have in their training?[49]

The loss of Tom turned Sherman away from his wife and children. "I can never have a home again," the desolate general told Byers on the last day of June. "I must serve out my time, and turn my thoughts and feelings towards the Army, which responds at least with sympathy, instead of to my family which recognizes in every bishop and priest a superior to Father parent or general. This terrible and utterly unexpected act has broken up my family circle completely." Accordingly, Ellen stored the furniture, leased out for three years the St. Louis house "for a mere nominal sum which will pay taxes," and moved into the Ewing home, rented from Tom Ewing, in Lancaster. Sherman continued to Byers:

> And I doubt if we will ever have a Home in its English sense—I have no further object in laboring to build up such a home if any Catholic Priest can enter, and carry off at will, without my leave & consent any child that he wants to sacrifice for the objects of that Church.
>
> . . . I regard Tom as dead—and my feelings toward the Catholic Church which decoyed him away from allegiance to me, and his duty as a son, are such that the bare sight of a Priest, or of any Catholic emblem will be to me, as the red flag to an infuriated Bull. You can foretell the necessary consequences.
>
> Meantime I must go in the world, to enact my part, like an actor on the stage, rehearsing words, and yet with no heart in the play—I ask your sympathy and nothing more, and I want you to know the exact Truth.[50]

To Turner, who had taken offense at Sherman's remarks about the Catholic church, the general complained about the journal *Ave Maria,* which reported that Tom had sailed to England with his father's blessing. He wrote:

> I never consented & never can or will. . . . The Jesuit Father in St. Louis who provided Tom the means to be educated a Priest in England never even asked my leave.—I say such a man and such a society is a danger to the State in which he lives and I am forced into the Ranks of those who regard the Catholic church as one of our public enemies. . . . I know that this alienates me from Saint Louis, and this is one reason why I was and still am so cast down by the misfortune.[51]

By late July Sherman had cooled off. He spent a week with his family at Lancaster, where he and Ellen decided that on October 1 she would join him at the Ebbitt House. "Elly and Rachel are bright fine girls," Sherman bragged to Lizzie Cameron, "and Lizzie is as good as good can be, but I cannot recover from Toms desertion and his name was not even mentioned. . . . I have never spoken or written an unkind word to or of him—and I do detest the underhand means by which he has been enticed away."[52]

The most comforting words came from an old attorney friend, Samuel Bowman, who reminded Sherman that Tom had exercised "the right of a free man to select his own lawful calling." Long ago Tom had confided to Bowman that he "was not in love with law studies. And I could see he was not cut out for a successful lawyer. He had no relish for a *contest*. He had little knowledge of business, and the crooked ways of mankind. And when he went to the courts, he saw lawyers wrangling over petty questions of form, and he felt himself incapable of entering into any such employment. And unless he loved the profession and could enter into it with spirit he would have proved a failure."[53] Bowman could scarcely have known it, but Tom was as unsuccessful a priest as he probably would have been a lawyer.

— V —

As the months passed, Sherman mellowed toward Tom and Ellen. When Tom sailed away, Sherman forbade him to write, but by 1880 the two were exchanging letters.[54]

Involved with his other children, Sherman soon forgave his devoted wife of nearly thirty years, even though he told Schofield early in 1879, "I really want her to get out of the rut into which the Church has led her." Life at the Ebbitt, an old-fashioned but comfortable hotel on the southeast corner of 14th Street and F Street, was, young Cump remembered, "very sociable and pleasant." For a while Mary Miles stayed there with her daughter, Cecilia. The hotel was also the stopping place for army officers whose families were not in Washington, so Sherman always had plenty of company.

Sherman filled four evenings a week with social engagements, but he intentionally left three open so he could roam about. Usually this meant visiting the old National Theater, just in back of the hotel, where Sherman, accompanied by his young son, would spend evenings watching the performers and hobnobbing with them. One evening father and son were out front enjoying Joseph Jefferson as Bob Acres in *The Rivals* when the boy laughed so hard he began to choke. Sherman had to take him home.[55]

In May 1879 the family moved into a three-story house at 817 15th Street, on the corner of H Street. Stewart Van Vliet occupied the home next door, and adjacent to him lived James G. Blaine. Across the street resided Admiral Benjamin Franklin Sands. John Sherman's house was at 1319 K Street, a few blocks away.

One of the great joys for the small boys of the neighborhood, young Cump recollected, was to gather on mild evenings around Admiral Porter's front steps and entice him out to tell of great sea battles, of encounters with the fabled Flying Dutchman, and of his many hairbreadth escapes. Beginning to doubt that one person could live through so many adventures, the boy mentioned them to his mother, who broke the illusion by revealing that they were not supposed to be true. The admiral was "yarning." Porter later compiled some of these tales into two books, but they failed to make him a famous author.

Former Confederate generals were among the most frequent visitors to the house on 15th Street. General Joseph Johnston, remembered by young Cump as "rather small and prim, but eminently soldierly," often stopped by with his wife, and Sherman enjoyed his many long conversations with them. One evening when the Johnstons dropped in, Mrs. Johnston told Sherman: "Well, General, during the war I spent all my time running away from you; but now it seems that I am spending all my time running after you." Two of Sherman's favorites were Generals James Longstreet and Joseph Wheeler. In an effort to preserve Lee's reputation, Southern writers were blaming Longstreet for the disaster at Gettysburg, but Sherman and the other Union generals refused to believe these stories and praised him lavishly. Sherman grew particularly close to Wheeler, then serving in Congress, and in letters addressed him as "My dear friend." Sherman always insisted that Wheeler did at least half of the damage in Georgia, even though Southerners blamed it all on the Yankees.

By the late 1870s a certain camaraderie had developed between Northern and Southern generals. The former Confederate Henry Heth, a West Point graduate in the class of 1847, recalled a dinner party given by his classmate and close friend Ambrose Burnside, at which Sherman, Van Vliet, John G. Parke, and several other generals talked about the Civil War. Seated next to Heth, Sherman "good-naturedly" twitted him. "Stop, Sherman, and think," Heth answered, "if there are two men in the world that should go on their knees and thank the Almighty for raising up the rebels, those two men are Grant and yourself; but for the rebels you would now be teaching school in the swamps of Louisiana and Grant would be tanning bad leather at Galena." Placing his hand on Heth's shoulder, Sherman said: "That is so, old fellow."

During this stay in Washington, Sherman's hair and beard changed color. His hair turned from dark red to dark brown, without the slightest trace of gray. His beard, however, went from light red to white. Like nearly all the men in the family, Sherman never shaved. Since California days, he let his beard grow because his skin was thin and shaving caused prolonged bleeding and soreness. About this time Sherman began wearing glasses for reading. Farsighted, he had trouble seeing close up. But his eyes remained a light hazel.[56]

In 1879 congressional matters dominated Sherman's official thoughts. The previous December, Burnside, now a senator from Rhode Island, introduced on behalf of a congressional committee a bill that reorganized the army but kept the number of enlisted men at 25,000. It also specified, to the chagrin of the staff officers in Washington who exercised great power, that commands must be issued through Sherman and not from the War Department to the troops, as Belknap had done. To Schofield, Sherman complained:

> I doubt if a dozen Senators or Members of Congress have read the Bill itself, . . . but all read the short paragraphs which have appeared simultaneously all over the Country, that you and I want absolute and dictatorial powers, that we made use of the Committee to this end, that Burnside owns shares in arms Manufactuies & therefore wants rifles manufactured thereat, and the most bold & palpable lies, than which I can recall none worse in any former cases of army legislation. . . . We have lost the influence of the Civil War, and this I feared, when Genl Grant would not put things on the right course in 1869, when he might so easily have done it.

To Sheridan, Sherman complained similarly: "The young staff officers here are as busy as bees, saying that I and the Generals want to usurp the Power of the President, Sec of War, Congress and of the Government itself."[57]

After killing the Burnside bill, the Democrats in Congress tried to add to the Army Appropriations Act a rider prohibiting the use of troops during elections, a sore point during Reconstruction. The debate became so intense that Congress adjourned without appropriating money for the army. Hayes thereupon called the legislature into special session.

The proceedings dismayed Sherman. "Politics are now awfully mixed," the general informed Byers. The Democrats, a majority of whom were Southerners, controlled both branches of Congress. "So at this minute the Rebels have conquered us, and we are at their mercy. Who would have thought this in 1865? Our papers announced yesterday the election of a Clerk of the Senate, with the recommendation that he had served *faithfully* on Lee's staff. Little by little it has come about and we find that it is popular to have belonged to the Confederate army, and correspondingly suspicious to have served in the Union army."[58]

During the struggle with Congress, Hayes vetoed five bills aimed at prohibiting federal supervision of elections. "To me it is simply amazing that so soon after our terrible Civil War that Congress should renew the angry debates of 1832–3—and of 1859–60, as it were ignoring the epoch 1861–5," Sherman complained to the Reverend William G. Eliot of St. Louis. "Indeed I have myself been told by men of real intelligence and seeming honesty that all public events and legislation since 1861 had been a mistake, and that the country must go back and begin where the Democrats left off when Mr Lincoln became President. Of course this will be madness & folly combined—Still I hope that the present war will be a war of words, but I agree with you that every man should be ready for the worst."[59]

After Hayes signed a compromise measure that barred the use of troops at polling places, things quieted down. In July, Eliot suggested that Sherman might be needed to run for president. Sherman answered:

> The office of President of the U. S. has never had the least attraction to me. It was my fortune to be somewhat behind the curtain in Tay-

lor's administration. I witnessed the fearful agonies and throes of that Good and Great Man Lincoln, and saw General Grant who never swerved in War, bend & twist and writhe under the appeals, and intrigues from which there was no escape, so that I look upon the office as beyond human endurance—each year becoming worse & worse.

. . . The country is full of men of average honesty & ability, who not only seek the office, but will labor, scheme, intrigue and do crime to reach the object—Our salvation & honor as a nation must depend on the System—not the goodness or badness of the agents.—In Hayes' position I would likely do pretty much as he does,—certainly no better. The Country is full of his Equals, and I propose to leave the office to them. In no event, and under no combination of circumstances will I allow the use of my name in that connection—Realizing finally that Time will accomplish all good things, I have little fear of the reaction of 1879—which is nearly expended, so that the pendulum is now going back.[60]

— VI —

In January 1880 an old feud resurfaced. A young man came to the War Department and complained to Sherman that Boynton had been slandering his father, Eugene H. Cowles of the *Cleveland Leader*. Asked about Boynton, Sherman went wild: "Everybody knows him to be a notorious slanderer. You could hire him to do anything for money. . . . He is entirely without character. Why, for a thousand dollars he would slander his own mother. . . . I would not bother with such vermin as he. It would take all my time and accomplish nothing." On January 15 the *Leader* published these comments under the headline: "Brevet Liar Boynton."[61]

When Boynton, fresh from a controversy with Howard, saw the Sherman interview, he demanded a retraction. Sherman responded by repeating his charges. Boynton thereupon requested that the new secretary of war, Alexander Ramsey, court-martial Sherman. Ramsey wisely refused, advising Boynton to sue Sherman in a civil court if he wished.[62]

Sherman hoped Boynton would sue. Both Ben Butler and Senator Matthew Carpenter of Wisconsin had offered to take Sherman's case free. "I want Boynton on the stand under oath," Sherman informed Church, "and Matt Carpenter will screw out of him the whole combination. . . . What I want to find out is the names & motives of those who employed Boynton."[63]

The approaching marriage of Elly and Lieutenant Alexander M. Thackara of the navy presented a different problem. Elly was Catholic, but Thackara was not. Ellen asked James Cardinal Gibbons of Baltimore for permission to have the wedding performed in a Catholic church, but the cardinal, following the practice toward mixed marriages, refused. Elly's wedding was therefore held on May 5 at the Sherman home. Smaller than Minnie's wedding, it was attended nonetheless by President and Mrs. Hayes, Porter, the Blaines, and John

Sherman and his wife, Cecelia. While the bride and groom were honeymooning at Niagara Falls, Sherman confided to Byers about the navy: "Elly is the best of my children for such a vagrant life."[64]

That August, Sherman made his most famous public utterance. For years P. Tecumseh Sherman denied that his father ever said "War is hell," arguing that the closest he ever came to it was "War is cruelty," written to the mayor of Atlanta on September 12, 1864, when he ordered the removal of civilians. Just after the outbreak of the First World War, the *New York Times* also looked for Sherman's statement. Unable to find the phrase, the paper put Sherman's words into the category of Grover Cleveland's "Public officials are the trustees of the people," which somehow became "Public office is a public trust."[65]

Three years before, however, the *Army and Navy Journal* and the *Ohio State Journal* (Columbus), searching jointly, unearthed the quote. On August 11, 1880, called on by 5,000 veterans at the fairgrounds in Columbus to say something after a formal speech by Hayes, Sherman came forward and said: "The war is away back in the past, and you can tell what books cannot. When you talk you come down to practical realities, just as they happened. . . . There is many a boy here to-day who looks on war as all glory, but boys, war is all hell. . . . I look upon war with horror; but if it has to come, I am there."[66]

In 1914 a writer to the *Times* recalled sitting with Sherman at a dinner. After the meal, while the men consumed punch and cigars, someone asked Sherman about the quote. "Gen. Sherman's reply was substantially that, ever since the Mexican war of 1847, he had many times expressed the opinion among men friends, especially during and since the conflict of 1861–5, that war is hell."[67]

Late August brought news of Tom. Having finished his course in England, he sailed for home and study at the seminary at Woodstock, Maryland. Rachel was to pick Tom up in New York and accompany him to Washington and the house on 15th Street. He would stay with Sherman for a few days before going with Rachel to Altoona, where his mother was spending the summer.[68]

Rachel left a picture of what happened late in the afternoon of August 23:

> When Tom reached Washington with me we were horribly agitated not knowing how my father would receive him. He was not at the depot & we were met by his orderly (Pat) & the carriage. At the house our old nurse Emily opened the door & motioned to the parlor door which was slightly open. Tom went in & with a cry my father threw his arms about him & I left them standing, clasped in each other's arms. I closed the door & went to my room. We later dined together at the Riggs House & he [Sherman] introduced my brother to all the senators & representatives who I must say looked half frightened & then so relieved. Every one knew of his distress & sorrow on his leaving. But he had the tenderest heart & loved us devotedly & he could never bear malice toward any one.[69]

Tom left in a happy mood, but Sherman still brooded. He instructed Elly:

I want you and Thackara to work out your own problem of life, for I regard mine as ended. Had Tom remained I would & could have laid a splendid foundation for you all in St. Louis, but he has deserted if not to the enemy, to a different institution to waste his life, in a cloister worse than death—ignoring this world for which our human bodies and natures were fabricated, and we must do the best we can without his help—We must eat, and drink.—We must live out our time on this earth, trusting to the Great Creator to provide for the future,—and for my few remaining years I want to help my children all I can.[70]

To Byers, Sherman depicted Tom as "some sort of a Catholic Divine—not a Priest—but employed in one of the Catholic Educational establishments near Baltimore—This all directly antagonistic to my ideas of Right—He ought to be in some career to assist us, and to take part in the Great Future of America.— I feel as though his life was lost, and am simply amazed he does not see it as I do."[71]

Politics added to the torment. To Grant, then in Tokyo while touring the world, Sherman described in 1879 "the cruel position in which Destiny" seemed to be pushing him. Hayes had declined to run for another term, and John Sherman and Grant loomed as rivals in the coming Republican convention. How could Sherman favor one over the other? With tears in his eyes, Grant told his traveling companion, the journalist John Russell Young: "Read this letter from Sherman. People may wonder why I love Sherman. How could I help loving Sherman—And he has always been the same during the thirty years I have known him. He was so at West Point."[72]

But neither Grant nor John received the Republican nomination. It went instead to Senator James A. Garfield of Ohio, who had served during the war on Rosecrans's staff. The Democrats, in turn, nominated General Winfield Scott Hancock, Sherman's friend for four decades. Sherman admired both candidates, but, he told Elly just after Garfield's election, he preferred the Republican "because his coming in will not make radical changes, which would have been forced on Hancock by clamorous Democrats, South and North. I dont want to pile on the South further humiliation, but I do think they should be a little more modest after involving us in a bloody Civil War, and getting such a good thrashing."[73]

Sherman and Rachel spent the September and October before the election touring the Far West with Hayes. "Every minute of time was taken up by the eager crowds which have thronged our way to see a Live President," Sherman informed Ellen. "He acquits himself admirably, and all our party is cheerful, strong, and seemingly well pleased with the varied scenes, and people by the way."[74]

Returning to Washington, Sherman found himself arguing with Hayes. Wishing to promote some of his friends before he left office, Hayes desired to retire some of the generals who had turned sixty-two. To Sherman's dismay, Hayes eyed Ord, who commanded the Department of Texas but had chased marauders across the border without respect for Mexican sovereignty. "I have lost confidence in his motives," Sheridan complained to Sherman about Ord in 1877, "and his management of his department is a confusion which is demoralizing to his subordinates." Denouncing Ord's "eccentricity of character and the devious methods he employs to accomplish his ends," Sheridan accused him in late 1879 of stirring up "revolutions, raids, murders and thefts" to avoid troop reductions in Texas.[75]

Trying to save his friend, Sherman argued that if anyone should go it should be Irvin McDowell, who was older and wealthier than Ord. Hayes countered by retiring Ord and Van Vliet. Ord's star went to Miles, but by acclamation Congress allowed him to leave as a major general, thereby giving him $1,000 more a year. Both Van Vliet and Ord took the news of their forced retirements hard.[76]

Sherman himself contemplated retirement. Sheridan had waited long enough and deserved his chance to command the army. "Had Tom remained to us," Cump lamented to Ellen in May 1881, "I would not have hesitated in choosing St. Louis for him & Cump—But now I hardly can." Perhaps, he suggested, they should stay in Washington. Kilpatrick, Garfield's minister to Chile, had bought a lot on 14th Street. So had Bacon. Sherman knew of a good lot on the corner of 14th Street and Kennesaw Avenue. "In a few years that will be one of the most healthy and pleasant places in Washington."[77]

20

Extreme Unction

— I —

FOR SHERMAN the year 1881 brought reverberations other than the retirements of Ord and Van Vliet. On April 6 and 7, the nineteenth anniversary of Shiloh, Sherman appeared at the Society of the Army of the Tennessee meeting in Cincinnati, where he read a paper in which he disputed the argument that the Union army had been surprised there and that Buell had saved the day. After he concluded, numerous participants in the battle rose to second Sherman's account. One of them, General Ralph P. Buckland, Hayes's neighbor in Fremont, Ohio, challenged Whitelaw Reid's assertion that the men of his brigade had been surprised in their tents. They were, on the contrary, in line and ready for Sidney Johnston's assault. Unfortunately, Buckland asserted, Reid's version had been copied into the histories of the war, although "there is not a word of truth in it." "Certainly not," Sherman seconded, "not one word of truth. It was written at Cairo and not on the field at all." In his paper, the *New York Tribune*, Reid objected only mildly to the criticism, but Boynton immediately issued a statement calling Reid's account more accurate than the version in Sherman's *Memoirs*.[1]

On May 7, 1881, exactly one month after the Cincinnati meeting, Sherman issued his most important order as general-in-chief. Aimed at revamping military education in the United States, it established at Fort Leavenworth an advanced army learning center, the School of Application for Infantry and Cavalry. In a real sense, the school constituted a memorial to Sherman's friend, Colonel Emory Upton, who, for a reason that escaped his relatives and associates, had killed himself that March.[2]

Before 1881 the army possessed but two advanced training centers, one for engineers and another for artillery. In articles and interviews Sherman challenged the notion, prevalent among cadets at the Military Academy, that the engineers constituted an elite branch. "So deep rooted is this preference for the Engineers," he wrote Howard, "that it will take some time to convince Cadets that it is more honorable to command men, than to build Forts and improve Rivers and harbors, and until Cadets themselves reach this conclusion I see no first reason to compel them to choose what they believe to be an inferior service."[3]

Upton set the tone for the new school. Graduating from West Point in 1861 with the class that produced Kilpatrick and Wheeler, he rose during the Civil War to the rank of brigadier general of volunteers. In 1875, after serving as commandant of cadets at West Point for five years, Upton resolved to study the armies of the world. With Sherman's help, he traveled about and then returned home to write two books, *The Armies of Asia and Europe* and *The Military Policy of the United States from 1775*, the latter published twenty-three years after his death.

In his writings Upton concluded that an army existed for an obvious reason: to wage war. Its officers should be professionals, not volunteers more civilians than soldiers. In organization, the U.S. army was far behind others, headed as it was not by a chief of staff but by a general-in-chief, whose role, as Sherman repeatedly complained, was not defined. Staff officers, men like Sherman, should plan, not lead in battle.

Upton's stress on officers as trained and admired professionals had an almost immediate impact. Young officers clamored to take the advanced courses offered at the new school. To Upton's writings and Sherman's enthusiasm could be traced, as one student of the subject has put it, "much of the feeling of intellectual vigor that permeated the ranks of the officer corps in the late nineteenth century."[4]

—— II ——

In 1881 another death shook the country. In July a disgruntled office seeker shot President Garfield, who died on September 19. Chester A. Arthur became the new president. "In three months all these 'startling' events will be forgotten," Sherman scoffed to Ellen, "and we will have the same old political squabbles of the past—I pity Arthur—and his proverbial 'good feeling' is the best proof that he will be victimized."[5]

That November, attending the Cotton Exposition in Atlanta at the invitation of the two senators from Georgia, Sherman encountered his first unpleasant incident in the South since the war. Clark Howell, the editor of the *Atlanta Constitution,* was supposed to greet the guests at the railroad station, but he left word that he went to see his grandmother in Alabama. In reality, Howell was scared off by an editorial in "a dirty evening paper" asserting that Sherman was coming to Atlanta to gloat over and celebrate the anniversary of its burning. "Howell was a moral coward," Sherman later observed, but Senator Joseph E. Brown was not, for he spent the entire next day escorting the general about.[6]

Late 1881 and early 1882 brought other deaths. John W. Draper, the historian, chemist, and inventor of daguerreotype, had read and advised Sherman on all his writings. But the harshest blow was the death on December 16, 1881, of Henry S. Turner, mourned by Sherman as "my best friend on Earth."[7]

Having served as head of the army since 1869, Sherman realized that he must soon retire. In addition to a full general, the army contained one lieutenant general, Sheridan, who commanded the Midwest, and three major generals—Hancock, governing the East; McDowell, in charge of the Pacific Coast; and Schofield, recently the commandant of West Point. Since the army consisted of three divisions, one of which Sheridan led, one major general had to command a unit not fitting his rank. "I think McDowell should voluntarily retiree so as to make room for you," Sherman told Schofield, "but in my opinion he is the impersonation of selfishness, and has got the Pacific Senators to represent to the President his great popularity, and his peculiar fitness for the place by reason of his great wealth and consequent ability to entertain distinguished strangers." If McDowell refused to leave, "then there is no alternative but for me to retire, let Sheridan come to Washington & you to succeed him at Chicago."[8]

In June 1882 Congress solved the problem. It passed a law retiring Sherman on full pay and allowances on or before February 8, 1884, his sixty-fourth birthday. "This is liberal and exceptional," Sherman confessed to Ellen, "and is all I or any one should ask." Sherman suggested three possible places for their retirement: Washington, where they now lived; St. Louis, where Ellen "can have access to her Church and plenty of Catholics who think and feel as she does," where Rachel and Lizzie could "find congenial society," and where young Cump "if he can escape the Cloisters of the church may earn a living after I am gone"; and Yonkers, the beautiful New York City suburb to which Sherman's cousin, Colgate Hoyt, had recently moved. "As to my happiness that is not to be considered for since Tom left us, committed suicide in fact so far as this world is considered, I dont consider myself as concerned in the least—I want to make a good home for the children, so that when I go they and you can manage the rest."[9]

By the summer of 1882 Minnie had five children and Elly one. Ellen decided to rent a summer place large enough to accommodate the brood in Oakland, Maryland. There, early in July, the family decided to move back to St. Louis and the Garrison Avenue house.[10]

But the summer that began with a Fourth of July celebration ended tragically. Located at the top of the Allegheny Mountains, Oakland had hot days and cool nights that proved too much for two of Minnie's daughters, Maria, eight months old, and Kate, two years. They developed dysentery and died. Overwhelmed, the family scattered.[11]

Among army officers, Sherman's projected retirement, and that of McDowell on October 15, 1882, unleashed a mad dash for promotion. Pope, Terry, Howard, Crook, and even Miles began maneuvering for the vacant major generalship. Forced to retire, McDowell, Sherman's commander at Bull Run, was angry. "Ever since the Ord affair McDowell has withheld from me his personal friendship," Sherman confided to Schofield, "and I am glad of it, for now he can expect nothing of me. I have known him since a child, and can recall no one with such opportunities who has less personal friends and admirers."[12]

The promotion of Pope did not quench the ambition of some of the others. "Mackenzie and Miles are troublesome," Sherman reported to Ellen in 1883 from Santa Fé. "They count the days till age will compel the retirement of all above them, that they may be in Chief Command. That is a long way off and no man is wise enough to guess what may happen. Meantime, yet they fret & chafe over it like young horses in harness."

That December Mackenzie, in command of Texas, suffered a mental breakdown. "Poor Mackenzie," Sherman commiserated to Grierson, "has for fifteen years tortured his friends & correspondents and fretted himself to such a degree that he succeeded in his ambition to be a Brig General but has exhausted his brain & nervous power to such an extent that in all probability he will be the inmate of an asylum the remainder of his life."[13]

As retirement approached, Sherman's chief concern became not the size of his salary, which the Republican administration had reduced from $19,000 to $14,000 a year, but whether Ellen would entice their remaining son into the clergy. "If Cump will only take a fancy to being a Mechanic, Merchant or Farmer, and not a Priest, I will be reasonably content," he advised his wife, "but if he like Tom runs off into the Church, I will not answer for the consequences. I still believe and ever will that the Church when it took our oldest living son away from the legitimate work cut out for him, committed a crime of such magnitude, that the blood of a hundred martyrs cannot wash it out."[14]

Ellen reassured her husband. Young Cump's deafness would disqualify him for both the army and the priesthood, "so you need have no fears on that score. . . . When the good God gives you faith you will feel differently about Tom."[15]

—— III ——

To enable Sheridan to move to Washington before winter set in, Sherman relinquished command of the army on November 1, 1883. Subleasing the house in Washington to Slocum, now a congressman from Brooklyn, Sherman moved back to St. Louis. Tom, stationed nearby at the Jesuit college that is now St. Louis University, visited frequently, and Minnie lived with her family at Côte Brilliante, Sherman's six-acre farm two or three miles out from Garrison Avenue.[16]

Almost as soon as Sherman arrived in St. Louis, John Sherman, Miles, and Schofield asked whether he would accept the Republican presidential nomination. "John Sherman is of the same mind as you," he responded to Schofield, "that if the Country calls I will not be at liberty to decline even the office of President.—In my judgment the Country cannot call—A party by its convention may call. . . . I shall decline with an emphasis which cannot be misconstrued—You may therefore address me always to 912 Garrison Avenue till you hear I am safely laid away at Bellefontaine Cemetery."[17]

During the Republican convention of 1884, Sherman authorized his neighbor and former associate on the Indian Commission, ex-senator John B. Henderson, to speak for him. To Byers he described what happened:

> I do *all* I can to keep out of the newspapers, but they keep paid spies to catch one's chance expressions to circulate over the earth as substantial news.—Recently I was informed by parties of national fame that in the Chicago Republican Convention in case of a dead-lock between Blaine and Arthur my name would be used—I begged to be spared the humiliation but was answered that no man *dared* refuse a call of the People.—I took issue that a political party convention was not the people of the U. S.—and that I was not a bit afraid and would decline a nomination in such language as would do both the convention & myself harm—Fortunately Blaine & Logan were nominated and they are fair representatives of the Republican Party.—Next month another set of fellows will meet at Chicago and will nominate Jeff Davis, Ben Butler, Tilden, Grover Cleveland, or some other fellow—No matter whom—and the two parties can fight it out—Fortunately, and thanks to the brave Volunteer Soldiers & Sailors the ship of state is now anchored in a safe Harbor, and it makes little difference who is the Captain.[18]

That same month Sherman learned that Grant had gone bankrupt. "I dont assume to myself extraordinary wisdom or virtue," he explained to Orlando Poe's wife, "and I do feel for Genl Grant, though he did not deal by me fairly or generously, for the rock on which he is shipwrecked was his love & faith in his children, and a greediness for wealth not earned by the sweat of the brow, or by patient saving.—I would rather go out on my little farm in Illinois and live on hog & hominy, than be the slave as he now is of Vanderbilt."[19]

— IV —

St. Louis's most prominent citizen, Sherman was much in demand. "I am a sort of 'show-man,' " he joshed in October 1884 to Spencer F. Baird of the Smithsonian Institution, on whose board both sat, "and must appear one day as a Scotsman—next an Irish-man—then a Simon pure descendant of the Pilgrims of New England,—as well as a carriage builder,—'corrections & charities' and Wholesale Druggists.—Now I am fairly impressed as Presiding Officer at a Banquet of Cattle men for November 20th."[20]

Even with appearances at dinners and conventions, Sherman's life in St. Louis was relaxed and carefree. Young Cump recalled with pleasure the family dinners at which Sherman and Ellen engaged in friendly repartee: "It was clear that my father and mother both superlatively enjoyed their conversations, with freedom from all restraints."[21]

Besides religion, only two issues fomented quarrels. One was newspaper reporters, whom Sherman still despised. Ellen often urged diplomacy, but her words merely brought a grunt from her husband, who never changed his opinion.

The other was financial. Sherman sometimes growled that they were "headed for the poorhouse," but these complaints were rarer than one might expect of a former banker. From her father Ellen had inherited $17,000 plus a good deal of property, most of which she gradually sold, donating the proceeds to charities or to needy friends. When the family moved to St. Louis, she had but two parcels of land left. These she persuaded her husband to buy from her. On each lot Sherman built a house, giving one to Lizzie and the other to Rachel. Needing money for charities, Ellen demanded payments from her husband long before they were due, something Sherman considered the height of extravagance.[22]

The summer of 1885 was among the pleasantest the Shermans ever spent. Along with Poe's family, Ellen, Lizzie, Rachel, and Cumpy vacationed at Lake Minnetonka, Minnesota, as guests of Tourtellotte, a bachelor. Near the end of August, Sherman arrived and escorted the family to a weeklong reunion of his surviving brothers and sisters at John Sherman's house in Mansfield. Present were Elizabeth Reese of Mansfield, Lampson and Hoyt Sherman of Des Moines, and Fanny Moulton of Cincinnati. Young Cump recalled that

> Uncle John Sherman, my father, Aunt Fannie Moulton and my mother kept the conversation animated and generally witty, the others being generally listeners. Uncle John was then at his best—jocular and inclined to tease. Although reserved in public, Uncle John was always gay, chatty and belligerent—he had to leave school when he was 13 because he "licked" the teacher—whereas, in contrast, my father in his youth was studious and reserved—despite a very red head—but became social and belligerent later.[23]

Meanwhile, on July 23, 1885, Grant died of throat cancer. He "had some human infirmities and weaknesses which would have clouded any Public character of less strength," observed Sherman. "He played Poker and Boston all through his Presidential career for money." Grant, moreover, encouraged the telling of obscene jokes by laughing at them. "And when he was at the White House he had as his intimates men that I could not have tolerated—the very men who Iago-like excited his suspicions against his friends."[24]

That September, writing with his usual haste, Sherman made one of the great literary blunders of his life. To Colonel Robert N. Scott, then compiling for the government the official war records, Sherman compared Grant with General Charles F. Smith. "Had C. F. Smith lived," he observed, "Grant would have disappeared in history after Donelson." But Smith, he recalled, skinned his leg while stepping into a yawl and soon could not mount a horse. Grant was then given command of the army at Pittsburg Landing.[25]

Three months later Sherman noticed the indiscreet sentence in an article on Grant published in the *North American Review* and written by General James

B. Fry, who had been Buell's adjutant at Shiloh. He complained to the magazine that he had never written such a thing. Reminded that he had, he tried to extricate himself gracefully. "It seems to me funny," he lamented to Eliot, "that I who was so true & faithful to Grant should be placed on the 'defensive' as against Fry—a provost marshal—who came to us on Shiloh Field after the real Battle was over and *then* claimed all the honors of rescuing us from certain destruction. He was one of the most persistent of Grants 'Maligners' from 1862 to 1884, and now for pay, he assumed the character of panegyrist at the expense of Grants steadfast friends."[26]

As much as he loved Grant, Sherman ridiculed the notion of building memorials to him all over the country. "I have already bought and paid $500 for a place to bury my-self," he scoffed to Miles, "and I have to maintain 6 children, 7 Grandchildren and hundreds of dependents, and the question is shall I turn these out to public charity that I may see my name on subscription lists for superfluous monuments to Grant—I have no objection to every city, town, and Hamlet having its monument provided the citizens thereof pay for it, but I do honestly think it would be better for all to unite on one, and that one over his grave at Riverside on the Hudson."[27]

— V —

Answering a correspondent who invited him to address the New-York Historical Society, Sherman insisted he could not

> come to New York without opening the flood gate which would very soon make me envy General Grant in his guarded tomb on the banks of the Hudson. . . . I have already over an hundred similar calls to fulfill which would necessitate the enlargement of the year to embrace a thousand days instead of 365, and am at this moment advertised like Barnum's Circus to be at Grand Rapids, Mich—Dubuque, Iowa—Kirksville and St. Joe, Missouri and Topeka, Kansas, all points for which you Knickerbockers may feel a sovereign contempt, but which esteem themselves your equals and a little better.[28]

In retirement, Sherman became convinced he had stumbled onto the secret of a long life. On a day in October that Joseph Jefferson, the actor, was coming to the Garrison Avenue house for lunch, Sherman noted to Eliot that most of his wartime comrades were dead, "nearly all prematurely by anxiety, disappointment, or worryment—so I will court amusements & recreation and live out my time as easily as possible."[29]

Still, in 1885 and 1886, Sherman prepared the second edition of his *Memoirs*. He added an introduction of six pages and an appendix, principally documents supporting his arguments. He left alone the statements about Logan and Blair, but for some reason he revised ninety-one words about Hooker. While not enlarging his account of Hooker's role in the Atlanta campaign, he took out two damaging comments. The first said that Hooker believed Thomas and Sherman to be "jealous" of him. The second noted that Hooker, on reaching Cincinnati from Atlanta, predicted disaster for the Union army, something Halleck had told Sherman in September 1864. In place of these Sherman substituted a comment about Hooker proving his reputation as a "fighter" by his good work at Chattanooga and New Hope Church.[30]

Sherman had intended to spend his remaining days in St. Louis, but two events changed all that. Late in 1884, Will Fitch's firm, the Harrison Wire Company, failed. The following March Sherman's house at Côte Brilliante, in which the Fitches lived, burned down. This double calamity induced Fitch to move to Pennsylvania, where steel for wire was cheaper.[31]

Their first-born gone, Sherman was heartbroken. "Minnie is now at Pittsburg," he told Eleanor Poe in late 1885, "and will never return to us. . . . Tom is swallowed up by that modern Moloch, the Catholic church. Lizzie is the same self denying girl. . . . Rachel still has her string of beaux principal of which is that Mr Gordon of St Paul who was with her so much at Lake Minnetonka."

The most important news, however, involved young Cump, who decided to attend Yale that fall. But, Sherman continued, "spite of all I can do his Mama will follow him on the theory that his health needs her supervision though really to watch him lest his faith be shaken. She would rather have him dead than a Protestant. So that I shall not be astonished if next year we should break up here to go to New York, to be near him."[32]

Ignorant of these family matters, newspaper reporters played up something else. In St. Louis, Sherman felt persecuted by the city government. After he spent $12,000 on improvements for his house, Sherman received a new tax assessment. Then, early in 1884, the city paved Garrison Avenue. The work was done sloppily and had to be redone. Sherman was assessed for both jobs. Next came trouble with the Water Department. When the family moved into the house, it paid an annual water bill of $80. But one day an inspector noticed the hired man washing the sidewalk with a hose. The result was a bill for $225 extra, a dollar for each foot of sidewalk. Sherman swore he would not pay and was vilified by the *St. Louis Post-Dispatch* for his poor civic spirit. Ellen possessed more sense. Accompanied by a lawyer, she marched into the office of the Water Department and forced officials to admit that the original bill was sufficient.[33]

Yet when the time came to move, Sherman became blue. "I dont want to leave St. Louis," he told Eleanor Poe, "but I find myself a mere waif. Cump is offered a partnership at Law with the son of Wm M. Evarts.—Rachel dont like St Louis,—so Mrs. S. Lizzie and I would be left alone in this house which cant be maintained at less than $15,000 a year.—We three who are left could board at Paris, London, Vienna or New York for half this—& therefore our conclusion."[34]

Moving to New York in late June 1886, the family settled into three rooms on the second floor of the old Fifth Avenue Hotel, on the corner of Fifth Avenue and Twenty-third Street. This setup enabled Lizzie and Rachel to come and go as they pleased. Meantime, young Cump attended Yale. "He has made a solemn promise not to follow Tom's example," Sherman wrote Lizzie Cameron, "and I believe him to be made of sterner stuff."[35]

Tom was now teaching rhetoric at Detroit College, a Jesuit institution. Still a "scholastic," he led a Spartan life, rising at 4:30 or 5:00 A.M. and passing the day praying and teaching. In Detroit he frequently visited the Poes, who lived there. "Of course I still feel that he did a great wrong in abandoning us for a church which makes use of him for its ends," Sherman confided to Mrs. Poe, "simply holding out the promise of eternal salvation for relinquishing his worldly advantages—He seems content & happy, but a man should help his father to maintain an expensive family." After serving in Detroit, Tom planned to go back to Woodstock to prepare for his ordination.[36]

Sherman was as popular in New York as he had been in St. Louis. He attended first nights at the theater and dinners about four times a week. "The beacon-lights of life," he told the author James Howard Bridge, "are its friendships."

Wherever Sherman went, he was greeted with "Marching Through Georgia." "He never went anywhere," Theodore Roosevelt remembered, ". . . that some idiot was not struck with the happy idea of starting up 'Marching Thru Georgia' as a special and delicate compliment to the General; whereupon the latter, who had heard the tune on several million previous occasions, and was a straightforward old gentleman, used almost to jabber with rage." Sherman sometimes threatened to take refuge in the South so that he would be free of the nuisance.[37]

The 1880s was the decade of Civil War statues, and Sherman was asked to speak at the dedications of many of them. With pleasure he attended those honoring friends like Thomas, McPherson, and Phil Kearny. But he felt it galling to be forced to contribute $50 toward the equestrian statue of Logan, "who in Congress cut down my pay from $18,000 plus to $13,500—nearly $5000 less a year than Scott and Grant received for the same office, when money had more value than it has now." The city fathers of St. Louis, moreover, wanted him to attend the dedication of the Grant statue, to which he had contributed $20. "To get to St. Louis," he complained to Ellen, "will cost me a hundred dollars, of which no account is taken. I have written them that I cannot go, that I am at the end of my rope, will attend my own funeral, but must be excused from others."[38]

Knowing Sherman's indifference to being preserved in art, his friends pushed him to sit for a bust by the sculptor Augustus Saint-Gaudens. At first Sherman told the architect Stanford White that he refused to be pestered by any more "d——d sculptors." Then Whitelaw Reid got the idea of having Rachel persuade him. Sherman finally consented to give Saint-Gaudens the sittings, which, the sculptor promised, would be only twice a week during January 1888. In March the general found himself still sitting.[39]

Sherman's posing led to a newspaper story that Saint-Gaudens's biographer has repeated but which is probably untrue. One day Robert Louis Stevenson, the author, and his wife were visiting Saint-Gaudens, who mentioned he was working on a bust of Sherman. A great admirer of the general, Stevenson asked to see him. The sculptor said he would try to arrange something, but he warned that Sherman was "a little dotty." Told Stevenson wanted to meet him, Sherman purportedly answered: "Robert Louis Stevenson? Was he one of my boys?"

At Sherman's hotel, Stevenson and his wife supposedly found the general lounging on a sofa. Sherman rambled on about the difference between saber cuts, which "make you look done-up without doing you much harm," and bullet wounds, "which went into you, 'zip.'" As he spoke, he leaned forward and dug a finger into Fanny Stevenson.

For two reasons this story seems far-fetched. In letters and speeches Sherman gave little indication of being "a little dotty." He was, moreover, a fan of Stevenson, having read and reread all of his important works, and would have instantly recognized the name.[40]

Another tale that circulated about Sherman was also untrue. The *New York World* reported that one day, while roaming about West Point, Sherman accompanied the officer of the day on an inspection of the cadet quarters. Entering a familiar room, he poked a scabbard up the fireplace, removed a brick, and took out a pipe and some tobacco he had secreted there as a cadet. The only thing wrong with the story was that the North and South Barracks of his day no longer existed, having been demolished in the late 1840s and early 1850s.[41]

In August of 1888, finding it too expensive to board his son at the hotel, Sherman began searching for an apartment. Finding nothing, he looked at houses. Within a short time he saw six "admirably suited" for the family, settling for one at 75 West Seventy-first Street, near Central Park. A four-story brownstone with a finished basement, which Sherman and his secretary, James M. Barrett, used as an office, it was "valued at $36,000—but will cost me much less," Sherman informed Tourtellotte, "as the Builder is hard up." Selling their St. Louis home, Sherman and Ellen put fifty percent down on the new one, assuming a mortgage of five percent on the other half.[42]

Ellen's room was large and sunny, extending the width of the house. It looked south over Seventy-first Street. But by September 24, when the family moved into the home, Ellen could not walk up the steps. She had to be carried to her room in a portable chair and never again left the floor.[43]

Since January 1888 Ellen suffered from what Sherman called "languor and a feeling of suffocation." Coming from a wealthy family, Ellen always had servants and was spared from many of the chores allotted to poorer women. Consequently, as the years rolled by, she put on considerable weight. That February Sherman described her to the svelte Lizzie Cameron as "too fat. . . . Your Aunt Ellen rather likes to be feeble and unused," he scoffed. "Nothing but exercise and work" would help, but these she "will not do."[44]

In the new house Ellen seemed, Sherman told Tourtellotte, "perfectly happy." Sherman's army surgeon and a Philadelphia physician whom Tom Ewing recommended attended her. But in mid-November she grew worse, declining until "she sank without pain into her final sleep—I have seen death in many forms, but hers was the easiest of all. In her last hours she seemed twenty years younger . . . and as such I shall ever remember her—To her the world was a day—Heaven Eternity—and could I, I would not bring her back." Dying on Thanksgiving Day, November 28, Ellen was buried in Calvary Cemetery in St. Louis near her beloved Willy. "I want it understood," Sherman ordered Schofield, "that when I am summoned that my body must repose at the same spot, and that no one be called on for a cent for a monument or other expense."[45]

Adding to the gloom, Sheridan and Moulton also died that year. But at his office in the army building at Houston and Green Streets and at his home, the general busied himself. He wrote numerous magazine articles, answered a huge amount of mail, and welcomed friends like Fred Grant and the actors Lawrence Barrett and Billy Florence. "It seems almost absurd that I should survive all contemporaries," he observed to Tourtellotte, "but so it is, and I see no reason to resort to Suicide when I have children and grand children dependent on me, and when I seem to possess my usual faculties."[46]

To cheer her father, Lizzie Sherman arranged a series of birthday dinners for him. Attending the first, on February 8, 1889, were many of his generals—Howard, Slocum, Dodge, Swayne, Corse—and the brother-in-law whose loyalty to Sherman knew no bounds, Tom Ewing.

In his office at home Sherman arranged on one wall the photos of his favorite subordinates. On the left he placed a picture of McPherson above one of Howard, in the center one of himself over that of Thomas, and on the right Schofield over Slocum. "And thus will leave them," Sherman advised Howard, "when summoned to the 'Unknown.' "[47]

The death of Ellen made Sherman even more conscious of his duty to provide for his unmarried children. Lizzie, who devoted her early life to him, was comfortable, having $2,600 drawing interest in a bank, an additional $5,000 in Pittsburgh, and a house in St. Louis, worth $12,500 and rented for $1,000 a year. After graduating from Yale in 1888, P. Tecumseh Sherman began attending Columbia Law School and working in Secretary Evarts's law office. "In two years he ought to be self maintaining," Sherman confided to Tourtellotte. "Rachel is the only extravagant one. She runs with a rich and extravagant set, and it would require the U. S. Treasury to supply her wants."[48]

Superficially, Tom's relations with his father seemed pleasant. Much to Tom's disappointment, John Sherman failed to get the Republican nomination for president in 1888. Selected instead was Benjamin Harrison, one of Sherman's colonels on the marches of 1864 and 1865. After winning the election, Harrison dispensed political plums to Sherman's friends. "I am delighted to see that Col. Grant has been given a good mission," Tom wrote his father, "and that Mr. Reid goes to Paris. The next thing I expect to hear is that Rachel is spending a few weeks in Paris with her friend Mrs. Reid. Did you succeed in keeping for Gen. Joe Johnston the office that you obtained for him? He is so little of a politician either way that he might well be left without having his head cut off."[49]

But even after a decade Sherman still resented the decision of his eldest son. "Had Tom not bolted ten years ago," he informed Eleanor Poe, "I should

have been spared these ten years of trial." When, on July 7, 1889, Tom was ordained a Jesuit priest in Philadelphia, his father did not attend, taking instead
a trip to San Francisco.[50]

That December, Sherman went to Washington, where several Senators
asked his opinion of a bill to make Schofield, who had succeeded Sheridan as
head of the army, a lieutenant general. "My answer was most emphatic," Sherman told Miles, "that Congress should be ashamed to keep Schofield a Maj
Gen and to pay him as such when he is doing the work of a Lieut General; the
present army being equal to a Corps, the legitimate command of a Lt Genl."[51]

In February 1890, on his seventieth birthday, Sherman invited sixteen close
friends, all his dining room could hold, to celebrate. "The dinner will be purely
private," he promised Schofield. "No speaking other than conversational. No
newspaper reporters visible or invisible—already these pestiferous fellows have
been here to pick up items but have generally left unsatisfied."[52]

— VI —

In January 1891 Sherman's asthma grew worse. He put off all entertaining. On
February 5 he and Rachel attended a wedding, but on February 8, his seventy-
first birthday, he folded down a page of Dickens's *Great Expectations,* which he
was reading for the fourth or fifth time, and took to his bed. The next day
Sherman awakened with a severe case of erysipelas. He soon developed pneu-
monia.

On the ninth Dr. Charles T. Alexander, the army surgeon, was alarmed
enough to ask Sherman's children to notify the other members of the family:
Uncle John, Minnie, Elly, and Tom, who was at a Jesuit seminary on the Isle
of Jersey. Sherman still possessed his senses, for early the next morning he recognized John, Elly, and Thackara when they visited him.[53]

But Minnie, arriving that morning, found her father rambling. Father Taylor, the local priest, came and, Minnie remembered, said "he would give Papa
conditional absolution if we would let him see him. Indeed he would gladly
give him Extreme Unction."

Returning from mass on the morning of the eleventh, Minnie found her father worse. He lay on the bed, his eyes shut, his swollen face painted with io-
dine. He was scarcely recognizable. When he opened his eyes, she asked: "Do
you know me?" He made no response.

A while later Minnie returned to Sherman's room. After a time, Sherman
again opened his eyes and responded to her question: "I know you, Minnie!"
During the afternoon he spoke quite a bit, especially about his four girls, whom
he loved so deeply. He asked if the inscription was on his monument and
pleaded: "Put 'Faithful & honorable; faithful & honorable!' "

That evening Sherman grew much worse. One by one the children went
in to see him. At eleven in the evening Minnie and Lizzie decided it was time
for Father Taylor and asked Dr. Alexander if there was any objection to ad-
ministering the sacraments. "The Dr. said No," Minnie recalled, "nothing will

make any difference now. . . . When Fr. Taylor anointed Papa we all knelt around the bed. The Dr. sat by the fire. Papa was perfectly unconscious. He did not move or open his eyes once. After Fr. Taylor was through he asked the Dr. if 'it would disturb the Gen'l if he said the beads.' He said them and we responded, he went into the front room when he finished."[54]

On the morning of Friday the thirteenth, John Sherman noticed a distasteful article in the *New York Times.* "Your reporter intimates," he answered the paper, "that advantage was taken of my temporary absence to introduce a Catholic Priest into Gen. Sherman's chamber to administer the rite of Extreme Unction to the sick man in the nature of a claim that he was a Catholic." John and his brother were not Catholics, but the general was "too good a Christian and too human a man to deny his children the consolation of their religion." If present, John would have assented to any request by his brother's children, "whether called a prayer or Extreme Unction, and whether uttered by a priest or a preacher or any other good man who believed what he spoke and had an honest faith in his Creed."[55]

The same day, amidst public concern over Sherman's condition, an acquaintance wrote to him. "You have been a good friend to me," the letter read, "& I, like all the rest of this nation, grieve to think that the kindest heart & the most noble spirit that exist to-day are about to be taken away from us. These words will not come to your eye, but I had to say them for the love I bear you & so long have borne you." The letter was signed "Mark Twain."[56]

Although Sherman died at 1:50 P.M. on February 14, the funeral was delayed for five days, enabling Tom to return from England on the *Majestic*. At the family's request Slocum and Howard handled the arrangements and led the procession in New York. The brief funeral service took place at the Sherman home at noon of the nineteenth. Tom and Father Taylor officiated, assisted by Father George Deshon, the Paulist priest who had graduated from West Point in 1843, and Father Neil H. McKennon, a Jesuit. Immediately after it, Tom informed the *Times:* "The service was Catholic." His father, he made himself believe, had been baptized a Catholic, had married in a Catholic church, and had attended a Catholic church until the outbreak of the war. Since then, Sherman had not gone to church, but, Tom insisted, "he has repeatedly told me that if he had any regular religious ideas they were Catholic." A week ago Sherman had received absolution and extreme unction from Father Taylor. "He was unconscious at the time, but that has no important bearing, for the sacraments can properly be administered to any person whose mind can be interpreted as desirous of receiving them."[57]

Clearly Sherman's children had done to the dying man what he never wished to do himself. Despite Ellen's numerous attempts, he had refused to convert to Catholicism. Since 1878, moreover, he had not hidden from his friends and relatives his feelings about the church that, as he saw it, had stolen his son. So bitter was Sherman that he made out a will disinheriting Tom. He later mellowed and destroyed it, never making out another.[58]

From St. Louis in 1886 Sherman described to Howard why he belonged to no religious group:

You know the earnest attachment of my family to the Catholic Church which demands a faith and submission which I cannot give, and for me to ally myself to another church less exacting would create dissension which I hate. Some of my best and most intimate friends here and elsewhere are Protestant clergymen . . . with whom I am constantly brought in contact in works of charity, and I have such abundant Faith in the one God, Maker of Heaven and Earth, who can read the hearts of men, that I will risk the final decree.[59]

In St. Louis, Sherman's funeral was held on the twenty-first at the Catholic church on the corner of Grand Avenue and Pine. Burial took place in Calvary Cemetery. Hayes, Schofield, Howard, and Slocum were there. John Tourtellotte came from Minnesota, the Hoyts from New York, Nelson Miles from the Rockies, and David Boyd from the Kentucky Military Institute. Standing on the steps of Sherman's house after the casket had been brought out, Joe Johnston, one of the pallbearers, stood in the bitter cold with his head uncovered. Warned he would catch cold, he answered: "If I were in his place and he standing here in mine, he would not put on his hat." Johnston caught cold at the funeral and died the next month.[60]

Read by Tom Sherman, the Catholic service startled Sherman's army friends. Asking John Sherman why such rites were given to a non-Catholic, Howard was told "that this was a comfort to his children." Four days after Sherman's burial, a letter to the *Times* decried the statements of Tom Sherman that "would place his father in a wrong position before the world." Signed "A Friend of the General," the letter came from Brooklyn, Slocum's home.[61]

In his autobiography, published in 1902, George S. Boutwell, who while serving as Grant's secretary of the treasury spent many evenings at the Sherman home playing billiards and talking, noted that the general frequently spoke "with hostility and bitterness of the Catholic Church." Referring to the practice of not eating meat on Friday, Sherman once told Boutwell: "I know better than these priests what I want to eat." Boutwell saw "no honor in the attempt to enroll his name among its devotees now that he is dead and cannot speak for himself."[62]

— VII —

After Sherman's death, his children could find no will. To raise money Tom conceived of publishing his father's *Memoirs* in a cheap edition, costing two dollars instead of five. But the edition, which was supposed to contain an introduction by Blaine, never caught on, partly because other houses rushed out hastily written biographies of Sherman. When his frustrated brother accused a partner of Webster & Company, which published the cheap edition, of "sharp practice" and "breach of contract," Tom warned him about such language. "I trust you will never forget the danger in which you stand by reason of the nature which we have both inherited, a nature military, imperious & commanding, therefore *very offensive* to others. . . . A little more diplomacy wont hurt us."[63]

A month after Sherman's death, some of his wealthy friends raised money and arranged with Saint-Gaudens for an equestrian statue of the general. After three years, the allotted time, Saint-Gaudens had gotten nowhere. He had made numerous sketches, none of which satisfied him, and he refused to be pushed by the members of the statue committee, many of whom were old and wished to see the work completed before they died.

Finally, in 1896 or 1897, Saint-Gaudens sent word to P. Tecumseh Sherman that he had finished a model. With General Miles, young Cump went to see it. When they disputed the position of one of the horse's forelegs, Saint-Gaudens got a huge mallet and without blinking an eye demolished the model. Told that Sherman had ridden a thoroughbred, he borrowed the hurdle racer Iroquois and completed a work that satisfied everyone. As the model for Winged Victory, who leads Sherman, the sculptor used Lizzie Cameron.

A controversy then developed over the site of the statue. Saint-Gaudens preferred the esplanade of the Grant monument along Riverside Drive in New York, but General Dodge, a trustee of the Grant Monument Association and a leading member of the Sherman statue committee, vetoed the proposal. Finally, on May 30, 1903, the magnificent work was unveiled in a beautiful grove of trees at the south end of Central Park, close to its present site.[64]

Amidst these pleasant experiences, misfortune seemed to haunt the men of the family. James Sherman had died a drunk, and Uncle Charles had died irrational. Both of Sherman's brothers in Des Moines, Lampson and Hoyt, were plagued by "dizziness and the fear of falling. Sometimes in walking around," Lamp explained, "this feeling comes over me, and I have to grasp a tree, fence or some permanent structure to keep from falling. In a few minutes it leaves me and I can go along."[65]

John Sherman's breakdown was more complete. Appointed Secretary of State in 1897 by President William McKinley, he deteriorated mentally and was replaced. In June 1900 his wife Cecelia died, and several months later he returned to Washington shattered in mind and body. Taking a last glimpse of Mansfield, he was bewildered, not knowing the place and muttering: "Where are they going to take me?" He died on October 22, 1900, at the age of seventy-seven.[66]

John Sherman lived a fruitful life, even if its end was unpleasant. Tom Sherman's remaining years can only be described as tragic. His constant fights with superiors and his feeling of unworthiness led in 1911 to a suicide attempt. Violent, Tom spent a period in a state insane asylum, where Lizzie and Rachel found him in rags and, Rachel wrote, in a physical condition "beyond words to describe." His blood was "chiefly water." While in a mental hospital in Brookline, Massachusetts, he often silently gazed out through the barred windows, an immense sadness in his eyes. Spending much of his remaining life in institutions, Father Sherman died on April 29, 1933.[67]

From their youngest son, Sherman and Ellen would have derived much satisfaction. For two years P. Tecumseh Sherman served on the New York City

Board of Aldermen and from 1905 to 1907 he was commissioner of labor for New York State. "When growing deafness forced him from the political world," recorded his niece, Eleanor Sherman Fitch, "he devoted himself to Workman Compensation Laws—and Casualty Insurance. He worked long hours & untiringly—, & always for the betterment of his fellow man." On December 6, 1941, the day before the Japanese bombed Pearl Harbor, Cump died of a heart attack. He never married.[68]

The four sons of General and Mrs. Sherman, two of whom died at young ages, thus left no children to carry on the name. Looking down from His perch in the sky, God perhaps had grown weary of the family's squabbles over religion.

Sherman: A Brief Assessment

ASSESSING SHERMAN as a general is difficult, for one can make the case for him being a great general and a bad general. As Joseph McCullagh frequently joshed, it is hard to find a battle that Sherman won. Chickasaw, Missionary Ridge, Kennesaw, and Bentonville show no great ability on Sherman's part. Rather, on long campaigns, such as the one that ended with the capture of Atlanta, his organizational skills and his ability to swing armies about stand out. Sherman, moreover, seemed to have a penchant for allowing enemy troops to escape: Johnston escaped from Jackson, Hood and Hardee from Atlanta, and Hardee again from Savannah.

In a memoir now in the Library of Congress, John M. Schofield hinted at Sherman's chief liability as a tactician. Because of his impulsiveness—the characteristic that often led him to dash off letters critical of his subordinates—Sherman, according to Schofield, often mistrusted his own judgment. Who among us, after reading stories of one's insanity in newspapers, would not? Perhaps that is why at places like Peachtree Creek and Ezra Church Sherman rode off or stood by and let his subordinates handle the fighting.

But being a general is not all battles, and it is Sherman's marches that make him unique. Today few people travel over the territory traversed during the Atlanta campaign. But each summer thousands of tourists, thick guidebooks in hand, follow the route of the March to the Sea. The march to Jackson, in the broiling July heat of 1863, and the march through the icy, tangled swamps of lower South Carolina were enormous achievements. If it is difficult to imagine Sherman planning Lee's victory at Chancellorsville, it is equally hard to imagine Lee leading an army through the Salkehatchie swamps in winter.

On race, Sherman also presented a dual picture. In theory, he believed whites to be superior to blacks. But on a personal level he was gracious, friendly, and never superior or haughty. Who can forget the picture presented by the historian of the 104th Illinois of Sherman, on the first day of the great march, "sitting in the passageway between two ends of a cabin, a dozen or two negroes standing around and staring at him with wonder and awe"? Of all generals he was the most approachable and most informal.

The same might be said of Sherman's relations with his wife. From his days in Charleston, Sherman left evidence that he was attracted to lovely women. Throughout his adult life he enjoyed teasing them and flirting with them. But absolutely no evidence exists to show that he carried on with them. Sherman and Ellen quarreled over religion, over rearing their children, and over politics. They frustrated one another. But their letters to each other reveal an unending devotion and closeness. Perhaps their youngest son, writing of the days in St. Louis in the 1880s, best captured the relationship between these two strong-willed people:

> My happiest recollections of our life then are of our family, when my father and mother were both present, without strangers to restrain their intimacy. . . . My father had a keen wit, a fund of reminiscences and much vividness in expression, whereas my mother was a fountain of good humor and knew how to draw my father out and to direct the conversation in most interesting channels. They differed in opinions enough to occasion some lively arguments with sharp repartees. It was clear that my father and mother both superlatively enjoyed their conversations, with freedom from all restraints. Once in a while my father would be too depressed to carry on, in which case my mother would most tactfully avoid irritating discussions. And in later years, with her advancing illness, my mother less and less frequently sat at the table and became more and more a listener; but she never ceased to derive much happiness from listening to free and easy talks by my father.

In this day before women were supposed to possess rights, Sherman showed his regard for Ellen another way. From her father, Ellen inherited a small fortune, largely in land in St. Louis and Kansas. Like all of the Sherman men, the general never tried to control his wife's property. Left to her own devices, Ellen sold almost all of it, a parcel at a time, donating the proceeds to charities and to needy friends and relatives. When she was down to two parcels, Ellen, as young Cump described it, "made my father buy them from her on credit, installments to be payable on demand." To Sherman's displeasure, Ellen then demanded rapid payments. By the time she died, she had no money at all, having given it all away. On each of the parcels he had bought, Sherman built a house. One he gave to Lizzie, the other to Rachel.[1]

There are thus many Shermans. To Georgians and South Carolinians he remains a beast, intent on destroying not soldiers but civilians. Inspired by the slurs in Sherman's *Memoirs*, followers of Thomas, like Boynton, and of Buell, like Fry, attacked Sherman as an egotist. Biographers have also viewed Sherman differently. Lloyd Lewis saw him as "a fighting prophet," John F. Marszalek as a seeker of "order." God and devil, hero and villain, genius and madman, Sherman remains today, as Colonel Lyman put it in 1865, "the concentrated quintessence of Yankeedom," exemplifying the contradictions and strengths of the country that produced him.

Appendix

Patton and Sherman

T HE WORLD WAR TWO GENERAL most commonly compared to Sherman is George S. Patton Jr. In a memorandum, the British military analyst B. H. Liddell Hart, who in the 1920s had written a book on Sherman's campaigns, recalled two discussions he had with Patton just before the Allied invasion of France in 1944. Liddell Hart wrote of the first meeting:

> We had a very good talk, and found ourselves in the closest agreement about tank tactics. But I was rather disconcerted to find him saying he did not think, when the Allied armies got to France, they would be able to repeat the kind of armoured drives the Germans had achieved in 1940. He felt that we should have to go back to 1918 methods. While questioning this, I felt it best to put the contrary arguments in the form of an "indirect approach." He had told me that before the war he had spent a long vacation studying Sherman's campaigns on the ground in Georgia and the Carolinas, with the aid of my book. So I talked of the possibilities of applying "Sherman methods" in modern warfare—moving stripped of impediments to quicken the pace, cutting loose from communications if necessary, and swerving past opposition, instead of getting hung up in trying to overcome it by direct attack. It seemed to me that by the development and exploitation of such Sherman methods, on a greater scale, it would be possible to reach the enemy's rear and unhinge his position—as the Germans had already done in 1940.
>
> I think the indirect argument made some impression. At any rate, when I spent another evening with him in June, just before he went over to Normandy, he was no longer talking about 1918 methods, but on much bolder lines. The way that, after the break-through, he actually carried out his plans, in super-Sherman style, is a matter that all the world knows.[1]

Notes

— 1. Of Raymonds and Streets, Hoyts and Shermans —

1. Genealogy of the Sherman Family, reel 13, cont. 23, William T. Sherman Papers, Manuscript Division, Library of Congress.

2. William T. Sherman to C. Alfred Jones, New York, November 5, 1888, reel 48, cont. 98, ibid.; *Army and Navy Journal* 21 (December 29, 1885): 435; *John Sherman's Recollections of Forty Years in the House, Senate and Cabinet* (Chicago: Werner, 1895), 1:2–5; George F. Hoar, *Autobiography of Seventy Years* (New York: Charles Scribner's Sons, 1906), 1:18–19.

3. John Sherman, "Memoir of Life of Charles R. Sherman & Pedigree of Hoyt Family," February 1847, roll 9, William T. Sherman Family Papers, University of Notre Dame Archives, South Bend, Indiana; Genealogy attached to Jared W. Young to Philemon Tecumseh Sherman, New York, July 2, 1928, box 9, William T. Sherman Papers, Ohio Historical Society, Columbus.

4. Sherman, "Memoir of Life of Charles R. Sherman"; *John Sherman's Recollections*, 1:15, 25.

5. David W. Hoyt, *A Genealogical History of the Hoyt, Haight, and Hight Families* (Providence: Providence Press, 1871), 376; Sherman, "Memoir of Life of Charles R. Sherman."

6. Sherman, "Memoir of Life of Charles R. Sherman."

7. Genealogy attached to Young to P. T. Sherman; Samuel E. Raymond, *Raymond Genealogy* (Seattle: Seattle Genealogical Society, 1970), 60–61.

8. Francis F. Spies, "Inscriptions Copied from Graveyards in Norwalk Township," unpublished manuscript, in Genealogy Room, New York Public Library, 1924, 1:85, 110.

9. Ellen E. Sherman to William Sherman, Lancaster (Ohio), May 16, 1860, roll 4, Sherman Family Papers; Ellen Sherman to William Sherman, n.p., end of 1861, roll 4, ibid.; Ellen Sherman to William Sherman, Lancaster (Ohio), January 8, 1862, roll 4, ibid.; John Sherman to William Sherman, Mansfield (Ohio), October 10, 1869, reel 15, cont. 27, William Sherman Papers, Library of Congress. On John Sherman's mental condition, see *New York Times*, August 11, 1897.

10. Samuel Raymond, *Genealogies of the Raymond Families of New England, 1630–1 to 1886* (New York: J. J. Little, 1886), 6, 12–13; Spies, "Inscriptions Copied from Graveyards in Norwalk Township," 1:85.

11. *John Sherman's Recollections*, 1:12–13; *Memoirs of General William T. Sherman* (New York: Charles L. Webster, 1892), 1:10–11.

12. Sherman, "Memoir of Life of Charles R. Sherman"; *Memoirs of General William T. Sherman*, 1:11.

13. *John Sherman's Recollections*, 1:18; *Memoirs of General William T. Sherman*, 1:11.

14. *John Sherman's Recollections*, 1:20; *The Americanization of Edward Bok* (New York: Charles Scribner's Sons, 1923), 217.

15. *John Sherman's Recollections*, 1:25–26; Spies, "Inscriptions Copied from Graveyards in Norwalk Township," 1:110.

16. *John Sherman's Recollections*, 1:9, 18–20.

17. William J. Reese, "Sketch of the Life of Judge Charles R. Sherman," 6, reel 51, cont. 109, William Sherman Papers, Library of Congress; Lloyd Lewis, *Sherman, Fighting Prophet* (New York: Harcourt, Brace, 1932), 18, 24.

18. *Cincinnati Commercial*, October 27, 1871.

19. *Americanization of Edward Bok*, 216; "Sherman Ancestry," box 9, William Sherman Papers, Ohio Historical Society; Note by Eleanor Sherman Fitch, December 1945, attached to Maria Gillespie Blaine to Ellen Sherman, Brownsville (Pa.), April 13, 1864, roll 1, Sherman Family Papers.

20. Ellen Ewing Brown, "Notes on the Boyhood of Philemon Beecher Ewing and William Tecumseh Sherman," unpaged, roll 14, Sherman Family Papers; Anna McAllister, *Ellen Ewing, Wife of General Sherman* (New York: Benziger, 1936), 5.

21. McAllister, *Ellen Ewing*, 6.

22. *Americanization of Edward Bok*, 216; Brown, "Notes on the Boyhood of Philemon Beecher Ewing and William Tecumseh Sherman."

23. Lloyd Lewis to Thomas Ewing III, Chicago, April 28, 1930, box 154, Thomas Ewing Family Papers, Manuscript Division, Library of Congress; Thomas Ewing to George Ewing, Lancaster (Ohio), April 19, 1827, box 157, ibid.

24. *John Sherman's Recollections*, 1:20, 23.

25. *Memoirs of General William T. Sherman*, 1:13–14; *John Sherman's Recollections*, 1:23.

26. Ellen E. Sherman, "Recollections for My Children," 3, October 23, 1880, box 9, William Sherman Papers, Ohio Historical Society; William Sherman to William Henry Smith, St. Louis, June 26, 1885, reel 47, letterbook in cont. 97, William Sherman Papers, Library of Congress; Lampson P. Sherman to My Dear Niece, Des Moines (Iowa), February 26, 1892, reel 42, cont. 83, William Sherman Papers, Library of Congress.

27. Brown, "Notes on the Boyhood of Philemon Beecher Ewing and William Tecumseh Sherman"; Ellen Sherman, "Recollections for My Children," 1–2; *John Sherman's Recollections*, 1:26.

28. Henry Stoddard to Thomas Ewing, n.p., March 21, 1830; Jacob Parker to Thomas Ewing, Mansfield (Ohio), April 16, 1830; Charles Hoyt to Thomas Ewing, New York, May 22, 1830, all in box 158, Ewing Family Papers.

29. Brown, "Notes on the Boyhood of Philemon Beecher Ewing and William Tecumseh Sherman."

30. William Sherman to Henry S. Turner, n.p., November 15, 1854, box 2, William Sherman Papers, Ohio Historical Society.

31. *John Sherman's Recollections*, 1:30–33.

32. Ibid., 1:33–34; Ellen Sherman, "Recollections for My Children," 3.

33. Ellen Sherman, "Recollections for My Children," 3–4; *Memoirs of General William T. Sherman*, 1:14–15.

34. Ellen Sherman, "Recollections for My Children," 3–4; Thomas Ewing to Lewis Cass, Lancaster (Ohio), August 1, 1835, roll 1, Sherman Family Papers.

35. William Sherman to Lewis Cass, Lancaster (Ohio), April 4, 1836, roll 1, Sherman Family Papers; Ellen Sherman, "Recollections for My Children," 3–4.

36. William Sherman to Maria Ewing Boyle, Washington City, June 2, 1836, roll 1, Sherman Family Papers; *Memoirs of General William T. Sherman*, 1:15–16.

37. Albert E. Church, *Personal Reminiscences of the Military Academy from 1824 to 1831* (West Point, N.Y.: U.S.M.A. Press, 1879), 14, 19–22.

38. Ibid., 9, 24–26, 63.

39. Ibid., 45–46; *Official Register of the Officers and Cadets of the U.S. Military Academy, June 1841* (N.p.: n.p., n.d.), 5.

40. Church, *Personal Reminiscences*, 61–62.

41. William Sherman to Hugh B. Ewing, Fort Moultrie (S.C.), January 25, 1844, box 1, William Sherman Papers, Ohio Historical Society.

42. William Sherman to Thomas Ewing, West Point (N.Y.), September 12, 1836, box 154, Ewing Family Papers.

43. Church, *Personal Reminiscences*, 14, 19; *Cullum Memorial Edition, Register of Cadets and Former Cadets, 1802–1980* (West Point, N.Y.: Association of Graduates, 1980), 231–34; *Army and Navy Journal* 21 (August 4, 1883):15. For the grades and averages of the cadets, see "Register of Merit," unpublished and unpaged volume, United States Military Academy Archives, West Point, New York.

44. *Cullum Register of Cadets*, 233; *Army and Navy Journal* 21 (August 4, 1883):14–15; Bernarr Cresap, *Appomattox Commander: The Story of General E. O. C. Ord* (San Diego: A. S. Barnes, 1981), 1–7.

45. *Army and Navy Journal* 20 (June 16, 1883): 1042; *Cullum Register of Cadets*, 234.

46. *Army and Navy Journal* 21 (August 4, 1883): 15; William T. Sherman, "The Militia," *Journal of the Military Service Institution of the United States* 6 (March 1885): 7–8.

47. Richard O'Connor, *Thomas: Rock of Chickamauga* (New York: Prentice-Hall, 1948), 60.

48. William Sherman to Philemon Ewing, West Point (N.Y.), September 30, 1837, and November 5, 1837, box 1, Philemon B. Ewing Papers, Ohio Historical Society, Columbus.

49. W. McCrory, "Early Life and Personal Reminiscences of General William T. Sherman," *Glimpses of the Nation's Struggle: A Series of Papers Read before the Minnesota Commandery of the Military Order of the Loyal Legion of the United States* (New York: D. D. Merrill, 1893), 3:314–315.

50. *New York Evening Post*, March 10, 1866.

51. "Register of Merit," United States Military Academy Archives.

52. *Memoirs of General William T. Sherman*, I, 17; "Register of Delinquencies," 124, United States Military Academy Archives.

53. McAllister, *Ellen Ewing*, 17–18; Rachel Sherman Thorndike, ed., *The Sherman Letters: Correspondence between General and Senator Sherman from 1837 to 1891* (New York: Charles Scribner's Sons, 1894), 4–5.

54. *Cullum Register of Cadets*, 235–237; *New York Times*, February 22, 1875.

55. William Sherman to Philemon Ewing, West Point (N.Y.), October 13, 1838, box 1, Philemon Ewing Papers.

56. William Sherman to Philemon Ewing, West Point (N.Y.), May 8, 1839, box 1, ibid.; "Register of Merit," United States Military Academy Archives.

57. William Sherman to Philemon Ewing, West Point (N.Y.), December 1, 1839, and January 26, 1840, box 1, Philemon Ewing Papers; "Register of Merit," United States Military Academy Archives.

58. *John Sherman's Recollections*, 1:35–37, 47–50.

59. Thorndike, *Sherman Letters*, 11–12.

60. "Register of Merit," June 1939 and June 1940, United States Military Academy Archives.

61. James M. Merrill, *William Tecumseh Sherman* (Chicago: Rand McNally, 1971), 42.

62. Philemon Ewing to Maria Boyle Ewing, Philadelphia, June 21, 1840, roll 1, Sherman Family Papers.

63. *Memoirs of General William T. Sherman*, 1:17.

64. Richard Delafield to Joseph G. Totten, West Point (N.Y.), September 22, 1840, and September 24, 1840, roll 1, Sherman Family Papers; Totten to Richard Delafield, Washington, D.C., September 26, 1840, roll 1, ibid.

65. William Sherman to Maria Ewing, Fort Columbus (N.Y.), October 2, 1840, roll 1, ibid.

66. Grady McWhiney, *Braxton Bragg and Confederate Defeat* (New York: Columbia University Press, 1969), 31; *Memoirs of General William T. Sherman*, 1:17–19.

___ 2. Beside the Still Waters ___

1. *Memoirs of General William T. Sherman* (New York: Charles L. Webster, 1892), 1:19–20; William T. Sherman to Philemon B. Ewing, Fort Pierce (Fla.), October 24, 1840, box 1, Philemon B. Ewing Papers, Ohio Historical Society, Columbus.

2. Erasmus D. Keyes, *Fifty Years' Observation of Men and Events* (New York: Charles Scribner's Sons, 1884), 163.

3. William Sherman to Philemon Ewing, Fort Pierce (Fla.), October 24, 1840, box 1, Philemon Ewing Papers.

4. John K. Mahon, *History of the Second Seminole War, 1835–1842* (Gainesville, Fla.: University of Florida Press, 1967), 298–99; *Memoirs of General William T. Sherman*, 1:23–26; William Sherman to Philemon Ewing, Fort Pierce (Fla.), July 23, 1841, box 1, Philemon Ewing Papers.

5. William Sherman to John Sherman, Fort Pierce (Fla.), July 14, 1841, reel 1, cont. 1, William T. Sherman Papers, Manuscript Division, Library of Congress; "Diary of Thomas Ewing," *American Historical Review* 18 (October 1912): 97–98, 110–12.

6. William Sherman to Ellen Ewing, Picolata (Fla.), January 12, 1842, roll 2, William T. Sherman Family Papers, University of Notre Dame Archives, South Bend, Indiana.

7. William Sherman to Philemon Ewing, Picolata (Fla.), February 7, 1842, box 3, Philemon Ewing Papers.

8. William Sherman to Philemon Ewing, Fort Moultrie (S.C.), August 4, 1842, box 3, ibid.

9. *San Francisco Argonaut*, April 5, 1879, clipping, reel 51, cont. 109, William Sherman Papers, Library of Congress; Keyes, *Fifty Years' Observation*, 178.

10. William T. Sherman, "Old Shady, With A Moral," *North American Review* 148 (October 1888): 364–365; Clyde N. Wilson, ed., *The Papers of John C. Calhoun* (Columbia, S.C.: University of South Carolina Press, 1987), 17:358.

11. Keyes, *Fifty Years' Observation*, 174. For Sherman's views, see his letters to Philemon Ewing, Fort Moultrie (S.C.), August 4, 1842, and November 5, 1842, box 3, Philemon Ewing Papers.

12. *New York Times*, February 22, 1865, and May 31, 1925; *New York Tribune*, May 20, 1879.

13. William Sherman to Mrs. A. A. Draper, Savannah (Ga.), January 15, 1865, box 1, William T. Sherman Papers, United States Military Academy Library, West Point, New York.

14. William Sherman to Ellen Ewing, Fort Moultrie (S.C.), March 12, 1843, roll 2, Sherman Family Papers.

15. Keyes, *Fifty Years' Observation*, 177.

16. William Sherman to Ellen Ewing, Fort Moultrie (S.C.), November 28, 1842, roll 2, Sherman Family Papers.

17. *Memoirs of General William T. Sherman*, 1:29–30; Anna McAllister, *Ellen Ewing, Wife of General Sherman* (New York: Benziger, 1936), 35–37.

18. William Sherman to Ellen Ewing, Fort Moultrie (S.C.), February 8, 1844, roll 2, Sherman Family Papers.

19. William Sherman to Philemon Ewing, Marietta (Ga.), February 20, 1844, box 3, Philemon Ewing Papers; William Sherman to Hugh B. Ewing, Marietta (Ga.), March 10, 1844, box 1, William T. Sherman Papers, Ohio Historical Society, Columbus.

20. *Memoirs of General William T. Sherman*, 1:31–32.

21. William Sherman to Philemon Ewing, Fort Moultrie (S.C.), June 12, 1844, and October 20, 1844, box 3, Philemon Ewing Papers.

22. William Sherman to Ellen Ewing, Fort Moultrie (S.C.), June 14, 1844, roll 2, Sherman Family Papers; William Sherman to Thomas Ewing, Fort Moultrie (S.C.), June 17, 1844, box 154, Thomas Ewing Family Papers, Manuscript Division, Library of Congress.

23. William Sherman to John Sherman, Fort Moultrie (S.C.), October 24, 1844, reel 1, cont. 1, William Sherman Papers, Library of Congress; *John Sherman's Recollections of Forty Years in the House, Senate and Cabinet* (Chicago: Werner, 1895), 1:92.

24. William Sherman to Hugh Ewing, Marietta (Ga.), March 10, 1844, box 1, William Sherman Papers, Ohio Historical Society.

25. William Sherman to Hugh Ewing, Fort Moultrie (S.C.), October 1, 1844, box 1, ibid.; *Army and Navy Journal* 39 (June 14, 1902): 1029.

26. William Sherman to Thomas Ewing, Fort Moultrie (S.C.), March 13, 1845, box 154, Ewing Family Papers.

27. William T. Sherman, "Personal Recollections of California," 216, reel 49, cont. 103, Sherman Papers, Library of Congress; William Sherman to Ellen Ewing, Fort Moultrie (S.C.), June 9, 1845, roll 2, Sherman Family Papers.

28. William Sherman to Ellen Ewing, Fort Moultrie (S.C.), November 19, 1845, roll 2, Sherman Family Papers.

29. William Sherman to Ellen Ewing, Fort Moultrie (S.C.), January 31, 1846, roll 2, ibid.

30. William Sherman to Ellen Ewing, Fort Moultrie (S.C.), June 9, 1845, and January 31, 1846, roll 2, ibid.

31. *John Sherman's Recollections,* 1:84; William Sherman, "Personal Recollections," 216–218.

32. William Sherman to Ellen Ewing, Pittsburgh, June 30, 1846, roll 2, Sherman Family Papers.

33. William Sherman to Ellen Ewing, On Board *Lexington,* July 12, 1846, roll 2, ibid.

34. *Memoirs of General William T. Sherman* (New York: Da Capo, 1984), 1:12–15; William Sherman to Ellen Ewing, Rio de Janeiro, September 16, 1846, roll 2, Sherman Family Papers. Note the use here, and for the rest of this chapter, of the reprint of the first edition of Sherman's *Memoirs,* which, when published in 1875, covered events in Sherman's life beginning in 1846.

35. M. A. DeWolfe Howe, ed., *Home Letters of General Sherman* (New York: Charles Scribner's Sons, 1909), 63, 68.

36. *Memoirs of General William T. Sherman,* 1:16–18, 23–24; Howe, *Home Letters,* 86.

37. William Sherman to Ellen Ewing, Monterey (Calif.), March 12, 1847, roll 2, Sherman Family Papers.

38. *Memoirs of General William T. Sherman,* 1:24.

39. William Sherman to Richard C. McCormick, New York, February 17, 1890, reel 48, letterbook in cont. 98, William Sherman Papers, Library of Congress.

40. Ibid.; *Memoirs of General William T. Sherman,* 1:25–27.

41. William Sherman to Ellen Ewing, Monterey (Calif.), October 8, 1847, roll 2, Sherman Family Papers.

42. Henry B. Judd to William Sherman, Camp Near Monterrey, Mexico, February 26, 1848, reel 1, cont. 2, William Sherman Papers, Library of Congress.

43. *Memoirs of General William T. Sherman,* 1:32–33; *Army and Navy Journal* 6 (July 10, 1869): 742.

44. *Memoirs of General William T. Sherman,* 1:40.

45. Ibid., 1:46–47. See also Robin Pennock, "Sherman and Old Monterey," *True West* 41 (February 1994): 50–55.

46. William Sherman to John Sherman, Monterey (Calif.), August 24, 1848, reel 1, cont. 2, William Sherman Papers, Library of Congress.

47. *Memoirs of General William T. Sherman,* 1:57–60; William Sherman to Edward O. C. Ord, Camp on American Ford, October 28, 1848, and November 14, 1848, in *The California Gold Fields in 1848: Two Letters from Lt. W. T. Sherman, U.S.A.* (New Haven, Conn.: Beinicke Library, n.d.), passim.

48. John Sherman to William Sherman, Mansfield (Ohio), May 2, 1847, reel 1, cont. 1, William Sherman Papers, Library of Congress.

49. Mary Hoyt Sherman to William Sherman, Mansfield (Ohio), November 12, 1848, roll 1, Sherman Family Papers; *John Sherman's Recollections,* 1:53, 89–90.

50. "Register of Merit," June 1848, United States Military Academy Archives, West Point, New York; Ellen Ewing to William Sherman, Lancaster (Ohio), January 19, 1849, and February 5, 1849, roll 4, Sherman Family Papers.

51. *Memoirs of General William T. Sherman,* 1:62–64; William Sherman to Charles W. Moulton, St. Louis, May 13, 1885, roll 1, Sherman Family Papers.

52. *Memoirs of General William T. Sherman*, 1:66–67, 74–77.

53. Ellen Ewing to William Sherman, Washington, D.C., February 5, 1849, and May 22, 1849, roll 4, Sherman Family Papers.

54. *Memoirs of General William T. Sherman*, 1:81–83; *New York Times*, June 21, 1874.

55. Elizabeth Sherman Reese to John Sherman, Philadelphia, January 15, 1850, reel 2, cont. 4, William Sherman Papers, Library of Congress.

56. William Sherman to John Sherman, Washington, D.C., April 29, 1850, and Lancaster (Ohio), July 1, 1850, reel 2, cont. 4, ibid.

57. Lampson Sherman to William Sherman, Fort Des Moines (Iowa), July 14, 1850, roll 1, Sherman Family Papers; William Sherman to John Sherman, August 12, 1850, reel 2, cont. 4, William Sherman Papers, Library of Congress.

58. William Sherman to James A. Hardie, New York, April 12, 1850, James A. Hardie Papers, Manuscript Division, Library of Congress.

59. Roy F. Nichols, ed., "William Tecumseh Sherman in 1850," *Pennsylvania Magazine of History and Biography* 75 (October 1951):424; Ellen Sherman to William Sherman, Philadelphia, November 22, 1857, roll 4, Sherman Family Papers.

60. *Memoirs of General William T. Sherman*, 1:85–86.

61. Nichols, "William Tecumseh Sherman in 1850," 430–431.

62. William Sherman to Robert C. Winthrop, New York, October 13, 1886, reel 48, letterbook in cont. 98, William Sherman Papers, Library of Congress.

63. William Sherman to Thomas Ewing, Lancaster (Ohio), September 12, 1850, box 154, Ewing Family Papers.

64. William Sherman to Ellen Sherman, St. Louis, September 22, 1850, roll 2, Sherman Family Papers.

65. William Sherman to Ellen Sherman, Jefferson Barracks (Mo.), October 8, 1850, and St. Louis, October 23, 1850, roll 2, ibid.; William Sherman to George Gibson, St. Louis, October 15, 1850, box 1, William T. Sherman Papers, Missouri Historical Society, St. Louis.

66. William Sherman to Hugh Ewing, St. Louis, January 5, 1851, box 1, William Sherman Papers, Ohio Historical Society.

67. William Sherman to Ellen Sherman, St. Louis, January 30, 1851, roll 2, Sherman Family Papers.

68. McAllister, *Ellen Ewing*, 69–70; William Sherman to John Sherman, St. Louis, May 19, 1851, reel 2, cont. 2, William Sherman Papers, Library of Congress.

69. McAllister, *Ellen Ewing*, 71; *Memoirs of General William T. Sherman*, 1:88–89.

70. William Sherman to John Sherman, St. Louis, September 23, 1851, reel 2, cont. 4, William Sherman Papers, Library of Congress.

71. William Sherman to John Sherman, St. Louis, May 19, 1851, and July 16, 1851, reel 2, cont. 4, ibid.

72. William Sherman to John Sherman, St. Louis, June 11, 1851, reel 2, cont. 4, ibid.

73. John Sherman to William Sherman, Mansfield (Ohio), February 29, 1852, reel 2, cont. 4, ibid.

74. William Sherman to John Sherman, St. Louis, September 2, 1851, reel 2, cont. 4, ibid.

75. *John Sherman's Recollections*, 1:25, 94; William Sherman to Ellen Sherman, St. Louis, September 30, 1852, roll 2, Sherman Family Papers.

76. William Sherman to Thomas Ewing Jr., September 17, 1852, box 154, Ewing Family Papers.

77. McAllister, *Ellen Ewing*, 77.

___ 3. "I Regret I Ever Left the Army" ___

1. *Memoirs of General William T. Sherman* (New York: Da Capo, 1984), 1:90–92; William T. Sherman to John Sherman, New Orleans, November 17, 1852, reel 2, cont. 4, William T. Sherman Papers, Manuscript Division, Library of Congress.

2. William Sherman to John Sherman, New Orleans, November 17, 1852, reel 2, cont. 4, William Sherman Papers, Library of Congress; Anna McAllister, *Ellen Ewing, Wife of General Sherman* (New York: Benziger, 1936), 80–81.

3. Henry S. Turner to William Sherman, St. Louis, December 7, 1852, reel 2, cont. 4, William Sherman Papers, Library of Congress.

4. *Memoirs of General William T. Sherman*, 1:92–93; William Sherman to John Sherman, New Orleans, March 4, 1853, reel 2, cont. 4, William Sherman Papers, Library of Congress.

5. William Sherman to John Sherman, New Orleans, March 4, 1853, reel 2, cont. 4, William Sherman Papers, Library of Congress.

6. Dwight L. Clarke, *William Tecumseh Sherman: Gold Rush Banker* (San Francisco: California Historical Society, 1969), 16–17; William Sherman to Ellen Sherman, San Francisco, April 12, 1853, roll 2, William T. Sherman Family Papers, University of Notre Dame Archives, South Bend, Indiana; *Memoirs of General William T. Sherman*, 1:94–100.

7. William Sherman to Ellen Sherman, San Francisco, April 12, 1853, roll 2, Sherman Family Papers.

8. William Sherman to John Sherman, San Francisco, June 3, 1853, reel 3, cont. 5, William Sherman Papers, Library of Congress.

9. William Sherman to Ellen Sherman, Marysville (Calif.), May 11, 1853, roll 2, Sherman Family Papers.

10. William Sherman to Ellen Sherman, San Francisco, July 14, 1853, roll 2, ibid.

11. William Sherman to Ellen Sherman, St. Louis, August 21, 1853, roll 2, ibid.

12. McAllister, *Ellen Ewing*, 85–89.

13. William Sherman to Hugh Ewing, Steamer *Star of the West*, September 29, 1853, box 1, William T. Sherman Papers, Ohio Historical Society, Columbus; McAllister, *Ellen Ewing*, 89–93.

14. *Memoirs of General William T. Sherman*, 1:107; McAllister, *Ellen Ewing*, 94–95, 98.

15. Clarke, *Gold Rush Banker*, 21; McAllister, *Ellen Ewing*, 98.

16. William Sherman to Henry S. Turner, San Francisco, September 29, 1854, box 2, William Sherman Papers, Ohio Historical Society.

17. McAllister, *Ellen Ewing*, 105–106; William Sherman to Philemon B. Ewing, San Francisco, January 31, 1854, and March 30, 1854, roll 9, Sherman Family Papers; William Sherman to James A. Hardie, San Francisco, February 10, 1854, James A. Hardie Papers, Manuscript Division, Library of Congress.

18. William Sherman to Philemon Ewing, San Francisco, January 31, 1854, roll 9, Sherman Family Papers.

19. William Sherman to Philemon Ewing, San Francisco, June 29, 1854, roll 9, ibid.; *Memoirs of General William T. Sherman*, 1:104.

20. William Sherman to Thomas Ewing, Jr., San Francisco, June 15, 1854, box 154, Thomas Ewing Family Papers, Manuscript Division, Library of Congress.

21. William Sherman to Hugh Ewing, San Francisco, July 15, 1854, box 1, William Sherman Papers, Ohio Historical Society; William Sherman to Henry S. Turner, San Francisco, August 15, 1854, box 2, ibid.

22. Clarke, *Gold Rush Banker*, 55–56.

23. *John Sherman's Recollections of Forty Years in the House, Senate and Cabinet* (Chicago: Werner, 1895), 1:103–104; William Sherman to Philemon Ewing, San Francisco, June 15, 1854, roll 9, Sherman Family Papers.

24. William Sherman to Thomas Ewing, San Francisco, December 8, 1854, box 154, Ewing Family Papers; William Sherman to Ethan A. Hitchcock, San Francisco, October 15, 1854, box 2, Ethan A. Hitchcock Papers, Manuscript Division, Library of Congress.

25. William Sherman to Philemon Ewing, San Francisco, October 31, 1854, and December 23, 1854, roll 9, Sherman Family Papers.

26. William Sherman to Henry S. Turner, San Francisco, September 15, 1854, box 2, William Sherman Papers, Ohio Historical Society; McAllister, *Ellen Ewing*, 116.

27. William Sherman to Henry S. Turner, San Francisco, February 25, 1855, and February 28, 1855, box 2, William Sherman Papers, Ohio Historical Society; Clarke, *Gold Rush Banker,* 116, 121–22.

28. William Sherman to Hitchcock, San Francisco, May 14, 1855, box 2, Hitchcock Papers.

29. *Memoirs of General William T. Sherman,* 1:116–17; William Sherman to Turner, San Francisco, March 8, 1855, box 2, William Sherman Papers, Ohio Historical Society.

30. McAllister, *Ellen Ewing,* 121, 127–31; Ellen Sherman to William Sherman, New York, May 13, 1855, roll 4, Sherman Family Papers.

31. Ellen Sherman to William Sherman, Cincinnati, May 23, 1855, roll 4, ibid.

32. Ellen Sherman to William Sherman, Lancaster (Ohio), July 14, 1855, roll 4, ibid.

33. William Sherman to Ellen Sherman, San Francisco, July 14, 1855, roll 2, ibid.

34. John T. Doyle to P. Tecumseh Sherman, Menlo Park (Calif.), November 21, 1891, roll 9, ibid.

35. M. A. DeWolfe Howe, ed., *Home Letters of General Sherman* (New York: Charles Scribner's Sons, 1909), 142.

36. Ellen Sherman to William Sherman, Lancaster (Ohio), July 21, 1855, roll 4, Sherman Family Papers.

37. Ellen Sherman to William Sherman, Lancaster (Ohio), September 15, 1855, roll 4, ibid.

38. John B. Purcell to Ellen Sherman, Cincinnati, November 7, 1855, roll 1, ibid.; Sketch of Thomas Ewing, Jr., box 288, Ewing Family Papers.

39. William Sherman to Ellen Sherman, San Francisco, September 18, 1855, roll 2, Sherman Family Papers; William Sherman to Philemon Ewing, San Francisco, October 5, 1855, roll 9, ibid.

40. William Sherman to Henry S. Turner, San Francisco, December 3, 1855, box 2, William Sherman Papers, Ohio Historical Society; Clarke, *Gold Rush Banker,* 170–179.

41. *John Sherman's Recollections,* 1:115–137.

42. William T. Coleman, "San Francisco Vigilance Committee," *Century* 43 (November 1891): 137, 145; Clarke, *Gold Rush Banker,* 203–204; "Sherman and the San Francisco Vigilantes," *Century* 43 (December 1891): 197.

43. William Sherman to Henry S. Turner, San Francisco, May 18, 1856, and May 20, 1856, box 1, William T. Sherman Papers, Missouri Historical Society, St. Louis; Clarke, *Gold Rush Banker,* 206–217; Coleman, "San Francisco Vigilance Committee," 137.

44. William Sherman to Ethan A. Hitchcock, San Francisco, June 19, 1856, box 2, Hitchcock Papers.

45. John Sherman to William Sherman, Washington, D.C., July 15, 1856, reel 4, cont. 7, William Sherman Papers, Library of Congress.

46. William Sherman to Henry S. Turner, San Francisco, August 3, 1856, reel 4, cont. 7, ibid.

47. William Sherman to John Sherman, San Francisco, August 3, 1856, reel 4, cont. 7, ibid.

48. *John Sherman's Recollections,* I, 139; William Sherman to Henry S. Turner, San Francisco, October 19, 1856, box 2, William Sherman Papers, Ohio Historical Society.

49. McAllister, *Ellen Ewing,* 154–155; William Sherman to Henry S. Turner, San Francisco, October 19, 1856, box 2, William Sherman Papers, Ohio Historical Society.

50. William Sherman to John Sherman, San Francisco, December 4, 1856, reel 4, cont. 7, William Sherman Papers, Library of Congress; William Sherman to Turner, San Francisco, December 18, 1856, box 2, William Sherman Papers, Ohio Historical Society.

51. William Sherman to Henry S. Turner, San Francisco, January 3, 1857, box 2, William Sherman Papers, Ohio Historical Society; Clarke, *Gold Rush Banker,* 273–274.

52. William Sherman to Henry S. Turner, San Francisco, January 18, 1857, box 2, William Sherman Papers, Ohio Historical Society.

53. George H. Thomas to William Sherman, Fort Yuma (N. Mex. Terr.), March 15, 1855, reel 3, cont. 5, William Sherman Papers, Library of Congress; Braxton Bragg to William Sherman, Thibodaux (La.), February 10, 1856, reel 3, cont. 6, ibid.; Clarke, *Gold Rush Banker,* 300.

54. William Sherman to Thomas Ewing, San Francisco, March 22, 1857, box 154, Ewing Family Papers.

55. McAllister, *Ellen Ewing*, 158–159; *Memoirs of General William T. Sherman*, 1:134.

56. William Sherman to John Sherman, New York, August 22, 1857, reel 4, cont. 7, William Sherman Papers, Library of Congress; McAllister, *Ellen Ewing*, 160.

—— 4. A Yankee in Rebeldom ——

1. Dwight L. Clarke, *William Tecumseh Sherman: Gold Rush Banker* (San Francisco: California Historical Society, 1969), 318–319.

2. Address by General W. T. Sherman at Unveiling of the McPherson Statue, Clyde, Ohio, reel 47, letterbook in cont. 95, William T. Sherman Papers, Manuscript Division, Library of Congress; *Army and Navy Journal* 39 (June 14, 1902): 1029.

3. William Sherman to Ellen E. Sherman, New York, July 29, 1857, roll 2, William T. Sherman Family Papers, University of Notre Dame Archives, South Bend, Indiana.

4. Ellen Sherman to William Sherman, Lancaster (Ohio), August 10, 1857, roll 4, ibid.

5. William Sherman to John Sherman, New York, September 4, 1857, reel 5, cont. 8, William Sherman Papers, Library of Congress; William Sherman to Thomas Ewing, St. Louis, November 17, 1857, box 154, Thomas Ewing Family Papers, Manuscript Division, Library of Congress; John Sherman to William Sherman, Mansfield (Ohio), August 29, 1857, reel 4, cont. 7, William Sherman Papers, Library of Congress.

6. William Sherman to Ellen Sherman, New York, September 28, 1857, roll 2, Sherman Family Papers.

7. William Sherman to Henry S. Turner, New York, October 6, 1857, box 2, William T. Sherman Papers, Ohio Historical Society, Columbus; William Sherman to Ellen Sherman, New York, October 6, 1857, roll 2, Sherman Family Papers.

8. William Sherman to Ellen Sherman, St. Louis, October 23, 1857, roll 2, Sherman Family Papers.

9. Ellen Sherman to William Sherman, Lancaster (Ohio), November 30, 1857, roll 4, ibid.

10. Lloyd Lewis, *Captain Sam Grant* (Boston: Little, Brown, 1950), 347; Statement of Colonel Henry C. Hodges, n.d., box 1, William Conant Church Papers, Manuscript Division, Library of Congress.

11. William Sherman to John Sherman, Lancaster (Ohio), December 16, 1857, reel 4, cont. 7, William Sherman Papers, Library of Congress.

12. William Sherman to Henry S. Turner, San Francisco, February 18, 1858, box 2, William Sherman Papers, Ohio Historical Society.

13. William Sherman to Thomas Ewing, San Francisco, March 3, 1858, and April 2, 1858, box 154, Ewing Family Papers.

14. William Sherman to Thomas Ewing, San Francisco, April 15, 1858, box 154, ibid.

15. William Sherman to Philemon Ewing, San Francisco, June 3, 1858, reel 4, cont. 7, William Sherman Papers, Library of Congress.

16. *Memoirs of General William T. Sherman* (New York: Da Capo, 1984), 1:139.

17. Ellen Sherman to William Sherman, Mansfield (Ohio), September 20, 1857, and Lancaster (Ohio), June 15, 1858, roll 4, Sherman Family Papers.

18. William Sherman to John Sherman, Lancaster (Ohio), August 9, 1858, reel 4, cont. 7, William Sherman Papers, Library of Congress.

19. William Sherman to Thomas Ewing, Jr., Lancaster (Ohio), August 9, 1858, reel 4, cont. 7, ibid.

20. William Sherman to Ellen Sherman, Leavenworth (Kans. Terr.), September 18, 1858, roll 2, Sherman Family Papers; Henry L. Patterson to William Sherman, St. Louis, October 10, 1858, reel 4, cont. 7, William Sherman Papers, Library of Congress.

21. William Sherman to Ellen Sherman, Leavenworth (Kans. Terr.), September 14, 1858, roll 2, Sherman Family Papers.

22. William Sherman to Ellen Sherman, Leavenworth (Kans. Terr.), September 17, 1858, September 18, 1858, and October 12, 1858, roll 2, ibid.

23. William Sherman to Ellen Sherman, Leavenworth (Kans. Terr.), October 1, 1858, and October 10, 1858, roll 2, ibid.; *Memoirs of General William T. Sherman*, 1:140.

24. William Sherman to Ellen Sherman, Leavenworth (Kans. Terr.), October 10, 1858, and October 12, 1858, roll 2, Sherman Family Papers.

25. Ellen Sherman to William Sherman, Lancaster (Ohio), October 13, 1858, roll 4, ibid.

26. William Sherman to Ellen Sherman, Leavenworth (Kans. Terr.), October 12, 1858, roll 2, ibid.

27. William Sherman to John Sherman, Leavenworth (Kans. Terr.), October 19, 1858, reel 4, cont. 7, William Sherman Papers, Library of Congress; Lloyd Lewis, *Sherman: Fighting Prophet* (New York: Harcourt, Brace, 1932), 102–103.

28. Anna McAllister, *Ellen Ewing, Wife of General Sherman* (New York: Benziger, 1936), 168.

29. William Sherman to John Sherman, Leavenworth (Kans. Terr.), November 16, 1858, reel 4, cont. 7, William Sherman Papers, Library of Congress.

30. Ibid.; William Sherman to Hugh Ewing, Leavenworth (Kans. Terr.), January 20, 1859, box 1, William Sherman Papers, Ohio Historical Society.

31. William Sherman to John Sherman, Leavenworth (Kans. Terr.), December 8, 1858, reel 4, cont. 7, William Sherman Papers, Library of Congress; Rachel Sherman Thorndike, ed., *The Sherman Letters: Correspondence between General and Senator Sherman from 1837 to 1891* (New York: Charles Scribner's Sons, 1894), 65–66.

32. *Washington National Intelligencer,* January 18, 1859, in reel 4, cont. 8, William Sherman Papers, Library of Congress; William Sherman to John Sherman, Leavenworth (Kans. Terr.), January 6, 1859, reel 4, cont. 7, ibid.; William Sherman to H. C. Nutt, New York, December 24, 1888, reel 47, letterbook in cont. 97, ibid.

33. William Sherman to Hugh Ewing, Leavenworth (Kans. Terr.), January 27, 1859, box 1, William Sherman Papers, Ohio Historical Society.

34. William Sherman to Thomas Ewing, Leavenworth (Kans. Terr.), February 12, 1859, box 154, Ewing Family Papers.

35. William Sherman to Thomas Ewing, Leavenworth (Kans. Terr.), March 4, 1859, March 21, 1859, and March 25, 1859, box 154, ibid.

36. McAllister, *Ellen Ewing,* 170; William Sherman to Ellen Sherman, Indian Creek (Kans. Terr.), April 3, 1859, roll 2, Sherman Family Papers.

37. William Sherman to Ellen Sherman, Indian Creek (Kans. Terr.), April 3, 1859, roll 2, Sherman Family Papers; *Army and Navy Journal* 15 (December 29, 1877): 331.

38. Ellen Sherman to William Sherman, Lancaster (Ohio), April 7, 1859, roll 4, Sherman Family Papers.

39. William Sherman to Ellen Sherman, Indian Creek (Kans. Terr.), April 15, 1859, roll 2, ibid.

40. William Sherman to Thomas Ewing, Leavenworth (Kans. Terr.), May 19, 1859, and May 29, 1859, box 154, Ewing Family Papers.

41. *Memoirs of General William T. Sherman*, 1:142–143.

42. William Sherman to John Sherman, Leavenworth (Kans. Terr.), April 30, 1859, and May 27, 1859, reel 4, cont. 8, William Sherman Papers, Library of Congress.

43. William Sherman to Ellen Sherman, Leavenworth (Kans. Terr.), June 1, 1859, roll 2, Sherman Family Papers.

44. Ellen Sherman to William Sherman, Lancaster (Ohio), June 3, 1859, roll 4, ibid.

45. Ellen Sherman to William Sherman, Lancaster (Ohio), June 6, 1859, roll 4, ibid.

46. Ellen Sherman to William Sherman, Lancaster (Ohio), June 8, 1859, roll 4, ibid.

47. Ellen Sherman to William Sherman, Lancaster (Ohio), June 20, 1859, roll 4, ibid.

48. William Sherman to Hugh Ewing, Leavenworth (Kans. Terr.), July 5, 1859, and July 6, 1859, box 1, William Sherman Papers, Ohio Historical Society; Don Carlos Buell to William Sherman, Washington, D.C., June 17, 1859, reel 4, cont. 8, William Sherman Papers, Library of Congress.

49. William Sherman to Hugh Ewing, Leavenworth (Kans. Terr.), July 22, 1859, box 1, William Sherman Papers, Ohio Historical Society.

50. *New Orleans Picayune,* March 25, 1875.

51. William Sherman to Hugh Ewing, Lancaster (Ohio), August 13, 1859, box 1, William Sherman Papers, Ohio Historical Society.

52. William Sherman to G. Mason Graham, Lancaster (Ohio), September 7, 1859, roll 10, Sherman Family Papers; William T. Sherman, "Reminiscences," 287, reel 49, cont. 103, William Sherman Family Papers, Library of Congress.

53. Ellen Ewing to William Sherman, Lancaster (Ohio), October 5, 1859, roll 4, Sherman Family Papers.

54. Ellen Sherman to William Sherman, Lancaster (Ohio), October 21, 1859, and October 27, 1859, roll 4, ibid.

55. William Sherman to Henry S. Turner, St. Louis, October 26, 1859, box 1, William Sherman Papers, Ohio Historical Society; William Sherman to Thomas Ewing, St. Louis, October 26, 1859, box 154, Ewing Family Papers.

56. William Sherman to Ellen Sherman, Steamer *L. M. Kennett,* October 29, 1859, roll 2, Sherman Family Papers.

57. William Sherman to Ellen Sherman, Seminary of Learning, November 12, 1859, roll 2, ibid.; Ellen Sherman to William Sherman, Lancaster (Ohio), November 25, 1859, roll 4, ibid.

58. Walter L. Fleming, ed., *General W. T. Sherman as College President* (Cleveland: Arthur H. Clark, 1912), 52–53.

59. *Memoirs of General William T. Sherman,* 1:145; William Sherman to Ellen Sherman, Seminary of Learning, November 25, 1859, roll 2, Sherman Family Papers.

60. John Sherman to William Sherman, Mansfield (Ohio), November 18, 1859, reel 4, cont. 8, William Sherman Papers, Library of Congress.

61. Allan Nevins, *The Emergence of Lincoln* (New York: Charles Scribner's Sons, 1950), 1:116–123; *John Sherman's Recollections of Forty Years in the House, Senate and Cabinet* (Chicago: Werner, 1895), 1:178; William Sherman to Ellen Sherman, Seminary of Learning, December 18, 1859, roll 2, Sherman Family Papers.

62. *Memoirs of General William T. Sherman,* 1:148–150.

63. William Sherman to Thomas Ewing, Seminary of Learning, November 27, 1859, box 154, Ewing Family Papers.

64. William Sherman to Ellen Sherman, Seminary of Learning, December 23, 1859, roll 2, Sherman Family Papers.

65. William Sherman to G. Mason Graham, New Orleans, December 2, 1859, December 12, 1859, and December 25, 1859, roll 10, ibid.; Fleming, *Sherman as College President,* 74–75, 91–93.

66. Thomas Ewing to William Sherman, Lancaster (Ohio), December 23, 1859, reel 4, cont. 8, William Sherman Papers, Library of Congress.

67. William Sherman to Ellen Sherman, Seminary of Learning, December 16, 1859, roll 2, Sherman Family Papers.

68. Ellen Sherman to William Sherman, Lancaster (Ohio), December 20, 1859, and December 26, 1859, roll 4, ibid.

69. William Sherman to Ellen Sherman, Seminary of Learning, December 28, 1859, and January 4, 1860, roll 2, ibid.

70. *Army and Navy Journal* 47 (December 25, 1909): 466.

71. William Sherman to Thomas Ewing, Seminary of Learning, January 8, 1860, box 154, Ewing Family Papers.

72. William Sherman to Ellen Sherman, Seminary of Learning, January 27, 1860, roll 2, Sherman Family Papers.

73. Fleming, *Sherman as College President,* 137–142; William Sherman to Ellen Sherman, Seminary of Learning, February 10, 1860, roll 2, Sherman Family Papers; *Official Register, Louisiana State Seminary of Learning* (Alexandria: Louisiana Democrat, 1860), 4–5.

74. G. Mason Graham to Thomas O. Moore, Alexandria (La.), February 9, 1860, and February 11, 1860, reel 4, cont. 8, William Sherman Papers, Library of Congress.

75. William Sherman to Thomas Ewing, Seminary of Learning, February 12, 1860, box 154, Ewing Family Papers.

76. William Sherman to John Sherman, Seminary of Learning, February 12, 1860, reel 4, cont. 8, William Sherman Papers, Library of Congress.

77. William Sherman to Ellen Sherman, Baton Rouge (La.), February 16, 1860, and February 17, 1860, roll 2, Sherman Family Papers.

78. Telegram, Ellen Sherman to William Sherman, Lancaster (Ohio), February 21, 1860, roll 4, ibid.; William Sherman to Ellen Sherman, New Orleans, February 21, 1860, roll 2, ibid.

79. Fleming, *Sherman as College President*, 190–193; William Sherman to John Sherman, Lancaster (Ohio), March 12, 1860, reel 4, cont. 8, William Sherman Papers, Library of Congress.

80. William Sherman to Hugh Ewing, Seminary of Learning, April 15, 1860, box 1, William Sherman Papers, Ohio Historical Society.

—— 5. The Insanity of the South—and of Uncle Charles ——

1. Walter L. Fleming, ed., *General W. T. Sherman as College President* (Cleveland: Arthur H. Clark, 1912), 193, 201; William T. Sherman to Ellen Sherman, Seminary of Learning, April 15, 1860, and May 8, 1860, roll 2, William T. Sherman Family Papers, University of Notre Dame Archives, South Bend, Indiana.

2. William Sherman to John Sherman, Seminary of Learning, May 8, 1860, reel 4, cont. 8, William T. Sherman Papers, Manuscript Division, Library of Congress.

3. Ellen Sherman to William Sherman, Lancaster (Ohio), May 16, 1860, and May 31, 1860, roll 4, Sherman Family Papers; David W. Hoyt, *A Genealogical History of the Hoyt, Haight, and Hight Families* (Providence: Providence Press, 1871), 509.

4. Ellen Sherman to William Sherman, Lancaster (Ohio), June 5, 14, 17, and 23, 1860, roll 2, Sherman Family Papers.

5. William Sherman to Thomas Ewing Jr., Seminary of Learning, June 21, 1860, box 154, Thomas Ewing Family Papers, Manuscript Division, Library of Congress.

6. Ellen Ewing to Thomas Ewing, Lancaster (Ohio), June 20, 1860, roll 2, Sherman Family Papers.

7. William Sherman to Ellen Sherman, Seminary of Learning, June 28, 1860, roll 2, ibid.

8. Ellen Sherman to William Sherman, Lancaster (Ohio), July 3, 1860, and July 10, 1860, roll 4, ibid.; Emerson David Fite, *The Presidential Campaign of 1860* (New York: Macmillan, 1911), 123, 131.

9. Ellen Sherman to William Sherman, Lancaster (Ohio), July 17, 1860, roll 4, Sherman Family Papers.

10. Fleming, *Sherman as College President*, 255–256, 258–259.

11. *Memoirs of General William T. Sherman* (New York: Da Capo, 1984), 1:150; Fleming, *Sherman as College President*, 260.

12. Walter Fleming, "General William T. Sherman as a History Teacher," *Educational Review* 40 (October 1910): 235–238; *Army and Navy Journal* 49 (January 13, 1912): 594.

13. Fleming, *Sherman as College President*, 280–281, 289.

14. William Sherman to John Sherman, Lancaster (Ohio), October 3, 1860, reel 5, cont. 8, William Sherman Papers, Library of Congress.

15. Ellen Sherman to William Sherman, Lancaster (Ohio), October 18, 1860, roll 4, Sherman Family Papers; William Sherman to Thomas Ewing, Seminary of Learning, November 14, 1860, box 154, Ewing Family Papers.

16. *Memoirs of General William T. Sherman*, 1:152–153; Fleming, "Sherman as a History Teacher," 235–236.

17. William Sherman to Ellen Sherman, Seminary of Learning, November 29, 1860, roll 2, Sherman Family Papers.

18. William Sherman to John Sherman, Seminary of Learning, December 1, 1860, reel 5, cont. 8, William Sherman Papers, Library of Congress.

19. Ellen Sherman to William Sherman, Lancaster (Ohio), December 5, 1860, roll 4, Sherman Family Papers.

20. William Sherman to Ellen Sherman, Seminary of Learning, December 16, 1860, roll 2, ibid.

21. David F. Boyd to Philemon Tecumseh Sherman, Farmdale (Ky.), February 15, 1891, and December 7, 1891, roll 9, ibid.

22. William Sherman to John Sherman, Seminary of Learning, December 18, 1860, reel 5, cont. 8, William Sherman Papers, Library of Congress.

23. William Sherman to Hugh Ewing, Seminary of Learning, December 18, 1860, box 1, William T. Sherman Papers, Ohio Historical Society, Columbus; William Sherman to Ellen Sherman, Seminary of Learning, December 23, 1860, roll 2, Sherman Family Papers; Fleming, *Sherman as College President*, 316.

24. William Sherman to Ellen Sherman, Seminary of Learning, January 5, 1861, roll 2, Sherman Family Papers.

25. William Sherman to Ellen Sherman, Seminary of Learning, January 8, 1861, roll 2, ibid.

26. *Memoirs of General William T. Sherman*, 1:154–155; William Sherman to John Sherman, Seminary of Learning, January 16, 1861, reel 5, cont. 8, William Sherman Papers, Library of Congress.

27. Ellen Sherman to William Sherman, Lancaster (Ohio), January 16, 1861, roll 4, Sherman Family Papers.

28. William Sherman to Ellen Sherman, Seminary of Learning, January 20, 1861, roll 2, Sherman Family Papers; *Memoirs of General William T. Sherman*, 1:155.

29. Ellen Sherman to William Sherman, Lancaster (Ohio), January 29, 1861, and February 6, 1861, roll 4, Sherman Family Papers.

30. William Sherman to Ellen Sherman, Seminary of Learning, February 16, 1861, roll 2, ibid.

31. *Memoirs of General William T. Sherman*, 1:92, 163.

32. Pierre G. T. Beauregard to G. Mason Graham, New Orleans, January 14, 1866, in Joseph Rubinfine Catalog, 1991, West Palm Beach, Florida.

33. *Washington Sunday Herald*, May 19, 1889; Grady McWhiney, *Braxton Bragg and Confederate Defeat* (New York: Columbia University Press, 1969), 151–152.

34. William Sherman to Ellen Sherman, On Boat from Columbus, Ky., to Cairo, Ill., February 25, 1861, roll 2, Sherman Family Papers; David F. Boyd to Philemon Tecumseh Sherman, Farmdale (Ky.), October 12, 1891, roll 9, ibid. See also Germain M. Reed, *David French Boyd, Founder of Louisiana State University* (Baton Rouge and London: Louisiana State University Press, 1977), 26–30.

— 6. Hamlet —

1. William T. Sherman to John Sherman, Lancaster (Ohio), March 9, 1861, reel 5, cont. 9, William T. Sherman Papers, Manuscript Division, Library of Congress; William T. Sherman diary, March 2, 1861, roll 12, William T. Sherman Family Papers, University of Notre Dame Archives, South Bend, Indiana.

2. *Memoirs of General William T. Sherman* (New York: Da Capo, 1984), 1:167–168; *John Sherman's Recollections of Forty Years in the House, Senate and Cabinet* (Chicago, Werner, 1895), 1:241–242; William Sherman diary, March 6, 1861, roll 12, Sherman Family Papers.

3. Charles Ewing to William Sherman, St. Louis, March 13, 1861, roll 1, Sherman Family Papers; William Sherman to John Sherman, Lancaster (Ohio), March 9, 1861, reel 5, cont. 9, William Sherman Papers, Library of Congress.

4. William Sherman to John Sherman, Cincinnati, March 22, 1861, reel 5, cont. 9, William Sherman Papers, Library of Congress.

5. John Sherman to William Sherman, Mansfield (Ohio), April 3, 1861, ibid.

6. Anna McAllister, *Ellen Ewing, Wife of General Sherman* (New York: Benziger, 1936), 180–181; William Sherman to Montgomery Blair, St. Louis, April 8, 1861, reel 5, cont. 9, William Sherman Papers, Library of Congress.

7. William Sherman to John Sherman, St. Louis, April 8, 1861, reel 5, cont. 9, William Sherman Papers.

8. McAllister, *Ellen Ewing*, 181–182; Ellen E. Sherman to Philemon B. Ewing, St. Louis, April 15, 1861, roll 9, Sherman Family Papers.

9. John Sherman to William Sherman, Washington, D.C., April 14, 1861, reel 5, cont. 9, William Sherman Papers, Library of Congress.

10. *Memoirs of General William T. Sherman*, 1:171.

11. William Sherman to John Sherman, St. Louis, April 22, 1861, reel 5, cont. 9, William Sherman Papers, Library of Congress.

12. Ibid.; William Sherman to Thomas Ewing Jr., St. Louis, April 26, 1861, box 154, Thomas Ewing Family Papers, Manuscript Division, Library of Congress.

13. Tom Ewing to William Sherman, April 24, 1861, reel 5, cont. 9, William Sherman Papers, Library of Congress.

14. William Sherman to Tom Ewing, St. Louis, April 26, 1861, box 154, Ewing Family Papers.

15. *Memoirs of General William T. Sherman*, 1:169–170; James Peckham, *Gen. Nathaniel Lyon and Missouri in 1861: A Monograph of the Great Rebellion* (New York: American News Company, 1866), 29–31.

16. Tom Ewing to William Sherman, Washington, D.C., May 5, 1861, reel 5, cont. 9, William Sherman Papers, Library of Congress; William Sherman to Simon Cameron, St. Louis, May 8, 1861, reel 5, cont. 9, ibid.

17. Tom Ewing to William Sherman, Washington, D.C., May 8, 1861, reel 5, cont. 9, ibid.; William Sherman to Tom Ewing, St. Louis, May 23, 1861, box 154, Ewing Family Papers.

18. William Sherman to Tom Ewing, St. Louis, May 11, 1861, box 154, Ewing Family Papers; McAllister, *Ellen Ewing*, 186; *Memoirs of General William T. Sherman*, 1:172–174.

19. William Ernest Smith, *The Francis Preston Blair Family in Politics* (New York: Macmillan, 1933), 2:390; William Sherman to Tom Ewing, St. Louis, May 23, 1861, box 154, Ewing Family Papers.

20. Tom Ewing to William Sherman, Washington, D.C., May 17, 1861, roll 1, Sherman Family Papers.

21. William Sherman to Thomas Ewing, St. Louis, May 27, 1861, box 154, Ewing Family Papers.

22. Schuyler Hamilton to William Sherman, Washington, D.C., May 31, 1861, reel 5, cont. 9, William Sherman Papers, Library of Congress; Charles T. Sherman and Tom Ewing to William Sherman, n.p., June 5, 1861, reel 5, cont. 9, ibid.; William Sherman diary, June 7, 1861, roll 12, Sherman Family Papers.

23. William Sherman to Tom Ewing, St. Louis, June 3, 1861, box 154, Ewing Family Papers; William Sherman to Ellen E. Sherman, Pittsburgh, June 8, 1861, roll 2, Sherman Family Papers.

24. William Sherman to John Sherman, Pittsburgh, June 8, 1861, reel 5, cont. 9, William Sherman Papers, Library of Congress; William Sherman to Ellen Sherman, Pittsburgh, June 8, 1861, roll 2, Sherman Family Papers.

25. William Sherman to Ellen Sherman, Washington, D.C., June 12, 1861, roll 2, Sherman Family Papers.

26. *Memoirs of General William T. Sherman*, 1:175–178; William Sherman to Ellen Sherman, Washington, D.C., June 12, 1861, and June 17, 1861, roll 2, Sherman Family Papers.

27. *Independent* 51 (June 15, 1899): 1611.

28. *Army and Navy Journal* 39 (January 4, 1902): 715; *John Sherman's Recollections*, 1:250; *Memoirs of General William T. Sherman*, 1:177–178.

29. *Memoirs of General William T. Sherman*, 1:178.

30. William Sherman to Ellen Sherman, Washington, D.C., June 23, 1861, roll 2, Sherman Family Papers; *Memoirs of General William T. Sherman*, 1:178–179.

31. *Memoirs of General William T. Sherman*, 1:179.

32. See the following letters from William Sherman to Ellen Sherman, roll 2, Sherman Family Papers: Washington, D.C., June 23, 1861; Fort Corcoran (Va.), July 6, 1861; Opposite Georgetown, July 15, 1861.

33. Lloyd Lewis, *Sherman: Fighting Prophet* (New York: Harcourt, Brace, 1932), 168; Thomas S. Allen, "The Second Wisconsin at the First Battle of Bull Run," *War Papers, Commandery of the State of Wisconsin, Military Order of the Loyal Legion of the United States* (Milwaukee: Burdick, Armitage & Allen, 1892), 1:382.

34. William C. Davis, *Battle at Bull Run: A History of the First Major Campaign of the Civil War* (Garden City, N.Y.: Doubleday, 1977), 252; William Todd, *The Seventy-ninth Highlanders New York Volunteers in the War of Rebellion, 1861–1865* (Albany, N.Y.: Brandow, Barton, 1886), 16.

35. William Sherman to Thomas Ewing, Louisville, September 15, 1861, box 154, Ewing Family Papers; *Memoirs of General William T. Sherman*, 1:180; H. B. Jackson, "From Washington to Bull Run and Back Again," *War Papers, Commandery of the State of Wisconsin, Military Order of the Loyal Legion of the United States* (Milwaukee: Burdick & Allen, 1914), 4:234.

36. Davis, *Bull Run*, 74–75.

37. Ibid., 76–77; William Sherman to Ellen Sherman, Opposite Georgetown, July 16, 1861, Sherman Family Papers.

38. Davis, *Bull Run*, 96–97; Allen, "Second Wisconsin at the First Battle of Bull Run," 379–381; Todd, *Seventy-ninth Highlanders*, 20–21.

39. William Sherman to Ellen Sherman, Camp 1 Mile West of Centreville (Va.), July 19, 1861, in M. A. DeWolfe Howe, ed., *Home Letters of General Sherman* (New York: Charles Scribner's Sons, 1909), 201–202.

40. Allen, "Second Wisconsin at the First Battle of Bull Run," 382.

41. *Memoirs of General William T. Sherman*, 1:181; Davis, *Bull Run*, 122–123; Allen, "Second Wisconsin at the First Battle of Bull Run," 383–384.

42. Davis, *Bull Run*, 158–160; *Army and Navy Journal* 33 (August 22, 1896): 914.

43. *Memoirs of General William T. Sherman*, 1:186; William Sherman to Ellen Sherman, Fort Corcoran (Va.), July 28, 1861, roll 2, Sherman Family Papers.

44. Todd, *Seventy-ninth Highlanders*, 33; William Sherman to Ellen Sherman, Fort Corcoran (Va.), July 28, 1861, roll 2, Sherman Family Papers.

45. *The War of the Rebellion: A Compilation of the Official Records of the Union and Confederate Armies* (Washington, D.C.: Government Printing Office, 1880–1901), ser. 1, vol. 2, 372 (hereafter cited as *O.R.*); *Memoirs of General William T. Sherman*, 1:183, 186; William Sherman to Ellen Sherman, Fort Corcoran (Va.), July 28, 1861, roll 2, Sherman Family Papers; Todd, *Seventy-ninth Highlanders*, 44. "The Rebels at 2PM were beaten & took refuge in a forest," Sherman later commented, "and had we simply moved beyond the range of their rifles towards Manassas Depot they would have been defeated." See William Sherman to John W. Draper, St. Louis, July 19, 1867, cont. 6, John W. Draper Papers, Manuscript Division, Library of Congress.

46. Davis, *Bull Run*, 217; *New York Times*, July 22, 1861.

47. *O.R.*, ser. 1, vol. 2, 369–371; Davis, *Bull Run*, 217–220; Allen, "Second Wisconsin at the First Battle of Bull Run," 389–390.

48. *Memoirs of General William T. Sherman*, 1:186; William Sherman to Ellen Sherman, Fort Corcoran (Va.), July 28, 1861, roll 2, Sherman Family Papers; *O.R.*, ser. 1, vol. 2, 405–407; Allen, "Second Wisconsin at the First Battle of Bull Run," 387.

49. Jackson, "From Washington to Bull Run and Back Again," 243–245.

50. Lewis, *Sherman*, 178; Todd, *Seventy-ninth Highlanders*, 43–44.

51. William Sherman to Ellen Sherman, Fort Corcoran (Va.), July 24, 1861, and July 28, 1861, roll 2, Sherman Family Papers.

52. Todd, *Seventy-ninth Highlanders*, 52–53.

53. *Memoirs of General William T. Sherman*, 1:188; William Sherman to Thomas Ewing, Louisville, September 15, 1861, box 154, Ewing Family Papers.

54. Todd, *Seventy-ninth Highlanders*, 53–54.

55. William Sherman to Ellen Sherman, Fort Corcoran (Va.), August 15, 1861, roll 2, Sherman Family Papers.

56. Newton Martin Curtis, *From Bull Run to Chancellorsville: The Story of the Sixteenth New York Infantry* (New York: G. P. Putnam, 1906), 44–45; William Sherman to Ellen Sherman, Washington, D.C., August 6, 1861, roll 2, Sherman Family Papers.

57. William Sherman to Ellen Sherman, Fort Corcoran (Va.), August 15, 1861, and Washington, D.C., August 17, 1861, roll 2, Sherman Family Papers.

58. William Sherman to Ellen Sherman, Washington, D.C., August 17, 1861, and Fort Corcoran (Va.), August 19, 1861, roll 2, ibid.

59. *Memoirs of General William T. Sherman*, 1:192–193.

60. Henry Coppée, *General Thomas* (New York: D. Appleton, 1893), 319–320.

61. William Sherman to Ellen Sherman, Louisville, September 18, 1861, roll 2, Sherman Family Papers.

62. See *Army and Navy Journal* 33 (August 22, 1896): 914.

63. William Sherman to John Sherman, Muldraugh's Hill (Ky.), October 5, 1861, in Howe, *Home Letters*, 131–132; Samuel M. Bowman and R. B. Irwin, *Sherman and His Campaigns: A Military Biography* (New York: Charles B. Richardson, 1865), 37.

64. *Memoirs of General William T. Sherman*, 1:197–198; *Cincinnati Commercial*, September 23, 1861.

65. *Memoirs of General William T. Sherman*, 1:198–199.

66. *Cincinnati Commercial*, September 24, 1861; Richard W. Johnson, *A Soldier's Reminiscences in Peace and War* (Philadelphia: J. B. Lippincott, 1886), 266–269.

67. *Cincinnati Commercial*, September 26, 1861; *Independent* 51 (June 15, 1899): 1611–1612.

68. *O.R.*, ser. 1, vol. 4, 278–279; Johnson, *A Soldier's Reminiscences*, 269.

69. Johnson, *A Soldier's Reminiscences*, 271.

70. Ellen Sherman to William Sherman, Lancaster (Ohio), September 29, 1861, and October 4, 1861, roll 4, Sherman Family Papers; William Sherman to Ellen Sherman, Muldraugh's Hill (Ky.), October 6, 1861, roll 2, ibid.

71. *O.R.*, ser. 1, vol. 4, 296–297; *Memoirs of General William T. Sherman*, 1:199; *Cincinnati Commercial*, October 9, 1861.

72. *O.R.*, ser. 1, vol. 4, 306–307.

73. William Sherman to Ellen Sherman, Louisville, October 12, 1861, roll 2, Sherman Family Papers.

74. *Memoirs of Henry Villard, Journalist and Financier, 1835–1900* (Boston: Houghton Mifflin, 1904), 1:209–211.

75. *Memoirs of General William T. Sherman*, 1:200–203; *Army and Navy Journal* 29 (November 21, 1891): 222, and 39 (March 22, 1902): 715; William T. Sherman diary, October 17, 1861, roll 2, Sherman Family Papers.

76. William Sherman to Ellen Sherman, Louisville, October 20, 1861, roll 2, Sherman Family Papers.

77. William Sherman to Ellen Sherman, Louisville, November 1, 1861, ibid. See also Judson W. Bishop, *The Story of A Regiment: Being A Narrative of the Service of the Second Regiment, Minnesota Veteran Volunteer Infantry* (St. Paul, Minn.: n.p., 1890), 28.

78. *Army and Navy Journal* 29 (November 21, 1891): 222, and 53 (July 1, 1916): 1420; Allen, "The Second Wisconsin at the First Battle of Bull Run," 392.

79. *Cincinnati Commercial*, October 25, 1861; J. Cutler Andrews, *The North Reports the Civil War* (Pittsburgh: University of Pittsburgh Press, 1955), 117; Louis M. Starr, *Bohemian Brigade: Civil War Newsmen in Action* (New York: Alfred A. Knopf, 1954), 174.

80. *Memoirs of Henry Villard*, 1:211–213; John F. Marszalek, *Sherman's Other War: The General and the Civil War Press* (Memphis, Tenn.: Memphis State University Press, 1981), 58–60.

81. George B. McClellan to William Sherman, Washington, D.C., November 8, 1861, roll 1, Sherman Family Papers.

82. *O.R.*, ser. 1, vol. 4, 350–351, 353–354; William Sherman to Robert Anderson, Louisville, November 3, 1861, vol. 14, Robert Anderson Papers, Manuscript Division, Library of Congress.

83. A. K. McClure, *Abraham Lincoln and Men of War Times* (Philadelphia: Times Publishing Co., 1892), 212–213.

84. Frederick E. Prime to Thomas Ewing, Louisville, November 8, 1861, roll 1, Sherman Family Papers.

85. Ellen Sherman to John Sherman, Louisville, November 10, 1861, reel 5, cont. 9, William Sherman Papers, Library of Congress; Ellen Ewing diary, November 8–11, 1861, roll 13, Sherman Family Papers.

86. Ellen Sherman diary, November 9, 10, 11, and 15, 1861, roll 13, Sherman Family Papers.

87. John Sherman to William Sherman, Camp Buckingham (Ohio), November 17, 1861, roll 9, ibid.

88. William Sherman to John Sherman, Louisville, November 21, 1861, reel 5, cont. 9, William Sherman Papers, Library of Congress.

89. *O.R.*, ser. 1, vol. 8, 391–392.

90. *Memoirs of General William T. Sherman*, 1:215; Ellen Sherman to Charles Ewing, St. Louis, December 2, 1861, box 6, Charles Ewing Papers, Manuscript Division, Library of Congress.

91. *New York Times*, December 9, 1861; *Cincinnati Commercial*, December 11, 1861.

92. Ellen Sherman to John Sherman, Lancaster (Ohio), December 12, 1861, reel 5, cont. 10, William Sherman Papers, Library of Congress; *Cincinnati Commercial*, December 13, 1861.

93. John Sherman to Ellen Sherman, Washington, D.C., December 14, 1861, roll 9, Sherman Family Papers.

94. Ellen Sherman to John Sherman, Lancaster (Ohio), December 12, 1861, December 16, 1861, and December 17, 1861, reel 5, cont. 10, William Sherman Papers, Library of Congress.

95. William Sherman to Ellen Sherman, St. Louis, December 17, 1861, roll 2, Sherman Family Papers; Ellen Sherman to William Sherman, Lancaster (Ohio), December 19, 1861, roll 4, ibid.

96. *O.R.*, ser. 1, vol. 8, 459; Ellen Sherman to William Sherman, Lancaster (Ohio), December 20, 1861, roll 4, Sherman Family Papers.

97. Quoted in Ellen Sherman to William Sherman, Lancaster (Ohio), December 22, 1861, roll 4, Sherman Family Papers.

98. Ibid.

99. Ellen Sherman to William Sherman, n.p., end of 1861, roll 4, ibid.

100. William Sherman to Ellen Sherman, Benton Barracks (Mo.), January 1, 1862, roll 3, ibid.

—— 7. The Same Game as at Bull Run ——

1. William T. Sherman to John Sherman, Benton Barracks (Mo.), January 4, 1862, reel 5, cont. 10, William T. Sherman Papers, Manuscript Division, Library of Congress.

2. Thomas Ewing Jr. to Ellen E. Sherman, Cincinnati, March 18, 1862, roll 1, William T. Sherman Family Papers, University of Notre Dame Archives, South Bend, Indiana; William Sherman to John Sherman, Benton Barracks (Mo.), January 8, 1862, reel 5, cont. 10, William Sherman Papers, Library of Congress. See also *O.R.*, ser. 1, vol. 4, 356–360.

3. Ellen Sherman to William Sherman, Lancaster (Ohio), January 8, 1862, roll 4, Sherman Family Papers.

4. Ellen Sherman to Abraham Lincoln, Lancaster (Ohio), January 10, 1862, copy, reel 5, cont. 10, William Sherman Papers, Library of Congress.

5. Ellen Sherman to William Sherman, Lancaster (Ohio), January 11, 1862, roll 4, Sherman Family Papers.

6. Ellen Sherman to William Sherman, Lancaster (Ohio), January 13, 1862, and February 6, 1862, roll 4, ibid.

7. Ellen Sherman to William Sherman, Lancaster (Ohio), January 15, 1862, roll 4, ibid.

8. Ellen Sherman to William Sherman, Washington, D.C., January 29, 1862, roll 4, ibid.

9. *The Story of the Fifty-fifth Regiment Illinois Volunteer Infantry in the Civil War, 1861–65* (Clinton, Mass.: W. J. Coulter, 1887), 18–39, 40; James Howard Bridge, *Millionaires and Grub Street* (Freeport, N.Y.: Books for Libraries Press, 1968), 132–139.

10. *Memoirs of General William T. Sherman* (New York: Da Capo, 1984, I, 1:218–222; *O.R.,* ser. 1, vol. 8, 628.

11. *Personal Memoirs of U. S. Grant* (New York: Da Capo, 1982), 161; *O.R.,* ser. 1, vol. 7, 555.

12. *O.R.,* ser. 1, vol. 7, 637, 682–684. Sherman later explained to John W. Draper of New York University: "The success at Forts Henry & Donelson are due to Grant. But I know that Halleck designed him without an hours delay to follow it up by a lodgement on the Charleston & Memphis Road somewhere near the head of the Tennessee (then in a fine stage of water), but Hallecks orders were not received in time and Grant went up the Cumberland to Nashville." See William Sherman to John W. Draper, St. Louis, July 19, 1867, cont. 6, John W. Draper Papers, Manuscript Division, Library of Congress.

13. John K. Duke, *History of the Fifty-third Regiment Ohio Volunteer Infantry during the War of the Rebellion, 1861 to 1865* (Portsmouth, Ohio: Blade Printing Co., 1900), 6; *Memoirs of General William T. Sherman,* 1:225; William Sherman to Ellen Sherman, Paducah (Ky.), February 17, 1862, and March 6, 1862, roll 3, Sherman Family Papers.

14. William Sherman to Ellen Sherman, Paducah (Ky.), February 21, 1862, roll 3, Sherman Family Papers.

15. *O.R.,* ser. 1, vol. 7, 666; William Sherman to Ellen Sherman, Paducah (Ky.), February 26, 1862, and March 6, 1862, roll 3, Sherman Family Papers.

16. William Sherman to Ellen Sherman, Savannah (Tenn.), March 12, 1862, roll 3, Sherman Family Papers.

17. John Y. Simon, ed., *The Papers of Ulysses S. Grant* (Carbondale and Edwardsville, Ill.: Southern Illinois University Press, 1972), 4:379–381; Bruce Catton, *Grant Moves South* (Boston: Little Brown, 1960), 212–214; William Sherman to Ellen Sherman, Pittsburg Landing (Tenn.), March 17, 1862, roll 3, Sherman Family Papers.

18. Charles Ewing to William Sherman, Alton (Ill.), February 11, 1862, box 6, Charles Ewing Papers, Manuscript Division, Library of Congress; Ellen Sherman to John Sherman, n.p., February 20, 1862, reel 5, cont. 10, William Sherman Papers, Library of Congress; Ellen Sherman to William Sherman, n.p., February 21, 1862, and February 22, 1862, roll 3, Sherman Family Papers.

19. Ellen Sherman to Charles Ewing, Lancaster (Ohio), April 13, 1862, box 6, Charles Ewing Papers.

20. William Sherman to W. F. Smith, St. Louis, May 11, 1885, reel 47, letterbook in cont. 97, William Sherman Papers, Library of Congress; *O.R.,* ser. 1, vol. 10, pt. 1, 28.

21. William Sherman to Thomas Ewing Jr., Camp Shiloh (Tenn.), April 4, 1862, roll 1, Sherman Family Papers.

22. Joseph H. Parks, *General Leonidas Polk, C.S.A., the Fighting Bishop* (Baton Rouge: Louisiana State University Press, 1962), 223–230; William Conant Church, *Ulysses S. Grant and the Period of National Preservation and Reconstruction* (New York: G. P. Putnam's Sons, 1897), 124–125.

23. *O.R.,* ser. 1, vol. 10, pt. 1, 89–91; Alfred T. Andreas, "The 'Ifs and Buts' of Shiloh," *Military Essays and Recollections: Papers Read before the Commandery of the State of Illinois, Military Order of the Loyal Legion of the United States* (Chicago: Dial Press, 1891), 1:112.

24. *Lew Wallace: An Autobiography* (New York and London: Harper & Brothers, 1906), 1:484–485; *O.R.*, ser. 1, vol. 10, pt. 1, 90, 93. Wallace included Ricker's memoir in his book to justify his actions that day.

25. E. C. Dawes, "My First Day Under Fire at Shiloh," in W. H. Chamberlain, ed., *Sketches of War History 1861–1865: Papers Prepared for the Ohio Commandery of the Military Order of the Loyal Legion of the United States* (Cincinnati: Robert Clarke, 1896), 4:1–22; James Lee Mc-Donough, *Shiloh—in Hell before Night* (Knoxville: University of Tennessee Press, 1977), 55–56.

26. *Army and Navy Journal* 35 (October 16, 1897): 123; Charles A. Morton, "A Boy at Shiloh," in A. Noel Blakeman, ed., *Personal Recollections of the War of the Rebellion: Addresses Delivered before the Commandery of the State of New York, Military Order of the Loyal Legion of the United States* (New York: G. P. Putnam's Sons, 1907), 3:57–60.

27. Arthur L. Wagner, "Hasty Intrenchments in the War of Secession," *Papers of the Military Historical Society of Massachusetts* (Boston: Military Historical Society of Massachusetts, 1913), 13:131–132, 135–136; *Memoirs of General William T. Sherman*, 1:229.

28. Duke, *History of the Fifty-third Regiment Ohio Volunteer Infantry*, 42–43.

29. Morton, "A Boy at Shiloh," 54, 58–62; Carlton L. Smith, "A Promising Son Is Lost," *Civil War Times Illustrated* 24 (March 1985): 26, 30, 33, 35.

30. William J. McCaffrey, "Shiloh: A Case Study in Surprise," Master of Military Art and Science Thesis, U.S. Army and General Staff College, Fort Leavenworth, 1970, 60; Wiley Sword, *Shiloh, Bloody April* (New York: William Morrow, 1974), 174; Duke, *History of the Fifty-third Regiment Ohio Volunteer Infantry*, 26–27; *O.R.*, ser. 1, vol. 10, pt. 1, 248–250.

31. John T. Taylor, "Reminiscences of Services as an Aide-de-Camp with General William Tecumseh Sherman," *War Talks in Kansas: A Series of Papers Read before the Kansas Commandery of the Military Order of the Loyal Legion of the United States* (Kansas City: Franklin Hudson, 1908), 132.

32. Catton, *Grant Moves South*, 228; Duke, *History of the Fifty-third Regiment Ohio Volunteer Infantry*, 27; *O.R.*, ser. 1, vol. 10, pt. 1, 249–250.

33. *O.R.*, ser. 1, vol. 10, pt. 1, 250; Sword, *Shiloh*, 209.

34. *Personal Memoirs of U. S. Grant*, 173, 178.

35. McDonough, *Shiloh*, 124–125; *Memoirs of General William T. Sherman*, 1:244–245; *Personal Memoirs of U. S. Grant*, 173–174.

36. McDonough, *Shiloh*, 114; William Sherman to Maria Boyle Ewing, Camp Shiloh (Tenn.), April 22, 1862, roll 1, Sherman Family Papers.

37. William Sherman to Whitelaw Reid, Washington, D.C., April 21, 1881, reel 46, letterbook in cont. 94, William Sherman Papers, Library of Congress; *Army and Navy Journal* 35 (October 6, 1897): 123.

38. Morton, "A Boy at Shiloh," 63–65; Catton, *Grant Moves South*, 229, 236.

39. William Sherman to Philemon B. Ewing, Corinth (Miss.), May 16, 1862, box 154, Thomas Ewing Family Papers, Manuscript Division, Library of Congress.

40. Elijah C. Lawrence, "Stuart's Brigade at Shiloh," *Civil War Papers Read before the Commandery of the State of Massachusetts, Military Order of the Loyal Legion of the United States* (Boston: The Commandery, 1900), 2:489–494.

41. Ibid., 494–495; *O.R.*, ser. 1, vol. 10, pt. 1, 104, 258–259; McDonough, *Shiloh*, 126.

42. *O.R.*, ser. 1, vol. 10, pt. 1, 250; *Memoirs of General William T. Sherman*, 1:245; Matilda Gresham, *Life of Walter Quintin Gresham, 1832–1895* (Chicago: Rand McNally, 1919), 1:185.

43. *O.R.*, ser. 1, vol. 10, pt. 1, 292, 323, 328; Catton, *Grant Moves South*, 237, 239; William Sherman to John W. Draper, St. Louis, September 24, 1867, cont. 6, Draper Papers; William B. Hazen to William Conant Church, Washington, D.C., July 4, 1881, William Conant Church Papers, Manuscript Division, Library of Congress.

44. *O.R.*, ser. 1, vol. 10, pt. 1, 292, 324, 334, 355; William Sherman to John W. Draper, St. Louis, September 24, 1867, cont. 6, Draper Papers.

45. *Army and Navy Journal* 31 (December 10, 1893): 317.

46. *O.R.*, ser. 1, vol. 10, pt. 1, 170, 331–332; Morton, "A Boy at Shiloh," 65; William Sherman to Ulysses S. Grant, St. Louis, February 5, 1885, reel 47, letterbook in cont. 97, William Sherman Papers, Library of Congress.

47. D. W. Reed, *The Battle of Shiloh and the Organizations Engaged* (Washington, D.C.: Government Printing Office, 1903), 23.

48. Marie Caroline Post, *The Life and Memoirs of Comte Régis de Trobriand* (New York: E. P. Dutton, 1910), 504; Sword, *Shiloh*, 430–431.

49. For Grant's report, see *O.R.*, ser. 1, vol. 10, pt. 1, 109–111.

50. James G. Smart, ed., *A Radical View: The "Agate" Dispatches of Whitelaw Reid, 1861–65* (Memphis: Memphis State University Press, 1976), 1:129–130; Royal Cortissoz, *The Life of Whitelaw Reid* (New York: Charles Scribner's Sons, 1921), 1:87; Catton, *Grant Moves South*, 252–256.

51. Catton, *Grant Moves South*, 253–256; Smart, *A Radical View*, 129–131; *O.R.*, ser. 1, vol. 10, pt. 1, 253, 261–266.

52. William Sherman to Ellen Sherman, Camp Shiloh (Tenn.), April 24, 1862, roll 3, Sherman Family Papers.

53. William Sherman to Charles Ewing, Camp Shiloh (Tenn.), April 25, 1862, box 6, Charles Ewing Papers. See also William Sherman to Alfred P. Goodman, 10 miles west of Pittsburg Landing (Tenn.), May 1, 1862, Huntington Manuscripts, Henry E. Huntington Library, San Marino, California.

54. *Army and Navy Journal* 34 (June 19, 1897): 783.

55. *O.R.*, ser. 1, vol. 10, pt. 1, 113–116.

56. William Sherman to Thomas Ewing, Camp Shiloh (Tenn.), April 27, 1862, box 154, Ewing Family Papers; William Sherman to Ellen Sherman, camp before Vicksburg (Miss.), April 23, 1863, roll 3, Sherman Family Papers.

57. William Sherman to Philemon Ewing, Corinth (Miss.), May 16, 1862, box 154, Ewing Family Papers; *O.R.*, ser. 1, vol. 10, pt. 1, 258.

58. *Personal Memoirs of U. S. Grant*, 207; William Sherman to Philemon Ewing, Corinth (Miss.), May 16, 1862, box 154, Ewing Family Papers; *O.R.*, ser. 1, vol. 10, pt. 1, 259.

59. *O.R.*, ser. 1, vol. 10, pt. 1, 639–641; Speech of General Sherman, Reunion of the Society of the Army of the Tennessee, April 6, 1881, in vol. 105, Grenville M. Dodge Papers, State Historical Society of Iowa, Des Moines.

60. Speech of General Sherman, Reunion of the Society of the Army of the Tennessee, April 6, 1881, vol. 105, Dodge Papers.

61. *O.R.*, ser. 1, vol. 10, pt. 1, 644–645; William Sherman to Ellen Sherman, Camp Shiloh (Tenn.), April 14, 1862, roll 3, Sherman Family Papers.

62. Ellen Sherman to John Sherman, Lancaster (Ohio), February 25, 1862, reel 5, cont. 10, William Sherman Papers, Library of Congress; Ellen Sherman to William Sherman, Lancaster (Ohio), February 24, 1862, roll 4, Sherman Family Papers.

63. William Sherman to Ellen Sherman, Camp Shiloh (Tenn.), April 14, 1862, roll 3, Sherman Family Papers.

64. William Sherman to Charles Ewing, Camp Shiloh (Tenn.), April 25, 1862, box 6, Charles Ewing Papers; Ellen Sherman to Charles Ewing, Lancaster (Ohio), April 13, 1862, ibid.

65. Ellen Ewing to Charles Ewing, Lancaster (Ohio), June 3, 1862, box 6, ibid.

66. William Sherman to Maria Boyle Ewing, Camp Shiloh (Tenn.), April 22, 1862, roll 1, Sherman Family Papers.

67. Ellen Sherman to William Sherman, Lancaster (Ohio), April 26, 1862, roll 4, ibid.; William Sherman to Ellen Sherman, camp before Corinth (Miss.), May 6, 1862, roll 3, ibid.

68. *Memoirs of General William T. Sherman*, 1:249–250.

69. Wagner, "Hasty Intrenchments in the War of Secession," 136–137; *O.R.*, ser. 1, vol. 10, pt. 1, 744. Wagner was being sarcastic, for Napoleon defeated the Austrians at Ulm in October 1805 with a series of quick marches.

── 8. Bad Day at Chickasaw ──

1. *New York Times*, September 10, 1885; *Memoirs of General William T. Sherman* (New York: Da Capo, 1984), 1:254; William T. Sherman to Ellen E. Sherman, camp before Corinth, June 2, 1862, roll 3, William T. Sherman Family Papers, University of Notre Dame Archives, South Bend, Indiana.

2. *New York Times*, September 10, 1885.

3. Compare *New York Times*, September 1, 1889, with the story in *Memoirs of General William T. Sherman*, 1:254–255. See also Bruce Catton, *Grant Moves South* (Boston: Little, Brown, 1960), 274–275.

4. M. A. DeWolfe Howe, ed., *Home Letters of General Sherman* (New York: Charles Scribner's Sons, 1909), 227–228; John Y. Simon, ed., *The Papers of Ulysses S. Grant* (Carbondale and Edwardsville, Ill.: Southern Illinois University Press, 1973), 6:141–142; William Sherman to Ellen Sherman, Chewalla (Tenn.), June 6, 1862, roll 3, Sherman Family Papers. Involved with Sherman in California railroad ventures, Baker was killed at Ball's Bluff in 1861.

5. *O.R.*, ser. 1, vol. 10, pt. 1, 745–746; *Memoirs of General William T. Sherman*, 1:256.

6. Samuel M. Bowman and R. B. Irwin, *Sherman and His Campaigns: A Military Biography* (New York: Charles B. Richardson, 1865), 71–72; *Cincinnati Commercial*, August 4, 1862; *O.R.*, ser. 1, vol. 17, pt. 2, 18–20.

7. William Sherman to John Sherman, Memphis, August 13, 1862, Edwin B. Janes Collection, Henry E. Huntington Library, San Marino, California; Bowman and Irwin, *Sherman and His Campaigns*, 73–74.

8. William Sherman to Benjamin Stanton, Chewalla (Tenn.), June 10, 1862, roll 10, Sherman Family Papers.

9. William Sherman to Charles Ewing, camp before Corinth (Miss.), May 23, 1862, box 6, Charles Ewing Papers, Manuscript Division, Library of Congress.

10. Ellen Sherman to William Sherman, Lancaster (Ohio), May 29, 1862, and June 1, 1862, roll 4, Sherman Family Papers.

11. Ellen Sherman to William Sherman, June 20, 1862, roll 4, ibid.

12. William Sherman to Thomas Ewing Sr., camp at Chewalla (Tenn.), June 7, 1862, box 6, Charles Ewing Papers; Ellen Sherman to William Sherman, Lancaster (Ohio), June 14, 1862, and July 17, 1862, roll 4, Sherman Family Papers.

13. Ellen Sherman to William Sherman, Lancaster (Ohio), June 12, 1862, roll 4, Sherman Family Papers.

14. *Memoirs of General William T. Sherman*, 1:265.

15. William Sherman to Ellen Sherman, Memphis, August 5, 1862, roll 3, Sherman Family Papers.

16. *Cincinnati Commercial*, August 5, 1862, August 11, 1862, and August 14, 1862.

17. Ibid., August 5, 1862, and August 11, 1862.

18. Ibid., August 5, 1862, and August 26, 1862.

19. Ibid., August 5, 1862.

20. Walter B. Stevens, "Joseph B. McCullagh," *Missouri Historical Review* 25 (April 1931): 427–428. See also William S. McFeely, *Grant: A Biography* (New York: W. W. Norton, 1981), 124.

21. Howe, *Home Letters of General Sherman*, 232.

22. *Cincinnati Commercial*, August 5, 1862; Albert D. Richardson, *The Secret Service, the Field, the Dungeon, and the Escape* (Hartford, Conn.: American Publishing Company, 1865), 264. See also Sherman's comment about "the commercial enterprise of Jews" in *Memoirs of General William T. Sherman*, 1:264.

23. William Sherman to John Sherman, Memphis, August 13, 1862, Janes Collection. This letter also appeared in *New York Tribune*, February 17, 1891, and *Huntington Library Quarterly* 8 (November 1944): 105–109.

24. *New York Times*, February 28, 1891.

25. Matilda Gresham, *Life of Walter Quintin Gresham, 1832–1895* (Chicago: Rand McNally, 1919), 1:183–185; *Army and Navy Journal* 15 (April 6, 1878): 559.

26. *New Orleans Times-Union*, quoted in *New York Times*, February 20, 1891.

27. William Sherman to Ellen Sherman, Memphis, August 5, 1862, roll 3, Sherman Family Papers; *O.R.*, ser. 1, vol. 17, pt. 2, 113, 158–160; William Sherman to Lewis B. Parsons, Memphis, August 30, 1862, box 11, Lewis B. Parsons Papers, Illinois State Historical Library, Springfield.

28. William L. B. Jenney, "With Sherman and Grant from Memphis to Chattanooga— A Reminiscence," *Military Essays and Recollections: Papers Read before the Commandery of the*

State of Illinois, Military Order of the Loyal Legion of the United States (Chicago: Cozzens and Beaton, 1907), 4:192–196.

29. John Sherman to William Sherman, Mansfield (Ohio), August 24, 1862, reel 6, cont. 11, William Sherman Papers, Library of Congress.

30. William Sherman to John Sherman, Memphis, September 3, 1862, reel 6, cont. 11, ibid.

31. Ellen Sherman to William Sherman, Lancaster (Ohio), August 13, 1862, and August 17, 1862, roll 4, Sherman Family Papers.

32. Ellen Sherman to William Sherman, Lancaster (Ohio), August 24, 1862, and October 1, 1862, roll 4, ibid.

33. William Sherman to Ellen Sherman, Memphis, September 12, 1862, and September 22, 1862, and December 6, 1862, roll 3, ibid.

34. William Sherman to Ellen Sherman, Memphis, September 4, 1862, roll 3, ibid.; Ellen Sherman to Thomas Ewing, Memphis, November 5, 1862, roll 2, ibid.

35. William Sherman to Ellen Sherman, Memphis, September 25, 1862, roll 3, ibid.; Ellen Sherman to William Sherman, Mansfield (Ohio), September 28, 1862, roll 4, ibid.

36. Ellen Sherman to Thomas Ewing, Memphis, November 5, 1862, roll 2, ibid.

37. William L. B. Jenney, "Personal Recollections of Vicksburg," *Military Essays and Recollections: Papers Read before the Commandery of the State of Illinois, Military Order of the Loyal Legion of the United States* (Chicago: Dial Press, 1899), 3:247–248.

38. *Personal Memoirs of U. S. Grant* (New York: Da Capo, 1982), 220–222; Donn Piatt and Henry V. Boynton, *General George H. Thomas: A Critical Biography* (Cincinnati: Robert Clarke, 1893), 235–240; Simon, *Papers of Ulysses S. Grant,* 6:288–289.

39. William Sherman to John Sherman, College Hill (Miss.), December 6, 1862, in Rachel Sherman Thorndike, ed., *The Sherman Letters: Correspondence between General and Senator Sherman from 1837 to 1891* (New York: Charles Scribner's Sons, 1894), 170–171.

40. Jenney, "Personal Recollections of Vicksburg," 248–249.

41. Ibid., 249; William Sherman to John Sherman, College Hill (Miss.), December 6, 1862, in Thorndike, *Sherman Letters,* 171.

42. *Personal Memoirs of U. S. Grant,* 223; *Memoirs of General William T. Sherman,* 1:281–282; William Sherman to John W. Draper, St. Louis, November 24, 1867, box 6, John W. Draper Papers, Manuscript Division, Library of Congress.

43. William Sherman to Ellen Sherman, Memphis, December 14, 1862, roll 3, Sherman Family Papers.

44. Ellen Sherman to William Sherman, Lancaster (Ohio), December 23, 1862, roll 4, ibid.

45. Reply of Lewis B. Parsons to Charles A. Dana's *Recollections of the Civil War,* 7–9, box 38, Parsons Papers; Lewis B. Parsons to Lucinda H. Parsons, St. Louis, December 21, 1862, box 31, ibid.; *O.R.,* ser. 1, vol. 17, pt. 2, 399.

46. William Sherman to David D. Porter, Memphis, November 3, 1862, and November 12, 1862, William T. Sherman Papers, Henry E. Huntington Library, San Marino, California; David D. Porter, "First Meeting of Admiral Porter and Sherman," *Magazine of American History* 25 (April 1891): 298–299.

47. *O.R.,* ser. 1, vol. 17, pt. 1, 605–606; Asa B. Munn et al., *Military History and Reminiscences of the Thirteenth Regiment of Illinois Volunteer Infantry in the Civil War in the United States, 1861–1865* (Chicago: Woman's Temperance Publishing Association, 1892), 237.

48. F. H. Mason, *The Forty-Second Ohio Infantry: A History* (Cleveland: Cobb, Andrews, 1876), 152–153; William Sherman to John W. Draper, St. Louis, November 24, 1867, box 6, Draper Papers.

49. William Sherman to Frank Blair, near Vicksburg, February 3, 1863, reel 7, cont. 12, William Sherman Papers, Library of Congress.

50. *Confederate Veteran* 15 (May 1907): 197; *Missouri Democrat,* January 5, 1863, clipping in Ulysses S. Grant Papers, addition, Manuscript Division, Library of Congress.

51. *O.R.,* ser. 1, vol. 7, pt. 1, 607–608; Mason, *Forty-second Ohio Infantry,* 143–144; D. Alexander Brown, "Battle of Chickasaw Bluffs," *Civil War Times Illustrated* 15 (July 1970): 46;

William Sherman to Ellen Sherman, Washington, D.C., October 26, 1866, roll 3, Sherman Family Papers.

52. George W. Morgan, "The Assault on Chickasaw Bluffs," in Robert Underwood Johnson and Clarence Clough Buel, eds., *Battles and Leaders of the Civil War* (New York: Thomas Yoseloff, 1956), 3:466–469.

53. Herman Hattaway, *General Stephen D. Lee* (Jackson: University Press of Mississippi, 1976), 72–73; *O.R.*, ser. 1, vol. 17, pt. 1, 608, 624–625, 638, 655–656, 682–683.

54. Apolline Blair to Francis P. Blair Sr., January 14, 1863, reel 1, cont. 1, Francis P. Blair Family Papers, Manuscript Division, Library of Congress; *O.R.*, ser. 1, vol. 17, pt. 1, 651.

55. Morgan, "The Assault on Chickasaw Bluffs," 468–469; William Sherman to John W. Draper, St. Louis, November 24, 1867, box 6, Draper Papers; Munn, *Thirteenth Regiment of Illinois Volunteer Infantry*, 270–271; *O.R.*, ser. 1, vol. 17, pt. 2, 890–891.

56. Munn, *Thirteenth Regiment of Illinois Volunteer Infantry*, 264–266.

57. See these reports in *O.R.*, ser. 1, vol. 17, pt. 1: 638 (Morgan), 652 (Steele), 658–659 (Thayer), 659–660 (Williamson). In his reminiscences, written almost sixty years later, Major Julius Pitzman, Sherman's aide and engineer, thus assessed the battle: "The failure was due to the fact that we had green troops and that General Sherman had no knowledge of the capacity of his generals. If we had our old Shiloh division to make the attack, we would have carried the heights successfully." See Julius Pitzman, "Vicksburg Campaign Reminiscences," *The Military Engineer* 15 (March–April 1923): 112.

58. Reply of Lewis Parsons to Charles Dana, 9, Parsons Papers.

59. Richard S. West Jr., *The Second Admiral: A Life of David Dixon Porter, 1813–1891* (New York: Coward-McCann, 1937), 193–194; Orville H. Browning to John A. McClernand, Washington, D.C., December 2, 1862, box 17, John A. McClernand Papers, Illinois State Historical Library, Springfield; Lyman Trumbull to John A. McClernand, Washington, D.C., December 1, 1862, box 17, ibid.; John A. McClernand to Orville H. Browning, Springfield, December 16, 1862, box 17, ibid.

60. William Sherman to John W. Draper, St. Louis, November 24, 1867, box 6, Draper Papers; Ellen Sherman to John Sherman, Lancaster (Ohio), January 8, 1863, reel 6, cont. 11, William Sherman Papers, Library of Congress; Ellen Sherman to William Sherman, Lancaster (Ohio), January 14, 1863, roll 4, Sherman Family Papers.

61. Extract from Admiral Porter's "Journal on Arkansas Post Expedition," reel 6, cont. 11, William Sherman Papers, Library of Congress; William Sherman to John W. Draper, St. Louis, November 24, 1867, box 6, Draper Papers.

62. *Memoirs of General William T. Sherman*, 1:294, 297–298; John T. Taylor, "Reminiscences of Services as an Aide-de-Camp with General William Tecumseh Sherman," *War Talks in Kansas: A Series of Papers Read before the Kansas Commandery of the Military Order of the Loyal Legion of the United States* (Kansas City: Franklin Hudson, 1908), 140–141.

63. L. M. Dayton to Ellen Sherman, Arkansas Post (Ark.), January 14, 1863, reel 6, cont. 11, William Sherman Papers, Library of Congress; *O.R.*, ser. 1, vol. 17, pt. 1, 704–709; Mason, *Forty-Second Ohio Infantry*, 172; *Cincinnati Commercial*, January 27, 1863.

64. William Sherman to John Sherman, Napoleon (Ark.), January 17, 1863, reel 6, cont. 11, William Sherman Papers, Library of Congress. For the reappearance of the insanity story, see Addison A. Stuart, *Iowa Colonels and Regiments: Being a History of Iowa Regiments in the War of Rebellion* (Des Moines, Iowa: Mills & Company, 1865), 120.

65. William Sherman to Ellen Sherman, camp near Vicksburg, January 24, 1863, roll 3, Sherman Family Papers.

___ 9. Vicksburg and Sherman's First March ___

1. William L. B. Jenney, "Personal Recollections of Vicksburg," *Military Essays and Recollections: Papers Read before the Commandery of the State of Illinois, Military Order of the Loyal Legion of the United States* (Chicago: Dial Press, 1899), 3:252.

2. Ibid.; John D. Winters, *The Civil War in Louisiana* (Baton Rouge: Louisiana State University Press, 1963), 175; William T. Sherman to Ellen E. Sherman, camp near Vicksburg,

January 28, 1863, roll 3, William T. Sherman Family Papers, University of Notre Dame Archives, South Bend, Indiana.

3. William Sherman to Ellen Sherman, headquarters before Vicksburg, February 4, 1863, roll 3, Sherman Family Papers.

4. Jenney, "Personal Recollections of Vicksburg," 252–253.

5. Walter George Smith, *Life and Letters of Thomas Kilby Smith, 1820–1887* (New York and London: G. P. Putnam's Sons, 1898), 279–280; Winters, *The Civil War in Louisiana*, 178–179.

6. For Halstead's letter see *New York Times*, September 30, 1885; *New York Sun*, January 23, 1887.

7. *Cincinnati Commercial*, January 17, 1863, and February 2, 1863.

8. *O.R.*, ser. 1, vol. 17, pt. 2, 580–581; Smith, *Life and Letters of Thomas Kilby Smith*, 269; *New York Herald*, January 15, 1863, and January 18, 1863; William T. Sherman to John Sherman, camp before Vicksburg, January 31, 1863, reel 6, cont. 11, William T. Sherman Papers, Manuscript Division, Library of Congress.

9. *O.R.*, ser. 1, vol. 17, pt. 2, 581–587.

10. Ibid., 889; William Sherman to Ellen Sherman, headquarters before Vicksburg, February 4, 1863, roll 3, Sherman Family Papers.

11. William Sherman to John Sherman, camp before Vicksburg, February 7, 1863, reel 7, cont. 17, William Sherman Papers, Library of Congress.

12. Thomas Ewing to Hugh B. Ewing, Lancaster (Ohio), March 12, 1863, box 3, Hugh B. Ewing Papers, Ohio Historical Society, Columbus; John Sherman to William Sherman, Washington, D.C., February 26, 1863, reel 7, cont. 12, William Sherman Papers, Library of Congress.

13. Ellen Sherman to William Sherman, Lancaster (Ohio), February 11, 1863, and February 22, 1863, roll 4, Sherman Family Papers.

14. *O.R.*, ser. 1, vol. 17, pt. 2, 889–895; J. Cutler Andrews, *The North Reports the Civil War* (Pittsburgh: University of Pittsburgh Press, 1955), 380–382; Louis M. Starr, *Bohemian Brigade: Civil War Newsmen in Action* (New York: Alfred A. Knopf, 1954), 178–182. See also Joseph H. Ewing, "The New Sherman Letters," *American Heritage* 38 (July/August 1987): 34–35.

15. William Sherman to John Sherman, n.p., April 7, 1863, roll 9, Sherman Family Papers.

16. John Sherman to William Sherman, Mansfield (Ohio), May 7, 1863, reel 7, cont. 12, William Sherman Papers, Library of Congress.

17. Jenney, "Personal Recollections of Vicksburg," 255–256; William Sherman to Ellen Sherman, camp before Vicksburg, March 30, 1863, roll 3, Sherman Family Papers.

18. Smith, *Life and Letters of Thomas Kilby Smith*, 285; Ellen Sherman to William Sherman, Lancaster (Ohio), March 26, 1863, April 7, 1863, and April 13, 1863, roll 4, Sherman Family Papers; William Sherman to Ellen Sherman, camp at Vicksburg, April 10, 1863, roll 3, Sherman Family Papers.

19. Ellen Sherman to William Sherman, Lancaster (Ohio), March 26, 1863, roll 4, Sherman Family Papers.

20. William Sherman to Ellen Sherman, camp before Vicksburg, April 6, 1863, roll 3, ibid.; William Sherman to John Sherman, camp before Vicksburg, April 10, 1863, reel 7, cont. 13, William Sherman Papers, Library of Congress.

21. William Sherman to Ellen Sherman, camp before Vicksburg, April 10, 1863, roll 3, Sherman Family Papers; Ellen Sherman to William Sherman, Cincinnati, April 18, 1863, ibid.

22. William Sherman to Ellen Sherman, camp before Vicksburg, April 10, 1863, roll 3, ibid.

23. Samuel M. Bowman and R. B. Irwin, *Sherman and His Campaigns: A Military Biography* (New York: Charles B. Richardson, 1865), 102–103; Isaac H. Elliott, *History of the Thirty-third Regiment Illinois Veteran Volunteer Infantry in the Civil War* (Gibson City, Ill.: The Association, 1902), 37.

24. William Sherman to Ellen Sherman, camp before Vicksburg, April 10, 1863, roll 3, Sherman Family Papers.

25. *Memoirs of General William T. Sherman* (New York: Da Capo, 1984), 1:317–318. See also the description in Elliott, *History of the Thirty-third Regiment Illinois Veteran Volunteer Infantry*, 37.

26. *Cincinnati Commercial*, May 5, 1863; William Sherman to Ellen Sherman, camp before Vicksburg, April 23, 1863, roll 3, Sherman Family Papers.

27. William Sherman to John Sherman, camp before Vicksburg, April 26, 1863, reel 7, cont. 13, William Sherman Papers, Library of Congress.

28. William Sherman to Ellen Sherman, before Vicksburg, April 29, 1863, roll 3, Sherman Family Papers.

29. *O.R.*, ser. 1, vol. 17, pt. 1, 752; *Cincinnati Commercial*, May 7, 1863, and May 8, 1863; Jenney, "Personal Recollections of Vicksburg," 258–259; William Sherman to Ellen Sherman, Milliken's Bend (Miss.), May 2, 1863, roll 3, Sherman Family Papers.

30. W. B. Droke, "Grant—the Logistician," *Army Logistician* (May–June 1990): 30–32; Julius Pitzman, "Vicksburg Campaign Reminiscences," *The Military Engineer* 15 (March–April 1923): 114.

31. *Memoirs of General William T. Sherman*, 1:321; Bowman and Irwin, *Sherman and His Campaigns*, 106–107; J. F. C. Fuller, *The Generalship of Ulysses S. Grant* (New York: Dodd, Mead, 1929), 147.

32. *O.R.*, ser. 1, vol. 24, pt. 1, 754; *Memoirs of General William T. Sherman*, 1:321–322.

33. *Memoirs of General William T. Sherman*, 1:322–324; Elliott, *History of the Thirty-third Regiment Illinois Veteran Volunteer Infantry*, 39–40.

34. *Memoirs of General William T. Sherman*, 1:323–324.

35. *O.R.*, ser. 1, vol. 24, pt. 1, 755; William Sherman to David D. Porter, Walnut Hills (Miss.), May 19, 1863, box 1, William T. Sherman Papers, Missouri Historical Society, St. Louis; Fuller, *The Generalship of Ulysses S. Grant*, 152.

36. William Sherman to Ellen Sherman, Walnut Hills (Miss.), May 19, 1863, Sherman Family Papers. Sherman obviously misdated this letter, for he talked of a battle "yesterday."

37. Bruce Catton, *Grant Moves South* (Boston: Little, Brown, 1960), 452; *O.R.*, ser. 1, vol. 24, pt. 1, 756–757; Fuller, *The Generalship of Ulysses S. Grant*, 153–154.

38. Pitzman, "Vicksburg Campaign Reminiscences," 115; John Y. Simon, ed., *The Papers of Ulysses S. Grant* (Carbondale and Edwardsville, Ill.: Southern Illinois University Press, 1979), 8:253; William Sherman to Ellen Sherman, Walnut Hills (Miss.), May 25, 1863, roll 3, Sherman Family Papers.

39. John A. McClernand to Richard Yates, near Vicksburg, May 28, 1863, box 24, John A. McClernand Papers, Illinois State Historical Library, Springfield.

40. Samuel H. Lockett, "The Defense of Vicksburg," in Robert Underwood Johnson and Clarence Clough Buel, eds., *Battles and Leaders of the Civil War* (New York: Thomas Yoseloff, 1956), 3:489–491.

41. F. H. Mason, *The Forty-Second Ohio Infantry: A History* (Cleveland: Cobb, Andrews, 1876), 226–230; *Cincinnati Commercial*, June 16, 1863, and June 30, 1863; William Sherman to Ellen Sherman, Walnut Hills (Miss.), June 11, 1863, roll 3, Sherman Family Papers; William P. Hopkins, *The Seventh Regiment Rhode Island Volunteers in the Civil War, 1862–1865* (Providence: Snow and Farham, 1903), 105; William H. Osborne, *The History of the Twenty-ninth Regiment of Massachusetts Volunteer Infantry in the Late War of the Rebellion* (Boston: Albert J. Wright, 1877), 240–242.

42. Simon, *The Papers of Ulysses S. Grant*, 8:384, 428–431; Jenney, "Personal Recollections of Vicksburg," 262–264; *O.R.*, ser. 1, vol. 24, pt. 1, 162–164.

43. William Sherman to Ellen Sherman, Walnut Hills (Miss.), June 21, 1863, roll 3, Sherman Family Papers.

44. Charles A. Dana, *Recollections of the Civil War* (New York: D. Appleton, 1909), 84–85; Mason, *The Forty-Second Ohio Infantry*, 231–232; William Sherman to Ellen Sherman, camp on Bear Creek (Miss.), June 27, 1863, roll 3, Sherman Family Papers.

45. Mason, *Forty-Second Ohio Infantry*, 231–232; *Memoirs of General William T. Sherman*, 1:329.

46. Catton, *Grant Moves South*, 469–470; Jenney, "Personal Recollections of Vicksburg," 264–265; Fuller, *The Generalship of Ulysses S. Grant*, 157.

47. William Sherman to John Sherman, Jackson (Miss.), July 19, 1863, reel 7, cont. 12, William Sherman Papers, Library of Congress.

48. Simon, *Papers of Ulysses S. Grant,* 8:461; Mason, *Forty-Second Ohio Infantry,* 233; William Sherman to Ellen Sherman, camp near Black River (Miss.), July 5, 1863, roll 3, Sherman Family Papers.

49. William Todd, *The Seventy-ninth Highlanders New York Volunteers in the War of Rebellion, 1861–1865* (Albany: Brandow, Barton, 1886), 309–311; Thomas H. Parker, *History of the 51st Regiment P. V. and V. V.* (Philadelphia: King & Baird, 1869), 343–344; Mason, *Forty-Second Ohio Infantry,* 234; Seth Alonzo Ranlett et al., *History of the Thirty-sixth Regiment Massachusetts Volunteers, 1862–1865* (Boston: Rockwell and Churchill, 1884), 59.

50. Asa B. Munn et al., *Military History and Reminiscences of the Thirteenth Regiment of Illinois Volunteer Infantry in the Civil War in the United States, 1861–1865* (Chicago: Woman's Temperance Publishing Association, 1892), 336; Parker, *History of the 51st Regiment of P. V. and V. V.,* 370.

51. Hopkins, *The Seventh Regiment Rhode Island Volunteers,* 109–111, 117; Edward O. Lord, ed., *History of the Ninth Regiment New Hampshire Volunteers in the War of the Rebellion* (Concord, N.H.: Republican Press Association, 1895), 301.

52. *O.R.,* ser. 1, vol. 24, pt. 2, 522–523, 535; William L. B. Jenney, "With Sherman and Grant from Memphis to Chattanooga—A Reminiscence," *Military Essays and Recollections: Papers Read before the Commandery of the State of Illinois, Military Order of the Loyal Legion of the United States* (Chicago: Cozzens & Beaton, 1907), 4:210.

53. Seth Alonzo Ranlett, "The Capture of Jackson," *Civil War Papers, Read before the Commandery of the State of Massachusetts, Military Order of the Loyal Legion of the United States* (Boston: The Commandery, 1900), 1:263–265.

54. Ranlett, *History of the Thirty-sixth Regiment Massachusetts Volunteers,* 66–67.

55. William Sherman to Ellen Sherman, before Jackson, July 15, 1863, roll 3, Sherman Family Papers.

56. *O.R.,* ser. 1, vol. 24, pt. 2, 527–528, 530, 536–537; William Sherman to John Sherman, Jackson (Miss.), July 19, 1863, reel 7, cont. 12, William Sherman Papers, Library of Congress. See also Edwin C. Bearss, *The Siege of Jackson, July 10–17, 1863* (Baltimore: Gateway Press, 1981), 70.

57. Parker, *History of the 51st Regiment of P. V. and V. V.,* 359; Hopkins, *Seventh Regiment Rhode Island Volunteers in the Civil War,* 115; *O.R.,* ser. 1, vol. 24, pt. 2, 530–531.

58. M. D. Gage, *From Vicksburg to Raleigh; or, A Complete History of the Twelfth Regiment Indiana Volunteer Infantry and the Campaigns of Grant and Sherman* (Chicago: Clarke, 1865), 92.

59. *O.R.,* ser. 1, vol. 24, pt. 2, 530–531. See also Gilbert E. Govan and James W. Livingood, *A Different Valor: The Story of General Joseph E. Johnston, C.S.A.* (Indianapolis: Bobbs-Merrill, 1956), 220–221.

60. Parker, *History of the 51st Regiment of P. V. and V. V.,* 366, 368; Hopkins, *Seventh Regiment Rhode Island Volunteers in the Civil War,* 115; *O.R.,* ser. 1, vol. 24, pt. 2, 537.

61. John Sherman to William Sherman, Mansfield (Ohio), July 18, 1863, reel 7, cont. 12, William Sherman Papers, Library of Congress.

62. In 1921, Major General Peter C. Hains, who as a young first lieutenant of engineers helped map out the strategy of the Vicksburg campaign, lavishly praised Grant, Sherman, and McPherson. "To what then can we reasonably attribute the magnitude of the victory?" he asked. "First and foremost it was due to the fact not known to everybody at that time that the Army of the Tennessee was commanded by one of the greatest generals in history, and had two of the best corps commanders that the Civil War produced." See Peter C. Hains, "The Vicksburg Campaign," *The Military Engineer* 13 (May–June 1921): 194.

___ 10. Willy, Chattanooga, and Knoxville ___

1. William Conant Church, *Ulysses S. Grant and the Period of National Preservation and Reconstruction* (New York: G. P. Putnam's Sons, 1897), 189–190; J. F. C. Fuller, *The Generalship of Ulysses S. Grant* (New York: Dodd, Mead, 1929), 158–159.

2. David D. Porter to William T. Sherman, Cairo (Ill.), October 19, 1863, reel 7, cont. 13, William T. Sherman Papers, Manuscript Division, Library of Congress. Stephen Mallory was the Confederate secretary of the navy.

3. Church, *Ulysses S. Grant*, 190; Fuller, *The Generalship of Ulysses S. Grant*, 159.

4. William Sherman to John Sherman, camp on Big Black (Miss.), August 3, 1863, reel 7, cont. 12, William Sherman Papers, Library of Congress.

5. Ellen E. Sherman to William Sherman, Lancaster (Ohio), July 26, 1863, roll 5, William T. Sherman Family Papers, University of Notre Dame Archives, South Bend, Indiana.

6. Anna McAllister, *Ellen Ewing, Wife of General Sherman* (New York: Benziger, 1936), 262–264; William Sherman to James B. McPherson, camp on Big Black (Miss.), August 15, 1863, box 2, William T. Sherman Papers, United States Military Academy Library, West Point, New York.

7. William Sherman to John Sherman, camp on Big Black (Miss.), September 9, 1863, reel 7, cont. 13, William Sherman Papers, Library of Congress; McAllister, *Ellen Sherman*, 264–265; William Sherman to Albert M. Landon, St. Louis, January 22, 1875, roll 1, Sherman Family Papers; James Grant Wilson, "War Horses of Famous Generals," *Century* 86 (May 1913): 54–55.

8. Fuller, *The Generalship of Ulysses S. Grant*, 160–161; Church, *Ulysses S. Grant*, 191.

9. *Memoirs of General William T. Sherman* (New York: Da Capo, 1984), 1:347–348.

10. Ibid., 348; Ellen Sherman to William Sherman, Lancaster (Ohio), October 16, 1863, roll 5, Sherman Family Papers.

11. *Memoirs of General William T. Sherman*, 1:348; Ellen Sherman to William Sherman, Iuka (Miss.), October ?, 1863, roll 5, Sherman Family Papers.

12. William Sherman to Ellen Sherman, Iuka (Miss.), October 19, 1863, roll 3, ibid.

13. William Sherman to Ellen Sherman, Fayetteville (Tenn.), November 8, 1863, roll 3, ibid.

14. William Sherman to Thomas E. Sherman, n.p., n.d., roll 6, ibid.

15. Wilbur F. Hinman, *The Story of the Sherman Brigade* (N.p.: The Author, 1897), 448; Oliver O. Howard, "Grant at Chattanooga," in James Grant Wilson and Titus Munson Coan, eds., *Personal Recollections of the War of the Rebellion: Addresses Delivered before the New York Commandery of the Loyal Legion of the United States, 1883–1891* (New York: The Commandery, 1891), 245–247.

16. Asa B. Munn et al., *Military History and Reminiscences of the Thirteenth Regiment of Illinois Volunteer Infantry in the Civil War in the United States, 1861–1865* (Chicago: Woman's Temperance Publishing Association, 1892), 350–351; William Sherman to Ellen Sherman, Collierville (Tenn.), October 12, 1863, Corinth (Miss.), October 14, 1863, and Iuka (Miss.), October 19, 1863, roll 3, Sherman Family Papers; William L. B. Jenney, "With Sherman and Grant from Memphis to Chattanooga—A Reminiscence," *Military Essays and Recollections: Papers Read before the Commandery of the State of Illinois, Military Order of the Loyal Legion of the United States* (Chicago: Cozzens & Beaton, 1907), 4:211–213. On Duke, see William Sherman to E. F. Andrews, New York, November 7, 1888, Rutherford B. Hayes Papers, Rutherford B. Hayes Library, Fremont, Ohio.

17. William Sherman to Ellen Sherman, Corinth (Miss.), October 14, 1863, roll 3, Sherman Family Papers; *O.R.*, ser. 1, vol. 21, pt. 2, 570.

18. William Sherman to Ellen Sherman, Iuka (Miss.), October 28, 1863, roll 3, Sherman Family Papers.

19. Howard, "Grant at Chattanooga," 245–247.

20. *Memoirs of General William T. Sherman*, 1:357–359. See also Peter Cozzens, *The Shipwreck of Their Hopes: The Battles for Chattanooga* (Urbana and Chicago: University of Illinois Press, 1994), 109–110.

21. William Sherman to Ellen Sherman, Fayetteville (Tenn.), November 8, 1863, and Bridgeport (Ala.), November 14, 1863, roll 3, Sherman Family Papers; William Wirt Calkins, *The History of the One Hundred and Fourth Regiment of Illinois Volunteer Infantry, War of the Great Rebellion, 1862–1865* (Chicago: Donohue & Henneberry, 1895), 166.

22. William Sherman to Ellen Sherman, Fayetteville (Tenn.), November 8, 1863, and Bridgeport (Ala.), November 14, 1863, roll 3, Sherman Family Papers.

23. William Sherman to Ellen Sherman, Bridgeport (Ala.), November 14, 1863, roll 3, ibid.

24. *O.R.*, ser. 1, vol. 31, pt. 2, 571; *Memoirs of General William T. Sherman*, 1:361.

25. Howard, "Grant at Chattanooga," 248–249. Howard also told this story, with slight variations, in *Autobiography of Oliver Otis Howard* (New York: Baker & Taylor, 1907), 1:473–476. On the smoking habits of Grant and Sherman, see *Cincinnati Commercial*, June 16, 1863.

26. William Sherman to William F. Smith, St. Louis, March 4, 1886, reel 48, letterbook in cont. 48, William Sherman Papers, Library of Congress.

27. Bruce Catton, *Grant Takes Command* (Boston: Little, Brown, 1968), 65; James Harrison Wilson, *Life and Services of William Farrar Smith in the Civil War* (Wilmington: John W. Rogers, 1904), 75–76; William F. Smith to William Sherman, Wilmington (Del.), March 6, 1886, reel 36, cont. 39, William Sherman Papers, Library of Congress.

28. *Memoirs of General William T. Sherman*, 1:363; *O.R.*, ser. 1, vol. 31, pt. 2, 572.

29. *Memoirs of Henry Villard, Journalist and Financier, 1835–1900* (Boston: Houghton Mifflin, 1904), 2:242–243; *Memoirs of General William T. Sherman*, 1:363.

30. *Memoirs of Henry Villard*, 2:242–244; James Harrison Wilson, *Under the Old Flag* (New York: D. Appleton, 1912), 1:290.

31. *O.R.*, ser. 1, vol. 31, pt. 2, 572; *Memoirs of Henry Villard*, 2:242; M. D. Gage, *From Vicksburg to Raleigh; or, A Complete History of the Twelfth Regiment Indiana Volunteer Infantry and the Campaigns of Grant and Sherman* (Chicago: Clarke, 1865), 138.

32. *The Story of the Fifty-fifth Regiment Illinois Volunteer Infantry in the Civil War, 1861–1865* (Clinton, Mass.: W. J. Coulter, 1887), 280–281; John K. Duke, *History of the Fifty-third Regiment Ohio Volunteer Infantry during the War of the Rebellion, 1861 to 1865* (Portsmouth, Ohio: Blade Printing Co., 1900), 125–126; John W. Storrs, *The "Twentieth Connecticut": A Regimental History* (Ansonia, Conn.: Naugatuck Valley Sentinel, 1886), 130.

33. James Lee McDonough, *Chattanooga—A Death Grip on the Confederacy* (Knoxville: University of Tennessee Press, 1984), 110–113; Howard, "Grant at Chattanooga," 249–250.

34. *Story of the Fifty-fifth Regiment Illinois Volunteer Infantry*, 282–285; *O.R.*, ser. 1, vol. 31, pt. 2, 572–573; Edwin W. Payne, *History of the Thirty-fourth Regiment of Illinois Volunteer Infantry* (Clinton, Iowa: Allen Printing, 1902), 82. See also Cozzens, *The Shipwreck of Their Hopes*, 148.

35. Wilson, *Under the Old Flag*, 1:294–295; *O.R.*, ser. 1, vol. 31, pt. 2, 573; McDonough, *Chattanooga*, 120–122; *Story of the Fifty-fifth Regiment Illinois Volunteer Infantry*, 284; Howell and Elizabeth Purdue, *Pat Cleburne, Confederate General* (Tuscaloosa, Ala.: Portals Press, 1977), 143–144.

36. William F. Smith to William Sherman, Wilmington (Del.), February 17, 1886, and February 22, 1886, and March 6, 1886, reel 36, cont. 69, William Sherman Papers, Library of Congress; William Sherman to William F. Smith, St. Louis, February 25, 1886, and March 9, 1886, reel 48, letterbook in cont. 48, ibid.

37. *O.R.*, ser. 1, vol. 31, pt. 2, 574–575; *Story of the Fifty-fifth Regiment Illinois Volunteer Infantry*, 285–287. Consult also John Bowers, *Chickamauga and Chattanooga: The Battles That Doomed the Confederacy* (New York: HarperCollins, 1994), 218–220.

38. Frederick Bancroft and William A. Dunning, eds., *The Reminiscences of Carl Schurz* (New York: Doubleday, Page, 1913), 3:75.

39. *O.R.*, ser. 1, vol. 31, pt. 2, 575; William Wirt Calkins, *The History of the One Hundred and Fourth Regiment of Illinois Volunteer Infantry, War of the Great Rebellion, 1862–1865* (Chicago: Donohue & Henneberry, 1895), 175.

40. *Story of the Fifty-fifth Regiment Illinois Volunteer Infantry*, 286–287; Calkins, *History of the One Hundred and Fourth Regiment of Illinois Volunteer Infantry*, 176; Purdue and Purdue, *Pat Cleburne*, 147–149.

41. Thomas J. Wood, "The Battle of Missionary Ridge," *Sketches of War History, 1861–1865: Papers Prepared for the Ohio Commandery of the Military Order of the Loyal Legion of the United States* (Cincinnati: Robert Clarke, 1896), 4:34–38.

42. Ibid., 39; Calkins, *History of the One Hundred and Fourth Regiment of Illinois Volunteer Infantry,* 178.

43. Wood, "The Battle of Missionary Ridge," 42; *Memoirs of General William T. Sherman,* 1:364; William Sherman to William F. Smith, St. Louis, February 25, 1886, reel 48, letterbook in cont. 48, William Sherman Papers, Library of Congress.

44. Wood, "The Battle of Missionary Ridge," 42.

45. Hinman, *Story of the Sherman Brigade,* 458–460. See also McDonough, *Chattanooga,* 163–169.

46. Samuel H. Hurst, *Journal-History of the Seventy-third Ohio Volunteer Infantry* (Chillicothe, Ohio: n.p., 1866), 95.

47. *O.R.,* ser. 1, vol. 31, pt. 1, 576; *Story of the Fifty-fifth Regiment Illinois Volunteer Infantry,* 288–289; Purdue and Purdue, *Pat Cleburne,* 153–157.

48. *Memoirs of General William T. Sherman,* 1:366–367; *Autobiography of Oliver Otis Howard,* 1:490–491.

49. *Story of the Fifty-fifth Regiment Illinois Volunteer Infantry,* 290; Duke, *History of the Fifty-third Regiment Ohio Volunteer Infantry,* 121–122.

50. Hurst, *Journal-History of the Seventy-third Ohio Volunteer Infantry,* 99–102.

51. Bancroft and Dunning, *Reminiscences of Carl Schurz,* 3:78–80; William Sherman to Oliver O. Howard, Chattanooga (Tenn.), December 18, 1863, Oliver O. Howard Papers, Bowdoin College Library, Brunswick, Maine.

52. William Marvel, *Burnside* (Chapel Hill: University of North Carolina Press, 1991), 330–332; Gage, *From Vicksburg to Raleigh,* 150–151.

53. *Memoirs of General William T. Sherman,* 1:367–368.

54. *Memoirs of General William T. Sherman,* 1:368; Ulysses S. Grant to William Sherman, Washington, D.C., January 29, 1876, reel 46, cont. 92, William Sherman Papers, Library of Congress.

55. Bancroft and Dunning, *Reminiscences of Carl Schurz,* 3:80–81; Gage, *From Vicksburg to Raleigh,* 151–153; Hurst, *Journal-History of the Seventy-third Ohio Volunteer Infantry,* 105.

56. William Sherman to John Sherman, Lancaster (Ohio), December 29, 1863, reel 7, cont. 13, William Sherman Papers, Library of Congress.

57. *O.R.,* ser. 1, vol. 31, pt. 3, 339–345; Walter H. Hebert, *Fighting Joe Hooker* (Indianapolis: Bobbs-Merrill, 1944), 268–269.

58. William Sherman to John Sherman, Lancaster (Ohio), December 29, 1863, reel 7, cont. 13, William Sherman Papers, Library of Congress; Ellen Sherman to John Sherman, Lancaster (Ohio), January 25, 1864, reel 7, cont. 13, ibid.

59. Ellen Sherman to John Sherman, Lancaster (Ohio), February 11, 1864, reel 7, cont. 13, ibid.

60. William Sherman to John Sherman, Vicksburg (Miss.), February 1, 1864, reel 7, cont. 13, ibid.

61. *Memoirs of General William T. Sherman,* 1:385.

62. *O.R.,* ser. 1, vol. 32, pt. 2, 278–281.

— 11. Commander of the Armies —

1. *Memoirs of General William T. Sherman* (New York: Da Capo, 1984), 1:386, 388–390; Grenville M. Dodge to John J. Rider, Council Bluffs (Iowa), December 10, 1910, in Dodge Records, vol. 21, 493–494, Grenville M. Dodge Papers, State Historical Society of Iowa, Des Moines; William T. Sherman to Ellen E. Sherman, U.S. Gunboat *Juliet,* January 5, 1864, roll 3, William T. Sherman Family Papers, University of Notre Dame Archives, South Bend, Indiana.

2. Grenville M. Dodge, *Personal Recollections of President Abraham Lincoln, General Ulysses S. Grant, and General William T. Sherman* (Council Bluffs, Iowa: Monarch Printing Company, 1914), 139–140.

3. Ibid., 141–142; Grenville M. Dodge, "Tribute to A Hero, General Sherman," vol. 105, Dodge Papers. On the phrase "War is cruelty," see *Memoirs of General William T. Sherman* (New York: Da Capo, 1984), 2:126; *Army and Navy Journal* 45 (May 16, 1908): 995.

4. James M. Merrill, *William Tecumseh Sherman* (Chicago: Rand McNally, 1971), 239.

5. William Sherman to John Sherman, Lancaster (Ohio), December 30, 1863, reel 7, cont. 13, William T. Sherman Papers, Manuscript Division, Library of Congress.

6. William Sherman to Ellen Sherman, U.S. Gunboat *Juliet*, January 5, 1864, roll 3, Sherman Family Papers.

7. William Sherman to Ellen Sherman, Memphis, January 11, 1864, roll 3, ibid.

8. Albert Castel, *Decision in the West: The Atlanta Campaign of 1864* (Lawrence: University Press of Kansas, 1992), 41–42; *O.R.*, ser. 1, vol. 32, pt. 1, 174–175, 177, and pt. 2, 258–260.

9. William Sherman to Ellen Sherman, Gunboat *Silver Cloud*, January 19, 1864, roll 3, Sherman Family Papers; *Memoirs of General William T. Sherman*, 1:388–390.

10. *O.R.*, ser. 1, vol. 32, pt. 2, 260–261. Benjamin was actually born in St. Croix.

11. Ibid., pt. 1, 175; *Indianapolis American Tribune*, March 16, 1888. The latter contains the reminiscences of Thomas H. Harris, McPherson's adjutant.

12. R. L. Howard, *History of the 124th Regiment Illinois Infantry Volunteers, Otherwise Known as the "Hundred and Two Dozen"* (Springfield, Ill.: H. W. Bokker, 1880), 185–186; *Indianapolis American Tribune*, March 16, 1888.

13. Howard, *History of the 124th Regiment Illinois Infantry Volunteers*, 187–190.

14. William M. Polk, *Leonidas Polk, Bishop and General* (New York: Longmans, Green, 1893), 2:304–307; William Sherman to John Sherman, near Atlanta, July 31, 1864, reel 7, cont. 13, William Sherman Papers, Library of Congress.

15. *O.R.*, ser. 1, vol. 32, pt. 1, 176.

16. Howard, *History of the 124th Regiment Illinois Infantry Volunteers*, 195–196.

17. *O.R.*, ser. 1, vol. 32, pt. 1, 176; William Sherman to William Sooy Smith, St. Louis, July 11, 1875, reel 46, letterbook in cont. 92, William Sherman Papers, Library of Congress. See also William Sherman to Willard Warner, Washington, D.C., May 31, 1880, William T. Sherman Papers, Illinois State Historical Library, Springfield.

18. William Sooy Smith to Grenville M. Dodge, Medford (Ore.), December 14, 1910, Dodge Records, vol. 21, 509–511, Dodge Papers.

19. Edward A. Davenport, ed., *History of the Ninth Regiment Illinois Cavalry Volunteers* (Chicago: n.p., 1888), 92–93; *O.R.*, ser. 1, vol. 32, pt. 1, 252; Thomas S. Cogley, *History of the Seventh Indiana Cavalry Volunteers* (LaPorte, Ind.: Herald Company, 1876), 78–79.

20. Cogley, *History of the Seventh Indiana Cavalry Volunteers*, 90; Stephen D. Lee, "Sherman's Meridian Expedition and Sooy Smith's Raid to West Point," *Southern Historical Society Papers* 8 (February 1880): 54; *O.R.*, ser. 1, vol. 32, pt. 1, 256–257, 351, 353–354; Davenport, *History of the Ninth Regiment Illinois Cavalry Volunteers*, 94–95.

21. Howard, *History of the 124th Regiment Illinois Infantry Volunteers*, 205; *O.R.*, ser. 1, vol. 32, pt. 1, 177.

22. William Sherman to Ellen Sherman, aboard Steamboat *West Moreland*, March 10, 1864, roll 3, Sherman Family Papers.

23. William Sherman to Ellen Sherman, Vicksburg, February 28, 1864, roll 3, ibid.

24. David F. Boyd to William Sherman, Natchez (Miss.), February 13, 1864, reel 7, cont. 13, William Sherman Papers, Library of Congress; William Sherman to Ellen Sherman, aboard Steamboat *West Moreland*, March 10, 1864, roll 3, Sherman Family Papers; W. McCrory, "Early Life and Personal Reminiscences of General William T. Sherman," *Glimpses of the Nation's Struggle: Papers Read before the Minnesota Commandery of the Military Order of the Loyal Legion of the United States, 1889–1892* (New York: D. D. Merrill, 1893), 3:335–336.

25. William Sherman to Ellen Sherman, aboard Steamboat *West Moreland*, March 10, 1864, roll 3, Sherman Family Papers.

26. *Memoirs of General William T. Sherman*, 1:397.

27. William Sherman to Ellen Sherman, Memphis, March 12, 1864, roll 3, Sherman Family Papers.

28. Ellen Sherman to William Sherman, Lancaster (Ohio), February 16, 1864, roll 5, ibid. On the Mass, see the notes of Eleanor Sherman Fitch on John B. Purcell to Ellen Sherman, Cincinnati, November 7, 1855, roll 1, ibid.

29. *Memoirs of General William T. Sherman*, 1:398–400.

30. *Personal Memoirs of U. S. Grant* (New York: Da Capo, 1982), 359.

31. Dodge, *Personal Recollections*, 69–70, 143–144; James F. Rusling, *Men and Things I Saw in Civil War Days* (New York: Eaton & Mains, 1899), 110–111.

32. *O.R.*, ser. 1, vol. 32, pt. 3, 221; *Memoirs of General William T. Sherman*, 2:7–8, 14.

33. *Memoirs of General William T. Sherman*, 2:8; Ulysses S. Grant to William Sherman, Washington, D.C., April 4, 1864, reel 8, cont. 13, William Sherman Papers, Library of Congress.

34. William Sherman to John Sherman, Nashville, April 22, 1864, reel 8, cont. 14, William Sherman Papers, Library of Congress; Castel, *Decision in the West*, 93. Sherman had ordered the abandonment of Fort Pillow before he left for Meridian. "I don't know what these men were doing at Fort Pillow," he telegraphed Grant. *O.R.*, ser. 1, vol. 32, pt. 3, 367.

35. William Sherman to Hugh B. Ewing, near Memphis, January 20, 1864, box 1, William T. Sherman Papers, Ohio Historical Society, Columbus; Hugh Ewing to William Sherman, Lancaster (Ohio), February 7, 1865, box 4, Hugh B. Ewing Papers, Ohio Historical Society, Columbus.

36. William Sherman to Ellen Sherman, Nashville, April 7, 1864, roll 3, Sherman Family Papers.

37. *Memoirs of General William T. Sherman*, 2:9.

38. *O.R.*, ser. 1, vol. 32, pt. 3, 311; Jesse C. Burt, "Sherman, Railroad General," *Civil War History* 2 (March 1956); 46–49; George W. Herr, *Nine Campaigns in Nine States: The History of the Fifty-ninth Regiment Illinois Veteran Volunteer Infantry* (San Francisco: Bancroft, 1890), 271–272. Especially useful is James G. Bogle, "The Western & Atlantic Railroad in the Campaign for Atlanta," in Theodore P. Savas and David A. Woodbury, eds., *The Campaign for Atlanta and Sherman's March to the Sea* (Campbell, Calif.: Savas Woodbury, 1994), 313–340.

39. Jared W. Young, ed., "General Sherman on His Own Record," *Atlantic Monthly* 108 (September 1911): 294; Armin E. Mruck, "The Role of Railroads in the Atlanta Campaign," *Civil War History* 7 (September 1961): 266–267.

40. William Sherman to John Sherman, Nashville, April 11, 1864, reel 8, cont. 13, William Sherman Papers, Library of Congress; *O.R.*, ser. 1, vol. 32, pt. 3, 220, 301, 489–490.

41. *O.R.*, ser. 1, vol. 32, pt. 3, 220, 434, 489–490, 503, 539, 548.

42. Burt, "Sherman, Railroad General," 47–50; *O.R.*, ser. 1, vol. 32, pt. 3, 503.

43. Rusling, *Men and Things I Saw in Civil War Days*, 111. Studying the Union preparations for the coming campaign, Colonel James J. Cooke has recently reiterated the adage that good logistics, rather than good tactics, wins wars. "The Atlanta campaign, planned and implemented by William T. Sherman in 1864, was not only a masterpiece in its relentless pursuit of an enemy deep into Georgia," Colonel Cooke noted, "it was also a model for future logistical preparation and implementation." Assembling food and supplies for his vast army and forage for his horses and mules, Sherman "then moved them over bad roads in rugged, mountainous terrain with a less-than-adequate, well-worn railroad." Hauling "mountains of supplies deep into Georgia," he "fed his men and gave them the ammunition and equipment to do the job." See James J. Cooke, "Union Logistics in the Campaign for Atlanta," in Savas & Woodbury, *The Campaign for Atlanta*, 97–98, 114. Colonel Cooke's observations, it seems to me, are an antidote to the historians who ignore logistics and denounce Sherman for being a general who disliked to fight.

44. John Y. Simon, ed., *The Papers of Ulysses S. Grant* (Carbondale and Edwardsville, Ill.: Southern Illinois University Press, 1982), 10, 354–355; *O.R.*, ser. 1, vol. 32, pt. 3, 521.

45. William Sherman to Ellen Sherman, Chattanooga, May 4, 1864, roll 3, Sherman Family Papers.

—— **12. "We Must Kill Those Three Hundred Thousand"** ——

1. *Army and Navy Journal* I (May 28, 1864): 665.

2. Henry Stone, "The Atlanta Campaign," in *Papers of the Military Historical Society of Massachusetts* (Boston: Military Historical Society of Massachusetts, 1910), 8:335; *Autobiography of Oliver Otis Howard* (New York: Baker & Taylor, 1907), 1:504; *Cincinnati Commercial*, May 13, 1864.

3. Thomas B. Van Horne, *The Life of Major-General George H. Thomas* (New York: Charles Scribner's Sons, 1882), 220–221.

4. Grenville M. Dodge, *Personal Recollections of President Abraham Lincoln, General Ulysses S. Grant, and General William T. Sherman* (Council Bluffs, Iowa: Monarch Printing Company, 1914), 46–47; *O.R.*, ser. 1, vol. 37, pt. 4, 306.

5. Stone, "Atlanta Campaign," 359–360; *O.R.*, ser. 1, vol. 38, pt. 4, 35, 38–40; Roy Morris Jr., and Phil Noblitt, "The History of a Failure," *Civil War Times Illustrated* 27 (September 1988): 39–40.

6. *O.R.*, ser. 1, vol. 38, pt. 3, 375–376; Stone, "Atlanta Campaign," 360–363.

7. Morris and Noblitt, "The History of a Failure," 41; *O.R.*, ser. 1, vol. 38, pt. 4, 682.

8. *O.R.*, ser. 1, vol. 38, pt. 4, 111.

9. William T. Sherman to John Sherman, Acworth (Ga.), June 9, 1864, reel 8, cont. 14, William T. Sherman Papers, Manuscript Division, Library of Congress; Stone, "Atlanta Campaign," 366; Albert Castel, *Decision in the West: The Atlanta Campaign of 1864* (Lawrence: University Press of Kansas, 1992), 182–185.

10. *Cincinnati Commercial*, May 20, 1864; *O.R.*, ser. 1, vol. 38, pt. 1, 627, 735–736; Stone, "Atlanta Campaign," 381–383.

11. *Cincinnati Commercial*, May 20, 1864; Stone, "Atlanta Campaign," 383–384; *Autobiography of Oliver Otis Howard*, 1:515–516.

12. *O.R.*, ser. 1, vol. 38, pt. 4, 196; *Autobiography of Oliver Otis Howard*, 1:519.

13. John M. Schofield, "Comments on Sherman's Memoirs," 22, box 95, John M. Schofield Papers, Manuscript Division, Library of Congress; James Lee McDonough, *Schofield, Union General in the Civil War and Reconstruction* (Tallahassee, Fla.: Florida State University Press, 1972), p. 74.

14. Oliver O. Howard to Lizzie Howard, near Cassville (Ga.), May 22, 1864, Oliver O. Howard Papers, Bowdoin College Library, Brunswick, Maine; *Cincinnati Commercial*, May 30, 1864.

15. *Army and Navy Journal* 54 (January 13, 1917): 647.

16. *Autobiography of Oliver Otis Howard*, 1:524, 529.

17. Ibid., 1:524; Jacob D. Cox, *Atlanta* (New York: Blue & Gray Press, n.d.), 56; *O.R.*, ser. 1, vol. 38, pt. 3, 615–616. See also the account in Craig L. Symonds, *Joseph E. Johnston: A Civil War Biography* (New York: W. W. Norton, 1992), 293–295.

18. *Autobiography of Oliver Otis Howard*, 1:535–536, 539.

19. *O.R.*, ser. 1, vol. 38, pt. 4, 294; George R. Agassiz, ed., *Meade's Headquarters, 1863–1865: Letters of Colonel Theodore Lyman from the Wilderness to Appomattox* (Boston: Atlantic Monthly Press, 1922), 125–136.

20. John W. Storrs, *The "Twentieth Connecticut": A Regimental History* (Ansonia, Conn.: Naugatuck Valley Sentinel, 1886), 130–131.

21. William Sherman to John Sherman, Kingston (Ga.), May 21, 1864, reel 8, cont. 14, William Sherman Papers, Library of Congress; *Cincinnati Commercial*, May 28, 1864, and May 30, 1864; *Memoirs of General William T. Sherman* (New York: Da Capo, 1984), 1:42.

22. Edmund R. Brown, *The Twenty-Seventh Indiana Volunteer Infantry in the War of the Rebellion* (N.p.: n.p., 1899), 485; Stone, "Atlanta Campaign," 406–407; Cox, *Atlanta*, 68.

23. Brown, *Twenty-Seventh Indiana*, 485–486; Stone, "Atlanta Campaign," 408–409; *O.R.*, ser. 1, vol. 38, pt. 1, 862–863.

24. *O.R.*, ser. 1, vol. 38, pt. 1, 862–863; Brown, *Twenty-Seventh Indiana*, 488–489.

25. Brown, *Twenty-Seventh Indiana*, 486; Castel, *Decision in the West*, 226; *O.R.*, ser. 1, vol. 38, pt. 4, 312.

26. *Autobiography of Oliver Otis Howard*, 1:550–558; *O.R.*, ser. 1, vol. 38, pt. 3, 724–726, and pt. 4, 323. See also Jeffrey S. Dean, "The Battle of Pickett's Mill," in Theodore P. Savas and David A. Woodbury, eds., *The Campaign for Atlanta and Sherman's March to the Sea* (Campbell, Calif.: Savas Woodbury, 1994), 343–373.

27. Castel, *Decision in the West*, 243–246; *Autobiography of Oliver Otis Howard*, 1:559–560; *O.R.*, ser. 1, vol. 38, pt. 3, 95–96.

28. *O.R.*, ser. 1, vol. 38, pt. 4, 326–327, 352, 357.

29. Ibid., 366–367, 385, 408.

30. Brown, *Twenty-Seventh Indiana*, 503.

31. *O.R.*, ser. 1, vol. 38, pt. 4, 403, 415, 418, 454–455; *Cincinnati Commercial*, June 15, 1864, and June 21, 1864.

32. William Sherman to John Sherman, Acworth (Ga.), June 9, 1864, reel 8, cont. 14, William Sherman Papers, Library of Congress.

33. *O.R.*, ser. 1, vol. 38, pt. 4, 445–446, 459; Stone, "Atlanta Campaign," 418–419.

34. William Sherman to Ellen Sherman, Big Shanty (Ga.), June 12, 1864, reel 3, William T. Sherman Family Papers, University of Notre Dame Archives, South Bend, Indiana.

35. Oliver Howard to Lizzie Howard, near Marietta (Ga.), June 12, 1864, Howard Papers.

36. Joseph H. Parks, *General Leonidas Polk, C.S.A., the Fighting Bishop* (Baton Rouge: Louisiana State University Press, 1962), 382; *Autobiography of Oliver Otis Howard*, 1:563–564.

37. Lloyd Lewis, *Sherman: Fighting Prophet* (New York: Harcourt, Brace, 1932), 373–374; G. S. Bradley, *The Star Corps; or, Notes of an Army Chaplain during Sherman's Famous "March to the Sea"* (Milwaukee: Jermain & Brightman, 1865), 162.

38. See Stanley's report, *O.R.*, ser. 1, vol. 38, pt. 1, 223; Stone, "Atlanta Campaign," 419; Alexis Cope, *The Fifteenth Ohio Volunteers and Its Campaigns* (Columbus, Ohio: the author, 1916), 484; Castel, *Decision in the West*, 276, 280–281.

39. Walter Q. Gresham to Tillie Gresham, Kennesaw Mountain (Ga.), June 21, 1864, vol. 2, Walter Q. Gresham Papers, Manuscript Division, Library of Congress.

40. Brown, *Twenty-seventh Indiana*, 504–505.

41. Edwin E. Bryant, *History of the Third Regiment of Wisconsin Veteran Volunteer Infantry, 1861–1865* (Madison, Wis.: Veteran Association of the Regiment, 1891), 243.

42. *O.R.*, ser. 1, vol. 38, pt. 1, 877, and pt. 4, 492, 498.

43. Ibid., pt. 4, 507–508; William Sherman to Ulysses S. Grant, In the Field, June 18, 1864, William T. Sherman Papers, Henry E. Huntington Library, San Marino, California.

44. Castel, *Decision in the West*, 285. See also Stone, "Atlanta Campaign," 414–415.

45. On McCullagh, who served as John Sherman's secretary late in the war, see Walter B. Stevens, "Joseph B. McCullagh," *Missouri Historical Review* 25 (January 1931): 251–252; Charles C. Clayton, *Little Mack: Joseph B. McCullagh of the St. Louis Globe Democrat* (Carbondale and Edwardsville, Ill.: Southern Illinois University Press, 1969), 39–40. For Schofield's attitude see especially in the Sherman Papers, Huntington Library, the numerous letters exchanged between the two generals in 1884 and 1885 during a heated argument.

46. *O.R.*, ser. 1, vol. 38, pt. 4, 537–538.

47. Bryant, *History of the Third Regiment of Wisconsin Veteran Volunteer Infantry*, 246–248; *Autobiography of Oliver Otis Howard*, 1:572; Castel, *Decision in the West*, 294–295.

48. Walter H. Hebert, *Fighting Joe Hooker* (Indianapolis: Bobbs-Merrill, 1944), 39–41, 278; Lloyd Lewis, *Captain Sam Grant* (Boston: Little, Brown, 1950), 309; *O.R.*, ser. 1, vol. 31, pt. 2, 340, and vol. 38, pt. 5, 857; William Sherman to Charles W. Moulton, St. Louis, May 13, 1885, reel 47, letterbook in cont. 97, William Sherman Papers, Library of Congress.

49. *O.R.*, ser. 1, vol. 38, pt. 4, 561–563, 569.

50. Ibid., 558–561.

51. Ibid., 559–560.

52. Hebert, *Fighting Joe Hooker*, 280–281.

53. *O.R.*, ser. 1, vol. 38, pt. 4, 589; William Sherman to Ellen Sherman, near Marietta, June 26, 1864, roll 3, Sherman Family Papers.

54. *O.R.*, ser. 1, vol. 38, pt. 1, 68, and pt. 4, 588.

55. Castel, *Decision in the West*, 303–304; Stone, "Atlanta Campaign," 480–481.

56. Stone, "Atlanta Campaign," 422, 480–481; *Autobiography of Oliver Otis Howard*, 1:586–588; Charles Royster, *The Destructive War: William Tecumseh Sherman, Stonewall Jackson, and the Americans* (New York: Alfred A. Knopf, 1991), 296–316; John F. Marszalek, *Sherman: A Soldier's Passion for Order* (New York: Free Press, 1993), 272–273.

57. Nixon B. Stewart, *Dan McCook's Regiment: 52nd O.V.I.* (N.p.: the author, 1900), 118–123.

58. Ellen Sherman to William Sherman, Lancaster (Ohio), July 20, 1864, roll 5, Sherman Family Papers.

59. *O.R.*, ser. 1, vol. 38, pt. 4, 616–618; Cox, *Atlanta*, 130.

60. Stone, "Atlanta Campaign," 423; *O.R.*, ser. 1, vol. 38, pt. 5, 3, 15, 20; Cox, *Atlanta*, 132.

61. *Autobiography of Oliver Otis Howard*, 1: 593–597; *O.R.*, ser. 1, vol. 38, pt. 5, 29–31.

62. *Autobiography of Oliver Otis Howard*, 1:593–597; Charles A. Partridge, ed., *History of the Ninety-sixth Regiment Illinois Volunteer Infantry* (Chicago: Historical Society of the Regiment, 1887), 373–374; *O.R.*, ser. 1, vol. 38, pt. 5, 51.

63. *O.R.*, ser. 1, vol. 38, pt. 5, 55–59, 68–69, 73; Stone, "Atlanta Campaign," 423.

64. *O.R.*, ser. 1, vol. 38, pt. 5, 91–93; McDonough, *Schofield*, 86–88.

65. Dodge, *Personal Recollections*, 149–152; Interview with Lt. Edward Jonas, December 22, 1886, Dodge Records, vol. 4, 1183–1184, Grenville M. Dodge Papers, State Historical Society of Iowa, Des Moines. See also Philip Shipman, "Sherman's Pioneers in the Campaign to Atlanta," in Savas & Woodbury, *The Campaign for Atlanta*, 255–256, 261–262.

66. Dodge, *Personal Recollections*, 150; *O.R.*, ser. 1, vol. 38, pt. 5, 73, 76–77; *Confederate Veteran* 14 (July 1906): 296, and 14 (November 1906): 512–513.

67. Stanley F. Horn, *The Army of Tennessee* (Norman: University of Oklahoma Press, 1952), 340; William Sherman to Orlando M. Poe, St. Louis, January 15, 1866, cont. 11, Orlando M. Poe Papers, Manuscript Division, Library of Congress.

68. Edward O. Bartlett, *The "Dutchess County Regiment" in the Civil War* (Danbury, Conn.: Danbury Medical Printing Co., 1907), 98–99; W. H. Chamberlain, *History of the Eighty-first Regiment Ohio Infantry Volunteers During the War of the Rebellion* (Cincinnati: Gazette Steam Printing House, 1865), 126–127.

69. William E. Merrill to William Sherman, Nashville, November 9, 1865, reel 10, cont. 17, William Sherman Papers, Library of Congress; Willard Warner to John Sherman, near Marietta, July 9, 1864, vol. 73, John Sherman Papers, Manuscript Division, Library of Congress; George W. Herr, *Nine Campaigns in Nine States: The History of the Fifty-ninth Regiment Illinois Veteran Volunteer Infantry* (San Francisco: Bancroft, 1890), 212–214; Errol MacGregor Clauss, "Sherman's Rail Support in the Atlanta Campaign," *Georgia Historical Quarterly* 50 (December 1966): 415. On the maps, see Keith F. Davis, *George N. Barnard: Photographer of Sherman's Campaign* (Kansas City, Missouri: Hallmark Cards, 1990), 224.

70. John Sherman to William Sherman, Mansfield (Ohio), July 24, 1864, reel 8, cont. 14, William Sherman Papers, Library of Congress; Ellen Sherman to William Sherman, July 20, 1864, roll 5, Sherman Family Papers.

71. Stone, "Atlanta Campaign," 435–436; *O.R.*, ser. 1, vol. 38, pt. 5, 175–178, 185–186.

72. Grenville M. Dodge, "The Late J. M. Schofield," *Confederate Veteran* 15 (October 1907): 460–461; Grenville M. Dodge, "The Secret Service in the Civil War," Dodge Records, vol. 99, 16–18, Dodge Papers; Symonds, *Joseph E. Johnston*, 270–273, 311.

73. Castel, *Decision in the West*, 371–372; *O.R.*, ser. 1, vol. 38, pt. 3, 630–631, 698–699, 870–872.

74. Stone, "Atlanta Campaign," 441–443; *O.R.*, ser. 1, vol. 38, pt. 3, 630–633, 698–699, and pt. 5, 211.

75. *O.R.*, ser. 1, vol. 38, pt. 5, 196–197, 208; Castel, *Decision in the West*, 379–380.

76. Stone, "Atlanta Campaign," 449; Julian Wisner Hinkley, *A Narrative of Service with the Third Wisconsin Infantry* (N.p.: Wisconsin History Commission, 1912), 134–135.

77. John Bell Hood, *Advance and Retreat: Personal Experiences in the United States and Confederate Armies* (Bloomington: Indiana University Press, 1959), 173; Castel, *Decision in the West*, 385–387.

78. Stone, "Atlanta Campaign," 444–445; *O.R.*, ser. 1, vol. 38, pt. 5, 223–227, 231.

79. *O.R.*, ser. 1, vol. 38, pt. 1, 72; Castel, *Decision in the West*, 393; William E. Strong, "The Death of General James B. McPherson," *Military Essays and Recollections: Papers Read before the Commandery of the State of Illinois, Military Order of the Loyal Legion of the United States* (Chicago: Dial Press, 1891), 1:323–328. Strong's article must be used with caution. Sherman questioned the times given by Strong, and both Sherman and Logan believed he overemphasized his own role in the episode. See William Sherman to John A. Logan, Washington, D.C., July 21, 1876, reel 46, letterbook in cont. 92, William Sherman Papers, Library of Congress; William Sherman to William Conant Church, Washington, D.C., July 25, 1876, box 1, William Conant Church Papers, Manuscript Division, Library of Congress.

80. *O.R.*, ser. 1, vol. 38, pt. 3, 369–371, 475–477.

81. Strong, "Death of General James B. McPherson," 323–328.

82. William Sherman to Hugh Hastings, Washington, D.C., August 16, 1881, reel 47, letterbook in cont. 95, William Sherman Papers, Library of Congress.

83. Charles E. Putnam to Grenville M. Dodge, Cedar Rapids (Iowa), December 17, 1910, Dodge Records, vol. 21, 523, Dodge Papers. Lieutenant Colonel William Hempstead also noticed McPherson as "he rode by our front alone; and five minutes later he was killed." See his "Little Things About Big Generals," *Personal Recollections of the War of the Rebellion: Addresses Delivered before the Commandery of the State of New York, Military Order of the Loyal Legion of the United States* (New York: G. P. Putnam's Sons, 1907), 3:162.

84. *Confederate Veteran* 11 (March 1903): 118–119; *New York Times*, July 4, 1875.

85. William W. Belknap to Frank P. Blair Jr., near Atlanta, July 25, 1864, cont. 105, Dodge Papers.

86. *Memoirs of General William T. Sherman*, 2:77–78; Schofield, "Comments on Sherman's Memoirs," 26, box 95, Schofield Papers.

87. Walter Lord, "General Sherman and the Baltimore Belle," *American Heritage* 9 (April 1958): 102–104. Lord, the distinguished author, was Hoffman's grandnephew.

88. Ellen Sherman to William Sherman, Lancaster (Ohio), July 25, 1864, roll 5, Sherman Family Papers.

89. Schofield, "Comments on Sherman's Memoirs," 29–30, box 95, Schofield Papers.

90. *O.R.*, ser. 1, vol. 38, pt. 5, 234–235; *Autobiography of Oliver Otis Howard*, 2:11, 13–14.

91. William Sherman to John K. Shellaberger, Washington, D.C., May 13, 1881, reel 46, letterbook in cont. 46, William Sherman Papers, Library of Congress; Dodge, *Personal Recollections*, 160; James P. Jones, *"Black Jack": John A. Logan and Southern Illinois in the Civil War* (Tallahassee, Fla.: Florida State University Press, 1967), 193; James P. Jones, "The Battle of Atlanta and McPherson's Successor," *Civil War History* 7 (December 1961), 399–400. For the Logan-Thomas quarrel, see *O.R.*, ser. 1, vol. 32, pt. 3, 490, 521–522.

92. Dodge, *Personal Recollections*, 159–160.

93. Hebert, *Fighting Joe Hooker*, 284–285; *O.R.*, ser. 1, vol. 38, pt. 5, 272–273.

94. *Cincinnati Commercial*, August 4, 1864; Oliver Howard to Lizzie Howard, near Atlanta, August 11, 1864, Howard Papers; *O.R.*, ser. 1, vol. 38, pt. 5, 857.

95. William Sherman to Ellen Sherman, near Atlanta, August 2, 1864, roll 3, Sherman Family Papers; Milo M. Quaife, ed., *From the Cannon's Mouth: The Civil War Letters of General Alpheus S. Williams* (Detroit: Wayne State University Press and the Detroit Historical Society, 1959), 349–350; Samuel M. Bowman to William Sherman, New York, July 10, 1867, reel 12, cont. 21, William Sherman Papers, Library of Congress.

96. *O.R.*, ser. 1, vol. 38, pt. 3, 40; *Autobiography of Oliver Otis Howard*, 2:18–19; *The Story of the Fifty-fifth Regiment Illinois Volunteer Infantry in the Civil War, 1861–1865* (Clinton, Mass.: W. J. Coulter, 1887), 344–345.

97. *Autobiography of Oliver Otis Howard*, 2:20–21.

98. *O.R.*, ser. 1, vol. 38, pt. 3, 41, 104–105; *Story of the Fifty-fifth Regiment Illinois Volunteer Infantry*, 346–347; *Autobiography of Oliver Otis Howard*, 2:24; Castel, *Decision in the West*, 434.

99. Stone, "Atlanta Campaign," 450; *O.R.*, ser. 1, vol. 38, pt. 1, 75–77.

100. William Sherman to Ellen Sherman, near Atlanta, August 9, 1864, roll 3, Sherman Family Papers; William Sherman to John Sherman, St. Louis, February 24, 1867, reel 11, cont. 20, William Sherman Papers, Library of Congress.

101. William Sherman to John A. Spooner, near Atlanta, June 30, 1864, box 1, William T. Sherman Papers, Missouri Historical Society, St. Louis.

102. William Sherman to Ellen Sherman, near Atlanta, August 6, 1864, roll 3, Sherman Family Papers; William Sherman to William M. McPherson, n.p., n.d., Huntington Manuscripts, Henry E. Huntington Library, San Marino, California.

103. Wilbur F. Hinman, *The Story of the Sherman Brigade* (N.p.: the author, 1897), 585; Bartlett, *The "Dutchess County Regiment" in the Civil War,* 109, 115.

104. Bartlett, *The "Dutchess County Regiment" in the Civil War,* 109–110; Hinman, *Story of the Sherman Brigade,* 584–585; Bryant, *History of the Third Regiment of Wisconsin Veteran Volunteer Infantry,* 263–264.

105. Bryant, *History of the Third Regiment of Wisconsin Veteran Volunteer Infantry,* 264–265; Partridge, *History of the Ninety-Sixth Regiment Illinois Volunteer Infantry,* 98.

106. Hinman, *Story of the Sherman Brigade,* 585–590.

107. James F. Rusling, *Men and Things I Saw in Civil War Days* (New York: Eaton & Mains, 1899), 113–114.

108. Edwin W. Payne, *History of the Thirty-fourth Regiment of Illinois Volunteer Infantry* (Clinton, Iowa: Allen Printing, 1902), 133–134; Brown, *Twenty-Seventh Indiana,* 504, 510–511.

109. Hinman, *Story of the Sherman Brigade,* 590.

110. *O.R.,* ser. 1, vol. 38, pt. 5, 482; Castel, *Decision in the West,* 455–458.

111. Stone, "Atlanta Campaign," 451; Cope, *The Fifteenth Ohio Volunteers* 545; *O.R.,* ser. 1, vol. 38, pt. 5, 486–489, 547, 557.

112. *O.R.,* ser. 1, vol. 38, pt. 5, 629, 631, 980–982; Castel, *Decision in the West,* 473–475.

113. *Autobiography of Oliver Otis Howard,* 2:30–33; *O.R.,* ser. 1, vol. 38, pt. 5, 639, 691.

114. Herr, *Nine Campaigns in Nine States,* 281; *O.R.,* ser. 1, vol. 38, pt. 3, 700, and pt. 4, 990–994, 998.

115. *Story of the Fifty-fifth Regiment Illinois Volunteer Infantry,* 366–369; *O.R.,* ser. 1, vol. 38, pt. 3, 700, 764, 773–774.

116. *O.R.,* ser. 1, vol. 38, pt. 3, 701, and pt. 5, 718–719.

117. Ibid., pt. 1, 214–215, 932, and pt. 5, 745–746, 749–750.

118. Stone, "Atlanta Campaign," 456–457; *O.R.,* ser. 1, vol. 38, pt. 5, 746, 749, 751.

119. *Memoirs of General William T. Sherman,* 2:108; *O.R.,* ser. 1, vol. 38, pt. 5, 764, 765, 767–778.

120. Castel, *Decision in the West,* 533, 539; *O.R.,* ser. 1, vol. 38, pt. 5, 777.

121. *O.R.,* ser. 1, vol. 38, pt. 5, 791–794.

122. Ibid., 856–857.

123. William Sherman to Ellen Sherman, Atlanta, September 17, 1864, roll 3, Sherman Family Papers.

13. "A Scene I Pray My ― Eyes May Never See Again" ―

1. Adin R. Underwood, *The Three Years' Service of the Thirty-third Mass. Infantry Regiment, 1862–1865* (Boston: A. Williams, 1881), 233; Julian Wisner Hinkley, *A Narrative of Service with the Third Wisconsin Infantry* (N.p.: Wisconsin History Commission, 1912), 141–143.

2. *Cincinnati Commercial,* October 13, 1864.

3. *Memoirs of General William T. Sherman* (New York: Da Capo, 1984), 2:111; *Cincinnati Commercial,* September 17, 1864; Underwood, *The Three Years' Service of the Thirty-third Mass. Infantry Regiment,* 235.

4. *Cincinnati Commercial,* September 20, 1864, and September 22, 1864; John Bell Hood, *Advance and Retreat: Personal Experiences in the United States and Confederate Armies* (Bloomington: Indiana University Press, 1959), 229–236.

5. Edward O. Bartlett, *The "Duchess County Regiment" in the Civil War* (Danbury, Conn.: Danbury Medical Printing, 1907), 121–122; Hinkley, *A Narrative of Service with the Third Wisconsin Infantry*, 142. See also Lee Kennett, *Marching Through Georgia: The Story of Soldiers and Civilians During Sherman's Campaign* (New York: HarperCollins, 1995), 213–215.

6. *Cincinnati Commercial*, October 13, 1864; William T. Sherman, "An Address on General Ransom," in James Grant Wilson and Titus Munson Coan, eds., *Personal Recollections of the War of the Rebellion: Addresses Delivered before the New York Commandery of the Loyal Legion of the United States, 1883–1891* (New York: The Commandery, 1891), 1:115.

7. Thomas E. G. Ransom to Grenville M. Dodge, East Point (Ga.), September 13, 1864, Dodge Records, vol. 4, Grenville M. Dodge Papers, State Historical Society of Iowa, Des Moines.

8. George E. Spencer to Grenville M. Dodge, Kingston (Ga.), September 25, 1864, Dodge Records, vol. 4, 1447–1448, ibid.

9. *New York Herald*, October 7, 1864, and October 8, 1864; *Cincinnati Commercial*, October 10, 1864; William Wirt Calkins, *The History of the One Hundred and Fourth Regiment of Illinois Volunteer Infantry, War of the Great Rebellion, 1862–1865* (Chicago: Donohue & Henneberry, 1895), 240–241.

10. *O.R.*, ser. 1, vol. 39, pt. 2, 481, 503; Charles Royster, ed., *Memoirs of General William T. Sherman* (New York: Library of America, 1990), 1012–1026. This edition is cited only in this footnote.

11. John R. McBride, *History of the Thirty-third Indiana Veteran Volunteer Infantry During the Four Years of Civil War* (Indianapolis: Wm. B. Buford, 1900), 138; Underwood, *The Three Years' Service of the Thirty-third Mass. Infantry Regiment*, 236–238; Edwin E. Marvin, *The Fifth Regiment Connecticut Volunteers* (Hartford, Conn.: Wiley, Waterman & Eaton, 1889), 337.

12. Henry Hitchcock to Mary Hitchcock, Kingston (Ga.), November 4, 1864, Henry Hitchcock Papers, Manuscript Division, Library of Congress.

13. Ellen E. Sherman to William T. Sherman, South Bend (Ind.), October 11, 1864, roll 5, William T. Sherman Family Papers, University of Notre Dame Archives, South Bend, Indiana.

14. Ellen Sherman to William Sherman, Cincinnati, October 4, 1864, and South Bend (Ind.), October 11, 1864, roll 5, ibid.

15. William Sherman to Ellen Sherman, Summerville (Ga.), October 19, 1864, roll 3, ibid.

16. Calkins, *History of the One Hundred and Fourth Regiment of Illinois Volunteer Infantry*, 240–241; *Army and Navy Journal* 53 (June 17, 1916): 351; William Sherman to George H. Thomas, Atlanta, September 27, 1864, and September 28, 1864, box 2, William T. Sherman Papers, United States Military Academy Library, West Point, New York.

17. *O.R.*, ser. 1, vol. 39, pt. 3, 3; William Sherman to Oliver O. Howard, Atlanta, October 2, 1864, Oliver O. Howard Papers, Bowdoin College Library, Brunswick, Maine.

18. *Memoirs of General William T. Sherman*, 2:146–50; Alonzo L. Brown, *History of the Fourth Regiment of Minnesota Infantry Volunteers during the Great Rebellion, 1861–1865* (St. Paul, Minn.: Pioneer Press, 1892), 306–310; *O.R.*, ser. 1, vol. 39, pt. 1, 748–749.

19. Brown, *History of the Fourth Regiment of Minnesota Infantry*, 310–314, 324.

20. William Sherman to Richard Rowett, Washington, D.C., May 27, 1882, reel 47, letterbook in cont. 95, William T. Sherman Papers, Manuscript Division, Library of Congress. See also Phil Gottschalk, "The Battle of Allatoona Pass," in Theodore P. Savas and David A. Woodbury, eds., *The Campaign for Atlanta and Sherman's March to the Sea* (Campbell, Calif.: Savas Woodbury, 1994), 117–155.

21. *O.R.*, ser. 1, vol. 39, pt. 3, 162; *Memoirs of General William T. Sherman*, 2:152.

22. *O.R.*, ser. 1, vol. 39, pt. 3, 324–326, 357; *Cincinnati Commercial*, October 21, 1864, and October 24, 1864.

23. *Cincinnati Commercial*, November 12, 1864; Riley F. Ennis, "General Sherman on Supply Versus Mobility," *Infantry Journal* 37 (September 1930): 300.

24. *O.R.*, ser. 1, vol. 39, pt. 3, 222; Samuel M. Bowman to William Sherman, Wilmington (Del.), February 7, 1865, reel 9, cont. 15, William Sherman Papers, Library of Congress.

25. *O.R.*, ser. 1, vol. 39, pt. 3, 304–305; *Memoirs of General William T. Sherman*, 2:156.

26. *O.R.,* ser. 1, vol. 39, pt. 3, 357–358.

27. William Sherman to Ellen Sherman, Gaylesville (Ala.), October 27, 1864, roll 3, Sherman Family Papers.

28. Ellen Sherman to William Sherman, Lancaster (Ohio), October 31, 1864, roll 5, ibid.

29. *Army and Navy Journal* 51 (July 4, 1868): 733.

30. *New York Times,* December 28, 1894; *O.R.,* ser. 1, vol. 39, pt. 2, 502.

31. William Sherman to Joseph R. Hawley, Washington, D.C., January 11, 1880, reel 46, letterbook in cont. 94, William Sherman Papers, Library of Congress; Henry Van Ness Boynton to Orville E. Babcock, Washington, D.C., June 16, 1875, Ulysses S. Grant Papers, Manuscript Division, Library of Congress; Babcock to Boynton, Long Branch (N.J.), June 19, 1875, ibid.; Ulysses S. Grant to William Sherman, City Point (Va.), November 1, 1864, reel 8, cont. 15, William Sherman Papers, Library of Congress; *Army and Navy Journal* 6 (October 10, 1868): 118–119.

32. William Sherman to John McLaughlin, St. Louis, December 14, 1883, reel 47, letterbook in cont. 96, William Sherman Papers, Library of Congress.

33. William Sherman to Thomas T. Gantt, St. Louis, June 8, 1886, reel 48, letterbook in cont. 98, ibid.

34. George E. Spencer to Grenville M. Dodge, Rome (Ga.), November 1, 1864, Dodge Records, vol. 4, 1474–1477, Dodge Papers.

35. *O.R.,* ser. 1, vol. 39, pt. 3, 203; *Cincinnati Commercial,* October 27, 1864; William Sherman to John Sherman, Kingston (Ga.), October 11, 1864, reel 8, cont. 14, William Sherman Papers, Library of Congress.

36. John Sherman to William Sherman, Mansfield (Ohio), September 4, 1864, reel 8, cont. 14, William Sherman Papers, Library of Congress.

37. William Sherman to Ellen Sherman, Rome (Ga.), October 29, 1864, roll 3, Sherman Family Papers; *O.R.,* ser. 1, vol. 39, pt. 3, 493.

38. *O.R.,* ser. 1, vol. 39, pt. 3, 613–614, 658–660.

39. Ibid., 740.

40. J. Cutler Andrews, *The North Reports the Civil War* (Pittsburgh: University of Pittsburgh Press, 1955), 576–577; John Y. Simon, ed., *The Papers of Ulysses S. Grant* (Carbondale and Edwardsville, Ill.: Southern Illinois University Press, 1984), 12:403–404; *New York Times,* November 10 and 11, 1864.

41. *O.R.,* ser. 1, vol. 39, pt. 3, 740.

42. Simon, ed., *Papers of Ulysses S. Grant,* 12:410–411.

43. Calkins, *History of the One Hundred and Fourth Regiment of Illinois Volunteer Infantry,* 255; *Memoirs of General William T. Sherman,* 2:176–177.

44. *Atlanta Post-Appeal,* November 23, 1881; Underwood, *The Three Years' Service of the Thirty-third Mass. Infantry Regiment,* 239.

45. Aaron Dunbar, *History of the Ninety-third Regiment Illinois Volunteer Infantry* (Chicago: Blakely Printing, 1898), 144; Edwin E. Bryant, *History of the Third Regiment of Wisconsin Veteran Volunteer Infantry, 1861–1865* (Madison, Wis.: Veteran Association of the Regiment, 1891), 276.

46. Calkins, *History of the One Hundred and Fourth Regiment of Illinois Volunteer Infantry,* 257.

47. William Sherman to John K. Duke, Washington, D.C., June 6, 1883, reel 47, letterbook in cont. 96, William Sherman Papers, Library of Congress.

48. Bryant, *History of the Third Regiment of Wisconsin Veteran Volunteer Infantry,* 278–280; Underwood, *The Three Years' Service of the Thirty-third Mass. Infantry Regiment,* 244–245; Judson W. Bishop, *The Story of a Regiment: Being a Narrative of the Service of the Second Regiment, Minnesota Veteran Volunteer Infantry* (St. Paul, Minn.: n.p., 1890), 160–162.

49. Underwood, *The Three Years' Service of the Thirty-third Mass. Infantry Regiment,* 244–245; M. A. DeWolfe Howe, ed., *Marching with Sherman: Passages from the Letters and Campaign Diaries of Henry Hitchcock* (New Haven, Conn.: Yale University Press, 1927), 69.

50. Bryant, *History of the Third Regiment of Wisconsin Veteran Volunteer Infantry,* 280–281.

51. Eliot Norton, "Tales at First Hand," *Blackwood's* 233 (January 1933): 37–39.

52. Howe, *Marching with Sherman,* 76–77, 86–87, 131.

53. John J. Hight, *History of the Fifty-eighth Regiment of Indiana Volunteer Infantry* (Princeton, Ind.: Press of the Clarion, 1895), 419; Burke Davis, *Sherman's March* (New York: Vintage Books, 1980), 42.

54. Bryant, *History of the Third Regiment of Wisconsin Veteran Volunteer Infantry*, 281.

55. Alf G. Hunter, *History of the Eighty-second Indiana Volunteer Infantry* (Indianapolis: Wm. B. Burford, 1893), 138–139; Hartwell Osborn, *Trials and Triumphs: The Record of the Fifty-fifth Ohio Volunteer Infantry* (Chicago: A. C. McClurg, 1904), 176–177; Bishop, *The Story of a Regiment*, 158.

56. Underwood, *The Three Years' Service of the Thirty-third Mass. Infantry Regiment*, 243; Bryant, *History of the Third Regiment of Wisconsin Veteran Volunteer Infantry*, 281–282; Thomas M. Stevenson, *History of the Seventy-eighth Regiment O.V.V.I.* (Zanesville, Ohio: Hugh Dunne, 1865), 314.

57. David P. Conyngham, *Sherman's March Through the South* (New York: Sheldon and Company, 1865), 276–277.

58. Calkins, *History of the One Hundred and Fourth Regiment of Illinois Volunteer Infantry*, 260; Hight, *History of the Fifty-eighth Regiment of Indiana Volunteer Infantry*, 416.

59. Bishop, *The Story of a Regiment*, 159–160.

60. Calkins, *History of the One Hundred and Fourth Regiment of Illinois Volunteer Infantry*, 216; Davis, *Sherman's March*, 51–56.

61. Bryant, *History of the Third Regiment of Wisconsin Veteran Volunteer Infantry*, 278; *Memoirs of General William T. Sherman*, 2:185; Henry J. Aten, *History of the Eighty-fifth Regiment, Illinois Volunteer Infantry* (Hiawatha, Kans.: n.p., 1901), 246–247.

62. G. S. Bradley, *The Star Corps; or, Notes of an Army Chaplain during Sherman's Famous "March to the Sea"* (Milwaukee: Jermain & Brightman, 1865), 190; Underwood, *The Three Years' Service of the Thirty-third Mass. Infantry Regiment*, 246–247; Bryant, *History of the Third Regiment of Wisconsin Veteran Volunteer Infantry*, 282–284.

63. *Memoirs of General William T. Sherman*, 2:189–190; *O.R.*, ser. 1, vol. 39, pt. 3, 358; *Army and Navy Journal* 53 (May 6, 1916): 1150.

64. Davis, *Sherman's March*, 58–59; George Ward Nichols, *The Story of the Great March from the Diary of a Staff Officer* (Williamstown, Mass.: Corner House, 1972), 57–58.

65. Samuel H. Hurst, *Journal-History of the Seventy-third Ohio Volunteer Infantry* (Chillicothe, Ohio: n.p., 1866), 157–158; Bradley, *Star Corps*, 191–192.

66. Bryant, *History of the Third Regiment of Wisconsin Veteran Volunteer Infantry*, 284–285; Marvin, *The Fifth Regiment Connecticut Volunteers*, 355; Underwood, *The Three Years' Service of the Thirty-third Mass. Infantry Regiment*, 246–247.

67. Robert C. Black III, *The Railroads of the Confederacy* (Chapel Hill: University of North Carolina Press, 1952), 259–260; Bryant, *History of the Third Regiment of Wisconsin Veteran Volunteer Infantry*, 286.

68. Hunter, *History of the Eighty-second Indiana Volunteer Infantry*, 139; Howe, *Marching with Sherman*, 124; James Moore, *Kilpatrick and Our Cavalry* (New York: W. J. Widdleton, 1865), 180–182.

69. Stevenson, *History of the Seventy-eighth Regiment O.V.V.I.*, 316–317; Underwood, *The Three Years' Service of the Thirty-third Mass. Infantry Regiment*, 251–252; Hurst, *Journal-History of the Seventy-third Ohio Volunteer Infantry*, 159–160.

70. Stevenson, *History of the Seventy-eighth Regiment O.V.V.I.*, 161.

71. Bryant, *History of the Third Regiment of Wisconsin Veteran Volunteer Infantry*, 288–289; Underwood, *The Three Years' Service of the Thirty-third Mass. Infantry Regiment*, 252–253; Hurst, *Journal-History of the Seventy-third Ohio Volunteer Infantry*, 159–160.

72. Underwood, *The Three Years' Service of the Thirty-third Mass. Infantry Regiment*, 252.

73. Hight, *History of the Fifty-eighth Regiment of Indiana Volunteer Infantry*, 426–427, 432; James C. Bonner, "Sherman at Milledgeville in 1864," *Journal of Southern History* 22 (August 1956): 286.

74. Charles D. Kerr, "From Atlanta to Raleigh," in Edward D. Neill, ed., *Glimpses of the Nation's Struggle: A Series of Papers Read before the Minnesota Commandery of the Military Order of*

the *Loyal Legion of the United States* (St. Paul, Minn.: St. Paul Book and Stationery Company, 1887), 1:215–216; *Memoirs of General William T. Sherman*, 2:244–245.

75. Edwin W. Payne, *History of the Thirty-fourth Regiment of Illinois Volunteer Infantry* (Clinton, Iowa: Allen Printing, 1902), 172; Calkins, *History of the One Hundred and Fourth Regiment of Illinois Volunteer Infantry*, 272; Hurst, *Journal-History of the Seventy-third Ohio Volunteer Infantry*, 163.

76. *Memoirs of General William T. Sherman*, 2:194; Howe, *Marching with Sherman*, 161–164; William Sherman to F. Y. Hedley, Lake Minnetonka (Minn.), August 25, 1885, reel 47, letterbook in cont. 97, William Sherman Papers, Library of Congress; Charles C. Jones, *The Siege of Savannah* (Albany, N.Y.: Joel Munsell, 1874), 126.

77. *Memoirs of General William T. Sherman*, 2:194–195; Payne, *History of the Thirty-fourth Regiment of Illinois Volunteer Infantry*, 172.

78. *Memoirs of General William T. Sherman*, 2:195–196; Dunbar, *History of the Ninety-third Regiment Illinois Volunteer Infantry*, 153.

79. Howe, *Marching with Sherman*, 178; *Memoirs of General William T. Sherman*, 2:197–198.

80. Howe, *Marching with Sherman*, 178–181; Jeffrey Mosser, "Gateway to the Atlantic," *Civil War Times Illustrated* 33 (November–December 1994): 68.

81. William B. Hazen, *A Narrative of Military Service* (Boston: Ticknor and Company, 1885), 333–334; Mosser, "Gateway to the Atlantic," 68–70.

82. *Memoirs of General William T. Sherman*, 2:202–203.

83. Calkins, *History of the One Hundred and Fourth Regiment of Illinois Volunteer Infantry*, 272–273: Hurst, *Journal-History of the Seventy-third Ohio Volunteer Infantry*, 163; Underwood, *The Three Years' Service of the Thirty-third Mass. Infantry Regiment*, 254.

84. Maxwell Van Zandt Woodhull, "A Glimpse of Sherman Fifty Years Ago," in *War Papers: Military Order of the Loyal Legion, Commandery of the District of Columbia* (N.p.: n.p., 1914), 7–12.

85. Ibid., 12–16; *Memoirs of General William T. Sherman*, 2:206.

86. William Sherman to Ellen Sherman, Savannah (Ga.), December 16, 1864, roll 3, Sherman Family Papers.

87. *Memoirs of General William T. Sherman*, 2:210–218, 231; Nathaniel Cheairs Hughes Jr., *General William J. Hardee: Old Reliable* (Baton Rouge: Louisiana State University Press, 1965), 264–268; Underwood, *The Three Years' Service of the Thirty-third Mass. Infantry Regiment*, 255.

88. Underwood, *The Three Years' Service of the Thirty-third Mass. Infantry Regiment*, 254–255.

—— 14.   "Gone to Join Willy" ——

1. *Times* (London), December 3, 1864, in *Army and Navy Journal* 2 (December 24, 1864): 279.

2. *New York Times*, December 15, 1879. See also John Y. Simon, ed., *The Papers of Ulysses S. Grant* (Carbondale and Edwardsville, Ill.: Southern Illinois University Press, 1985), 13:148–149, 153–154.

3. Simon, *Papers of Ulysses S. Grant*, 13:131–132.

4. *Memoirs of General William T. Sherman* (New York: Da Capo, 1984), 2:224–228.

5. William T. Sherman to George H. Thomas, Savannah (Ga.), December 25, 1864, William T. Sherman Papers, Henry E. Huntington Library, San Marino, California.

6. Henry J. Aten, *History of the Eighty-fifth Regiment, Illinois Volunteer Infantry* (Hiawatha, Kans.: n.p., 1901), 263–264; Samuel Toombs, *Reminiscences of the War, Comprising a Detailed Account of the Experiences of the Thirteenth Regiment New Jersey Volunteers* (Orange, N.J.: The Journal, 1878), 192–194.

7. John J. Hight, *History of the Fifty-eighth Regiment of Indiana Volunteer Infantry* (Princeton, Ind.: Press of the Clarion, 1895), 451–452.

8. Aten, *History of the Eighty-fifth Regiment, Illinois Volunteer Infantry*, 264; Charles D. Kerr, "From Atlanta to Raleigh," in Edward D. Neill, ed. *Glimpses of the Nation's Struggle:*

A Series of Papers Read before the Minnesota Commandery of the Military Order of the Loyal Legion of the United States (St. Paul, Minn.: St. Paul Book and Stationery Company, 1887), 1:217.

9. M. A. DeWolfe Howe, ed., *Home Letters of General Sherman* (New York: Charles Scribner's Sons, 1909), 319; Henry Hitchcock to Mary Hitchcock, Savannah (Ga.), December 24, 1864, Henry Hitchcock Papers, Manuscript Division, Library of Congress.

10. Thomas Ewing to William Sherman, Washington, D.C., December 18, 1864, letterbook in cont. 166, Thomas Ewing Family Papers, Manuscript Division, Library of Congress; Hugh B. Ewing to William Sherman, Louisville, December 10, 1864, roll 1, William T. Sherman Family Papers, University of Notre Dame Archives, South Bend, Indiana; Ellen E. Sherman to Her Aunt, South Bend (Ind.), December 11, 1864, roll 9, Sherman Family Papers.

11. Ellen Sherman to John Sherman, South Bend (Ind.), December 26, 1864, reel 8, cont. 15, William T. Sherman Papers, Manuscript Division, Library of Congress.

12. William Sherman to Ellen Sherman, Savannah (Ga.), December 31, 1864, roll 3, Sherman Family Papers.

13. Ellen Sherman to William Sherman, South Bend (Ind.), December 30, 1864, roll 5, ibid.

14. Ellen Sherman to William Sherman, December 29, 1864, and January 4, 1865, roll 5, ibid.

15. William Sherman to Ellen Sherman, Savannah (Ga.), January 15, 1865, roll 3, ibid.

16. William Sherman to Thomas E. Sherman, Savannah (Ga.), January 21, 1865, roll 6, ibid.

17. Ellen Sherman to John Sherman, South Bend (Ind.), December 26, 1864, reel 8, cont. 15, William Sherman Papers, Library of Congress; Ellen Sherman to William Sherman, South Bend (Ind.), January 3, 1865, roll 5, Sherman Family Papers.

18. Ellen Sherman to William Sherman, South Bend (Ind.), December 29, 1864, and January 10, 1865, roll 5, Sherman Family Papers; William Sherman to Ellen Sherman, Savannah (Ga.), January 21, 1865, roll 3, ibid.

19. William Sherman to Ellen Sherman, Savannah (Ga.), January 21, 1865, roll 3, ibid.; William Sherman to George Thomas, Savannah (Ga.), January 20, 1865, copy, box 4, Hugh B. Ewing Papers, Ohio Historical Society, Columbus; Hugh Ewing to William Sherman, Lancaster (Ohio), February 7, 1865, box 4, Hugh Ewing Papers.

20. Howe, *Home Letters of General Sherman*, 326–327; Unpublished Memoirs of William T. Sherman, 52–56, reel 50, cont. 106, William Sherman Papers, Library of Congress.

21. *Memoirs of General William T. Sherman*, 2:237–238.

22. William Sherman to David D. Porter, Savannah (Ga.), December 31, 1864, William Sherman Papers, Huntington Library; *Memoirs of General William T. Sherman*, 2:241–242; *Personal Memoirs of U. S. Grant* (New York: Da Capo, 1982), 507–508; *New York Times*, January 31, 1865.

23. William Sherman to John Sherman, Savannah (Ga.), January 19, 1865, reel 9, cont. 15, William Sherman Papers, Library of Congress.

24. Hight, *History of the Fifty-eighth Regiment of Indiana Volunteer Infantry*, 452–453.

25. *Memoirs of General William T. Sherman*, 2:242–243; O.R., ser. 1, vol. 42, pt. 2, 35–36.

26. Hight, *History of the Fifty-eighth Regiment of Indiana Volunteer Infantry*, 456–458.

27. *O.R.*, ser. 1, vol. 44, 836–837; Henry W. Halleck to William Sherman, Washington, D.C., December 30, 1864, reel 8, cont. 15, William Sherman Papers, Library of Congress.

28. Salmon P. Chase to William Sherman, Washington, D.C., January 2, 1865, reel 8, cont. 15, William Sherman Papers, Library of Congress.

29. *Memoirs of General William T. Sherman*, 2:244–245; Paul M. Angle, ed., *Three Years in the Army of the Cumberland: The Letters and Diary of Major James A. Connolly* (Bloomington: Indiana University Press, 1959), 373.

30. Josef C. James, "Sherman at Savannah," *Journal of Negro History* 39 (April 1954): 127–133; *Memoirs of General William T. Sherman*, 2:245.

31. *Army and Navy Journal* 3 (February 10, 1866): 394; O.R., ser. 1, vol. 47, pt. 2, 60–62; *New York Times*, October 25, 1994.

32. William Sherman to John Sherman, January 19, 1865, cont. 15, William Sherman Papers, Library of Congress.

33. *Times* (London), February 23, 1865.

34. *O.R.*, ser. 1, vol. 47, pt. 2, 36–37.

35. *Memoirs of General William T. Sherman*, 2:252.

36. William Sherman to John Sherman, Savannah (Ga.), January 19 and January 22, 1865, reel 9, cont. 15, William Sherman Papers, Library of Congress; *O.R.*, ser. 1, vol. 47, pt. 2, 103–104.

37. Howe, *Home Letters of General Sherman*, 327.

38. *Times* (London), April 5, 1865.

39. William Sherman to Ellen Sherman, Savannah (Ga.), January 21, 1865, roll 3, Sherman Family Papers.

40. *Memoirs of General William T. Sherman*, 2:253–256; Aten, *History of the Eighty-fifth Regiment, Illinois Volunteer Infantry*, 267–269.

41. Simon, *The Papers of Ulysses S. Grant*, 13:296, 349–350.

___ 15.   The Carolinas ___

1. *Memoirs of General William T. Sherman* (New York: Da Capo, 1984), 2:268–269.

2. Ibid.; John J. Hight, *History of the Fifty-eighth Regiment of Indiana Volunteer Infantry* (Princeton, Ind.: Press of the Clarion, 1895), 467.

3. John M. Schofield, "Essay on Sherman's March," 3–4, box 95, John M. Schofield Papers, Manuscript Division, Library of Congress.

4. Manning F. Force, "Marching Across Carolina," in *Sketches of War History, 1861–1865: Papers Read before the Ohio Commandery of the Military Order of the Loyal Legion of the United States* (Cincinnati: Robert Clarke, 1883), 1:1–4; *O.R.*, ser. 1, vol. 47, pt. 1, 19; Alonzo L. Brown, *History of the Fourth Regiment of Minnesota Infantry Volunteers during the Great Rebellion, 1861–1865* (St. Paul, Minn.: Pioneer Press, 1892), 369.

5. Hight, *History of the Fifty-eighth Regiment of Indiana Volunteer Infantry*, 467–468; *Autobiography of Oliver Otis Howard* (New York: Baker & Taylor, 1907), 2:113–114.

6. Joseph B. Foraker, *Notes of A Busy Life* (Cincinnati: Stewart & Kidd, 1916), 1:53.

7. Hight, *History of the Fifty-eighth Regiment of Indiana Volunteer Infantry*, 467–468; *New York World*, June 17, 1875; Charles Elihu Slocum, *The Life and Services of Major-General Henry Warner Slocum* (Toledo: Slocum Publishing Company, 1913), 254–257; Foraker, *Notes of a Busy Life*, 1:53; Joseph T. Glatthaar, *The March to the Sea and Beyond: Sherman's Troops in the Savannah and Carolinas Campaigns* (New York: New York University Press, 1985), 142; Adin B. Underwood, *The Three Years' Service of the Thirty-third Mass. Infantry Regiment, 1862–1865* (Boston: A. Williams, 1881), 258–260.

8. *Army and Navy Official Gazette* 2 (April 18, 1865): 665.

9. Underwood, *The Three Years' Service of the Thirty-third Mass. Infantry Regiment*, 261–262; *Memoirs of General William T. Sherman*, 2:273–274.

10. Underwood, *The Three Years' Service of the Thirty-third Mass. Infantry Regiment*, 263; *O.R.*, ser. 1, vol. 47, pt. 1, 20.

11. *Autobiography of Oliver Otis Howard*, 2:110–111; *Memoirs of General William T. Sherman*, 2:275–276.

12. Frank H. Putney, "Incidents of Sherman's March Through the Carolinas," in *War Papers Read before the Commandery of the State of Wisconsin, Military Order of the Loyal Legion of the United States* (Milwaukee: Burdick & Allen, 1903), 3:385–386; Oliver O. Howard to William T. Sherman, Washington, D.C., April 12, 1866, Oliver Howard Papers, Bowdoin College Library, Brunswick, Maine; *"Our Women in the War": The Lives They Lived; The Deaths They Died* (Charleston, S.C.: News and Courier, 1885), 206; William B. Hesseltine and Larry Gara, "Sherman Burns the Libraries," *South Carolina Historical Magazine* 55 (July 1954): 141.

13. Marion Brunson Lucas, *Sherman and the Burning of Columbia* (College Station: Texas A. & M. University Press, 1976), 47–50; *O.R.*, ser. 1, vol. 47, pt. 1, 20.

14. *Autobiography of Oliver Otis Howard,* 2:119; *Memoirs of General William T. Sherman,* 2:278–279; Lucas, *Sherman and the Burning of Columbia,* 143. See also Charles Royster, *The Destructive War: William Tecumseh Sherman, Stonewall Jackson, and the Americans* (New York: Alfred A. Knopf, 1991), 13.

15. Lucas, *Sherman and the Burning of Columbia,* 49–50; William T. Sherman to John Sherman, St. Louis, April 2, 1866, reel 10, cont. 18, William T. Sherman Papers, Library of Congress.

16. J. P. Carrol, "The Burning of Columbia, South Carolina—Report of the Committee of Citizens Appointed to Collect Testimony," *Southern Historical Society Papers* 8 (May 1880): 204–205; Sherman's Comments, accompanying copy of General Order 26, reel 9, cont. 15, William Sherman Papers, Library of Congress; *O.R.,* ser. 1, vol. 47, pt. 1, 264–265.

17. Burke Davis, *Sherman's March* (New York: Vintage Books, 1980), 160; William Sherman to Joseph C. Breckinridge, New York, June 27, 1887, reel 48, letterbook in cont. 98, William Sherman Papers, Library of Congress.

18. William Sherman to John Sherman, St. Louis, April 2, 1866, reel 10, cont. 18, William Sherman Papers, Library of Congress; Oliver O. Howard to William Sherman, Washington, D.C., April 12, 1866, Howard Papers; Carrol, "Burning of Columbia," 205.

19. Lucas, *Sherman and the Burning of Columbia,* 164; Brown, *History of the Fourth Regiment of Minnesota Infantry,* 377.

20. Lucas, *Sherman and the Burning of Columbia,* 164; Sherman's Comments, accompanying copy of General Order 26, reel 9, cont. 15, William Sherman Papers, Library of Congress; Carrol, "Burning of Columbia," 208.

21. *Autobiography of Oliver Otis Howard,* 2:120; Brown, *History of the Fourth Regiment of Minnesota Infantry,* 373–374.

22. *Memoirs of General William T. Sherman,* 2:281, 284–286; Carrol, "Burning of Columbia," 205–206.

23. Carrol, "Burning of Columbia," 206.

24. *Memoirs of General William T. Sherman,* 2:286; Lucas, *Sherman and the Burning of Columbia,* 98.

25. Brown, *History of the Fourth Regiment of Minnesota Infantry,* 378; Richard Harwell and Philip N. Racine, ed., *The Fiery Trail: A Union Officer's Account of Sherman's Last Campaign* (Knoxville: University of Tennessee Press, 1986), 129; Carrol, "Burning of Columbia," 208–209.

26. Charles R. Woods to L. M. Dayton, near Longtown (S.C.), February 21, 1865, reel 9, cont. 16, William Sherman Papers, Library of Congress; Lucas, *Sherman and the Burning of Columbia,* 162–166.

27. Thomas M. Stevenson, *History of the Seventy-eighth Regiment O.V.V.I.* (Zanesville, Ohio: Hugh Dunne, 1865), 331.

28. Lucas, *Sherman and the Burning of Columbia,* 160–167.

29. Ibid., 99.

30. Carrol, "Burning of Columbia," 209–210; *"Our Women in the War,"* 209–210.

31. S. Sosnowski, "Scenes and Incidents during the Burning of Columbia, South Carolina," unidentified clipping, reel 51, cont. 109, William Sherman Papers, Library of Congress; Julian A. Selby, *Memorabilia and Anecdotal Reminiscences of Columbia, S.C.* (Columbia, S.C.: R. I. Bryan, 1905), 163.

32. *"Our Women in the War,"* 209–210.

33. Mother Superior to William Sherman, Columbia (S.C.), May 15, 1865, reel 9, cont. 16, William Sherman Papers, Library of Congress.

34. *Louisville Courier-Journal,* July 8, 1875; *Army and Navy Journal* 12 (July 17, 1875): 778.

35. William Sherman to Joseph C. Breckinridge, New York, June 27, 1887, reel 48, letterbook in cont. 98, William Sherman Papers, Library of Congress.

36. Stevenson, *History of the Seventy-eighth Regiment O.V.V.I.,* 332; Underwood, *The Three Years' Service of the Thirty-third Mass. Infantry Regiment,* 268.

37. Underwood, *The Three Years' Service of the Thirty-third Mass. Infantry Regiment,* 269; *The Story of the Fifty-fifth Regiment Illinois Volunteer Infantry in the Civil War, 1861–65* (Clinton, Mass.: W. J. Coulter, 1887), 411.

38. Hight, *History of the Fifty-eighth Regiment of Indiana Volunteer Infantry*, 485, 487.

39. Ibid., 487–488.

40. C. Vann Woodward, ed., *Mary Chesnut's Civil War* (New Haven, Conn.: Yale University Press, 1981), 745–746; Manly Wade Wellman, *Giant in Gray: A Biography of Wade Hampton of South Carolina* (New York: Charles Scribner's Sons, 1949), 169.

41. *Confederate Veteran* 12 (December 1904): 582; *O.R.*, ser. 1, vol. 47, pt. 1, 860; Aaron Dunbar, *History of the Ninety-third Regiment Illinois Volunteer Infantry* (Chicago: Blakely Printing, 1898), 175.

42. *Confederate Veteran* 12 (December 1904): 582.

43. *Army and Navy Official Gazette* 2 (April 18, 1865): 665; Slocum, *Life and Services of Major-General Henry Warner Slocum*, 263.

44. *O.R.*, ser. 1, vol. 47, pt. 2, 596–597.

45. Cornelius Cadle Jr., "The Recollections of an Adjutant in the War of the Rebellion," vol. 101, 19, Grenville M. Dodge Papers, State Historical Society of Iowa, Des Moines; *O.R.*, ser. 1, vol. 47, pt. 2, 649–650; Stevenson, *History of the Seventy-eighth Regiment O.V.V.I.*, 333.

46. *Memoirs of General William T. Sherman*, 2:290.

47. *Story of the Fifty-fifth Regiment Illinois Volunteer Infantry*, 411–412.

48. *Memoirs of General William T. Sherman*, 2:291; Henry J. Aten, *History of the Eighty-fifth Regiment, Illinois Volunteer Infantry* (Hiawatha, Kans.: n.p., 1901), 280.

49. *Memoirs of General William T. Sherman*, 2:291–292; Underwood, *The Three Years' Service of the Thirty-third Mass. Infantry Regiment*, 276.

50. *Memoirs of General William T. Sherman*, 2:292; Underwood, *The Three Years' Service of the Thirty-third Mass. Infantry Regiment*, 276.

51. William Sherman to John W. Draper, Washington, D.C., March 15, 1870, cont. 6, John W. Draper Papers, Manuscript Division, Library of Congress; *Army and Navy Journal* 34 (June 19, 1897): 583, and 54 (March 10, 1917): 885.

52. *Memoirs of General William T. Sherman*, 2:292; Foraker, *Notes of a Busy Life*, 1:55.

53. Dunbar, *History of the Ninety-third Regiment Illinois Volunteer Infantry*, 179–181.

54. E. L. Wells, "A Morning Call on General Kilpatrick," *Southern Historical Society Papers* 12 (March 1884): 125–127; Aten, *History of the Eighty-fifth Regiment, Illinois Volunteer Infantry*, 283–284.

55. Wells, "A Morning Call on General Kilpatrick," 128; Davis, *Sherman's March*, 155.

56. Edwin W. Payne, *History of the Thirty-fourth Regiment of Illinois Volunteer Infantry* (Clinton, Iowa: Allen Printing, 1902), 196–197; F. M. McAdams, *Every-Day Soldier Life; or, A History of the One Hundred and Thirteenth Ohio Volunteer Infantry* (Columbus, Ohio: Charles M. Cott, 1884), 141–142.

57. *Confederate Veteran*, 12 (April 1904): 177; 12 (December 1904): 588–589; 13 (July 1905): 315; 13 (October 1905): 456.

58. McAdams, *Every-Day Soldier Life*, 142; *Memoirs of General William T. Sherman*, 2:294–295.

59. Samuel H. M. Byers, "A Historic War Song," in *War Sketches and Incidents as Related by Companions of the Iowa Commandery, Military Order of the Loyal Legion of the United States* (Des Moines, Iowa: P. C. Kenyon, 1895), 1:393–397; Samuel H. M. Byers, *With Sword and Fire* (New York: Neale Publishing Co., 1911), 190; Samuel H. M. Byers, "Personal Recollections of General Sherman," *McClure's* 3 (August 1894): 218.

60. *Memoirs of General William T. Sherman*, 2:295; *The Countess Pourtales* (N.p.: S & H Publishing Co., 1915), 7–8, 45–51.

61. *Memoirs of General William T. Sherman*, 2:294–295; Eli J. Sherlock, *Memorabilia of the Marches and Battles of the One Hundredth Regiment of Indiana Infantry Volunteers* (Kansas City: Gerard-Woody, 1896), 207.

62. Byers, "Personal Recollections of General Sherman," 218.

63. *Memoirs of General William T. Sherman*, 2:298–299; William Sherman to Ellen Sherman, Fayetteville (N.C.), March 12, 1865, roll 3, Sherman Family Papers.

64. Edwin E. Bryant, *History of the Third Regiment of Wisconsin Veteran Volunteer Infantry, 1861–1865* (Madison, Wis.: Veteran Association of the Regiment, 1891), 315–316; Samuel Toombs, *Reminiscences of the War, Comprising a Detailed Account of the Experiences of the Thirteenth Regiment New Jersey Volunteers* (Orange, N.J.: The Journal, 1878), 209–210.

65. Toombs, *Reminiscences of the War,* 210–213; Bryant, *History of the Third Regiment of Wisconsin Veteran Volunteer Infantry,* 316–317.

66. Bryant, *History of the Third Regiment of Wisconsin Veteran Volunteer Infantry,* 317; M. A. DeWolfe Howe, ed., *Marching with Sherman: Passages from the Letters and Campaign Diaries of Henry Hitchcock* (New Haven, Conn.: Yale University Press, 1927), 283.

67. Nathaniel Cheairs Hughes Jr., *General William J. Hardee: Old Reliable* (Baton Rouge: Louisiana State University Press, 1965), 285–286; Bryant, *History of the Third Regiment of Wisconsin Veteran Volunteer Infantry,* 320; *Memoirs of General William T. Sherman,* 2:301–302; William Sherman to Mrs. A. A. Draper, Savannah (Ga.), January 15, 1865, William T. Sherman Papers, United States Military Academy Library, West Point, New York.

68. *Memoirs of General William T. Sherman,* 2:299–301; Payne, *History of the Thirty-fourth Regiment of Illinois Volunteer Infantry,* 198; Howe, *Marching with Sherman,* 288–290; *Autobiography of Oliver Otis Howard,* 2:141.

69. *Memoirs of General William T. Sherman,* 2:302–303.

70. Slocum, *Life and Services of Major-General Henry Warner Slocum,* 274–276; *Memoirs of General William T. Sherman,* 2:303.

71. Bryant, *History of the Third Regiment of Wisconsin Veteran Volunteer Infantry,* 321–322; Hughes, *General William J. Hardee,* 287.

72. Slocum, *Life and Services of Major-General Henry Warner Slocum,* 276–278; Dunbar, *History of the Ninety-third Regiment Illinois Volunteer Infantry,* 183; Leslie Anders, *The Eighteenth Missouri* (Indianapolis and New York: Bobbs-Merrill, 1968), 314; Henry Slocum, "Sherman's March from Savannah to Bentonville," *Century* 34 (October 1887): 937; Lansing H. Beach, "The Civil War Battle of Bentonville," *The Military Engineer* 21 (January–February 1929): 25–28.

73. Slocum, *Life and Services of Major-General Henry Warner Slocum,* 278–280, 288–289; Foraker, *Notes of a Busy Life,* 1:64. In October 1861, Sherman's friend Colonel Edward D. Baker stumbled into an ambush at Ball's Bluff, Virginia, and was killed.

74. Bryant, *History of the Third Regiment of Wisconsin Veteran Volunteer Infantry,* 323–324; Toombs, *Reminiscences of the War,* 214–215; McAdams, *Every-day Soldier Life,* 146–147.

75. Slocum, "Sherman's March from Savannah to Bentonville," 938; Slocum, *Life and Services of Major-General Henry Warner Slocum,* 289.

76. Anders, *The Eighteenth Missouri,* 315–316; *Autobiography of Oliver Otis Howard,* 2: 144.

77. Anders, *The Eighteenth Missouri,* 317–321; *Autobiography of Oliver Otis Howard,* 2: 149.

78. *Autobiography of Oliver Otis Howard,* 2:149–151; *Memoirs of General William T. Sherman,* 2:304–305. See also Glatthaar, *The March to the Sea and Beyond,* 168–172.

79. Schofield, "Essay on Sherman's March," 8–9.

80. *Memoirs of General William T. Sherman,* 2:304–305; Charles D. Kerr, "From Atlanta to Raleigh," in Edward D. Neill, ed., *Glimpses of the Nation's Struggle: A Series of Papers Read before the Minnesota Commandery of the Military Order of the Loyal Legion of the United States* (St. Paul, Minn.: St. Paul Book and Stationery Company, 1887), 1:221.

81. Bryant, *History of the Third Regiment of Wisconsin Veteran Volunteer Infantry,* 326–327; Kerr, "From Atlanta to Raleigh," 222.

82. McAdams, *Every-day Soldier Life,* 147; Brown, *History of the Fourth Regiment of Minnesota Infantry,* 394; Bryant, *History of the Third Regiment of Wisconsin Veteran Volunteer Infantry,* 327; Foraker, *Notes of a Busy Life,* 1:68–69.

83. Force, "Marching Across Carolina," 10; Kerr, "From Atlanta to Raleigh," 222.

84. William Sherman to William M. McPherson, Goldsboro (N.C.), March 24, 1865, Huntington Manuscripts, Henry E. Huntington Library, San Marino, California.

85. McAdams, *Every-day Soldier Life,* 148; Davis, *Sherman's March,* 245–246.

16.   "I Will Take a Regiment of
___ My Old Division and Clear Them All Out" ___

1. Joseph B. Foraker, *Notes of a Busy Life* (Cincinnati: Stewart & Kidd, 1916), 1: 65–66.

2. John. Y. Simon, ed., *The Papers of Ulysses S. Grant* (Carbondale and Edwardsville, Ill.: Southern Illinois University Press, 1985), 14:172–175; *Memoirs of General William T. Sherman* (New York: Da Capo, 1984), 2:311–313.

3. John M. Schofield, "Essay on Sherman's March," 4–5, box 95, John M. Schofield Papers, Manuscript Division, Library of Congress; William T. Sherman to George P. A. Healy, Washington, D.C., January 13, 1868, box 2, William T. Sherman Papers, United States Military Academy Library, West Point, New York.

4. *Memoirs of General William T. Sherman*, 2:324, 334; William Sherman to George P. A. Healy, Washington, D.C., January 13, 1868, box 2, William Sherman Papers, United States Military Academy Library; *O.R.*, ser. 1, vol. 47, pt. 1, 29; William T. Sherman to I. N. Arnold, Washington, D.C., November 28, 1872, William T. Sherman Papers, Chicago Historical Society; John Y. Simon, ed., *The Personal Memoirs of Julia Dent Grant* (New York: G. P. Putnam's Sons, 1975), 135–136.

5. William Sherman to George P. A. Healy, Washington, D.C., January 13, 1868, box 2, William Sherman Papers, United States Military Academy Library; William T. Sherman to John W. Draper, St. Louis, November 27, 1868, cont. 6, John W. Draper Papers, Manuscript Division, Library of Congress. Admiral Porter always maintained he was at the conference, but Sherman could not remember him being there.

6. William Sherman to George P. A. Healy, Washington, D.C., January 13, 1868, box 2, William Sherman Papers, United States Military Academy Library; *Memoirs of General William T. Sherman*, 2:325–328.

7. George R. Agassiz, ed., *Meade's Headquarters, 1863–1865: Letters of Colonel Theodore Lyman from the Wilderness to Appomattox* (Boston: Atlantic Monthly Press, 1922), 327; *Personal Memoirs of P. H. Sheridan* (New York: Charles L. Webster, 1888), 2:131–133.

8. William Sherman to Thomas Ewing, Goldsboro (N.C.), April 5, 1865, box 154, Thomas Ewing Family Papers, Manuscript Division, Library of Congress; William Sherman to Ellen E. Sherman, Goldsboro (N.C.), April 5, 1865, roll 3, William T. Sherman Family Papers, University of Notre Dame Archives, South Bend, Indiana.

9. *Memoirs of General William T. Sherman*, 2:333; William Sherman to Ellen Sherman, Goldsboro (N.C.), April 5, 1865, roll 3, Sherman Family Papers.

10. *Memoirs of General William T. Sherman*, 2:342–344; *O.R.*, ser. 1, vol. 47, pt. 1, 30; Simon, *Papers of Ulysses S. Grant*, 14:352–353.

11. William Sherman to Ellen Sherman, Goldsboro (N.C.), April 10, 1865, roll 3, Sherman Family Papers.

12. Edwin E. Bryant, *History of the Third Regiment of Wisconsin Veteran Volunteer Infantry, 1861–1865* (Madison, Wis.: Veteran Association of the Regiment, 1891), 328–329; *Memoirs of General William T. Sherman*, 2:343–344; Henry Hitchcock to Mary Hitchcock, Raleigh (N.C.), April 14, 1865, Henry Hitchcock Papers, Manuscript Division, Library of Congress.

13. *O.R.*, ser. 1, vol. 47, pt. 1, 30–31; Henry Hitchcock to Mary Hitchcock, Raleigh (N.C.), April 14, 1865, Hitchcock Papers.

14. *O.R.*, ser. 1, vol. 47, pt. 1, 31; *Memoirs of General William T. Sherman*, 2:346–347.

15. Simon, *Papers of Ulysses S. Grant*, 14:418; *O.R.*, ser. 1, vol. 47, pt. 3, 221.

16. William Sherman to John W. Draper, St. Louis, November 6, 1868, cont., 6, Draper Papers.

17. *Memoirs of General William T. Sherman*, 2:347–348.

18. William Sherman to John W. Draper, St. Louis, November 8, 1868, cont. 6, Draper Papers.

19. *Memoirs of General William T. Sherman*, 2:350–352.

20. William Sherman to John W. Draper, St. Louis, November 8, 1868, cont. 6, Draper Papers; *Memoirs of General William T. Sherman*, 2:352–357.

21. *O.R.*, ser. 1, vol. 47, pt. 3, 243–244.

22. M. A. DeWolfe Howe, ed., *Home Letters of General Sherman* (New York: Charles Scribner's Sons, 1909), 344–345.

23. Frederic Bancroft and William A. Dunning, eds., *The Reminiscences of Carl Schurz* (New York: Doubleday, Page, 1913), 3:114-15.

24. Henry Hitchcock to Mary Hitchcock, Washington, D.C., April 21, 1865, Hitchcock Papers; *O.R.*, ser. 1, vol. 47, 263–264, 285–286; Benjamin P. Thomas and Harold Hyman, *Stanton: The Life and Times of Lincoln's Secretary of War* (New York: Alfred A. Knopf, 1962), 405–407; Howard K. Beale, ed., *Diary of Gideon Welles, Secretary of the Navy Under Lincoln and Johnson* (New York: W. W. Norton, 1960), 2:294–296.

25. *Memoirs of General William T. Sherman*, 2:358–359; *O.R.*, ser. 1, vol. 47, pt. 3, 302.

26. *O.R.*, ser. 1, vol. 47, pt. 3, 313; *Memoirs of General William T. Sherman*, 2:363–364.

27. *New York Times*, April 24, 1865; Jacob Dolson Cox, *Military Reminiscences of the Civil War* (New York: Charles Scribner's Sons, 1900), 2:499–500, 511. For Stanton's doctoring of Halleck's message on Davis and plunder, compare *O.R.*, ser. 1, vol. 47, pt. 3, 277 and 286.

28. George C. Gorham, *Life and Public Services of Edwin M. Stanton* (Boston and New York: Houghton Mifflin, 1899), 2:187–188; Cox, *Military Reminiscences*, 2:501–506.

29. Cox, *Military Reminiscences*, 2:507–508; *O.R.*, ser. 1, vol. 47, pt. 3, 301–302, 311; Simon, *The Papers of Ulysses S. Grant*, 14:431–432; *New York Times*, April 26, 1865.

30. Thomas and Hyman, *Stanton*, 408–410.

31. Bancroft and Dunning, *The Reminiscences of Carl Schurz*, 3:116–117.

32. *Memoirs of General William T. Sherman*, 2:365–367.

33. Cox, *Military Reminiscences*, 2:510–511; *O.R.*, ser. 1, vol. 27, pt. 5, 791.

34. *O.R.*, ser. 1, vol. 47, pt. 3, 221, 245.

35. Ibid., 311–312, 454; Henry W. Halleck to Edwin M. Stanton, Richmond, April 26, 1865, box 1, William T. Sherman Papers, Missouri Historical Society, St. Louis; *New York Times*, April 28, 1865; Cox, *Military Reminiscences*, 2:511.

36. *Times* (London), April 5, 1865; *New York Times*, April 26, 1865; Thomas Ewing Jr. to William Sherman, Washington, D.C., May 1, 1865, letterbook in cont. 167, Ewing Family Papers.

37. Raoul S. Naroll, "Lincoln and the Sherman Peace Fiasco—Another Fable?" *Journal of Southern History* 20 (November 1954): 459–483; Foraker, *Notes of a Busy Life*, 1:68; Cox, *Military Reminiscences*, 2: 517–518.

38. Jacob D. Cox, "The Surrender of Johnston's Army and the Closing Scenes of the War in North Carolina," in *Sketches of War History, 1861–1865: Ohio Commandery of the Military Order of the Loyal Legion of the United States* (Cincinnati: Robert Clarke, 1888), 2:247–257.

39. Ellen Sherman to William Sherman, Lancaster (Ohio), April 25, 1865, roll 5, Sherman Family Papers.

40. Tom Ewing to William Sherman, Washington, D.C., May 1, 1865, letterbook in cont. 167, Ewing Family Papers.

41. *Memoirs of General William T. Sherman*, 2:369; *O.R.*, ser. 1, vol. 47, pt. 1, 38.

42. *New York Tribune*, February 22, 1891; *O.R.*, ser. 1, vol. 47, pt. 3, 410–411.

43. William Sherman to Henry W. Halleck, Morehead City (N.C.), May 7, 1865, William T. Sherman Papers, Henry E. Huntington Library, San Marino, California.

44. William Sherman to Ellen Sherman, Steamer *Russia*, May 8, 1865, roll 3, Sherman Family Papers.

45. Henry W. Halleck to William Sherman, Richmond, May 9, 1865, reel 9, cont. 16, William T. Sherman Papers, Manuscript Division, Library of Congress.

46. *O.R.*, ser. 1, vol. 47, pt. 3, 454–455.

47. William Sherman to Ellen Sherman, camp opposite Richmond, May 10, 1865, roll 3, Sherman Family Papers; William Sherman to Elizabeth Halleck, Washington, D.C., March 16, 1873, reel 46, letterbook in cont. 92, William Sherman Papers, Library of Congress.

48. William Sherman to Ulysses S. Grant, camp opposite Richmond, May 10, 1865, reel 9, cont. 16, William Sherman Papers, Library of Congress.

49. William Sherman to Elizabeth Halleck, Washington, D.C., March 16, 1873, reel 46, letterbook in cont. 92, ibid.; Henry J. Aten, *History of the Eighty-fifth Regiment, Illinois Volunteer Infantry* (Hiawatha, Kans.: n.p., 1901), 312–313.

50. *O.R.*, ser. 1, vol. 47, pt. 3, 478.

51. *Memoirs of General William T. Sherman*, 2:375; William Wirt Calkins, *The History of the One Hundred and Fourth Regiment of Illinois Volunteer Infantry, War of the Great Rebellion, 1862–1865* (Chicago: Donohue & Henneberry, 1895), 321.

52. Henry C. Morhaus, *Reminiscences of the 123d Regiment N.Y.S.V.* (Greenwich, N.Y.: People's Journal Book and Job Office, 1879), 185–187; Bryant, *History of the Third Regiment of Wisconsin Veteran Volunteer Infantry*, 331–332; Adin B. Underwood, *The Three Years' Service of the Thirty-third Mass. Infantry Regiment, 1862–1865* (Boston: A. Williams, 1881), 296–297.

53. Ellen Sherman to William Sherman, Lancaster (Ohio), May 17, 1865, roll 5, Sherman Family Papers.

54. *Memoirs of General William T. Sherman*, 2:375–376; Henry Hitchcock to Mary Hitchcock, camp near Washington, May 26, 1865, Hitchcock Papers.

55. Thomas and Hyman, *Stanton*, 415; George Ward Nichols, *The Story of the Great March from the Diary of a Staff Officer* (Williamstown, Mass.: Corner House, 1972), 350–382.

56. Aten, *History of the Eighty-fifth Regiment, Illinois Volunteer Infantry*, 320–321; John Richards Boyle, *Soldiers True: The Story of the One Hundred and Eleventh Regiment Pennsylvania Veteran Volunteers in the War for the Union, 1861–1865* (New York: Eaton & Mains, 1903), 306.

57. *Autobiography of Oliver Otis Howard* (New York: Baker & Taylor, 1907), 2:210–212.

58. *New York Times*, May 25, 1865; Boyle, *Soldiers True*, 309.

59. *New York Times*, May 25, 1865; Boyle, *Soldiers True*, 309–310; Calkins, *History of the One Hundred and Fourth Regiment of Illinois Volunteer Infantry*, 325.

60. *New York Times*, May 25, 1865; Boyle, *Soldiers True*, 309.

61. Henry Hitchcock to Mary Hitchcock, camp near Washington, May 26, 1865, Hitchcock Papers. Mrs. Grant noted that Sherman "shot" a "defiant and angry glance" toward Stanton. Simon, *The Personal Memoirs of Julia Dent Grant*, 159.

62. *New York Times*, May 29, 1865. For the denials by Stanton's son and Dana, see Gorham, *Life and Public Services of Edwin M. Stanton*, 2:198; *New York Sun*, June 15, 1875.

63. William Sherman to John M. Schofield, camp near Washington, May 28, 1865, William Sherman Papers, Huntington Library.

64. *O.R.*, ser. 1, vol. 47, pt. 3, 576; Simon, *The Papers of Ulysses S. Grant*, 15:98–99.

65. *O.R.*, ser. 1, vol. 47, pt. 3, 634–637; William Sherman to Tom Ewing, n.p., June 21, 1865, box 154, Ewing Family Papers; William Sherman to Elizabeth Halleck, Washington, D.C., March 16, 1873, reel 46, letterbook in cont. 92, William Sherman Papers, Library of Congress.

___ 17.   "Whatever We Do Here Causes Death" ___

1. *New York Times*, June 4, 1865, and June 5, 1865.

2. Ibid., June 7, 1865; Charles King, "A Boy's Recollections of Our Great Generals," in *War Papers Read before the Commandery of the State of Wisconsin, Military Order of the Loyal Legion of the United States* (Milwaukee: Burdick & Allen, 1903), 3:126, 134–135.

3. *New York Times*, June 17, 1865; Hartwell Osborn, *Trials and Triumphs: The Record of the Fifty-fifth Ohio Volunteer Infantry* (Chicago: A. C. McClurg, 1904), 217–218.

4. Marie Caroline Post, *The Life and Memoirs of Comte Régis de Trobriand* (New York: E. P. Dutton, 1910), 503; William T. Sherman to Thomas Ewing, Lancaster (Ohio), June 25, 1865, Thomas Ewing Family Papers, Manuscript Division, Library of Congress.

5. Working Sheet of Officers, St. Louis, March 15, 1866, reel 10, cont. 18, William T. Sherman Papers, Manuscript Division, Library of Congress.

6. William Sherman to Ellen E. Sherman, St. Louis, July 16, 1865, roll 3, William T. Sherman Family Papers, University of Notre Dame Archives, South Bend, Indiana.

7. John Sherman to William Sherman, Philadelphia, July 29, 1865, reel 9, cont. 17, William Sherman Papers, Library of Congress.

8. William Sherman to John Sherman, Lancaster (Ohio), August 3, 1865, reel 9, cont. 17, ibid.

9. William Sherman to John Sherman, Lancaster (Ohio), August 9, 1865, reel 9, cont. 17, ibid.; William Sherman to Thomas Ewing Jr., Lancaster (Ohio), August 10, 1865, box 154, Ewing Family Papers.

10. John Sherman to William Sherman, Mansfield (Ohio), August 13, 1865, reel 9, cont. 17, William Sherman Papers, Library of Congress.

11. William Sherman to Thomas Ewing, St. Louis, December 23, 1865, box 154, Ewing Family Papers; Charles Anderson to William Sherman, Columbus (Ohio), November 16, 1865, reel 10, cont. 17, William Sherman Papers, Library of Congress; Daniel Butterfield to Ulysses S. Grant, New York, February 15, 1866, reel 10, cont. 18, Sherman Papers, Library of Congress.

12. John Sherman to William Sherman, Mansfield (Ohio), August 13, 1865, reel 9, cont. 17, William Sherman Papers, Library of Congress; William Sherman to Tom Ewing, Lancaster (Ohio), August 10, 1865, box 154, Ewing Family Papers; William Sherman to John Sherman, St. Louis, August 18, 1865, and September 21, 1865, reel 9, cont. 17, William Sherman Papers, Library of Congress.

13. Ellen Sherman to Charles Ewing, Lancaster (Ohio), September 14, 1865, box 6, Charles Ewing Papers, Manuscript Division, Library of Congress.

14. Ellen Sherman to "My Very Dear Cousin," St. Louis, December 16, 1865, roll 9, Sherman Family Papers.

15. *Memoirs of General William T. Sherman* (New York: Charles L. Webster, 1892), 2:411–412; Robert G. Athearn, "General Sherman and the Western Railroads," *Pacific Historical Review* 34 (February 1955): 40; Dwight L. Clarke, *William Tecumseh Sherman: Gold Rush Banker* (San Francisco: California Historical Society, 1969), 99, 378.

16. William Sherman to Ulysses S. Grant, St. Louis, December 22, 1865, Ulysses S. Grant Papers, Manuscript Division, Library of Congress; William Sherman to John Sherman, St. Louis, December 28, 1865, reel 10, cont. 17, William Sherman Papers, Library of Congress.

17. Rachel Sherman Thorndike, ed., *The Sherman Letters: Correspondence between General and Senator Sherman from 1837 to 1891* (New York: Charles Scribner's Sons, 1894), 261; William Sherman to Willard Warner, St. Louis, January 16, 1866, William T. Sherman Papers, Illinois State Historical Library, Springfield.

18. William Sherman to Charles Ewing, St. Louis, January 4, 1866, and February 14, 1866, box 6, Charles Ewing Papers; Tom Ewing to William Sherman, Washington, D.C., February 6, 1866, letterbook in cont. 167, Ewing Family Papers; William Sherman to Thomas Ewing, St. Louis, February 23, 1866, box 154, Ewing Family Papers.

19. William Sherman to Thomas Ewing, St. Louis, February 23, 1866, box 154, Ewing Family Papers.

20. William Sherman to Edward O. C. Ord, St. Louis, March 1, 1866, box 1, William T. Sherman Papers, Missouri Historical Society, St. Louis.

21. Samuel M. Bowman to William Sherman, New York, March 1, 1866, reel 10, cont. 18, William Sherman Papers, Library of Congress.

22. Daniel Butterfield to William Sherman, New York, February 27, 1866, reel 10, cont. 18, and Washington, D.C., May 13, 1866, reel 10, cont. 19, ibid.

23. Ulysses S. Grant to William Sherman, n.p., January 16, 1866, reel 10, cont. 18, ibid.; William Sherman to Ulysses S. Grant, Niagara (N.Y.), July 27, 1866, Grant Papers; William Sherman to Tom Ewing, Washington, D.C., August ?, 1866, box 154, Ewing Family Papers.

24. Grenville M. Dodge, *Personal Recollections of President Abraham Lincoln, General Ulysses S. Grant, and General William T. Sherman* (Council Bluffs, Iowa: Monarch Printing Co., 1914), 184, 186.

25. Athearn, "General Sherman and the Western Railroads," 41; William Sherman to Ulysses S. Grant, Niagara (N.Y.), July 26, 1866, Grant Papers.

26. Robert G. Athearn, *William Tecumseh Sherman and the Settlement of the West* (Norman: University of Oklahoma Press, 1956), 59; Robert M. Utley, *Frontier Regulars: The United States Army and the Indian, 1866–1891* (New York: Macmillan, 1973), 2–3; William Sherman to Ellen Sherman, Fort Laramie (Wyo. Terr.), September 1, 1866, roll 3, Sherman Family Papers;

Blacksmith and Wheelwright (June 1885): 277, in scrapbook, reel 51, cont. 109, William Sherman Papers, Library of Congress.

27. William Sherman to Ellen Sherman, Fort Laramie (Wyo. Terr.), August 30, 1866, roll 3, Sherman Family Papers.

28. William Sherman to Ellen Sherman, Denver, October 10, 1866, roll 3, ibid.; Athearn, *William Tecumseh Sherman and the Settlement of the West*, 71–75.

29. James F. Rusling, *Men and Things I Saw in Civil War Days* (New York: Eaton & Mains, 1899), 119–120.

30. Athearn, *William Tecumseh Sherman and the Settlement of the West*, 77–78; Robert Wooster, *The Military and United States Indian Policy, 1865–1903* (New Haven, Conn.: Yale University Press, 1988), 108.

31. William Sherman to Ellen Sherman, Fort Garland (N.Mex. Terr.), September 20, 1866, roll 3, Sherman Family Papers.

32. Rusling, *Men and Things I Saw in Civil War Days*, 122.

33. William Sherman to Ellen Sherman, Denver, October 10, 1866, and Fort Ellsworth (Kans.), October 12, 1866, roll 3, Sherman Family Papers; William Sherman to John Sherman, St. Louis, October 20, 1866, reel 11, cont. 19, William Sherman Papers, Library of Congress.

34. William Sherman to Ellen Sherman, Washington, D.C., October 26, 1866, roll 3, Sherman Family Papers; Albert Castel, *The Presidency of Andrew Johnson* (Lawrence, Kans.: Regents Press of Kansas, 1979), 96–97.

35. William Sherman to Ellen Sherman, Havannah [*sic*], Cuba, November 18, 1866, roll 3, Sherman Family Papers.

36. William Sherman to Ellen Sherman, New Orleans, December 21, 1866, roll 3, ibid.; William Sherman to Ulysses S. Grant, St. Louis, December 30, 1866, Grant Papers.

37. E. S. Plumb to William Sherman, New Orleans, February 2, 1867, reel 11, cont. 20, William Sherman Papers, Library of Congress; William Sherman to Thomas Ewing, St. Louis, January 25, 1867, box 154, Ewing Family Papers.

38. Ellen Sherman to Thomas Ewing, St. Louis, January 20, 1867, roll 2, Sherman Family Papers.

39. William Sherman to Edward O. C. Ord, St. Louis, April 23, 1867, box 1, William Sherman Papers, Missouri Historical Society.

40. John Sherman to William Sherman, Washington, D.C., January 6, 1867, March 7, 1867, and March 14, 1867, reel 11, cont. 20, and March 24, 1867, reel 11, cont. 21, William Sherman Papers, Library of Congress; Charles H. Hoyt to William Sherman, Washington, D.C., March 16, 1867, reel 10, cont. 20, ibid.; Samuel M. Bowman to William Sherman, New York, March 10, 1867, reel 10, cont. 20, ibid.

41. William Sherman to John Sherman, St. Louis, March 14, 1867, reel 11, cont. 20, ibid.; William Sherman to Christopher C. Augur, St. Louis, February 28, 1867, box 1, Christopher C. Augur Papers, Illinois State Historical Library, Springfield; William Sherman to Grenville M. Dodge, St. Louis, January 16, 1867, and February 20, 1867, vol 105, Grenville M. Dodge Papers, State Historical Society of Iowa, Des Moines.

42. William Sherman to William Scott, St. Louis, April 6, 1867, box 1, William T. Sherman Papers, United States Military Academy Library, West Point, New York; William Sherman to Edward O. C. Ord, St. Louis, April 23, 1867, box 1, William Sherman Papers, Missouri Historical Society.

43. William Sherman to Edward O. C. Ord, St. Louis, May 28, 1867, box 1, William Sherman Papers, Missouri Historical Society; William Sherman to M. S. Branch, St. Louis, May 26, 1867, box 1, ibid.

44. William Sherman to John Sherman, St. Louis, September 28, 1867, reel 12, cont. 21, William Sherman Papers, Library of Congress.

45. William Sherman to Ellen Sherman, North Platte (Nebr.), September 19, 1867, roll 3, Sherman Family Papers.

46. Henry M. Stanley, *My Early Travels and Adventures in America and Asia* (New York: Charles Scribner's Sons, 1895), 1:197–216.

47. Ulysses S. Grant to William Sherman, Washington, D.C., September 18, 1867, reel 12, cont. 21, William Sherman Papers, Library of Congress.

48. William Sherman to Ellen Sherman, Washington, D.C., October 7, 1867, roll 3, Sherman Family Papers.

49. William Sherman to Thomas Ewing, St. Louis, October 18, 1867, box 154, Ewing Family Papers.

50. *Memoirs of General William T. Sherman,* 2:421; Benjamin P. Thomas and Harold M. Hyman, *Stanton: The Life and Times of Lincoln's Secretary of War* (New York: Alfred A. Knopf, 1962), 567.

51. Thomas and Hyman, *Stanton,* 568–569; William Sherman to Ellen Sherman, Washington, D.C., January 13, 1868, roll 3, Sherman Family Papers.

52. William Sherman to John M. Schofield, St. Louis, October 28, 1885, reel 41, letterbook in cont. 97, William Sherman Papers, Library of Congress; Stewart Van Vliet to William Sherman, Baltimore, February 13, 1868, reel 12, cont. 21, ibid.

53. William Sherman to Ellen Sherman, Washington, D.C., January 15, 1868, roll 3, Sherman Family Papers.

54. William Sherman to Thomas Ewing, Washington, D.C., January 25, 1868, box 154, Ewing Family Papers; Hans L. Trefousse, *Andrew Johnson: A Biography* (New York: W. W. Norton, 1989), 300; Thomas Ewing to William Sherman, n.p., January 25, 1868, reel 12, cont. 22, William Sherman Papers, Library of Congress.

55. William Sherman to Thomas Ewing, St. Louis, February 14, 1868, box 154, Ewing Family Papers.

56. William Sherman to Thomas Ewing, St. Louis, February 22, 1868, box 154, ibid. On the arrest of Thomas's daughter, see Ellen Sherman to William Sherman, Lancaster (Ohio), January 11, 1862, roll 4, Sherman Family Papers.

57. Trefousse, *Andrew Johnson,* 314, 317; John Sherman to William Sherman, Washington, D.C., February 23, 1868, reel 12, cont. 22, William Sherman Papers, Library of Congress.

58. Ellen Sherman to Thomas Ewing, St. Louis, March 5, 1868, roll 2, Sherman Family Papers; Tom Ewing to William Sherman, Washington, D.C., April 15, 1868, reel 12, cont. 22, William Sherman Papers, Library of Congress.

59. Athearn, *William Tecumseh Sherman and the Settlement of the West,* 196–197.

60. Ibid., 200–202; William Sherman to Ellen Sherman, Fort Laramie (Wyo. Terr.), May 10, 1868, roll 3, Sherman Family Papers; William Sherman to John Sherman, Denver, May 17, 1868, reel 13, cont. 23, William Sherman Papers, Library of Congress. This latter letter is misdated June 17, 1868.

61. Proceedings of the Council, May 28, 29, and 30, 1868, reel 13, cont. 23, William Sherman Papers, Library of Congress; William Sherman to John Sherman, Fort Union (N.Mex. Terr.), June 11, 1868, reel 13, cont. 23, ibid. See also the touching account of what happened to the agreement in John L. Kessell, "General Sherman and the Navajo Treaty of 1868: A Basic and Expedient Misunderstanding," *Western Historical Quarterly* 12 (July 1981): 251–272.

62. William Sherman to Ellen Sherman, Santa Fe (N.Mex. Terr.), June 7, 1868, roll 3, Sherman Family Papers.

63. William Sherman to John Sherman, Omaha (Nebr.), August 21, 1868, reel 13, cont. 23, William Sherman Papers, Library of Congress; William Sherman to G. Douglas Brewerton, Washington, D.C., March 11, 1880, reel 46, letterbook in cont. 94, ibid.

64. William Sherman to Mary Sherman, Fort Laramie (Wyo. Terr.), May 10, 1868, box 4, Nelson A. Miles Papers, Manuscript Division, Library of Congress; Virginia Weisel Johnson, *The Unregimented General: A Biography of Nelson A. Miles* (Boston: Houghton Mifflin, 1962), 32; William Ernest Smith, *The Francis Preston Blair Family in Politics* (New York: Macmillan, 1933), 2:390; William Sherman to Ellen Sherman, St. Louis, July 11, 1868, roll 3, Sherman Family Papers.

65. William Sherman to Ulysses S. Grant, St. Louis, June 7, 1868, and June 14, 1868, box 54, James William Eldridge Collection, Henry E. Huntington Library, San Marino, California;

William Sherman to Willard Warner, St. Louis, June 23, 1868, William Sherman Papers, Illinois State Historical Library.

66. Ellen Sherman to William Sherman, St. Louis, July 17, 1868, and July 19, 1868, roll 5, Sherman Family Papers.

67. Dodge Memorandum, July 26 and 28, 1868, vol. 105, Dodge Papers; Dodge, *Personal Recollections,* 187–190.

68. William Sherman to Ellen Sherman, Omaha (Nebr.), August 22, 1868, roll 3, Sherman Family Papers; William Sherman to John Sherman, St. Louis, September 25, 1868, reel 13, cont. 24, William Sherman Papers, Library of Congress.

69. Samuel F. Tappan to William Sherman, Washington, D.C., September 29, 1868, reel 13, cont. 24, William Sherman Papers, Library of Congress. On the Indian war, see William H. Leckie, *The Military Conquest of the Southern Plains* (Norman: University of Oklahoma Press, 1963), 88–93.

70. John Sherman to William Sherman, Washington, D.C., September 13, 1868, reel 13, cont. 24, William Sherman Papers, Library of Congress; William Sherman to John Sherman, St. Louis, September 23, 1868, and September 25, 1868, reel 13, cont. 24, ibid.

71. William Sherman to John Sherman, St. Louis, November 23, 1868, reel 13, cont. 24, ibid.

72. William Sherman to John Sherman, St. Louis, December 20, 1868, reel 13, cont. 24, ibid.; *Memoirs of General William T. Sherman,* 2:437–440.

73. Ellen Sherman to Thomas Ewing, St. Louis, January 11, 1869, roll 2, Sherman Family Papers; Ulysses S. Grant to William Sherman, Washington, D.C., January 5, 1869, box 9, William T. Sherman Papers, Ohio Historical Society, Columbus; Hamilton Fish, et al., to William Sherman, New York, March 3, 1869, box 9, William Sherman Papers, Ohio Historical Society; William Sherman to Christopher C. Augur, Washington, D.C., April 18, 1870, box 1, Augur Papers.

74. William Sherman to John M. Schofield, March 29, 1869, box 28, Hiram Barney Collection, Henry E. Huntington Library, San Marino, California.

—— 18. At War with Grant ——

1. P. Tecumseh Sherman, "Reminiscences of Early Days," 2–3, roll 14, William T. Sherman Family Papers, University of Notre Dame Archives, South Bend, Indiana; *Washington Evening Star,* July 18, 1942; Joseph T. Durkin, *General Sherman's Son* (New York: Farrar, Straus, 1959), 21–22.

2. Minnie Sherman Fitch, "Washington Society of 1869–1870," 2, roll 14, Sherman Family Papers.

3. Ibid., 3–4.

4. Sherman, "Reminiscences of Early Days," 4.

5. Fitch, "Washington Society," 4: Sherman, "Reminiscences of Early Days," 4–5.

6. *Memoirs of General Williams T. Sherman* (New York: Charles L. Webster, 1892), 2:443–444; *History of the Fifteenth Regiment, Iowa Veteran Volunteer Infantry* (Keokuk, Iowa: R. B. Ogden, 1887), 24–26.

7. William T. Sherman to Charles H. Hoyt, Washington, D.C., October 8, 1869, box 1, William T. Sherman Papers, Missouri Historical Society, St. Louis; William Sherman to John Sherman, Washington, D.C., October 5, 1869, reel 15, cont. 27, William T. Sherman Papers, Manuscript Division, Library of Congress; John Sherman to William Sherman, Mansfield (Ohio), October 10, 1869, reel 15, cont. 27, William Sherman Papers, Library of Congress.

8. Thomas B. Van Horne, *The Life of Major-General George H. Thomas* (New York: Charles Scribner's Sons, 1882), 432–443; John Russell Young, *Around the World with General Grant* (New York: American News Company, 1879), 2:296.

9. Gail Hamilton, *Biography of James G. Blaine* (Norwich, Conn.: Bill Publishing Co., 1895), 243–244; William Sherman to Orlando M. Poe, Washington, D.C., January 6, 1870, box 11, Orlando M. Poe Papers, Manuscript Division, Library of Congress.

10. William Sherman to William Conant Church, Washington, March 16, 1870, box 1, William Conant Church Papers, Manuscript Division, Library of Congress; William Sherman to Christopher C. Augur, Washington, June 9, 1870, box 1, Christopher C. Augur Papers, Illinois State Historical Library, Springfield.

11. William Sherman to John Sherman, Washington, D.C., July 27, 1870, reel 15, cont. 28, William Sherman Papers, Library of Congress; William Sherman to Ulysses S. Grant, Washington, D.C., July 27, 1870, Ulysses S. Grant Papers, Manuscript Division, Library of Congress; William Sherman to Edward O. C. Ord, Washington, D.C., August 1, 1870, box 1, William Sherman Papers, Missouri Historical Society; Sherman, "Reminiscences of Early Days," 3.

12. William Sherman to John Sherman, Washington, D.C., August 5, 1870, reel 15, cont. 28, William Sherman Papers, Library of Congress.

13. John Sherman to William Sherman, Mansfield (Ohio), October 21, 1870, reel 16, cont. 29, ibid.

14. William Sherman to John Sherman, Washington, D.C., October 23, 1870, reel 16, cont. 29, ibid.

15. John Sherman to William Sherman, Mansfield (Ohio), October 27, 1870, reel 16, cont. 29, ibid.

16. William Sherman to John M. Schofield, Washington, D.C., March 29, 1871, box 28, Hiram Barney Collection, Henry E. Huntington Library, San Marino, California.

17. William Sherman to Ellen Sherman, New Orleans, April 21, 1871, roll 3, Sherman Family Papers; Joseph G. Dawson III, *Army Generals and Reconstruction: Louisiana, 1862–1877* (Baton Rouge: Louisiana State University Press, 1982), 108.

18. *New York Times,* April 27, 1871, and April 29, 1871.

19. *Army and Navy Journal* 8 (June 10, 1871): 685; *New York Times,* June 9, 1871.

20. William H. Leckie, *The Military Conquest of the Southern Plains* (Norman: University of Oklahoma Press, 1963), 147–155; William Sherman to Ellen Sherman, San Antonio, April 29, 1871, Fort Concho (Tex.), May 10, 1871, and Fort Richardson (Tex.), May 18 and 20, 1871, roll 3, Sherman Family Papers; *Army and Navy Journal* 8 (July 8, 1871): 737.

21. William Sherman to Thomas E. Sherman, Fort Sill (Okla. Terr.), May 29, 1871, roll 6, Sherman Family Papers.

22. J'Nell Pate, "Indians on Trial in a White Man's Court," *Great Plains Journal* 14 (Fall 1974): 56–71, is a captivating article.

23. William Sherman to Thomas Ewing, Washington, D.C., July 8, 1871, box 154, Thomas Ewing Family Papers, Manuscript Division, Library of Congress.

24. William Sherman to John Sherman, Mansfield (Ohio), July 16, 1871, reel 16, cont. 30, William Sherman Papers, Library of Congress.

25. *Philadelphia Press* and *Catholic Telegraph,* undated clippings, roll 14, Sherman Family Papers; Ellen Sherman to Jane Ewing Latimer, Washington, D.C., November 29, 1871, roll 1, ibid.

26. "General Sherman's Tour of Europe," *Century* 57 (March 1899): 729.

27. William Sherman to Ellen Sherman, Cádiz, December 14, 1871, roll 3, Sherman Family Papers.

28. William Sherman to Ellen Sherman, Madrid, January 6, 1872, roll 3, ibid.

29. William Sherman to Ellen Sherman, Rome, February 18, 1872, roll 3, ibid.

30. William Sherman to Henry S. Turner, Naples, March 1, 1872, box 3, William T. Sherman Papers, Ohio Historical Society, Columbus.

31. *Army and Navy Journal* 16 (February 8, 1879): 477.

32. William Sherman to Ellen Sherman, Cairo, March 24, 1872, roll 3, Sherman Family Papers; William Sherman to Thomas Sherman, Cairo, March 29, 1872, roll 6, ibid.; Sherman, "Reminiscences of Early Days," 3.

33. William Sherman to Henry S. Turner, Sebastopol, April 25, 1872, box 3, William Sherman Papers, Ohio Historical Society; "General Sherman in Russia," *Century* 57 (April 1899): 871–875.

34. John Bigelow, *Retrospections of an Active Life* (Garden City, N.Y.: Doubleday, Page, 1913), 5:33–34.

35. "Sherman on Franco-Prussian Battle-Fields," *Century* 58 (May 1899): 279.

36. William Sherman to Ellen Sherman, Paris, July 7, 1872, roll 3, Sherman Family Papers; William Sherman to Thomas Haines Dudley, Paris, July 7, 1872, and July 14, 1872, Thomas H. Dudley Papers, Henry E. Huntington Library, San Marino, California.

37. William Sherman to Ellen Sherman, near Glasgow, August 25, 1872, roll 3, Sherman Family Papers; Philemon B. Ewing to Jane Latimer, Lancaster (Ohio), July 28, 1873, roll 1, ibid.; Thomas Ewing Family Record, box 293, Thomas Ewing Family Papers, Manuscript Division, Library of Congress.

38. Henry B. Reese to William Sherman, Louisville, September 15, 1872, reel 18, cont. 33, William Sherman Papers, Library of Congress; William Sherman to John Sherman, Washington, D.C., September 25, 1872, reel 18, cont. 33, ibid.; *New York Times*, December 27, 1872.

39. Sherman, "Reminiscences of Early Days," 4. At the inauguration Sherman disgusted his staff by wearing a pair of bright yellow kid gloves. See Ben: Perley Poore, *Perley's Reminiscences of Sixty Years in the National Metropolis* (Philadelphia: Hubbard Brothers, 1886), 296.

40. Robert M. Utley, *Frontier Regulars: The United States Army and the Indian, 1866–1891* (New York: Macmillan, 1973), 198–207.

41. William Sherman to John M. Schofield, Washington, D.C., April 24, 1873, box 28, Barney Collection; Richard Allen Andrews, "Years of Frustration: William T. Sherman, the Army and Reform, 1869–1883" (Ph.D. diss., Northwestern University, June 1968), 109–110; William Sherman to Stephen A. Hurlbut, Washington, D.C., May 26, 1874, reel 46, letterbook in cont. 92, William Sherman Papers, Library of Congress.

42. William Sherman to Edward O. C. Ord, Washington, D.C., May 23, 1874, box 1, William Sherman Papers, Missouri Historical Society.

43. William Sherman to William Conant Church, Washington, D.C., July 18, 1874, box 1, Church Papers.

44. *Memoirs of General William T. Sherman*, 2:453–454; Wedding invitation, Maria Ewing Sherman, roll 6, Sherman Family Papers.

45. William Sherman to Thomas Sherman, St. Louis, October 23, 1874, roll 6, Sherman Family Papers.

▬ 19. Of Lizzie and Tom ▬

1. P. Tecumseh Sherman, "Reminiscences of Early Days," 9, roll 14, William T. Sherman Family Papers, University of Notre Dame Archives, South Bend, Indiana.

2. Ibid., 10–11.

3. Ibid., 12–13.

4. Ibid., 14; John B. Hood to William T. Sherman, New Orleans, April 20, 1871, reel 16, cont. 30, William T. Sherman Papers, Manuscript Division, Library of Congress. In 1875 Sherman, hearing that Hood was in St. Louis, "called on him at his Hotel, & had him to dine with my family & a few friends." He was convinced, he told Professor Charles Davies of West Point, that bitterness in the South was "manifested" not "by the active combatants" but by "women & boys grown up since the War." See William Sherman to Charles Davies, St. Louis, February 26, 1875, Charles Davies Papers, United States Military Academy Library, West Point, New York.

5. Sherman, "Reminiscences of Early Days," 16.

6. William Sherman to William Conant Church, St. Louis, January 26, 1875, box 1, William Conant Church Papers, Manuscript Division, Library of Congress; William Sherman to William Scott, St. Louis, January 23, 1875, box 1, William T. Sherman Papers, Missouri Historical Society, St. Louis; William Sherman to Thomas E. Sherman, St. Louis, January 16, 1875, roll 7, Sherman Family Papers.

7. William Sherman to John Sherman, St. Louis, May 25, 1875, reel 20, cont. 39, William Sherman Papers, Library of Congress.

8. *New York Times,* May 28, 1875; Henry W. Slocum to William Sherman, Brooklyn, May 20, 1875, reel 20, cont. 39, William Sherman Papers, Library of Congress; William Sherman to John Sherman, St. Louis, May 25, 1875, reel 20, cont. 39, William Sherman Papers, Library of Congress.

9. Judson Kilpatrick to the *New York Times,* clipping, reel 51, cont. 109, William Sherman Papers, Library of Congress; William Sherman to William Conant Church, St. Louis, October 3, 1875, box 1, Church Papers; William Sherman to Orlando M. Poe, St. Louis, November 30, 1875, box 11, Orlando M. Poe Papers, Manuscript Division, Library of Congress.

10. *Confederate Veteran* 5 (March 1897): 120; Henry Van Ness Boynton to Whitelaw Reid, Washington, D.C., October 10, 1875, and October 18, 1875, cont. 76, Whitelaw Reid Papers, Manuscript Division, Library of Congress; William Sherman to John W. Draper, St. Louis, November 19, 1875, cont. 6, John W. Draper Papers, Manuscript Division, Library of Congress.

11. H. V. Boynton, *Sherman's Historical Raid: The Memoirs in the Light of the Record* (Cincinnati: Wilstach, Baldwin, 1875), passim; Henry Van Ness Boynton to Orville E. Babcock, Washington, D.C., June 16, 1875, Ulysses S. Grant Papers, Manuscript Division, Library of Congress; Memo on Boynton's Book by John W. Draper, undated, cont. 6, Draper Papers.

12. William Sherman to C. H. Grosvenor, St. Louis, July 13, 1875, reel 46, letterbook in cont. 92, William Sherman Papers, Library of Congress.

13. C. W. Moulton, *The Review of General Sherman's Memoirs Examined* (Cincinnati: Robert Clarke, 1875); Richard Allen Andrews, "Years of Frustration: William T. Sherman, the Army and Reform, 1869–1883" (Ph.D. diss., Northwestern University, 1968), 139–140; William Sherman to John W. Draper, St. Louis, December 17, 1875, cont. 6, Draper Papers.

14. William Sherman to John Sherman, St. Louis, May 14, 1886, reel 36, cont. 70, William Sherman Papers, Library of Congress.

15. William Sherman to John Sherman, St. Louis, March 4, 1876, reel 22, cont. 42, ibid.; Andrews, "Years of Frustration," 144–145.

16. William Sherman to David D. Porter, St. Louis, March 15, 1876, box 1, William Sherman Papers, Missouri Historical Society.

17. William Sherman to Thomas Sherman, St. Louis, March 15, 1876, and March 30, 1876, roll 7, Sherman Family Papers.

18. Andrews, "Years of Frustration," 147–150; William Sherman to Thomas Sherman, Washington, D.C., April 23, 1876, roll 7, Sherman Family Papers.

19. Sherman, "Reminiscences of Early Days," 9; William Sherman to Ellen Sherman, May 23, 1876, and May 27, 1876, roll 3, Sherman Family Papers.

20. William Sherman to Ellen Sherman, Washington, D.C., June 1, 1876, roll 3, Sherman Family Papers.

21. William Sherman to Thomas Sherman, Washington, D.C., June 3, 1876, roll 7, ibid.; *New York Times,* May 10, 1878.

22. Ellen Sherman to William Sherman, Fort Leavenworth (Kans.), May 8, 1876, roll 5, Sherman Family Papers; William Sherman to Ellen Sherman, Washington, D.C., May 13, 1876, roll 3, ibid.

23. Ellen Sherman to William Sherman, St. Louis, June 21, 1876, roll 5, ibid.

24. William Sherman to Samuel F. Tappan, Washington, D.C., July 21, 1876, reel 46, letterbook in cont. 92, William Sherman Papers, Library of Congress. See also *Army and Navy Journal* 13 (July 29, 1876): 821.

25. William Sherman to Nelson A. Miles, Washington, D.C., July 29, 1876, box 4, Nelson A. Miles Papers, Manuscript Division, Library of Congress.

26. William Sherman to Mary Sherman Miles, Washington, D.C., August 20, 1876, box 4, ibid.

27. William Sherman to Nelson A. Miles, Washington, D.C., October 20, 1876, box 4, ibid.

28. William Sherman to Nelson A. Miles, Washington, D.C., December 4, 1876, box 4, ibid.

29. John E. Tourtellotte to William Sherman, North Grosvenor Dale (Conn.), July 8, 1876, reel 23, cont. 44, William Sherman Papers, Library of Congress; Thomas Sherman to William Sherman, St. Louis, October 13, 1876, roll 7, Sherman Family Papers; William Sherman to Ellen Sherman, Washington, D.C., March 3, 1877, roll 4, Sherman Family Papers.

30. William Sherman to Ellen Sherman, Washington, D.C., March 3, 1877, roll 4, Sherman Family Papers.

31. William Sherman to John M. Schofield, Washington, D.C., March 13, 1877, box 28, Hiram Barney Collection, Henry E. Huntington Library, San Marino, California.

32. William Sherman to Nelson A. Miles, Washington, D.C., April 23, 1877, box 4, Miles Papers.

33. William Sherman to Nelson A. Miles, Washington, D.C., June 26, 1877, box 4, Miles Papers; William Sherman to J. Donald Cameron, Tongue River (Mont.), July 17, 1877, ibid.

34. Hugh L. Scott, *Some Memories of a Soldier* (New York and London: Century, 1928), 52–53.

35. William Sherman to Ellen Sherman, Steamboat *Rosebud*, Mouth of Big Horn, July 25, 1877, and Fort Ellis (Mont. Terr.), August 3, 1877, roll 4, Sherman Family Papers; William Sherman to Edward D. Townsend, Fort Ellis (Mont. Terr.), August 3, 1877, Edward D. Townsend Papers, Henry E. Huntington Library, San Marino, California.

36. William Sherman to Ellen Sherman, Walla Walla (Wash. Terr.), September 19, 1877, roll 4, Sherman Family Papers.

37. William Sherman to Nelson A. Miles, Washington, D.C., November 13, 1877, box 4, Miles Papers; William Sherman to Willard Warner, Washington, D.C., December 6, 1877, William T. Sherman Papers, Illinois State Historical Library, Springfield.

38. William Sherman to Nelson A. Miles, Washington, D.C., January 9, 1878, box 4, Miles Papers; William Sherman to F. V. Greene, Washington, D.C., January 13, 1878, reel 46, letterbook in cont. 92, William Sherman Papers, Library of Congress.

39. William Sherman to Lizzie Sherman, Washington, D.C., April 1, 1878, box 4, Miles Papers.

40. *New York Times*, May 10, 1878; Arline Boucher Tehan, *Henry Adams in Love: The Pursuit of Elizabeth Sherman Cameron* (New York: Universe Books, 1983), 39–41. See especially Julia Stoddard Parsons, *Scattered Memories* (Boston: Bruce Humphries, 1938), 56.

41. Ellen Sherman to William Sherman, St. Louis, May 13, 1878, roll 5, Sherman Family Papers; Thomas Sherman to William Sherman, St. Louis, May 20, 1878, roll 7, ibid.; *New York Times*, October 6, 1878, and October 13, 1878; Tehan, *Henry Adams in Love*, 16, 41, 63, and 156. Into such society, which was far beyond the reach of Tom, the accomplished General Sherman fit admirably. One night at a dinner at the Camerons, Mrs. Adams found herself sitting next to a bore. From across the table she caught "the merry blue eyes" of the general, asking something about his war experiences. That was all Sherman needed. Using knives and forks, he explained the story of his great achievements, sweeping "the rebel army off the tablecloth with a pudding knife to the amusement of his audience." See Tehan, *Henry Adams in Love*, 63.

42. Ellen Sherman to William Sherman, St. Louis, May 25, 1878, roll 5, ibid.; Ellen Sherman to Minnie Sherman Fitch, St. Louis, May 21, 1878, roll 6, ibid.

43. Ellen Sherman to William Sherman, Lancaster (Ohio), June 15, 1858, roll 4, ibid.; Ellen Sherman to William Sherman, South Bend (Ind.), January 4, 1865, roll 5, ibid.

44. Ellen Sherman to Minnie Fitch, St. Louis, May 30, 1878, roll 6, ibid.; Sketch of Major Henry S. Turner, 1, box 1, Henry Smith Turner Papers, Missouri Historical Society, St. Louis; William Sherman to Henry S. Turner, Washington, D.C., May 27, 1878, box 3, William T. Sherman Papers, Ohio Historical Society, Columbus.

45. William Sherman to John M. Schofield, Washington, D.C., May 28, 1878, box 28, Barney Collection.

46. William Sherman to Charles Ewing, Washington, D.C., May 29, 1878, box 7, Charles Ewing Papers, Manuscript Division, Library of Congress; John Tracy Ellis, *The Life of James Cardinal Gibbons, Archbishop of Baltimore, 1834–1921* (Milwaukee: Bruce Publishing Company, 1952), 1:193.

47. Thomas Ewing III to Basil Liddell Hart, n.p., March 5, 1930, box 154, Thomas Ewing Family Papers, Manuscript Division, Library of Congress.

48. William Sherman to Eleanor M. Sherman, Washington, D.C., June 4, 1878, box 1, William Sherman Papers, Ohio Historical Society; William Sherman to Samuel H. M. Byers, Washington, D.C., June 30, 1878, Samuel H. M. Byers Papers, State Historical Society of Iowa, Des Moines; Jack J. Detzler, "The Religion of William Tecumseh Sherman," *Ohio History* 75 (Winter 1966): 29.

49. John Cardinal Farley, *The Life of John Cardinal McCloskey, First Prince of the Church in America, 1810–1885* (New York: Longmans, Green, 1918), 344–345; William Sherman to John Cardinal McCloskey, Washington, D.C., June 3, 1878, reel 46, letterbook in cont. 93, William Sherman Papers, Library of Congress; William Sherman to John M. Schofield, Washington, D.C., June 5, 1878, box 28, Barney Collection; Thomas Sherman to Minnie Fitch, New York, June 4, 1878, roll 6, Sherman Family Papers.

50. William Sherman to Samuel H. M. Byers, Washington, D.C., June 30, 1878, Byers Papers.

51. William Sherman to Henry S. Turner, Washington, D.C., June 28, 1878, box 3, William Sherman Papers, Ohio Historical Society; *Army and Navy Journal* 15 (July 13, 1878): 795 and 15 (July 20, 1878): 809. See also Ellen Sherman's letter to Father Daniel E. Hudson, the editor of *Ave Maria,* Lancaster (Ohio), July 16, 1878, roll 1, Sherman Family Papers.

52. William Sherman to Lizzie Sherman Cameron, Washington, D.C., August 3, 1878, and August 7, 1878, box 4, Miles Papers.

53. Samuel M. Bowman to William Sherman, Baltimore, July 4, 1878, reel 25, cont. 48, William Sherman Papers, Library of Congress.

54. Thomas Sherman to Ellen Sherman, London, October 24, 1878, and May 9, 1880, roll 7, Sherman Family Papers.

55. William Sherman to John M. Schofield, Washington, D.C., April 25, 1879, box 28, Barney Collection; Sherman, "Reminiscences of Early Days," 24.

56. Sherman, "Reminiscences of Early Days," 25, 28–30; James L. Morrison Jr., ed., *The Memoirs of Henry Heth* (Westport, Conn.: Greenwood Press, 1974), 209–210.

57. Andrews, "Years of Frustration," 208–212; William Sherman to John M. Schofield, Washington, D.C., January 19, 1879, Barney Collection; William Sherman to Philip H. Sheridan, Washington, D.C., January 19, 1879, reel 17, cont. 39, Philip H. Sheridan Papers, Manuscript Division, Library of Congress.

58. Andrews, "Years of Frustration," 214–216; William Sherman to Samuel H. M. Byers, Washington, D.C., March 22, 1879, Byers Papers.

59. William Sherman to William G. Eliot, May 26, 1879, box 2, William G. Eliot Papers, Missouri Historical Society, St. Louis.

60. William Sherman to William G. Eliot, Washington, D.C., August 3, 1879, box 2, ibid.

61. William Sherman to William Conant Church, Washington, D.C., January 25, 1880, box 1, Church Papers; *Cleveland Leader,* January 15, 1880.

62. *New York Tribune,* January 31, 1880, and February 25, 1880.

63. William Sherman to Rutherford B. Hayes, Washington, D.C., February 17, 1880, Rutherford B. Hayes Papers, Rutherford B. Hayes Library, Fremont, Ohio; William Sherman to William Conant Church, Washington, D.C., February 3, 1880, and February 25, 1880, box 1, Church Papers.

64. Ellis, *The Life of James Cardinal Gibbons,* 2:466–467; *New York Times,* May 6, 1880; William Sherman to Samuel H. M. Byers, Washington, D.C., May 11, 1880, Byers Papers.

65. *Army and Navy Journal* 48 (March 25, 1911): 880, and 45 (May 16, 1908): 995; *New York Times,* September 8, 1914.

66. *Army and Navy Journal* 48 (May 6, 1911): 1068–1069.

67. *New York Times,* September 12, 1914.

68. Ellen Sherman to William Sherman, Cresson (Pa.), August 5, 1880, and Altoona (Pa.), August 19, 1880, and August 23, 1880, roll 5, Sherman Family Papers.

69. Comments of Rachel Sherman Thorndike, attached to William Sherman to Ellen Sherman, Washington, D.C., August 24, 1880, roll 4, ibid.

70. Joseph T. Durkin, *General Sherman's Son* (New York: Farrar, Straus, 1959), 67–68; William Sherman to Elly Thackara, Washington, D.C., May 24, 1881, box 1, William Sherman Papers, Ohio Historical Society.

71. William Sherman to Samuel H. M. Byers, Washington, D.C., January 2, 1881, Byers Papers.

72. John Russell Young to William Sherman, London, February 14, 1880, reel 46, cont. 94, William Sherman Papers, Library of Congress.

73. William Sherman to Elly Thackara, Washington, D.C., November 14, 1880, box 1, William Sherman Papers, Ohio Historical Society.

74. Memorandum of Proposed Trip, Hayes Papers; William Sherman to Ellen Sherman, Portland, October 2, 1880, roll 4, Sherman Family Papers; William Sherman to John M. Schofield, Washington, D.C., November 7, 1880, box 28, Barney Collection.

75. Robert M. Utley, *Frontier Regulars: The United States Army and the Indian, 1866–1891* (New York: Macmillan, 1973), 350–356; Bernarr Cresap, *Appomattox Commander: The Story of General E. O. C. Ord* (San Diego and New York: A. S. Barnes, 1981), 315–316, 323–324.

76. William Sherman to Rutherford B. Hayes, Washington, D.C., November 18, 1880, Hayes Papers; William Sherman to Ellen Sherman, Washington, D.C., January 21, 1881, and January 26, 1881, roll 4, Sherman Family Papers.

77. William Sherman to Ellen Sherman, Washington, D.C., May 26, 1881, roll 4, Sherman Family Papers.

—— 20. Extreme Unction ——

1. *Army and Navy Journal* 18 (April 8, 1881): 753; William T. Sherman to Whitelaw Reid, Washington, D.C., April 16, 1881, reel 46, letterbook in cont. 94, William T. Sherman Papers, Manuscript Division, Library of Congress; *New York Tribune*, April 8, 1881, and April 9, 1881; Henry Van Ness Boynton to James Harrison Wilson, Washington, D.C., September 26, 1881, cont. 4, James Harrison Wilson Papers, Manuscript Division, Library of Congress.

2. Richard Allen Andrews, "Years of Frustration: William T. Sherman, the Army and Reform, 1868–1882" (Ph.D. diss., Northwestern University, 1969), 261–264, 275; Stephen E. Ambrose, *Upton and the Army* (Baton Rouge: Louisiana State University Press, 1964), 149–150.

3. William Sherman to Oliver O. Howard, Washington, D.C., December 29, 1881, Oliver O. Howard Papers, Bowdoin College Library, Brunswick, Maine.

4. Ambrose, *Upton and the Army*, 96–109; Peter S. Michie, *The Life and Letters of Emory Upton* (New York: D. Appleton, 1885), 298–303. Quoted is Andrews, "Years of Frustration," 266.

5. William Sherman to Ellen Sherman, Washington, D.C., September 23, 1881, roll 4, William Sherman Family Papers, University of Notre Dame Archives, South Bend, Indiana.

6. William Sherman to P. A. Stovall, New York, October 21, 1888, reel 48, letterbook in cont. 98, William Sherman Papers, Library of Congress; *New York Times*, November 23, 1881.

7. William Sherman to Daniel Draper, Washington, D.C., January 6, 1882, cont. 6, John W. Draper Papers, Manuscript Division, Library of Congress.

8. William Sherman to John M. Schofield, Washington, D.C., February 14, 1882, box 28, Hiram Barney Collection, Henry E. Huntington Library, San Marino, California.

9. William Sherman to Ellen Sherman, Washington, D.C., June 19, 1882, and June 22, 1882, roll 4, Sherman Family Papers; William Sherman to Elly Thackara, Washington, D.C., May 17, 1882, box 1, William T. Sherman Papers, Ohio Historical Society, Columbus.

10. Anna McAllister, *Ellen Ewing, Wife of General Sherman* (New York: Benziger, 1936), 357; William Sherman to W. W. Jarvis, July 6, 1882, box 1, William T. Sherman Papers, Missouri Historical Society, St. Louis.

11. Ellen Sherman to William Sherman, Oakland (Md.), August 7, 1882, and August 8, 1882, roll 5, Sherman Family Papers; William Sherman to Samuel H. M. Byers, Washington, D.C., November 7, 1882, Samuel H. M. Byers Papers, State Historical Society of Iowa, Des Moines.

12. William Sherman to John M. Schofield, Washington, D.C., September 29, 1882, reel 47, letterbook in cont. 75, William Sherman Papers, Library of Congress.

13. William Sherman to Ellen Sherman, Santa Fé, September 16, 1883, roll 4, Sherman Family Papers; *New York Times,* December 27, 1883; William Sherman to Benjamin H. Grierson, St. Louis, December 28, 1883, box 7, Benjamin H. Grierson Papers, Illinois State Historical Library, Springfield.

14. William Sherman to Ellen Sherman, Santa Fé, September 16, 1883, roll 4, Sherman Family Papers.

15. Ellen Sherman to William Sherman, St. Louis, September 20, 1883, roll 5, ibid.

16. *Army and Navy Journal* 20 (June 30, 1883): 230–231; P. Tecumseh Sherman, "Reminiscences of Early Days," 33, roll 14, Sherman Family Papers.

17. William Sherman to Nelson A. Miles, St. Louis, December 19, 1883, box 4, Nelson A. Miles Papers, Manuscript Division, Library of Congress; William Sherman to John M. Schofield, St. Louis, December 3, 1883, box 28, Barney Collection.

18. Sherman, "Reminiscences of Early Days," 38–39; William Sherman to Samuel H. M. Byers, St. Louis, June 21, 1884, Byers Papers.

19. William Sherman to Eleanor Poe, St. Louis, June 2, 1884, cont. 11, Orlando M. Poe Papers, Manuscript Division, Library of Congress.

20. William Sherman to Spencer F. Baird, St. Louis, October 25, 1884, box 52, William Jones Rhees Papers, Henry E. Huntington Library, San Marino, California.

21. Sherman, "Reminiscences of Early Days," 37.

22. Ibid., 37–38; Ellen Sherman to William Sherman, Philadelphia, April 4, 1887, roll 5, ibid.

23. Sherman, "Reminiscences of Early Days," 40.

24. William Sherman to William G. Eliot, St. Louis, September 12, 1885, reel 47, cont. 97, William Sherman Papers, Library of Congress; Sherman, "Reminiscences of Early Days," 36.

25. William Sherman to Robert N. Scott, St. Louis, September 6, 1885, reel 47, cont. 97, William Sherman Papers, Library of Congress.

26. James B. Fry, "An Acquaintance with Grant," *North American Review* 141 (December 1885): 551; Allen Thorndike Rice, "Sherman on Grant," *North American Review* 142 (January 1886): 111–113; William Sherman to William G. Eliot, St. Louis, February 7, 1886, box 2, William G. Eliot Papers, Missouri Historical Society, St. Louis.

27. William Sherman to Nelson A. Miles, St. Louis, August 14, 1885, box 4, Miles Papers.

28. William Sherman to Benjamin H. Field, St. Louis, September 15, 1885, reel 47, letterbook in cont. 97, William Sherman Papers, Library of Congress.

29. William Sherman to William G. Eliot, St. Louis, October 15, 1885, box 2, Eliot Papers.

30. William Sherman to Charles W. Moulton, St. Louis, May 13, 1885, and May 19, 1885, reel 47, letterbook in cont. 97, William Sherman Papers, Library of Congress. For Halleck's statement, see *O.R.,* ser. 1, vol. 38, pt. 5, 856–857.

31. Sherman, "Reminiscences of Early Days," 41; William Sherman to John E. Tourtellotte, St. Louis, October 5, 1884, box 1, William T. Sherman Papers, Missouri Historical Society, St. Louis; William Sherman to Eleanor Poe, St. Louis, March 22, 1885, cont. 22, Poe Papers.

32. William Sherman to Eleanor Poe, St. Louis, December 23, 1885, cont. 11, Poe Papers.

33. Sherman, "Reminiscences of Early Days," 41–42; William Sherman to Laura V. Harbaugh, St. Louis, January 26, 1886, box 1, William Sherman Papers, Missouri Historical Society.

34. William Sherman to Eleanor Poe, St. Louis, June 21, 1886, cont. 11, Poe Papers.

35. Sherman, "Reminiscences of Early Days," 42; William Sherman to Lizzie Cameron, New York, March 6, 1888, box 4, Miles Papers.

36. *Army and Navy Journal* 24 (January 1, 1887): 585; William Sherman to Eleanor Poe, New York, September 29, 1886, cont. 11, Poe Papers.

37. Thomas T. Gantt to Henry Jackson Hunt, St. Louis, February 6, 1886, box 4, Henry Jackson Hunt Papers, Manuscript Division, Library of Congress; James Howard Bridge, *Millionaires and Grub Street* (Freeport, N.Y.: Books for Libraries Press, 1968), 132; Elting E. Morison, ed., *The Letters of Theodore Roosevelt* (Cambridge, Mass.: Harvard University Press, 1952), 6:1337.

38. William Sherman to Ellen Sherman, New York, September 16, 1888, roll 4, Sherman Family Papers.

39. Royal Cortissoz, *The Life of Whitelaw Reid* (New York: Charles Scribner's Sons, 1921), 2:379; William Sherman to Lizzie Cameron, New York, March 6, 1888, box 4, Miles Papers.

40. Sherman, "Reminiscences of Early Days," 45; Louise Hall Tharp, *Saint-Gaudens and the Gilded Age* (Boston and Toronto: Little, Brown, 1969), 214–215.

41. *Army and Navy Journal* 39 (June 14, 1902): 1029.

42. William Sherman to John E. Tourtellotte, New York, August 7, 1888, roll 1, Sherman Family Papers; Sherman, "Reminiscences of Early Days," 45.

43. Sherman, "Reminiscences of Early Days," 46.

44. William Sherman to Lizzie Cameron, New York, February 10, 1888, box 4, Miles Papers; William Sherman to Oliver O. Howard, New York, January 11, 1888, Howard Papers.

45. William Sherman to John E. Tourtellotte, New York, December 6, 1888, roll 1, Sherman Family Papers; William Sherman to John M. Schofield, New York, December 5, 1888, box 28, Barney Collection.

46. William Sherman to John E. Tourtellotte, New York, December 6, 1888, roll 1, Sherman Family Papers; John Sherman to Lizzie Cameron, n.p., January 24, 1888, box 4, Miles Papers.

47. Sherman, "Reminiscences of Early Days," 46; William Sherman to Oliver O. Howard, New York, March 1, 1889, Howard Papers.

48. William Sherman to John E. Tourtellotte, New York, February 5, 1889, roll 1, Sherman Family Papers; William Sherman to John E. Tourtellotte, New York, November 6, 1889, William T. Sherman Papers, United States Military Academy Library, West Point, New York.

49. Thomas E. Sherman to William Sherman, Woodstock (Md.), March 23, 1889, roll 7, Sherman Family Papers.

50. William Sherman to Eleanor Poe, New York, February 8, 1889, cont. 11, Poe Papers; Joseph T. Durkin, *General Sherman's Son* (New York: Farrar, Straus, 1959), 109–110; Sherman, "Reminiscences of Early Days," 47.

51. William Sherman to Nelson A. Miles, New York, December 29, 1889, box 4, Miles Papers.

52. William Sherman to John M. Schofield, New York, February 5, 1890, box 20, Barney Collection; Unidentified interview with Sherman, reel 51, cont. 109, William Sherman Papers, Library of Congress.

53. Mary Elizabeth (Lizzie) Sherman diary, February 5–10, 1891, roll 14, Sherman Family Papers; Sherman, "Reminiscences of Early Days," 48.

54. Minnie Sherman Fitch, "Account of Last Illness & Death of General Sherman," 1–4, box 9, William Sherman Papers, Ohio Historical Society; Lizzie Sherman diary, February 11, 1891, roll 14, Sherman Family Papers.

55. John Sherman to the Publishers of the *New York Times*, February 13, 1891, roll 9, Sherman Family Papers.

56. Mark Twain to William Sherman, Hartford (Conn.), February 13, 1891, reel 42, cont. 83, William Sherman Papers, Library of Congress.

57. *New York Times*, February 18, 1891, and February 20, 1891; Sherman, "Reminiscences of Early Days," 48.

58. Rachel Sherman to John Sherman, New York, February 24, 1891, reel 42, cont. 83, William Sherman Papers, Library of Congress.

59. William Sherman to Oliver O. Howard, St. Louis, January 7, 1886, reel 48, letterbook in cont. 98, ibid.

60. David R. Francis to William K. Bixby, White Sulphur Springs (W.Va.), April 16, 1919, box 1, William Sherman Papers, Missouri Historical Society; Sherman, "Reminiscences of

Early Days," 49; *Autobiography of Oliver Otis Howard* (New York: Baker & Taylor, 1907), 2:553–554.

61. *Autobiography of Oliver Otis Howard,* 2:553; *New York Times,* March 1, 1891.

62. George S. Boutwell, *Reminiscences of Sixty Years in Public Affairs* (Greenwich, Conn.: Greenwood Press, 1968), 2:243–244, 258.

63. Tom Sherman to John Sherman, New York, February 24, 1891, and February 25, 1891, reel 42, cont. 83, William Sherman Papers, Library of Congress; Tom Sherman to Oliver O. Howard, March 4, 1891, and March 9, 1891, Howard Papers; Tom Sherman to P. Tecumseh Sherman, St. Louis, September 28, 1891, and October 10, 1891, roll 9, Sherman Family Papers.

64. Sherman, "Reminiscences of Early Days," 43–44. See also Charles Royster, *The Destructive War: William Tecumseh Sherman, Stonewall Jackson, and the Americans* (New York: Alfred A. Knopf, 1991), 366–369.

65. Lampson Sherman to My Dear Niece, Des Moines (Iowa), February 26, 1891, reel 42, cont. 83, William Sherman Papers, Library of Congress.

66. Theodore E. Burton, *John Sherman* (Boston and New York: Houghton Mifflin, 1906), 416–417; *New York Times,* August 11, 1897.

67. Durkin, *General Sherman's Son,* 196–202, 208–223, 233–238; *New York Times,* May 1, 1933.

68. *New York Times,* December 7, 1941; Note of Eleanor Sherman Fitch at the end of Sherman, "Reminiscences of Early Days."

—— Sherman: A Brief Assessment ——

1. P. Tecumseh Sherman, "Reminiscences of Early Days," 37–38, roll 14, William T. Sherman Family Papers, University of Notre Dame Archives, South Bend, Indiana.

—— Appendix: Patton and Sherman ——

1. B. H. Liddell Hart, "Notes on Two Discussions with Patton, 1944," February 20, 1948, box 6, George S. Patton Jr. Papers, United States Military Academy Library, West Point, New York.

Manuscripts Cited

Robert Anderson Papers, Manuscript Division, Library of Congress.

Christopher C. Augur Papers, Illinois State Historical Library, Springfield.

Hiram Barney Collection, Henry E. Huntington Library, San Marino, California.

Francis P. Blair Family Papers, Manuscript Division, Library of Congress.

Samuel H. M. Byers Papers, State Historical Society of Iowa, Des Moines.

William Conant Church Papers, Manuscript Division, Library of Congress.

Charles Davies Papers, United States Military Academy Library, West Point, New York.

Grenville M. Dodge Papers, State Historical Society of Iowa, Des Moines.

John W. Draper Papers, Manuscript Division, Library of Congress.

Thomas H. Dudley Papers, Henry E. Huntington Library, San Marino, California.

James William Eldridge Collection, Henry E. Huntington Library, San Marino, California.

William G. Eliot Papers, Missouri Historical Society, St. Louis.

Charles Ewing Papers, Manuscript Division, Library of Congress.

Hugh B. Ewing Papers, Ohio Historical Society, Columbus.

Philemon B. Ewing Papers, Ohio Historical Society, Columbus.

Thomas Ewing Family Papers, Manuscript Division, Library of Congress.

Ulysses S. Grant Papers, Manuscript Division, Library of Congress.

Walter Q. Gresham Papers, Manuscript Division, Library of Congress.

Benjamin H. Grierson Papers, Illinois State Historical Library, Springfield.

James A. Hardie Papers, Manuscript Division, Library of Congress.

Rutherford B. Hayes Papers, Rutherford B. Hayes Library, Fremont, Ohio.

Ethan A. Hitchcock Papers, Manuscript Division, Library of Congress.

Henry Hitchcock Papers, Manuscript Division, Library of Congress.

Oliver O. Howard Papers, Bowdoin College Library, Brunswick, Maine.

Henry Jackson Hunt Papers, Manuscript Division, Library of Congress.

Huntington Manuscripts, Henry E. Huntington Library, San Marino, California.

Edwin B. Janes Collection, Henry E. Huntington Library, San Marino California.

John A. McClernand Papers, Illinois State Historical Library, Springfield.

Nelson A. Miles Papers, Manuscript Division, Library of Congress.

Lewis B. Parsons Papers, Illinois State Historical Library, Springfield.

George S. Patton Jr. Papers, United States Military Academy Library, West Point, New York.

Orlando M. Poe Papers, Manuscript Division, Library of Congress.

Registers of Merit and Delinquencies, United States Military Academy Archives, West Point, New York.

Whitelaw Reid Papers, Manuscript Division, Library of Congress.

William Jones Rhees Papers, Henry E. Huntington Library, San Marino, California.

John M. Schofield Papers, Manuscript Division, Library of Congress.

Philip H. Sheridan Papers, Manuscript Division, Library of Congress.

John Sherman Papers, Manuscript Division, Library of Congress.

William T. Sherman Family Papers, University of Notre Dame Archives, South Bend, Indiana.

William T. Sherman Papers, Chicago Historical Society.

William T. Sherman Papers, Henry E. Huntington Library, San Marino, California.

William T. Sherman Papers, Illinois State Historical Library, Springfield.

William T. Sherman Papers, J. P. Morgan Library, New York City.

William T. Sherman Papers, Manuscript Division, Library of Congress.

William T. Sherman Papers, Missouri Historical Society, St. Louis.

William T. Sherman Papers, Ohio Historical Society, Columbus.

William T. Sherman Papers, United States Military Academy Library, West Point, New York.

Francis F. Spies Collection, Genealogy Room, New York Public Library.

Edward D. Townsend Papers, Henry E. Huntington Library, San Marino, California.

Henry Smith Turner Papers, Missouri Historical Society, St. Louis.

James Harrison Wilson Papers, Manuscript Division, Library of Congress.

Index

459

About the Author

Stanley P. Hirshson is a professor of history at Queens College of the City University of New York. He is also the author of *The Lion of the Lord, Grenville M. Dodge,* and *Farewell to the Bloody Shirt: Northern Republicans and the Southern Negro, 1877–1893.* Mr. Hirshson earned his Ph.D. in history from Columbia University. He lives in Closter, New Jersey.